Praise for

THE OUTLIER

A *New York Times Book Review* Editors' Choice

An Amazon Editors' Pick for Best History

"An 'outlier' among politicians, Carter shows what democratic politics could be, if the power-hungry, dishonest figures would just get out of the way. [Kai] Bird's book offers a rich and compelling account of Carter's sincere efforts to make American policies match the nation's ideals."

—*The Washington Post*

"Important . . . Bird is able to build a persuasive case that the Carter presidency deserves this new look. [This] landmark presidential biography . . . explains why American presidents continue to learn as much from President Carter's mistakes as from his many achievements."

—*The New York Times Book Review*

"Bird's nuanced study not only sets the record straight on Carter's misunderstood presidency, it brings him to life in a way that few other biographers have been able to thus far."

—*Variety*

"In Kai Bird's latest masterpiece, a book that models the virtues of the biographer's craft, Jimmy Carter receives his due. Deeply empirical and exquisitely sculpted . . . *The Outlier* is a landmark. . . . Bird's treatment gives Carter's presidency the deep analysis it deserves."

—*Foreign Policy*

"A bracing reminder that the 39th president was a man of probity, decency, high hopes, and high moral standards . . . Bird's take on . . . 'our most enigmatic president' is relentlessly fair-minded. [*The Outlier*] redeems [Carter's] presidency and reminds us of how callous we might have been during his years in office."

—*The Boston Globe*

"Immense with historical detail buoyed by Washington intrigue . . . *The Outlier* paints a detailed portrait of the man and his legacy."

—*The Atlanta Journal-Constitution*

"*The Outlier* seeks to renovate the legacy of the Carter administration in the only way likely to succeed: by adding to the scales of judgment an enormous amount of research and a refreshing lack of partisanship."

—*The Christian Science Monitor*

"This in-depth biography, well served with huge amounts of recently released classified data (especially including significant personal diaries), tells an extraordinary, sometimes shocking, but nuanced story. Bird's phenomenal research and artful interviews . . . [do] not disappoint."

—*The Decatur Daily*

"Incisive . . . Bird is a keen biographer of political figures, and he offers a welcome reminder that Carter's liberal impulses were correct while his missteps were often the result of events he could not fully control. . . . [*The Outlier* is] the best study to date of the Carter era and a substantial contribution to the history of the 1970s."

—*Kirkus Reviews* (starred review)

"A readable, masterful biography of a complex leader . . . Bird does a magnificent job characterizing the many strong and fiery personalities in the Carter administration, making them all individuals with virtues and flaws."

—*Booklist* (starred review)

"It is said that biography is the most challenging of the writing arts. Kai Bird's brilliant new work on the life and presidency of the elusive but consequential Jimmy Carter demonstrates that this gifted writer has more than met the challenge. The depth and detail of his research, his grasp of a story played out mostly in the complicated culture of South Georgia, and his elegant and nuanced writing combine to make a terrific read, and a literary gem. He cites the flaws as well as glimpses of greatness at points in Carter's presidency, with emphasis on his early and steadfast commitment to human rights. It's time that Jimmy Carter gets his due, and Kai Bird's biography is a giant step in that direction."

—RICHARD MOE, author of *Roosevelt's Second Act*

"A grand work of revisionist history . . . I, for one, will never again be able to look on the Carter presidency as a 'failed' one. Prodigiously researched, gracefully written, *The Outlier* tells the story of a singular man and a unique presidency at a critical turning point in American and world history."

—DAVID NASAW, *New York Times* bestselling author of *The Last Million*

"Books about presidents are often fat and dull—not this one. Bird has talked to everybody and written a compelling account of the most underrated president in American history."

—THOMAS POWERS, Pulitzer Prize–winning journalist and author of *The Killing of Crazy Horse*

"Kai Bird's brilliant biography doesn't just capture Jimmy Carter's decency and courage. It reminds us what America can still learn from him today."

—PETER BEINART, author of *The Crisis of Zionism*

BY KAI BIRD

The Outlier: The Unfinished Presidency of Jimmy Carter

The Good Spy: The Life and Death of Robert Ames

*Crossing Mandelbaum Gate: Coming of Age Between the
Arabs and Israelis, 1956–1978*

*American Prometheus: The Triumph and Tragedy of
J. Robert Oppenheimer,* with Martin J. Sherwin

*The Color of Truth: McGeorge Bundy and William Bundy:
Brothers in Arms*

*Hiroshima's Shadow: Writings on the Denial of History and
the Smithsonian Controversy,* edited with Lawrence Lifschultz

*The Chairman: John J. McCloy & The Making of
the American Establishment*

THE
OUTLIER

Candidate Jimmy Carter

THE
OUTLIER

The Unfinished Presidency of
JIMMY CARTER

Kai Bird

CROWN
NEW YORK

LIBRARY OF CONGRESS CATALOGING-IN-PUBLICATION DATA
Names: Bird, Kai, author.
Title: The outlier / Kai Bird.
Description: First edition. | New York: Crown, [2021] | Includes
bibliographical references and index.
Identifiers: LCCN 2021004350 (print) | LCCN 2021004351 (ebook) |
ISBN 9780451495242 (trade paper) | ISBN 9780451495259 (ebook)
Subjects: LCSH: Carter, Jimmy, 1924– | Presidents—United States—
Biography. | United States—Politics and government—1977–1981. | United
States—Foreign relations—1977–1981. | Plains (Ga.)—Biography.
Classification: LCC E873 .B48 2021 (print) | LCC E873 (ebook) |
DDC 973.926092 [b]—dc23
LC record available at lccn.loc.gov/2021004350
LC ebook record available at lccn.loc.gov/2021004351

Printed in Canada on acid-free paper

crownpublishing.com

2 4 6 8 9 7 5 3 1

Book design by Simon M. Sullivan

SUSAN GOLDMARK

Not merely a muse, but a rabbi for life's imponderables

Contents

PART 3: THE POST-PRESIDENCY

THE
OUTLIER

Prologue

THE NINETY-ONE-YEAR-OLD EX-PRESIDENT and Nobel Peace Prize winner walks briskly through the back hallway of the Maranatha Baptist Church in Plains, Georgia, and enters the overflow room behind the church sanctuary. Waiting to catch a glimpse are more than forty people, mostly tourists from various parts of America, who could not squeeze into the main sanctuary. They have all come to hear Jimmy Carter teach Sunday school. He's wearing his Sunday best—dark slacks, a rumpled brown tweed jacket, a purple-and-white plaid shirt. A bolo tie adorned with a turquoise clasp hangs around his neck. His black shoes are scuffed and unshined. Notoriously frugal, Carter buys some of his clothes from the local Dollar General store. "Tight as bark on a tree," quipped Dot Padgett, the president's old Georgia friend who organized Carter's famous "Peanut Brigade" of roving campaign supporters in 1976.

Standing only five feet seven inches, Carter was never a physically imposing man. In his prime, he projected an unassuming, mild-mannered demeanor. His style was studiously unpretentious. In the White House, he aspired to a distinctly austere, nonimperial presidency. Even in his nineties, his translucent blue eyes sparkle so sharply that he seems slightly intimidating.

"Thank you for your service, Mr. President," exclaims someone.

"Oh, well," Carter replies, "I'm still having a good time. In fact, this week we're going to Argentina, fishing."

Grinning broadly, Carter takes a few questions as he waits to be introduced into the main sanctuary. Suddenly, from the front row, a woman asks, "Do you still hear from Mary Fitzpatrick?" Slightly startled by the query, Carter, eyebrows raised, answers, "Yes, she lives with us. She lives here in Plains and works for us five days a week." He pauses and looks quizzically at the stranger, who then offers, "Well, I was her lawyer."

Carter turns to the crowd and explains, "Mary Fitzpatrick was in prison for life when I was governor." A murmur rises from the crowd as Carter continues, "She went to the governor's mansion to help us, and she's been with us ever since. When I was elected president, I got permission from the prison board to be her parole officer, so she went to the White House and lived there with us. She's a wonderful person." And then, as an afterthought, he adds in a matter-of-fact tone, "She was innocent."

Mary Prince Fitzpatrick was a convicted murderer when in 1977, at the age of thirty-one, she moved into a bedroom on the third floor of the White House living quarters. For the next four years she served as the governess to the president's daughter, Amy. And when the Carters left the White House, defeated by the Hollywood film star–turned–California governor Ronald Reagan, their African American nanny moved back with them to Plains, where she lives in a home bought for her by the Carters. Mary has worked ever since as the ex-president's housekeeper. Her story tells us something essential about the character and religious values of our strangely perplexing thirty-ninth president. But it also highlights an enduring mystery about how a product of the Old South, a white boy reared in a highly segregated, conservative rural society, came to personify decency and an uncommon humanitarianism in the White House.

CARTER IS PERHAPS our most enigmatic president. He is often celebrated for what he has achieved in his four-decade-long post-presidency. Conservatives and liberals alike accord him the accolade of "the best ex-president." But most citizens and the punditocracy routinely label his a "failed" presidency, ostensibly because he failed to win reelection. But in truth, Carter is sometimes perceived as a failure simply because he refused to make us feel good about the country. He insisted on telling us what was wrong and what it would take to make things better. And for most Americans, it was easier to label the messenger a "failure" than to grapple with the hard problems. Ultimately, Carter was replaced by a sunny, more reassuring politician who simply promised that he would "make America great again."

Conventional wisdom has not given high marks to Carter's presidency. One historian described him as an "utter failure as a national leader." Another historian labeled his a "mediocre presidency." He was "long on good intentions," complained this historian, "but short on know-how." Gore Vidal called him "a decent man if an inept politician."

He is also perceived as a "weak" or hapless executive—the victim of runaway inflation, a militant ayatollah, and even a "killer rabbit." Much of this is a simplistic caricature. No modern president worked harder at the job and few achieved more than Carter in his one term in office. Both his domestic legislative record and his radical foreign policy initiatives made his presidential term quite consequential. As a politician, most of the time he was a nonpolitician, uninterested in the cajoling and dealmaking of Washington. This made him both an outsider and an *outlier*—"a person or thing situated away or detached from the main body or system."

Far from being weak or indecisive, Carter repeatedly demonstrated his willingness to make tough decisions despite the predictable political consequences. It may have been naïveté, but he invariably rebuffed his advisers when they cautioned him to do something because it was politically popular. They knew he was just as likely to do the opposite. Indeed, he displayed in the Oval Office an unbending backbone and moral certitude in dealing with such politically fraught issues as the Israeli-Palestinian conflict, the Panama Canal, nuclear weapons, the environment, and consumer protection. His greatest foreign policy triumph—the Camp David Accords, which led to a peace treaty between Israel and Egypt—never would have happened but for Carter's vision.

His insistence on lecturing the Soviet apparatchiks about human rights contributed more to the disintegration of the Soviet system than did Ronald Reagan's reckless spending on Star Wars. He anticipated the end of the Cold War and proclaimed an end to our "inordinate fear of communism." He asked us to think critically about the hubris of American exceptionalism. In the aftermath of defeat in Vietnam he asked us to beware of foreign interventions. Carter refused to take us to war—even when the Iran hostage crisis posed an existential threat to his own reelection.

He was, as Garry Wills has argued, the "first American president to take seriously the entire postcolonial era that has remade the globe since

World War II." This was why he was willing to ram through the unpopular Panama Canal Treaty; he understood that America could not engage with this new postcolonial world without relinquishing its own colonial outpost in the Panama Canal Zone.

Against the advice of his inner circle, he hired Paul Volcker to strangle inflation, knowing full well that the Princeton-educated economist intended to make the economy scream as he faced reelection. Carter antagonized entrenched corporate interests by deregulating the airlines, the trucking industry, and railroads. Deregulation benefited millions of consumers—but it also tended to weaken labor unions, a core constituency of the Democratic Party. He forced through auto-safety and fuel-efficiency standards over the opposition of the Detroit auto companies. Seatbelts and airbags would become mandatory—and save thousands of lives each year. Environmentalists cheered when he placed millions of acres of Alaskan wilderness under federal protection—even as he accepted that most Alaskans were outraged. For Carter, it was simply the right thing to do.

Carter stubbornly spent much of his political capital in his first term, acting as if he were a second-term president, which helps to explain the outcome of the 1980 election. His relentless pursuit of what he thought was a virtuous agenda made him political enemies. Southern conservatives turned on him for his determination to remake the judiciary, elevating more African Americans and women to the federal bench than all previous presidents combined. Carter's obvious compassion and affinity for the poor, disenfranchised Blacks of his South Georgian childhood made many white working-class citizens uneasy. If race is the third rail in American society, Carter never hesitated to touch it. He was a southern white man—but he was the first president to feel entirely comfortable worshipping and speaking in a Black church.

Core constituencies within the Democratic Party did not understand this southern man and distrusted his political pedigree. He presented himself not as a liberal per se but just as a good-government progressive. He promised never to lie and campaigned on the notion that the country needed a government as good as the American people. His message was integrity.

All of this sounded suspiciously naïve. Many in the Washington pundit class ridiculed his soft Georgian twang and peanut farmer persona. It was an unfortunate cultural disconnect—as if Carter had arrived from a foreign country. His religion was also seen by the establishment as a curiosity. He personally disapproved of abortion, but he always defended a woman's right to choose and lobbied for passage of the Equal Rights Amendment. He criticized busing as a tool of integration but ardently supported affirmative action. He was a Southern Baptist who believed in the separation of church and state—and so he refused to subsidize private Christian academies schooling all-white student bodies.

His social liberalism was tainted by a small-town fiscal provincialism, but Carter's political sensibilities as a liberal on social issues were authentic. Historically, he was a product of the southern populist outlook that helped to build Franklin Roosevelt's New Deal coalition. He was a southern liberal quietly but adamantly opposed to segregation, and as governor of Georgia he proclaimed an end to racial discrimination minutes after taking the oath of office.

During the 1976 campaign, the *New York Times* columnist Anthony Lewis found himself listening to Carter on the stump and concluded, "Jimmy Carter really does see himself fighting entrenched power, the status quo. He resents privilege, official arrogance, unfairness. He thinks of himself as one of the outsiders, those without power in society." Lewis thought Carter was channeling an authentic "modern voice of that old American strain, Populism."

Carter presented himself as an outsider, running against Washington. In 1976, in the wake of the Watergate scandal that brought down Richard Nixon, this populist branding aided his rise to power. His timing was impeccable. At no other moment in American political history could such an improbable candidate have won the presidency. But governing was another matter. No one understood it at the time, but the mid-1970s marked a turning point in the country's political economy. The 1973 Middle East oil embargo led to surging energy costs and stimulated inflation. Simultaneously, global markets expanded dramatically, leading to the export of manufacturing jobs to the less developed world. Deindustrialization began to eliminate middle-class American jobs. In retrospect, it is clear that the liberalism of the New Deal era was under siege. The grand liberal coalition was falling apart—just as Carter was dealt the most difficult economic hand of any post–World War II American president.

His response was complicated. He was for the poor and underprivileged. But his fiscal instincts were conservative. As a pragmatist and an engineer, he paid more attention to details and facts than to politics and ideology. He valued competency and expertise. He read all the papers and concluded—as did most economists—that the country faced a unique situation: a dismal combination of rising budget deficits, rising unemployment, and rising inflation. As stagflation persisted, Carter insisted the right response was to prioritize the fight against inflation by cutting the federal budget deficit. Inflation, he insisted, hurt the working classes more than the investor class. Following this logic, he was willing to sacrifice some social programs—but not the defense budget—in an effort to control what he thought were inflationary budget deficits. Naturally, this proved to be extremely unpopular with the liberal base of the Democratic Party—and in retrospect, history suggests that the American economy could have sustained much larger deficits. Liberals complained that he could have spent more on social programs to stimulate job creation and less on a defense budget still premised on Cold War assumptions.

In any case, Carter was not adept at selling his fiscally conservative policies. He didn't have the personality of a natural politician. He tended to think that he was the smartest fellow in the room. And he probably was. But he also had a stubborn streak and a surprising audacity. His self-confidence bordered on arrogance. As a Southern Baptist he was painfully self-aware that his pride was the deepest of sins. And so he tried to compensate for his overweening intelligence by working hard to be humble and transparent. But inevitably this cauldron of pride, self-confidence, and principled problem solving came across as sanctimonious.

Republicans and Democrats alike were annoyed when he refused to barter with them. Liberal Democrats controlled both the House and the Senate and expected a conventionally liberal presidency—one that would endorse federal spending on a broad range of domestic programs, from pork-barrel water projects to national healthcare. But Carter looked at the budget numbers and determined that the country could no longer afford each and every liberal program. In his memorable but gloomy "malaise" speech he lectured Americans that "too many of us now tend to worship self-indulgence and consumption." And when he said no to the liberals, he was accused of being a bland technocrat, self-righteous, and simply not a team player.

His arguments with the liberals in his own party came to a head over the fundamental issue of healthcare. By 1978, the idea that every American deserved national health insurance became a key issue within the Democratic Party. Senator Edward Kennedy championed this cause and used it to challenge Carter for the 1980 party nomination. Carter was as committed as Kennedy to the New Deal dream of bringing national healthcare to every American. But he looked at the numbers and made the political calculation that the liberal senator's universal-healthcare bill didn't have the votes. Neither did he think Kennedy had the tax dollars to fund it without fueling inflation. Carter offered to crack the door open to universal healthcare with a bill to provide universal *catastrophic* care to every American. Kennedy, the labor unions, and the liberal wing of the Democratic Party rejected this compromise, and the senator from Camelot announced his run for the presidency.

Initially, Kennedy and his supporters were confident that they would prevail. But they had not reckoned with the unbridled self-confidence of the Georgian peanut farmer. Carter announced that he was going to "whip his ass." And he did, ruthlessly doing what was politically necessary to turn back the challenge. *Rolling Stone*'s gonzo journalist, Hunter S. Thompson, once described Carter as one of the "meanest men" he had ever met. By this Thompson meant that he saw in Carter a man marked by a certain righteous determination.

Carter fended off the Kennedy challenge from his left—but he was not able to defeat the rising challenge from his right. The tragedy for this decent politician who believed in the power of government to help people was that he was eventually defeated by Ronald Reagan—who upon taking the oath of office proclaimed that "government is not the solution to our problems; government is the problem." The Carter White House years thus turned out to be a tipping point toward a profoundly conservative era. To Carter's enduring regret, America became more partisan and more unequal. His presidency was all about personal character and decency. But instead of becoming transformational, Jimmy Carter's presidency marked a transition to decades of divisive politics.

History will judge Carter as a president ahead of his time. In an age of limits he asked us to conserve energy. He put solar panels on the roof of the White House before they were economical. He talked about climate change before it was ever fashionable. He was a "premature" environmentalist.

After the scandals of Watergate, he scorned the trappings of an imperial presidency. Most Americans in the 1970s were not ready for this spartan vision of limits.

Carter understood that the country had not recovered from the divisiveness of the sixties. "These wounds are very deep," he told us. "They have never been healed."

Neither was the country ready for his message on the core issue of racism. As a white boy growing up in South Georgia, Jimmy Carter lived a childhood steeped in segregation and a culture of white supremacy. And yet his childhood playmates were mostly African Americans. His only neighbors were Black tenants. He experienced from the ground the great chasm between America's beliefs about itself and the reality of inequality, poverty, and racism.

His distinctive southern sensibilities and his Southern Baptist religiosity left him open to the revelation that America was hobbled by its myths. "The American Negro has the great advantage of having never believed that collection of myths to which white Americans cling: that their ancestors were all freedom-longing heroes, that they were born in the greatest country the world has ever seen, or that Americans are invincible in battle and wise in peace." James Baldwin wrote these words in his small but powerful book *The Fire Next Time,* published in 1963, just as Carter began his political career. The two men had nothing in common. Baldwin was a New York intellectual, a Black gay man who had turned his back on the Christian church of his youth.

But Carter was the rare southern white man who saw what African Americans saw—that America was not that "city on a hill." Carter understood that the myths were myths and that America, both North and South, was in fact a country in need of serious healing. This was his strength as a politician and ultimately the source of his unpopularity in 1980. America was not ready for a politician who could engage in such truth telling. Indeed, as evidenced by the country's reaction to the "malaise" Camp David retreat, many Americans were perplexed and even unnerved to see a president willing to engage in such ruthless introspection and self-criticism. His efforts to persuade the country to confront its original sins were somehow both heroic and ill-fated.

"Our society is steadily growing more racially and economically polarized," Carter wrote in 1996. "One reason is that many poor and minority Americans are convinced, with good reason, that the basic system of justice and law enforcement is not fair." He said exactly the same thing in his famous "Law Day" speech in Georgia in 1974. Few listened.

Sadly, a far more divided America is today having to deal with many of the issues Carter grappled with forty years ago: environmental limits, national healthcare, our racial divide, income inequality, Middle East wars, and an excess of presidential powers. His was a decidedly unfinished presidency, in practical terms but also philosophically. If Carter as president was ahead of his time, both his post-presidency and the story of his White House years now seem all too relevant.

This is a presidential biography, largely focused on Carter's White House years. But early in the writing, I found it impossible to explain his presidency without exploring his upbringing as a southerner. I write about that journey, but I have endeavored to describe Carter's life in this unique geography and history through the lens of how the American South shaped Carter's presidency. One cannot begin to understand Carter's presidential decisions without an accounting of his extraordinary quest for the presidency. It is a very American story about a most complex man.

Part 1

THE PRE-PRESIDENCY

Jimmy Carter on his horse Lady

Chapter 1
The Past Is Never Dead

We had too much money to be ostracized.
—Miss Lillian

Ruth, Miss Lillian, and Jimmy
JIMMY CARTER PRESIDENTIAL LIBRARY AND MUSEUM

J AMES EARL CARTER, Jr., was always an outlier—as a president and as a boy decades earlier in rural South Georgia. Born on October 1, 1924, in a small hospital in Plains, Georgia, Jimmy grew up on his father's 360-acre farm two and a half miles down the road in the tiny hamlet of Archery. The Carter family home was a three-bedroom single-story house assembled from a Sears, Roebuck kit. The structure lacked electricity and insulation and had no running water until 1935, when Carter's father bought a small windmill to pump water from the backyard well into a water tank. Until then, the family used an outdoor privy with four holes. The family's shower was made by punching nail holes in the bottom of a bucket suspended from a water pipe in the wood ceiling.

The village of Plains, population 479, had electricity "most of the hours of the day," provided by a large one-cylinder engine. Every time it hit a stroke, the engine blew a smoke ring up in the air. Everyone in town could hear the engine pounding away—until, periodically, it would break down and there would be no electricity at all. Although electricity came to Atlanta in 1884, it took more than a half century to reach Archery in 1938. Carter later recalled wryly, "The greatest day in my life was not being inaugurated president, [and] it wasn't even marrying Rosalynn—it was when they turned the electricity on because that totally transformed our lifestyle." Most of the streets of Plains were not paved until 1954. But if Jimmy's boyhood home was spartan and surrounded by abject poverty, his childhood was nevertheless comfortable and relatively privileged.

Archery was a throwback to the nineteenth century. Jimmy's father, James Earl Carter, Sr., had a tenth-grade education before dropping out to join the army. In 1903, when Earl was only ten years old, his father, William Archibald Carter, was shot dead during a violent brawl with a business rival. They had been arguing over who was the rightful owner of a desk. Earl was certainly not country "white trash"—but neither was he part of the southern plantation aristocracy. By the late 1920s, he made more than a comfortable living growing peanuts, corn, and cotton and drawing "rents" from his Black tenants. He managed to expand his farm acreage even during the boll weevil blight of the 1920s, which wiped out many cotton farmers.

"Daddy was a very aggressive, competent farmer," Jimmy recalled. He was always trying to turn any harvest into cash. One year he planted ten acres of tomatoes, and they turned out beautifully. But so did everyone else's tomato patches all over Georgia that year. "I remember a man named Mr. Rycroth and I loaded his truck with tomatoes," Jimmy said, "and we rode all over Georgia, trying to sell the tomatoes. We couldn't sell them at all. So, we came back home and told Daddy and he decided to make ketchup out of those tomatoes." Earl was unusually entrepreneurial. "We had sheep," Jimmy said, "and Daddy would send the wool off to some central manufacturing place, I never knew where, and get blankets back, and we would sell blankets in our local store. We grew beef cattle. We milked twelve cows at most. . . . Daddy would process the milk, either making vanilla or chocolate milk to sell in little 5-cent bottles that he would haul around and put in different grocery stores." They grew sugarcane that Earl turned into a syrup and bottled under the label "Plains Maid," with a picture of a pretty girl on the label. They plucked the down from a flock of geese to make down comforters and pillows. "Everything Earl Carter touched turned to money," said his nephew Hugh Carter.

A short, stocky man, Earl dressed in store-bought suits, wore a fedora in the winter and a straw hat in the summer, and drove a Model T Ford and later a 1937 Oldsmobile. He sometimes taught Sunday school at the Baptist church—but he refused to sit for the sermons because he thought them boring. Earl had an easygoing side to him. But over his wife's objections, he refused to give up his Friday-night poker games. He enjoyed playing tennis on a red clay court he had constructed immediately adjacent to his Sears, Roebuck home. Earl was a "very accomplished tennis player," Carter recalled—and by the time he was thirteen years old, so too was Jimmy. Earl bought Jimmy his own riding horse, a Shetland pony named Lady, a ping-pong table, and plenty of books. Some years later, Earl built a three-bedroom guesthouse on a nearby property, complete with a swimming pond. They called this family retreat the "Pond House." Earl tightly controlled the family's monthly budget, and eventually he owned five thousand acres of prime farmland, a grocery in Plains, a fire insurance agency, and a peanut warehouse and brokerage business. Upon Earl's death in 1953, his net worth was a quarter million dollars—or about $2.4 million in today's dollars.

Growing up in Archery, Jimmy was barefoot from early April until the cold arrived in October: "There was always an argument which my parents always won about how early I could take my shoes off and how early I had to put them back on." Every autumn Jimmy had plenty of time to go hunting with his friends for squirrels, rabbits, and quail. When it was too wet to work in the fields, he would hike down to Chucahatcha Creek with his mostly Black playmates. They'd catch catfish and eels. Occasionally, the boys played baseball. There were only three whites on the team, Jimmy and the Watson boys, and the rest of the team was Black.

Jimmy's closest boyhood friend was A. D. Davis, whose relatives were tenants on the Carter farm. "Jimmy and them [the Carter brood] were raised up with nothin' but colored people," A.D. later told a reporter. "He ain't never acted like he was more'n somebody because he was white." They played together in the fields and worked together. And sometimes Jimmy's mother, born Bessie Lillian Gordy—whom everyone called "Miss Lillian"—took them to the Rylander Theatre in Americus to watch movies, seating Jimmy with his Black friend in the "white-only" downstairs section. But as A.D. grew older, he'd insist on sitting in the segregated "black-only" balcony seats. That was the way things were.

Some two hundred people lived in Archery, but aside from a railroad foreman, the Carters were the only whites in the hamlet—and most of the Blacks depended on Earl for their subsistence livelihood, working as day laborers. Aside from Earl, the leading figure in the community was an African American preacher, William Decker Johnson. Born in 1869, Johnson was ordained as a bishop in the African Methodist Episcopal Church. In 1911, he moved to Archery and founded a vocational school, the Johnson Home Industrial College. He regularly preached at the St. Mark Church in Archery. Bishop Johnson was a singular influence, a rare Black man who owned property, drove his own car, and traveled across the country. Miss Lillian enjoyed talking to him and scandalized her husband by inviting the bishop into her home to chat. Jimmy occasionally heard the bishop preach at St. Mark's Church and listened to the Black choir.

Most of young Jimmy's childhood playmates were the sons of his father's Black tenants, and they spent their days roaming the woods, hunting, and fishing. He had one white friend, Rembert Forrest, who sometimes rode his horse out from Plains to visit Jimmy. If his parents were away in Atlanta on business, young Jimmy would spend the night in the nearby wooden cabin occupied by Jack and Rachel Clark, sleeping on a pallet on the floor. Jack Clark was Earl's foreman, the only Black tenant who received monthly wages. Jimmy followed Jack around the farm "like a puppy dog and bombarding him with questions." Jack often took Jimmy into the woods to hunt raccoons and possums. Rachel sat with Jimmy, watching him fish in the creek and telling him folktales to while away the hours. Though illiterate, Rachel was a poised and dignified woman. Jimmy thought of her as an "aristocrat" and a "queen." In the evenings they often played checkers or seven-up, a two-player, trick-taking gambling card game popular in the nineteenth century. Rachel was a small woman—and the best worker on the farm. She could pick 300 to 350 pounds of cotton a day—a hundred pounds more than anyone else, including Jimmy, even when he was seventeen or eighteen years old. "Rachel was not the kind of woman that Mother would ever have asked to do housework," Carter said. "I don't know what Rachel would have done if Mother asked her. She probably would have said, 'Yes, ma'am.' But Rachel was a little too aristocratic to do that kind of work."

She taught Jimmy to fish, but she usually handled seven fishing poles at once and often caught three fish to every one Jimmy caught. But it wasn't a competition. "She was nice and gentle," Carter recalled. Rachel was just very self-assured and independent. In her later years, she'd walk around with Maccoboy snuff in her lip. She always wore a long apron with a can of beer stuffed in the pocket.

"More than anyone else in my family," Carter wrote in his evocative childhood memoir, *An Hour Before Daylight,* "perhaps even including my father, I could understand the plight of the black families, because I lived so much among them. During most of the year they ate only two meals a day, usually cornmeal, fatback, molasses, and perhaps sweet potatoes from our common field. . . . I don't remember any of the tenant family members being the slightest bit overweight." For most of Jimmy's childhood the family cook was a young African American girl named Annie Mae, who began working for them when she was only eleven years old. Jimmy's sister Gloria, born twenty months after him, later said of Annie Mae, "She more or less raised us, all of us. . . . We always had a cook and we always had a man—the foreman [Jack Clark] would come in the wintertime and build fires. He'd build a fire in the stove. . . . He would build a fire in my mother and father's bedroom. . . . And then the cook would come in and fix breakfast." The family ate meat three times a day, fried steak and pork, but also grits, gravy, biscuits, eggs, and all the milk they wanted. Miss Lillian ventured into the kitchen herself only to cook Sunday dinners, usually freshly slaughtered fried chicken with homemade rolls, potato salad, and butter beans.

Jimmy's only real connection to the world outside Archery was the family's battery radio. They listened only occasionally, to such popular radio programs as *Little Orphan Annie, Fibber McGee and Molly,* and *Amos 'n' Andy.* It was a sound from another world.

The terrible albatross of race and the legacy of the "War Between the

States" was a constant reality. William Faulkner, later one of Carter's favorite novelists, described his homeland as a "deep South dead since 1865 and peopled with garrulous outraged baffled ghosts." Carter later read all of Faulkner's novels, and he said that "on many occasions I've read them aloud to my children." He thought Faulkner had captured the struggle between "good and evil . . . perhaps better than any other Southern writer." This southern novelist, he said, understood the "self-condemnation resulting from slavery, the humiliation following the War Between the States." More than most white southerners, the rural folk of South Georgia had defied assimilation and loyally clung to their native culture as a matter of principle. They had their own vernacular and distinctive accent. And they had their own religion, an unvarnished, evangelical southern Protestantism that affirmed the supremacy of the white race in society and patriarchy at home.

Two generations had passed since the Civil War, but that conflagration continued to define their collective identity. "The past is never dead. It's not even past"—so says Gavin Stevens, a character in Faulkner's novel *Requiem for a Nun*. Curtis Wilkie, a celebrated journalist from Mississippi who later covered the Carter administration, wrote in his memoirs, "We deliberately set ourselves apart from the rest of America during the Civil War and continue, to this day, to live as spiritual citizens of a nation that existed for only four years in another century." The South had lost the Civil War, but most if not all white southerners unashamedly celebrated what they revered as the "Lost Cause." On the eve of the Civil War, Georgia was the South's leading slave state, with some 462,000 slaves, or nearly 45 percent of the population. It was also the last southern state to rejoin the Union, in July 1870. It was all about slavery. The South was preoccupied with a history heavily laden with questions about guilt, evil, and sin. History mattered to these Georgians.

"I grew up in one of the families whose people could not forget that we had been conquered," Carter wrote, "while most of our neighbors were black people whose grandparents had been liberated in the same conflict."* Segregation of the races, particularly after adolescence, "was

---

* Carter's great-great-grandfather Wiley Carter died in 1864, leaving forty-three slaves in his will to his twelve children. Many of these nameless slaves are still buried in an unmarked mass grave in the Carter family cemetery.

an accepted fact, never challenged or even debated." Jimmy attended an all-white school in Plains, a village where more than 50 percent of the residents were descendants of slaves.

Earl was a confirmed segregationist. "Jimmy Carter's daddy, I knew him before he died," recalled Bobby Rowan, once a state senator from Enigma, Georgia. "He was a redneck, hard-nosed, hard-driving Southern plantation owner." He called his African American tenants "niggahs." But years later, Miss Lillian staunchly defended her late husband. "Oh, he said things," she told a reporter in 1976. "He believed in the black man's inferiority, but he was no different from all those people around here and all over the country who are now trying to pretend they were never prejudiced. Earl would have changed. . . . It annoys me to hear people denounce him when he was simply a Southern man who lived at a certain time."

When Jimmy was fourteen years old, his father set the family radio on the windowsill to listen to a much-anticipated world heavyweight championship boxing match between the German national Max Schmeling and Joe Louis, at the time America's best-known Black athlete. The event before a crowd of seventy thousand boxing fans in New York's Yankee Stadium was being broadcast on national radio. It was the evening of June 22, 1938, and Earl knew that all his Black sharecropper neighbors were intensely interested in the fight, a rematch of the 1936 bout in which Louis had lost to Schmeling. The German's publicist had brazenly announced that no "Negro" could defeat his Aryan client. Schmeling's winnings, he boasted, would be used to build tanks in Nazi Germany. A major sporting event had thus taken on political overtones, with Schmeling being dubbed by reporters as the "Great White Hope." Earl sat down in his red leather chair near the window to listen to the match. "We didn't have electricity then," Jimmy recalled, "and we hooked the radio up to a battery out of the car."

Dozens of their African American tenants gathered under the big mulberry tree right outside the window and listened quietly to the rematch. "Daddy was so happy that Max Schmeling was going to beat Joe Louis . . . and when Joe Louis almost killed Schmeling, Daddy was despondent." Louis pummeled Schmeling to the floor three times in the first round; the fight was over after just two minutes and four seconds. A disappointed Earl snapped the radio off, and the Black audience gathered outside his window noiselessly walked away. "The blacks walked all the way out of the yard and across the road," Jimmy recalled, and only then did they burst out cheering. "You could have heard them five miles celebrating Louis's victory. . . . That was quite an interesting experience."

Jimmy's childhood was steeped in the Old South. It was then, and arguably has struggled to remain, a nation within a nation, a foreign province that just happens to exist within the boundaries of the Yankee realm. A conquered territory. In the words of W. J. Cash, the author of the deeply melancholic 1941 classic *The Mind of the South,* "the South is another land." Carter himself read the book in the late 1940s. Cash wrote in the anguished voice of a southern intellectual from South Carolina, and his critical portrait of the states that embraced the doomed Confederacy is heartfelt and sadly poignant. He wrote of the South's capacity for violence, its inherent intolerance and "attachment to fictions and false values." But the region's greatest vice, he argued, was its "attachment to racial values and a tendency to justify cruelty and injustice in the name of those values . . . and despite changes for the better, they remain its characteristic vices today."

Cash was writing in the late 1930s, describing precisely the "sleepy old hamlets" and cotton fields that were the scenery of Jimmy Carter's childhood. A belief in white supremacy permeated the red-baked clay earth of South Georgia. It defined the culture of Plains and all other small towns across the Old South. It was a culture that could foster both moments of gentleness and episodes of what the Mississippi journalist Willie Morris labeled "unthinking sadism." Like Faulkner, Morris was one of a legion of astute southern writers who spent their writing lives exploring the curious gulf between the region's "manners and morals, the extraordinary apposition of its violence and kindliness."

That was the way things were and, it seemed, always had been. The defining mystery of the future president's childhood was how he nevertheless was molded into something quite alien from his South Georgian racist culture. He became an outsider from an early age—under the influence of his mother, and less so of his father. Both Earl and Lillian shaped their son's character, providing him and his siblings with a nurturing, if sometimes challenging, environment. But it was Miss Lillian who obviously influenced Jimmy's evolving political instincts, particularly on the central issue of race.

Earl was just a very ordinary southern man who, like virtually all his neighbors, upheld the reigning social order—but in that time and place this meant he believed whites to be superior to Blacks. His relationship to his Black employees and sharecroppers was drenched in patriarchy and condescension—and sometimes compassion. One February day Miss Lillian was called to the shack of Joe Johnson, an African American tenant on the farm. His two-week-old newborn son was terribly sick. Diphtheria was a common affliction. Miss Lillian did what she could, but the baby soon died. The baby's elder sister, Ruth Ann, recalled years later, "After my brother passed, well, her husband [Earl], he came out there that morning and took it upon himself to make one of the most beautiful little old boxes." Earl lined the baby casket with silk. Ruth Ann remembered coming into the room where her baby brother was lying and Miss Lillian telling her, "Ruth Ann, you [can] touch him. . . . There's nothing to be afraid of." She had gathered a bouquet of jonquils, and when Miss Lillian saw this, she took the flowers and tied them together with a red ribbon. After the burial, Joe asked, "Well, what do I owe you for all this?"

"Nothing," Miss Lillian replied. "You don't owe us anything. It's something that I like to do for everybody in our community."

That was the story as told from the memory of Ruth Ann Jackson. Jimmy's sister Gloria remembered the same incident from the other side. Gloria saw Earl working one morning on something outside the farm store. "My Daddy was not a carpenter," Gloria said. But he was building a little casket. He was putting the finishing touches on it, lining it with cotton and then some blue cloth. "And I remember that he was doing that with tears coming down his eyes." Earl was a southern man who could also be moved to tears by the death of a Black baby.

But like nearly all of his white neighbors in Plains, Earl was a "Talmadgist"—a supporter of the populist Georgia politician Governor Eugene Talmadge, an ardent segregationist. "We in the South love the Negro in his place," Talmadge once said, "but his place is at the back door." Jimmy was eight years old in the spring of 1933 when Governor Talmadge spent the night in the Carters' Archery home after giving the commencement address at Plains High School. A year later Earl took his son to a Talmadge campaign barbecue, where they heard "Ol' Gene" rail against the Atlanta establishment. "I can carry any county that ain't got streetcars," Talmadge said. Over the years his blatant race-baiting and demagoguery symbolized the region's cruelest instincts. Lynchings in the South—defined as the extrajudicial killing of Blacks by hanging, shooting, or bludgeoning to death—were not uncommon. Between 1877 and 1950, Georgia was the scene of 589 lynchings—outranked only by Mississippi. Gene Talmadge was undoubtedly one of the worst of Georgia's racist politicians.

Even as a southern Democrat, Talmadge launched fiery attacks on President Franklin Roosevelt's New Deal programs. Earl Carter was of the same view; after the 1932 election, he never again voted for Roosevelt. "He turned against Roosevelt quite bitterly," Carter recalled, "after the government made farmers kill their hogs and plow up their cotton. Daddy thought that was an excessive interference in the freedom of American farmers."

Earl's wife, however, remained a staunch supporter of Roosevelt. Born in 1898, Miss Lillian was always unconventional. Her liberal views on race probably came from her father, a postmaster who had no hesitation about sharing a meal with a Black man. Trained as a nurse, Miss Lillian worked long hours at the local Plains hospital, the Wise Sanitarium, and often paid house visits to both white and Black patients. The sanitarium paid her $4 for a twelve-hour day—the equivalent of about $60 today. Always outspoken, she was not afraid to defend Abraham Lincoln—a singular opinion in South Georgia at the time.

All her life she simply ignored the social boundaries of racial segregation. "She was the first white lady I've seen come into a black people's home," recalled Ruth Jackson, an African American neighbor. Miss Lillian's white neighbors either ignored her transgressions or explained them away as the behavior of an unconventional but privileged southern matriarch. "It seems to me," the president later wrote of his mother, "that the South has a tradition of accommodating eccentrics, as long as they are self-confident, strong enough, or immune to social ostracism." Carter loved his mother and deeply admired her outlier eccentricities. She was a Dodgers baseball fan and traveled to attend their games in the summer. One day, she was in the stadium when Jackie Robinson hit one of his first home runs. Excited, she jumped up and cheered loudly while Earl was pulling on her and saying, "Lily, sit down, sit down! Look around you!" Earl said she was the only white person standing up. "I didn't care," she said. "He hit a home run. He's a person, just like me."

Miss Lillian was regarded by everyone as an outspoken eccentric. She smoked cigarettes and occasionally drank wine, and late at night she and Earl regularly shared a bourbon nightcap. Raised a Methodist, Miss Lillian joined the Plains Baptist Church—but often skipped the services, just like her husband. Some parishioners made it known that they were scandalized by her fraternization with African Americans. But Miss Lillian didn't give a damn. "We had too much money to be ostracized," she recalled. "We were the biggest contributors." Her nephew Hugh Carter recalled, "She was considered the most flamboyant woman of the community, doing what she wanted to do even if it was against the tide of opinion." Miss Lillian broke the norms, particularly when it came to race. She encouraged Jimmy to play outdoors with the sons of their African American neighbors. This alone was regarded as "almost a taboo thing in Plains." But she also invited these young Black boys to sit at the dining table with him, play in his room—and "even lie on his bed."

Like many white families, the Carters always employed an African American woman to do most of the cooking, particularly since Miss Lillian worked long hours outside the home. She made a habit of leaving a note on a little black side table, reminding Jimmy to sweep the yard, haul in some stove wood, and feed the chickens. Her absence was such that Jimmy began teasing her that he thought that desk was his mother for the longest time. He knew this aggravated her. Miss Lillian used to deny how much time she spent out of the home nursing patients. "But the strong memory in my mind," Jimmy recalled, "is coming home and Mother not being here."

In the evenings when the family gathered for dinner, everyone but Earl brought a book to the table. This was Miss Lillian's habit, and she expected her children to use the time not for dinner-table chat but to read. "We weren't allowed to talk at the table," Jimmy's sister Gloria recalled. "People would come to see us, you know, and we'd sit at the table and we'd have our food and they always thought, 'Well, what's wrong?' " Reading was mandatory. Miss Lillian got her books from the Book of the Month Club. "Every Christmas when I was asked by Santa Claus what I wanted," Jimmy recalled, "I always said books." He had a complete collection of Victor Hugo, many of the Tom Swift books, and eleven of Edgar Rice Burroughs's Tarzan adventure novels. He was eleven years old when he first read Tolstoy's *War and Peace*. And she made a point of never interrupting any child who was reading—not even to nag them about their chores. Hugh Carter—known as Cousin Beedie—recalled dining with the Carters, but because he had no book with him, "I would study my plate and just look around while everyone else read. After Jimmy ate, he would throw himself down on the couch and read a little more until his food digested. Then he would jump up and we would go out and continue our games."

The towering mulberry tree growing near the house seemed to exist only so children could climb it. "We could take a running start bare-footed," said Gloria, "and hit the top of the tree before we opened our eyes." Jimmy was a resilient, athletic boy, but accidents did happen. He broke his arm twice. And when he was six years old, he was playing with a friend three doors down from the Plains home of Rosalynn Smith—his future wife, who was then only three—when he crossed the dirt road and was run over by the local school bus. The driver was Sonny Fair-cloth, an employee of Rosalynn's daddy. "I saw the bus coming and I tried to turn around, but I slid, and the school bus wheels ran over both my feet." The bones in both feet were broken. "For several months," Carter recalled, "I could only walk on my heels." He told this frightening story only once, many decades later, and spoke nothing of the trauma of this near-death experience. But perhaps the incident speaks to a certain fatalistic resilience in the young boy's character.

Jimmy and Cousin Beedie sometimes would sell bags of boiled pea-nuts outside the one bank in "downtown" Plains. In the summers they would sell three dips of homemade ice cream for a nickel. Rosalynn's first memory of speaking to Jimmy was when he sold her an ice cream cone in the old bank building. Cousin Beedie would make Jimmy walk up and down the dirt street shouting, "I scream, you scream, we all scream for ice cream!" Then they'd wander down to Will Kennedy's gro-cery store late at night and buy a half pound of hamburger meat, a loaf of white bread, and some onions. "We would mix the meat with the squished-up bread and onions," Carter recalled, "and we sold our ham-burgers for five cents each." These were the Depression years and money was scarce. But Jimmy saved his nickels and later bought five bales of cotton for five cents a pound. When the price of cotton hit eighteen cents per pound, Carter sold his cotton bales and in 1940 bought five dilapidated shacks. At the age of fifteen, he was a landlord, renting out the shacks for $2 a month.

As a teenager, Jimmy helped his father make sausage every winter. Earl had his own spicy flavoring. It was an elaborate operation. "We'd go in there," Carter said, "and shoot twenty hogs [with a .22-caliber rifle], string them up by their hind legs, cut out their entrails, separate the intestines. . . . The women would start washing them, turn them wrong side outwards for sausage casing, and separate the heart, which the blacks on the place always wanted. . . . Daddy would save the brains. We had brains and eggs for breakfast." Every Fourth of July the family would slaughter three or four hogs and a couple of goats, and Earl would invite everybody in Archery for a free barbecue.

Earl and Lillian had three more children: Gloria, born in 1926, Ruth, born in 1929—and Billy, who came along as an afterthought in 1937. Earl nicknamed Billy "Buckshot." Gloria was "GoGo," and pretty, golden-haired Ruth was "Boop-a-Doop." Earl indulged these offspring in a way he did not with his firstborn son. He had expectations for Jimmy. And because his wife was often out of the house nursing patients, he was the disciplinarian and always a looming presence. He made sure his young son rose early and worked hard after school hours, picking cotton or stacking peanut plants. Earl was a stern and demanding father; he never praised his son—whom he called "Hot Shot." Earl whipped him exactly six times between the ages of four and fifteen. Jimmy vividly remembered each whipping—and the instrument used: a long and thin peach tree switch. "Daddy's spankings were not anything to be scoffed at." He later wrote a revealing poem about his father entitled "I Wanted to Share My Father's World."

> *This is a pain I mostly hide,*
> *But ties of blood, or seed, endure,*
> *And even now I feel inside*
> *The hunger for his outstretched hand,*
> *A man's embrace to take me in,*
> *The need for just a word of praise.*
> *I despised the discipline.*

Earl was also a stickler for being on time. He once walked out of a physician's office because the doctor was five minutes late for his appointment. Jimmy later ran White House meetings with the same unforgiving exactness.

The Carters kept farmers' hours. The farm's foreman, Jack Clark, rang a heavy iron bell early every morning. Jimmy was awakened by the ringing of that bell an hour before dawn—a habit he kept for the rest of his life. At sundown, after working in the fields, somebody would shout "sundown" and Jimmy would run home, clean up, and eat supper, and then everyone went to bed. Except Jimmy often stayed up a little longer, lying down in front of the fireplace in wintertime. "At eight o'clock I would turn on the radio for fifteen minutes and listen to Glenn Miller. . . . Usually, I was the last one in bed. And that was 8:15 PM. That was sun time." Things changed when they finally got electricity.

The absolute worst job on the farm was what they called "mopping cotton." Poison had to be applied to each bud of cotton to fight off the boll weevils and boll worms. Earl mixed up a horrible yellow concoction of molasses, water, and arsenic in a gallon bucket. And then Jimmy had to walk through the fields with a three-foot stick with a rag mop attached to the bottom. Jimmy remembered, "You would dip your mop in the bucket and then put your mop in the bud of every cotton plant and this poison would kill the boll weevils. And, of course, it didn't take you long walking down the cotton rows until your pants were covered with syrup . . . and the flies would come from a hundred yards away, you know, attracted by the molasses. And your legs would be covered with molasses and by the end of the day, the molasses would get hard, like sugar. You'd take your pants off at night and you'd have to stand your pants in the corner. They wouldn't bend. And then, to get up the next morning and put those sticky, hard-coated pants on was, you know, a very icky feeling."

Jimmy was only twelve years old when he started driving his father's pickup truck. Earl sent him from time to time on errands to pick up seed or fertilizer. And by thirteen, he was using the pickup to go on dates. Social life revolved around events sponsored by the Baptist Young People's Union. His first sweetheart was a girl named Eloise Ratliff, though everyone called her "Teenie." It didn't last, if only because a boy from out of town moved into Plains, and he had both a car and a motorcycle and stole Teenie away from Jimmy. There were other girlfriends.

One day when Jimmy was twelve years old, his father called him into the bathroom and closed the door. Earl sat down on the commode and said, "Jimmy, I got something very serious I want to talk to you about." Carter knew that when his father called him "Jimmy" he was in trouble. "I thought he was going to tell me about sex or something like that. I said, 'Yes sir.'"

"There's a promise I want you to make to me," said Earl.

"Daddy, I'll promise you anything."

"I want you to promise that you won't smoke a cigarette until you're twenty-one years old."

Jimmy replied, "I promise."

As an incentive, Earl said he would give him a gold watch if he didn't smoke until he was twenty-one. Jimmy was already an extremely disciplined boy, and he kept his promise. On the day he turned twenty-one, he bought a pack of cigarettes and took one puff. Disgusted, he never touched another cigarette. Earl smoked three packs a day. He had tried to quit but never succeeded.

Jimmy was a bright and emotionally intelligent child. And stubborn. One day in the fifth grade, his teacher, Mrs. Jeanette Davis, left the room momentarily and upon returning discovered that someone had swept her belongings off the desk and into the trash. She accused Jimmy and demanded that he retrieve her stuff from the trash. "I refused because I hadn't done it." When she threatened him with a bad grade, he was unmoved. "It was a big deal in my life," Carter recalled, but he wasn't going to be cowed. Mrs. Davis talked with his father, and eventually she conceded that Jimmy probably was innocent—but she still insisted that he had to be the one to retrieve her belongings from the trash. Jimmy agreed, but he "wasn't going to do it as long as she was insinuating that I was the one that threw it in the trash." Jimmy had stood his ground and his teacher backed down.

The Plains School never had more than three hundred students, grades one through eleven. It was all white, but it had a mix of relatively well-off children like the Carters and some students from very poor families. Times were hard. "I went to school one whole year without a pair of shoes to wear," recalled one student from the 1930s. "My old feet would crack open and I'd have to go home crying at night and get tallow that we had by the fireplace." Jimmy always had shoes in the winter. Classes averaged twenty-five students.

Miss Julia Coleman was the school's long-standing superintendent. She taught English literature and made her students participate in weekly debates and one-act plays. "I don't care how black the clouds looked out there," said one of her students, "she could make you see that pretty blue. . . . She believed in poetry and she believed in seeing the beauty of the world." A "spinster" from Mississippi, Miss Coleman was born with one leg shorter than the other. She gave Jimmy special attention. "She was always challenging me to read classical books and to learn about great painters." Jimmy thought her "an extraordinary teacher." She made him listen to symphonies and operas and then would quiz him on the names of the composers. Even as an adult, when listening to any music, he made a habit of always memorizing the names of the composers.

Schoolwork also exposed him to basic science—and this naturally led to "a nagging degree of skepticism about the relationship between my faith and the scientific point of view." At the age of eleven, while attending a local revival service, Carter had "decided to accept Christ." And accordingly, the following Sunday he was baptized. This was pretty much what all young Baptist boys did at that age. It was tradition. But later he had to explain that he had not been "born again" at the age of eleven. That was to come later; being born again was "an evolutionary thing."

As a boy, Carter just took it for granted that whites and Blacks attended separate schools. One day when he was about fourteen years old, he and two Black friends were walking back from working in the fields north of Archery, and as the boys approached the pasture gate, Carter was startled to see his two friends stop and make a show of holding the gate open so he could pass through first. For a moment, he worried that they were playing some trick on him, but then he realized that their parents had probably told them "that the time had come to conform to the racial distinctions that were strictly observed among adults." It was a minor incident, but Carter would never forget that moment.

*   *   *

ON SUNDAY, DECEMBER 7, 1941, seventeen-year-old Jimmy was lying in
a hammock under a large chinaberry tree right outside his bedroom in
Archery when he heard on the radio that Pearl Harbor had been attacked by Japanese aircraft. The outbreak of war only renewed his long-
standing ambition to attend the Naval Academy in Annapolis. He always
knew he wanted to go to college, but he assumed for financial reasons
that he would either have to attend a local state university or gain admit-
tance to West Point or Annapolis. His mother's young brother, Uncle
Tom, had joined the navy and used to send Jimmy postcards from his
seafaring life. This relationship inspired Jimmy to think about the navy.
Decades later he would recall, "So if anyone asked me, even as early as
six or seven years old, 'What would you like to do when you grow up?'
instead of saying, 'I want to be a fireman' or something like that, I always
said, 'I want to go to Annapolis.'"

Earl made it happen. As Jimmy was graduating from Plains High
School, Earl lobbied their local congressman, Representative Stephen
Pace (D-GA), to nominate Jimmy for admission to the Academy. Jimmy
spent the next two years in a community college in Americus and at
Georgia Tech in Atlanta, studying engineering, but he was finally accepted for the class of 1947—and so left for Annapolis on June 26, 1943.
Earl was proud of his eighteen-year-old son—but also anxious. After all,
his firstborn son was going off to the navy in the midst of a world war.
"After Jimmy's noon departure," wrote the biographer and historian
E. Stanly Godbold, Jr., "Earl drove to pick up his friend Raymond Sullivan, went to an isolated pond, and drank whiskey until dark. Taking her
own automobile, Lillian drove alone to a different pond, where she
fished and wept."

AS A NAVAL Academy plebe, Midshipman Carter, 4th Class, had to endure the usual period of hazing. When some upperclassmen ordered
him to sing "Marching Through Georgia"—a battle hymn that celebrated
General William T. Sherman's scorched-earth march through Georgia
in late 1864—Carter flatly refused. Sherman was anathema for any
southerner. For this defiance he was called a "cracker" and required to

sit awkwardly at his mess table without touching his chair. Jimmy was stoic. "My main trouble," he wrote in his diary, "was that I smiled too much." His superiors were constantly telling him to "wipe it off." In the eyes of his peers, Carter seemed overly eager, and too stoic for a wiry, boyish man who weighed only 130 pounds.

Many of his classmates were southerners, and all were white. The following year, Carter befriended Wesley Brown, the sole African American, a midshipman from New York. The two young men ran together on the Academy's cross-country team. "I ran with you," Carter later wrote to Brown, but "you were better." Not surprisingly, Brown was subjected to relentless harassment. On one occasion, he was forced by an upperclassman to do three sets of forty-nine push-ups, and when he emerged looking shaken and downcast, Jimmy intercepted him, put his arm around him, and said something encouraging. As he walked away, Brown heard another midshipman refer to Jimmy as a "goddamn nigger lover."

Carter graduated from the Naval Academy on June 11, 1946, one year early owing to an accelerated wartime schedule. Just a few weeks later, Navy ensign Carter married Rosalynn Smith in Plains. They had known each other slightly all their lives. "When we got married," Rosalynn said, "I think I was kin to everybody that Jimmy wasn't. Once we got married, we were kin to everybody in town." Rosalynn was the best friend of Jimmy's sister Ruth—who had conspired to put them together. They had begun dating and corresponding only the previous year. "I always said," Rosalynn recalled, "I fell in love with a photograph of him on her bedroom wall. My mother said it must have been his white uniform." Rosalynn was just eighteen years old when Jimmy found himself back in Plains on a few weeks' break from Annapolis. Jimmy dialed 6-1-1—the three-digit phone number for the Smith home in Plains—and asked to speak to the girl he called "Rosie." "She was remarkably beautiful," Jimmy later wrote, "almost painfully shy, obviously intelligent, and yet unrestrained in our discussions on the rumble seat of the Ford Coupe." He proposed to her in February 1946 and initially she put him off. She had wanted to attend college—but in May she agreed, and on July 7, 1946, they were married in a private ceremony at the Plains Baptist Church. They were both virgins.

"Rosie" was disarmingly enchanting, a pretty young woman with high cheekbones, dark eyes, and a demure smile. The novelist Norman

Mailer later described her with colorful language: "With her heart-shaped face, her large eyes, her direct features, her absence of patrician hesitation to approve or judge, she could have been a hostess or waitress, but a most marvelous, intelligent and attractive waitress—a movie star of a waitress in a good 1930's film—the sort who gives you cheer about the future of the human condition."

They began married life on various navy bases on the East Coast, until early 1949, when Jimmy was posted to Pearl Harbor. They spent fifteen delightful months in Hawaii. By then he had graduated from submarine school, an elite and arduous service. One night off the coast of China, Carter was standing night duty on the deck of a surfaced submarine, the USS *Pomfret* (SS-391), when he suddenly saw a mammoth wave approaching. Carter ducked down and wrapped his arms around a rail—but the wave buried the submarine under a wall of water and Carter was swept from the bridge into the ocean. He later wrote that this was his "first experience with impending death." But improbably, when the wave receded, Carter found himself landing back on the rear deck, where he managed to cling to a five-inch mounted gun. He was just damn lucky.

His weeks at sea left him longing for his young wife. "Oh, Rosalynn, my darling, I love you so very, very much," he wrote her on August 23, 1949. "It's funny, but when I first leave you, I miss more than anything your mouth and breasts and body and the way you feel and smell to me when we're making love. But after a day or so those things become less and less important to me, and I want to touch your hair and hold your hand or look at you across the room. . . . I feel lonely and lost, and it seems that I am not really living but just waiting to live again when you are with me."

For two years Carter was assigned as the ranking officer after the executive officer aboard one of the navy's new attack submarines, the SS K-1. The boat was particularly sleek and claustrophobic. "When I was lying on my back [in my bunk]," Carter recalled, "there was not enough space for a paperback book to be opened on my chest." Carter actually reveled in work that demanded close attention to detail—and extreme punctuality.

Carter was aboard one of his submarines in 1948 when President Harry Truman issued an executive order ending segregation in the armed forces. Out of sixty-one officers training that year to be submariners, he had been the only officer openly supporting Truman in the 1948 presidential election. "I didn't think he had a chance to win," Carter recalled. "But I was a staunch Truman supporter." One day his commander overheard Carter engaging in a heated discussion about politics with his fellow junior officers. Soon afterward, Carter was summoned, and the commander poked a flashlight forcefully into his chest and said angrily, "Either choose the navy or politics." Carter was stunned at this insulting treatment from an officer he found lacking in any leadership qualities. His morale sank and he began to wonder whether he'd made a "dreadful mistake" in choosing a naval career.

But he stuck it out, and three years later, Carter found himself serving aboard another boat with a lone African American submariner, a popular sailor named Russell. One day, after the submarine anchored in Nassau harbor, the British governor-general invited the Americans to an official ballroom dance. But when word was sent that nonwhite crewmen were not welcome, Carter persuaded his fellow crew members to turn down the invitation. Later that year, when visiting his parents on home leave, Carter mentioned the incident. Earl reacted by silently leaving the room, and Miss Lillian explained, "Jimmy, it's too soon for our folks here to think about black and white people going to a dance together." Rosalynn remembers that Jimmy and Earl "disagreed so much on politics . . . they'd get very upset and so they just didn't talk about it." Perhaps he was simply revolting against his father's racism. In any case, the young naval officer was painfully aware of his own provincialism.

In June 1952, Carter was promoted to full lieutenant; he might someday command his own submarine. But ever ambitious, Carter then applied for admission to the navy's highly secret program to construct two state-of-the-art nuclear submarines, the *Nautilus* and the *Seawolf.* The program was headed by Captain Hyman G. Rickover, a brilliant, pugnacious, and often rudely irascible officer later promoted to rear admiral in 1953. "Sharp-tongued Hyman Rickover spurred his men to exhaustion, ripped through red tape, drove contractors into rages. He went on making enemies," reported *Time* magazine in 1953. But he nevertheless "won a reputation as a man who gets things done." Carter would never forget his searing two-hour interview. Rickover's style was to intimidate; he made an unknowing Carter sit in a chair with two front legs shortened—so the young man had the odd sensation of feeling himself sliding off the chair for the entire interview. Rickover began by asking Carter to select a topic for discussion—submarine strategy, current politics, electronics—and then the admiral bored in with questions to show that Carter knew less than he thought. They discussed Herman Wouk's novel *The Caine Mutiny*, Shakespeare, William Faulkner, and Ernest Hemingway. Finally, Rickover asked Carter if he had always done his best in the Naval Academy. Carter was about to answer in the clear affirmative but hesitated and then replied truthfully, "No, sir, I didn't always do my best."

Rickover stared at him intensely and finally asked, "Why not?" Then Rickover turned his back and began shuffling through some papers on his desk. Carter waited a few minutes to be dismissed and then quietly got up and left the room, convinced that he had been rejected.

Instead, Rickover soon assigned Carter to work on the early design of a high-capacity prototype reactor for the USS *Seawolf,* the nation's second nuclear-powered submarine. His duties included studying theoretical nuclear physics at Union College.* Few naval officers were given such elite training in nuclear engineering. In the midst of his studies, Carter was ordered in December 1952 to assist in the emergency disassembly of a heavy-water reactor at Chalk River in Canada. Due to an accidental loss of water coolant, the reactor core had experienced a meltdown and hydrogen explosions. Intense radioactivity required the cleanup crews—including Carter and his navy team—to don white protective suits and masks; even so, each man could spend no more than ninety seconds inside the reactor core building, hastily removing a bolt or pipe. Slowly and methodically, the crews succeeded in dismantling the damaged core, and two years later the reactor was brought back online. The experience did nothing to lessen Carter's belief in the efficiency of nuclear power generation—and it would inform his own handling as president in 1979 of another nuclear accident, Three Mile Island.

Carter admired Rickover in the same way he admired his father—from a distance. "We feared and respected him and strove to please him," Carter later said of his time with Rickover. "I do not in that period remember his ever saying a complimentary word to me. . . . Rickover was not dissimilar from my father. He scared me." But what Carter particularly revered about Rickover was the officer's willingness to buck the navy

---

* In 2005, the navy commissioned a high-tech version of the *Seawolf* class of nuclear submarine and named it the USS *Jimmy Carter* (SSN-23); Rosalynn Carter christened the boat.

establishment in the interest of doing the right thing. As one of Carter's early biographers, Peter Bourne, observed, "Being right was for Rickover a legitimate substitute for being political. It was a perspective on government that to some extent rubbed off on his subordinate Jimmy Carter."

BY 1953, LIEUTENANT Carter had every reason to believe that he was headed for a distinguished naval career. That spring, Admiral Rickover recommended him for promotion, praising his "excellent progress in learning the technical aspects of nuclear engineering." But then in April Jimmy got a phone call from his cousin Don Carter, reporting that Daddy Earl was gravely ill. By June, Lillian conveyed the sad news that Earl had been diagnosed with terminal pancreatic cancer. Jimmy took two weeks of emergency family leave to visit his dying father. Earl was in pain but fully cognizant. Sitting by his bed, Jimmy later wrote, he had "the longest and most thorough conversations I had ever had with him." Jimmy had been absent from Plains almost continuously for the past decade, but now he was getting to know his father through the eyes of an adult. What he saw was a father more complicated—and more benevolent—than the stern, distant father of his childhood. He had always felt emotionally torn and ambivalent about his father. Earl's racism and provincialism were traits that the now well-traveled navy officer clearly found distasteful. But during this last visit he saw in Earl a moral fiber that mirrored his own values.

Earl had secured his family's fortune—and in the last decade he had devoted himself to social welfare and politics. He served on the country school board, helped to build Sumter County's first school for African American children, and worked to bring electricity to rural southwest Georgia. In 1951, he won a seat in the state legislature, running as a loyal "Talmadgist"—this time loyal to the son of "Ol' Gene," Governor Herman Talmadge. But to his surprise Jimmy learned from a stream of visitors to this father's deathbed, most of them African Americans, that Earl had also become an anonymous philanthropist, giving away money to the poorest of the rural poor, Black and white.

Earl died on July 22, 1953, at the age of fifty-nine, cradled in the arms of Annie Mae Hollis, his former house cook, and surrounded by his family. Jimmy later wrote that as his father took his "last tortured breath," Annie Mae "never flinched when she was covered with his black vomit."

Chapter 2
A Peculiar Heritage

Jimmy is so naïve, so naïve.
—MISS LILLIAN

Carter shoveling peanuts
JIMMY CARTER PRESIDENTIAL LIBRARY AND MUSEUM

EARL'S EARLY DEATH precipitated what Carter would call "one of the strangest and most unexpected events in my life." Within weeks, he made a precipitate decision to abandon his promising career in the navy and return to Plains. Rosalynn was aghast and even furious. "I argued," Rosalynn wrote later. "I cried. I even screamed at him. I loved our life in the Navy and the independence I had finally achieved. . . . Plains had too many ghosts for me." By some accounts, she even threatened

Jimmy with divorce. "She almost quit me," Carter said. But Jimmy was determined. His decision was spurred by a mosaic of feelings, some stemming from new insights about his father's benevolent role in the Plains community but others from a growing unease about dedicating his life to a military bureaucracy. "God did not intend for me to spend my life working on instruments of destruction to kill people." Carter confided this to his friend Dr. Peter Bourne in August 1976—just one month after his selection as the Democratic Party's nominee for president. He was not a pacifist. But with his father's death he had come to realize that he had made the wrong career choice. At the age of twenty-nine, it took enormous courage—and self-confidence—to walk away from the navy.

On the other hand, when he told his mother of his decision, Miss Lillian was not surprised. "He had to come back," she said. "Everything we had was on the line." Jimmy had to learn how to be a farmer. This red-soil farmland had been tilled by Carters since 1833—and Jimmy felt he could not abandon it. He had been gone a decade. And to be sure, traveling north, and indeed all over the world with the U.S. Navy, had been transformational. The boy from Plains could now see the South through cosmopolitan eyes. But the southerner in him would always be there. And like many other southern expatriates, he was emotionally drawn back to the place.

Willie Morris, another southern liberal who left and came back, described his emotions in his elegiac 1967 memoir *North Toward Home:* "I had the most over-whelming sense of coming home, to some place that belonged to me; I was not merely stunned by its beauty, for this was not new to me; I was surprised to feel so settled inside, as if nothing, no matter how cruel and despairing, could destroy my belonging." Morris could admit that he came from "the most brutal part of America." He was writing about coming home to Mississippi—but there was plenty of cruelty and despair in southern Georgia when Jimmy Carter came home in the early 1950s. Whites still treated their Black neighbors with a disturbing blend of gentle paternalism and criminal unkindnesses.

Sumter County had been the scene of five documented lynchings in the years from 1898 through 1920. All five lynchings occurred before Carter's birth in 1924, but all took place well within the collective memory of his kin. These things were talked about, often in whispers—but talked about and remembered. And then, a few years before Carter came home to Plains, newspapers around the country reported on the particularly gruesome murders of two African American couples at Moore's Ford Bridge, near Monroe, Georgia—about forty miles east of Atlanta in Walton County. On July 25, 1946—just two weeks after Jimmy and Rosalynn were married in Plains—a mob of twenty white males, none of them masked, stopped a car on a lonely stretch of road, pulled out the two Black men, bound them with ropes, and dragged them off to the side of the dirt road. One of the Black women sitting in the car then loudly cursed the name of a man she recognized in the mob. Hearing her curses, the mob's leader was heard to order, "Get those bitches too." The two women had to be pried out of the car, but soon they too were dragged down to the river.

All four were then summarily executed with three rounds of gunfire. The mob's primary target, a twenty-four-year-old sharecropper named Roger Malcom, had just been released on bail, having been charged eleven days earlier with stabbing and wounding his landlord, Barnette Hester, during a drunken scuffle. The young Black sharecropper and his white landlord were childhood friends. They had worked alongside each other in the fields for years. Another victim, who just happened to be in the car, George W. Dorsey, twenty-eight, was a decorated army veteran who had fought in the Pacific during World War II. His wife, Mae Murray Dorsey, was twenty-three years old. And his sister, Dorothy Dorsey, twenty years old, was living with Malcom and called herself "Mrs. Malcom." All four victims were known to the people, white or Black, of Walton County. And so were their killers.

It was the first lynching in Georgia in three years, and it made headlines across the country. Five thousand people gathered in New York's Madison Square Garden to protest the lynchings. Thousands more protesters marched in Pittsburgh, Boston, Tampa, Detroit, and other cities. Four days after the murders, *The New York Times* reported that "President Truman was horrified by the lynching of four Negroes in Georgia last week." The president ordered the FBI to investigate the crime—but the *Times* soon reported that the investigation was being hampered by a "reluctance of Walton County citizens to talk about the affair." The local Walton County sheriff, E. S. Gordon, said that federal officers "are better qualified to handle this case than we are." The Grand Dragon of the

Georgia Knights of the Ku Klux Klan, Dr. Samuel Green of Atlanta, solemnly issued a statement denying that the KKK had any part in the massacre. Former Georgia governor Eugene Talmadge—who had just won the Democratic nomination to be reelected governor—issued a statement saying that "such atrocities" as these lynchings would be "at a minimum" in his upcoming term in office. Even at the time, it was clear to everyone that Talmadge had no interest in apprehending the killers. *The Washington Post* published a Herblock cartoon depicting a southern sheriff toting a shotgun, walking through the crime site, and saying to his buddy, "It's okay—Ol' Gene Will Be Back Soon." To no one's surprise, Talmadge won the November 1946 election—and then he died suddenly in December.

Decades after his death, evidence emerged that Talmadge may have personally played a role in instigating the infamous Monroe lynchings. FBI records revealed that Talmadge allegedly offered immunity to anyone "taking care of [the] negro" who was accused of stabbing and wounding the white farmer. The FBI sent twenty-five agents into Walton County and spent four months investigating the murders; they interviewed 2,790 people, and 106 individuals testified before a grand jury. Fifty-five suspects were identified, but to this day, the Moore's Ford Bridge lynchings remain unsolved and the grand jury transcripts remain sealed.

The 1946 lynchings stunned America and compelled President Truman to jump-start a national conversation on race. A 1947 presidential commission on civil rights eventually recommended federal antilynching laws, the elimination of the poll tax, and various other reforms, none of which were passed at the time but which became key demands of a reinvigorated civil rights movement in the 1950s. On July 26, 1948—two years after the Moore's Ford Bridge massacre—Truman issued Executive Order 9981, desegregating the military. A defiant Truman talked about the infamous lynchings during his 1948 presidential campaign, saying, "When the mob gangs can take four people out and shoot them in the back, and everybody in the country is acquainted with who did the shootings and nothing is done about it, that country is in a pretty bad fix. I am going to try to remedy it, and if that ends up in my failure to be elected, that failure will be in a good cause." Southern politicians decried

Truman's criticisms of the South. Georgia's junior senator, Richard Russell, said, "Mr. Truman's unwarranted attack on our Southern civilization has made me sick at heart." The Moore's Ford Bridge massacre signaled the end of the Jim Crow era and instigated the modern civil rights movement.

Carter must have read about the lynchings in that summer of 1946—and the controversy it stirred across the nation. By then he was back up north, stationed in Norfolk, Virginia, with his bride, focused on his career in the navy. But he knew all about "Ol' Gene" Talmadge—and he was an ardent supporter of Truman's in the 1948 election. When he left the navy and came home to Plains in 1953, he knew he was returning to a sometimes violent land imbued with a racist culture. "We love it and we hate it," Willie Morris wrote about the South. "And we cannot turn our backs on it."

WHEN EARL DIED, his farm had one pickup truck; mules and horses were still the engines of motion. Cotton was still being picked by hand, and likewise the peanuts. This was still the agrarian South, not far removed from the nineteenth century and described by the great southern historian C. Vann Woodward as "the one-horse farmer, one-crop agriculture, one-party politics, the sharecropper, the poll tax, the white primary, the Jim Crow car, the lynching bee." But this life was already disappearing. Woodward noted that in 1930, 5.5 million southerners were employed on the farm—but by 1950 this figure had declined to 3.2 million. Blacks and whites alike were moving to the cities. And in the aftermath of World War II, nearly a half million African American veterans came home to the South, proud of their national service and determined to upend southern social norms. The New South was being born.

Carter discovered that he was land rich but cash poor. He was also only one of five heirs, and most of the estate's cash went to pay back taxes. He and Rosalynn moved into public housing, and he had to take out a loan for $10,000. That first year they sold three thousand tons of fertilizer in one-hundred- and two-hundred-pound bags—all on credit to local farmers. "I loaded every ton of it myself," Carter recalled. They also sold seed and other supplies to South Georgia farmers, but their gross income that first year was a mere $280. The following year, how-ever, the harvest was plentiful, and they collected $5,000 on their ac-counts. They plowed all their profits back into the peanut-seed business. The navy engineer in Carter soon designed his own peanut-shelling plant "to treat every peanut as though it was a fragile egg. . . . It got so that we couldn't grow enough peanuts to supply the farmers who wanted our seed."

Jimmy loved his new-old life in Plains. It was where he belonged. The tiny sunbaked town was really no more than a sleepy, bucolic commu-nity. A surprising number of its rambling wooden houses, nearly all painted white, were about fifty years old. The ample front lawns were green and shaded by oak, pecan, and elm trees. There was one gas sta-tion, a general store, a shabby barbecue shack, and a one-room train station adjacent to the train tracks that crossed the main street. The most substantial buildings in town were the Plains High School and not one but several Baptist and Methodist churches. Plains was not even a small town; it was a hamlet, a place where everyone literally knew every-one. Carter joined the Lions Club and volunteered for the local hospital and public library. Later, he was elected chairman of the Sumter County School Board. He even became a scoutmaster for the local Boy Scouts. It was a life idealized by Norman Rockwell's drawings in *The Saturday Eve-ning Post*.

Except it was rural southwest Georgia—and so one summer day in 1955 a dozen of Carter's peanut warehouse customers paid him a visit and suggested that he join the White Citizens' Council—basically the Klan in business suits. When he politely declined, they offered to pay on his behalf the $5 annual membership fee. At this, Carter lost patience, angrily took out his own $5 bill, and announced that he'd sooner "flush it down the toilet" than give it to the White Citizens' Council. That eve-ning, he mentioned the incident to Rosalynn, who winced. As book-keeper, she worried about their cash flow and feared a boycott. "I was really worried," she later told a reporter. "But I was also very proud of Jimmy. Those people were ugly. They were all wrapped up in small, mean things and I was so proud that he had stood up to them; I think Jimmy was proud of himself, too." Later, someone placed a handwritten sign on the Carter Peanut Warehouse reading "Coons and Carters Go Together."

South Georgia, and Sumter County in particular, were hotbeds of racism. The leading citizens of nearby Americus were members of an active chapter of the John Birch Society. The Americus newspaper, the *Times-Recorder,* featured a regular Birch Society column on its editorial page. This was Klan country—which made it all the more striking that one of Carter's neighbors, Dr. Clarence Jordan, had decided to establish an interracial commune on a 440-acre farm just seven miles down the road from Plains. Jordan was reared in South Georgia, but he nevertheless grew up to be one of those stalwart liberal activists, a rare but defiant strain in southern culture.

Born in 1912, Jordan earned a degree in agriculture from the University of Georgia in 1933—and then obtained a doctorate in Greek New Testament studies from the Southern Baptist Theological Seminary in Louisville, Kentucky. His biographer, Dallas Lee, wrote that he was a bundle of contradictory virtues: "He was a gentle man who thundered, a nonviolent man who was known to have stared down a Ku Kluxer or two, a man with much to say who listened patiently, a genuinely humble man who could walk into the home of an affluent person and say: 'Nice piece of plunder you have here.' He was a dirt-farming aristocrat, a good ol' Georgia country boy with a doctor's degree, a teacher with manure on his boots, a scholar in working clothes." He was a soapbox preacher who always read the Bible in the Greek. In 1942 Jordan and his wife founded Koinonia Farm, so named after the earliest of Christian communes, where everyone shared all things in common. In defiance of virtually all of his neighbors in South Georgia, Clarence was determined to build a truly Christian farming community where whites and Blacks lived together, farming the land and dining at a common table.

In the early 1950s, a young Martin Luther King, Jr., heard about Jordan's interracial commune and invited him to speak at the Dexter Avenue Baptist Church in Montgomery, Alabama. "It was shocking and inspiring," King recalled, "and sounded too good to be true. Here was a son of the Old South, a white Baptist preacher doing what we were just talking about doing. I went to Koinonia later to see it for myself and couldn't wait to leave because I was sure that Klan would show up and kill us both." King later described Clarence as "my friend, my mentor, and my inspiration." The two preachers occasionally corresponded with each other during the 1950s, and in June 1962 Jordan heard King preach in nearby Albany in the midst of that city's highly contentious voter reg-istration drive.*

Not surprisingly, Jordan and his Koinonia Farm became targets. One evening, Klansmen drove by the farm and raked it with machine-gun fire. Its roadside produce stand was dynamited. On another occasion, three hundred apple, peach, and pecan trees were chopped down. In 1956–57, Klansmen, known as night riders, repeatedly fired bullets into Koinonia and dynamited the property. One night, the Klan erected a large wooden cross wrapped with oil-saturated burlap and set it afire. The attacks became so routine that the community of forty-five white people and fifteen African Americans felt compelled to appoint some-one each night to serve as a watchman with a flashlight.

Segregationists organized a long-standing boycott of the radical com-mune. Only one local businessman, Herbert Birdsey, the owner of the Birdsey Flour and Feed Store, attempted publicly to defy the boycott, writing to Jordan that his store would sell him cattle feed. But at 1:00 A.M. on May 19, 1957, a bomb ripped through the Birdsey store in Ameri-cus, completely destroying it. "Violence is foreign to our way of life and thinking," intoned an editorialist for the *Americus Times-Recorder*. "Re-gardless of how we feel toward Koinonia, this violence, from whatever source it comes, must be stopped." The "peace-loving" and "church-going" people of Americus may have been in denial about the Klan-inspired attacks, but the Birdsey explosion signaled to the local establishment that things were getting out of hand.

A week after the explosion, an ad hoc group of ten prominent Ameri-cus citizens asked for a meeting with Jordan. The mayor of Americus, the president of the local Chamber of Commerce, the president of the largest bank, a prominent medical doctor, and an attorney from a local law firm, among others, gathered in his living room at Koinonia. Jordan must have realized that this would be an extraordinary encounter, so he tape-recorded the conversation.

---

* Jordan did not always agree with King's views, and by the mid-1960s he expressed his disappointment that King had become less of a spiritual leader and more of a politician. He thought King's nonviolence was not enough: "You don't love your enemy because you want to convert him. . . . You love your enemy in order to be a son of God."

After a bit of polite chitchat, Charles Crisp, the president of Americus's Bank of Commerce, turned to the problem at hand: "Now your experiment has provoked the sensibilities of a vast majority of our people." Crisp said he understood that Jordan and his colleagues were dedicated Christians. "You say you are, and we accept that." Unfortunately, he said, the experiment had not created brotherly love: "It has set brother against brother; it has created bitterness; it has created hatred.... It is our belief that unless this experiment is moved to other fields that tempers will get to such a point that somebody is going to be hurt." Crisp concluded with a plea that Jordan should "move and leave us in peace."

Jordan responded by calmly asking why they couldn't hire a detective to discover exactly who had been carrying out these attacks. But he was told, "There's no way in the world for us to furnish you police protection out here and we don't have any control over these folks slipping around at night and throwing a stick of dynamite."

The men argued a bit longer, some of them clearly feeling uncomfortable jousting with a man so well versed in Christian verse. "Before all this terrorism started," Jordan said softly, "I had a feeling of friendship with all of you." Jordan was clearly unmoved: "I don't believe as many people are against us as appears on the surface."

As the meeting drew to an end, Jordan laid down a quiet challenge: "If strong men, men of Christian courage, can stand up and say: 'We're going to believe in religious freedom—'"

Someone interrupted, "It has gone too far."

"We haven't planted any dynamite," replied Jordan.

A few weeks later, another meeting was held and once again the Americus elders said there was but one solution, and that was for Koinonia to move elsewhere. Jordan recalled, "We then emphatically reaffirmed our intention to remain."

The boycott against Koinonia continued, and so too did the violence. Local authorities ignored the violence and instead convened a grand jury in the spring of 1957 to investigate the farm's connections to communists. Clarence Jordan and other Koinonians were forced to give testimony, but in the end the grand jury failed to issue any indictments. The jury nonetheless reported its suspicions that the farm was a communist front dedicated to keeping African Americans in a state of

"brain-washed peonage." Such public calumnies and the economic effects of the boycott took a hard toll. By the end of 1959, dozens of Koinonians had abandoned the commune, leaving a core of just three families
and a handful of transient guests.

CARTER KNEW ALL about Koinonia, and he knew Clarence Jordan as a
casual acquaintance long before the dynamite sticks or the boycott. In a
small way, Jordan was inadvertently responsible for Rosalynn switching
her allegiance from the Methodist to the Baptist church in the summer
of 1954. Jimmy and Rosalynn were at a Baptist revival meeting one weekend when a visiting preacher named Ben Grenade happened to remark,
"I am delighted to see my good friend Clarence Jordan in the congregation." Upon hearing Jordan's name, a large number of people walked out.
"About a third of the people got up and walked out," Carter recalled.
"That was the first time I knew anything about Koinonia." The Carters
stayed. Rosalynn liked Jordan and found herself charmed by his jovial
personality. Miss Lillian, however, recalled that her late husband Earl
had once told Jordan that he and the Koinonia farmers were not welcome at Plains Baptist Church. "He'd heard that there were colored and
whites living together," Miss Lillian said, and Earl disapproved. The
Carters were told that the commune harbored radicals. "They said it was
Communist," Rosalynn recalled.

   Later, when things got ugly for Koinonia, Carter never offered Jordan
public support. "I went there several times in the fifties and sixties,"
Carter said. "They couldn't get anyone else to shell seed for them, and I
did." He also tried to sell Jordan fertilizer. Jordan turned him down, explaining that he bought his fertilizer wholesale from a northern factory.
Carter said he went "a couple of times" to talk to Jordan, but he generally
kept his distance from the nearby commune, knowing that any fraternization with the Koinonia radicals invited trouble.* Much later, he told

---

* Clarence Jordan's wife, Florence, later insisted that she had never met Carter. "He has
never come over here; he has never helped; neither has his mother." But Rosalynn Carter
admired Jordan, and when a little boy whose father worked on the farm died of leukemia, she attended the burial on the farm and brought a baked ham. Afterward, she drove
back to Plains and angrily remonstrated with her Baptist preacher for refusing to preside
at the graveside service. The dead boy's father, Jack Singletary, commented, "That's a
little insight into the kind of person she is, and I'm sure that Jimmy was with her."

the journalist Robert Scheer that he thought the shootings and dynamiting of Koinonia had been carried out by "fringe elements."

Carter was keeping his head down, but he was also quietly breaking the boycott, if only by agreeing to shell peanut seeds for Koinonia. When this became known, the Carter warehouse was itself briefly boycotted. Carter nevertheless conceded, "We never did anything heroic." Indeed, he was silent. In the autumn of 1960, Americus High School refused to admit children from Koinonia, arguing that their presence would incite violence. The Koinonians filed suit in federal district court to force the Sumter County School Board to admit their children. The school board, chaired by Carter, fought the case—and lost. A federal judge ordered the children, all white, to be admitted. There is no record of where Carter stood on this case. Perhaps he was outvoted by other school board members. But neither did he publicly oppose the board.

He was no radical. Any public support for the Koinonia experiment would have spelled certain financial ruin for the Carter Warehouse. Even then, Carter probably knew that he harbored political ambitions, and so he decided to steer clear of any public association with the burgeoning civil rights movement. The decision was a calculated political act. Decades later, the journalist Nicholas Dawidoff would perceptively observe, "His ambition caused him to miss the seminal, transformative social event of his lifetime." Carter was absent. But his absence from the civil rights struggle in South Georgia left the door open for him to play a role on a grander stage years later. As a southerner, Carter could not walk away from his "peculiar" heritage, but as a southern liberal he fully embraced the notion that the South's "peculiar culture"—Jim Crow and segregation—was morally discredited.

Still, Clarence Jordan's radical life touched the life of the future president in several ways. Carter later wrote that he was "a man who had great influence on my life." For one thing, he explained, Koinonia was "the birthplace of the self-help movement known today as Habitat for Humanity." In 1968, Millard Fuller, a wealthy Alabama entrepreneur, gave away all his assets and joined the Koinonia commune—and later founded Habitat for Humanity, a charity that sponsored house-building events for the poor around the world. In 1982, after returning to Plains, Carter gave a speech in which he fully embraced Koinonia: "I am proud to be a neighbor of Koinonia . . . and to have seen, from perhaps too

great a distance, the profound impact of Clarence Jordan on this country . . . and to have known this quiet man who demonstrated in his own
life an image of Christ. . . . I think I will be a better Christian because of
Clarence Jordan, Koinonia and Habitat." It was a late endorsement—but
also an admission that he had kept his distance from the Koinonia experiment.

Perhaps more important, Clarence had a nephew, Hamilton Jordan,
who would someday write the strategy paper that would propel Carter
into the White House. Hamilton grew up in Albany, Georgia—knowing
that his Uncle Clarence was "the black sheep of the family."

CARTER BRIEFLY CONSIDERED abandoning Plains. "When Rosalynn
and I talked it over," he recalled, "we thought we were going to have to
leave Plains." He had a standing job offer from the Electric Boat Company in New London, Connecticut. But in the end, they decided to
"stick it out." Racial tensions were always an issue. And these tensions
escalated after the 1954 Supreme Court decision ordering desegregation of schools. The Carters were not politically active and certainly
did nothing to participate in the burgeoning civil rights movement of
the 1950s and early '60s. But they voted for Democratic presidential
candidate John F. Kennedy in 1960, and everyone knew that Jimmy
and Rosalynn Carter held socially progressive views. Everyone in
Plains except the Carters opposed school integration. "It was a cut and
dried issue and you didn't discuss it," Carter said. "We thought blacks
and whites ought to be treated the same, and so you just didn't discuss
it. It was a tough time." When the owner of the only service station in
Plains refused to sell him gasoline for his pickup truck, Jimmy installed his own underground tank and pumping station on the farm.
He just made do. "It was a hard time for us," Rosalynn said. "I remember going to church when people wouldn't speak to you, you're kind of
outcasts." They had only a few friends in Americus—and practically
none in Plains.

But as the years passed, the family business prospered, selling peanut
seeds and fertilizer all over Georgia. In 1960, the Carters bought a 2.4-
acre lot on the outskirts of town, hired an architect, and built a simple
but comfortable four-bedroom ranch house at 209 Woodland Drive for
about $10 a square foot. They needed the space for their three boys, Jack,

Chip, and Jeff.* Carter's book-lined study was simply furnished with an old table that had once belonged to Earl. They dragged it from the peanut warehouse, and Jimmy refinished the tabletop with fine leather and brass corners. He hung a bright fluorescent light from the ceiling. They kept a small liquor cabinet, and occasionally in the early evenings they might share a "toddy" with Miss Lillian. By then, the Carters were certainly among the wealthiest residents of tiny Plains. Later, they bought the entire surrounding farm of 170 acres and left it in its wooded natural state.

One morning in the autumn of 1962, Jimmy changed out of his khaki work pants and put on a jacket and tie. When Rosalynn asked if he was going to a funeral, Jimmy said no, he had decided to file papers at the county courthouse as a candidate for the Georgia state senate. "It seems inconceivable to me now," he later acknowledged, "but I had not consulted her about my plans." Rosalynn was nevertheless pleased—and with the election just two weeks hence, she threw herself into the affair, designing a campaign poster and calling friends to lend their support. The campaign became a family project.

Carter had always been interested in politics. He had served on the Sumter County School Board, and now he couldn't hide his ambition. But he also told himself that politics could be an extension of his Christian devotion. When a visiting revival preacher challenged him, "How can you, as a Christian, a deacon, and a Sunday school teacher, become involved in politics?" Carter replied, "I will have 75,000 people in my Senate district. How would you like to have a congregation that big?"

Miss Lillian thought her thirty-eight-year-old son's sudden foray into politics was motivated by his boredom with the peanut business. Earlier that spring he had read in the newspapers that a three-member panel of federal judges had declared illegal Georgia's "county unit" system, which heavily favored rural voters in sparsely populated rural counties and grossly discounted voters in Atlanta and other urban areas with large African American populations.

---

* John "Jack" William Carter was born in 1947. James Earl Carter III was born in 1950, when his parents were stationed in Honolulu. He got his nickname because his baby bracelet read "Chip Carter"—"Chip" translates as "baby" in a Hawaiian dialect. Donnel Jeffrey "Jeff" Carter was born in 1952.

The judge who wrote the decision striking down the "county unit" decision was Griffin Boyette Bell, age forty-six—who just happened to be a distant cousin of Rosalynn's. Carter didn't know it, but Judge Bell would have an enduring influence over his political life. At first glance, Judge Bell was a typical product of the Old South. Bell was a country boy, born and bred in Americus, just down the road from Plains. His father ran a gas station and appliance store in Americus. Bell himself never left Georgia, or even visited Atlanta, until he served in the U.S. Army during World War II. After the war, he used his GI Bill benefits to attend Mercer Law School in Georgia and eventually became a successful trial lawyer with the influential Atlanta law firm King & Spalding. In 1960, Bell was cochairman of Senator John F. Kennedy's Georgia presidential campaign—and Kennedy won more votes in Georgia than he did in Massachusetts. President Kennedy then rewarded Bell with an appointment to the Federal Court of Appeals for the Fifth Circuit in 1961.

The "county unit" case was one of Judge Bell's earliest judicial decisions, and it marked him as a southern reformer—not necessarily a liberal, but a southerner who understood that the Supreme Court's 1954 desegregation decision was inaugurating a new political order. Judge Bell later reminisced that his decision "was not a shock to the political establishment." Rather, the white power establishment that had profited so long from the system recognized that things had to change: "The new day was coming, but it had not yet taken form." Later, long after President Jimmy Carter had appointed him U.S. attorney general, Judge Bell was asked by a critic if he was part of the "establishment." He replied in his heavy South Georgia drawl, "I don't know if I'm part of the establishment or not, but I do know I've spent most of my life trying to get into it."

In the autumn of 1962, Carter calculated that a virtual political newcomer like himself might win the straight popular vote in one of the newly drawn state senate districts. He astutely campaigned on the vague notion of "good government" and his own personal qualifications— avoiding the acrimonious issue of race. But on the day of the Democratic Party primary he received reports from friends that a local political boss, Joe Hurst, was blatantly rigging the vote in Quitman County. And indeed, when the results were announced, Carter lost the primary election by a margin of 139 votes: 3,063 to 2,924. But Carter saw that in Quitman County alone, he had lost by 360 to 136—though only 333 citizens had registered to vote.

Carter quickly decided to contest the results in court—even though he overheard his mother saying, "Jimmy is so naïve, so naïve." He drove every day to Quitman County to collect affidavits from voters who might have witnessed fraud. This did not go unnoticed. "He was followed from the moment he crossed the county line," Rosalynn recalled, "and when he got out of the car to talk to anyone, two men followed not more than ten feet away, listening to his conversation, and making notes." Rosalynn was alarmed by anonymous threats to her husband's life. But Carter was not to be intimidated. Realizing that he needed to challenge the outcome, he had his cousin Don Carter make a few phone calls. In short order, Carter was referred to Charles Kirbo, a partner at King & Spalding. Kirbo's best friend at the time was none other than Judge Bell—and almost overnight the King & Spalding lawyer became not only Carter's consigliere but also his closest personal friend and his most trusted political adviser.

Seven years older than Jimmy, Charles Hughes Kirbo played the part of a classic southern country trial lawyer. Dressed in expensive but baggy suits, his prematurely graying hair slicked back, the sleepy-eyed lawyer looked the part of a country gentleman. His corporate clients in Atlanta might be Coca-Cola and Delta Air Lines, but Charlie still drove a dented, weathered pickup truck to work. He had grown up in spartan circumstances on a small farm outside of Bainbridge, south of Plains, near the Florida state line.

The Kirbos had emigrated long ago from French Alsace-Lorraine; they were largely poor, white, and illiterate. Neither of Charlie's parents had more than a third-grade education, though his father later passed the Georgia bar examination and became a clerk in the county court. Kirbo grew up steeped in the segregated culture of South Georgia. "When I was a little boy," Kirbo told freelance writer Kandy Stroud, "a good many of the people we knew were in the Ku Klux Klan, and they were constantly putting pressure on Papa to join. He didn't, and I didn't understand it at the time. He was the only one I'd seen that shook hands with black people."

Kirbo graduated from the University of Georgia law school in 1939 and then served as an infantry officer, surviving combat on D-Day in Normandy. After the war, he opened his own law office in Albany and then back in Bainbridge and built a reputation as a winning trial lawyer. In 1960 he was recruited as a partner in Atlanta's largest law firm, King & Spalding. But Charlie insisted on living on a 175-acre farm just outside Atlanta with his wife, three daughters, a son, two hundred head of Black Angus cattle—and a mule. He also owned more than three thousand acres of wooded land in South Georgia, and he later acquired a chain of building-supply stores, Stone, Inc., that grossed $2 million to $3 million in sales annually.

King & Spalding strove hard to keep its corporate clients out of court. But when that failed, the firm needed one good trial lawyer like Kirbo. "Trial work is his ace," said Kirbo's brother Bruce, also a lawyer. "Juries catch it right away: he talks so slow and easy and he tries never to complicate things, and I believe people just look at him and listen to him and say, 'Well, now, by God, there's an honest man.'" One friend compared his demeanor and measured gravitas to Atticus Finch, the trial lawyer in Harper Lee's 1960 novel *To Kill a Mockingbird*.*

Kirbo's soft southern drawl was so halting and slow that when he spoke in court, jurors often sat on the edge of their seats, straining to hear. "No one speaks more slowly than Charlie Kirbo," Carter later wrote. "His words come out just two or three at a time, punctuated by long silent intervals, giving the impression that he doesn't quite understand his own subject." But Kirbo was nevertheless seen as a "big gun." When Kirbo agreed to meet with him, Carter immediately drove the three hours to Atlanta and walked into King & Spalding's lavish corporate offices dressed in his work clothes, wearing dusty high-top brogans. "He appeared to have just climbed off of a tractor," said one of Kirbo's junior partners.

"I recollect that he [Carter] looked mighty tanned, very young," Kirbo said. "And he seemed a friendly sort of fellow, the kind you'd probably like right off. But I remember he was what you might call timid, maybe

* Years later Gregory Peck, the actor who played Atticus Finch in the 1962 film, was at a Georgetown dinner party when he asked Eden Rafshoon, the wife of Carter's White House communications director, "Does Carter listen to anyone?" Eden replied, "Why, yes, he listens to Charlie Kirbo, who is very much like Atticus Finch."

bashful or shy—I don't know. At any rate, he asked if I was going to help him or not." Kirbo frankly told Carter that "he didn't have much of a chance, that they more than likely had put fresh ballots in there, the exact number that they withdrew—and unless there was some flaw in the ballots he could detect, we didn't have a chance."

But Kirbo drove himself to Georgetown in Quitman County and managed to find the ballot box and have it delivered before Superior Court judge Carl E. Crow. "When we opened up the ballot box," Kirbo recalled, "I nearly fainted." They found loose ballots—but also a batch of more than a hundred ballots rolled up and bound by a rubber band. Missing were any ballot stubs and the required list of people who had voted. Kirbo reminded Judge Crow that Georgia politicians had stolen past elections "just like chicken thieves dragging a bush behind them to wipe out their tracks." In this case, Kirbo argued that because the county officials had trashed the receipts that would show how many valid votes had been placed in the ballot box, the only solution was to throw out all the votes from the incriminating box. Judge Crow stared at Kirbo, then slowly turned his head and spat tobacco juice into a spittoon.

After the formal arguments, as everyone was walking out of the courtroom, Kirbo sidled up to Judge Crow and said, "I know your normal practice, to just go by the count."

"Absolutely right," responded Judge Crow.

Kirbo pressed him. "I never knew you to tolerate fraud, though."

"That bothers me," replied the judge.

"Ask your wife what she thinks," Kirbo said.

A few days later, Judge Crow ruled that the votes from the Georgetown precinct ballot box would not be counted. The ruling tipped the balance. Carter's opponents still tried to challenge the decision, but in the end a dogged Jimmy Carter had won his first Democratic primary race for elected office by sixty-five votes. In those years, winning the Democratic primary amounted to winning the election.

That night, Jimmy and his friends celebrated by passing around a bottle of Old Crow bourbon—in honor of Judge Crow. "Now," Kirbo said, "I believe that as a result of that case they passed a law that disqualified anybody from votin' who'd been dead for more than two years." Such was the beginning of Carter's long relationship with Charlie Kirbo. "After it was all over," Kirbo recalled, "I felt like I had gotten to know an unusual person. He [Jimmy] was a person who exuded more confidence and consequence than anybody I had ever known . . . just sort of a gut feeling I had. He was simple, but then he was also sophisticated. . . . I had never seen a family work together the way they worked, and yet they lived very simply. They had a lot of nice things, but he was tight and very careful with his money." Kirbo's legal fee was $2,500. "I don't believe," Kirbo later said with measured understatement, "he [Carter] thinks that was, uh—uh, exorbitant."

Kirbo admired Carter's diligence and intelligence. "He was organized to a 'T,'" Kirbo said. If Jimmy was interested in a subject, he would pick up the phone and start calling people. "He would learn all there was to know about it. . . . It slowed him down some, but he seldom agreed to anything that he didn't think he understood. He knew how to find information, even when he was living in Plains." Kirbo saw Carter as both a workaholic and a playaholic: "His work and his play are organized so he gets more out of it. Jimmy doesn't waste time." Kirbo was also impressed by how Carter handled the issue of race. "He was the only fellow I knew who could talk to [his neighbors] and tell them they were wrong, that he disagreed with them, and that they were going to have to adjust in part on a religious basis." But for Kirbo, the astonishing thing was that "they wouldn't get mad at him."

Kirbo's regard for Carter was reciprocated. "Going to see Charlie Kirbo that day was probably one of the smartest things I ever did in my life," Carter later said. Carter knew Kirbo was more conservative than he, and though their difference in age was only seven years, Kirbo seemed older—a man with gravitas who understood human nature. He was earthy and irreverent. His humor was self-deprecating. These were all character traits absent in Carter's own personality, but Jimmy nevertheless was drawn to men who lived life unabashedly. Kirbo, he knew, was always authentic. And his southern-style aphorisms were endearing. Kirbo loved to talk about his mule: "Now, I regard the mule as a unique specimen. I don't mean in a biological sense. I mean in the sense that a mule is not fixin' to do anything he hasn't decided is the thing he ought to do. That's not like a lot of folks, you know. Folks tend to do things—and then think about whether they ought to or not—and folks, as you know, tend to get in trouble, sometimes. But you take a mule now. He very seldom gets into trouble."

Decades later, Carter would write an entire book just about his 1962 Georgia state senate race, aptly entitling it *Turning Point*. It was indeed a tipping point into his political career, and the beginning of a lifelong friendship with Kirbo. But it also marked a change in the dynamics of his marriage with Rosalynn—who to his surprise stepped out of her shy demeanor and embraced the political life. "I liked being a political wife," Rosalynn later wrote. She was good at it. She got people to confide in her and enjoyed managing all the petty details of arranging press interviews, travel, and even fundraising. "She liked the entire political process more than I did," Carter recalled.

For the next two years, Carter's service as a state senator broadened his horizons. The South was changing, and both Jimmy and Rosalynn were excited by what was happening around them. They made new friends, including Marvin Shoob, a Jewish lawyer from Savannah, and William Gunter, a Gainesville lawyer who had served in the Georgia House of Representatives. Shoob's wife, Janice, became a good friend of Rosalynn's, and the three couples often dined together. Carter thought Gunter "brilliant and very liberal. . . . He saw I needed some education— that I was very parochial in my attitudes."

Carter was still a voracious reader. Not surprisingly, as a southerner he was deeply moved by James Agee's *Let Us Now Praise Famous Men*— a journalistic account of the lives of impoverished sharecropper families in Alabama. During a slow day at the peanut warehouse, Carter was reading an anthology of poetry and stumbled across a poem by Dylan Thomas, "A Refusal to Mourn the Death, by Fire, of a Child in London." He was baffled by the final line, "After the first death, there is no other." "That struck me," he later said. "I didn't understand it." He checked out from the library a book of Thomas's poems, and "as a family exercise we would read his poems and try to figure them out." Later, he bought some audio records of Thomas reading his poems. He had become an ardent fan, to the point that in the summer of 1964, during a special session of the Georgia legislature, Carter most improbably cajoled several other state senators to sit down and listen to the Welsh poet. Carter's intellect was a bit rich for most Georgians. One day he used a Thomas poem in a speech about the environment, only to be mocked by *The Atlanta Con-*

stitution. "I learned," he later said, "to be more careful about what poems I quoted."

In retrospect, however, it is astounding that the Carters and their progressive circle of friends could forge any kind of viable political life. They were stunned and sorrowful when President John F. Kennedy was assassinated. But when the news was announced in their son Chip's high school classroom in Plains, the teacher exclaimed, "That's good!" and students cheered. Shocked by this display, Chip stood up and threw his desk at the teacher. He was suspended for three days. Chip was a fighter. "I got beat up every day at school," he recalled. One day his classmates "tied me upside-down from the volleyball net and threw the football at me while I spun around." The boy knew why he was being bullied: "I was really voraciously against everybody that was racist, and I let them know. . . . I was kind of raised in a liberal . . . non-racist culture, mostly because I think of the way my grandmother treated people all of her life and Dad kind of picked it up from her." It all went back to Miss Lillian.

Oddly, no one bothered to run against State Senator Carter in 1964; perhaps the word had spread that the man was tenacious. That summer President Lyndon Johnson signed the landmark Civil Rights Act, acknowledging as he did so that he was probably delivering the South to the Republican Party. Indeed, that autumn most Georgians voted for the Republican nominee, Senator Barry Goldwater, who campaigned on a platform of states' rights. Most of Carter's friends supported Goldwater. But not the Carters. Miss Lillian controversially volunteered to run the Johnson-for-President campaign office in Americus. For her troubles, she sometimes found her Cadillac windshield smeared with soap and the antenna tied in a knot.*

"People hated Johnson down here," Miss Lillian said, "because of his stand on civil rights and it got very ugly, but I was never afraid, not even when they threw things at my car and yelled 'Nigger lover, nigger lover' at me. . . . Didn't bother me a damned bit; stupidity is something I grew up with." The following year, Carter's fellow deacons at Plains Baptist Church proposed a rule prohibiting African Americans from entering the church. Carter led the debate against the proposition—but only six

---

* Miss Lillian attended the 1964 Democratic Party convention in Atlantic City as a Johnson delegate—where she was thrilled to meet Bobby Kennedy.

people, five of them members of the Carter family, voted against the measure. Fifty-four church members voted for the racial ban. Carter was appalled but not surprised; he knew he was right, and he decided to remain in the church. Afterward he received phone calls from some church members who had abstained on the vote but nevertheless told him privately that they understood that integration was inevitable.

Carter's calm demeanor allowed him to sail unscathed through the hot tempers of the time. He naturally deflected controversy. People knew his views, and while they disagreed, they did not disapprove of *him*. In the spring of 1966, Carter brazenly announced his candidacy for a U.S. congressional seat, and when his Republican opponent dropped out to run for governor, Carter was assured of election. But ever ambitious, he soon had second thoughts and decided he too should set his sights on the governorship. It was a mistake. Running as a moderate liberal, he lost the Democratic primary that September to the right-wing segregationist Lester Maddox, who went on to become governor. Kirbo had urged him to stick with the congressional race, but this time Carter had ignored his advice. Characteristically, he had expected to win. "It hurt to lose," Rosalynn recalled. "The idea that Lester Maddox would beat Jimmy—I couldn't believe it."

For the first time in his life, Carter had failed, and this precipitated a personal crisis. He had been "accustomed to accomplishing almost every goal I had sought." He later wrote that he was "deeply disappointed and disillusioned" and overcome with "bitterness and despair." He was tempted to "abandon my faith altogether." In secular terms, his psychiatrist friend Dr. Peter Bourne suggested that Carter had experienced "an acute reactive depression." Miss Lillian said he had "cried like a baby." Perhaps. But Carter himself plainly remembered that he was just "taken aback because the man who defeated me was a racist. . . . I could not believe that God, or the Georgia voters, would let this person beat me and become governor of our state."

But in subsequent years Carter also acquiesced in the notion that he had journeyed through a spiritual crisis, and one that had ended with a "born-again" cathartic experience. The actual story is probably more mundane than he allowed.

In the late autumn of 1966, after his defeat, Jimmy was visited by his sister Ruth Carter Stapleton, by then a rising Christian lay preacher-cum-therapist with a popular following across the country. (Her personal ministry, Behold, Inc., incorporated old-fashioned "sawdust Christianity" with modern new age psychotherapy.) An attractive blond woman who wore dark eye shadow and gold rings in her pierced ears, Ruth was a striking star on the evangelical circuit.* Billy Graham and Oral Roberts often made appearances at her evangelical camp in Tyler, Texas. One day Ruth and Jimmy went for a walk in the piney woods outside Plains, and she recited biblical scriptures that spoke to the topic of human failure and disappointment. Carter listened. And decades later he wrote, "She advised me to forget about myself for a while, strengthen my religious faith, learn from my political defeat, and become stronger." But Ruth, speaking to *Washington Post* reporter Myra MacPherson ten years after the event, gave a slightly different cast to the conversation. In her version, Ruth pressed her brother, asking if he could give up everything to Jesus Christ: "What about all political ambitions?"

"Ruth!" Jimmy replied. "You know I want to be Governor. I would use it for the people."

"No, Jimmy," Ruth replied, arguing that the whole point was to give up all earthly desires. Ruth claimed that Jimmy had finally broken down and even cried, saying, "I would really rather have the fullness of Christ in my life than be President."

Soon after MacPherson published this controversial interview, Carter was asked about it by Jules Witcover, a reporter with *The Washington Star.* Carter said the story was "accurate, basically." But he bluntly denied that he had cried or promised Ruth that he would give up his political ambitions. By his own account, he and Ruth had sat under a pine tree and she listened while he "bemoaned my misfortune, deplored the poor judgment and racist tendencies of my fellow Georgians, and vented my anger toward God. . . . God has rejected me through the people's vote." Ruth argued that "out of this defeat can come a greater life." Carter bitterly responded, "Ruth, you and I both know that this is nonsense. There is no way I can build on such an embarrassing defeat."

Rosalynn confirmed that Jimmy's "born-again" experience was

---

* By the mid-1970s, the Stapletons owned a vacation home on the Portuguese coast and a country cabin in Georgia.

"blown out of all proportion by news reporters." In 1976 she said, "I've heard people talk about Jimmy after he lost, having his 'experience' with Ruth and all. I don't remember any of that. He doesn't either." Later, in her 1984 memoir, she insisted that there were "no flashing lights, no weeping, no trauma or emotional scene, just a quiet acceptance of God." If anything, Jimmy's 1966 political disappointment merely led to a calm intellectual rededication to long-held, basic religious beliefs—and a determination to prevail in the next election.

That same autumn of 1966, Carter heard his pastor, Robert Harris, ask his congregation, "If you were arrested for being a Christian . . . would there be enough evidence to convict you?" Carter was personally troubled by the question. He felt drawn to and comforted by his childhood Christian beliefs—but he remained intensely ambitious in the secular world. He had actually told Ruth that politics was the one thing in his life that he could not give up. And indeed, Rosalynn says that a month after his 1966 defeat Jimmy had already decided to make another run for the governorship in four years.

Like most everything in his life, Carter's approach to his Southern Baptist heritage was decidedly cerebral. He had been taught, like all Southern Baptists, to accept the doctrine of the "Priesthood of the Believer"—which simply meant that no priest or pastor could stand between the believer and his relationship to Christ. Theoretically, each Southern Baptist could read and interpret the Bible on their own. Carter took this quite literally, and particularly during his navy years, when he had hours of solitary time at sea, he read the scriptures and came to his own conclusions. Unlike most churchgoing Baptists, he was not following the lead of his local pastor, let alone the Baptist hierarchy. As a result, he embraced a certain religiosity, but in the words of one scholar, he "remained an idiosyncratic believer throughout his life." He was always wrestling with what he called "my continuing doubts about the biblical accounts of miracles."

He read books by theologians and philosophers, including Paul Tillich, Søren Kierkegaard, and the Lutheran pastor Dietrich Bonhoeffer, who was murdered in a Nazi concentration camp. He took to quoting Tillich on how "religion is a search." From Karl Barth he accepted the notion that the Bible could not be read literally. He read the Jewish philosopher Martin Buber. In 1965, his good friend William Gunter lent him a copy of *Reinhold Niebuhr: On Politics*—essays that ratified what he already believed: that he could be both a successful politician and a good Christian. He told Gunter that Niebuhr (1892–1971) was "the most amazing thing" he had ever read and took to describing *On Politics* as his "political Bible." Niebuhr—the favorite theologian of the "vital center" East Coast foreign policy establishment—became his philosopher of choice, a politically astute choice for a future president. But it made Jimmy Carter into a Niebuhrian Southern Baptist—a rather singular church of one. "One of my greatest regrets," Carter later said, "was not meeting Niebuhr before he died." He took to quoting Niebuhr's aphorism that it is "the sad duty of politics to establish justice in a sinful world." To Carter, that meant focusing on "justice."

In May 1968, nearly two years after his defeat, Carter traveled briefly with a Southern Baptist mission team to Lock Haven, a small industrial town in working-class Pennsylvania. As an act of faith, he had decided he needed to proselytize. Carter went door to door for a week, urging people to have faith in Jesus Christ. "I was nervous and somewhat embarrassed," Carter later admitted. But he was accompanied by a plain-spoken Texan farmer, Milo Pennington, "a simple, relatively uneducated man, blessed with supreme self-assurance." They shared a $3-a-day hotel room at the local YMCA. Carter let Pennington be the "primary witness" and was emotionally moved by his stories. In one memorable encounter, they spent two hours listening to the life story of a young woman who turned out to be the "madam" of the local whorehouse.

Such encounters with fragile human actors fueled the pragmatic nature of Carter's religiosity. He wanted to help, and he defined his faith as a search for solutions to human problems. To be sure, he believed in the separation of state and church—but his own personal reading of the scriptures (and Niebuhr's writings) had convinced him that politics and good governing could actually be a more effective path to ministry. When he prayed, he explained to a reporter, he was just thinking "quietly about what ought to be done." There was nothing mystical about this. "There was no wave of revelation that came over me, no blinding flash of light or voices of God or anything." It was just this navy engineer turned politician figuring out what needed to be done: "Being born again is a new life, not of perfection but of striving, stretching, and searching." For Carter, prayer was actually a cerebral exercise. "Some people relate religion with lack of masculinity and being a sissy," explained Kirbo. "But Jimmy is tough."

Carter was a complicated man, and his religiosity was not without genuine introspection. He had examined his own life and he was self-aware. In the language of Southern Baptists, he knew he was guilty of the "number one sin"—defined as pride, arrogance, or certitude. "I have a tendency to exalt myself," Carter once confessed. "I am a much better father and businessman and farmer and politician . . . than a Christian." He knew that he was always susceptible to certain feelings of superiority. Aware of his intelligence—and proud of it—Carter believed his Baptist faith could be a humbling antidote to his innate pride. Judge Gunter, the friend who had introduced him to Niebuhr's essays, wryly intimated that Carter's faith had given him a "modicum of humility."

Oddly enough, this faith in turn empowered his driving political ambitions. It was a contradiction the future president could live with. Niebuhr gave him permission to satiate his ambitions by pursuing power—because only with power could one govern wisely and dispense justice. He concluded that "the teachings of Christ could be applied to a secular existence." Carter soon began quoting Niebuhr in his stump speeches on the theme of how "love must be translated into justice in order to be effective." It would become his mantra and his sense of mission. This blend of religiosity and politics would move many citizens—but others saw only a maddening piety. Carter himself acknowledged that this could be annoying: "I had adopted . . . an attitude of piety that aggravated some people."

Chapter 3
The Populist from Plains

He [Carter] is a nice fella, Hamilton, but he is just a politician.
—CLARENCE JORDAN

Candidate Carter and Governor George Wallace
CHARLES NESBITT, *THE BIRMINGHAM NEWS*

AFTER FOUR YEARS in the marines, Billy Carter had returned to Plains in 1966 to manage the Carter family peanut warehouse, leaving Jimmy and Rosalynn more time for politics. Billy turned out to be a good businessman, and with Rosalynn still managing the books, the warehouse grew into a multimillion-dollar operation over the next few years. Early that year, Miss Lillian dropped by the warehouse and asked her two sons, "Do y'all love me?" Jimmy quickly responded, "Mama, you know that we love you." But Billy asked, "Mama, what the hell are you gonna do now?" Miss Lillian, sixty-seven, then explained that she had just volunteered to join the Peace Corps. She had asked to be sent to a country "where it's warm, people have dark skins, and need a nurse's service." In mid-December 1966, she flew to India, where she lived for the next two years in a small industrial town outside Bombay, working in a birth control clinic. She saw poverty in India worse than anything in the Deep South. But despite the hardships, she wrote home that she had learned "what life is all about. . . . If I had one wish for my children, it would be that each of you dare to do the things . . . that have meaning for you as individuals . . . but not worrying if you don't please everyone." Upon her return, she went around the country speaking about her experiences in the Peace Corps—and a few years later the irrepressible Miss Lillian was invited more than once onto television talk shows with Johnny Carson, Merv Griffin, and Phil Donahue.

While Miss Lillian was in India, Rosalynn, age forty, gave birth on October 19, 1967, to a fourth child, Amy Lynn. The Carters were delighted to have a daughter. By then their three sons were nearly all grown. Their eldest, Jack, was a college student in Atlanta, and like many young people in the sixties, he joined protests against the Vietnam War. Jack was particularly disturbed that it seemed as if only the sons of poor, rural families were being drafted to serve in the unpopular war. In 1968, Jack, after wrecking his car, dropped out of college, joined the navy, and was posted to Vietnam. He saw no combat—but in December 1970 he was caught smoking marijuana and the navy released him with a general discharge. "Dad was not appreciative," Jack observed sardonically, "but he was sort of involved in his own things by that time." Carter was an exacting father—just like Earl—so he was troubled when his sons seemed to do less than their "best." Not surprisingly, the Carter boys sometimes pushed back. "In my view," Jack Carter said, "whenever you do one thing to the exclusion of something else, you get very, very good at it, but you exclude everything else. And so that has been sort of a philosophical difference that I've had with him for quite some time."

Carter was running for governor, and his position on the war was purposefully vague. Carter was determined to win in 1970—and he knew from his 1966 defeat that he could not triumph if he was perceived as either an antiwar candidate or a clear proponent of integration. So he defined himself as a "conservative progressive." No one knew what that meant. When asked in 1966 whether he was a liberal or a conservative— left or right—Carter had responded, "I believe that I'm a more compli- cated person than that." Borrowing a page from "Ol' Gene" Talmadge, Carter decided to run as a populist against the "Atlanta establishment"— meaning both "the big-shots that own the Atlanta newspapers" and the city's corporate elite. But unlike Talmadge, he would not overtly play the race card. In his view, class politics could trump racial politics. It was a daring but astute political gamble.

One day one of his affluent supporters, Carol Muldawer, a white lib- eral from Atlanta, introduced him to Andrew Young, one of the late Martin Luther King, Jr.'s legendary aides. Young knew Carter came from Sumter County, and he mentioned the name of the Albany sheriff, Lau- rie Pritchett, who had once arrested King. Both men knew Chief Pritch- ett's reputation as an ardent segregationist. To Young's surprise, Carter responded, "He's not that bad. He probably was more afraid of you than you were of him." Young thought this an unexpected "sympathetic un- derstanding of a sinner." Carter was clearly not a "converted redneck" and displayed no embarrassment or guilt. Young found Carter's self- confidence about the tinderbox of race refreshing and reassuring.

Carter was unflagging. "I drove all over Georgia for four years," Carter recalled later. "I'd work all day at the warehouse and on the farm. In the late afternoon, I'd drive all over the state giving speeches." Driving home, "I'd dictate on a hand-held dictaphone the names of people I met." He often traveled in the company of David Rabhan, a well-heeled business- man who owned a string of nursing homes and other business ventures across Georgia. Rabhan had heard Carter speak several times during the failed 1966 campaign, and afterward he had called him up and volun- teered his services if he ran again. Carter sometimes had this effect on people. "Dad really isn't an orator," his son Jack observed. "But what he can do, when he speaks with moral intensity, he makes you believe it."

Rabhan believed in Carter enough to fly him all over Georgia in his new twin-engine Cessna 310. Rabhan was a skilled but perhaps danger- ously fearless pilot. The Carters nicknamed him "Captain Midnight." With his shaved head and grungy blue jumpsuits, Rabhan, age forty- four, cut a colorful, even eccentric figure. Some thought this "flying entrepreneur" was part con man, part charming rogue.* But Rabhan contributed at least $8,600 to Carter's campaign—the single largest individual contribution—and also lent him the use of a well-furnished, high-end apartment in downtown Atlanta. They became good friends, and Rabhan got to know the entire Carter clan, often staying with Miss Lillian when he visited Plains. Of Jewish Iranian descent, Rabhan had been raised in a devout Orthodox Jewish family in Savannah, but as a young man he had broken with organized religion. And like Miss Lillian, he could be acerbic and irreverent. Carter didn't mind, even when Rabhan one day exclaimed, "I do not know how an educated person like you can believe all that stuff." Carter rarely argued when challenged about his faith; instead, he typically just sat in silence and listened. But he genuinely liked Rabhan and enjoyed his humor: "He's an unbelievable pilot, artist, sculptor, businessman and bull-shit artist." Chip Carter later told Dr. Peter Bourne, one of his father's advisers on health issues, and later the author of the 1997 biography *Jimmy Carter,* that Rabhan had "packed his father's head with liberal ideas." (The British-born Bourne was himself a cosmopolitan, liberal influence on Carter. Trained as a psychiatrist at Emory University, Bourne became a close friend of Rosalynn's and advised her and Jimmy about public-health issues.)

Rabhan had more Black than white friends; civil rights activists like Ralph Abernathy used to come by his apartment in Atlanta late at night and talk into the early-morning hours over a few drinks. So perhaps it was no surprise that one day he persuaded Carter to pay a visit to Martin Luther King, Sr.—the father of the recently assassinated civil rights leader. The local press noted that Carter was the first white gubernatorial candidate to visit the mostly Black Ebenezer Baptist Church. Rabhan later swayed a skeptical "Daddy" King to endorse Carter in the 1970 gubernatorial race.

Kirbo nevertheless thought Rabhan was a bad influence on Carter.

---

* Rabhan was arrested in Iran in 1979 while on a business trip, was falsely charged with being an American spy, and spent more than eleven years in a Tehran prison. Iranian authorities probably arrested him because of his association with Carter. He was released only in 1990, after Carter persuaded the PLO's Yasir Arafat to intercede. In 2003, Rabhan was convicted of bank fraud on a Georgia loan and spent another four and a half years in a federal prison.

And Rabhan thought the same of Kirbo: "Black people were not his favorite people," Rabhan alleged years later. Two days after introducing
Carter to "Daddy" King, Rabhan met Kirbo in his Atlanta law office. The
two men understood instantly that they didn't care for each other. According to Rabhan, Kirbo bluntly told him, "I don't want you to be
bringing your *nigger* friends here. . . . You deal with them and if they
have any problems you come to me." Rabhan always remembered the
language; Kirbo was talking to him coarsely as one white southerner to
another. But he was sure at the time that Kirbo would never talk like that
in front of Jimmy. Kirbo was skeptical of the political wisdom of trying
to appeal to Black voters: "Over the objections of some of our staff,"
Kirbo later said, "he [Carter] would go right to all the black beer joints
and everything, shaking hands. The TV followed him, and they would
show it on TV. All the TV stations and newspapers were against him."
Carter must have known that such images carried certain political risks.
But he was determined to win, and he had a sophisticated and clever
strategic plan. He walked a thin line, running as a populist, tacking to
both the right and the left of his political enemies.

His main opponent was former governor Carl Sanders, a man perceived as more liberal, more cosmopolitan, and more likely to win the
race. Sanders would likely get more Black votes and more liberal, urban
votes. As governor, he had been relatively tolerant on racial issues, saying he would uphold civil rights laws—though he had also testified
against the 1964 Civil Rights Act. But Sanders was actually as racist as
most Georgia politicians, making it clear that he personally disapproved
of integration. (He once described the interracial marriage of the African American Charlayne Hunter [-Gault] with a white college classmate
as a "disgrace" and a "shame.") Though Sanders was not born wealthy, he
had become a prosperous corporate lawyer since his first term as governor. Carter might be flying around in Rabhan's Cessna, but Sanders actually owned his own private plane. Carter thought the "nouveau riche"
Sanders was a hypocritical limousine liberal. He inveighed against Sanders's "close connections with . . . the Atlanta establishment" and repeatedly called his opponent "Cuff Links" Carl.

This line of attack was clearly inspired by Charlie Kirbo. "I believe I
know white people in rural Georgia as well as anybody," Kirbo later
wrote. "I've worked in the fields with them, I've worked on the hog rows,

I've been hungry and pore [*sic*] as hell, and now I've done better." Intellectuals, he thought, didn't understand poor people. Intellectuals "want to talk about being Left and Right, liberal or conservative." But Kirbo thought the important thing to know was that "most people in a way have a sort of inferiority complex. They are status conscious. They like people that are friendly. If you ever give the impression that you think you are better than they are, that you think they are inferior in some respect, then you have committed an unpardonable sin. . . . There are people who will fall out with you over petty things like cuff links and wearing silk stockings." Kirbo knew that Sanders was vulnerable to this kind of populist resentment.

Carter's 1970 campaign benefited from the brilliant talents of a young New York advertising genius named Gerald Rafshoon. Carter had first employed Rafshoon during the 1966 campaign, and the two men had bonded. "I liked this guy Carter," Rafshoon explained. "He seemed thoughtful. He could properly say the word 'Negro.'" (Many white southerners at the time tended to slur the word to make it sound like the epithet.) Jerry Rafshoon had moved to Atlanta to make his fortune, founding his own ad agency. "I was impressed," recalled Rafshoon, "by how bad Carter's advertising was." Brash and very liberal, Rafshoon approached Carter with a hundred-page report outlining a modern media campaign. Carter hired him, and soon the two men could be seen drinking beer together in taverns, plotting out radio and television ads.

Up until then, candidates had sat behind a desk with an American flag on one side and a Georgia state flag on the other and spoken directly into the camera about what they were going to do for Georgia. It was very wooden and static. Rafshoon had another idea: "Let's take a camera and go down and follow him around." It was the first cinema verité campaign advertising in Georgia. But when he first proposed this approach, Carter's advisers vigorously protested. As the argument escalated with raised voices, Rafshoon suddenly felt himself being kicked under the table. "I looked over and there was this smiling face looking at me with a grin, and he kind of gave me a look like 'shut up.'"

After everyone left, Carter said, "Don't argue with these people. I need these people. Go ahead and do the campaign. I'm the only person you have to satisfy." Carter and Rafshoon clicked, perhaps because Rafshoon had a mischievous streak, like Kirbo. "I think there's a flaw in my character," Carter once told Rafshoon, "but I like having you around. I don't know why." Rafshoon quickly realized that Carter was at his best when he was speaking extemporaneously. "He could not stand to work with a text," Rafshoon recalled. "I tried to do more town meetings and Q and A's, about which one never had to worry with Jimmy Carter. Speeches were different. There was something about a teleprompter . . . that made him so boring." Forced to read a speech, Carter's voice, oddly enough, invariably stepped up an octave, sounding slightly high-pitched and reedy. One reporter described his voice as high-timbred, "almost Elizabethan in its inflections, that curious rise on the penultimate syllables." Reading a text, he often seemed uncomfortable and impatient. "It's not nervous," Rafshoon said. "I can never think of Jimmy Carter as nervous." But as Rafshoon got to observe Carter on the stump, he realized that his candidate had a certain disdain for oratory. "I think he thinks that the time for rhetoric is over. I think he equates it with a Kennedy. You think about it, all his political life his adversaries have been much better orators. Carter couldn't do with a crowd what George Wallace or Lester Maddox or Ted Kennedy could do with a crowd." Rafshoon urged him, "More preacher, less engineer. When you're a preacher, you're great. When you're an engineer you put me to sleep."

Rafshoon's most effective television ad opened with a fancy wooden door closing and a voiceover saying, "This is the door to an exclusive country club, where big-money boys play cards, drink cocktails, and raise money for their candidate, Carl Sanders." Then the camera pans to a close-up of a man wearing an elegant dress shirt with French cuffs and glittering cuff links, signing a check. The commercial ends with a scene of Jimmy Carter talking to an "ordinary working person," and the narrator intones, "Vote for Jimmy Carter, our kind of man, our kind of governor." The ad conveyed raw, pure populism. It was not racist, but few Georgians were likely to miss the message sent by the phrase "our kind of man"—the familiar campaign slogan of neighboring Alabama governor George Wallace. Rafshoon's antiestablishment ads were brilliantly negative—and Carter himself was perfectly comfortable with this portrayal of himself as a lonely, relentless populist.

Carter ran on his personality and character, appealing to voters to support him for his integrity, his smarts, and his peanut-farmer roots. But he also was not above sending signals to working-class, rural white voters that he understood their fears about the pace of integration. He portrayed himself as an "intellectual red-neck." When a newspaper reported that he was opposed to private schooling, Carter responded, "I am convinced that there is a permanent and important place in Georgia education for private schools." He also took a hard line on "law and order," condemning violent antiwar protests on college campuses. "I have a son in Vietnam and I wish the war there could be honorably ended." He frankly explained to a reporter from *The Atlanta Constitution* that he had "no trouble pitching for Wallace votes and the black votes at the same time." In Carter's eyes, they were all just "average working people" in need of a governor "who understands their problems." He was not being phony or disingenuous, just shrewd. "I told people," he later explained, "that conservatism did not mean racism. But if I had gone in and said, 'All of you are wrong. You shouldn't have done what you did. I'm better than you are,' . . . I wouldn't have been elected."

Carter's strategy was to be all things to all people; he was running not on issues but on character and values. "Jimmy can and does appeal to the Wallace voter, but not on the racial thing," said Charlie Kirbo. "Jimmy is a populist." Asked if Carter was a liberal or a conservative, Kirbo liked to say, "That's always a tough question." Kirbo himself claimed not to be political in an ideological sense. "Charlie doesn't care much about politics and he doesn't give a damn about government," observed a fellow lawyer. "All he cares about is Jimmy." Kirbo just thought Carter was "a remarkable campaigner . . . he had the capacity to deal with people who differed with him on major concerns."

Another friend, Thomas Bertram "Bert" Lance, a Georgia banker who became a close adviser to Carter during this campaign, observed, "He was a moderate to moderates, a conservative to conservatives, and a liberal to liberals." Vietnam veteran and Georgia state senator Max Cleland saw Carter on the stump and recalled, "He could charm the scales off a snake." Carter campaigned hard, and some of his critics later accused him of campaigning dirty, specifically with the circulation of anonymous "fact sheets" attacking Sanders. Someone distributed leaflets with a photograph of a Black member of the Atlanta Hawks basketball team pouring champagne over Sanders, a part owner of the team. In the context of the times, this was a not-so-subtle reminder not only of Sanders's wealth but also of his supposed liberal views on race. (The

Sanders campaign retaliated with a photograph of Carter and civil rights activist Hosea Williams.) Such incidents underscored Carter's willingness to engage in the rough-and-tumble of hardball politics. He was indeed a liberal by any measure—but he was determined not to be labeled one. He would always try to keep Sanders to his left. This was not only disingenuous but consciously devious. As Carter confessed to Vernon Jordan, then an up-and-coming Black Atlanta lawyer, "You won't like my campaign, but you will like my administration." Carter even met with Roy Harris, a former chairman of the White Citizens' Council, and won his endorsement.

His campaign platform included language on education, for instance, calculated to appeal to white voters worried about being forced to send their children to integrated schools. He pledged "to establish and maintain the highest standards of quality in the public schools and colleges of Georgia, in spite of any obstacle brought about by integration, court rulings, local apathy or other causes." The dog whistle to race was subtle, but it was there: "in spite of any obstacle brought about by integration." He conveyed a similar message by talking about how he would do "everything" he could for private schools—seeming to imply the segregated white "academies" springing up all over the state.

Such clear-eyed ruthlessness was not appreciated in some quarters. "He's somebody who was willing to dip on the dark side to get elected," observed Georgia state representative Julian Bond. Even decades later, Bond could not suppress his distaste for what he thought Carter had done. "He wanted badly to get elected. This is what he chose. To me, it was an awful thing to do." And yet Bond would wryly concede, "A good man had a couple of bad days."

HAMILTON JORDAN, AGE twenty-five, served as campaign chairman. When Dorothy "Dot" Padgett, a local volunteer, first met Jordan, she thought to herself, "Good grief, this campaign is being run by a kid." Padgett noticed immediately that the handsome young man radiated an exaggerated sense of old-fashioned southern courtesy. He addressed her as "ma'am," opened doors for women, and politely stood up when elders entered the room. Born in Albany, a small town in southwestern Georgia, William Hamilton McWhorter Jordan had a comfortably middle-class childhood. His father, Richard, was a hardworking insurance agent, but his mother, Adelaide, suffered from multiple sclerosis and his younger sister Helen had survived a bout of polio. The Jordans belonged to the local country club and socialized with the business community of Albany. Hamilton had grown up accepting southern racial conventions—segregation was a way of life—but even as a young boy he had sensed that "things had been falling apart all around us for years." At seventeen, Hamilton watched from the sidewalk as Martin Luther King, Jr., marched arm in arm with a youthful Andrew Young and other civil rights activists down the streets of Albany. Hamilton and his father were shocked to see the family's maid, Hattie, marching at the back of the throng of protesters. On that day, Hamilton stood on the sidelines as overzealous policemen forced some of the marchers into a narrow alley, where they staged a sit-in and were arrested. Hattie spent the night in jail, as did King. Hamilton's parents had told him that these people were troublemakers and outside agitators intent on destroying their way of life. But witnessing the protest up close gave the young man pause: "I felt real shame for the first time in my life, standing by and merely watching while decent people—including our own dear Hattie—were herded into an alley and treated like animals."

Jordan's views were also influenced by clandestine chats with his controversial uncle Clarence Jordan, the founder of South Georgia's only interracial communal farm. While still in high school, unbeknownst to his parents, Hamilton used to drive over to Koinonia to chat with his uncle a couple of times each year. He also remembered Uncle Clarence dropping by their home in Albany frequently during the summer of 1962. Only later did Clarence tell him that he was actually visiting Albany to see his friend "Martin."

"Change came hard to the South—and to the Jordan family," Jordan later wrote. "My father could never bring himself to say 'Negro' properly, but he stopped saying 'nigger' around us and usually used the words 'colored' or 'nigra' which was the 'polite' compromise between 'nigger' and 'Negro.'"

At the age of nineteen, Hamilton spent the summer of 1963 in Washington, DC, working as a summer intern for Georgia's Senator Richard Russell, an ardent segregationist. But he also got a chance to visit the White House that summer and was exhilarated to hear President John F. Kennedy give a short speech on the South Lawn. That August, he witnessed Martin Luther King, Jr.'s historic speech during the March on Washington. "I was not proud of myself that day," Jordan wrote. "I was still straddling the fence." He felt great loyalty toward Senator Russell, but was troubled that this put him politically in the company of George Wallace, Strom Thurmond, and J. Edgar Hoover—"men whose actions and opinions were despicable."

In 1966, Jordan was a junior at the University of Georgia when he happened to hear Carter speak at an Elks Club. Jordan was intrigued. A self-described "political animal," Jordan sensed that this was one South Georgian politician who was speaking a different, more egalitarian language on racial issues. That was the key. A political science major, Hamilton decided he might want to volunteer for Carter's 1966 campaign. Significantly, it was his uncle Clarence Jordan who initiated the introduction to Carter by calling up a mutual friend, Hugh Gaston, who had designed Carter's house in Plains. Carter phoned Hamilton and asked if he'd become his "youth coordinator" for $50 a week. When Hamilton responded that he already had a summer job spraying mosquitoes, Carter quipped that "if killing insects was more important," well, perhaps he should withdraw from the governor's race. Hamilton joined the campaign.

When Carter lost the 1966 race, young Hamilton went on to graduate from the university. His roommate, Jay Beck, reported that Hamilton had spent much of college just having a good time. He wasn't a scholar. "We were the class of *American Graffiti*," Beck said, "and we were shielded from an understanding of the significant issues of the day. I guess you might say our generation was a bridge between James Dean and the hostilities of the late 1960s. Frankly, we didn't think seriously about much during college."

The war in Vietnam would change that. But for a leg injury that left him physically disqualified, Jordan might have been drafted into the army and sent to Vietnam. Instead, Jordan found a way to go to Vietnam on his own, as a $120-a-month employee for the humanitarian nonprofit group International Voluntary Services, helping to relocate refugees in the Mekong Delta. He arrived in late 1967 and survived the January 1968 Tet Offensive before falling ill with dengue fever. After being shipped back stateside, Jordan looked up his uncle Clarence and told him he thought he would go to work again for Carter. "He is a nice fella, Hamilton, but he is just a politician," his uncle told him. Clarence was feeling discouraged that day and confided in his nephew, "We have made progress, but not much. . . . We have survived, a tiny light in a sea of hate." Six months later, in the midst of the Carter campaign, Hamilton received a phone call informing him that Clarence had suffered a heart attack. Friends had called for medical help, but according to Hamilton, "no doctor would risk coming to Koinonia, particularly not to save Clarence Jordan's life." Clarence was dead at the age of fifty-nine. But Koinonia Farm would survive until the present.

By his own account, Hamilton deeply admired his uncle. He thought of him as a "great man I had barely known but who had brushed against my own life." For obvious reasons, Hamilton never referred to his controversial uncle while campaigning for Carter. At the time, virtually no one made the connection between Hamilton Jordan and his uncle—the antiestablishment, antisegregationist, and wholly radical Christian rebel. But the lesson Jordan took from Uncle Clarence's quixotic life story was that hardball politics mattered. The acquisition of real power mattered. As a young man in his mid-twenties, with thick coal-black hair, dark eyes, and a muscular frame, Jordan was a handsome figure. Unlike his boss, he was affable, self-deprecating, and unpretentious. But he was an absolutely ruthless political operator, willing to do whatever was necessary to win. He could be merciless in the service of a greater cause. Jordan was disarmingly roguish—and Jimmy Carter liked to surround himself with young men who were both idealistic and rough-hewn.

JODY POWELL WAS another young man in the same mold. Powell was raised on a five-hundred-acre farm in Dooly County, South Georgia, just twenty-five miles from Plains. His father, Joe, was a peanut farmer and his mother, June, was a high school civics teacher. June filled the house with books—and unlike most of their neighbors, she understood that racial segregation was on its way out. When the local public schools were finally desegregated in 1970, June Powell was one of a handful of white teachers who chose to remain. Jody recalled that his father had taught him "the most important things—how to drink beer, drive a tractor and shoot a gun."

The sandy-haired boy had a playful, mischievous nature. Extremely bright, Powell made it into the U.S. Air Force Academy, only to be expelled one semester before graduation because he had foolishly cheated on an exam. "You don't know what loneliness is," he said, "until you drive into your driveway at home, in the Deep South, on Christmas Eve, having just had your ass booted out of a military academy." His mother thought he never would have taken to military discipline anyway. "He's always been such a cluttered person," she recalled. "He constantly topped the list of those paying for lost library books." Powell himself later joked about his expulsion: "After getting kicked out for cheating, politics seemed like the next best thing." Powell rebounded by finishing his bachelor's degree at Georgia State University, and then he enrolled in a graduate degree program at Emory University in Atlanta.

"Jody was a serious South Georgia redneck," recalled Peter Bourne, who admitted he never got along with the younger man. Powell and his college friend Herky Harris loved fast cars and pretty women. Jody owned a Corvette. Like many proud southerners, Powell was an amateur historian on the "War Between the States." At Emory, he chose to write his thesis on the career of segregationist George Wallace. But when he met Carter in 1969, Powell found himself enchanted and volunteered his services. "My part of the state," Powell said, "had turned out a lot of bombastic, racist politicians, and I felt Jimmy Carter might be able to change that." He became Carter's personal assistant and driver. "We soon found that we were quite different," Carter later said. "I was punctual." Powell was not. But if Powell didn't show up on time, Carter just left for his next appointment—and Jody would hitchhike. This happened several times, until finally one day Powell hired a taxicab to catch up, and the candidate, of course, had to pay the cab fare. Carter was not only punctual, he was also cheap, so after this incident, Carter recalled, "we worked out a better arrangement so that we could leave on time."

Powell was smart, quick-witted, and pugnacious. The two men, so different, nevertheless bonded during their long drives around Georgia. They talked a lot about the timeless issue of race. Carter told him that there were two ways to talk to people about race. "You can tell people, 'Look, you are all a bunch of ignorant racists, and you have been wrong and your granddaddy and daddy were wrong.' . . . Or you can say, 'We have always known that was not what we learned at church, that was not what Christianity taught us. . . . Now is the time to do what we have always known was the right thing.' " Powell was impressed; Carter made him think he would do the right thing—but always with the "understanding that people are complicated folks."

By the end of the 1970 gubernatorial campaign, Powell had become Carter's press secretary. They made an odd couple. Carter was circumspect where Powell was brash. Carter disapproved of tobacco, but Jody chain-smoked True Blue cigarettes. Jody was hard-drinking, while Carter might indulge in a fine Scotch, a single shot of Chivas, on a rare day off. Jody was combative and bristled with nervous energy. While reading the morning newspaper or talking on the phone, he couldn't help but gnaw his fingernails down to the quicks. Carter meticulously planned his days. Powell was "totally disorganized," Jordan later said, and was notorious for never returning phone calls. And yet, Carter would later admit, "Outside of Rosalynn, Jody understands me best."

But still, it was Kirbo who ran the campaign, budgeting fifteen cents per voter in each county. And it was Kirbo who was the only one who could bluntly reprimand the candidate. After hearing rumors that Carter had been impatient and "rude" to some reporters, Kirbo wrote him a firm note, telling him, "This is a mistake. . . . It makes me think you are tired and need some rest. Maybe when you get back from your vacation you can behave better."

CARTER SPENT $700,000 on the race—a lot of money by Georgia standards. He received contributions—all legal—from large corporations like Coca-Cola ($6,200), Delta Air Lines ($4,995), and Cox Broadcasting Company ($26,500). Ironically, Cox owned *The Atlanta Constitution* and *The Atlanta Journal*, whose influence Carter had excoriated in his campaign stump speeches. Probably a quarter million dollars came from businessmen, lawyers, and bankers—and another quarter million was raised from small contributors. But Carter probably spent around $200,000 of his own money—a considerable portion of his own net worth. One Saturday before the election, Jimmy and Rosalynn went for a walk on their farm, and he suddenly turned to his wife and asked if she would be willing to sell their land if they had to pay campaign debts. Rosalynn agreed: "If we had lost the election, we probably would have lost our farms as well."

* * *

CARTER WON THE Democratic primary in September 1970 with 48 percent of the vote; Sanders got just 37 percent, and two weeks later Carter
triumphed in the runoff with 63 percent. The press called it a "stunning
upset." The outgoing governor, Lester "Axe-handle" Maddox, personally
despised Carter but had nevertheless supported him in the runoff. "I
believe the peanut farmer is the right man," Maddox said in his endorsement. And Carter reciprocated by saying, "Lester Maddox is the embodiment of the Democratic party." Carter easily won the November
general election against a lackluster Republican opponent. Maddox was
elected lieutenant governor with 70 percent of the vote.

At the time, Carl Sanders was bitter and angry; he called Carter an
"unprincipled grinning chameleon." Two decades later, Sanders coolly
observed that Carter had won by drawing "more of a class distinction
than a race distinction. I think he postured himself as a peanut farmer
from outside Atlanta and . . . he pictured me as a corporate lawyer in
Atlanta . . . representing fat cats and he was out there representing the
average citizen. That's a pretty tough thing to overcome." Carter had
beaten Sanders running as a southern populist, hiding his liberal agenda.
He never lied, but some might think him guilty of guile. A telling statis-
tic is the fact that Carter won only 5 percent of the Black vote. Rafshoon
later boasted that they had consciously decided to win by losing Black
voters: "To win in politics you had to decide whose vote you didn't
want. . . . Once you decide who you can do without, the black vote [for
example], you can go ahead and win." When a colleague gently chided
him, "I wish you hadn't picked just that example," Rafshoon replied, "I
picked that example because that's just what we did in 1970."

One day, just before the November election, Carter was flying with
Rabhan from Brunswick to Newnan, Georgia. As usual, Carter was in
the copilot's seat, and while Rabhan snoozed, Carter was at the controls
when suddenly the engines stopped. Carter frantically nudged Rabhan
with his elbow, but the pilot was slow to respond. As the Cessna rapidly
lost altitude, Rabhan casually leaned over and flipped a switch to open
the plane's standby fuel tanks. The engines roared back to life and Rabhan laughed merrily. Carter was initially quite angry at his friend's nonchalance. But after a few minutes, he regained his composure and they

began talking about the future. Both men were confident that Carter was about to become governor. Feeling a sense of gratitude for all that his friend had done in the campaign, Carter asked Rabhan if there was anything he could do for him.

Rabhan grabbed an aviator's map and asked Carter to scribble in the margins as he dictated one sentence: "The time for racial discrimination is over in Georgia," he said. "This is what I want you to say when you are inaugurated." Carter hesitated only for a moment, and then signed the aviator's map and handed it back to Rabhan.

Charlie Kirbo had actually prompted Carter to have this conversation with Rabhan. "I told Jimmy to make a deal and get rid of that loon Rabhan." But when Kirbo learned what had happened, he was incensed. "From my perspective, it was political suicide."

For once, Kirbo was wrong. Carter knew this was what he wanted to say. He knew it was the right thing to do. He knew he had to transform himself by distancing himself from the campaign he had just run. As Kirbo soon realized, the governor-elect was making a larger political calculation. Georgia governors are allowed only one term in office. So even before he took the oath of office, Carter was already thinking about his potential for national political office. Soon after the election, Carter must have confided to his friend that he had national ambitions, because on November 23, 1970, Kirbo wrote him a revealing memo, warning him, "I think you should be careful not to say anything that would indicate you are running for vice-president or president. . . . You ought to state emphatically that you have a job to do here." Kirbo suggested that he should say that it would be "presumptuous for you to think about running for vice-president, president or whatever else is in the offing and that you are perfectly happy to live here and work at home."

Carter wasn't even governor yet, and Kirbo was already telling him how to couch his language for a national run. In the past, he pointed out, some southern politicians had made remarks "critical of some of our traditions in an effort to make themselves acceptable on a national scale." Kirbo thought this would be a mistake. "I don't believe this is politically wise on a local or national scale. I think the public will respect and admire a man who is proud of his own state and proud of his own people and doesn't go around belittling them." It was a thin line, but if

Kirbo thought he could talk Carter out of condemning segregation, he was wrong.

On January 12, 1971, James Earl Carter, Jr., was sworn in as Georgia's new governor. His inaugural address was only eight minutes long. He prefaced his remarks with a confession: "I realize that the *test of a leader is not how well he campaigned* [emphasis added] but how effectively he meets the challenges and responsibilities of the office." This was almost an apology, but not quite. "This is a time for truth and frankness. . . . I say to you quite frankly that the time for racial discrimination is over." There were audible gasps and a few groans when he uttered the words promised to Rabhan. Lieutenant Governor Maddox, sitting on the platform, was stunned, and soon denounced him as a liar. Jody Powell retorted, "Being called a liar by Lester Maddox is like being called ugly by a frog." Carter despised Maddox. And Maddox returned the sentiment: "He's cold, cunning and cruel, and will destroy anything or anyone who stands in his way. . . . He told me in January 1971 that if I crossed him on any issue, he would work to destroy me with the full resources at his command. . . . I was never so shocked."

Carter was showing his true colors. This heartened liberals and shocked conservatives. "I always thought he was a progressive man and had these notions," said one Black state legislator, "yet couldn't say them and get elected." Less than a year later, Newt Gingrich, then a young history professor at West Georgia College, wrote in an opinion piece in *The Atlanta Journal* that Carter's Republican opponent, Hal Suit, a local radio and television personality, "lacked the experience to tear away at the phony image and reveal the liberal heart under the blue-collar picture."

Harsh words. Governor Carter never responded to these criticisms. But some sources reported that he "felt bad" about the campaign. *The New York Times*'s James Wooten later wrote in his account of the campaign that Carter had called Sanders and personally apologized. Carter denied this in 1976. Wooten also reported that Carter told Rosalynn that "he would never go through such a campaign again."

Carter nevertheless rationalized that he had run "a working man's campaign" and now he had the opportunity to do good. He would govern as a Southern Baptist Niebuhrian. Immediately after being sworn in, Carter turned around and swore in Charlie Kirbo as his chief of staff—

actually an unpaid, ceremonial position. Hamilton Jordan became his executive assistant and Jody Powell was appointed press secretary. Jerry Rafshoon continued to provide media advice.

In a private memo to the governor-elect, Kirbo urged his friend to govern as a populist. "It is important that you retain your populist appeal and your contact with the average people." He reminded Carter that they had campaigned on the idea that they were going to "give the little people a greater part in government." And while these "little people are not very sophisticated in their thinking, they are judging government by the results." Kirbo counseled a strategy of confrontation with the legislature: "a veiled threat that if the legislature and politicians don't listen to the people they are all going to get thrown out themselves." Kirbo's country-lawyer demeanor sometimes led people to assume that he was more conservative than his protégé. But Kirbo had a sophisticated understanding of the undue influence of corporate power. He warned Carter that "business elements" in all communities were invariably "better organized" to lobby government to spend money on expensive buildings such as Atlanta's proposed coliseum when such funds were probably better spent on "vital needs" in the "ghettos, law enforcement, rapid transit," and cleaning up pollution in Georgia's rivers. Kirbo was in sync with Carter's own populist instincts. The savvy Atlanta lawyer and the ambitious peanut farmer from Plains had forged a remarkably close partnership that was both a genuine friendship and a political alliance. Their story was only just beginning.

Chapter 4
Jimmy Who?

Don't pay any attention to that smile. That don't mean a thing.
That man is made of steel, determination, and stubbornness.

—STATE SENATOR BEN FORTSON

Rosalynn and Jimmy Carter, 1976
RICK DIAMOND/GETTY IMAGES

CARTER'S INAUGURAL DECLARATION that "the time for racial discrimination is over" had made national news. *The New York Times*
ran a front-page news story describing Carter as "a 45-year-old peanut
farmer who bears a strong physical resemblance to President Kennedy."
Noting that four other relatively liberal governors had been elected in
the South that season, the editors at *Time* magazine decided that spring
to assign a cover story on the "New South." Rafshoon persuaded the
magazine's team of reporters to make their base in Atlanta—where, he
wagered, they would end up spending a lot of time with Governor
Carter. *Time* could have pictured any one of the four other governors or
all of them on the cover—but as Rafshoon had hoped, the reporters

ended up spending more time with Carter, and he naturally got more copy in the story. It didn't hurt that J. Paul Austin, the CEO of Coca-Cola Company, headquartered in Atlanta, called up his friend Andrew Heiskell, the chairman of Time Inc., and urged him to feature Carter alone on the cover of the May 31, 1971, issue under the headline "Dixie Whistles a Different Tune." Suddenly, Jimmy Carter was a national political figure. Charlie Kirbo told him, "Some of those close to you will be promoting you for all kinds of damned jobs in the next year or so." But he bluntly warned him not to think about running for a national office.

THE CARTERS MOVED from Plains to the governor's mansion in Atlanta, built on eighteen acres just three years earlier at a cost of $2 million. By Georgia tradition, all the servants and gardeners working on the grounds were "trusties," convicted felons serving out their time from the state penitentiary. Prisoners selected for the "trusty" program had to be deemed reliable and trustworthy.

One such prisoner assigned to the mansion was an amiable twenty-five-year-old African American woman named Mary Prince Fitzpatrick. Born in Richmond, Georgia, just thirteen miles from Plains, Mary Prince was reared in a family with few resources and little education. She never knew her father, and her stepfather left when she was nine years old. "Mother raised vegetables," she said, "but there were times when we were hungry, and a lot of the time we just had bread, butter and syrup." She dropped out of school in seventh grade and spent her adolescence listening to rhythm and blues, dreaming of a career as a singer. By the time she was twenty, she had already given birth to two sons. Eventually, Mary found a job as a motel maid—and she worked part time in the evenings as a bar girl.

Life got even tougher one evening in April 1970 when she visited a bar in Lumpkin, Georgia, with a cousin, Aniemaude Perry. An argument occurred, and Cousin Aniemaude pulled a gun on a man, perhaps an ex-boyfriend. "I went outside and heard a shot," Mary later told a reporter from *People* magazine. "Aniemaude and this woman were fighting over Aniemaude's gun. I don't know anything about guns, but I tried to take it away and it went off. We didn't know it had hit anyone." A bullet hit and killed Aniemaude's ex-boyfriend. Mary was arrested, even though some eyewitnesses said she had not pulled the trigger. After four months in jail, Mary was assigned a court-appointed defense attorney. "I saw him twice for ten or fifteen minutes." The white lawyer quickly persuaded her to plead guilty to what she thought was a manslaughter charge, assuring her that this would get her a light punishment. Only later did she realize she had pled guilty to a murder charge, and the judge sentenced her to life imprisonment. "She was young, black, and penniless," Rosalynn Carter wrote, "and so she did as he [the lawyer] told her and got a life sentence in return."

The Carters learned of Mary's story only gradually. In December 1970, just before the Carters moved into the governor's mansion, Mary was selected by prison authorities to serve as a trusty. She was interviewed briefly by Rosalynn, who asked if she could take care of Amy. "She was just three," Mary later said, "and she took to me right away. She liked me to sing 'Swing Low, Sweet Chariot' to her every night, and I would rub her back and lie down with her. She would even cry at night because she hated to see me leave."

By the end of the year, Mary had become what they called a "friendly" in the governor's mansion. But even so, she still had to sleep each night in Fulton County Jail, together with other trusties. Rosalynn visited the jail and found the conditions so "deplorable" that afterward she couldn't sleep well. The Carters were fully cognizant of the pitfalls of southern justice and believed that Mary had been unfairly convicted. "She convinced us of her innocence," Jimmy later wrote. And ever since, Mary "has been an integral part of our family."

AS GOVERNOR, CARTER kept workaholic hours, arriving at his office in the Capitol every morning by 7:15. He insisted on punctuality and hated to waste time in meetings. He was a perfectionist, and while he could be brusque, he was willing to delegate authority—but always "with faint praise for those who use it well and icy stares for those who do not." He wanted data—not counsel. He spent his days reading memos and responding in writing. Most days he ate lunch alone at his desk, and only occasionally invited Hamilton Jordan, Bert Lance, or Charlie Kirbo to share lunch—as long as they paid for their own sandwiches. Kirbo and Carter were always on the same page. "I usually know," Kirbo said, "what he's going to do before he does it." The always discreet Kirbo saved his counsel for Carter's ears. "Kirbo speaks only to Carter," gibed an aide, "and Carter speaks only to God." Interestingly, as a Southern Baptist who believed in a clear separation of church and state, Carter canceled any religious services in the governor's mansion.

Early in his term Carter offered to appoint Kirbo to a vacant U.S. Senate seat, but Kirbo declined. He preferred to exert his influence behind the scenes, and without fanfare. "People wouldn't know whether I was acting on my own or whether it was Jimmy talking." Much of their relationship was conducted via memos, and "most of it was political advice." When President Nixon announced in July 1971 his diplomatic rapprochement with communist China, Kirbo wrote to Carter, "It was a sound move, and it will help strengthen his position in the months to come. I suspect that they are even now negotiating with China about the Vietnam war and they are likely to come up with a solution within nine months." He thought neither Democrats nor Carter in particular could score political points by criticizing Nixon's China policy: "If any criticism is made it should be that he has made the move too late."

Kirbo deeply admired Carter, but sometimes he felt he was there to compensate for Carter's utter transparency. "He had a policy I didn't like," Kirbo said, "of being open with everything. If he had a problem or scandal of some type, he would just lay it out. I spent about half my time patching up holes that were created by this openness. A lot of times, it served no purpose and was nonproductive. It helped nobody, but that was his policy."

Gradually, Carter also came to rely on Bert Lance, whom he had appointed, on Kirbo's recommendation, as state highway director. Lance began showing up early in the morning to discuss politics, and he often played tennis with Carter in the late afternoons. Born in 1931, Thomas Bertram Lance had grown up in Young Harris, a rural Appalachian community in northeastern Georgia, where his father was president of a liberal arts college. Later, his father became a Georgia public school superintendent and moved the family to Calhoun, another small town north of Atlanta. In sixth grade, Bert fell in love with a classmate, LaBelle David, the daughter of a local banker. They were married at nineteen. After three years at Emory University and then the University of Georgia, Bert dropped out of college and went to work in 1951 as a $90-a-month teller at the Calhoun First National Bank. LaBelle's grandfather was president of the bank. In 1963, Bert became president of the family bank. Ironically, arithmetic had never been Bert's long suit. "I don't use numbers if I can help it," he once said. But he was a charmer and good with people. And he could be candid with Carter. One day in the governor's office, Carter abruptly ended a meeting with a curt dismissal, telling everyone to "get back to work." As the aides filed out, Lance remained, and then calmly remonstrated: "You know, every once in a while, you might say 'Thank you' to these people."

Lance was instrumental in helping Carter to achieve his major legislative priority, a massive reorganization and reform of the state bureaucracy, consolidating various agencies and trimming budgetary waste under a "zero-based" budgetary policy. For Carter, it was just good governance, a matter of restructuring an "antiquated government." Georgia state legislators thought his reforms were high-handed—but Carter nevertheless pushed his proposals relentlessly. He wanted to consolidate more than three hundred state agencies into twenty-two departments. "I'm going to get it because it is right," he told reporters. Literally at the midnight hour, on the last night of the state senate's mandatory adjournment, Carter got his bill passed by a vote of twenty-nine to twenty-six. "Don't pay any attention to that smile," commented Georgia Secretary of State Ben Fortson. "That don't mean a thing. That man is made of steel, determination, and stubbornness. Carter reminds me of a South Georgia turtle. He doesn't go around a log. He just sticks his head in the middle and pushes and pushes until the log gives way."

By law, the state was required to run a balanced budget, and to this end, the governor had the right to strike any budget item from final bills. The state legislature convened for no more than forty-five days in alternating years, so a Georgia governor—unlike a president—possessed nearly unfettered executive powers. Naturally, Carter "took full advantage of this authority." As governor, he became accustomed to ignoring the legislative branch, an instinct that would not serve him well in the White House. One day he complained to Kirbo, "If one more legislator walks through that door and asks for some trade-off deal, so help me God, I think I'll throttle him." Carter's adversaries in Atlanta sensed his attitude. "He was always so right about everything," said one legislator. "Always so goddamned right, and righteous. That's what it was. That's what I didn't like about the little bastard." One of his conservative adversaries, House Speaker Thomas Murphy, quipped,

"He liked to run the state like he was still commanding a submarine." State senator Julian Bond complained, "I have never seen a man so rigid, and it was not on a question of high principle. Carter just wouldn't give in."

An impatient man, Carter was determined to get things done. "You could get in to see him," said one aide, "but when you got in, you better have something to say." Carter unilaterally doubled the number of African Americans on the state payroll and appointed fifty-three Blacks to various state committees, including parole boards. With Ku Klux Klansmen protesting outside, the governor ostentatiously hung a portrait of Martin Luther King, Jr., in the Georgia statehouse. Carter knew this piece of political theater would offend some whites, but he didn't care. When Kirbo expressed his trepidation about eliminating some of Maddox's people from the state payroll, Carter responded, "Hell, I couldn't wait to get in there."

Carter's other priorities included prison reform, equal education, reform of the judiciary, and legislation to protect the environment. It was a liberal tilt with an eye on watching the budget. He hired a noted criminologist and champion of prison reform to run the Georgia correctional system. Ellis MacDougall insisted on hiring prison wardens with college degrees and implemented in-prison vocational instruction, work-release, and rehabilitation programs. Under MacDougall, the number of Georgia parolees doubled. At the same time, Carter reluctantly signed a bill that reinstated the death penalty for certain crimes. Privately, he was relieved that no one was executed during his four-year tenure. He also opposed local prohibition laws, telling Georgians, "It is important for Baptists and others to realize that just because a county is dry doesn't mean that liquor isn't being sold."

In another unpopular move, he joined a lawsuit filed by the Koinonia communal farm against the Sumter County Board of Education, charging the board members with a bias against public education. Carter knew he was suing his neighbors, but he didn't care because he hated "to see my own county have the worst school situation in Georgia." Koinonia lost the case. Carter also vetoed plenty of popular pork-barrel legislation, including an Army Corps of Engineers dam that would have tamed a popular rafting river. He opposed unbridled commercial development, favored tough regulations to protect Georgia's coastal wetlands, and endorsed the creation of two major seashore and river parks. He took every opportunity to appoint liberals as state judges, including the first Jewish judge to the Georgia Court of Appeals.

Racial animosities always threatened to upset Carter's gubernatorial agenda. In September 1971 the Black and white citizens of the small town of Sparta, Georgia, population 8,759, suddenly began arming themselves. Seventy percent of Hancock County was Black, but the county seat, Sparta, population 478, was a majority-white township. Black voters had recently won control of the county government, and using funds from a Ford Foundation grant, the county administrator was aggressively trying to promote Black-owned businesses. The sudden shift in political power so frightened the county's outnumbered whites that Sparta's mayor, T. M. "Buck" Patterson, decided to announce that he had purchased ten submachine guns for his six white deputies. The Black county administrator, John McCown, promptly issued a public notice announcing that "sporting rifles" could be purchased by anyone joining a hunting club. Governor Carter was informed that purchase orders for thirty machine guns had been submitted by McCown. Carter moved quickly to defuse the situation, dispatching a three-member mediation team to Sparta and ordering them to buy back any machine guns. It took seven hours of tense negotiations, but finally Sparta's mayor agreed to surrender his machine guns. McCown credited Governor Carter's "personal intervention" for de-escalating the situation.

Carter had run against the Atlanta establishment—and of course, that meant the legislators too. Jody and Hamilton were the tip of the governor's spear. "Here were these 25-year-old kids—and you have to remember how young Hamilton and Jody were at the time—telling grizzled old state legislators where to shove it," one state official told the reporter Joe Klein. "There were stories that Jody would stand right in front of Lester Maddox, the lieutenant governor, and blow smoke in his face." Jody was practically channeling Jimmy Carter; they were that close. Carter treated him like a son. "Jody knows Jimmy better than anyone," observed a mutual friend. Both men had an impish desire to stick it to the establishment. They thought of themselves as outliers. "Jody—and Jimmy—really enjoyed that role," said one journalist who wrote about

Carter's governorship. "The outsider on the white horse. The battler against special interests. They loved controversy."

Carter also knew how to deflect controversy. In the spring of 1971, Lieutenant William L. Calley, Jr., was convicted by court-martial of murdering twenty-two Vietnamese civilians at My Lai, South Vietnam. More than three hundred unarmed civilians had been killed on March 16, 1968—and the U.S. Army managed to cover up the massacre for eighteen months. In due course, however, Calley and twenty-five other soldiers were charged with murder. But only Calley was convicted, and on March 31, 1971, he was sentenced to life imprisonment. Just one day later, responding to public sentiment, President Nixon ordered Calley transferred from Fort Leavenworth and placed under "house arrest" in Fort Benning, south of Atlanta.

Many Georgians thought Calley was being unfairly singled out for crimes carried out in the fog of war. Carter knew better. "I never thought Calley was anything but guilty," he later said. "I never felt any attitude toward Calley except abhorrence." But the Georgian commander of the Veterans of Foreign Wars held a press conference and challenged the governor to declare an official day of support for the convicted mass killer. Lieutenant Governor Maddox publicly called on Nixon to pardon Calley.

Under enormous political pressure, Carter held a press conference on April 2, 1971, and flatly stated that Calley had become a "scapegoat" and his commanding officers should "receive the same treatment as Calley." He went on to suggest that antiwar critics were using the Calley conviction "to cheapen and shame the reputation of American servicemen." But instead of paying tribute to the convicted officer with a "William Calley Day," Governor Carter proclaimed April 5 "American Fighting Men's Day." He then asked Georgians to honor military servicemen on that day by turning on their auto headlights while driving. Critics of the war were appalled by Carter's pandering to those who would come to the defense of a mass killer. But there were not many antiwar critics in Georgia—and not many people elsewhere paid much attention to the Georgia governor's words.

Carter had managed to signal a nod to the Right for his Georgia constituency while evading the full focus of the more liberal national media.

Carter's close adviser and friend Dr. Peter Bourne concluded, "It was a skillful and successful ploy that defused the situation."* Interestingly, Carter's closest adviser, Charlie Kirbo, told him that he differed in his position on Calley. "While I disagree with your position on the Calley thing, I believe that politically, it has reoriented you with the conservative element out over the state." Kirbo thought that was a good thing, because he was already worried that Governor Carter was getting too much press exposure as a liberal who was beginning to cozy up to the Atlanta establishment: "If you let them, they will love you." Kirbo warned him that his press clips were tending to identify him with the "upper bracket." He advised him to get his photo taken with his coat off, sitting on a tractor or fishing. In these divisive times, Kirbo was particularly attuned to the optics of his protégé's position on the Vietnam War.

Carter's stance on the war was vague. Kirbo was telling him that spring that many voters had come to regard Vietnam as a "mistake." But at the same time, Kirbo warned against "playing politics with the question of the war." Democrats like former Democratic presidential candidate Eugene McCarthy might be calling for an "immediate withdrawal," but, Kirbo told Carter, "I think we should stay away from the war issue right now, but if it has to be discussed I do not believe it's safe to talk about fixing a date to withdraw."

Kirbo was generally very cautious about the war. He realized that most Americans had come to the conclusion that it had been one big mistake—and yet his instincts told him that voters might still punish an antiwar politician like Senator George McGovern while Americans were still dying on the battlefield. He told Carter that in the public's mind it was the Democrats and Lyndon Johnson who had gotten us into the war—and therefore it looked "ridiculous or irresponsible to criticize Nixon about being slow to get us out of a mess that the public thinks the Democrats got us in." Kirbo advised backing the commander in chief so long as "he is trying to get out of Vietnam." This positioned Carter well to the right of his fellow Democrats. But Kirbo didn't mind if Carter sounded "a bit conservative" compared to other Democrats, because

---

* Calley remained under house arrest, but after a series of court appeals, his life sentence was cut to ten years, and he was freed in 1974 after serving only three and a half years. Most of this confinement was in his own apartment at Fort Benning.

"remember that we feel like the national opinion is somewhat similar to Georgia's opinion—which is conservative." Carter seemed to agree.

By 1972, CARTER was already signaling to the national media that his political ambitions were not confined to Georgia. As Democrats assembled in Miami to select a nominee for president, Carter was being labeled as a moderate critic of the presumptive nominee, Senator George McGovern.* But astonishingly, this first-term governor was clearly jockeying to position himself as a possible vice presidential pick. On the eve of the convention, Kirbo advised Carter to "remain moderate and progressive" and therefore "attractive" to "anyone who is . . . interested in you on the national ticket."

Carter followed this advice by formally nominating Senator Henry "Scoop" Jackson—but he also kept his distance from George Wallace, signaling to the McGovern forces that a "moderate progressive" southern governor like him might be an astute pick for the veep slot. Carter even asked the civil rights leader Andrew Young, who was running for an Atlanta congressional seat that year, to suggest his name to McGovern. But it was not to be. McGovern named Missouri senator Tom Eagleton as his vice presidential candidate—but then Eagleton had to withdraw when it was discovered he had undergone electroshock therapy for depression.

Seeing an opening, Jimmy sent Rosalynn over to see Dr. Peter Bourne, who had close ties to the McGovern camp. Rosalynn urged Bourne to call his friends and recommend Carter as Eagleton's replacement on the ticket. Simultaneously, Jimmy got a somewhat reluctant state representative, Julian Bond, to do the same thing. Bourne and Bond failed to persuade anyone in McGovern's camp—but clearly, Carter wanted to run for national office, even if it was on the same ticket with the much more liberal George McGovern. He was both audacious and tenacious—and too early.

That summer Jody Powell wrote to Carter that he thought "it was

---

* To Carter's surprise, his middle son, Chip, had organized Democrats in Georgia's Third Congressional District to attend the convention as McGovern delegates. Carter had to bargain with Chip, who gave up his own slot as a delegate but in return got his father to promise him all expenses and credentials for the convention.

important to make it 'perfectly clear' that you are not down on McGovern just because he is anti-establishment. Point out that you were the same sort of candidate. In many ways, your campaign organization in Georgia was a mix of Wallace and McGovern. You fought and are still fighting the established economic, social and political leadership in Georgia." Powell's notion that Carter was a "mix of Wallace and McGovern" was itself an audacious idea—but prescient.

By early autumn, Carter and his advisers correctly assumed that McGovern would be trounced by President Richard Nixon. Now certain of Carter's ambitions, Bourne sent the governor a ten-page memorandum, urging him to run for the presidency in 1976. "Once you have made a decision to compete nationally," Bourne argued, "you have to take positions that will alienate a lot of people in the South. . . . What is critical is the psychological and emotional decision to take the risk." Carter passed Bourne's memo to Hamilton Jordan, who then proceeded to flesh out the rationale for a Carter campaign. Interestingly, Bourne, Jordan, and others in his inner circle were talking about *how* Carter could win the nomination—but there was little discussion on the question of *why*.

Carter firmly revealed his decision to run to only a handful of confidants at an early-morning meeting in the governor's mansion. The date was October 17, 1972. In attendance were Dr. Bourne, Jordan, Powell, Rafshoon—and a thirty-one-year-old Atlanta real estate developer, Landon Butler, who had become an informal adviser to Carter on environmental issues. (Butler was first a friend of Jordan's older brother, Lawton, and had become Hamilton's deputy early in 1971.) Carter told these men that he and Rosalynn were committed. Walking out of the meeting, Rafshoon turned to Jordan and said, "The son of a bitch, he wants it." Rosalynn wanted it too. "She wants to be first lady as bad as he wants to be president," Jordan later remarked. "Hell, she wants it worse than he does."

After the November election debacle, the Carter family spent a relaxed Thanksgiving on the Georgia coast, interrupted only by the arrival of Jordan, who came with a confidential fifty-two-page memo laying out in considerable detail how Carter could win the presidency in 1976. Jordan argued that Carter could win the nomination, even in a crowded field of candidates, by running hard in all the early primaries. Precisely because the media would peg Carter as a southern regional candidate, Jordan argued that they needed to have "a strong surprise showing in New Hampshire and a victory in Florida." Jordan assumed that Carter's two major opponents for the nomination would be Senator Ted Kennedy and ex-governor George Wallace. If Kennedy ran, he thought, few if any other liberal Democrats would be willing to run. But quite audaciously, Jordan advised Carter that he thought "it would be very difficult for Senator Kennedy to win a national election, as the unanswered questions of Chappaquiddick run contrary to this national desire for trust and morality in government." Jordan therefore actually thought Carter could defeat Kennedy in the primaries.

Defeating George Wallace was another issue. "In my opinion," Jordan wrote, "a serious national effort by George Wallace in 1976 would preempt your candidacy." Jordan saw Wallace as a credible candidate in the South. Interestingly, Kirbo disagreed. While Kirbo agreed with much of Jordan's thinking, he did not believe that Wallace "had any possibility of being elected President." Kirbo advised Carter, "I think we are sort of over-sensitive to the Wallace problem since he is so near us and so many of our Georgia people support him so loudly. . . . If it is not him, it will be somebody else. There will be plenty of people in the field and if we are going to make the trip, we need to plan to go over, through or around whoever happens to get in the way." Running against Wallace might even work to Carter's benefit. "He [Wallace] knows that Jimmy can appeal to groups who he cannot reach." In short, Kirbo thought Carter could do to Wallace what he had done to Carl "Cuff Links" Sanders in 1970.

In preparation for the coming campaign, both Jordan and Kirbo thought Carter would need to burnish his foreign policy credentials with a trip or two abroad. As an afterthought, Jordan advised him to read *The New York Times* every day, despite "its liberal orientation and bias."

By Christmas 1972, Jimmy was telling his sons and the rest of the family that he was running for president. Miss Lillian initially responded, "President of *what*?"

IN JANUARY 1973, Governor Carter gave a speech at the National Press Club in Washington. There was no formal announcement, but reporters could speculate that the Georgian was testing the national waters. Andrew Young happened to be sitting in the audience, and as Carter spoke, he jotted a quick note and passed it to Dr. Peter Bourne: "I'll be damned if he isn't running for president."

Early in the new year, Kirbo began writing occasional memos, quietly advising Carter on campaign strategy. On domestic affairs, he thought Carter should run on a theme of "benevolent conservatism." He told him, "You did a great job with this during the [gubernatorial] campaign and I believe you can handle it effectively on a national scale." Kirbo had in mind an ideologically eclectic program that would appeal to both Wallace and McGovern Democrats. Kirbo wanted to wed the notion of local control—meaning states' rights—with a fiscally lean and efficient federal government. "We need an administration that understands the individual states, their problems, their limitations and their capacity."

Nearly a decade after LBJ's Great Society programs had been enacted, conservatives were getting away with labeling liberal Democrats as wasteful, inefficient spendthrifts. Kirbo's instinct was to package Carter as a neoliberal candidate, a politician who "believes in or will implement these [liberal] programs but is a conservative businessman and will see that the programs are properly administered in a business-like manner." He gave as an example the "foolish policy of selecting blacks because they had to deal with blacks when they were absolutely incompetent." Kirbo cited the practice of putting tenants in public housing projects in charge of running housing boards "when every one of them are ignorant, have no experience and are mostly on welfare." While this might give such people "an opportunity to be heard, it also screws up the program where it becomes ridiculous and the whole project has to be abandoned." Kirbo understood that this "cannot be said in many places without appearing to be racist, but I believe for example if you were speaking to a group of liberal Jews in New York or California . . . you could speak frankly about this, and they are all good businessmen and they like to win and I believe they will understand."

To be sure, Kirbo was no segregationist. He wanted Carter to "work with all races and without race being the dominant consideration." He just wanted Carter to make sure that his audiences "know that you are a businessman and a nuclear engineer and are aware that sound, ambitious and compassionate programs can fail unless they are conservatively managed and efficiently carried out."

Kirbo's views on foreign affairs were less developed, but his instincts were similarly neoliberal in tone. President Nixon and his national security adviser, Henry Kissinger, had finally negotiated an end to the Vietnam War on January 23, 1973. Two weeks later, Kirbo wrote to Carter that he thought "the peace we have is rather thin." The world was still a complicated and dangerous place, "and in all events, we must continue to be the number one military power." The energy crisis had hit the country "without any careful planning," but it made clear that it was the federal government's responsibility to see that people had "adequate fuel and energy, particularly as they related to some of the simple necessities of life."

Meanwhile, Richard Nixon's presidency was beginning to crumble. By the spring of 1973 the White House's inept efforts to cover up the administration's role in the Watergate break-in were unraveling. "The Watergate fuss," Kirbo advised Carter on May 23, 1973, "may require us to do some re-thinking and careful planning about your role and what you say in your speeches in the future." Kirbo advised Carter to keep his distance from the "Washington crowd." Anyone running for president, he said, was going to have trouble if he was too closely identified with Washington. The public's mood now was to "throw the bastards out," and so Kirbo thought an outsider with no connections to Washington stood a good chance of capturing the Democratic nomination. He even suggested that Carter should start thinking about developing a stump speech, "somewhat along the line that people were demanding law and order and ought to have law and order with respect to blacks, the poor etc. but we need law and order on a high plane in government, in politics, in big business and in all the affairs of man." Carter should call for "new moral standards in all these areas."

This was astute political advice, if somewhat cynical. But Carter still had to pay attention to his "day job" as governor for the next two years. Few suspected that he was already preparing a national campaign. Fortuitously, he soon received a phone call from Robert Strauss, an influential corporate lawyer from Texas. A political ally of Lyndon Johnson's, Strauss had just been elected chairman of the Democratic Party. Strauss said he wanted to meet with Carter. Kirbo joined them at a meeting in the governor's mansion where Strauss asked if Carter would help elect Democrats in the upcoming 1974 midterm elections. Carter jumped at

the offer, though he later confessed he had "kind of pretended to be reluctant and then I agreed to do it." Soon afterward Hamilton Jordan flew
to Washington, DC, where he became the executive director of the
Democratic National Committee's 1974 Congressional and Gubernatorial Campaign Committee.* Carter served as chairman, giving him an
inside seat on the Democratic Party's campaign apparatus. Strauss had
no inkling that the relatively obscure Georgia governor had already decided to seek the party's presidential nomination. "Bob was an innocent
victim," Kirbo later said. Carter and Jordan made the most of this opportunity, making thousands of contacts around the country, all the
while learning the nuts and bolts of how to run a national campaign.
Committee staffers jokingly referred to Jordan as "the Trojan peanut."

One night in Washington, Jordan left his office in the Democratic
National Committee and forgot to refile a copy of his 1972 strategy
memo, leaving it out open on his desk. Early the next morning an aide
to Strauss read the seventy-two-page document outlining how Carter
could win the presidency. The blunt Strauss later confronted Jordan: "Is
this yours?"

"Yeah," Jordan admitted.

"So Carter is going to run for president?" Strauss said with a chuckle.

Jordan mumbled in the affirmative, and Strauss told him, "Don't
worry, I'm not going to tell anybody because they'll think I'm crazy."

Strauss was a shrewd operator, a man who knew how to straddle different worlds. He knew Texas, and so he knew the Old South and the
potential of the rising New South. But he also knew how to grease the
wheels of the Washington establishment, connecting lobbyists, lawyers,
and journalists to elected officials on Capitol Hill and powerful civil servants in the federal bureaucracy. He was a bridge. And while he was
highly skeptical of Carter's ambitions in 1973, he would not get in his
way. Strauss would let things take their course.

That same spring of 1973, Carter received another fortuitous invitation, this time from David Rockefeller. The powerful New York financier
wanted a token politician from the rising New South to join his recently
formed Trilateral Commission, a semiannual gathering of corporate ex-

---

* Initially, Jordan was paid so poorly that he complained to Carter, "I personally cannot
afford to go deeper and deeper in debt."

ecutives, academicians, scientists, and a handful of politicians from America, Europe, and Japan. Initially, there were no more than fifty members on the commission, and Carter was one of only two U.S. governors invited. Rockefeller's hope was that their private debates would forge a degree of harmony on critical global issues, including trade, the environment, and management of the West's Cold War rivalry with the Soviet Union. It was partly a rich man's discussion group, modeled after the Bilderberg Meeting, a similar body funded by the CIA in the 1950s to stimulate consensus building between American and European elites.

Carter attended his first Trilateral Commission meeting in October 1973 and became a regular participant, conversing with men like Cyrus Vance, Michael Blumenthal, and Harold Brown—all three of whom he would later appoint to cabinet positions. Carter used the commission's seminars in Washington, New York, Tokyo, and elsewhere to broaden his contacts and burnish his credentials on foreign policy but also macroeconomic issues. In the spring of 1974, for instance, he received a detailed tutorial on the global economy and the problem of inflation from a New York economist named Paul Volcker—whom Carter later appointed to be chairman of the Federal Reserve. The Trilateral Commission issued short policy papers on international issues, and Carter "studied those things like a Bible."

The Trilateral Commission gave the Georgia governor some foreign policy chops. But more important, he was introduced to Zbigniew Brzezinski and Cyrus Vance, two rising stars of the American foreign policy establishment. Carter was impressed by both men.

Brzezinski, a professor at Columbia University, was the Trilateral Commission's executive director. Born in Warsaw, Poland, in 1928, Brzezinski had landed in New York when he was ten years old. He was not a refugee but the privileged son of a Polish diplomat assigned as consul general in Montreal. He spent the war years in Canada, knowing that his homeland had been occupied, first by the Nazis and after the war by the communists. It was a bitter lesson in geopolitics. As a young college student at McGill University in Montreal in the late 1940s, he was already known for his stridently anticommunist views. "My homeland was denied to me after the end of World War II," Brzezinski recalled, "and I craved something I could identify with."

By 1950 he was studying international relations at Harvard. He became an American citizen in 1958, but he still spoke English with a Polish accent. At Harvard he formed a not-so-subtle intellectual rivalry with Henry Kissinger. And when in 1959 Kissinger, five years older, received a tenured position as an associate professor, a disappointed Brzezinski moved to Columbia University. Like Kissinger, he used his academic position to influence policy makers in Washington. He floated in and out of the ivory tower. He was an active member of the Council on Foreign Relations. In 1960, he was an informal foreign policy adviser to the John Kennedy presidential campaign, and he similarly advised President Lyndon Johnson during the 1964 campaign. He advertised himself as a Democrat's alternative to the Republican Kissinger. But he was pretty much a hawk on most issues. During the 1962 missile crisis, he cabled his White House friend Arthur Schlesinger, Jr.: "Any further delay in bombing missile sites fails to exploit Soviet uncertainty." As a Cold Warrior, he supported the Vietnam War, arguing that it was necessary to contain communism in Asia. By the early 1970s, he was criticizing the détente policies of Kissinger and President Richard Nixon, suggesting that détente was merely helping to prop up a weakened Soviet empire. At the Trilateral Commission he advanced the notion that a policy of engagement and liberalization could loosen the Kremlin's hold over Eastern Europe. For Brzezinski, what mattered most was getting the Russians out of his native Poland.

Precise and sharp-witted, Brzezinski impressed Carter with his passion and his knowledge of foreign policy. The two men clicked and began to exchange handwritten notes. Before long, "Zbig" found himself drafting speeches for the Georgia governor.

Cyrus Vance was a wholly different personality: calm, diplomatic in manner and speech, and ever thoughtful. Hamilton Jordan described him as "solid as a rock and completely predictable." Vance had served eight years as a high-ranking Defense Department official in the Kennedy and Johnson administrations. He personified the gravitas of a hardworking member of the foreign policy establishment. A graduate of Yale Law School, Vance later became a partner in the New York law firm of Simpson, Thacher & Bartlett. Working in Washington at the height of the Vietnam War had also taught him a healthy skepticism about the use of military force. He had quietly resigned in June 1967, unhappy with the Johnson administration's escalation of the bombing of North Vietnam.

That same summer, Brzezinski was advocating an escalation of the war. Their differences over Vietnam were striking.

Brzezinski, of course, had known Vance for years in New York City, interacting with him at meetings of the Council on Foreign Relations and more recently at the Trilateral Commission. But they were not especially close. Brzezinski thought Vance had become too much of a dove in the aftermath of the Vietnam War. He also thought Vance had an "overoptimistic" view of détente and the Russians. Indeed, he thought of him as a weak exemplar of the old white Anglo-Saxon Protestant establishment, a dying breed. In short, Brzezinski suspected Vance lacked a certain toughness—which led him to think that he could always handle the soft-spoken lawyer.

Carter first met Vance during a brief meeting in Atlanta in 1971. They next encountered each other at a meeting of the Trilateral Commission. They were only acquaintances, but Carter found himself impressed by Vance's humility and low-key demeanor.

Brzezinski, Vance, and other members of the Trilateral Commission gave this southern outsider a window onto the foreign policy establishment. He was fraternizing with powerful men—and finding himself at ease doing so. One day in December 1974 Carter was listening to a discussion group led by Secretary of State Henry Kissinger when an elderly British diplomat stood up and asked a long-winded, meandering nonquestion. When after five long minutes the British gentleman finally sat down and Kissinger rose to respond, Governor Carter interjected in his Georgia drawl, "Mr. Secretary, would you mind repeating the question?" The audience erupted with laughter.

ON THE EVENING of January 21, 1974, Carter and his family drove to the Omni, Atlanta's new arena, to attend a rock concert featuring Bob Dylan and The Band. Carter had been a fan of Dylan's lyrics since at least 1965. Back in his navy days he had been obsessed with classical music. "Then I started to listen to Bob Dylan's music primarily because of my sons, but I got to like it and I used to spend three or four hours a day listening to Paul Simon, Bob Dylan and the Allman Brothers. At home, I'd study government reorganization or budgeting techniques while I listened to rock." His favorite Dylan album was the 1966 release *Blonde on Blonde*.

It was a memorable show; Dylan and The Band played such classics as "Blowin' in the Wind" and "Knockin' on Heaven's Door" and closed with "Like a Rolling Stone." Afterward, Dylan and his fellow musicians drove out to the governor's mansion, where Carter had invited them a month earlier for a postconcert party. Carter gave Dylan a tour of the mansion and the two men chatted quietly in hushed tones. "First thing he did was quote my songs back to me," Dylan recalled. "He put my mind at ease by not talking down to me." Carter later said he thought Dylan was "painfully timid." The bard never initiated a conversation, but "he'll answer a question if you ask him."

Also invited that evening was Gregg Allman—who showed up only after all the other guests had just departed. Allman sheepishly apologized to the police officer manning the gate and was about to turn around when the guard received a phone call from the mansion. It was Carter calling, and he insisted that Allman come up to the mansion. "I thought I was going to get a federal butt-chewing," Allman recalled, "so we drive up, and I see the silhouette of this guy standing on the porch. He didn't have on a shirt, he didn't have any shoes on, and he had on this old pair of Levi's, and they were seasoned down perfect, man—they were almost white. I thought, 'Who's this bum they're letting hang out at the governor's mansion?' But dadgum! It was him! So we get out, go inside, and after meeting all the ladies, he gets everybody out of the room but me and him. So he goes to the cupboard, gets a bottle of J&B scotch, and we sit there and pretty well finish off the jug."

Allman was charmed. At one point, Carter turned to Allman and said, "Gregory—can I call you Gregory? I'm going to be president." Allman nearly spit his drink all over the room and replied, "Sir, not being a smartass, but there hasn't been a Southern president since 1842."

"That's gonna change," replied Carter.

Allman was won over by this brashness—and the following year he and his band played at benefit concerts to raise funds for Carter's campaign.

Three months later, on May 4, 1974, Senator Ted Kennedy was invited by the University of Georgia in Athens to give the keynote address at an event billed as "Law Day." Governor Carter was asked to give the luncheon talk at the same event. Carter nearly declined but decided to accept because he knew his son Jack, by then a third-year law student, would be in the audience. Curious to size up Kennedy, Carter invited the senator to stay at the governor's mansion the night before the event. "Everyone thought he was going to be the next president," Carter recalled. But Carter was not impressed. His son Jack was in the mansion that evening, and he thought Kennedy was "just very bland." The next morning, the two politicians treated each other with cold, polite deference. "Jimmy Carter baffled me," Kennedy recalled decades later. "I believed then and now that he reserved a special place in his animus toward me." Their personal chemistry was awkward. In an effort to extend the Boston politician a touch of southern hospitality, Carter initially told Kennedy he could have use of his official plane to fly to Athens, where the Law Day event was scheduled. But the next morning, for some reason, the plane was not available—so Carter brusquely withdrew the offer, without explanation. Kennedy was deeply annoyed. If Carter noticed, the incident would only have confirmed his perception that this last of the famous Kennedy brothers lived a life of entitlement.

Hunter S. Thompson, the late, great inventor of gonzo journalism, happened to be traveling with Kennedy that day and observed the chilly encounter between the two men. Thompson immediately noticed "the relaxed and confident way" Carter handled himself with Kennedy, who was "sitting there looking stiff and vaguely uncomfortable." Thompson had stayed up late drinking with Jack Carter, but he had decided to spend the night in a motel. When he showed up hungover the next morning at the governor's mansion, Thompson thought Carter was "not an imposing figure in any way. . . . He could pass for a Fuller Brush man on any street in America." Thompson assumed that Carter was just another slick, two-faced southern cracker. But later that day he began to change his mind.

Late that morning Kennedy gave his speech—and Carter realized that it "was basically the same speech I was going to make." So he threw away his own prepared remarks and hastily scribbled out some notes on a yellow legal pad. He began his off-the-cuff remarks by noting the presence of the powerful and rich Massachusetts senator. He pointed out that he had spoken for free the previous evening to an audience that had paid $10 that night to hear Senator Kennedy speak. And then he joked that the luncheon tickets for his speech were $3.50—enough to "salvage part of my ego."

Because the occasion was Law Day and many lawyers might be in the audience, Carter decided to vent his heartfelt disgust with the inequities of the criminal justice system. Perhaps he was inspired by the personal circumstances of Amy's nanny, Mary Fitzpatrick. But instead of Mary's story, Carter recounted the story of a poor, illiterate African American woman who was swindled out of her land on the Georgia coast by a corrupt sheriff. Seeking justice, the woman had hired a lawyer, only to learn later that the man failed to file the necessary claims by the legal deadline—and so she had lost all rights to her only property. Carter told her story with unaccustomed passion. At one point, he candidly told this roomful of lawyers, "I don't know, it may be that poor people are the only ones who commit crimes, but I do know that they are the only ones who serve prison sentences." Carter explained that, not being a lawyer, he had nevertheless learned a bit about law and society by reading Reinhold Niebuhr. "The other source of my understanding about what's right and wrong in this society is from a friend of mine, a poet named Bob Dylan. . . . I grew up as a landowner's son. But, I don't think I ever realized the proper interrelationship between the landowner and those who worked on a farm until I heard Dylan's record, 'I Ain't Gonna Work on Maggie's Farm No More.'"

Thompson was sipping iced tea spiked with whiskey, and only vaguely listening to Carter's speech, when he suddenly noticed that the room had gone quiet. "It was the anger in his voice that first caught my attention," Thompson wrote. "They had not come there to hear lawyers denounced as running dogs of the status quo." Afterward, Thompson ran after Carter and asked him for a transcript.

"There is no transcript," Carter replied. He showed Thompson a page and a half of handwritten notes and said that was all he had.

"Jesus Christ," Thompson exclaimed. "That was one of the damnedest things I've ever heard. You mean you just winged it all the way through?"

Carter smiled and admitted, "I guess I was a little surprised at how it came out."

Years later, he reminisced with Peter Bourne about the Law Day speech: "I went in and just let my hair down to that crowd in a totally extemporaneous way. . . . I think it was probably the best speech I ever made." His son Jack agreed: "I get chill bumps thinking about it."

Thompson thought it was "a king hell bastard of a speech, and by the time it was over he had rung every bell in the room." Two years later,

Thompson wrote about it in a cover story for *Rolling Stone* in which he endorsed Carter for president. By then, Thompson had concluded that Carter was "one of the most intelligent politicians I've ever met, and also one of the strangest." He also thought Carter was one of the "meanest men" he had ever met. By that Thompson meant "functional meanness," which he defined as the ability to get from A to B or Z. "I saw him push Teddy Kennedy around in Athens, Georgia. . . . I was stunned." The literary lion Norman Mailer had a similar reaction to Carter, calling him a "political genius." Mailer generally had a low opinion of politicians. He wrote that politics was "a dance where you need not do more than move from right to left and left to right while evading the full focus of the media." Mailer thought the skill was in the timing—and Carter seemed elegantly adept at this public dance. But an even more astute political observer, Garry Wills, noted that the whole point of Carter's speech was to prove that he could "hold his own" against a Kennedy: "Carter cut him down that day, deftly, politely, but unmistakably." It was the beginning of a fateful public rivalry.

AS THE GOVERNOR contemplated a national campaign, Hamilton Jordan crafted a lengthy questionnaire, asking his potential candidate to spell out his positions. Hamilton was prepping his candidate. Carter provided succinct, handwritten answers to most of Jordan's 137 questions. Critics later would accuse candidate Carter of being extraordinarily vague, but Jordan's private questionnaire revealed a candidate who knew exactly what he believed on a wide variety of domestic and foreign policy issues. If he had a vision, it was pragmatic—socially liberal on domestic issues and moderately dovish on foreign policy. To his analytical mind, the positions he staked out were all about common sense. It was all very utilitarian.

In response to a question about school busing, Carter wrote, "Mandatory busing of children to distant schools, against the wishes of the child or its parents should not be required." But "busing students who desire to attend another school, providing the busing increases integration, seems to work ok." He favored an extension of the 1965 Voting Rights Act. He favored registration of all handguns and a prohibition of "Saturday night specials." He favored making marijuana possession a misdemeanor offense. Asked about inflation, Carter said he would "restrain

[the] growth in money supply." In principle, he favored reduced trade barriers. He thought teachers, firemen, and policemen should have the right to freely organize in public employee unions—but "binding arbitration would be preferable to the right to strike." On energy, he wanted to reduce foreign imports of oil by at least one million barrels a day— and he would make this happen through increased prices coupled with a tax rebate for the poor. If necessary, he would adopt a national ration program to force reduced consumption of natural gas and gasoline. He favored the elimination of the oil depletion allowance. Offshore oil drilling should be minimized for environmental reasons. But he favored a "TVA type" quasi-governmental corporation to explore for domestic oil. He added sarcastically, "After all, the Corps of Engineers may need something to do when they quit building unnecessary dams." He flatly opposed any relaxation of auto emissions standards. He favored more investment in a mass transportation system. Air- and water-pollution standards "should be raised as technology permits." He favored strict controls on strip mining. He favored the creation of a national health insurance program run by the federal government. The nation's welfare system should be "simple and understandable." Recipients of welfare should be encouraged to work—and the system should include "aspects of publicly financed employment." The space program, he noted, was "not a top priority for me." But he thought federal funding of the arts should be increased. Public and educational television should be "improved and strengthened with minimal government censorship and control. . . . News analysis of controversial subjects, for instance, should be encouraged."

He supported amnesty for those who refused to serve in the Vietnam War. Asked about pornography, Carter wrote, "Just need an understandable and permanent Supreme Court ruling." He was against "euthanasia." And he was "not familiar" with the goals of the gay liberation movement. But he favored decriminalization of "homosexual conduct between consenting adults." Asked about the controversial issue of abortion, Carter wrote that the Supreme Court's recent decision in *Roe v. Wade* "suits me." He was also against mandatory prayer in schools.

Turning to foreign policy, Carter thought America's NATO allies should be contributing more to defense spending. But he thought the Southeast Asia Treaty Organization (SEATO) could be safely disbanded.

He favored withdrawing America's 26,000 troops from Thailand, and the 40,000 troops stationed in South Korea could also be sent home. In fact, he wanted to shutter many of America's "222 foreign military bases." He thought Castro's Cuba should be allowed to join the Organization of American States (OAS). He favored full diplomatic relations with mainland China—but he also favored normal relations with Taiwan.

On defense issues, Carter was decidedly dovish. He wanted to reduce the defense budget and cut tactical nuclear weapons by 50 percent. He thought the limits on nuclear weapons set in the SALT (Strategic Arms Limitation Talks) treaty were "too high." He complained that "we are still accumulating excessive nuclear weapons." He favored the cancellation of the proposed B-1 strategic bomber. He wished to propose to the Soviets a treaty to drastically reduce the number of nuclear weapons—with the ultimate goal being the "complete elimination of nuclear weapons."

Asked where he placed himself on the political spectrum, and specifically, "Are you closer to George McGovern or George Wallace?" Carter replied evasively, "I have no desire to place myself on any political spectrum." But if his handwritten answers to Jordan's questionnaire had leaked to the press, most political pundits would have concluded that the Georgia governor was a thoughtful but decidedly nonideological maverick. Needless to say, Jordan kept Carter's frank answers locked away in his personal files.

Early in 1974, Carter persuaded Atlanta lawyer Stu Eizenstat to produce more than two dozen succinct policy papers on various issues for the Democratic Party's Congressional Campaign Committee. When, in October, the lanky, self-effacing young lawyer had finished this task, Eizenstat invited the governor to lunch at a restaurant near the state capitol and pitched to him what he thought was a brazen idea. In the wake of the Watergate scandal, Eizenstat said, he thought the Democrats would do well in the November congressional elections, and Carter, as chairman of the Campaign Committee, would probably get some credit for this victory. Looking ahead to the 1976 presidential primaries, Eizenstat suggested Carter might run and win a few southern state primaries—and thus earn a spot on the national ticket as vice president. Carter grinned and responded, "Stu, I have already decided to run, but I am going to be the Democratic candidate for president, not vice president. Would you like to join my campaign?"

Carter formally announced his candidacy for the presidency on December 12, 1974. *The New York Times* reported the early announcement the following morning and described Carter as "a Southern Kennedy." By then, both Senators Ted Kennedy and Walter Mondale had dropped out, leaving the race wide open. Carter was certainly a fresh face, and his life story reeked of gritty authenticity. When he announced, "I'll never lie to you," and incorporated this promise as part of his stump speech, people took note. But Kirbo told him, half seriously, "You're going to lose the liar vote." His former Georgia rival Lester Maddox told reporters, "The reason he says he never lies is because he thinks the truth originates with him."

Miss Lillian was asked by Kandy Stroud, a Washington reporter for *Women's Wear Daily,* if her son really had never told a lie. Annoyed, Miss Lillian replied, "Well, maybe a little white lie every now and then." Microphone in hand, Stroud leaned forward and asked, "What do you mean by a white lie?" Miss Lillian replied, "Honey, do you remember a few minutes ago when I met you at the door and said that you looked very nice and that I was glad to see you? That was a white lie."

A key part of Carter's campaign stump speech was a declaration that he wanted a government "as good as the American people." Often he expanded on this phrase by saying, "I want a government that is as good, and honest, and decent, and truthful, and fair, and competent, and idealistic, and compassionate, and as filled with love as are the American people." Reporters heard the line so often, they groaned. *Washington Post* reporter Jules Witcover observed, "He recited this sequence almost as if it were his personal rosary, and, crowd after crowd, it worked."

If vague, it nevertheless appealed to voters emotionally drained by the Watergate scandal. But he also spoke a populist language, labeling the tax system unfair and a "disgrace to the human race." He called for universal voter registration and endorsed both the Equal Rights Amendment and universal, mandatory national health insurance—but only "as revenues permit." He pledged to create a Department of Education. But in general, he refrained from endorsing any big-budget spending programs. He criticized government waste and attacked congressional pork-barrel projects. He portrayed himself as a peanut farmer who favored energy conservation and regulations to protect the environment. But he also said he was a fiscal conservative.

Kandy Stroud concluded he was a maddening "enigma," even after following him around for much of two years on the campaign trail. "Carter is not just complex," Stroud wrote, "he is contradictory. His paradoxes are multiple. He is at once vain and humble, sensitive and ruthless, soft-hearted and tough, conservative and liberal, country boy with city wisdom, spiritual and pragmatic, loving and cold. He can be fascinating and dull. His sister Gloria once told me, 'He's the most boring person I ever listened to.'"

Still, not many pundits thought the obscure, soon-to-be-ex-governor had much of a chance. Carter ran a methodical, grassroots campaign. He traveled all the time, often sleeping in his Jockey shorts on the couches of local supporters. He dressed simply, alternating between a navy-blue polyester jacket and a gray plaid suit. He breakfasted on black coffee and orange juice and ate burgers and other fast food at campaign events. He needed little sleep. Rosalynn told a reporter, "He never had a sleepless night in the campaign. He goes right to sleep, and he wakes up wide awake. That really bothers me!"

Carter focused initially on the Iowa Democratic Party caucus and the New Hampshire primary, both scheduled for early 1976. He was running early and closely followed Hamilton Jordan's script. His would be an autobiographical campaign; he was running not so much on issues but on his life story, his integrity, and his populist, antiestablishment persona. Oddly for a politician, he avoided partisanship. "Certain politicians feel they represent this group or that group," explained a senior aide. "But Jimmy feels he can represent all groups."

Running on his biography, Carter personally wrote the campaign book that served to introduce himself to voters: "I am a Southerner and an American. I am a farmer, an engineer, a father and a husband, a Christian, a politician and a former governor, a planner, a businessman, a nuclear physicist, a naval officer, a canoeist, and among other things a lover of Bob Dylan's songs and Dylan Thomas' poetry."

As Jordan had calculated, voters, soured by the Watergate scandal, Ford's unseemly pardon of Nixon, and the Vietnam War, were attracted by a candidate running against the Washington establishment. They wanted an outsider. But as Carter began to win primaries, many fixtures of Washington society did not know what to make of the surging candidate from Plains, Georgia. The influential columnist Joe Alsop—a hawkish Cold Warrior and Georgetown society snob—told intimates that he had nothing but contempt for Carter. After Carter won the New Hampshire primary on February 24, 1976, Averell Harriman, the grand old man of Washington's foreign policy establishment, was overheard at a cocktail party grumbling, "He can't be president; I don't even know him!" Arthur Schlesinger, Jr., the eminent historian and former aide to President Kennedy, noted in his diary in early 1976, "I tend to regard Carter as an intelligent, ambitious opportunist. . . . He continues to turn me off—his steely eyes, fixed grin, righteousness and ambiguity on issues." He conceded that Carter was "the only candidate to ring any kind of bell in the black community." Still, he could not refrain from writing to his good friend Ursula Niebuhr, the widow of the theologian whom Carter so admired, that Carter "seems to me a humorless, ungenerous, cold-eyed, crafty, rigid, sanctimonious and possibly vindictive man." Predictably, Schlesinger thought Ted Kennedy "would make the best president."

Bill Moyers, the television host and former aide to President Lyndon Johnson, was also skeptical. After interviewing Carter for his syndicated television show, Moyers called up Schlesinger and said that he found Carter "cold, tough, terrifyingly self-confident." Moyers said of his fellow Southern Baptist, "He's not a real Baptist. I know the Baptists. He's Calvinist. I recognize the type. . . . He's the sort who would burn people at the stake." Moyers confessed he was highly ambivalent: "I don't dislike him. I respect him, and I'm afraid of him. He never seems to relax—always businesslike, always the consummate politician." What startled Moyers most about Carter was his steely self-confidence. When he asked him, "What drives you?" Carter replied, "I don't know exactly how to express it. I feel I have one life to live. I feel like God wants me to do the best I can with it. And that's quite often my major prayer. Let me live my life so that it will be meaningful." Such calm religiosity was refreshing and reassuring to some but disconcerting to secular ears.

Carter was an enigma, and oddly, the closer he got to power and the more the media put him in the spotlight, the more enigmatic he seemed. Hunter Thompson had certainly spotted Carter's "functional meanness," his inner determination, when he first encountered him at the May 1974 Law Day speech. *The Washington Post*'s Sally Quinn discerned the same weird toughness in one of her earliest profiles of the candidate when she wrote, "The conventional image of a sexy man is one who is hard on the outside and soft on the inside. Carter is just the opposite." The candidate's toothy smile masked an inner relentlessness and cool resolve.

Liberals accused him of "fuzziness" on the issues. Shortly before the crucial Pennsylvania primary, Carter hired Bob Shrum, an excellent speechwriter with impeccable liberal credentials. The thirty-three-year-old political consultant had worked for George McGovern. But only days after coming aboard the campaign, Shrum began to have serious doubts. After only ten days on the job, Shrum suddenly quit, writing to the candidate, "I am not sure what you truly believe in, other than yourself." Shrum thought Carter was saying one thing in public and just the opposite in private. "I was disturbed," Shrum wrote, "to discover that you might favor a substantial increase in the defense budget in spite of your previous pledge to reduce that budget in the range of five to seven percent."

It was certainly true that Carter didn't want to be pinned down too much on specifics. When Powell learned of Shrum's resignation, he told Jules Witcover of *The Washington Post,* "He's made a very hasty judgment about people he doesn't know or understand." Shrum was adamant and told Witcover, "I really believe it would be bad for this person to be president." Shrum's public resignation raised a lot of eyebrows in liberal circles and seemed to confirm their suspicions that Carter was not really part of the liberal fold. (Shrum later went to work for Ted Kennedy, a politician much more to his liking.)

Schlesinger was mystified by Carter, particularly his evangelical Christianity. A Gallup poll suggested that nearly one-third of Americans claimed to be "born again"—but this was far afield from the Harvard-trained professor's cultural experience. After meeting him in a small group that included the actress Elizabeth Taylor, Schlesinger conceded that Carter was clearly a man of "very considerable intelligence, confidence and competence." But still, "He does not move one to rush to the barricades." Carter lacked the Kennedy charisma that Schlesinger sorely missed. His unassuming physical presence seemed unpresidential. Dressed in his pale gray-blue suit, Carter often spoke and looked like a sales manager pitching his products at a trade convention. In the wake of the sixties' sexual revolution, Carter was an anomaly, a "sexual conservative" married to his hometown sweetheart for three decades.

Schlesinger's loyalties, quite obviously, were always with Ted Kennedy. As Carter won the Democratic nomination in July, Schlesinger noted in his diary that there was a "certain sadness" about Ted. History was passing him by: "Now it looks as if Jimmy Carter, whom no one ever heard of, will be President for the next eight years." Schlesinger was mollified only by the thought that Kennedy could serve as the "ideological conscience" of the coming Carter regime. "Ted is quite clearly prepared to go into the opposition if he feels that Carter is moving too far to the right." This would prove to be prescient.

Much of the establishment's reticence was stoked by a latent contempt for Carter's southern roots. Former senator Eugene McCarthy snidely called Carter "the liberals' pet Cracker." The cultural divide between North and South was deep and enduring. Ex-president Lyndon Johnson complained bitterly in his 1971 memoir, *The Vantage Point,* "I was not thinking just of the derisive articles about my style, my clothes, my manner, accent, and my family. I was thinking of a more deep-seated and far-reaching attitude—a disdain for the South that seems to be woven into the fabric of Northern experience." He was convinced that one reason "the country could not rally behind a Southern president" was that the East Coast press establishment "would never permit it." Carter had the same worries. Once, during the campaign, he turned to Greg Schneiders, then his personal advance man, and asked, "Do you think northerners can ever take me seriously?"

Many elite northern opinion leaders simply could not hide what amounted to prejudice against Carter, another southern white man. The accent grated on their ears. The image of the peanut farmer brought on a smirk. If he came from southern Georgia, he must be conservative, and if Carter himself seemed intelligent—he claimed to be a "nu-cu-lar" engineer—well, his entourage of rednecks were not so smart. When a reporter visiting Plains cornered Alton "Buddy" Carter, the octogenarian brother of the candidate's late father, Earl, and asked him what the white folks of Plains thought of Black folks today, Uncle Buddy replied, "They think there's a place for 'em, but they'd still like to see 'em stay in their place. But they don't hate 'em. Just don't associate with 'em, that's all, 'ceptin sometimes. Like when Earl died, his nigguhs went to the funeral. All two hundred of 'em. Jimmy? He don't worship with 'em neither, but he considers 'em folk. He's more liberal with the nigguhs than anyone else down here."*

Northerners could see plenty about Carter's roots that confirmed their own stereotypes about the South. But this blinded them to the South's other possibilities, rooted in a paradoxical populist, and even progressive, tradition. Willie Morris, a Mississippi-born journalist who often made it his mission to explain the South to the North, published a widely read op-ed in *The New York Times* in July 1976 entitled "Of Northern Fears, Southern Realities and Jimmy Carter." Why, asked Morris, with Carter on the verge of winning the Democratic nomination, were so many "well-meaning people" still so suspicious of this Georgia politician? Morris believed part of the answer lay in the fact that most northerners had "practically no knowledge of, much less direct experience with, the complexity and pluralism of the South, of the nobilities which have existed there, or of that strain in its uncommon past which has endowed it with an enlightened humanitarian legacy." Northerners still saw the South as a segregated, racist society—"ignoring the fact that a combination of the Federal presence and its own best instincts have transformed it in the last fifteen years into the most racially integrated region in America." This transformation explained why Carter was able to defeat George Wallace. Northerners had not begun to "acknowledge the liberalism, often with populist overtones, which has undergirded much of the South for generations, or those Southerners, often at physical hazard, who have stood for something opposite to the Bilbos, the Faubuses and the Wallaces." Carter, Morris argued, was the heir to this humanitarian impulse. Readers of *The New York Times* remained skeptical.

Even those northerners who got a chance to observe Carter up close came away perplexed: "The real wonder about Carter," noted one of his own speechwriters, "is that he spent all those years in a little South Georgia town—and didn't get [to be] like them. An unsatisfactory an-

---

* When Uncle Buddy died in January 1978, Carter flew to Plains to attend the funeral. He later wrote that his uncle had been "like a father to me during my years after leaving the U.S. Navy. He was a shrewd country philosopher, with a wonderful sense of humor." And yet Carter obviously never shared Uncle Buddy's racial views.

swer." James Wooten, the *New York Times* reporter assigned to cover his campaign, later remarked on the enigma of the man from Plains: "It was so damned hard to bracket the man. . . . He was a quicksilver bubble, a living, breathing, grinning paradox, maddening for those who tried to define him."

Confronted by these southern stereotypes, Carter and his people often responded with a defiant defensiveness. Sometimes they proudly followed the hackneyed script, burnishing their image as unsophisticates, as southern rebels—as unabashed outliers. Jordan and Powell, the two young men closest to Carter, bore their southern heritage as a badge of honor. Powell believed, "Even if we win, they're not ever going to accept us."

Jordan sometimes went out of his way to offend. When Ann Pincus, a well-known Washington hostess, bumped into Jordan in a hotel elevator one day, she introduced herself and said, "We'll be getting to know each other much better in Washington. . . . By the way, are you called Jordan or *Jerdan*?"

"My friends call me *Jerdan*," he replied with a grin, "but you can call me Jordan."

Carter's speechwriter during the campaign, Patrick Anderson, thought Jody and Hamilton looked "like a couple of raw-boned narrow-eyed South Georgia thugs. There was always a hint of violence about them." Anderson had the two Georgians in mind when he later quipped, "Our candidate may have been a saint, but he surrounded himself with sinners." Anderson later described Carter's team as being as "hard-drinking, fornicating, pot-smoking, free-thinking a group as has been seen in higher politics." Another campaign aide said of Powell and Jordan, "That country-boy act is as phony as a three-dollar bill. They're tough cookies." Anderson didn't get along with Jordan and Powell—and he didn't last long as speechwriter. But he was always impressed by Carter's unnerving self-confidence. One day he was astonished when the candidate pulled into the driveway of his simple ranch house in Plains and remarked, "There's just one more house I want to live in. Then I'll settle down here for good."

Sometimes, of course, the Georgians actually were clueless. "A lot of people in Washington are just names to us," confessed Powell. During the autumn campaign, Rafshoon, Carter's publicity wizard, drew up a list of major media personalities. At the top of the list was *Washington Post* syndicated columnist David Broder—whom Rafshoon aptly described as the "dean" of the Washington press corps. A few days later Rafshoon and Charlie Kirbo were invited to a fancy Georgetown dinner party where the guests included Broder. Rafshoon told Kirbo that he should seat himself next to Broder. "But then I overheard Charlie addressing Broder as 'Dean.' So I lean in and whisper, 'Charlie, his name is "David," not "Dean." Didn't you get my memo?' Kirbo replied, 'Oh, I thought you meant his name was *Dean.*'" Perhaps Kirbo could be excused for not being a regular reader of *The Washington Post*. But the incident underscored the cultural disconnect.

Carter and his South Georgia boys were running against Washington in order to take power in Washington. Shortly before the election, Jordan told the press, "If, after the inauguration, you find Cy Vance as Secretary of State and Zbigniew Brzezinski as head of National Security, then I would say we failed. And I'd quit."

THE CARTER CLAN were colorful fodder for the press covering the 1976 campaign. One sister, Ruth Stapleton, was a nationally known evangelical lay preacher. The other sister, Gloria Spann, owned a Harley-Davidson motorcycle franchise in Atlanta and regularly drove her Harley on cross-country road trips.*

And then there was Billy. When a reporter observed to Billy Carter that he seemed rather eccentric, Billy riposted, "I've got one sister who spends all her time on a motorcycle, another who is a Holy-Rolly preacher, a mother who was in the Peace Corps when she was seventy years old, and my brother thinks he's going to be President of the United States. Which one of our family do *you* think is normal? Hell," he declared, "I'm the only sane one in the bunch." Billy actually harbored some deep-seated sibling rivalry. He flaunted his lack of a college degree and his "good ol' boy" demeanor. "Yes, I'm a real Southern boy," he boasted. "I got a red neck, white socks and *Blue Ribbon* beer." He was also a Republican and more or less an open segregationist. "I'm not an integrationist," he told a reporter covering the campaign. When his brother, as governor, one day entered Billy's house, accompanied by a

---

* Gloria Spann's tombstone reads, "She rides in Harley heaven."

Black state trooper, Billy admitted, "It was very hard for me at first—that was the first black that was ever in our house."

He also made sure that people understood that he was the Carter managing the family business: "I made more money for the business than Jimmy ever did." Billy also went out of his way to tell reporters of his dislike for his cousin Hugh Carter—"a sorry son of a bitch"—who owned a ramshackle hardware and "antique" store across the street. Billy was actually a smart, self-taught man who read widely and devoured the newspapers each morning. Much of his good ol' boy act was part of his self-deprecating southern defiance—a performance put on for the northern foreigners. During the '76 campaign, however, he drowned his resentments in alcohol, often drinking nine beers by midnight. "Billy drinks too much," Miss Lillian said. "He's a wonderful boy and he's really my favorite son. But he drinks too much. Jimmy never tells him off for it and neither do I. But he does."

When a British television correspondent asked Miss Lillian why some voters seemed to be perplexed by her son, she smiled and replied, "Some people are just dumb." She confided to another reporter, "I hate to use the word ruthless, but Jimmy's going to win or bust. He expects victory. He'll go through hell to get what he wants." Reporters loved Miss Lillian's unscripted remarks. "Sometimes," she told one interviewer, "when I look at my children, I wish I had remained a virgin."

The candidate remained a southern enigma for many reporters. Some—like Kandy Stroud—were unnerved when Carter on occasion would greet her with "his soul stare." This entailed Carter reaching out, placing both hands on her shoulders, and staring "soulfully into my eyes without saying a word." Ethel Allen, an African American surgeon in Philadelphia, called this Carter greeting "his Jesus bit . . . another time, he'd cup my face with his hand, ever so gently, like he was the Messiah. It drives me crazy. . . . The thing is, it works. Most black people think it's fantastic." It was a southern thing, and a bit too weirdly personal outside the Deep South.

Carter was all about the South—but he was not by any definition a good ol' boy. Carter's aide, Greg Schneiders, told *The Boston Globe*'s Curtis Wilkie that he had observed that the three southern reporters covering the campaign were also the three reporters who wrote most critically about his candidate. "Behind that big smile," Wilkie wrote of Carter, "lay a cold and calculating mind."

Wilkie was from Mississippi, Jim Wooten was from Tennessee, and Eleanor Randolph had grown up in Pensacola, Florida. Schneiders thought all three were liberal southerners who were constantly frustrated by Carter's moderation. Wilkie conceded that Schneiders may have been right. These reporters held Carter to a higher standard and were constantly probing for inconsistencies. Wilkie admired Carter's forthright stance on racial issues—but he was frustrated that he could never get the candidate to comment on Koinonia, the interracial commune just down the road from Plains. Wilkie realized this was another of Carter's cold calculations: "I suppose he felt, as a Democratic candidate trying to regain the goodwill of the South, that some subjects were best left alone." If so, this was less an example of hypocrisy than sheer pragmatism. Wilkie knew it, and Carter knew this fellow southerner could see through what he was doing. Wilkie managed to needle Carter on even his little, mostly harmless exaggerations—such as reporting that he was wrong to call himself a "nuclear physicist" rather than a "nuclear engineer." Carter was particularly incensed by a story Wilkie ran in January 1976, reporting that the Georgia state payroll had actually increased by ten thousand civil servants during the Carter governorship.

After a few months on the campaign trail, Carter concluded that the irreverent Wilkie was a smartass—and he let him know it. One Sunday in Plains, Carter saw Wilkie walking into church services empty-handed. "Here," Carter said, handing him his Bible. "You probably need this more than anyone else."* Wooten and Randolph were equally hardnosed in their campaign reporting. And when they found it hard to categorize the candidate, they fell back on calling him an enigma. "Maybe it was better to say that Carter was an enigma," wrote Randolph in *Esquire,* "than to say directly, in the middle of the campaign, that he wasn't a particularly nice guy."

---

* Flipping through Carter's Bible, Wilkie saw it was dog-eared, heavily underlined, and annotated in the margins in the candidate's neat handwriting. "I had once laughed at Carter's piety," Wilkie later wrote. "But I found his Bible quite touching . . . and I regretted that I had ever mocked his faith."

Carter himself was often dangerously unscripted in his remarks to the press. One day in Ohio he told a reporter off the record, "I'm glad I don't have to kiss Teddy Kennedy's ass to be president." When confronted at a press conference as to whether he had actually said this, Carter just laughed and asked for the next question. Later in the day someone handed him a "Kiss My Ass" T-shirt, and the candidate gamely held it up and grinned. Reporters on the campaign trail naturally liked these moments of candor. But most of the time, inspired by Carter's "I'll never tell a lie" pledge, they were constantly digging for evidence of duplicity, however small or inconsequential. ABC television network reporter Sam Donaldson repeatedly got laughs when he made fun of the line in Carter's stump speech about how the country needed "a government as good as its people." Quipped Donaldson, "Jesus Christ, if we had a government as good as our people, this would be Italy!"

A full year before the 1976 New Hampshire primary, Hunter Thompson spent a weekend hanging out with the Carter family in Plains. He came away with six hours of taped interviews. They talked about everything from Bob Dylan to the "treachery of Richard Nixon." Carter enjoyed Thompson's roguish company. "Both Carter and his wife have always been amazingly tolerant of my behavior," Thompson wrote, "and on one or two occasions they have had to deal with me in a noticeably bent condition." Many years later, Carter himself would say, "Hunter Thompson was a delightful, unpredictable and unforgettable friend of mine for more than 30 years. He interviewed me for many hours, tape-recording extensive conversations about every conceivable subject, some of which were quite discomforting. Later, I learned, with some relief, that he had lost all the tapes." Not surprisingly, Thompson bonded most with Miss Lillian. Thompson loved the notion that "an almost totally unknown ex-governor of Georgia with no national reputation" could launch a viable campaign for the presidency. Both men wanted to stick it to the Washington establishment.

So too did Ralph Nader. The iconoclastic consumer movement activist had long searched for a sympathetic politician, and for a time he thought he had found one in Carter. The two men first met in Atlanta when Governor Carter told Nader of his frustration at not being able to get the Georgia state legislature to pass a consumer protection law. And during the 1976 campaign Carter called Nader more than once to ask for his advice on consumer protection and regulatory issues. After securing the nomination, Carter invited Nader to spend the night at his Plains ranch house. Nader famously umpired a softball game between the press corps and Carter's campaign staff, and later he ate black-eyed peas with Rosalynn and Jimmy. The next morning, Nader was served breakfast by the presidential candidate. Nader was impressed by Carter's intelligence and command of the issues.

And yet the campaign was all about Carter the man. After locking down the nomination, Carter was introduced at the New York convention via a slick film depicting his meteoric political rise. "We didn't need any big-name politician to introduce him," said Rafshoon, who crafted the film. "We choreographed it to the T." The humorous film used a series of graphic cartoons that featured his signature grin, including a full screen depicting his glowing white teeth in the dark, with a voiceover of Rosalynn saying, "Jimmy, cut it out and go to sleep!" Afterward, Carter himself strode through the convention hall, shaking hands on all sides, and then bounded up to the rostrum, where he grinned broadly and, echoing his stump speech, intoned, "My name is Jimmy Carter, and I'm running for president."

His short acceptance speech was "populist in tone," promising that it was time to kick out "a political [and] economic elite who have shaped decisions and never had to account for mistakes or to suffer from injustice. . . . It is time for us to take a new look at our own government, to strip away the secrecy, to expose the unwarranted pressure of lobbyists, to eliminate waste."

Carter the candidate was still his most effective in front of a small audience. Soon after winning the nomination, he flew out to California for a reception hosted by actor Warren Beatty. Guests at the Beverly Wilshire Hotel included such celebrities as Sidney Poitier, Peter Falk, Robert Altman, Faye Dunaway, Jon Voight, Hugh Hefner, Alan Pakula, Norman Lear, Tony Randall, and dozens of other Hollywood personalities. When someone asked if this was his first trip to California, Carter quipped, "It's the first time anyone ever noticed I was here." And when Beatty jocularly suggested that his presence at such a Hollywood gathering might reassure many secular-minded people about his Southern Baptist beliefs, Carter responded, "If I come to Warren Beatty's party, it should wipe out the issue." The celebrities laughed.

But then Carter took the opportunity to launch into an extemporane-ous sermon, telling this roomful of the rich and famous, "If you and I make a mistake, the chances are we won't actually go to prison, and if we don't like the public-school system, we put our kids in private schools. . . . When the tax structure is modified, which Congress does almost every year, you can rest assured that powerful people who are well organized, who have good lawyers, who have lobbyists in the Capitol in Washing-ton, they don't get cheated. But there are millions of people in this coun-try who do get cheated, and they are the ones who can't afford it. Public servants like me . . . have a special responsibility to bypass the big shots and to make a concerted effort to understand people who are poor, black, speak a foreign language, who are not well educated, who are in-articulate, who are timid, who have some monumental problem. At the same time, we must run the government in a competent way, well orga-nized, efficient, manageable, so that those services which are so badly needed can be delivered." This was vintage Carter, a South Georgia pop-ulist condemning "big-shot" lawyers and yet simultaneously pledging to run government in an efficient and competent manner.

Carter seemed indefatigable, but toward the end of what had become a twenty-two-month campaign, he began showing signs of human ex-haustion. Late that autumn, his speechwriter Patrick Anderson took a draft speech to the candidate's Pittsburgh hotel room. "I found him in jockey shorts and a T-shirt, stretched crossways across the bed, as if he'd thrown himself down and been too tired to straighten out." Handed the speech, Carter set it on the floor, his head hanging over the edge of the bed to read it. After he made a few perfunctory edits, Anderson picked up the speech from the floor and started to leave. Carter rarely offered his aides any compliments, but this time he whispered, "Thank you very much, Pat." Anderson was moved and later wrote, "This exhausted man, who literally hadn't the strength to raise his head, had thanked me. It was the most I ever liked him." But an hour later, Carter darted into the hotel ballroom and delivered an energetic speech, one of his best perfor-mances of the campaign.

As an antiestablishment candidate, Carter took every opportunity to cultivate his image as a "regular guy." This included a decision to grant five hours of interviews over three months to Robert Scheer, a freelance reporter for *Playboy* magazine. Scheer was legendary in the business, known for his relentless interrogations. Published in mid-September, the interview turned out to be a cultural and political bombshell, if only because Scheer got Carter to talk about his attitudes on sex and adultery. Carter was being frank and open. He thought he was using the interview to explain to a secular audience that just because he was "born again" didn't mean that he was self-righteous and judgmental—or just an "ignorant peanut farmer."

"The thing that is drummed into us all the time is not to be proud," he told Scheer, "not to be better than anyone else, not to look down on people." Carter earnestly explained to the reporter, "Christ set some impossible standards for us. Christ said, 'I tell you that anyone who looks on a woman with lust has already committed adultery.' I have looked on a lot of women with lust; I've committed adultery in my heart many times. This is something that God recognizes that I will do—and I have done it—and God forgives me for it. But that doesn't mean that I condemn someone who not only looks on a woman with lust but who leaves his wife and shacks up with somebody out of wedlock. Christ says, don't consider yourself better than someone else because one guy screws a whole bunch of women while the other guy is loyal to his wife." Perhaps the most startling thing he said came next: "I don't think I would ever take on the same frame of mind that Nixon or Johnson did—lying, cheating and distorting the truth. . . . I think that my religious beliefs alone would prevent that from happening to me."

Arguably, the news headlines should have highlighted a presidential candidate flatly talking about Nixon and Johnson "lying, cheating and distorting the truth." But naturally, the "lust" comment stole the headlines the next day. The interview set off alarm bells among both liberal and conservative skeptics, or as Jordan put it, the *Playboy* comments resurrected everyone's concerns about the "weirdo factor" in Jimmy Carter's personal biography. One pastor archly observed that *screw* was not a "good Baptist word" and Martin Luther King, Sr., gibed, "They can't kill you for lookin'."

When Rosalynn heard about the *Playboy* brouhaha, she dismissively remarked, "Jimmy talks too much." The whole episode was another reminder for Kirbo of how Carter's reflexive transparency, his urge to be "open with everything," could cause a whole lot of needless trouble. Miss Lillian had often told him to "quit that stuff about never telling a lie, and being a Christian, and how he loves his wife more than the day he met her. There are some things you don't have to go around saying." This time his openness and desire to explain his personal religious beliefs in a secular venue like *Playboy* nearly cost him the presidency. Patrick Anderson later wrote that the *Playboy* interview "destroyed his lead, soured his press relations, threw him on the defensive and his campaign into chaos, and probably cost him the big electoral victory he had expected." An angry Carter blamed Powell for persuading him to talk to Scheer.

Carter stumbled again during the first of three nationally televised debates with President Gerald Ford. Out of an excess of self-confidence, Carter refused any debate preparation or rehearsals. Not surprisingly, during the first debate he came off wooden, reeling off statistics and meandering through long-winded policy-wonky answers. But he did well in the two subsequent debates, using humor at one point to mollify voters about his "adultery in my heart" gaffe: "If I should ever decide in the future to discuss my deep Christian beliefs and condemnation and sinfulness, I'll use another forum besides *Playboy*." Ford blundered into his own gaffe when he said that he thought Eastern Europe was not under the domination of the Soviet Union.

Still, Carter's once-formidable lead in the polls shrank to a few points by Election Day, November 2. After voting in Plains early that morning, a relaxed and seemingly confident Carter stopped to chat with Jimmie Wallace, a local black laborer who had been a childhood friend. "Jimmie and I used to plow a mule together," he told reporter Kandy Stroud. That afternoon, Nader called Carter on his personal phone line and offered a premature accolade: "Let me be the first to congratulate you!" Referring to Carter's campaign book, *Why Not the Best?,* Nader warned him, "I'm going to hold you to it." Carter laughed and replied, "I want you to."

Late that evening, Carter sat in Atlanta's Omni International Hotel, holding hands with Rosalynn and watching the election returns. Charlie Kirbo was sipping a Fanta laced with Jack Daniel's. At 2:00 A.M. Jody Powell had to go downstairs and tell the restive crowd, "We have waited more than a hundred years for this moment. We can wait a few minutes more." The crowd of mostly southerners understood exactly what he meant and bellowed in approval. But it was another hour and a half before the voters of Mississippi finally gave Carter the necessary electoral votes. Carter won 49.9 percent of the popular vote against incumbent president Gerald Ford's 47.9 percent. It was a very narrow win. If fewer than ten thousand citizens in just two states, Ohio and Hawaii, had voted for Ford instead of Carter, Ford would have remained president. Curiously, he had won even though he was found to be "least acceptable among Northern liberals and Southern conservatives." Jimmy Carter had pulled off a miracle. He had come from nowhere and triumphed. Just ten years earlier, he had been knocking on doors, asking people to accept Christ. And now he was the president-elect who owed the establishment nothing.*

In a short victory speech, Carter called his opponent, Jerry Ford, a "good and decent man" and then said it was time to "tap a sense of brotherhood and sisterhood" and to make the nation "great once again." And then his entourage rushed to the Atlanta airport for a short flight back to Plains. To Carter's annoyance, the press bus was very late, and Jody Powell had to do some fast talking to persuade his always punctual boss not to fly off to Plains, leaving the reporters behind. They finally clambered aboard the plane, and just before takeoff Carter walked down the aisle, past Curtis Wilkie, Eleanor Randolph, Mary McGrory, and some of the other reporters who had covered his campaign for so many months. Wilkie couldn't resist one more wisecrack: "Governor," he said, "congratulations. It didn't take much to get Massachusetts, but I had to work like hell to deliver Mississippi."

Carter turned around and glared at Wilkie, and then said evenly, "If it weren't for people like you, this election would have been over at nine o'clock last night." The president-elect was tired but also obviously on edge about how close he had been to defeat.

At 5:30 a.m. Jimmy and Rosalynn arrived back in Plains, where hundreds of their neighbors had waited up all night. After hugging his mother, Jimmy tried to thank the crowd: "I came all the way through— through twenty-two months and I didn't get choked up until I . . . " With tears in his eyes he turned and embraced Rosalynn. This tearful, very private moment of victory was captured on television, and then Carter

---

* Carter ran his entire general campaign with public financing—which amounted to $21.8 million, a pittance even in 1976.

regained his composure and, turning to the crowd, made a confession: "The only reason we were close last night was because the candidate wasn't quite good enough as a campaigner. But I'll make up for that when I'm President." It was vintage Carter, a vow to improve and do his best. But it was not good enough for Arthur Schlesinger, who watched the Plains performance on television and then noted in his diary, "He really seems to me a total phony." Schlesinger could not bring himself to vote for Carter, and had instead just left the presidential space on his ballot blank. It was an omen.

Part 2

THE PRESIDENCY

Jimmy and Rosalynn Carter on the Truman Balcony
DENNIS BRACK/ALAMY

Chapter 5
Mr. Carter Goes to Washington

We were country bumpkins, and we won, and they didn't.
—Chip Carter

Jimmy and Rosalynn Carter walking down
Pennsylvania Avenue
RON GALELLA/GETTY IMAGES

GREG SCHNEIDERS, TWENTY-NINE years old, knew Carter probably as well as any of his campaign staff. He had spent months traveling with the candidate, carrying his bags, driving him from one campaign venue to another, and often sleeping in the same motel room. Just a few days after the election, Greg was sitting alone with Jimmy in the living room of the Carter home in Plains when the president-elect suddenly adopted a fatherly tone and asked Greg about his girlfriend, Marie, also a campaign worker. "By this time," Schneiders said, "everyone in Plains knew Marie and I were living together in a house down the road in Americus." Carter gently inquired whether he and Marie had ever thought about getting married. Schneiders replied that, yes, they had discussed marriage, and had thought they might do it in April because they both happened to have April birthdays. Carter then volunteered that he had heard some complaints about their living together out of wedlock.

"Oh, who is complaining?"

"Well, I heard this from both Charlie [Kirbo] and Rosalynn," Carter said. "So perhaps it would be better if you got married before the inauguration."

Greg married Marie on New Year's Eve. "The funny thing about this story," Greg recalled, "is that sometime later I ran into Mr. Kirbo and I made a point of apologizing for having 'upset' him. Kirbo looked at me quizzically and said, 'Hell, I don't care who you are shacking up with.'" No one was really surprised when this story made the rounds of his inner circle; this was just Carter gently nudging the people around him to do the right thing.

HAVING WON THE presidency, Jimmy Carter now had nearly three months to mold his administration. Typically, a president-elect appoints his White House staff by Thanksgiving and his cabinet secretaries by Christmas. This transition period is always marked by intense lobbying. It is a power struggle for the soul of the presidency.

Carter came more prepared than most presidents for this transition. Trained as a submariner, the engineer in Carter knew that careful planning was essential to launching this new ship of state. And so back in the spring of 1976, confident of ultimate victory, he had appointed Jack Watson, a thirty-seven-year-old law partner of Charlie Kirbo's, to head his transition team. Carter had known Watson since 1966, when Kirbo literally badgered Watson to pay a visit to Carter in Plains. Watson was industrious and diligent. Kirbo thought him "an extraordinary fellow, highly competent and well-educated." A southerner from Arkansas, Watson had attended both Vanderbilt University and Harvard Law School. Mentored by Kirbo at King & Spalding, he had also served as the chairman of Georgia's Department of Human Resources during Carter's term as governor. So Carter knew him well as a Kirbo protégé.

Watson put together a team of experts, and they produced a series of briefing books on various issues, culminating in a thick document that was handed to Carter shortly before the election. Watson was given a budget of about $150,000 for his team. David Rubenstein, a young aide who had worked on the campaign, recalled, "Watson had a real staff of some twenty professionals, people who had expertise in various issues. People with credentials. Not campaign people." Three days after the election, Watson gave Carter three large black binders. He'd done a meticulous job, but Carter didn't like it. He later told Eizenstat, "All of a sudden we found that Jack had put together a set of decisions in which neither I, nor you nor Hamilton or others were involved." Carter thought it smacked of "empire building." Jordan was outraged to see that Watson had budgeted only one staff member to work with him. Hamilton complained loudly, "What about us?" He meant all the people who had worked their asses off for nearly four years. Rubenstein recalled, "I think it only dawned on Hamilton on Election Day that Jack Watson's operation was a threat."

Watson—who thought correctly that Kirbo was pushing for him to be appointed chief of staff—was initially oblivious to what was happening, a power play by Jordan against him. Jordan told an aide that "JC is unhappy with [the] transition.... He wishes he hadn't gone on vacation." Within days, Carter let it be known that Jordan would be in charge of presidential appointments. Watson only found out on a flight down to Georgia when Vice President–elect Walter Mondale handed him an Evans & Novak column published in *The Washington Post* that morning that described tensions inside Carter's transition team. To his distress, Watson saw himself characterized as a "walking dead man." When he looked up, Mondale grinned broadly and said, "Welcome to Washington." Arriving in Plains, Watson was told by Carter that instead of becoming chief of staff, he would be given a nebulous job as "cabinet secretary," ostensibly a perch from which he could help to coordinate the administration.

Carter knew he wanted his Georgia boys in the White House. That meant familiar faces like Hamilton Jordan, Jody Powell, Stu Eizenstat, and Charlie Kirbo. He didn't want outsiders in his inner circle of advisers. Indeed, he thought it would have been "improper and inconsistent to bring an outsider in as a leader of all these people who had been with me since I was a young politician." He was also inclined not to appoint a chief of staff. "It was an over-reaction to Watergate," recalled Rafshoon. "He didn't want an H.R. Haldeman." Of course, there was no comparison between Hamilton Jordan and Nixon's notoriously sycophantic chief of staff. Carter nevertheless told Kirbo and others that he favored a "spokes of the wheel" style of management whereby his cabinet secretaries and other major appointees would all have direct access to the Oval Office.

Kirbo tried to talk him out of this notion, arguing that he needed a gatekeeper. He told Carter that "Hamilton ought to be his chief advisor on a sort of wild card [basis]." Kirbo understood that Hamilton had a special relationship to the president-elect and that he needed to be close by. Hamilton, he thought, "was dedicated. He was very smart. He was a great planner. He was a great writer. . . . He was absolutely loyal." But Charlie did not go on to say what he privately thought—that "Hamilton and Jody were young boys who hadn't fully developed." Charlie tried gently to advance the name of Jack Watson. "I thought Jack ought to have a very prominent—if not a leading—position on the staff. . . . Jack is more sophisticated and better organized and understands issues and knows more substantive people." But Kirbo later admitted that he hadn't made an explicit, strong argument on behalf of Watson, partly because he didn't want to be seen promoting his own law partner. Carter must have known what Charlie was implying, but this time he resisted Charlie's advice. Instead, Jimmy said the only chief of staff he would appoint would be Charlie.

Kirbo acknowledged that "part of his plan was for me to go to Washington." And initially, he was inclined to do so. But after the election, Kirbo got cold feet. He told friends that "if I had been independently wealthy," he'd have preferred to be "an advisor without any title." He wanted to be a "dollar-a-year-man," "sort of Chief of Staff without the responsibility of running the White House." Carter wanted him on any basis, and at one point he set aside Richard Nixon's hideaway office in the Old Executive Office Building for Kirbo's exclusive use. But Kirbo never used it, and in the end he turned down any official position in the Carter White House. Later he claimed that he just couldn't afford to abandon his corporate law practice. His King & Spalding law partner-ship was certainly well paid—but Kirbo owed several hundred thousand dollars and he needed that income to pay the interest on those loans. "I found out that I would have had to sell my home and my farms and ev-erything or I would get into serious trouble up there [in Washington] trying to service a debt." It was an unfortunate decision; Kirbo was the only "adult" in Carter's inner circle, literally the only person older than Carter himself and the only person close to the president-elect who had the gravitas and presence to be able to convey unwanted "truths."

Kirbo "felt a little guilty."

But if Kirbo wasn't going to Washington, everyone knew he was still Jimmy Carter's power broker, at least during the transition. It was Kirbo who had vetted Mondale for the vice presidency, telling Carter, "Gover-nor, I thought I could get rid of that fellah, but I didn't, and I don't think I will." Kirbo came away from his first encounter with Mondale liking the affable Minnesotan, and he knew his liberal credentials would help Carter win the November election. Now Kirbo served as the clearing-house for hundreds of résumés. Jack Watson was appointed cabinet secretary—not a pivotal position, but still in the White House. Carter already had Harold Brown slated for Defense, but he told Kirbo he was so worried about wasteful defense budgets that he wanted someone as deputy defense secretary who could be really tough on procurement is-sues. Kirbo recommended Charlie Duncan, a former Coca-Cola Com-pany president. "Why didn't I think of Charlie?" Carter exclaimed. Kirbo also recruited Baltimore lawyer Ben Civiletti as an assistant at-torney general and Juanita Kreps for commerce secretary.

Kirbo even influenced Carter in his choice of secretary of state, steer-ing him away from Zbigniew Brzezinski and toward Cyrus Vance: "I got a little concerned about Brzezinski." Kirbo thought Zbig knew a lot, and he realized he was a great briefer. But he thought Zbig "hasn't got the judgment that Vance had." Kirbo made a point of seeking Vance out and had lunch with him one day. "I had known Vance from a distance," Kirbo said, "but I liked what I saw. After I had lunch with him, I talked to Jimmy."

Carter reluctantly agreed with Kirbo; he conceded that Cy Vance was a "natural selection" for secretary of state. Carter had phoned Vance early in the campaign and invited him to join his group of foreign policy advisers, which included Brzezinski, Richard Gardner, Anthony Lake, and Richard Holbrooke. Vance knew all these men, and as he got to know Carter, he became impressed by his intelligence. Shortly before the election, Vance sent the candidate a memo setting out "specific goals and priorities for a Carter foreign policy." He spent Election Night with Dick Gardner, Brzezinski, and all their respective wives, watching the returns late into the night. After Carter's narrow victory was announced, Vance and Brzezinski left Gardner's apartment and strolled together in the chilly November early-morning hours, casually discussing whether they might both be working together in the new administration.

They did not know it, but Carter's preference for the slot of secretary of state was George Ball, who had previously served as under secretary of state during the Kennedy and Johnson administrations. Carter knew Ball had "spoken up when nobody else in government did about what was wrong with the Vietnam War." But he also sensed that Ball's similar "outspokenness on the Middle East would have made it difficult for him to pass confirmation hearings. So, I chose Cyrus Vance." On November 30, Carter invited Vance to spend the night in his Plains home. When Vance arrived, Carter himself prepared a simple meal of soup and sand-wiches, which they ate with Amy. Afterward, Amy went off to do her homework and the two men sat down for five hours of conversation about a whole gamut of foreign policy issues. Carter made it clear that his instinct was for bold, "comprehensive" initiatives—and not the "in-cremental" diplomacy practiced by Kissinger. Carter made a point of saying that a new SALT nuclear-arms-control agreement with the Sovi-ets was one of his highest priorities. Vance concurred, and both men agreed that détente with the Soviets was a necessity. "I felt a growing rapport with this earnest, intelligent man," Vance later wrote. Around midnight, Carter finally offered Vance the top job. "I accepted with grat-itude and a sense of optimism."

Carter asked Vance directly if he had any objections to appointing Brzezinski as his national security adviser. Vance replied diplomatically that he did not know Zbig well but that he thought they could work well together—so long as it was clear that he (Vance) would be the president's spokesman on foreign policy. Carter agreed.

But the president-elect knew Brzezinski was both "innovative and often provocative." Even Zbig's friends had cautioned Carter that he was "aggressive and ambitious, and that on controversial subjects he might be inclined to speak out too forcefully." Clark Clifford, a former secretary of defense and perennial presidential adviser dating back to the Truman administration, strongly advised Carter not to employ Brzezinski. He thought Brzezinski was "too much of an advocate and not enough of an honest broker. . . . Also, I was certain he would clash with the gentle and collegial Vance."

Richard Holbrooke, age thirty-five, had served as Carter's foreign policy coordinator during the previous summer, and Carter had come to like the brash young Foreign Service officer, writing to him, "I feel at ease with you." He would appoint Holbrooke to the State Department, where he became the youngest-ever assistant secretary of state. But when Carter called Holbrooke on Thanksgiving Day and asked for his opinion of Brzezinski, Holbrooke paused for a moment and then gently suggested, "Governor, I don't think that Vance and Brzezinski will make a good team. I think Brzezinski is too combative and has too strong a personal agenda for the job." There was a long silence on the phone line—and then Carter brusquely thanked Holbrooke and hung up. Clearly, he hadn't wanted to hear this criticism. Stu Eizenstat—who knew both Vance and Brzezinski—similarly advised Carter that either man would make a good addition to his foreign policy team, but he warned against appointing both men because they "held diametrically opposing views" on the Soviet Union. Carter hesitated for barely a second before responding, "I like hearing different opinions. I can handle it."

Carter felt comfortable around Brzezinski. They could joke with each other and freely debate issues. Brzezinski could be charming, gracious in his Polish aristocratic manners, and sometimes even playful. "He has, for all his sophistication, a certain childlike quality that can be appealing," wrote Elizabeth Drew in *The New Yorker*. "I was an eager student of Zbig's," Carter later said, "and I enjoyed being around him." He thought he also knew Brzezinski's political outlook. But he may not have realized just how conservative Brzezinski was on a host of issues. Carter had campaigned in part against the foreign policy record of Henry Kissinger. And yet in many ways, Brzezinski was to the right of Kissinger. He thought Kissinger's détente policies advantaged the Soviets, enabling them to reap geopolitical gains in the third world. He had defended the Vietnam War and criticized the New Left and the liberal-left McGovern faction of the Democratic Party. Intellectually, he was close to such neo-conservative thinkers as Daniel Bell, Nathan Glazer, Midge Decter, and Jeane Kirkpatrick. He found himself in sympathy with the views of Paul Nitze, Paul Wolfowitz, and other members of the Committee on the Present Danger. He admired Senator Scoop Jackson's foreign policy views, and, like Jackson's aide, Richard Perle, he favored higher defense spending and a hard line against the Soviet Union. Pointedly, he was a critic of the SALT II negotiations and believed Kissinger had conceded too much in those arms-control negotiations. "A schematic portrait of Brzezinski," wrote one of his biographers, Justin Vaïsse, "would seem to make him a perfect neoconservative." But Vaïsse would argue that there were some differences. Brzezinski instinctively rejected the bleak pessi-mism of the neoconservatives. Unlike Kissinger and Nitze, he did not believe America was a declining power, and this made him an optimist about America's role in the world. "I'm not a Utopian," he told Vaïsse many years later. "I'm not a Manichean, I don't think our side was always right, and I've been increasingly critical for example of [the] decisions to bomb Nagasaki and Hiroshima." Brzezinski could at times seem hard to categorize. He was certainly a Cold War liberal and, as Vaïsse concludes, "a fellow traveler of the neoconservatives." But he sold himself to Carter as a liberal contrarian, a fiercely independent intellectual who enjoyed a good argument.

Carter had always presumed that Zbig would be his national security adviser. He worried that Zbig could become another Henry Kissinger, but he also knew that Zbig would always have something interesting to say: "Zbig would be my favorite seatmate on a long-distance trip; we might argue, but I would never be bored." They were friends. And Carter was nothing if not loyal to his friends.

Observing their relationship, Hamilton Jordan thought Brzezinski and Vance represented two different sides of Carter's own personality. "Zbig represented his boldness. . . . Vance represented the more tradi-tional and methodical side of Jimmy Carter."

Carter heard plenty of criticisms of Brzezinski: "Knowing Zbig, I re-alized that some of these assessments were accurate." But he had nev-ertheless decided, "I wanted him with me in the White House." In late November, Carter phoned Brzezinski and teasingly asked his advice about "people and appointments"—but without offering him a job. Zbig played along, and at one point in their conversation he told Carter that he assumed he did not want to model his foreign policy team after the Nixon administration, where a strong president, assisted by a forceful national security adviser, overshadowed a weak secretary of state. Instead, Brzezinski urged Carter to construct a "balanced team" modeled on the Kennedy administration, where a strong president (Kennedy) was assisted by a "relatively secure" secretary of state (Dean Rusk) and "an equally confident and energetic" national security adviser (McGeorge "Mac" Bundy). Brzezinski, of course, was broadly hinting that he wished to play the role of Bundy. And yet Brzezinski must have known, if Carter did not, that Mac Bundy had run circles around Rusk and had essentially invented the Kissinger style of national security adviser.

Carter kept Brzezinski waiting—with "mounting impatience"—until he finally offered him the national security slot on December 15. Brzezinski would prove to be everything Carter hoped for and feared. The two men often strongly disagreed. Brzezinski quickly decided that it was his job to balance Carter's "more idealistic views" with his "realistic and hard-nosed advice." Nine days before the inauguration, Brzezinski was already noting in his diary, "I will try to sensitize [Carter] to the need to have somewhat more tough-minded a group in security and arms control-oriented areas." What he meant, of course, was that this Polish anticommunist Cold Warrior was going to be relentless in pursuing a hard line against the Soviets. Brzezinski was always a disruptive force. And in retrospect, his appointment was no doubt Carter's first major mistake.

Brzezinski spent the next few months—until he and his wife, Emilie Benes, bought their own home—living with Averell and Pamela Harriman in their magnificent Georgetown mansion on N Street. At eighty-five years of age, the tall, stoop-shouldered American aristocrat was still an elite power broker, and his fifty-seven-year-old wife, an English-born socialite once married to the son of Winston Churchill, was the virtual queen of Georgetown high society. Hosting the new president's designated national security adviser in their home gave the Harrimans immediate access to the Carter team. And it seemed to signal that the Washington establishment had given its blessing to Brzezinski. But there was, in fact, some underlying tension between the polished, aristocratic son of a Polish diplomat and Harriman, the son of one of America's great robber barons. As President Franklin Roosevelt's ambassador to wartime Moscow in the 1940s, Harriman thought of himself as Washington's foremost expert on Soviet-American relations. Like Carter, he strongly favored a policy of détente, believing the Russian regime was basically a conservative, defensive power—and not one bent on risking war in the nuclear era. Over time, Harriman believed, the communist dictatorship would evolve liberally or disintegrate economically. But in the meantime, he thought provoking the Soviet bear was pointless and dangerous. And he knew Brzezinski's instincts favored a far more confrontational and combative policy in dealing with the Soviets. Harriman was not a man to keep his opinions to himself. Inside the State Department, his code name on top secret cables was "Crocodile"—an apt moniker for a man known for his snappish wit. Just three years earlier, Harriman had publicly criticized Brzezinski, brazenly declaring that Zbig's Polish prejudices disqualified him from handling American-Soviet relations. Brzezinski thought Harriman naïve, and he had immediately replied with a private letter:

> Dear Mr. Harriman:
> I have been told by some friends that you expressed the view that my Polish background somehow disqualifies me from dealing objectively with the U.S.-Soviet relationship. . . . Since you are a blunt man, let me also say quite bluntly that I do not feel that Henry Kissinger's background disqualified him from dealing effectively with the Middle Eastern problem, nor do I think that your background as a millionaire capitalist prevents you from dealing intelligently with the Soviet communists.
> Yours sincerely
> Zbigniew Brzezinski

Harriman was no doubt charmed by this riposte, but it didn't alter his opinion about how to deal with the Soviets. And he knew that Cy Vance shared his opinion and not that of Brzezinski. It did not augur well for the new administration's foreign policy that it was already divided sharply on such a key issue.

"We don't owe anybody anything," said one of Carter's Georgia aides. This was true. The Georgia boys had won the White House without the

Democratic Party, without the East Coast establishment, and without Washington's Georgetown set. "We were country bumpkins," Chip Carter said, "and we won, and they didn't."

His father just wanted the best possible advice and the best people. He invited Ralph Nader back to Plains, and the two men sat for more than three hours, batting around ideas. As Nader expounded on his vision for various federal agencies, he noticed Carter assiduously taking careful notes. Nader was impressed. "I've never had anybody at the top level of politics do something like that." This was a president who could listen.

A witness to the scene was James Fallows, a twenty-seven-year-old Harvard graduate whom Carter would later sign up to be his chief speechwriter. A former editor of *The Harvard Crimson* and later a Rhodes Scholar at Oxford, Fallows was very bright—and very liberal. He was also one of "Nader's Raiders," having worked for the consumer advocate in Atlanta during the summer of 1970, just as Carter was making his second run for the governorship. Fallows understandably had a vivid memory of that campaign; he remembered it as "a very gloves-off and quasi-racist campaign." As he sat watching his former boss, Nader, and his new boss, the president-elect, Fallows thought the conversation "greatly illuminating." He knew Carter was complicated, and he realized that he had evolved from the 1970 campaign. Carter was now presenting himself to Nader as a southern liberal, a consumer-rights advocate, and an environmentalist. In fact, when Fallows had first met Carter in August 1976, the presidential candidate had made a point of saying that he had read Fallows's 1971 book *The Water Lords,* a Nader study-group report on water pollution in Savannah. Fallows was naturally impressed—but he was also wary. He later confessed to having an "oblique view of Carter." The young speechwriter's diffidence about Carter would gnaw at him for the next two years—and then lead to a terrible break. But for the moment, Fallows was eager for the experience of working in the White House.

Carter himself did not feel overwhelmed by the task ahead. He was nothing if not confident in his own muscular intelligence. He would coolly study each problem put before him, reach the most rational conclusion—and not look back. Throughout late November and December, he summoned various policy experts and potential appointees.

They would be bused into Plains from the Atlanta airport and meet with the president-elect in Miss Lillian's Pond House. Lunching on boxed fried chicken and coleslaw, these policy wonks from Harvard or Yale or various Washington think tanks came armed with elaborate position papers and talking points. And invariably, they were astonished by Carter's tenacity. He kept them holed up in the Pond House for sessions that often lasted four, five, and six hours. Carter grilled them relentlessly, demonstrating that he had read every position paper and knew how to ask the most penetrating questions. To some who participated in these marathon exercises, it seemed like the president-elect was showing off, and that he was not to be dismissed as a southern "cracker" or "redneck." But this was no show; it was just how Carter tackled problems.

Not surprisingly, Washington's political cartoonists were already having fun with the impending invasion of Georgians to the nation's capital. After *The Washington Star* devoted nearly a full page to a Pat Oliphant cartoon entitled "Fowah Mo' Years"—depicting an outhouse on the front lawn of the White House and a spare tire hanging from a nearby tree—hundreds of readers objected to this "pointless ridicule." The newspaper responded with a long editorial on the "Oliphant Flap," defending its decision to publish the cartoon. And needless to say, Oliphant and other political satirists would continue to target the president's southern heritage.

Carter spent most of his time during the transition months in Plains, but he shuttled up frequently for meetings in Washington, DC, where he'd stay in Blair House, kitty-corner from 1600 Pennsylvania Avenue. One November day he and Fritz Mondale were about to walk over to the White House to pay a courtesy call on President Ford when Carter quietly asked Fritz, "What's it like?"

"What are you talking about?" Mondale asked.

"The White House."

"You've never been in the White House?" Mondale replied. "It's a pretty nice place. I think you'll like it."

When a few days later Jimmy and Rosalynn were given a formal tour of the White House, the incoming First Lady asked the White House chef if they were familiar with southern cuisine. "Yes, ma'am, we've been fixing that kind of food for the servants for a long time."

At this early stage in the transition, Carter was trying to keep close to him the people he knew best. And he could become quite firm and even irritable when various Washington power brokers tried to push newcomers into his inner circle. It was a matter of loyalty. One day the Speaker of the House, Congressman Thomas "Tip" O'Neill, came by to urge the appointment of an experienced Hill staffer to serve as the assistant to the president for congressional liaison. Carter listened impatiently, knowing that he had long ago decided to retain Frank Moore for that slot. Moore had served him well as liaison to the Georgia legislature, and Carter thought Moore could do the same job on Capitol Hill. After O'Neill left, Carter got on the phone with Jack Watson, practically seething with fury: "Frank Moore is my man. He always has been and he always will be."

Born in the mountains of northeast Georgia, Moore had been working for Carter since 1966, when Carter was still a state senator. He described himself as Carter's "spear carrier." In his early forties, Moore was diligent, methodical, and absolutely loyal. He knew how to work the phones, and he knew Carter. Moore would always be a member of Carter's inner circle—but he would prove to be the one member of the Georgia mafia whose personal style never meshed with the Washington establishment. He was so low-key, so laid-back, that other men tended to dismiss him as a lightweight, an adman who had once marketed television commercials for Cap'n Crunch cereal.

People didn't realize that Moore had quit his promising career in advertising because one day he came home and saw that hungry children were there to watch him discard his sample boxes. "I saw these children just waiting for me to come home, and they'd scramble and get the Aunt Jemima pancake mix, dog food, whatever Quaker Oat products I would toss out of my car." Moore was shocked and resolved to do something about child poverty. By 1967, he found himself running the Head Start program in fourteen Georgia counties. Around this time Carter, then a recently defeated gubernatorial candidate, brought Moore fully into his political orbit. The two men bonded. Moore became Governor Carter's point man on his campaign to reorganize Georgia state agencies. And then Moore ran the presidential campaign for the old Confederate states. Carter trusted Moore precisely because Frank was so self-effacing and unpretentious. It was no surprise to any of the Georgia mafia that the president-elect had named Moore as his liaison to Capitol Hill.

One December day, Moore was sitting with Mondale outside the bedroom where Carter was interviewing prospective cabinet officers. Moore had been badgered recently by Senator John Stennis, the staunchly conservative Democrat from Mississippi, who wanted to know who Carter's pick for defense secretary would be. "What should I tell him?" Moore asked the vice president–elect. "Tell him Sam Brown [the anti–Vietnam War activist] is looking good," replied Mondale. "Then step away from the phone." Mondale always found a way to deflate tensions with his laid-back wit.

BY EARLY DECEMBER the Carter transition team was still scrambling to get the president-elect to sign off on the most basic appointments. Presidential transitions are by definition always a scramble, and the Carter transition was probably no worse or better than most. Infighting was partly to blame. Watson was still jockeying with Jordan, trying to turn his slated position as cabinet secretary into something more powerful than Carter intended. Jordan, meanwhile, was "feeling particularly cocky." He knew he had the inside track. Landon Butler, whom Jordan had selected as his deputy, had a ringside seat to this competition. Butler, age thirty-five, would soon prove himself to be one of the Carter White House's most effective and levelheaded aides. A graduate of Harvard Business School, Butler was older than most of the Georgia mafia. Butler had worldly experience; he had served a stint in the U.S. Marine Corps and had later built a business in Atlanta, developing real estate. Unlike Jordan, who had no savings and virtually no assets, Butler owned stocks and bonds worth more than $170,000—the equivalent of $730,000 in current dollars. But he was a social liberal and a principled environmentalist. He was low-key, insightful, and charming in a patrician manner, a man who could listen to an argument. "Landon was very competent," recalled Jerry Rafshoon. Aware that he was witnessing history, Butler kept an erratic but perceptive diary. "The transition is a complete bummer," Butler noted in December.

Butler had flown into Washington, DC, a week after the election to work on the transition. He was nervous, excited, and full of anticipation, noting in his diary, "I am overwhelmed by how different everyone looks: Ivy League, well-dressed. I'm also impressed with how nothing seems to work." Butler knew his fate was closely linked to Jordan's, and he was feeling "acute anxiety over the way things are going." Landon deeply admired Jordan, and early in the transition he saw him "shaping up as a defacto chief of staff." Hamilton, he observed, "keeps things moving, and has a grasp of a wide range of mechanical problems." But Landon was also aware that Hamilton "is a very unpredictable and secretive person. He is, after all, very young, and it would be a lot to expect him to be well-rounded." Landon also realized that Hamilton was poorly organized. It was a rare day that Hamilton returned all his phone calls—even to friendly congressmen. It soon dawned on Landon that part of his job as deputy was to compensate for Hamilton's chaotic management style. Already in mid-December Landon was hearing complaints from multiple sources about Hamilton's unresponsiveness. Fritz Mondale's very experienced chief of staff, Richard Moe, called him one evening to warn Landon that Hamilton was "on the verge of some bad press for the sloppy way his personal matters are handled."

Butler and Jordan disliked Watson. In fact, the personal chemistry was toxic. Butler described Watson as a "sycophant," noting that his nickname at King & Spalding was "Sugar"—"a perfect name for someone as hypocritically sweet as he is." Watson struck Hamilton as naïve and starry-eyed about Washington. Tim Kraft, who had served as national field director for the presidential campaign, thought of Watson as a "Boy Scout." In early December Kirbo came by Butler's transition office and spent an hour going over candidates for various administration slots. "He was in town, I think," Butler noted in his diary, "to do what he could to dampen down the Watson-Jordan clash."

Jordan was himself under enormous personal pressure. He and his wife, Nancy Konigsmark, then thirty-two years old, had been married since 1970, and they had been trying to have a child for years. Soon after the election, Hamilton told a few close friends that Nancy was pregnant. He was obviously happy about this—but then, on December 30, Nancy miscarried. It was a blow to the marriage. When Butler learned the sad news the following day, he noted with some bitterness in his diary, "Somehow staffers are assumed to have no family obligations—personal considerations are somehow considered taboo at the staff level, and not to be talked about. But this affects one's own judgment and pervades one's decisions."

Jordan's personal life was as chaotic and unpredictable as his office routine. His marriage was already troubled. "He treated Nancy terribly," recalled Dr. Peter Bourne, "sometimes insulting her in public." Nancy worked as a scheduler for Rosalynn Carter during the campaign, and Rosalynn intended to keep her in that role as First Lady. The Jordans were thus a working couple—but both were dedicated to the Carters. But it was Nancy who did the housework. "I'm neat, he's not. . . . I cook," Nancy told a *People* magazine reporter that spring. "If he comes home, okay. If not, okay." Bourne insists that even then Hamilton would "disappear often": he was "running off with other women." Perhaps the perception was unfair, but Carter's critics on the left thought his administration had a problem with women.

Martha "Bunny" Mitchell, an African American woman in her early thirties, was appointed "special assistant to the president for special projects." The title was vague, but in reality, Mitchell would be the only Black woman in the White House, responsible for liaison with the African American community. Some thought it an odd selection. Mitchell's previous experience was as a low-level information officer for the Drug Abuse Council. Carter's first pick for a special assistant on minority affairs had been Eleanor Holmes Norton, a highly qualified, well-known African American lawyer and civil rights activist, trained at Yale Law School. But according to Bourne, Hamilton advised Carter, "We'll never be able to control Norton." So Mitchell got the job. Norton was instead made chairman of the Equal Employment Opportunity Commission.

Mitchell was a rarity in those days—a well-educated Black feminist who knew Washington. Born in Gary, Indiana, she had earned both a BA and an MA at Michigan State University and moved to Washington in 1968. Mitchell had first met Carter during the campaign at a small dinner party hosted by Peter Bourne and his wife, Mary King. Mitchell knew Bourne from her work at Washington's Drug Abuse Council, and she was intrigued that evening when she met Carter: "I was not put off that he was a southern white guy." Shortly afterward, Mitchell had campaigned in Pennsylvania with the "peanut brigade." And after the election she had met with Carter in his Plains home, along with Gloria Steinem, Midge Costanza, and other feminist activists.

When Jordan hired Mitchell in January 1977, he never explained what her job was to be. "Special projects could encompass anything," she recalled. "But it was like, well, she is Black, so she will handle all the Black issues." She had met Jordan during the campaign. "He was not my cup of tea," Mitchell said. "The way he talked, the words he used, his whole demeanor suggested nothing sophisticated. He and Jody both. They wanted to advertise that they were not from Washington. Personally, I resented that they wore Levi's into the White House. I thought it was demeaning. We had words about this. But Hamilton flaunted his outsider image. When I asked him about the Levi's, he just said, 'This is who we are.'" Bunny was thrilled to be working in the White House, but Jordan, Butler, Powell, and the other Georgia boys were sometimes hard to fathom. "Hamilton was not an easy person to like," she recalled, "if you were outside his milieu. He always seemed to be a bit tense and standoffish. But he could also be quite charming, but it was always on his terms."

Mitchell's tenure in the White House was always precarious. "The knives were always out for me," she said. During her very first week, she had to write a memo to the president reporting that some prominent African American political figures, including the Urban League's Vernon Jordan, were unhappy with her selection. They wanted a meeting. "For these Black men, it was a slap in the face to see the president put a Black woman in the White House. They didn't know me, and they didn't think I gave them the access to Carter that they expected." When Mitchell handed Carter the memo, he quickly read it and looked up at her and merely nodded. But he was clearly annoyed with her critics and the whole situation. For the time being, he pushed back, telling anyone who asked about Mitchell that he would make his own staff picks. "But the issue never died," Mitchell recalled, "and someone was always talking to Hamilton to get me out of there." Bunny would be gone within two years.

PERHAPS THE BEST decision Carter made during the transition concerned his relationship with Fritz Mondale. The two men had spent very little time together during the campaign, but they bonded during the transition weeks, developing a relaxed trust. Early in December they met together with Mondale's longtime aide Richard Moe and talked frankly about the role of the vice presidency. Mondale spent a solid hour pitching his ideas. He began by noting that Hubert Humphrey's vice presidency had been painfully demeaning; President Johnson had repeatedly humiliated Humphrey and firmly kept him out of the loop.

Mondale said he "didn't want anything like that." Carter quickly agreed and surprised Mondale by observing, "I think some presidents in the past were uncomfortable with the presence of their own vice president. They were worried by their own mortality, and their vice president only reminded them of it. But that doesn't bother me." Carter indicated that he'd like to "use the vice president in a way that hasn't ever happened before."

After the election, Mondale asked his chief of staff, Moe, to give him a memo delineating what exactly he wanted from Carter. Moe's eleven-page memo was sent to Carter on December 9, and a few days later Mondale flew down to Plains to discuss it. He was a bit apprehensive, expecting Carter to negotiate point by point. Instead, Carter silently read the memo, tossed it onto his desk, and said, "This is fine." And then he added, "I also want you to be in the White House." Mondale had not asked for this; no vice president had ever had an office with any kind of physical proximity to the Oval Office. But Carter gave Mondale a West Wing layout and told him to pick out an office. Mondale chose a room next door to the office of national security adviser Brzezinski—just a short walk down the hallway from the Oval Office. Carter thought the vice presidency up until then had been a "wasted national asset," and he was determined to change the whole nature of the office. He agreed that Mondale should have full access to all classified documents and would be allowed to participate in any meeting he wished, whether it was in the Oval Office or elsewhere.

Moe's memo had also included a plea that Mondale be given at least one hour each week to meet privately with the president. Carter topped this by promising that they would have a private lunch every Monday when both men were in town. The Monday luncheons became a nearly sacrosanct part of the presidential calendar. Carter also decided to make Mondale's top aide, Moe, a member of the White House senior staff. More than a handful of Mondale's Senate aides received top positions—including David Aaron as deputy national security adviser and Bert Carp as a senior staffer on the White House Domestic Policy Council. Carp's appointment came about when Mondale called up Eizenstat and said he wanted Carp to serve as his deputy. When Eizenstat replied that he already had recruited David Rubenstein for this position, Mondale just laughed and said, "Stu, now you have two deputies!" The Georgia boys would dominate the White House inner circle, but the president-elect was making it very clear that Mondale and his liberal midwesterners were part of the team. By fully integrating Mondale into the chain of command, Carter set a new precedent. Henceforth, all vice presidents would insist on the prerogatives accorded Mondale. Together, Carter and Mondale invented the modern vice presidency.

BY EARLY JANUARY 1977, Carter had selected most of the senior aides who would occupy offices on the first floor of the West Wing. Susan Clough had been his personal secretary when he was governor, and now this blond thirty-two-year-old divorcée with two children would serve him again, sitting in the small room just outside the Oval Office. Hamilton Jordan, appointed assistant to the president, had the corner office overlooking the Rose Garden.* His deputy, Landon Butler, sat next door in a smaller office. "It's amazing," Butler jotted in his diary, "how the best reassurance is the floor plan!" National security adviser Zbigniew Brzezinski had another corner office, facing Pennsylvania Avenue. Press secretary Jody Powell also had his office facing Pennsylvania Avenue. His deputy, Rex Granum, a young reporter who had covered the Carter gubernatorial years for *The Atlanta Constitution,* sat nearby. Jack Watson was relegated to the second floor of the West Wing, along with Frank Moore, the president's congressional liaison. Also on the second floor sat the president's chief domestic policy adviser, Stuart Eizenstat, who had a corner office just above the Oval Office.

Stu Eizenstat had served up policy papers to Carter ever since the 1970 gubernatorial campaign, and now, at the age of thirty-four, he was director of policy planning for the transition. Eizenstat's father had owned an Atlanta shoe company. He graduated from the University of North Carolina and went on to get a law degree from Harvard in 1967. From Harvard, his first job was as a researcher and junior speechwriter for Joseph Califano, then a White House assistant to President Lyndon B. Johnson. In 1969, he joined a law firm back in

---

* When Jordan first walked into his new office, he found on the desk a bicycle wheel; most of the wheel's spokes were bent out of shape and twisted. Accompanying this gift was a note from his Republican predecessor, Dick Cheney: "Dear Hamilton, beware the spokes of the wheel."

Atlanta. Eizenstat was extremely disciplined, a liberal nuts-and-bolts policy thinker, and a savvy political operator. His youthful experience in the Johnson White House had tempered his strong social liberal instincts. "I like to think I come out of the progressive stream of the [Democratic] party," he told a *New York Times* reporter in 1976. "But we have learned many lessons from the Sixties—that things don't always work. I have a very strong sense that traditional liberalism has not really had a mandate since 1964, and it won't until the people are convinced that government can manage itself." He now called himself a "pragmatic progressive." Some friends called him a "disillusioned liberal" and others a "conservative liberal." Everyone admired his work ethic, but as one colleague wrote, some friends "perpetually worried Stu was the class grind."

"Stu was not fun," recalled his twenty-seven-year-old deputy, David Rubenstein. "Stu and I were both the only sons of Jewish parents. But Stu was Jewish in a way I was not. He could read Hebrew. I did my bar mitzvah, and that was it. . . . He was very hardworking. He carried a yellow legal pad into every meeting." Rubenstein had his office next door to Eizenstat, also overlooking the Rose Garden. Rubenstein quickly gained a West Wing reputation for being a workhorse. "He knew everything that was going on," said Frank Moore, Carter's legislative aide. "David was Stu's personal think tank," recalled Les Francis, another White House aide. "The guy was brilliant." Rubenstein's colleagues joked that he seemed to eat all his meals out of the vending machine. He was often in his office by 7:00 A.M., and sometimes he slept on the sofa. He had a studio apartment a few blocks from the White House, but four years later, when he was packing up his belongings, Rubenstein opened the door of his refrigerator to find it devoid of any food and completely encrusted with ice. As Eizenstat's right-hand man, Rubenstein was soon meeting with all sorts of national figures, powerful men—big shots. "The thing that's so surprising," he confided to another White House aide, "is how ordinary these guys are."

Robert J. Lipshutz, age fifty-five, was another Jewish member of the Georgia mafia. Born in Atlanta, Lipshutz first met Carter in 1966 and later served as the treasurer of his 1976 presidential campaign. A University of Georgia–trained lawyer, Lipshutz was low-key, reliable, and entirely bland. But Carter had spent many nights in Lipshutz's home in

Atlanta and he considered him a trusted personal friend. (He had even helped him to propose to his wife, Betty.) Carter appointed him White House counsel, with an office on the second floor of the West Wing, down the hall from Eizenstat and Rubenstein.

Carter had promised to appoint women to high-ranking positions in his administration, and by early January he was being publicly criticized by feminist leader Gloria Steinem and Congresswoman Barbara Mikulski (D-MD) for not having named a woman to his White House team. "There are several women more qualified than Hamilton Jordan by a long shot," complained Steinem. "A woman with his background would be laughed at and wouldn't get through the White House door." Jordan, when told of Steinem's remark, quipped, "My being unqualified has nothing to do with my being a man—I'm just unqualified."

In the event, Carter and Jordan selected a relatively unknown New York State politician, Midge Costanza, to be the president's assistant for public liaison. A fiery feminist—and at the time a closeted lesbian—Costanza was designated to handle women's issues from within the White House. As the first woman ever named as an assistant to the president, she was given an office in the West Wing, just four doors away from the Oval Office. Carter told her, "Midge, you're going to keep me straight. . . . I want you to help me do the right thing." When Landon Butler met with her for the first time on January 4, 1977, he noted, "Midge is a live-wire. . . . She'll be great." Costanza was an unusual feminist. A city councilwoman from Rochester, she made no effort to hide her working-class background. She compensated for her lack of a college education with a blunt, confrontational style. She laced her speeches with profanities and made it perfectly clear that she had no patience for Washington's snobbery. *The New York Times* described her as a "loud-mouthed pushy little broad." But Carter genuinely liked Costanza. They had first met in 1974 when Costanza was running for Congress. Carter came to upstate New York to campaign for her and was enthralled by her feisty speeches on the stump. When he first met her, he "kind of fell in love with her. . . . I knew increasingly that Midge had a mind of her own and she said provocative things, and she didn't back down under pressure. And those were the things that made her especially attractive to me." Costanza was another example of Carter's affinity for rough-hewn, plain-speaking personalities.

*   *   *

TIM KRAFT, THIRTY-FIVE, woke up on New Year's Day in San Juan, Puerto Rico, with a rum-soaked hangover. He felt like "some invisible giant was trying to batter" his head with a two-by-four. The bushy-haired and mustachioed Kraft had spent five days celebrating on the Caribbean island. He returned to Washington "without a clue" as to what he'd be doing in 1977. On January 4 he had breakfast with Jordan, who dropped "the bombshell right away": Carter was thinking of naming him appointments secretary. "Krafty," Jordan said, "you'd better go down to Plains and talk it over with him." Kraft arrived in Plains that same day. It was raining heavily. Kraft had never visited the Carter home: "Carter's study is warm, roomy and wood-paneled, with a comfortable strewn-with-books look about it." Jimmy greeted him dressed casually in jeans and a sweater. They talked for about twenty minutes, and the president-elect warned Kraft that "he can be exacting with staff and less than friendly." Kraft readily accepted the job.* For the next sixteen months this gregarious and colorful political operative from New Mexico would serve as the president's daily gatekeeper.

BY EARLY JANUARY 1977, Carter had filled all his cabinet posts. Joseph Califano was to become secretary of health, education, and welfare. W. Michael Blumenthal, the CEO of the Bendix Corporation, got the nod for Treasury. A relatively unknown Washington State congressman, Brock Adams, became secretary of transportation. James Schlesinger, a former defense secretary and CIA director, was named the president's assistant for energy issues, with the understanding that Schlesinger would lead the Department of Energy, if and when Carter created this new department. Cy Vance was anointed secretary of state. A former budget director, economist Charles Schultze, was made chairman of the Council of Economic Advisers. Idaho governor Cecil Andrus was named secretary of the interior. Harold Brown got Defense, and Brzezinski was made the president's national security adviser. Kirbo suc-

---

* Greg Schneiders had been slated for the job as appointments secretary, but during his security check the FBI discovered "a whole series of minor infractions—bad checks, repossessed cars, etc."

ceeded in having his law partner Griffin B. Bell named attorney general. Bell happened to be Rosalynn's cousin—though they were not particularly close. His appointment was briefly controversial because the press unearthed the fact that he belonged to a couple of Atlanta's private clubs that did not accept African Americans. But Carter knew Bell as a man with progressive instincts on race. Before Bell's confirmation, Jerry Rafshoon found himself seated next to Ethel Kennedy at a Georgetown dinner party. The outspoken widow of Bobby Kennedy abruptly turned to Rafshoon and said, "I think the Carter cabinet appointees are terrible. For instance, who is this Griffin Bell fellow?"

"Ethel," replied Rafshoon, "Bell was the man who got JFK elected president! Didn't you know that Bell was the man who persuaded the Kennedy campaign to get Martin Luther King Jr. out of jail when he was arrested in Georgia in 1960?"

But most of Carter's cabinet picks were relatively unknown and technocrats. Robert S. Bergland, a congressman from Minnesota, was named secretary of agriculture. Ray Marshall, a relatively unknown Berkeley-trained economist, was selected for labor secretary. Two women were offered cabinet posts: Juanita M. Kreps as commerce secretary and Patricia R. Harris as secretary of housing and urban development. Atlanta congressman Andrew J. Young was appointed United Nations ambassador, and another "Georgia boy," Bert Lance, was named director of the Office of Management and Budget (OMB).

Lance would turn out to be a critical selection. Carter knew him as a friend, frequent tennis partner, and trusted confidant from the gubernatorial years, when Lance had run the Georgia state Department of Highways. Lance was someone who could get things done, and he was the one Georgia boy—aside from Kirbo—who could tell Carter what he did not want to hear. Kirbo was one of seven people whose letters were delivered directly to Carter, unopened. The others were Miss Lillian; Billy Carter; his son Jack Carter; his two sisters, Ruth Stapleton and Gloria Spann; and Jerry Rafshoon. They were instructed to write the digits "611" on the envelope, Rosalynn's phone number when Jimmy was dating her in Plains. This code served to alert the White House mailroom that these letters should be sent directly to the president.

Every successful president needs to have at least a few confidants who can be counted on, when the facts warrant it, to say no. Lance was that man. He was congenial, loyal, and competent. "I had confidence in Bert," Kirbo recalled. "I assumed he was rich. He acted like a rich man. He was not gaudy or a braggart or anything like that. He had interests in a lot of banks, and people understood he was in good shape and was a fine banker." Carter confided to Kirbo that Lance had expressed a desire to become treasury secretary. But Kirbo advised instead that Lance be given the OMB directorship. Once again, Carter accepted Kirbo's counsel, but in doing so, he inadvertently planted a ticking time bomb inside the White House. As would become clear before long—and as a more serious vetting might have uncovered—Lance had financial and personal issues that would not escape the fine-tooth comb of a Senate confirmation process. One potential solution might have been making Lance chief of staff, since Kirbo had declined to move to Washington. But Carter had decided against even having a chief of staff. This too was probably a mistake.

Still, at the time, Washington insiders thought Carter had managed a pretty good transition. Sure, there was some of the usual chaos and some unexpected turns of events. But this was to be expected. *The New York Times* editorialized that the president-elect had "assembled a strong team." Butler, however, was unimpressed by most of Carter's cabinet picks. "I must say," he noted in his diary on December 19, 1976, "the Cabinet doesn't appear to be a very interesting bunch—except for Andy Young, we haven't done anything which shows boldness or imagination. Most of the choices are consensus candidates: solid choices, but none of them indicates that Carter has anything but a mainstream consensus point-of-view. The choices are all cautious choices." Butler was prescient. With the exception of Young, none of these cabinet picks represented a radical departure.

One selection became controversial so quickly that the nominee was never confirmed. Carter had met Theodore Sorensen during the summer of 1975 while campaigning in New York City. President John F. Kennedy's longtime aide and speechwriter took an instant liking to Carter and hosted his first major fundraising dinner in the city. Afterward, Carter spent the night in Sorensen's home. Sorensen later wrote some speeches for the campaign, and so it was not entirely unexpected that he might be offered a job in the new administration. But he was surprised when Jack Watson called him in early December and mentioned that

Carter wanted to nominate him as director of the Central Intelligence Agency. "No, that's not the job for me," Sorensen told Watson. But the president-elect soon invited him down to Plains and, after a perfunctory conversation, offered him the CIA job. Sorensen felt he couldn't decline, and the nomination was announced on December 23.*

The selection of a Kennedy family confidant like Sorensen was politically astute. The Georgia mafia needed to reach out to that iconic Democratic clan. And Sorensen was obviously qualified by his three years in the Kennedy White House, and perhaps equally so as a literate historian and biographer of the Kennedy administration. Sorensen, forty-eight years old, was a suave, cosmopolitan New York corporate lawyer whose friends and colleagues populated the East Coast establishment. These were precisely the members of the liberal establishment who viewed Carter with such skepticism and cultural disdain. Sorensen could serve as a bridge to this world, an emissary to the foreign policy establishment.

It all made sense—until Hamilton Jordan called Sorensen soon after the nomination was announced to ask if it was true that during World War II he had registered for the draft as a conscientious objector. Sorensen was surprised by the question, since he had assumed they had vetted him, and he had never hidden this piece of his personal biography. Indeed, it was a well-known fact; a decade earlier Senator Barry Goldwater had publicly attacked Sorensen on this very point. And Sorensen himself had disclosed it in his 1965 biography *Kennedy*. But now, of course, Sorensen's youthful, unorthodox views on nonviolence would be used by Republican senators to oppose the nomination of this Kennedy man as the nation's chief spymaster.

Sorensen's nomination quickly became contentious. Soon even some Democratic senators, like Henry "Scoop" Jackson, announced their opposition. (Ironically, even Senator Ted Kennedy, while sympathetic, felt constrained about publicly endorsing Sorensen, fearing that to do so would remind his critics that Sorensen had given him legal advice during the Chappaquiddick affair.) More than a dozen unnamed CIA offi-

---

* It had been obvious to Carter that George H. W. Bush had wanted to remain in his job as CIA director. "Of course, political history might have been different if I had said okay," Carter recalled. "But I wanted my own person in there."

cers spoke up against Sorensen, partly because of his critiques in print about the CIA's performance during the 1961 Bay of Pigs debacle, and partly because of Sorensen's sworn testimony before the 1975 Church Committee hearings that President Kennedy had never authorized or even spoken about assassinating foreign leaders. A retired intelligence officer was quoted as saying that Sorensen would be "about as well received at Langley," the CIA headquarters, "as Sherman was in Atlanta." Sorensen himself later wondered if these CIA veterans wanted to be sure that he never saw the Agency's records about Kennedy's assassination.

Worse was to come. Senator Joe Biden (D-DE) released an affidavit Sorensen had given in the trial of Daniel Ellsberg, the leaker of the Pentagon Papers in 1971. Sorensen's affidavit had been used by Ellsberg's defense lawyers to buttress their claims that the government routinely classified as secret documents that should be available to the public. Sorensen had further explained that in the 1960s government officials routinely took home classified documents—and that he had himself taken home seven boxes of classified papers upon his departure from the White House. He used them in his book on the Kennedy presidency. It didn't matter that this was not illegal at the time; retiring government officials routinely boxed up their papers when they left office. And it didn't matter that Sorensen's affidavit had been filed in defense of *The New York Times*'s First Amendment right to publish the Pentagon Papers. Sorensen's critics on Capitol Hill now charged that he could not be trusted with national security secrets. Senator Biden—who had initially praised Sorensen's nomination—now said, "Honestly, I'm not sure whether or not Mr. Sorensen could be indicted or convicted under the espionage statutes."

Sorensen's nomination battle had become a classic Washington feeding frenzy—nasty, irrational, and unwinnable. Jody Powell confided that he was startled to see "personal, catty, sniping stuff" from liberals who he had expected would be supportive. The president-elect faced his first major conundrum. Withdrawing the nomination would be perceived as a blow. But if he pressed forward with Sorensen's nomination, a rejection in the Senate would be regarded as an unprecedented defeat, early in his presidency. Carter waffled, at first telling Sorensen in a phone call that he was "behind" him. But he did not lobby the Senate on Sorensen's behalf, and the day before the scheduled confirmation hearing, he sent

Mondale and Jordan over to urge Sorensen to withdraw. Sorensen demurred, saying he realized where things were going, but he felt he needed to testify before the Senate committee and defend himself against the unfairness of these personal attacks on his integrity and beliefs. Jordan was clearly annoyed. Mondale was visibly emotional: "I have come closer to crying in the last two days," he told Sorensen, "than at any time in the eight years I have been in Washington. . . . You have been attacked unfairly. In a fair forum, you would win confirmation. But the Senate plays dirty, and Governor Carter and I are convinced that withdrawal is the only course." The meeting ended with everyone agreeing that Sorensen could have his day before the Senate—but would withdraw his nomination at the end of his testimony.

It was a bitter and sad ending—and foreshadowed political troubles to come. "I'll always wonder," Carter wrote to Sorensen on January 22, 1977, "if it would have been better to fight it out." *The New York Times* called it "a rare defeat for an incoming president" and blamed it on "timidity among Senate liberals and Democrats, and above all, misjudgments and an apparent failure of nerve by the new administration." If Carter had vociferously fought for the nomination, shaming the liberal Democratic senators into confirming Sorensen, Congress might have learned that this was a president who could not be pushed around.

AMID THE BATTLE over Sorensen's nomination, Carter alienated another powerful member of Washington's establishment. Carter knew that much of Washington presumed that he owed something to Robert Strauss, the chairman of the Democratic National Committee. Strauss was rich, influential, and connected. But for precisely that reason, Carter did not want to be seen rewarding such a man with a cabinet post. So one evening some weeks prior to the inauguration, Hamilton Jordan asked Joel McCleary, a twenty-six-year-old campaign advance man, to escort Bob Strauss over to Blair House to see the president-elect. McCleary sat with the gruff Texan in his limousine, and from their brief conversation it was clear that Strauss had high expectations. "Well, it was a disaster," McCleary recalled. "I took him into Blair house, and Carter offered him basically nothing: 'I really appreciate everything you have done, and now I'd like you to work on relations with Capitol Hill.' Strauss was expecting something much more, a cabinet position, perhaps Treasury. Afterwards, as we walked back to his limousine, he turned to me and said, 'It is very unfortunate that you have just watched me get fucked.' Strauss felt humiliated, and he would never forget it. I think he became a destructive force in the administration."

Strauss's relationship with Carter thereafter was marked by a resentful undertow. Some in Carter's inner circle knew that Strauss was a man who could make himself useful. "I thought, frankly," said Stu Eizenstat, "he should've gotten a more prominent position." At some point during the transition, Kirbo called Strauss and told him bluntly, "If you want something, you better ask for it. There's not much left." Weeks after the inauguration, Strauss was finally offered the post of special trade representative, a job they billed to him as "cabinet-level." Eager to be a player, Strauss ran with it, and by the end of the year he was negotiating ground-breaking trade deals with the Japanese and the Europeans. By late spring, the president was noting in his diary, "I believe he's one of the best appointments I've made." And yet Carter always had this lingering feeling that Strauss was one of his most "opportunistic" advisers. Indeed, over the next four years, Strauss would accumulate more power and prove the president's instincts to be on the mark. "I was a pain in the ass," Strauss said.

Strauss was intent on obtaining access to the Oval Office. He was relentless. One day he called Tim Kraft, demanding an appointment with Carter. Kraft put him off for two consecutive days. On the third day, Strauss called and again Kraft said there was no time in the president's schedule. "Kraft," Strauss said in his slow Texan drawl, "let me tell you something about this great country of ours. This is the only nation in the world where a rich, powerful, influential man like myself has to go through some two-bit-son-of-a-bitch like you to see the President of the United States." Strauss was only half kidding. As for Kraft, he knew his job as scheduler left no room for "false modesty, indecision or deference to rank." He'd have to do his best to "give the president an ordered work-day."

Nine days before the inauguration Kraft accompanied the president-elect from Plains up to Washington for two days of consultations. During the forty-mile drive to Albany, where they would board a Delta Air Lines charter plane, Carter provided "a running discourse on pecans, cypress swamps, Spanish moss, quail hunting, bird dogs and his guns . . .

but most about quail—what they're like, what they eat, what makes a good quail environment and the enjoyment of the hunt. He knows and loves this turf." Kraft thought his boss was in a good mood.

Two days later, they were driving back to Plains; Carter was tired and in a decidedly somber mood. He and Fritz Mondale had been up until one o'clock in the morning for briefings by Pentagon brass on defense issues. Carter told Kraft that he was trying to involve Mondale in everything so he could be fully informed, noting calmly, "I could be killed in an instant." But then, a few moments later, Carter leaned forward in the car and started chatting with Larry Sheaf, the Secret Service agent in the front seat, telling him that he was going to issue an executive order to curtail the air-freighting of the presidential armored limousine around the country—even for trips abroad. He wanted to save taxpayer funds. He then turned to Kraft and added that he was also going to terminate home-to-office limousine service for White House senior staff. Carter saw this as an extravagant perk.

"Except for the appointments secretary," Kraft deadpanned.

"Service in the White House," Carter said without a smile, "is voluntary."

It was a bright, cold, and sunny day in Plains on January 19 as Jimmy and Rosalynn prepared to leave their home on Woodland Drive and motor to Albany for the flight to Washington. Tim Kraft helped them to load suitcases into the car, including a sack of Amy's toys.

"Rosie, hurry up, let's go," Jimmy said.

"The schedule says I have till eleven fifteen," Rosalynn replied, "and I'm *almost* ready."

"Let's leave a little early," Jimmy said impatiently. "There's going to be a sort of rally in Albany."

But just as they were finally ready to walk out, Carter set his briefcase on the floor, walked back through the bedroom hallway, put on his reading glasses, and adjusted the thermostat down. Observing this, Kraft thought, "Incredible. Just like my old man."

Carter was determined to have a low-key, minimalist inauguration. After the excesses of Richard Nixon's imperial presidency, he wanted to send a message of simplicity, authenticity, and unadorned integrity. Taking the oath of office, he placed his left hand on both a family Bible and, beneath it, a Bible used by George Washington in his 1789 inauguration. Afterward, as he stepped forward to give his address, Carter gazed out on the magnificent scene. He felt "strangely calm." It was a brisk twenty-eight degrees Fahrenheit, but sunny with blue skies. His entire inaugural speech ran to only 1,228 words; read very slowly in his South Georgia drawl, it was over in less than fourteen minutes. It was one of the sparest inaugural addresses of any president. Reciting Micah 6:8, Carter reminded Americans about the need "to walk humbly with thy God." He then promised, "Our commitment to human rights must be absolute." He promised that this year the nation would take a step toward "our ultimate goal—the elimination of all nuclear weapons." And finally, he spoke of "limits"—a most un-American concept, but one that would become in retrospect a major theme of his entire presidency: "We have learned that 'more' is not necessarily 'better,' that even our great nation has its recognized limits, and that we can neither answer all questions nor solve all problems. We cannot afford to do everything. . . . We must simply do our best."

After the inaugural speech, President Carter was escorted back to the Senate's Magnussen Room, where he sat eating finger sandwiches and sipping coffee with Chief Justice Warren E. Burger, Vice President Mondale, Rosalynn, and Joan Mondale. After several minutes, Dick Keiser, the head of the president's Secret Service detail, beckoned Tim Kraft from a side door. "Tim, if we're going to depart in five minutes, you'd better ask the president-elect . . . uh, President Carter, to step in here and get dressed."

"Get dressed?" Kraft asked.

"The vest," replied Keiser.

A few moments later, Kraft watched in a small adjoining room as the new president shed his suit coat and white shirt—and then slipped on a bulletproof vest over his bare chest. "They want me to wear this," Carter explained to Kraft with a smile. "I told them I was going to walk about ten days ago, and they asked me to keep it quiet." Dressed, Carter then put on a black winter overcoat. It was a coat he had borrowed from—and never returned to—Jerry Rafshoon a year earlier during the wintry New Hampshire primary.

A few moments later, he emerged and explained to his family that he was going to walk down Pennsylvania Avenue. Miss Lillian showed her alarm, and so Carter sat on the armrest of the sofa chair where she was sitting, put his arm around her, and said, "Mother, I'm going to be fine; I'm going to walk among the people who voted for me."

The Secret Service was understandably nervous about Carter's desire to walk down Pennsylvania Avenue. Only thirteen years had passed since John Kennedy was shot riding in an open motorcade. And just seventeen months earlier President Ford had narrowly missed a bullet when Lynette "Squeaky" Fromme's pistol misfired. So Carter would have to wear a bulletproof vest. But the Secret Service also insisted that someone walk behind the president who could distinguish friends from strangers in the crowds lining the street. Carter pointed to Frank Moore and said, "Frank knows everybody I know."

Carter, Rosalynn, and nine-year-old daughter Amy entered the backseats of an armored presidential limousine and were driven toward the White House. But before the presidential caravan had even left the Capitol grounds, Carter asked the driver to stop. He got out of the black car, took Rosalynn's hand, and, waving to the crowds, walked the remaining mile to the White House. It was an electric scene. One of Carter's sons, Jack, later said, "I'll admit that walkin' down Pennsylvania Avenue past those big buildings I did feel a little bit like we were Caesar comin' into a conquered town." Carter himself noted in his diary that it was an emotional experience: "Many people along the parade route," when they saw that the new president was walking to his new home, "began to weep." Carter always cherished this memory of his stroll down Pennsylvania Avenue as "one of those few perfect moments in life when everything seems absolutely right."

Afterward the Carters sat in a solar-heated reviewing stand designed by their Atlanta friend and architect, Paul Muldawer, and watched the parade. The solar heat turned out to be rather inefficient, so they were all pretty cold. When it was finished, they began walking into the White House grounds, encircled by a bevy of reporters. Jody Powell instructed the family, "Stay close together, and don't any of you talk to the press." Miss Lillian whirled and said, "Jody, you can go to hell. I'll talk to whom I please." Turning to the television microphones, she was asked, "Miss Lillian, aren't you proud of your son?" Knowing his mama, President Carter leaned in to hear her answer: "Which one?"

Chapter 6
White House Life

I don't care if all 100 of them are against me. It's the right thing to do.

—PRESIDENT CARTER, January 20, 1977

Amy Carter
JIMMY CARTER PRESIDENTIAL LIBRARY AND MUSEUM

UPON ENTERING THE White House on the afternoon of January 20, 1977, the Carters were first escorted to the residence on the second floor of the mansion. But Carter spent only twenty minutes in the second-floor residence before he became restless: "Where I would work was much more interesting to me than where we would be sleeping." Taking the elevator to the ground floor, he realized he had no idea how to find the Oval Office. Casually turning to a Secret Service officer, he said, "I'm just going to the Oval Office." An agent then led the way under the South Arcade and opened the door to the Oval Office. It was 4:20 P.M.

Carter found himself alone, and, slightly awed, he wondered for a moment if he could touch anything. But then he strode across the room and jerked open the drapes to view the beautiful South Lawn of the White House.

Turning around, he sat down at the desk and immediately noticed that it was not the desk he had expected, the *Resolute* desk, famously photographed during the Kennedy years with the president's toddler, John F. Kennedy, Jr., peeping out from its lower door. Carved from the timbers of the British Arctic exploration ship HMS *Resolute,* the ornate oak desk was given by Queen Victoria to President Rutherford B. Hayes in 1880. It had since been used by every president until Kennedy's assassination in 1963, when it was loaned to the Smithsonian Museum. Carter associated the *Resolute* desk with the Oval Office. So his very first decision as president was to order its retrieval. It arrived the next day—and has remained in the White House ever since.

His next decision was more consequential; indeed, it would set the tone for how he governed over the next four years. Down the hallway a thirty-four-year-old disabled army veteran, Max Cleland, was sitting in his wheelchair in Hamilton Jordan's office, waiting to see the new president. Back in 1968, Captain Cleland had lost his legs and one arm to a hand grenade during the Battle of Khe Sanh. Two years later, he met Carter for the first time when Cleland introduced gubernatorial candidate Carter to a small crowd gathered at an abandoned gas station in Georgia. Cleland was running for state senate. "I thought he had no chance in hell," Cleland recalled. But both men won their races and became friends and political allies. By the time Carter was running for president, Cleland had moved to Washington, DC, to work on veterans' affairs as an aide to Senator Alan Cranston (D-CA). Cleland had been backstage at a Seattle convention of the American Legion the previous August when presidential candidate Carter pledged to "pardon" all Vietnam War–era draft evaders "to heal the nation's wounds." Cleland liked the idea, but he was shocked when the entire audience of veterans stood up in unison and booed Carter for three long minutes. Now, on the late afternoon of January 20, President Carter had summoned Cleland for a brief chat. It would be his first appointment as president in the Oval Office.

When Cleland rolled into the Oval Office at 4:35 P.M., he relished the memory of having been there once before, in the autumn of 1963, as a college student attending a seminar in the White House. President Kennedy's national security adviser, McGeorge Bundy, had graciously given him a tour of the Oval Office. Cleland immediately noticed—as Carter had—the absence of the famous *Resolute* desk. Carter greeted him warmly and then offered him the job of chief of the Veterans Administration. Cleland had known this might be in the offing and happily accepted.

But then he told Carter, "Senator Cranston asked me to warn you that there is growing opposition among members of the Senate to your plan to grant amnesty to draft dodgers." Without hesitation, Carter leaned over Cleland's wheelchair and said, "I don't care if all 100 of them are against me. It's the right thing to do." The next morning, Carter issued Executive Order 11967, providing a blanket presidential pardon for some 210,000 Vietnam-era draft evaders. He knew the news would be greeted by a firestorm of criticism in the press and on Capitol Hill. Republican senator Barry Goldwater denounced it as "the most disgraceful thing a president has ever done." Carter didn't care. He knew he had made the right decision; a pardon would heal some of the rancor over the Vietnam War. The controversy would soon pass, and perhaps even his critics would concede that carrying out an unpopular campaign promise was evidence of his strength as a political leader. This, his first major decision as president, was vintage Carter.

That afternoon the president's appointments secretary, Tim Kraft, was told by the Secret Service that Carter's code name had been changed from "Dasher" to "Deacon." Kraft wondered why, but few would doubt that "Deacon" was an apt moniker for a man devoted to the Niebuhrian principle of using political power for moral purposes.

IN THE EVENING, the Carters attended ten inaugural parties at various hotels and other venues and only retired to the White House residence at 12:30 A.M. Gregg Allman, who had raised considerable campaign funds playing at benefit concerts, was one of many celebrities in attendance, accompanied by his wife, Cher. Aretha Franklin, the "Queen of Soul," sang at one of the inaugural balls. But by and large, the Carter inaugural balls were staged for common folk. For sentimental reasons, but also to convey a message of frugality and simplicity, Rosalynn wore the same dress she had bought for their 1971 governor's inaugural ball. The press quickly took note of her "nonflamboyant style," and high-end fashion designers in New York were horrified to learn that the First Lady was bringing a sewing machine with her to the White House.

Sally Quinn, *The Washington Post*'s snarky "style" reporter, could not wait to make fun of the Carters' simple ways: "There is nothing royal or imperial about them. He signs his name 'Jimmy.' . . . She wears her un-fashionable 6-year-old evening dress from his gubernatorial ball for 'sentimental reasons.' . . . They pray openly and talk about Christ. He carries his own luggage. They hold hands in public, touch each other often, even kiss a lot. Really kiss." It was the first of Quinn's many broad-sides in the style section of the *Post*.* "The Carter people," she archly opined, "have yet to develop the proper cynicism." Quinn obviously har-bored a certain snobbish disdain for the Carters; but she also just seemed to think her job as the style-section sharpshooter was to humiliate ev-eryone outside Georgetown society. Years later, after suffering more than one such broadside from Quinn, Carter remained offended by what he remembered as a truly egregious error: "Sally insinuated that I did not know how to knot a bow tie. But every midshipman who gradu-ates from the Naval Academy has to wear a bow tie. And we have to tie it ourselves."

The next morning President Carter rose at 6:30 A.M.—he still kept farmer's hours. He was in the Oval Office by 7:00 A.M., reading the newspapers. At 8:30 A.M. he joined the whole Carter clan for their first breakfast in the residence. This included Rosalynn and Amy as well as his three sons and their wives—Chip and Caron Carter, Jeff and Annette Carter, Jack and Judy Carter—but also Miss Lillian and Rosalynn's mother, Allie Smith. Chip and Jeff, and their wives, had decided to live in the White House. Miss Lillian returned to Georgia that day—but not before scribbling a note to her son: "Dear Hot, I like your office . . . Goodbye! Ma."

Half an hour later, Carter walked downstairs to the Oval Office and

---

* In 1977, Quinn was living with *Washington Post* editor Ben Bradlee, and she already had a public persona for her irreverent profiles of Washington figures. Norman Mailer called her "Poison Quinn," and Henry Kissinger told *Post* publisher Katharine Graham, "Sally makes me want to commit suicide."

had his first briefing as president with Zbigniew Brzezinski, his national security adviser. This would become a morning ritual for the next four years. On his second day in office, Carter noted in his diary that Brzezinski would have "constant access to me several times a day, perhaps second only to Hamilton Jordan in frequency." The president was "determined to have Dr. Brzezinski be a constant source of stimulation for the Departments of Defense and State," but at the same time he did not want Zbig to "dominate members of the cabinet."

This would turn out to be a daily contradiction. Zbig would "stimulate" relentlessly—and scheme to dominate. "I got into a few heated exchanges with Brzezinski," recalled Tim Kraft. "There wasn't a personality problem or acrimony. It was just one very aggressive person vying for the president's time and somebody else trying to protect him." Brzezinski typically spent five hours each week with the president—more time than any other White House aide. At one point, later that spring, Kraft reprimanded Brzezinski, "Frankly, I think that, given your frequent access to the President, you have unconsciously devalued the importance of his time." Zbig was unrepentant, firing back to Kraft, "This note is outrageous in tone and substance. I do not accept it."

Early on, Carter made it clear to his schedulers that he needed the first couple of hours in the morning "free for his reading and study." Just five days into office, he wrote to Kraft, "I need more time alone early each morning. . . . Let's begin with Zbig's mtg at 8:30 AM." Carter sometimes rose as early as 5:00 A.M., but more often around 5:30 or 6:00 A.M. "I don't think Carter wakes up slow like most everyone else I know," Kraft noted in his diary. "I always looked forward to getting over to the Oval Office," Carter said, "even when I knew the day was going to be dismal and we were going to lose an important vote in the Congress, when I might be embarrassed by something, I still was eager to get over there. I just liked the administrative work."

After a quick glass of orange juice in the residence, he would retire to the small study situated just ten feet down a narrow hallway from the Oval Office. There he would sip a cup of coffee and read *The New York Times, The Atlanta Constitution, The Washington Post,* and various briefing papers. Carter relished his time alone in this small, intimate room, crowded with a six-foot couch and a large bookcase filled with his favorite history books and biographies. A large portrait of Rosalynn and Amy hung over the fireplace mantel, and a handcrafted flintlock rifle hung on the wall behind his desk. A *Flag Day* painting, one of a series by the Impressionist Childe Hassam (1859–1935), dominated the south wall. He quickly installed a high-fidelity sound system, and it was his personal secretary Susan Clough's job to change the 33 rpm records and keep the classical music flowing. Carter favored Beethoven and other classical composers—and he memorized the titles of everything he heard, listening to the music eight or ten hours a day. His favorite piece for a time was "Recuerdos de la Alhambra" by Francisco Tárrega.

Carter was always a stickler about time. One morning he was annoyed to notice that the antique grandfather clock in the Oval Office was running slow. He complained to Kraft and asked who was responsible for keeping it set. Kraft had to reprimand the White House electrician, who came and reset the clock. "So much for foreign policy," Kraft noted. "I thought I was going to write speeches." Kraft knew his boss was demanding. But he shared a surprisingly easygoing relationship with the president. And sometimes he brought out Carter's wry humor. "I'd say, 'Mr. President, a distinguished assembly awaits you in the Cabinet Room,' and he'd look up and say, 'What, did you change the schedule?' He'd just kill me with that stuff."

ON THE EVENING of January 22, 1977, the Carters adjourned downstairs to the White House theater and watched their first movie in a long time, *All the President's Men,* starring Dustin Hoffman and Robert Redford. Carter was "impressed" by the film's depiction of how the two *Washington Post* reporters had doggedly uncovered the Watergate scandal. But he noted in his diary that he "also felt strange occupying the same living quarters and position of responsibility as Richard Nixon, who had brought such disgrace on the White House and the presidency itself." He was determined that no such thing would happen on his watch. All members of the White House staff were subject to complete financial transparency. Any assets other than their residential real estate, savings certificates, and a standard checking account had to be placed in a blind trust run by a trustee authorized to "sell or buy without discussion with the government officer or anyone close to such officer." The president himself placed his peanut warehouse in a blind trust run by Kirbo—and four years later Carter would be shocked to discover that his family business was virtually bankrupt.

Initially, Rosalynn was dismayed to discover how expensive it was to live in the White House. The president and his family have always been required to pay for all the food and drink consumed in the private residence upstairs, and the bill for the last ten days of January came to more than $600. "It doesn't sound like very much," recalled Rosalynn, "but that was enormous to me back in '76. . . . Our food bill was always astronomical!"

Despite unusually frigid winter temperatures, Carter ordered the thermostats in the White House set at sixty-five degrees Fahrenheit during the day and a chilly fifty-five degrees at night. "I couldn't believe it," Rosalynn Carter later wrote. "I had been freezing ever since we moved in. My offices were so cold I couldn't concentrate, and my staff were typing with gloves on. . . . I pleaded with Jimmy to set the thermostats at 68 degrees, but it didn't do any good." Jimmy relented only the following winter, when both his mother and his wife complained about the cold.

Carter also disliked the hovering of the Secret Service officers; he firmly instructed them that he could open doors himself, without their assistance. He did not want agents lurking in every corridor. In a handwritten note to Dick Keiser, the special agent in charge of presidential security, Carter complained that he saw "no need for the extra guard you have placed outside my south office door." Upon learning that the stairwells to the second-floor residence were closed, requiring the presidential family to take the elevators, Carter ordered the stairways to be open except during public visiting hours.

"Jimmy Carter is a wonderfully sweet man," said Alice Rogoff, a White House staffer, "but extremely controlling." Carter wanted a spartan White House. That meant "more frugality, less ostentation, more accessibility to the press and public." Three days after the inauguration, he presided over a swearing-in ceremony for eight cabinet members. The president normally was greeted at such ceremonies by a marine band playing "Hail to the Chief." Carter dispensed with any such pomp: "In a nonmilitary ceremony," he noted in his diary, "I believe this is appropriate." He saved the federal government $12,000 annually by canceling such perks as limousine service for White House staff. Reporters noted that Jody Powell had begun arriving at 1600 Pennsylvania Avenue driving his battered, eleven-year-old blue Volkswagen Beetle. Powell wryly told Hedrick Smith of *The New York Times* that it was all about "depomping the Presidency."

The chronically late Powell soon became the affable face of the new administration. His demeanor was nonchalant and his humor droll and self-deprecating. One day, watching an air force jet fighter blast off the runway, Powell turned to a friend and remarked, "If I'd only learned not to lie and cheat, I'd be flying one of those things." When Jody presided over a press conference, the room was often filled with the sound of laughter. "His weapon of choice," said *Washington Post* columnist David Broder, "was his impish sense of humor." When asked to comment about a story reporting that a tribe of pygmies had attacked the government in Zaire—and that the U.S. government was shipping Coca-Cola into Zaire—Powell began his daily briefing, "I am specifically authorized to deny that the elite pygmy corps was high on Coke."

Over the next four years the press never caught him in an outright lie. Veteran ABC television correspondent Sam Donaldson sparred often with Powell in the press room. "He never lied to us," Donaldson recalled. "He never misled us. He dodged controversial issues once in a while. But he did it with grace and style. He'd laugh. He'd shuck. He'd jive. He'd pirouette. Even the fiercest of us, the legendary Helen Thomas, would laugh." Jody spoke slowly, with an air of studied nonchalance. He never seemed rattled. But when he had to dodge and weave, he signaled openly that this was what he was doing. After one particularly verbose and quite meaningless answer, Jody paused and said with a mischievous smirk, "Beat that one to death." (Laughter.) "Drown it in mush!"

A reporter responded, "I will beat it to death if I can put my hand on it and figure out what the hell it is." (Laughter.)

"If you can get your hands on that," Powell replied, "we will make you a Jell-O tester."

On another occasion, Jody observed, "Demagoguery in the Congress is something somebody else can worry about. Demagoguery in the press room is my problem." (Laughter.)

Early in March 1977, Joe Klein, then a reporter for *Rolling Stone*, came by the White House to interview Powell and Jordan. Jody took Klein into the president's private study and introduced him as "the first major threat to the administration." Carter laughed and told Jody, "Well, if that's the case, you're just going to have to lie."

Carter made Powell's job easier, if only because he made a point of being accessible to the press. In a radical contrast to previous presidents, Carter held regular, unscripted press conferences every two weeks, patiently taking questions from the press corps. He did so, some thought, with a confidence bordering on hubris. "Carter is always offering himself up in various forums to press questioning," complained one of his speechwriters. The president clearly prided himself on this transparency. The question-and-answer format of a press conference suited his style much better than giving a set speech, where he often sounded wooden and flat. Hugh Sidey, *Time* magazine's Washington bureau chief, observed of Powell, "If he is a success so far, it is because Carter runs an open White House. Certainly, Powell adds a dimension of humor and quick comeback. But if Carter should ever decide that he wants to close things down a bit, then all those jokes from Jody and his engaging ways would not mean a thing."

But over time, Carter developed an aversion to hanging out with members of the working press. He reluctantly agreed to speak at the White House Correspondents' annual banquet that first spring of 1977. But when Jody begged him to make a return appearance in 1978, Carter flatly refused, echoing Richard Nixon's flouting of this presidential tradition. He was determined not to subject himself to the roasting, telling Jerry Rafshoon, "Why should I spend all this time to prepare jokes to entertain your and Jody's friends?" Powell stood in for his boss, explaining that the president "wanted me to express his regrets. Unfortunately, time does not permit me to say all the things that are regrettable about the White House correspondents." Powell was joking, of course, but privately Carter noted in his diary that the press corps was "completely irresponsible and unnecessarily abusive."

THE PRESIDENT APPOINTED his thirty-four-year-old first cousin once removed, Hugh "Sonny" Carter, Jr., to manage the White House budget and ordered him to cut the frills. Hugh was actually highly qualified for the job, having earned a graduate degree from the Wharton School of Business at the University of Pennsylvania. He soon discovered that there were 325 television sets throughout the East and West Wings—and that the tab for magazine and newspaper subscriptions ran to $85,000 annually. Hugh immediately went on a rampage, throwing out 265 televisions, 175 radios, numerous typewriters, and any luxuries in the West Wing. "Cousin Cheap" canceled dozens of magazine and newspaper subscriptions. Powell complained loudly that "all the cuts and frills are being made by people who aren't responsible for carrying on day-to-day." Hugh Carter responded by sending Powell a tongue-in-cheek memo canceling *all* his newspaper subscriptions. "Since you are in touch with press people all the time, you should know all the news." Cousin Hugh also said Jody was banned from Air Force One "because it costs too much to filter all of your cigarette smoke out of the cabin."

Hugh also persuaded the president to sell the presidential yacht, the USS *Sequoia,* which was then costing the federal government $800,000 annually in maintenance and operation. (Jimmy noted dismissively in his diary, "I would never use [the yacht].") Hugh told reporters that the larger goal of all these cuts was to democratize the White House staff: "We just want to keep folks from getting too doggone exclusive."

During the first few months of the administration, Cousin Hugh also restricted the use of official cars. Zbig Brzezinski often left the White House late at night, steaming mad that the president's national security adviser was being forced to walk out into Washington's still-crime-ridden streets in search of a cab home.

The Carters were not teetotalers. But when Rosalynn mentioned to her husband that she had learned from the head usher, Rex Scouten, that previous presidents had spent as much as $1 million a year on alcohol, Jimmy decided to change things. Henceforth, wine would be served at official dinners, but no hard liquor would be offered to White House guests. If it was a matter of frugality, not Southern Baptist morality, nevertheless the public perception was that the president was banning alcohol on religious grounds. Rosalynn later thought this was a mistake, a "stereotype that we never lived down."

There was one perk that Carter embraced. In late February he and Rosalynn were driven in a motorcade to Camp David, the rustic presidential retreat nestled in Catoctin Mountain Park sixty-two miles northwest of Washington, DC. Built in 1938–39, the 120-acre camp was turned into a presidential retreat by Franklin Roosevelt in 1942. He called it his "Shangri-La." President Dwight D. Eisenhower later renamed the military-run facility after his grandson David. The grounds contained a dozen rustic cabins, stained or painted a moss-green hue. Guests could use either of two outdoor heated swimming pools, a sauna, tennis courts, two bowling alleys, a fishing stream, a skeet range, jogging trails, a single golf hole, and a trampoline. The Carters stayed in Aspen Lodge, a four-bedroom single-level home perched on a hill with scenic views of the Maryland countryside.* "It's secluded," Carter noted, "and is one of the perquisites of the White House that I intend to retain. I've asked Bert Lance [OMB chief] not even to let me know how much it costs to maintain Camp David." (It cost about $800,000 to operate, even with a bare-bones navy staff.)

Carter's obsession with frugality was matched only by his determination to avoid even the appearance of ethical scandal. After a visit to the White House by Muhammad Ali, the boxing champion sent the president two complimentary tickets to his next world heavyweight bout in Madison Square Garden. Carter immediately returned the $100 tickets with a handwritten note, thanking him for his "generosity" but saying, "I cannot accept so valuable a gift."

AMY CARTER, AGE nine, was undoubtedly the center of the family's personal life. Because her brothers were so much older, Amy grew up as if she were an only child. Her earliest memories were of living in the limelight of the governor's mansion, and from her child's perspective the White House was no different. She treated the White House as her home, roller-skating in the East Room and playing in a tree house her father designed and had built on the South Lawn. She made news sitting at state dinners, reading a book, oblivious to the adults. Her father encouraged her bookish behavior at the dinner table, saying it was the "Carter family habit. . . . My mother always read at the meal table; so did I . . . and we don't consider it to be rude." To the consternation of the Washington establishment, Amy was

---

* Camp David was also a nuclear bomb shelter. Chip Carter recalled opening the closet door in his Aspen Lodge bedroom and sliding the coat hangers to one side: "The wall opens and you take the circular stairs down into the bomb shelter—and 180 people could live down there for a year."

enrolled in the Thaddeus Stevens School, a historically African American elementary public school eight blocks from the White House.

"Amy's been much happier," Carter noted in his diary in late February, "since Mary Fitzpatrick got out of prison and came up to the White House to be with us." The Carters had invited Mary to attend the inauguration and cajoled the Georgia parole board to let her out of prison for a few days. Mary attended the swearing-in ceremony, watched the parade, and accompanied Amy to two inaugural balls. Before Mary returned to prison, Rosalynn asked if she'd like to work in the White House. "I said that if I got my parole this spring, I sure would," Mary told a reporter. "It would be just like old times again."

Jimmy promptly had himself named Mary's parole officer, and a month later Mary was living in the White House. Amy's nanny was receiving almost as much attention as the president's daughter. "I was worldwide news," recalled Fitzpatrick. "Going from prison to the White House." Her controversial past undoubtedly touched the hot button of race in America in the 1970s. Early that spring *Saturday Night Live* featured a skit in which Sissy Spacek played Amy and Garrett Morris played Mary in drag. But Amy thought of Mary as her playmate, and the Carters treated her like family.

One evening Mary was walking by the pool as Rosalynn was swimming laps. The First Lady paused and shouted, "Come on in! Just dive in in your uniform." Mary wasn't a swimmer, but she had been taking lessons with Amy, and so she kicked off her shoes and jumped in. Interviewed years later by Kate Andersen Brower, Mary recalled this as her fondest memory of her years in the White House, "just me and the first lady together out there swimming."

Carter's adult boys—Jack, Chip, and Jeff—had campaigned relentlessly for their father. After the election, Jack moved back to Georgia to practice law. But Chip and his wife, Caron Griffin, and Jeff and his wife, Annette Davis, decided to move into the third floor of the residence. Upon his arrival, Chip found a note in his bedroom from the previous occupant, Jack Ford: "Welcome, I hope you have as much fun here as I did!" Twenty-seven-year-old Chip got a part-time job working for the Democratic National Committee and spent much of his time traveling around the country, raising money for the party. Jeff, twenty-four years old, enrolled in George Washington University.

To their father's immense annoyance and concern, all three boys had acquired a cigarette habit. And not surprisingly for the 1970s, they smoked more than tobacco. One of the White House florists, Ronn Payne, recalled that when he tidied up their rooms, "I would regularly have to move bongs." Rosalynn had acknowledged during the campaign that her sons had "experimented" with marijuana, and Carter himself told Norman Mailer in 1976 that he knew that all of his sons had smoked weed. Chip liked to ascend to the White House roof and smoke a joint while gazing at the Mall. When Willie Nelson spent a night in the White House, Chip knocked on the door of the Lincoln Bedroom at the end of a long evening and invited the country-music legend to join him on the roof. Nelson had recently broken his foot, so he was on crutches. But he followed Chip up to the roof and sat there "with a beer in one hand and a fat Austin Torpedo in the other." Needless to say, Carter did not know about this incident, though he was certainly fond of Willie and his wife, Connie: "I like them very much," Carter noted in his diary. "They are at ease with us, and vice versa."*

Carter himself used to ascend to the White House roof on occasion late at night to watch Canada geese flying south. "There was something ghostly about it," he later told Paul Hendrickson, a *Washington Post* reporter. "Actually, we did lots of things like that that the American people never knew about." His son Jeff was an avid amateur astronomer, so sometimes Carter accompanied him up to the roof, where they gazed at the stars through a telescope.

ON THE MORNING of February 2, 1977, Carter woke up with the thought that he should name his Naval Academy classmate Admiral Stansfield Turner to be director of the CIA. Sorensen had been his first choice, but his second, surprisingly enough, had been Bill Moyers, the veteran CBS journalist and former aide to LBJ. *The New York Times* had reported in

---

* In 1977, possession of marijuana was a federal offense, subject to imprisonment of up to one year, plus a $1,000 fine. But eleven states had decriminalized the possession of small amounts of marijuana for personal use. Candidate Carter was on record as favoring decriminalization of marijuana.

late January that Moyers was under serious consideration for the intelligence post.

Moyers would have been almost as controversial a pick as Sorensen. A highly opinionated liberal pundit, Moyers had made plenty of political enemies in Washington. Carter had been interviewed during the campaign by Moyers, but they were not friends. And Carter knew that Moyers would have stirred controversy at the CIA, an agency still recovering from the Church Committee hearings two years earlier.* Carter liked the idea; he wanted an outsider to take control of the Agency. Landon Butler spent all morning on February 1 working up a nomination document on Moyers. After talking to some Washington insiders, Butler noted that Clark Clifford was "all for Moyers." Robert McNamara expressed "mixed emotions," and, not surprisingly, former secretary of state Dean Rusk was firmly against him. (Rusk had clashed with Moyers over Vietnam during the Johnson presidency.)

Butler thought the Moyers nomination would go forward, but the next morning Carter changed his mind. Perhaps the president thought Admiral Turner, age fifty-three, would be a safer choice, but more likely he just woke that morning and remembered that his classmate had become an admiral. The president hadn't even known Turner back in his Annapolis years. And when approached, Turner was not enthusiastic but told Carter he would do anything he wanted. "I decided right then," Carter noted in his diary, "that he would be the best director." Carter thought the CIA needed to be shaken up. "I think they're [the CIA professionals] going to resent Stan Turner's strength," he wrote. But Carter didn't care.

Turner would turn out to be an unpopular CIA director at Langley, largely because he decided to purge the Agency of hundreds of aging and ineffective clandestine agents. "Firing so many people right out of

---

* Soon after Moyers was approached about the CIA job, he was in Cuba interviewing Fidel Castro. When Moyers mentioned to Castro that he might head the intelligence agency that had once tried to assassinate him, Castro laughed and "offered to denounce him" if Moyers thought that would help. CBS broadcast Moyers's interview with Castro on the evening of February 9, and Castro expressed pleasure at Carter's election, calling him a man with a "sense of morals." By then, the Carter administration had already publicly suggested that it was prepared to discuss normalization of relations with Cuba.

the starting blocks was a grave mistake," said Jack Watson, Carter's cabinet secretary. Nevertheless, Turner was highly compatible with Carter's moral sensibilities. "The professionalism of the CIA has been a pleasant surprise to me," the president confided to his staff that spring. But when he went on to comment that it was "absolutely crucial" to maintain the Agency's covert action capabilities, Turner explained that covert action was "basically indecent." He described our sources abroad as "traitors" to their countries and then said, "There are limits to indecency beyond which we will not go." Carter seemed to agree, but many in the room were astonished by this expression of rectitude on the part of a CIA director. One aide present at this briefing noted in his diary, "Inconceivable that [Allen] Dulles—or even [William] Colby or [Richard] Helms—could have said such a thing or thought it." And neither would any previous president have shared Turner's moral qualms.

CARTER'S NATURAL INSULARITY—bordering on shyness—was perhaps compounded by the Georgia cast of his inner circle. Jack Watson passed on a note to the president from one of his female staffers, Jane Frank, who bluntly observed, "All of the inner circle involved in policy matters are white and male. . . . The inner circle lacks diversity. Most of the people are from Georgia. . . . With the exception of the Vice President, not one is a 'Washington insider.'"

Carter was something of an enigma even to those in the inner circle. Betty Rainwater, a deputy to Hamilton Jordan, had worked hard for the Carters throughout the campaign and admired them immensely. But even Rainwater observed that the president "has few what you'd call friends." She mused one day to speechwriter Jerry Doolittle that "the real wonder about Carter is that he spent all those years in a little South Georgia town and didn't get like them." Doolittle responded, "He didn't *get like* them, maybe, but he got *to like* them." Doolittle was thinking of Kirbo, Lance, Jordan, and Powell.

Others on Capitol Hill were disgruntled at the way in which the Georgia boys were flouting conventions. *The Washington Post* was already running stories about Hamilton Jordan's casual dress and lack of decorum in the White House. "Picture the second most powerful man in Washington," Sally Quinn wrote in the *Post*'s style section. "He is wearing a navy windbreaker, a plaid flannel shirt, corduroy trousers and boots. He is chewing gum. He looks like a high school football player on a class field trip to Washington. 'I always dress this way,' he shrugs. 'Uh oh. Guess I'll have to start cleaning up my act now that I'm in Washington.' " Quinn noted "just a trace of antagonism" in Jordan's voice. It was more like defiance. And some of it was an act. "Hamilton was the poster child for the wild young man," said Alice Rogoff, a young White House staffer, who later married David Rubenstein. "But in private he was not like that at all. He was the perfect southern gentleman. You never saw any bad-boy behavior in the daytime." Jordan played up the country-boy image. But his closest friends knew there was another side. "You'd never know it," recalled Les Francis, an aide to Frank Moore, "but he was a big ballet fan. He loved the ballet." Francis admired Jordan: "He was wicked smart, I mean, brilliant in his ability to perceive situations. But he had a wild streak."

One week into the administration, Jordan deputy Landon Butler noted in his diary that a *Newsweek* reporter, Jim Doyle, had told him over lunch at Sans Souci that "Ham's thumbing his nose at niceties will eventually hurt." Jordan was still feeling his way, and at times he was overwhelmed. "Ham is letting his desk become a bottleneck," Butler noted. Jordan confessed to Butler that he felt "depressed" and "disappointed" in the work: "If this was all there was to it, he didn't want to fool with it. Too many petty details." But Jordan's job was to pay attention to the details, and while he could grumble about it, he was also disciplined and smart. He typed his own memos and spent long hours in the office. He was working hard and sometimes partying hard in the evenings. And everyone knew it was taking a toll on his rocky marriage.

One day in early February, Kirbo came by the White House and made the rounds, chatting up people in his slow, deliberate manner. After a few hours of wandering around the West Wing, he told Carter that he thought Jordan was "overworked, bogged down with dozens of personnel appointments and that he needs some help returning his calls." Carter's response was to order his son Chip to go by Hamilton's office for several hours each day to work the phones. Carter always listened to Kirbo. "He has a way of absorbing complicated questions," Carter wrote, "and although he seems to talk about unimportant issues at times, the cumulative summary of his conversations is always one of guidance towards the right strategic objectives."

Kirbo had a message: "None of us would be any good to the president if we worked fourteen hours a day, and if our wives were unhappy." A few days later, Carter followed up by sending out handwritten notes, saying he was "concerned" about their family life. "We are going to be here a long time, and all of you will be more valuable to me & the country with rest and a stable home life." The problem, of course, was that the president himself set a grueling standard. During his first six weeks in office, Carter spent an average of seventy-one hours each week in the office—and that excluded his working hours in the residence or traveling outside Washington.

He also set a rigorous jogging schedule, running most afternoons at 4:30 P.M. for about four miles. On weekends or while in Georgia, he might stretch that to six miles. "I enjoy it," Carter told reporters. "I don't have any present intention of going above ten miles because of the time constraints. That takes me about an hour and a half." At fifty-two, Carter was in terrific shape, weighing about 150 pounds and with an ideal blood pressure of 120/80.

CARTER WAS IN many ways a gentle, diplomatic boss. But he was also a "tough guy," and sometimes awfully intimidating. "He was a solitary man with a fantastic ego," Jerry Rafshoon recalled. "Very controlled. I've never heard him raise his voice. To have those pale blue eyes bore into you, saying, 'You have failed,' is much worse than shouting."

That spring, James Wooten, the *New York Times* reporter who had covered the Carter campaign and was now assigned to the White House beat, wrote a front-page story drawing direct parallels between the personality and management style of Admiral Rickover and his onetime naval aide. Wooten's story was headlined "Carter's Style Making Aides Apprehensive." And when Powell and Jordan read it, they were not apprehensive but incensed. They generally admired Wooten as a reporter and regarded him as a friend. But in this instance, Wooten had not interviewed either Powell or Jordan. Instead, he cited a couple of anonymous, low-level White House aides agreeing with the notion that the president and the admiral shared some personality traits. Wooten suggested that both the "grim-faced admiral" and Carter could be "brutally brusque and sharp-tongued with those who displease him." Wooten read aloud to one of his sources a quote from Carter's campaign book describing Admiral Rickover: "We feared and respected him"—and yet Carter could not remember the admiral "ever saying a complimentary word to me." Upon hearing this, the unnamed Carter aide exclaimed, "That's Jimmy Carter." Another aide was quoted as saying, "Carter is such an intimidating man that it's very difficult to disagree with him."

None of this was particularly news—or surprising. But then Wooten ended the story with an anecdote about Carter showing "mounting jealousy about his power." Wooten alleged that when Jordan had disagreed with the president over some unspecified issue not long ago, Carter had snapped, "When you read as much of this as I do, then maybe you'll have the right to disagree." Wooten had not bothered to check the quote with Jordan. This did not sound at all like Carter—and Powell told reporters that afternoon that Wooten's story was "completely untrue." Jody had checked with Carter that morning and asked him if he had ever said such a thing to Jordan. Carter denied it. And Jordan denied it.

"Jody," asked one reporter at the press briefing, "why are you so uptight about this story? I am tempted to say that you protest too much."

"Without agreeing that I am uptight about the thing," Powell replied, "I think a story which implies that the president of the United States—that his senior staff members are dissatisfied, that he is not open to criticism, and that he is becoming reclusive and is brutal to his staff—is a fairly serious charge. And it happens to be the furthest thing from the truth."

Powell was right: Wooten's story had crossed the line; parts were simply inaccurate and, worse, rather unfair. But Wooten was not wrong to draw attention to Carter's admiration for Rickover and his gruff style. One reporter argued with Powell that Wooten's main point was that Carter admired the way Rickover dealt with people—and that the admiral never paid him a compliment. "So my question is," asked this reporter, "has the president ever on a specific occasion said to you, 'Jody, you did a nice job on this'?"

"I have never," Powell replied, "made any secret of the fact . . . that this particular president is not overly given to patting staff people on the back. And I would venture to say that if anybody that requires being patted on, stroked, or kissed on the ear in order to"—laughter—"in order to function effectively—"

"Which ear, Jody?" (Laughter.)

"—is in the wrong place and ought to work for somebody else."

Actually, the Wooten story, if anything, had things all backward. Carter had surrounded himself with men with large egos, like Zbig Brzezinski, Jim Schlesinger, and Joe Califano—men who constantly argued with him. And as for Powell and Jordan, they were on such close terms with the president that they felt no compunction about offering him frank criticism. Jordan routinely critiqued the president's performance, his speeches, and his tendency on occasion to be effusive to the point of exaggeration. But Carter listened when Jordan spoke up. One day, Bob Strauss—who was always trying to ingratiate himself with the president—turned to Carter and said of Jordan, "I wish he were my son." Carter replied, "You can't have him, Bob. He's mine."

Carter certainly expected his staff to work to exacting standards. He was also a stickler for both punctuality and the written word. He hated incorrect grammar and the sloppiness of the typo. "Watch the typos!" was a hand-scrawled message familiar to every White House aide. One day he spotted a typo in a memo from Terry Adamson, a Justice Department aide working for Attorney General Bell. Where Adamson had typed "Attorney Genetal" the president had mischievously circled "Genetal" and scribbled in the margin, "genital."

He thought most meetings in the White House were tedious and a waste of time. One day, he scheduled exactly fifteen minutes to meet with a group of trucking company executives to discuss a major bill to deregulate their industry. Carter listened impatiently to their vague and imprecise opening remarks, and then he said what he had to say, speaking almost abruptly. As the president stood to leave, one executive tried to get in one last word, but Carter told him, "I came in on time, so you should end on time."

It was not his finest performance, but Carter could not help himself, such was his obsession with punctuality. He strongly preferred getting his information from the written word, and consequently he ended up reading 250 pages of memoranda each day. One morning in early March, when he complained about his "enormous workload" at a senior staff meeting, his brash appointments secretary, Tim Kraft, suggested that Carter was himself the "culprit" because it was his own work habits that encouraged "so much paper flow." Carter jocularly responded, "You're fired."

Late one Friday afternoon, Kraft handed the president an "amended" schedule for the next morning, knowing that Carter was intent on leaving for Camp David by noon on Saturday. "I'm out of here by noon," Carter had insisted. Kraft's "amended" schedule had Carter meeting with an imaginary Native American tribal chief, a fundraiser, and "people he wouldn't want to see in a month of Sundays." Carter glanced at the spoof schedule and scrawled in the margin, "You can go to hell, or be president tomorrow. I'll see you on Monday."

In an effort to cope with a mountain of paper, he and Rosalynn began taking a weekly speed-reading course, inspired by Evelyn Wood, the author of a bestselling book on speed-reading. Jody Powell arranged it. "Stupid idea," commented a skeptical Butler. "Will JC begin to believe his own baloney?" It was a gimmick, but President Kennedy had also embraced Wood's fad, and it was only in character for Carter to seize upon another regimen in self-improvement. "Maybe," noted Carter, "I can cut down on the amount of time I have to spend each day reading." By early April, he claimed he had increased his reading speed fourfold while maintaining a "fairly constant level of comprehension."

This self-improvement dynamic had its human limits. David Rubenstein, the president's deputy domestic policy adviser, knew Carter was a fast reader. "But his biggest problem as president," observed Rubenstein, "was his willingness to read anything. Once, we gave him a 350-page memo on tax reform and he read the entire thing. We never should have subjected him to that—but he never should have read it." Carter routinely complained that his reading regimen was being interrupted by White House vermin. "I'm here at 5:30 A.M. trying to read briefing papers," he told Tim Kraft, "and there are mice scurrying around." Kraft and Jordan tried to take care of the problem but were met with a bureaucratic impasse: the Interior Department claimed they were responsible only for the White House exterior, and while the General Services Administration (GSA) serviced the interior, they had been told by the Environmental Protection Agency that poison traps were prohibited.

"What do the mice eat?" asked Jordan. Carter responded that he thought they were foraging for food in the basement mess. "Yeah," said Kraft, "so they come to your office to jog."

CARTER'S CLOSEST ADVISER was his lifelong partner. "The Carters don't have friends," quipped Stu Eizenstat. "They have each other." Frank Moore said much the same thing: "Friends aren't necessary to him. He's content to sit and read with Rosalynn beside him." Rosalynn was not what she seemed. In public, she appeared to be a strikingly pretty and demure southern woman. But alone with Jimmy, she was opinionated and often relentless: "I tell him what I think." At the time, few observers understood the extent of her influence. "If you ask me which were his ideas—or hers," Mondale later observed, "I couldn't tell you. They worked together." Their marriage was an ironclad partnership. Mary Finch Hoyt served as Rosalynn's press secretary and saw the relationship up close: "I think the Carters probably have one of the closest marriages I've ever seen."

Jimmy consulted his wife about most everything, and sometimes they disagreed. Over time, the press began to pick up on this aspect of their relationship, and sometimes she was called a "steel magnolia." Unlike Jimmy, Rosalynn was against capital punishment, and she strongly supported the right of women to choose to have an abortion—though she said personally she never would have made that choice. Both she and Jimmy supported passage of the Equal Rights Amendment. Her political instincts were sharp—and in some ways more sensitive than her husband's. Hoyt described her as "driving, pragmatic." She was more down-to-earth and she had learned to enjoy the game of politics. "I loved the politics," she later said, "and Jimmy never did." Often, she found herself pleading with Jimmy to postpone potentially divisive decisions, such as the Panama Canal Treaty or Middle East peace, until his second term. Invariably, Carter's response was that he could not succumb to political expediency: "I'll never do anything to hurt my country." Rosalynn would argue with him, sometimes loudly, saying, "The thing you can do to hurt your country most is not get reelected." She thought, for instance, that his early speeches urging the American people to conserve energy were "politically risky." She understood instinctively that this was not a message the electorate wanted to hear. Like any good wife of a politician, Rosalynn was trying to be protective. But often her pleas with him fell on deaf ears. This had not always been the case when Carter was governor. The presidency had somehow unleashed Carter's natural instinct to "do the right thing" regardless of the political costs.

Knowing how stubborn Jimmy could be on the path to righteousness only caused Rosalynn to become all the more vigilant in trying to protect him from political exigencies. It was a good marriage, and a powerful political partnership. Rosalynn was not a natural politician. Shy and initially insecure in the role of a political wife, she had forced herself to learn how to speak in public. "I hated to make speeches," she said, "but I think as you do these things, you develop a confidence and you learn." And now, more often than not, she was an effective speaker. She sounded authentic and connected emotionally with her audience.

In the governor's mansion, she had chosen mental health as her public cause. It was a very personal choice, and in her new role as First Lady she would not shy away from this emotionally charged issue. She said she wanted "to remove the stigma from mental health care so people will be free to talk about it and seek help." She got Jimmy to appoint her as the honorary chair of a new President's Commission on Mental Health. At the time, Carter nevertheless told the twenty-member panel, "There isn't going to be a lot of new money. You're going to have to make do with what you have." A dismayed Rosalynn told *The New York Times,* "I'll try to convince Jimmy of the need."

Rosalynn's interest in public health soon caused her to badger Joe Califano, the secretary of health, education, and welfare. Early in 1977, prompted by her friend Betty Bumpers, the wife of Senator Dale Bumpers, Rosalynn called Califano about a child-immunization program to eradicate measles. Califano promised he would meet with Bumpers, but Rosalynn also got her husband to send a note to the secretary, ordering him to fund the program. Within two years, the program had vaccinated 90 percent of the country's children. It would take another two decades, but by the end of the century measles was virtually eliminated in the United States. Califano learned over time to anticipate his encounters with Rosalynn with some trepidation. She was a "tough lady," observed the columnist Richard Reeves. "She may be soft-spoken, but people tend to underestimate her," Jody Powell told a reporter. "If you've ever been on the opposite side in a dispute, you've made a very serious mistake."

Rosalynn, now age forty-nine, spent many hours each day in her own home office in the White House, sitting at a Chippendale mahogany desk, making phone calls. David Rubenstein was delegated by Stu Eizenstat to brief Rosalynn on a regular basis about various White House initiatives. Early on, she peppered Carter with so many questions in the evenings that they agreed to schedule a working lunch every Wednesday at which Rosalynn would have a chance to be briefed by the president and query him about various issues of concern to her. She came to lunch with a brown leather folder stuffed with documents she wanted to discuss. They were a team, and Carter was highly dependent on her. Late in April 1977, Carter exhibited uncharacteristic fury when aides suddenly told him of a change in schedule. He had been planning to take Amy to the circus. "I've never seen him as put out," presidential aide Butler noted in his diary. Only later did Butler learn that Rosalynn had just had a nonmalignant lump removed from her breast. "That would explain his edginess."

In early June, Carter sent Rosalynn as his official envoy to meet with the leaders of Jamaica, Costa Rica, Ecuador, Peru, Brazil, Colombia, and Venezuela. Not since Eleanor Roosevelt had a First Lady been used in such a high-profile diplomatic mission. "I was determined to be taken seriously," Rosalynn said. Before leaving, she sat through more than a dozen two-hour briefings by Brzezinski and others on the various issues. She was told to emphasize the administration's human rights priorities—and its negative view of arms sales. Latin American diplomats were puzzled by the prospect of talking business with a woman. "I really can't think of her talking substance," said one ambassador from a country on her itinerary.

She called Jimmy each day, but it was the longest time the couple had been apart since he had left the navy. "Twelve days is just too long," Carter complained. Flouting protocol, Rosalynn skipped the usual First Lady visits to orphanages and schools and instead held face-to-face talks with heads of state.

In Brazil, she bluntly urged military dictator President Ernesto Geisel to halt his plans to build a plant capable of reprocessing nuclear fuel for weapons. She embarrassed Brazilian authorities by meeting with two

American missionaries and publicizing their allegations of mistreatment in a Brazilian jail. In Colombia, she passed on intelligence implicating a cabinet officer for accepting bribes from drug lords. She conducted sensitive talks with prickly leaders like Jamaica's prime minister Michael Manley. "It was a challenge," she later wrote, "to confront an argumentative leader in a friendly way about a controversial issue."

In general, the trip garnered accolades in the American press. But there was also criticism. "The question," wrote *Newsweek*'s Meg Greenfield, "is not whether Rosalynn Carter is capable of serving as an agent of her husband's government, but rather whether she should." *The New York Times* asked, "Who elected her?" As a guest on *Meet the Press* and other television shows, Rosalynn projected a polite, soft-spoken image. But her words were wholly feminist in substance: "What irritates me is that people in our country expect women to work now, but when the first lady tries to do something, she is criticized for it. It's ridiculous." More controversy ensued when she began to attend cabinet meetings. She sat on a chair against the wall, unobtrusively taking notes and never speaking up. Still, it was unprecedented to see a First Lady in the room. "There's no way I could discuss things with Jimmy in an intelligent way," she said, "if I didn't attend Cabinet meetings."

PRESS COVERAGE OF the Carter White House that first spring was generally positive. But some prominent members of Washington society, defined as the permanent establishment or the "Georgetown set," grumbled that they were not seeing enough of the new president. The Carters turned down many formal invitations to private dinner parties and rarely went out on the town. "I do not condemn the cocktail circuit," Carter noted. "It's just not natural for me to be a part of it." The Georgians in the new administration were more likely to socialize together over takeout pizza than to attend a fancy sit-down dinner in Georgetown. Katharine Graham was miffed. The publisher of *The Washington Post* had a weighty presence in the city. And she was not used to having her invitations ignored. After inviting a number of Carter aides to a soirée with a group of influential journalists, Graham noticed that Hamilton Jordan had declined and Jody Powell had failed to respond at all. "Thinking how stupid it was for the press secretary to ignore an event involving so many top editors," Graham later wrote in her memoirs, "I called his office and asked to speak to him. I was told he was in a meeting. I explained about the party and that I felt it would be useful for him to attend. Still no answer, and he didn't come."

The president was comfortable in his privacy. "If there is one thing Jimmy dislikes more than anything I can think of," Rosalynn said, "it is a cocktail party or reception or dinner every night." She later told Stu Eizenstat that she regretted this: "We would have been better off if we had cultivated some friends at one point in the social power game." Carter agreed. "I failed to make a proper introduction of myself to Graham and Ben Bradlee. But as far as my going to cocktail parties, it wasn't my way of life. I wasn't antagonistic towards them. I just didn't want to be part of it. That was a mistake on my part."

INSTEAD OF HOSTING cocktail parties, Carter brought popular musicians to the White House; Willie Nelson was a personal friend and frequent guest. So too were Gregg Allman and his Georgia blues rock-and-roll band, the Allman Brothers. One humid Sunday afternoon Carter invited some eight hundred people to the South Lawn to listen to Dizzy Gillespie, Mary Lou Williams, Sonny Rollins, Herbie Hancock, Lionel Hampton, Stan Getz, Cecil Taylor, and thirty other musicians to celebrate the twenty-fifth anniversary of the Newport Jazz Festival. Everyone drank beer or lemonade and ate from steaming black cast-iron pots of jambalaya shipped in from New Orleans.

"Whatever the political future of Jimmy Carter," wrote the *Village Voice*'s jazz critic, Gary Giddins, "cultural historians ought to note that on the evening of June 18, 1978, he was quite superb." The White House had never seen anything like this rollicking gathering of largely African American jazz artists, playing their uniquely American, home-brewed music. Carter stood before the crowd, wearing a casual white short-sleeved shirt and a bolo tie, and proclaimed that these musicians had been "heroes of mine for a long time." Observing that some of these jazz artists were celebrities abroad but not in America, he flatly blamed this unfortunate fact on "an element of racism"—because "most of the players are black." Jazz, he said, is "alive, aggressive, innovative . . . never compromising quality," and the assembled players were quite simply "some of the best musicians of the country, of the world." With that introduction, the president sat down on the grass to listen to what became a two-and-a-half-hour concert. He ignored the pungent smell of pot wafting across the South Lawn.

A NINETY-YEAR-OLD EUBIE Blake played "Boogie Woogie Beguine." Sonny Rollins played his "Sonnymoon for Two." In one poignant moment, everyone was asked to stand and acknowledge the presence of Charles Mingus, the legendary jazz composer and band leader recently diagnosed with Lou Gehrig's disease. Carter came over to Mingus's wheelchair, leaned down, and gave him a hug as the stricken musician wept softly. Later, jazz pianist Cecil Taylor stunned the audience with a frenetic seven-minute improvisation of creative mayhem, and when he abruptly left the stage without waiting for any applause, Carter sprang from his grass seat and ran after him into the bushes. Secret Service agents hastily followed and found Carter pumping Taylor's hand in congratulations: "I've never seen anyone play the piano that way." Later in the concert, the president walked onstage and proclaimed, "I don't believe that the White House has ever seen anything like this—and it's hard to believe, because as you can see, this is as much a part of the greatness of America as the White House or the Capitol building down the street." As the sun set, Carter said, "Anyone who wants to is free to go, but I'm gonna stay and listen to some more music." After spotting Pearl Bailey sitting in the audience, Rosalynn Carter requested that the Black actress sing "St. Louis Blues." Finally, Gillespie—sporting a funny-looking Sherlock Holmes cap—ended the lively evening by inviting "the President, his highness," onstage to sing "Salt Peanuts." Carter obliged, a little off the beat. At the end of the song, when Gillespie asked if Carter would like to join his band on their road tour, the president laughed and said, "I might have to after tonight."

The president had thoroughly enjoyed himself and later noted in his diary that this had been "the best party we've ever had." The guest list had included prominent African Americans like writers James Baldwin and Albert Murray—and the painter Sam Gilliam. Needless to say, Katharine Graham and most other members of the Georgetown set had not been invited.

Chapter 7
Life Is Unfair

The problem is that Jimmy Carter wants to be Mr. Clean.
—HOUSE MAJORITY LEADER JIM WRIGHT

President Carter and Speaker of the House Tip O'Neill
PETER BREGG/ASSOCIATED PRESS

CARTER WAS DETERMINED to be an innovative president. Shortly before the inauguration, he had "angrily" reprimanded his domestic affairs adviser, Stu Eizenstat, for having told *The New York Times* that the new administration would proceed slowly. "You shouldn't have said that," Carter said. "I'm going to be an activist president and I'm going to propose a lot of legislation." A week after his inauguration, Carter noted in his diary, "Everybody has warned me not to take on too many projects so early in the administration, but it's almost impossible for me to delay something that I see needs to be done."

He had an ambitious agenda, including a $50-per-head tax cut, national healthcare, a high-profile focus on human rights abroad, a Panama Canal treaty, Middle East peace, welfare reform, tax reform, and major initiatives to deregulate key sectors of the economy. But in the midst of an unusually harsh winter season, with much of the Eastern Seaboard suffering shortages in natural gas and heating oil, the new president wanted to make energy conservation a major priority.

Carter addressed the nation for the first time since his inauguration at 10:00 P.M. on February 2, 1977, in a televised speech focused on the need to conserve energy. It was thirty degrees Fahrenheit outside—and chilly enough inside the White House that Carter was wearing a beige wool cardigan. Rosalynn tried to persuade him to ditch the cardigan for a blue blazer, but Carter consciously chose to appear less presidential.

Earlier that evening he had signed the Emergency Natural Gas Act, his first piece of legislation, designed to address the sudden shortage of natural gas in the northeast part of the country. These shortages were actually wholly artificial—a consequence of convoluted government regulations that placed price controls only on domestic natural gas exported from producing states to nonproducing states. As a consequence, the price of natural gas that did not cross state lines was two to four times higher than the same product exported from Texas, for instance, to New York. Not surprisingly, such regulations gave the energy companies an incentive to sell their natural gas locally. It was insane, but that was how natural gas had been regulated for decades, and the energy companies were reaping enormous profits.

Some energy experts suggested that the rational thing to do would be to deregulate the price of natural gas nationally. But the oil companies opposed this, and so too did politicians from Big Oil states. Politicians from energy-poor states, like Massachusetts and New York, were also reluctant to see price controls lifted on natural gas. Seeking a middle ground, Carter had promised during the campaign to deregulate *new* natural gas production—leaving in place price controls on *old* natural gas. In the meantime, Carter's emergency law would allow the federal government to allocate interstate shipping of this commodity on a temporary, emergency basis.

Just before the taping, he asked one of the technicians how he looked and was told to look at the television monitor to see for himself. Satisfied, he sat down in a hard-backed wooden chair beside a roaring fireplace in his West Wing study and addressed the nation on live network television. The speech was memorable largely for its optics: The cardigan sent a message of simplicity and authenticity. *The New York Times* called his performance by the White House fireplace "masterful in ways he intended. His syntax matched the simplicity of his sweater.... Those who may have been misled by the narrow margin of his victory last November should know now that his hold on public opinion will be formidable." In later years, Republicans mocked the cardigan as somehow unpresidential, but Gallup polls in February gave Carter a 65 percent approval rating. And by April, his approval rating had soared to 75 percent.

Twenty days in office, Carter held his first press conference.* He appeared relaxed and open, speaking frankly about all the problems he was juggling, from staffing appointments to relations with sometimes taxing personalities on Capitol Hill. "We've made some mistakes," he freely admitted, and, pausing for a moment, he joked that he already understood "why Abraham Lincoln and some of the older presidents almost went home when they first got to the White House." As he walked out of the press room, Powell caught his eye and both men smiled broadly. "I felt completely at ease," Carter noted in his diary. *The New York Times*'s influential columnist James Reston called his performance "Carter at his best—open and honest, apologetic and hopeful."

Washington's establishment was beginning to think that this outsider from South Georgia might have the moxie to govern. Even David Broder, the *Washington Post* columnist, an early critic, seemed to be coming around: "In his first two months as President, Jimmy Carter has achieved a triumph of communications in the arena of public opinion. He has transformed himself from the very shaky winner of a campaign into a very popular President whose mastery of the mass media has given him real leverage with which to govern."

Former New York governor Averell Harriman, a formidable figure who personified the Georgetown set, had become an ardent fan of the new president. But to the surprise of some, Harriman had also bonded with Ham Jordan. The former governor hosted a lunch for Jordan on March 2 at his N Street mansion, and the two men spent the entire luncheon deep in conversation, primarily discussing the topic of nuclear disarmament. Harriman was keen to help with the impending confir-

---

* Carter would hold fifty-nine press conferences during his four years in office. By contrast, his successor held only forty-seven in eight years.

mation of his friend Paul Warnke as head of the Arms Control and Disarmament Agency. Warnke was perceived on Capitol Hill as a liberal dove on arms-control issues, a strong proponent of negotiating a drawdown of nuclear weapons with the Soviet Union. His critics included Senator Scoop Jackson—Carter's rival for the Democratic nomination—and such Cold War hawks as Paul Nitze, Richard Perle, and other members of the recently reconstituted Committee on the Present Danger, a neoconservative group opposed to détente with the Soviet Union. Nitze and Jackson aide Perle regarded Warnke as dangerously naïve and vigorously opposed his nomination. Carter was well aware that Warnke was a lightning rod, but characteristically, he didn't care. "The attacks on him," Carter noted in his diary, "which have been fairly rough, are primarily from those who don't want to see substantive reductions in nuclear weapons." Harriman agreed heartily and told Jordan over lunch that he admired Carter's "great choice." He also confided that he thought "the way the Cabinet had been put together was the most careful and successful he had ever seen. He said it was a miracle."

And yet, oddly, while Carter seemed to be winning over establishment figures like Broder, Reston, and Harriman, he was already becoming the target of sniping from the liberal Left. "To a surprising degree," wrote Richard Holbrooke in a late January *Newsweek* guest column, "Carter remains distrusted by many liberals. He is not one of them, and he is opposed by some on what seem to be stylistic grounds." Carter had brought a record number of women into top-level federal jobs, appointing Mary King,* for instance, as deputy director of ACTION, the federal domestic volunteer agency, Barbara Blum as deputy director of the Environmental Protection Agency, and Patricia Wald as an assistant attorney general for legislative affairs in the Justice Department. But expectations were high. "We cannot measure progress against Richard Nixon or Jerry Ford's record," said Mary Jean Tully of the National Organization for Women (NOW), "but against what Jimmy Carter promised."

Carter didn't assuage feminist concerns when he reiterated his longstanding opposition to federal funding of abortions "except when the woman's life is threatened or when the pregnancy was the result of rape

---

* King was married to Dr. Peter Bourne, the president's longtime adviser on health issues.

or incest." The question arose at a press conference soon after a Supreme Court decision that stipulated that the federal government was not obligated to pay for abortions for poor women. When asked at a press conference if this was fair to women who could not afford the procedure, Carter replied, "Well, as you know, there are many things in life that are not fair, that wealthy people can afford, and poor people can't. But I don't believe that the federal government should take action to try to make these opportunities exactly equal, particularly when there is a moral factor involved." Carter had always said that his religious beliefs compelled him personally to disapprove of abortions—but that as an elected official he would uphold the Supreme Court's *Roe v. Wade* decision guaranteeing a woman's right to choose abortion.

At the same time, he supported sex education (and contraceptives) for teenagers and federal funding of health programs for women that might minimize the number of abortions. He knew he was treading through an emotion-laden minefield, but his "own personal feeling is that the Supreme Court's rulings now are adequate, and they are reasonably fair." The president's position was complicated and, inevitably, deeply troubling to both abortion foes and advocates of a woman's right to choose. Feminist leader Gloria Steinem recalled, "During the campaign, the president once said that he personally would not have an abortion. That was my favorite statement!" Later that year, Steinem put a doctored photo of Carter on the cover of her feminist magazine, *Ms.,* showing the president with a pregnant belly under the headline "Carter Discovers 'Life Is Unfair.'"

Liberals were baffled by this outsider politician. In late March they were pleasantly surprised when Carter recommended to Congress a startling, radical package of electoral reforms, including universal same-day voter registration and the abolition of the undemocratic Electoral College. Not surprisingly, Republicans successfully lobbied against the reforms, labeling it a "Democratic power grab." Liberals generally liked Carter's instincts on social issues. They applauded his record number of appointments of African Americans and women to federal jobs, including an extraordinary number of such nominations to the federal bench. Liberal environmentalists were astonished by his appointment of Joan Claybrook, a lawyer and colleague of Ralph Nader's and a known critic of the auto industry, to head the National Highway Traffic Safety Administration. "Appalling," said a Chrysler auto executive when he heard the news. "She has always been against the industry." Claybrook, age thirty-nine, thrived on controversy. Before her appointment, she was called a "dragon-lady," if only because of her uncompromising advocacy for seatbelts and airbags, innovations long opposed by the auto industry as too costly.

Likewise, liberals were cheered by the appointment of Michael Pertschuk, forty-four, another Naderite and consumer activist, to chair the Federal Trade Commission. A Yale-trained lawyer, Pertschuk was already a legend on Capitol Hill for his crusade to require Big Tobacco companies to label their products with cancer health warnings. W. Harrison Wellford, one of the original "Nader's Raiders," was given a job as executive associate director of the Office of Management and Budget. Carter placed seventy-one-year-old Esther Peterson, a fiery labor and consumer activist, in the White House as his special assistant for consumer affairs. Peterson and Carter formed a particularly close friendship. Carter adored her, and she later said, "I can't underline strongly enough my belief in this man." Douglas M. Costle, a prominent environmentalist, was appointed administrator of the Environmental Protection Agency. Susan King, yet another Naderite, became commissioner of the Consumer Product Safety Commission. Carol Tucker Foreman became assistant secretary of food and consumer services at the Department of Agriculture.

All told, more than sixty consumer activists, most of them Nader acolytes, took jobs in the Carter administration. These quite radical appointments signaled that Carter was going to use the executive branch's regulatory powers to protect consumers from dirty air, dangerous automobiles, and big corporations. When a reporter asked Nader about these appointments, he replied rather sardonically, "They're not going to be compromised very much, and they're very experienced in consumer causes."

Claybrook moved quickly, forcing through an executive order on June 30, 1977, that required the auto industry to install both airbags and shoulder seatbelts in all standard models by 1982. One car company branded the decision a "multi-billion-dollar gamble with consumers' money." The cost was actually minimal, about $100 to $300 per airbag and $25 to $100 per seatbelt—and a good portion of this would be offset by a reduction in insurance costs. The decision would probably save at least nine thousand lives annually. Claybrook was ecstatic. She went on to persuade the administration to enact much tougher auto fuel-economy standards, and to apply auto safety standards to trucks as well as passenger cars. She also forced the standardization of vehicle identification numbers (VINs) on all vehicles, a measure opposed by auto companies because they understood that VINs would make it possible to hold individual companies liable for manufacturing errors and safety flaws. All these regulations were politically controversial, and often stridently opposed not just by Detroit but also by the United Auto Workers (UAW). But Claybrook persuaded Carter that millions of consumers would directly benefit. That spring, the president noted in his diary that Congressman John Dingell, the powerful Michigan Democrat, was "furious about our proposals on automobile emissions. . . . He blames my staff for being incompetent, rude." Carter refused to back down.

Carter also had to endure criticism from the Left. When late in 1977 Claybrook agreed to a temporary delay in the implementation of the airbag regulation, her old boss Nader publicly attacked her as a "cowardly defector from the consumer movement" and called for her resignation. Carter read Nader's harsh words in *The Washington Post* and immediately called up Claybrook and said, "Don't worry, Ralph is just mad; you are doing a great job."

NADER WOULD COME to realize that his influence over Washington reached its pinnacle during the Carter administration. Carter's instincts made him reflexively sympathetic to consumer rights. "I would never have dreamed," Nader later told Eizenstat, "that the Carter administration was our last chance." Carter and the Naderites agreed that too often federal regulations protected monopolistic businesses and kept costs artificially high for the average consumer. Carter thought being proconsumer meant paring down or eliminating altogether federal regulations on airlines, trucking, railroads, and communications. Nader agreed—so long as safety regulations were preserved. Ironically, the Business Roundtable and other probusiness lobbyists fought Carter's deregulation initiatives precisely because they were perceived as part of a radical consumer agenda. The commercial airline industry was a case in point. Historically, the Civil Aeronautics Board (CAB) controlled airfares and routing decisions. But the relationship between the CAB regulators and the industry was so cozy that the major airlines were not in competition. The CAB guaranteed them a 12 percent profit margin and awarded monopoly routes. Consumers had little choice—and fares were so high that few middle-class Americans flew. Carter decided he wanted to change all this.

In a surprise appointment, Carter named a little-known Cornell University economist, Alfred Kahn, as chairman of the CAB. The son of Russian immigrants, Kahn was an academic expert on federal regulation of public utilities. He displayed a wry wit in his dealings with the press. He was the first to admit that he knew nothing about the airline industry: "I really don't know one plane from the other. To me, they're all marginal costs with wings." But he was smart and relentless. He told Carter that he was outraged to learn that his predecessors had given the airlines "antitrust immunity." The CAB had also routinely refused to allow any carriers to enter new markets—effectively protecting the monopolies of existing carriers.

Kahn quickly moved to lift these restrictions and force the airlines into competition with one another. He also reached out to Nader's aviation consumer-action group to help fashion new legislation. Senator Edward Kennedy had held hearings on the airline industry in 1975, and one of his aides, Stephen Breyer—a future Supreme Court justice—helped to write the Airline Deregulation Act. The legislation was introduced in early 1978—and the airline industry lobbied hard to kill the bill. Tom Beebe, the chief executive officer of Delta Air Lines, headquartered in Atlanta, wrote Carter a stiff letter, promising that Delta would "expend whatever energy and resources we have available to us to fight deregulation." Carter nevertheless signed it into law in October 1978. The act revolutionized the industry, forcing airlines to compete directly over fares and routes. Average fares quickly declined by one-third, and over the next decade millions of middle-income Americans began flying for the first time. From 1971 to 1997, the percentage of American adults who traveled by air increased from 49 to 81 percent. Even Ralph Nader was happy with the president's airline legislation.

Carter thought airline deregulation was only the beginning. He told Eizenstat to get to work on the trucking industry. "After we'd notched this victory on airline deregulation," recalled Eizenstat, "we were in the

Roosevelt Room talking about what we'd do next, and I said, 'Mr. President, why don't we rest on laurels? I mean, this is a great win. If we try trucking deregulation, it's going to be infinitely harder. There are few airlines, but there are trucking firms all over the country, and the all-powerful Teamsters, who are going to be dead set against this.'" Carter ignored this advice. Two years later, after a hard-fought battle with the trucking industry and the Teamsters Union, Carter finally signed a sweeping bill to deregulate the industry. The bill opened the trucking business to independent operators, and as a result, shipping costs for businesses plunged. But so too did the wages of truck drivers, many of whom began working for nonunionized, independent, or family-owned carriers. On the whole, consumers benefited—but unionized truck drivers suffered. The same could be said of labor unions in the airline industry. There were always trade-offs, but Carter's political instinct was to favor consumers over trade unions. He had little empathy for class politics, epitomized, he believed, by labor's demands. This, of course, sowed unrest inside a traditional constituency for the Democratic Party.

One relatively obscure act of deregulation gave rise to a wholly new and wildly popular new industry all across America—craft breweries. It turned out that when Prohibition was lifted in 1933, home brewing of beer remained illegal under federal law. Carter thought this was ridiculous, and on October 14, 1978, he signed a law that allowed any adult to produce beer for personal and family use without having to pay federal excise tax. The old regulations had shut out small-scale producers and preserved for decades the monopolies of the big breweries like Coors and Anheuser-Busch. It took a few years, but home brewing soon spiked, and some of these ventures morphed into more than 1,500 high-quality craft beer operations in cities and small towns across the country. Budweiser suddenly had to compete with the likes of summer ales, black lagers, and honey orange wheat ales. It was a cultural renaissance for some beer lovers—but because these trends came long after Carter left office, he never got any political credit for this initiative.

IN EARLY APRIL 1977, a thirty-one-year-old policy analyst named Robert Greenstein went to the White House for a meeting about a proposed reform of the Food Stamp Act. A newly hired special assistant to the secretary of agriculture for domestic food assistance issues, Greenstein had ditched his blue jeans and backpack for a new suit. The lanky, bushy-haired, mustachioed Harvard graduate had previously worked as the associate editor of a newsletter published by the Community Nutrition Institute, an antihunger lobbying group. For several years he had been a hunger-policy activist, publicly critical of the Department of Agriculture. Now he was on the inside.

Until that year, if you were poor and hungry in America, you could use food stamps to subsidize the cost of food. But you still had to buy the stamps; a modest but meaningful cash outlay was necessary for most recipients of the program each month. In practice, that proved to be a barrier to millions of poor people who were otherwise qualified for the program.

Greenstein and his allies in the administration wanted to eliminate the purchase requirement. It was a simple reform but one that Greenstein knew would greatly expand the program and alleviate basic hunger, particularly for millions of poor African Americans in the rural South. Initially, Secretary of Agriculture Bob Bergland and Greenstein had persuaded Bert Lance, Carter's chief at the Office of Management and Budget (OMB), to support the reform. But at the urging of Georgia senator Herman Talmadge, chairman of the Senate Agriculture Committee, Carter rejected it.

"All these southern politicians opposed it. We got a note from Carter," Greenstein recalled, "saying he was opposed to the measure, but he was willing to reconsider if we had a good argument." A meeting was set up, and when Secretary Bergland, Assistant Secretary Carol Tucker Foreman, and Greenstein walked into the Cabinet Room, they saw the president, Secretary of Health, Education and Welfare Joe Califano, OMB director Lance, and White House aide Stu Eizenstat seated at the table. But Greenstein was surprised to see that *NBC Nightly News* anchor John Chancellor was also in the room with a television crew. They were filming a "day in the life of the president." With the cameras rolling, Carter explained that he didn't support the proposal to eliminate the purchase requirement and specifically mentioned Senator Talmadge's opposition. Bergland, Foreman, and Greenstein defended the proposal, but others remained silent. "Well, no one outside the three of us were going to argue with the president," Greenstein said, "while the TV cameras were in the room." Finally, Foreman passed a note to a White House press aide, and the aide asked Chancellor and his crew to leave. As soon as they were out the door, everyone jumped in and made their arguments on why this was a good proposal. Carter listened. "Among other things, we explained," Greenstein said, "that by eliminating the requirement to 'buy' the food stamps, we were actually simplifying the program and cutting administrative costs. Carter's instincts were always liberal; he wanted to help the poor. But he also wanted to cut any bureaucracy. He listened to us and changed his mind."

The measure passed Congress that summer, and in due course more than five million new beneficiaries were added to the program, many of them poor African Americans in the South. Greenstein reflected, "It was certainly one of the most significant anti-poverty measures since LBJ's war on poverty in the 1960s."

On the other hand, liberals distrusted Carter's talk about balancing the budget and "zero-based budgeting." Why, they asked, was this populist so antagonistic to federal spending? Nothing rankled veteran legislators more that spring of 1977 than Carter's adamant refusal to approve a slew of water projects, mostly small dams and river-diversion facilities, in dozens of congressional districts around the country. Carter labeled nineteen of these projects "pork-barrel" and slashed the $5 billion cost from the federal budget. Someone inside the administration leaked the list of doomed projects. In response, thirty-five members of Congress from both parties came to the White House. "They are raising Cain," Carter noted in his diary, "because we took those items out of their 1978 budget." It was a "rough meeting," but Carter initially refused to back down, saying that most of these dams and Army Corps of Engineers projects were ill-advised and costly. Vice President Mondale tried to warn him that some of this congressional "pork" was a relative thing: "In a democracy, someone's waste is another person's treasure." White House legislative aide Jim Free observed that it had turned into a "real mud fight." But against most everyone's expectations, Carter diligently assembled a veto-proof majority in the House and seemed ready to prevail.

But then Speaker Tip O'Neill called one day and proposed a compromise whereby some of the water projects were restored and in return Congress agreed to zero out the funding for Tennessee's Clinch River breeder reactor. Carter believed the Clinch River project was completely unnecessary, and even a potential hazard for nuclear proliferation. When O'Neill phoned to propose the deal, Carter listened and, after a long pause, finally agreed. Eizenstat happened to be in the president's study and overheard part of the conversation. When Carter said he'd agreed to O'Neill's deal, Eizenstat vigorously protested that their allies on the Hill would feel betrayed. Eizenstat thought the president had "literally grabbed defeat from the jaws of victory." Carter later regretted his decision. "Signing this act was certainly not the worst mistake I ever made, but it was accurately interpreted as a sign of weakness on my part." A year later, he vetoed a similar public-works bill, if only because it contained some of the same water projects. Legislators, including Democrats, were incensed. And even Carter admitted that "the battle left deep scars."

But he knew he was doing the right thing. Federal funding of water projects was often a waste of taxpayer funds. It was a boondoggle, often encouraged by the Army Corps of Engineers and the legislators who funded them. Carter knew this from his experience as governor in Georgia. But he also knew this from James Gustave Speth, a Yale-trained lawyer and Rhodes Scholar who in 1970 had cofounded the Natural Resources Defense Council, an early think tank and advocacy group on environmental issues. Early in his administration, Carter had appointed Speth, age thirty-five, to the president's Council on Environmental Quality. Speth minced no words, telling the president that these water projects were a "great waste of federal funds." Speth argued that dams and river-diversion projects usually harmed the environment and led to a loss of recreational use of wilderness lands, particularly in the western states. Such projects were usually capital intensive and rarely generated long-term jobs. "The subsidies are huge," Speth wrote, "and benefit primarily large business interests and construction firms." This populist, dollar-frugal argument was highly persuasive to Carter.* "Many of our wild rivers and streams are dammed unnecessarily," Carter later wrote.

---

* Speth continued to educate Carter about the environment, warning him on the dangers of acid rain, carbon dioxide buildup in the atmosphere, and the likely extinction of 100,000 species during the next quarter century. Just before leaving office, Carter published a prophetic report written by Speth, *The Global 2000 Report to the President*, that predicted "widespread and pervasive changes in global climatic, economic, social and agricultural patterns" if humanity continued to rely on fossil fuels.

"The Corps of Engineers was complicit in this ongoing scheme because this process had become one of the prime reasons for their popularity with appropriations committees."

"The problem is that Jimmy Carter wants to be Mr. Clean," observed House Majority Leader Jim Wright (D-TX). "He will not indulge in quid pro quo. He thinks it's tarnished and sordid. . . . I think deep down he has categorized patronage as being something corrupt." Carter was willing to compromise, but he tended to perceive some kind of moral turpitude if money was on the table. On Capitol Hill and elsewhere, the whole water bill fight created a perception of political incompetence. "It fed the emerging narrative," White House aide Les Francis recalled, "that these guys don't know what they're doing. They're not from Washington, so they don't know how the place works."

POLITICS IS ALMOST always about expectations. By the mid-1970s, liberal Democrats thought it was time for a reborn New Deal. Their expectations were all about a renewal of the federal government's social welfare compact. And yet economic realities clashed with these expectations. Unbeknownst to everyone, the great postwar boom was coming to a slow end. As the historian Jefferson Cowie later wrote of the 1970s, "White male workers' income had risen an astonishing 42 percent since 1960, but those incomes stagnated or fell for the next quarter century following the early seventies." It was Carter's political ill fortune, but the country was entering a period of oil price shocks, deindustrialization, and stagnation. The productivity gains of the last two decades suddenly slowed. Globalization and international trade weakened trade unions. Inequality was on the rise, and many working-class and middle-class Americans gradually experienced despair and disenchantment due to the loss of high-paying, unionized jobs.

As Carter came into office he faced two persistent but contradictory problems: unemployment and inflation. Early in that first spring of his presidency, Carter looked at the latest statistics and decided that the economy was heating up, and he began to worry less about unemployment and more about inflation. Persistent inflation was a new phenomenon in the 1970s, and Carter thought it particularly harmful to the poor. At the beginning of the decade inflation had hit 5 percent—but by 1974 it had spiked for a time to 11 percent. Inflation was initially spurred by deficit spending on the Vietnam War—but the spike in oil prices in 1971 and again during the Arab oil embargo of 1973 turned it into a persistent phenomenon. By the spring of 1977 it was nearly 7 percent. In January, when Carter still thought the economy sluggish, he had agreed to sponsor a quick tax rebate of $50 per person. With unemployment at 7 percent, Carter agreed to allot $30 billion in federal spending to stimulate the economy. The tax rebate bill quickly passed the House of Representatives with strong support from liberal Democrats, but as it was being debated in the Senate, the president suddenly began having doubts: "I'm becoming more concerned about inflation than I am about stimulation." Later in April, he decided to "bite the bullet" and informed congressional leaders that he was now opposed to the tax rebate. Without presidential support, the tax-rebate bill was dead.

Liberal legislators like Speaker O'Neill and Congressman John Brademas (D-IN) were infuriated by this flip-flop. The president's chief lobbyist for the Senate, Dan Tate, told Carter that Senator Robert Byrd (D-WV), a major powerhouse in the Senate, had warned him of "serious repercussions" over his handling of the tax rebate: "When you again ask congressional leaders to carry the ball on a controversial issue, some might not be willing to go to the wall, fearing that you might change your mind and leave them high and dry, embarrassed and battered politically."

Tactically, Carter's change of mind was bad politics. He looked indecisive. But his flip-flop on the $50 rebate also revealed an underlying contradiction in the president's impulses. Carter wanted to lower the number of unemployed, so he was willing to spend money on job training programs. But he also wanted to stop inflation, so he was simultaneously trying to balance the federal budget. Trying to execute both only produced a confusing political agenda. As Eizenstat later admitted, "One always knew that [Carter] wanted to spend as little money as possible, and yet at the same time he wanted welfare reform, he wanted national health insurance, he wanted job training programs."

O'Neill complained that the administration was "neglecting social programs in order to balance the budget in four years." Carter took "strong exception" to this critique and argued that his budget would maintain the social net for the neediest—but that "there's no way to have available financial resources in two or three years for better health care

and welfare reform if we don't put some tight constraints on unnecessary spending quite early." Battle lines were already being drawn
between the Democratic Party's traditional New Deal liberals and
Carter's blend of social populism and fiscal conservatism. "Carter will
adopt any idea, no matter how radical," quipped one pundit, "if only it
does not cost money."

Carter began dueling with Speaker O'Neill even before he was sworn
into office. O'Neill initially thought Carter was simply naïve about the
legislative process. The president, said O'Neill, "just didn't understand
Irish or Jewish politicians, or the nuances of city politics." Their relationship was a clash of both cultures and personalities—but also of geo-
graphical ideology. "Tip," Carter later recalled, "when I would criticize
the federal government as being overly bureaucratic and so forth, I think
Tip took that as kind of a personal reflection on him and on the House."
The Speaker wanted a stimulus package to address high unemployment
rates. That meant public service jobs, infrastructure projects paid with
federal dollars, a federal pay raise, and even an expansion of Social Security. High on O'Neill's list of priorities was a comprehensive national
health insurance bill—or at least a health bill that covered catastrophic
health events. O'Neill's agenda was the same as organized labor's. It was
a traditional New Deal agenda that would benefit the northeastern industrial belt—precisely O'Neill's constituency.

Carter's domestic wish list was quite different. When O'Neill's aides
met with Carter's domestic policy adviser, Stu Eizenstat, they were told
that Carter wanted regulatory reform, welfare reform, tax reform, and,
most important, a balanced federal budget by the end of his first term.
The latter goal would prove to be a major impediment in Carter's relations with his Democratic congressional allies. He had inherited from
the Ford administration a record federal budget deficit of $66 billion, or
about 4 percent of the gross domestic product. At the time, this was
considered to be excessive. In the 1950s and '60s, the federal budget deficit averaged 1 percent or less of GDP—which explains why Carter
thought a balanced federal budget was so important. He was determined
to generate a surplus by 1981. This meant less government, not more,
and, to the frustration of traditional New Deal and Great Society Democrats, less money for liberal public programs.

Ironically, contrary to the conventional wisdom at the time, the economy has proven itself able to sustain such deficit spending. The federal budget deficit has averaged more than 4 percent in the decades since Carter left the White House—suggesting that his concern for the size of the federal deficit was historically misplaced. In this sense, Carter's aversion to Keynesian deficit spending would prove to be a major political liability. (His successors, whether conservative Republicans or liberal Democrats, had no compunction about spending federal dollars, though with vastly different priorities.)

Carter also came into office wanting to simplify government regulations, particularly for small businesses. He wanted welfare recipients to work and the federal government itself to be streamlined and reorganized for the sake of efficiency. Carter believed his fight to reorganize the Georgia state government had been his greatest gubernatorial accomplishment, and he now wanted to replicate this on the federal level. To this end, he intended to introduce legislation to restore the president's powers to shutter federal agencies, transfer civil servants, and otherwise reorganize the federal government.

O'Neill didn't necessarily oppose this initiative, but he didn't much care for it either. But Carter warned him that if Congressman Jack Brooks (D-TX), the chairman of the House Government Operation Committee, tried to stall his reorganization bill, Carter would appeal directly to the American people. O'Neill blanched, and looking like he had been offered a glass of "strychnine on the rocks," he told Carter that would be a big mistake: "Jack doesn't get mad, he gets even. You don't know your throat is cut until you try to turn your head." "No," Carter told O'Neill, "I described the problem in a rational way to the American people. I'm sure they'll realize I'm right." O'Neill later said he "could have slugged" the president. "Carter used to think it should go on merit," O'Neill recalled. "He never looked at the political consequences." In this instance, Carter prevailed, and on March 31, 1977, he got his federal government reorganization bill passed—but the margin of victory came from Republican congressmen, a fact that was bound to annoy Speaker O'Neill.

"Tip took great offense to little things," recalled Jody Powell. O'Neill claimed he had been given "lousy" seats at a preinaugural Kennedy Center event. It was a misunderstanding, a mere kerfuffle. Neither did this Boston Irish politician understand why the new president served such modest fare at White House breakfast meetings. "I didn't get this way eating sweet rolls," he complained to Vice President Mondale. "I want a breakfast and I'm not coming back unless I get a meal!"

Speaker O'Neill was also personally offended by the appointment of a Massachusetts Republican, Elliot Richardson, as a special ambassador on maritime affairs. It was bad enough that the Speaker was given no warning of the decision, but O'Neill was also incensed because his own son was intending to run against Richardson for governor. O'Neill was being petulant, and early on he blamed these perceived snubs on Carter's young aides, particularly Jordan—whom he took to calling "Hannibal Jerkin." One day O'Neill phoned President Carter in the Oval Office and Carter asked him, "What can I do for you, Mr. Speaker?" O'Neill replied gruffly, "I would like you to go down the hall and ask Hamilton Jordan to return my call."

Similarly, O'Neill made it known to reporters that he thought Carter's congressional liaison aide, Frank Moore, was another bumbling "good ol' boy" from South Georgia. Moore became a useful target for a lot of criticism, largely unwarranted. He was a detail man, and after he got his shop up and running, it operated smoothly. If there was unhappiness on Capitol Hill with the White House, the source of the problem wasn't Moore but Carter. "They say it's that we're inept," Jordan told a reporter from *Newsday,* "and that the staff is naïve. But it's not ineptness and it's not a naïve staff—it's Carter. Instead of Carter bringing them down here slapping them on the back and offering them projects, he brings them down to the White House and offers them the merits of the bill. If Carter would play the patronage game, he'd be ahead today. . . . But that is not Carter."

O'Neill was also profoundly uncomfortable with Carter's Southern Baptist piety. Carter often said a brief grace, a prayer of thankfulness, at White House working breakfasts. The Catholic politician thought this out of place, a break with the separation of church and state. So his aides were surprised one morning when O'Neill opened a similar breakfast on the Hill with a prayer—and then he smiled mischievously and said, "That ought to last us for the year."

O'Neill's disdain for the Georgian boys was palpable. "They ran against the Tip O'Neills," he later said, "the cigar-smoking, whiskey-drinking Irish politicians. They [the Georgians] were all parochial. They were incompetent. They came with a chip on their shoulder against the entrenched politicians. Washington to them was evil."

Carter tried hard to like O'Neill. He invited the Speaker and his wife, Millie, to a private dinner in March with just him and Rosalynn. They had another dinner alone on June 1, 1977, and talked at length and afterward sat on the Truman Balcony, smoking cigars. On another occasion, the Carters had Tip and Millie over for a private supper, and they shared "a couple of good, strong drinks." O'Neill tried to impress upon Carter that the president was too involved in minutiae on too many pieces of legislation and that he should back off a bit and focus on just a few major items. "This is not something that I could accept," Carter noted in his diary that night. "But it was interesting to have his advice."

Over time, their relationship mellowed, and by the spring of 1978 Carter thought he had turned O'Neill into a firm ally. "He's so supportive of me in his speeches that sometimes it's almost embarrassing." The Irish American in O'Neill was particularly gratified when Carter announced the end of weapons sales to the Protestant-dominated Royal Ulster Constabulary, a police force in Northern Ireland that the British were using to repress the Catholic Irish. The British thought it a tactless intervention when Carter further insisted that any government in Northern Ireland had to "command widespread acceptance" from both the Catholic and the Protestant communities. Both O'Neill and Ted Kennedy found common cause with Carter on this change of policy and later came to regard it as a turning point in the Irish conflict.

ON PAPER, THIS Democratic president seemed to hold a strong hand on Capitol Hill. Democrats controlled the House, with 292 votes to only 143 Republicans; Senate Democrats possessed a filibuster-proof majority of 62 senators to only 38 Republicans. But the Democratic majority was itself split between liberals and conservatives, the latter invariably from the old Confederacy. In practice, Carter's legislative team had to work hard to build a majority coalition on any particular issue. To complicate the political dynamics, congressional liberals in the late 1970s were in a feisty mood and wary of executive powers, so even though Democrats controlled both the Senate and the House, Carter could not count on party loyalty to ram through his legislative agenda.

Carter blocked out plenty of time on his schedule to visit with a wide range of congressional leaders; on average, he met personally or had phone conversations with seventy-nine senators or congressmen each month. But most of these meetings were formal sessions in which he was telling legislators what he wanted. "He would never call somebody down from the Hill," said Mondale's aide Richard Moe, "just to put his feet up on the desk and bring out a bottle of Scotch and have a cigar. . . . He hated small talk of any form." Carter later described the process with disdain: "We had them over . . . in groups of thirty or forty ad nauseam. I mean, it was horrible. Night after night after night, after night, going through the same basic questions when I was absolutely convinced that the House members knew they ought to support the legislation."

Carter was stubbornly intellectual in his approach to governing. He wanted to do what was right. "Carter thought politics was sinful," recalled Mondale. "The worst thing you could say to Carter if you wanted to do something was that it was politically the best thing to do." When a slate of Pennsylvania congressmen sent word that they intended to vote against any Carter legislation unless he appointed their choice for U.S. attorney in Philadelphia, he "told them in a nice way to go to hell." Moe recalled the day one staffer raised a political obstacle, only to be rebuked by the president: "Stick to policy," Carter said. "I'll figure out the politics." Moe recalled that those "steely blue eyes could be very intimidating."

This was just the way Carter thought. Rosalynn tried sometimes to push him to be aware of the politics, but she later confessed to Dr. Bourne, "He's just not a politician." There was, of course, something admirable about this. But even his most loyal political operatives knew that it often meant Carter was his own worst nemesis. "JC not a politician," Eizenstat noted in one of his ubiquitous yellow legal pads. "JC simply [does] not like to be with other politicians; maybe felt he was better [than them]."

Jordan understood it was his job to protect his boss from making the right decision if it was not politically sustainable. Too often, he bluntly admonished Carter in one of his long "think piece" memos to the president, "We send proposals to the Congress which represent your own views and are probably correct technically, but they are not politically credible." Jordan cited Carter's decision on a farm bill in late March. With wheat farmers facing tumbling prices, candidate Carter had promised to back government price supports at least equal to thc price of production. But once in office, he changed his mind, simply because such price supports conflicted with his promise to balance the budget by 1981. After a meeting with farmers, Carter noted in his diary, "I'm going to be much more conservative on farm price supports than they anticipate."

Indeed, when Agriculture Secretary Bob Bergland proposed a small increase on farm price supports, Carter rejected it and ordered Bergland to submit a bill containing price supports lower than the existing market price for wheat. "You rejected his recommendation," Jordan observed, "and sent him to the Hill with a package that was not taken seriously by the Congress. When [Georgia senator] Herman Talmadge calls your farm bill 'a silly thing,' we have made a political mistake somewhere." As Jordan expected, a month later Congress voted for a bill with much more expensive price supports. Carter threatened to veto the bill—but the Senate promptly passed it by a vote of sixty-nine to eighteen, a veto-proof margin. The president got saddled with a farm bill costing not $1.6 billion a year but closer to $6.2 billion a year. Jordan's point was that they might have saved money, had the administration submitted a more politically viable bill in the first place. "Whenever you have to make a major domestic decision," he pleaded, "you should have Frank Moore, Mondale, myself and others in to talk about it. This is not happening now."

CARTER WAS NEVER afraid to take on controversy. And nothing was more contentious or complicated than the prices of gasoline, natural gas, and heating oil. In the midst of the October 1973 Arab-Israeli War, the Organization of Petroleum Exporting Countries (OPEC) had imposed an oil embargo. The price of a barrel of oil on the global market had risen from just under $2 in 1970 to more than $11 by the end of 1973. Americans, hooked on cheap gasoline, were suddenly spending hours waiting in gasoline lines. But with the end of the embargo in March 1974, energy prices had declined marginally, and by 1976, the nation's gross domestic product was growing at a phenomenal 5 percent per year. Thus, by the time Carter was inaugurated, oil prices had risen to $13 a barrel, but the political pressure to do something about energy issues had abated, at least temporarily.

The extraordinary oil embargo was, as Carter put it, "a crisis soon forgotten." In reality, the Arab oil embargo was mostly a symbolic gesture, affecting only about 5 percent of the global supply. But Carter nevertheless believed America's growing dependence on Saudi and other Middle Eastern oil imports was expensive, inflationary, and politically insecure. By 1977, America was importing nearly 50 percent of its oil. He thought it only prudent to manage a transition away from expensive imported oil. Americans were consuming 2.3 times the average per capita of other industrial nations. Carter thought this wasteful, and he was determined to lead the country toward an energy culture based on conservation and reliance on domestic coal, nuclear energy, natural gas—and whatever could be obtained from renewables like wind and solar power.

With hindsight, of course, his instincts were prescient. But the political hurdles were formidable. In principle, domestic energy supplies could be increased by the deregulation of natural gas and oil prices. Deregulation would be supported by the oil lobby but opposed by consumer advocates. Likewise, conservation and subsidies to stimulate renewable energy would be opposed by the auto and oil industries but supported by consumers—at least, as long as the alternatives did not cost more than oil and gas.

Carter was trying simultaneously to enact both deregulation and conservation, but it was nearly impossible to assemble a political coalition for both agendas. Such was the political logjam. But he was undeterred. He believed it was time to have a comprehensive national energy policy, and to this end he appointed James Schlesinger, a former defense secretary and former CIA director under Presidents Nixon and Ford, to be his energy czar. Working under a ninety-day deadline, Schlesinger quickly drafted legislation for a comprehensive energy policy that included the creation of a federal Department of Energy.

Carter was unhappy, however, with Schlesinger's early drafts. "Our basic and most difficult question," he wrote to Schlesinger, "is how to raise the price of scarce energy with minimum disruption of our economic system and greater equity in bearing the financial burden. I am not satisfied with your approach." This political dilemma would never be resolved, and neither would Schlesinger find a way to satisfy this president's desire for real reforms in the way the country shared its en-

ergy costs. Carter thought Schlesinger's initial proposal was too complicated: "I can't understand it. . . . A crucial element is *simplicity*. Even
perfect equity can't be sold if Americans can't understand it. Their distrust is exacerbated by complexity." Carter's note accurately described
the challenge at hand. But none of his energy proposals ever achieved
the clarity of simplicity.

Less than a hundred days after his inauguration, on April 18, 1977,
Carter gave another televised chat from the Oval Office in which he
began on a darkly frank note: "Tonight I want to have an *unpleasant* talk
with you about a problem that is unprecedented in our history." He proclaimed that the challenge facing the country was nothing short of "the
moral equivalent of war"—a phrase suggested to him by Admiral Rickover. His proposed 283-page National Energy Act (NEA) included a tax
on oversized, gas-guzzling cars, tax credits for home insulation, and federal research monies for alternative energy sources like solar and wind.
It was a complicated package, designed to encourage conservation and
raise prices—but also to tax excess profits earned by the oil companies.
Carter's proposed bill compromised on the politically sensitive issue of
natural gas deregulation by allowing price increases for independent
producers of newly discovered gas fields. Initially, his energy message
garnered broad popular support. *Newsweek* editorialized, "For the first
time, a strong activist president has seized the initiative on energy." Predictably, *The Wall Street Journal* referred to his "moral equivalent of
war" by the sarcastic acronym "MEOW."

Not surprisingly, Congress was slow to grapple with the legislation,
and Republican Party chairman Bill Brock accused the president of
"driving people out of their family cars." Carter also took some heat
from his own party. Congressman John Dingell (D-MI) told White
House aides that he thought it was an "asinine bill." But despite such
opinions, the House approved most of the energy package in early August by a vote of 244 to 177—including the creation of a stand-alone
Department of Energy. Rejected were Carter's request for a standby tax
on gasoline and a proposed tax rebate for consumers who bought small
cars. Carter would make another push a year later to gradually decontrol energy prices, including natural gas, but for the time being he could
claim a major legislative coup. But then the energy bill moved to the
Senate, where the big oil companies exercised much more political in-

fluence. By late September, the Senate was still deadlocked on the energy package. "The influence of the oil and gas industry is unbelievable," Carter complained, "and it's impossible to arouse the public to protect themselves."

By the end of 1977, it was clear that Congress would reject key provisions of the energy bill. One morning that December, Admiral Rickover called Carter to offer his encouragement. "You have not been a failure," Rickover told him. "[It] took about four hundred years for Lord Jesus Christ to have his message accepted. Up to that time he could have been considered a failure." An angry president was not consoled. "It's a bitch!" Carter told Rosalynn. "I know why no other president was willing to tackle it." Carter continued the fight, but he would not get an energy bill until October 1978, and even then it passed the House by a whisker vote of 207–206, with only eight Republican affirmative votes. While extremely complicated, the bill created a new Department of Energy, placed heavy penalties on the production of gas-guzzling automobiles, required higher efficiency standards for home appliances, encouraged the electric utilities to conserve energy, and provided tax incentives that supported the initial development of the wind and solar power industries. In an effort to shrink American dependence on imported oil, the bill also stimulated domestic production of coal and gasohol production.

In retrospect, the most consequential aspect of the energy package may have been the phased decontrol of natural gas prices and the creation of a competitive electric power industry through the Public Utilities and Regulatory Policies Act of 1978 (PURPA). Highly controversial at the time, phased deregulation eventually stimulated exploration for natural gas fields within the United States and created the market conditions decades later for the innovative fracking technology that would make the country a major supplier of liquefied natural gas (LNG). PURPA was intended to promote the use of waste fuels and cogeneration, but in practice it demonstrated that electric generation could be provided not only by conventional utilities but also by independent power producers. Ultimately, this gave rise to the deregulation of the electric industry in the 1990s.

Other components of the National Energy Act of 1978 were more problematic. For example, a key feature of the NEA was a provision called the Power Plant and Industrial Fuel Use Act, which required that any new power plant be fired by fuels other than oil or natural gas. In practice, that meant coal. Even older power plants that had once been coal-fired but had switched to oil fuels were required to switch back to coal. Environmentalists in the liberal wing of the Democratic Party were unhappy with this bias toward coal. But their concerns gave way to Congress's desire to lessen the nation's dependence on imported Arab oil. Over the next few years, Carter's policies actually resulted in a decline in the market for "clean" natural gas. Coal became king.

Carter generally believed in market-driven solutions. He stubbornly resisted pressures from Senator Kennedy and other liberals to consider imposing price controls on oil and gas. His policies pushed oil prices higher, which in turn promoted higher domestic oil production, and that eventually resulted in a decline in oil imports, from 50 percent in 1977 to 40 percent by 1980, a reduction of 1.8 million barrels per day. But Carter reaped no political dividends from this trend, and most Americans only grumbled about having to pay higher prices at the gas pump.

It is hard not to conclude that Carter's energy policies were a muddle. Politically speaking, he was criticized by liberals for enacting too much deregulation—while conservatives perceived him as a populist enemy of the oil and gas industry. It was a no-win during his presidency, and he is generally not given sufficient credit for creating the foundations for the enormous growth in U.S. energy supplies, coupled with a robust and competitive electric supply industry.

UNFORTUNATELY, CARTER'S OTHER legislative initiatives, on tax reform and welfare reform, completely stalled. During the 1976 campaign he had called the tax system "nothing less than a disgrace." Once in office, he had instructed Treasury Secretary Michael Blumenthal to craft a reform package that would create a simplified but more progressive tax code. He also wanted to limit business deductions and fully eliminate such perks as deductions for first-class travel and the proverbial "three-martini" business lunch.

Even more controversially for the business community, Carter instructed Blumenthal to include a proposal to tax the capital gains on investment income at the same rate as ordinary income. It was an unvarnished populist, even left-wing, set of guidelines. But Blumenthal didn't get the message. Three months later, the treasury secretary came back with what Carter called a "superficial" set of proposed "reforms" that actually favored the rich, including lowering the top tax rate from 70 to 50 percent. The president's domestic policy adviser, Stu Eizenstat, angrily objected, telling Carter that if he wanted progressive tax reform, "you will have to instruct Treasury to that effect."

Carter pushed Blumenthal during the summer of 1977, but when the administration finally took its tax proposal to Capitol Hill, Speaker O'Neill and other congressional leaders bluntly told the president he didn't have the votes. An embittered president reluctantly withdrew the legislation, calling it an "insidious game." Later, he wrote that he had concluded that any tax measure inevitably attracted "a pack of powerful and ravenous wolves, determined to secure for themselves additional benefits at the expense of other Americans."

One particularly egregious example of this was the foreign income tax credits claimed by large corporations, particularly Big Oil. When Carter realized that this long-standing loophole was allowing corporations to dodge billions of dollars in tax every year, he was outraged. He told Blumenthal that the loophole should be closed—and that the oil companies should be required to pay taxes on their overseas profits. This would mean that oil giants like the Arabian American Oil Company (ARAMCO) would have to pay tax on the royalties they forked over to Saudi Arabia. When the business community got wind of the president's intentions, their lobbyists on Capitol Hill worked overtime to defeat the proposal.

Carter himself took a phone call from J. Paul Austin, the CEO of Coca-Cola. A fellow Georgian, Austin had supported Carter for years. The Atlanta executive had regular access to the Oval Office. Austin made his pitch for keeping the foreign income tax credit loophole and told the president that Kirbo would also be weighing in on the issue. Carter listened politely and then hung up. But that night he noted in his diary, "I don't appreciate that kind of call." He knew it was a "less than subtle effort to derive financial benefit for his company from this personal relationship."

Notwithstanding the president's clearly expressed desires, Blumenthal did nothing. Finally, in 1979, Carter formally asked Congress to close this foreign tax credit loophole for the major oil companies. When

Congress refused, Carter imposed an oil import tax, but Congress then voted to override this executive order. Carter was relentless—but so too were the entrenched lobbyists on Capitol Hill. "The Business [Round-table] group was a waste of time, as could be predicted," Butler noted in his White House diary. "No give and take, just posturing. Before the meeting, the businesspeople told Blumenthal they were opposed to some of our tax reforms . . . and Blumenthal told them he agreed, but the president didn't: Carter was left as the heavy."

By late that spring of 1977, Kirbo was warning Carter that if he had "to tackle the vested interests, I think we should go about it very carefully." He was worrying that if the president challenged the "upper business establishment"—as might be warranted—it was important to send a signal to small businessmen that they weren't being lumped with the big fish. Unless warned, the small businessman "will put himself in the same general group of businessmen as the giants." Charlie said he didn't like the label "robber baron," but he thought Carter needed some such "modern term" to distinguish the "real culprits"—big corporations—from the small businessmen. He defined small businessmen as "companies that are closely held, partnerships and corporations doing a few million, say ten or fifteen million dollars a year."

Kirbo understood that a "public battle" between the president and the business community would be tough. But he nevertheless urged Carter to "stand firm." In this highly private advice to his president, Kirbo was wearing his populist heart on his sleeve. "I am inclined to believe your chances of being reelected would be better if you did this and did it in a visible way." No one outside the White House realized it, but the president's closest confidant, this easygoing, slow-talking country lawyer from Georgia, was urging the president to govern from the left as a country populist. Carter relied on Kirbo's sage advice. "His words were softer than the ice tinkling in his glass," the president recalled, "so I would bend close to hear the most complicated and important affairs of state explained with enough simplicity for a peanut farmer to understand."

Late in the spring of 1977, Kirbo spent two and a half hours with David Rockefeller, sixty-two, chairman of Chase Manhattan Bank and a grandson of one of America's most notorious robber barons. The meeting had been brokered at Rockefeller's request by Coca-Cola's Paul Austin. Rockefeller understood that Kirbo had the president's ear.

Kirbo had never met a Rockefeller, "but I was much impressed." Rockefeller came right to the point, though he was "very gentle and cool about what he said and seemed to have no personal distaste for anyone that was discussed." Rockefeller said he was concerned about the business community's poor relationship with the Carter administration. Specifically, Treasury Secretary Michael Blumenthal "had not gone over very well" and had been "very careless in his statements about the balance of trade." The main problem with the economy, Rockefeller said, was the price of energy. He was critical of the energy bill and thought energy czar James Schlesinger was "difficult to get along with and was not effective." He conceded that while he thought "we had one of the best cabinets on paper," he complained that "we had some very young, very liberal active people below them that were at the root of some of our problems." These young people, Rockefeller said, "irritated business." Having said this, the banker claimed he really wanted to help the president: "There was hardly anything he wouldn't do to help you and to help the country." He had tried to think of someone who could help in the field of energy, but the "only person who came to his mind" was George Shultz, a Bechtel Corporation executive who had served as treasury secretary under President Richard Nixon.

Kirbo responded to all this negativity by gently suggesting that Rockefeller could "help us by putting out the word that they were not getting anywhere by criticizing you and the administration." They agreed that perhaps Hamilton Jordan should regularly try to have a select number of prominent businessmen into the White House and listen to their views.

There is no record of the president's response to Kirbo's memo on Rockefeller, but the banker's criticisms could not have come as a surprise. Carter knew Rockefeller from his meetings in the early 1970s with the Trilateral Commission. Their relationship had always been formal and cool. And later the president would have cause to feel downright annoyed with the powerful banker.

THE ADMINISTRATION'S FIRST six months were not without substantial accomplishments on the domestic ledger. Economic growth for much of 1977 was running at a robust 5.2 percent. Early in May, Congress enacted Carter's $20.1 billion economic stimulus package, and soon afterward the president won a jobs bill for poverty-level youth and a one-year extension of the Comprehensive Employment and Training Act. Congress had also passed his request for presidential authority to streamline the federal bureaucracy under the Reorganization Act. In June 1977, he also introduced proposals for airline deregulation and signed a controversial law to regulate strip-mining practices by the coal industry. Lawmakers had dodged major tax reform, but they had at least agreed on a bill for tax-law simplification, as requested by the president. Progress had been achieved on auto-safety and fuel-efficiency standards, and the Agriculture Department had succeeded in greatly expanding the rolls of those eligible for food stamps.

Congress further authorized the expansion of the federal judiciary, creating 148 new federal judgeships—and Carter promptly began appointing record numbers of women and African Americans to the bench.* Carter was determined to remake the judiciary. A month before the inauguration, he met in Atlanta with Judge Griffin Bell and Mississippi's Senator James Eastland, known to be a stubborn opponent of racial integration. Charlie Kirbo also sat in on this critical meeting. Carter made it clear to Senator Eastland that he intended to nominate many more women and minorities to the federal bench. Eastland was chair of the Senate Judiciary Committee and could have used his power to block these appointments. Carter persuaded him not to do so. And in the spring of 1977, Carter instructed Attorney General Bell "to find at least one black federal judge for each of the states of the old Confederacy."

No president since Lyndon Johnson had achieved more legislative victories in his first year in office. Politicians on both sides of the aisle complained about Carter's aloofness and arrogance—but forgotten is the plain fact that this president nevertheless usually got what he wanted from Congress. More of his presidential initiatives became law than did those of presidents Eisenhower, Kennedy, Nixon, or Ford. Carter's success rate even approached that of Johnson. It was an extraordinary record.

---

* In early 1977, there were only eight female judges (1.4 percent), twenty African American judges (3.5 percent), and five Hispanic judges (0.9 percent). During the next four years, Carter appointed forty-one women, thirty-seven African Americans, and sixteen Hispanics to the federal bench—more minorities appointed to the federal bench than by all previous presidents combined.

Congress struggled to keep up with the president's long wish list of domestic initiatives. "You have proposed so much legislation," complained Speaker O'Neill, "we can't handle it all." Some of these languished, such as Carter's call for radical election reform, including a provision for universal voter registration and public financing of congressional elections. He angered labor unions by opposing a substantial hike in the minimum wage, arguing that it would only fuel inflation. Carter also ran into trouble with his proposals for substantial reforms of the country's complicated system of public welfare. Prior to the inauguration, Carter had asked Joe Califano, his designated secretary for the Department of Health, Education and Welfare (HEW), how early he could come up with a reform plan. Califano answered casually that he thought a package could be drawn up by May. The president held him to this schedule. But when Califano presented him with some options in March, the president rejected them all as too expensive.

"If you could start over, what would you do?" Carter asked. When Califano replied that he wasn't sure, Carter pressed him again, saying he wanted to "redesign the whole system from scratch" but spend the same amount of money.

"It will cost money to get a better system," Califano insisted.

The president stared coldly and reiterated, "I want a welfare reform program that doesn't cost anything more." The fiscal conservative in Carter wanted to cut welfare rolls by providing government jobs to those who could work and provide a "decent income" for the completely disabled and single parents with young children. But Carter didn't want to spend more tax dollars on welfare. "Are you telling me," an irate president complained, "there is no way to improve the present welfare system except by spending billions of dollars? In that case, to hell with it! We're wasting our time."

Afterward, Jordan—who had sat in on the meeting—wrote Carter a note: "Several things were obvious to me. You don't have a clear idea of what kind of program you want. . . . HEW has provided at best sketchy options." Jordan thought it not "humanly possible" to have a well-thought-out welfare proposal by May 1, Carter's self-imposed deadline. Predictably, the president reluctantly announced in early May that he would have to delay his welfare reform bill until August. After further jockeying among Califano, Eizenstat, and Labor Secretary Ray Marshall,

Carter concluded that the existing welfare system was "worse than we thought." It was not, he complained, a "coherent system," and, echoing conservative critics of welfare, he said the program was "overly wasteful, capricious and subject to fraud."

Finally, in early August, Carter submitted a welfare reform package—and Congress immediately began picking it apart. Ostensibly, the bill would have cut the welfare rolls by providing work incentives, but it was not clear who would be required to work. "It's so complicated," Carter groused to his diary, "that it's going to take at least a year to get the proposal through Congress." That turned out to be woefully optimistic. Conservatives like Senator Russell Long (D-LA) charged that the bill would actually add large numbers of people to the welfare rolls, while labor union leaders on the left warned that a government jobs program paying the minimum wage would threaten middle-class jobs. Carter was getting criticism from both sides. Califano archly observed that welfare reform was becoming "the Middle East of domestic politics." By the end of 1977 it was clear that welfare reform was dead. Carter would try again two years later with a $5.7 billion proposal that would have set a national minimum income, combined with a program to create as many as 1.4 million public-sector jobs. Carter claimed his bill would "abolish our existing welfare system." But even this relatively liberal program was too little for liberals and too much for congressional conservatives. The bill was going nowhere, and Carter admitted as much in his written message to Congress: "No legislative struggle had provided so much hopeful rhetoric and so much disappointment and frustration." The bill passed the House but died in the Senate.

CARTER'S FRUSTRATION WITH the welfare reform package carried over into his relations with his brash HEW secretary. The two men did not always get along. Califano later conceded that there was a "cultural chasm" between him and the president: "He was not comfortable in Washington." By contrast, Califano was the consummate insider, a Washington operative who knew every key player in town. Influential fixer Edward Bennett Williams was his law partner, Mondale had been his neighbor, Speaker O'Neill was a good friend, and Califano regularly attended Redskins football games with columnist Art Buchwald. He socialized with prominent media personalities like Phil Geyelin, David

Brinkley, Meg Greenfield, and Katharine Graham. "This was a world," Califano wrote in his memoirs, "that had little respect for Carter as president." Ed Williams had actually advised Califano not to join the Carter administration. "He's not our kind of person," said Williams. Before joining the administration, Califano had been earning more than $505,000 annually, representing *The Washington Post,* Pfizer Inc., Coca-Cola, and other well-paying clients. But unlike the president he served, Califano was a consummate political animal. As a young aide in the Johnson White House, he had not only possessed a front-row seat to the Great Society but had actually played a role in crafting key aspects of its antipoverty programs. He was still a believer in big government and now had a passion about making LBJ's programs work. "I wanted to prove that the Great Society programs could be managed." As HEW secretary he was running with gusto the federal government's largest non-military agency, with 145,000 employees and a budget of $181 billion. "The trouble with Califano," said one White House aide, "is that he was here before we got here, and he'll be here after we leave. He runs his own empire, and what makes it worse is that most of the time he is good at it."

Carter was pleased when Califano discovered that HEW was sitting on a billion dollars' worth of unpaid student loan bills. No one had bothered to send out invoices to the students, and records of the loans were being kept on index cards in shoeboxes. Califano solved the problem by hiring a data-processing team. This was a perfect example of how Carter thought government could be run more efficiently.

Califano certainly identified as a Great Society liberal—but he was also a Catholic, and as such, he agreed with Carter's position on abortion. He recognized *Roe v. Wade* as the law of the land—but he opposed using taxpayers' funds to finance abortions for poor women.

But Califano also had a knack for annoying the president—such as the day it was reported that the flamboyant HEW secretary had hired a "confidential assistant . . . to assist him in a broad range of personal services for personal activities." In truth, he had hired a personal chef. Carter was not pleased. Califano offered to fire the chef, but Carter told him, "Handle it your way. Whatever you do is fine with me." Califano kept the chef, and when Speaker O'Neill learned of this, he called up his friend and joshed, "Well, I've got some advice for you: Any guy in this town that hires a chef for twelve grand had better hire a food taster." Joe laughed it off; he was going to run his department his way.

Califano took the initiative on a host of issues, often without first consulting the White House. That first spring he promulgated new regulations requiring handicapped access to all federal buildings. He also strictly enforced Title IX of the 1972 law prohibiting sexual discrimination in educational programs. This controversial decision forced universities to spend millions of dollars expanding athletic programs for women. These measures stimulated a social revolution in how the country treated the handicapped and women.

But nothing Califano did generated more political heat than his decision in early 1978 to declare war on tobacco. Once a four-pack-a-day smoker, Califano described smoking as "slow-motion suicide" and banned tobacco from all HEW facilities. Tobacco company executives denounced Califano, and several southern governors of tobacco-growing states called upon Carter to fire the HEW secretary. But though the president knew the "war on tobacco" could only hurt his reelection bid in these states, he did not interfere. Indeed, he had asked Joe to mount a public-health awareness program based on preventive health measures—and it was hard to argue that cigarette smoking was not linked to cancer, heart ailments, and lung disease. Califano actually tried in 1979 to declare nicotine an addictive substance, a step that would have subjected the tobacco companies to stringent federal regulations. But the tobacco companies fought back, arguing that there was no evidence of nicotine's addictive qualities. They lied and were hiding the scientific data in company files that proved Califano's case. The consequences of these lies were quite deadly; at least six million people died prematurely over the next twenty years.

Carter did not hinder Califano's war on tobacco. But neither did he use the presidential bully pulpit to amplify his HEW secretary's message. Years later, Carter ran into Califano and confessed, "Joe, about smoking. You were right and I was wrong."

Carter often thought Califano was one of his best cabinet secretaries. He was energetic and efficient. "Califano does very well," the president noted in his diary in late 1977. "He's got a worse job than I have, and I sympathize with him." But there was still a cultural disconnect. One evening in early August 1978, the Carters invited *Washington Post* publisher Katharine Graham and some of her editors to dinner at the White House. Referring to her friendship with Califano, Graham told Carter, "Mr. President, we hear that Joe Califano is taking a bum rap in your administration. Because he worked so closely with us, he's blamed for many leaks." Graham assured Carter that it wasn't so.

"I'm very high on Joe," Carter replied. "I like Joe a lot. My staff is beginning to appreciate how good he is, and even Charlie Kirbo now likes him."

"Why wouldn't Charlie Kirbo like him?" Graham asked.

"Kirbo had problems with Joe," Carter said. "First, because he was so liberal coming out of the liberal Johnson administration with the Great Society. Then because he was Catholic, Italian, and a northerner. But Kirbo has come to respect him."

Graham and the other *Post* editors were stunned by Carter's simple candidness. But actually, the Posties were misreading Carter's southern politeness. Carter knew very well that there was friction between Califano and the Georgia boys. Kirbo thought Califano was "a strong man in a tough place." He might be doing a good job, but "he had his own kingdom. . . . He was sort of like Kissinger when he went out on a trip." Califano always traveled in style and with an "entourage." It was, Kirbo said, "a little different style than Carter liked."

Some in the White House called Califano a "megalomaniac." One White House aide, Les Francis, said, "Califano was a prick." Jordan and Powell positively disliked him. They always suspected him of leaking to the *Post*. They thought him imperious. One day, after reading in the papers about yet another hire Califano had made without clearing it through the White House, Jordan ripped the offending article out of the newspaper and scrawled on it, "Joe—I don't feel like I should have to read about these appts in the paper. The president asked that you clear these with me. You have been completely insensitive to our modest requests."

On occasion, Carter himself felt compelled to reprimand Califano. After Califano hired yet another white male as a senior aide, Carter wrote, "This can't go on. It is embarrassing to me."

Jordan and Powell wanted to get rid of Califano. But for the moment, there was not much they could do. "They would be wise not to get into a spitting match with Califano," said one unnamed official. "There is no doubt who would win." Or so it was thought.

CARTER'S ANTIDOTE TO political pressures from Capitol Hill was chatting with Kirbo. "Some mornings he would wake me up at 5:00 A.M.," Kirbo recalled. "He was bad about calling you early in the morning and saying, 'What the heck are you doing in bed at this time of day?' It was usually when he had a problem." Late that spring he went fishing with Kirbo at Blackbeard Island on the Georgia coast. Carter caught the largest bream he'd ever seen. Afterward, he noted in his diary, "I enjoyed talking with Kirbo about the problems I face as president, with big business, who are a greedy bunch; or the special interest groups; Congress; some of the foreign leaders. Quite often when I talk to him, this in itself is helpful, but in addition he's sometimes able to solve my problems. He has unique interrelationships both inside and outside of government, and he's close enough to understand me well, and very discreet." Kirbo poked his nose in just about anything that interested him. A few days before Carter made this diary entry, Kirbo wrote to the president about a meeting he had taken with a well-connected lobbyist, Jack Bridges, who was then working directly for the Saudi royal family. Kirbo claimed that Bridges was "working on an arrangement to furnish our oil reserve. . . . I was quite impressed by him." That same month, Kirbo also wrote to Carter to complain that too many businesses were charging 18 percent on their charge accounts—thus fueling inflation. Kirbo thought Carter could do something to force interest rates down.

That spring, after Andrew Young generated controversy from his new perch as United Nations ambassador, Kirbo reassured Carter, "I feel confident that after being bumped about a bit he will settle down and do the job you expected of him." An amateur constitutional lawyer, Kirbo wrote Carter a detailed brief on a proposed federal election law reform.

Carter trusted Kirbo implicitly, partly because he could impart unexpected advice. Delegated to study what could be done about the rising cost of federal pension programs, Kirbo later came back to the president and told him, "We've talked about it and reviewed it with statisticians, and I think the best thing is just sit on it."

"What!" exclaimed an incredulous president.

"Let it sit," Kirbo reiterated.

And Carter did. If Kirbo said nothing could be done, the president believed him. No one else could have persuaded Carter to just let something "sit."

Kirbo somehow lightened the president's burden. Carter could relax around Kirbo in a way he could not with others. One evening Carter invited a handful of reporters for an intimate dinner in the upstairs residence. It was supposed to be an off-the-record affair—a chance for seasoned journalists to chat with the president in an informal setting. But the president had failed to offer his guests anything to drink stronger than iced tea. Carter seemed stiff and wooden—until Kirbo flung open the door and strode into the room, whereupon Carter suddenly brightened, obviously delighted to see his old friend. "Charlie," he exclaimed, "get yourself a bourbon." The thirsty reporters were no doubt as glad as the president to see Kirbo.

Chapter 8
Lancegate

President Carter and Bert Lance

CHARLES HARRITY/ASSOCIATED PRESS

BESIDES CHARLIE KIRBO, Carter's only other truly intimate confidant was Bert Lance. The burly, six-foot-four-inch-tall OMB chief had nearly unfettered access to the president. They met every Tuesday afternoon in the Oval Office and usually had lunch together on Thursdays. The president also enjoyed playing tennis with Lance, who had a "vicious" serve. Lance quipped that on the tennis court he appeared to have the "size of an elephant and the grace of a gazelle." Carter considered the forty-five-year-old Lance to be "one of the closest friends I have in the world." Lance boasted that the president knew he was the kind of friend who would "be willing to chase hogs for you in the middle of the night." They talked on the phone a half dozen times a day. "Our conversations are wide-ranging," Lance told a *New York Times* reporter. "I can be a sounding board."

"It's a brotherly kind of thing," Jordan observed of their relationship. "Bert has more credibility to say no." The two men were complete opposites. Lance was gregarious and always jovial. He was one of the few people who could make Carter laugh. A reporter described him colorfully as "a friendly bear of a guy with the charm of an old song-and-dance man and the irrepressible guile of a safecracker." Kirbo recalled that Lance actually could sing pretty well; he was the kind of guy who could stop by the office holiday party and belt out Christmas carols. He kept a record of people's birthdays and made a habit of calling everyone he knew with his best wishes. Unlike Carter, he was not a detail man; he demanded one-page summaries from his staff and rarely read the accompanying bulky reports. But he knew how to cajole information and gossip from all sorts of Washingtonians—and he was genuinely liked. "He knew how to deal with big shots," Kirbo recalled, "and people who had money." Carter observed that his friend had "an easy, boyish way about him, and used his sense of humor effectively with all kinds of people. . . . Of all the Georgians I brought to the White House, he was the best at cementing ties with key members of Congress, with Cabinet members, and with business and financial leaders."

Lance was invaluable to a president who needed at least one person in the room who could tell him no, even if it was done in a good-natured manner. But Lance came to the White House with a personal vulnerability. His private finances were a smorgasbord of irregularities, peculiar but perhaps not uncommon for a small-town southern banker. The Calhoun First National Bank was essentially a family operation, owned and run by Lance's in-laws, the Davids. Back in the 1920s, A. B. David—the grandfather of Lance's wife, LaBelle David—had acquired a major interest in the bank. Its operations were minuscule, but the bank was nevertheless an important institution in a town of only six thousand people. When Grandfather David retired, he turned over the bank's presidency to a local country lawyer, Otto C. Langford—whose granddaughter Judy Langford later married Jack Carter, a son of the future president. Bert Lance paid his dues as a bank teller in the 1950s and later, in the 1960s, rose to become president. By that time, the bank and the David family fortunes were in decline. They looked to their charismatic son-in-law to turn things around—and for a time he did. By the 1970s, Lance was not as wealthy or solvent as his spending made him appear to both friends and the public. His banker's salary was never more than $60,000. Over the years, he had been successful on a small-town scale, growing Calhoun's assets from $11.9 million to $54.1 million. It was still a mom-and-pop operation. But Bert and LaBelle nevertheless lived in a sixty-room mansion surrounded by five hundred acres of rolling pastures near Calhoun. With twenty bedrooms, fifteen bathrooms, and three kitchens, their Calhoun home was an advertisement for ostentatious living.

Carter later defended his friend, citing "Bert's hometown friends," who explained that it had been his custom to make loans around Calhoun based on his "intimate knowledge of the borrowers." And he did not always demand the kind of collateral big-city bankers would have required. If banking regulators had looked, they probably would have deemed Lance's practices just sloppy and negligent—not criminal. Lance himself later quipped, "Country banks are different from city banks."

Despite his limited resources, Lance put on a good show, projecting an image of a solid, conservative banker, dressed in charcoal pinstripe suits and driving a bank-owned Lincoln Continental. LaBelle's spending sprees were legendary—but ostentatious only by small-town standards. The Lances were Calhoun's most prominent citizens, but also admired and well liked. Washington was a different universe. Not surprisingly, Bert acquired rivals inside Washington who soon found reason to undermine the affable small-town banker's influence with the president. It was Lance who convinced Carter in early 1977 to rescind the promised $50 tax rebate, arguing that the $10 billion savings could be used to pay down the federal deficit. And it was Lance who helped to persuade Carter to scuttle the congressionally popular B-1 bomber as too expensive. Lance also agreed with Kirbo that the administration should encourage the Federal Reserve to keep interest rates down. Lance could be seen as a fiscal conservative on budgetary issues, but he instinctively saw high interest rates as a threat to small-business growth. In one of his first nationally televised interviews, Lance had come out for a tax cut on the grounds that "the economy needs to be stimulated." This brought him into conflict with Treasury Secretary Michael Blumenthal, who agreed with the New York financial community that interest rates were too low.

Blumenthal also knew that Lance had ambitions to replace him as treasury secretary—or to become the next Federal Reserve chief. That spring, Blumenthal began leaking derogatory information about Lance's Georgia banking practices to *The New York Times*'s conservative columnist William Safire. The former Nixon speechwriter found plenty of grist for a series of columns on what he dubbed "Lancegate."

Unfortunately, during Lance's confirmation hearings he had promised a Senate committee that he would dispose of all his stock holdings in various Georgia banks in order to avoid any appearance of a conflict of interest. He said he would do this by October. But at the end of June 1977, Lance confided in the president that he would suffer heavy losses if he was compelled to sell large blocks of banking stocks all at once. Carter consulted with Kirbo, who inspected Lance's financial statement and firmly advised Lance that he ought to sell immediately all his bank stocks. "He did owe a good deal of money," Kirbo later said. "But the evaluations he had on his bank stock and other property still put him in a good position. But it turned out that the Calhoun bank stock really wasn't so hot." Lance argued that if he sold his stock that summer, the taxes on the capital gains "would nearly wipe him out."

Reluctantly, Kirbo agreed Lance should go back to the Senate committee and explain the situation and ask for more time to sell the stock— and in the meantime place his holdings in a blind trust. The Senate committee agreed to this arrangement, but soon the press got wind of the delay and reporters from *The Washington Post* and elsewhere began digging into Lance's finances. They found that Lance had taken out personal loans without adequate collateral and had been careless in observing banking regulations. The press stories led to more questions, and Lance had to answer further questions before a Senate committee at the end of July. "Bert just called me," Kirbo reported to Carter on July 25, "and seems to think things went well with the committee." Lance had also found a potential buyer for his bank stock—though the deal was not yet at the "handshaking stage." Kirbo was hopeful. As he left for a two-week vacation in Greece, he told Carter jokingly, "If you and Bert want to buy any banks, get in touch with me."

Hamilton Jordan, however, was seriously worried. In an "eyes only" memo, he told Carter that he was "shocked and frightened at the possibility that Bert might have serious problems." He went on to warn the president, "This unfortunate incident—which involves Georgians and close personal friends—could do great damage to your presidency if not handled properly. . . . You pledged that you would not tolerate wrongdoing or even the appearance of wrongdoing."

In late July the Treasury Department's comptroller of the currency, John Heimann, opened an investigation into the Calhoun bank. By mid-August, both the Senate committee and the comptroller announced they had found no illegal conduct. Heimann's report, however, while dry and understated, made it clear that Lance had made a mockery of sound banking practices. As he later explained, Lance had shuffled various loans from one account to another—though he had "never stuck it in his own pocket." The comptroller's report was hardly an exoneration. Unfortunately, that was how Carter's White House counsel, Bob Lipshutz, read it. Lipshutz sent the report to the president but slapped a cover note on it, asserting that Heimann had found no evidence of any fraud or illegality. Carter read the misleading cover note—and, in a rare exception, failed to read carefully the actual report.

Until then, Carter had carefully refrained from commenting on the investigation. But on August 18, he appeared at a press conference with Lance and released the comptroller's report, casting it as an unequivocal exoneration of his friend: "Bert Lance enjoys my complete confidence and support." Carter bluntly told reporters, "As far as I am concerned as president, the intensive investigation and the comptroller's report has answered the questions that were raised against Bert Lance." Concluding his remarks, the president turned to Lance and, smiling broadly, said, "Bert, I'm proud of you."

Carter's effusive praise was misplaced. "I almost died," recalled Heimann when he saw the president's performance. "I couldn't believe it. . . . I was sick, sick to my stomach." He blamed Lipshutz, who he said had "clearly misread it, and didn't recognize the obvious." Predictably, when reporters had a chance to examine the report, they found that while the comptroller had concluded that a prosecution was unwarranted, he had also discovered that Lance had made a practice of borrowing personal funds from correspondent banks where Calhoun First National Bank had recently opened accounts. While this wasn't technically illegal, "this recurring pattern of shifting bank relationships and personal borrowing raises unresolved questions as to what constitutes acceptable banking practices." The Calhoun bank, said Assistant U.S. Attorney Jeffrey Bogart, "was run like a piggy bank." Lance and his relatives were routinely running overdrafts on individual accounts ranging as high as $450,000. His wife, LaBelle Lance, had overdrafts fluctuating from $25,000 to $110,000 during the autumn of 1974—the same period in which Lance had been running for governor. The clear implication was that Lance had used unsecured bank overdrafts to finance his campaign. Lance himself had a $3.4 million loan from a Chicago bank—but according to the comptroller, $1.6 million of this loan was unsecured by any collateral. Again, while this was not illegal, reporters naturally raised numerous questions about the impropriety of such loans. They also asked pointed questions about Lance's use of the Calhoun bank's aircraft during his gubernatorial campaign—and whether the plane had also been used by Carter during the 1976 presidential campaign. Lance stonewalled, insisting that it would not be appropriate for him to comment about what was still an ongoing investigation. Lance tried to lighten the atmosphere by explaining that when he first joined Carter's political campaign, the man from Plains had assured him, "Bert, we're going to have a lot of fun." As time went by, Lance joked, "I realized that his definition of fun and mine might not be exactly the same." The assembled reporters laughed, but the optics were not good.

Afterward, Jordan came back to his office visibly upset and annoyed. He told Butler, "Bert had a chance to knock the ball out of the park, and he blew it." Butler agreed. He thought Lance had been "eaten alive" and had failed to defend himself "with the rigor and strength necessary to combat the press frenzy." Butler began to think Lance would have to go.

He thought that Bert had become "the victim of a press frenzy. . . . But I'm afraid that his defense of himself was probably just as sloppy as his personal banking. . . . Too much else came out that was minor but damaging." As ABC News characterized the comptroller's report, "Nothing Lance did was illegal, but maybe it should have been."

But oddly, the president didn't see it that way. Carter told Kirbo that he wanted to fight it. "He thought they were mistreating Bert, and they were." The president believed his friend was innocent. "The *Washington Post* is conducting a vendetta against Bert," Carter noted in his diary on September 1. "This morning, for instance, they had nine separate stories about Lance—headline stories—throughout the paper. In contrast, *The New York Times* didn't mention him."

Over the Labor Day weekend, things got worse. Senators Abraham Ribicoff and Charles Percy came to the White House and informed Carter that they had new evidence linking Lance to bank embezzlement. After seeing Carter in the Oval Office, the two senators made their accusations public in an impromptu press conference on the White House lawn. Embezzlement was a felony. Only later did it become clear that the charge was based on a statement from a convicted felon—who later recanted his story. The felon, Bill Campbell, had been convicted of embezzling hundreds of thousands of dollars from the Calhoun bank— and it turned out that it was Lance's testimony that had put him in prison for eight years. Of course, by the time this information was reported, the public had already seen headlines associating Lance with embezzlement.

In the end, Lance spent a total of twenty grueling hours testifying before a Senate committee. Some politicians, such as Senator John Glenn, voiced concerns that the investigation was going beyond the bounds of reason: "I think we've gone completely ethics happy around here. We've gone crazy." Even some reporters expressed doubts. Haynes Johnson, a well-respected *Washington Post* reporter, wrote, "Even some members of the press are speaking of a 'vendetta' atmosphere. . . . The press is either out to 'get' Carter and his Georgians by 'getting' Lance, or is trying to 'get' news rivals who may have triumphed in earlier competitive contests." It was certainly a media frenzy—but on the other hand, there was no denying that Lance's banking practices were liberal verging on shoddy. "Bert Lance has done nothing illegal," editorialized *The New Republic*. "That's what we're told, and we've seen nothing to contradict it." And yet the magazine nevertheless caricatured Lance as part of the "LBJ school of southern cronies, shabby but not indictable."

"I defended Bert early on," Landon Butler noted in his diary on September 4, 1977, "when the primary charge was that he had swapped [the Calhoun] bank's correspondent accounts for personal loans. That was defensible. And I also defended the overdrafts at the Calhoun Bank. But more and more keeps coming out—the double collateral, the bank's airplane and Bert's personal solvency." Things were getting too complicated, and Hamilton confided to Landon that "it didn't look good." Resignation was probably inevitable. Carter knew his closest aides were pessimistic. But in early September, the president "could not bring myself" to ask Bert to step down.

Lance wanted to fight the allegations and soon retained Clark Clifford to defend him in the court of public opinion. But the news only got worse. The White House conceded that the Carter campaign had failed to reimburse Lance's bank for five flights on a bank-owned airplane. Jody Powell announced that reimbursements worth $1,793.70 were an "oversight in campaign bookkeeping." A petty thing—but again, the optics were bad.

By mid-September, the press was reporting that Lance "may be broke." Back in January, Lance had submitted a financial statement showing assets of $8 million and liabilities of $5.4 million, for a net worth of $2.6 million. Unfortunately, most of Lance's assets were pledged as collateral to his loans. Worse, the assets were largely bank stocks that Lance had pledged to sell in order to take the OMB job. But selling off large blocks of depressed bank stocks was not going to be easy. A congressional investigator working for Senator Chuck Percy reported, "At this point in time, Lance is in a very precarious cash-flow situation. . . . The fact that virtually all of his assets are tied up as collateral casts serious doubt on his ability to meet his interest payments." Lance had dug himself into a hole so deep that he probably could not afford to remain in Washington, even if exonerated. "Lance is clearly on the ropes," Butler noted, "almost down for the count. . . . I still find myself very confused on the Lance issue." This was a sentiment shared by most everyone in the White House.

Needless to say, Lance failed to inform Carter of his dire finances and tried to sound upbeat about his prospects. One morning before another round of Senate testimony, Lance stopped by the White House and met with Carter in his private study adjoining the Oval Office. Brzezinski happened to walk into the study without knocking, as was his habit, and was taken aback to see the two old friends down on their knees, praying together. Slightly embarrassed, Brzezinski nevertheless thought it was "touching, really." Zbig knew Carter regarded Lance almost like a brother, and he realized that his president was personally distressed by the scandal. That afternoon, after watching Lance testify at the televised

Senate hearings, Carter again tried to talk himself into thinking that Lance could ride out the storm. "Rosalynn and I both decided it might be better for Bert to stay and fight it out." He even interrupted a morning staff meeting to demand that everyone be supportive of Bert. "I will fire anyone," he said, who criticizes the OMB chief.

But the next day, Sunday, September 18, after talking it over with Kirbo—who had flown up from Atlanta—he had a change of heart. "I talked to Kirbo, Fritz [Mondale], Ham and Jody, who unanimously feel that Bert has won a great victory and now should step down." That same afternoon, Carter had a long conversation with Senator Byrd, who reminded him that he had made personal morality and "honest government" a central feature of his presidential campaign—and so people naturally expected higher standards. Democrats in the Senate, Byrd advised, would not be disappointed if Lance now resigned. Kirbo himself, after calmly assessing the situation, told Lance, "Well, Bert, my primary responsibility is Jimmy, and I'm not sure your interest and his are compatible." Bert took this advice badly, and thereafter, Kirbo and Lance were never so close as before. But Kirbo's loyalty was to the president, so he had played the heavy.

Carter called Lance and asked him to come to the White House the next morning, Monday, September 19, at 6:15. Anxious and nervous, Carter clearly dreaded the meeting: "For one of the rare times in my life, I did not sleep much that night." That morning they had a long talk, and Carter tried to suggest that Bert had succeeded in turning things around. He had saved his reputation. His critics had suffered a setback, but nevertheless, his antagonists "were regrouping for another assault." The implication, gently hinted, was that now was the time to retire from the battlefield with dignity. Lance didn't argue, but he pushed back, pointing out that while his family's overdrafts were large, they were still less than the bank owed his wife in "undistributed earnings." Bert obviously thought he had done nothing wrong. But he agreed to think things over. He would need to talk to Clifford and LaBelle before making a final decision. "When he left," Carter later recalled, "I had no doubt that he would do what was right, for him and for me." That evening, Carter discussed the matter with Rosalynn, and they agreed that they were quite sure Bert would resign.

The president, of course, was juggling all sorts of issues, including sensitive talks with Israel's foreign minister, Moshe Dayan, about getting all the parties to the Arab-Israeli conflict into negotiations in Geneva. Early the next morning, Tuesday, September 20, Carter again came into his private office, and Kraft observed that he had "that red-eyed campaign-fatigue look." But after a full day of meetings, that afternoon Carter took time out to play a ninety-minute tennis match with Lance, Ham Jordan, and speechwriter Jim Fallows. Afterward, Bert and Jimmy sat on a courtside bench and talked for forty-five minutes. Lance intimated that he wanted to resign. "I didn't argue with him," Carter noted in his diary.

But the next day turned out to be excruciating, "probably one of the worst days I've ever spent." It began and ended badly. Carter was awakened at 5:30 A.M. and came into his private study adjoining the Oval Office a half hour later. The ever-punctual president had arranged to see Bert at 6:15 A.M.—but he arrived a full hour late, "which was not like him." That morning, Bert had risen at 5:30 A.M. and prepared a breakfast tray for LaBelle. As was his habit, he placed a fresh-cut rose on the bedside table. LaBelle and Bert had known each other as children, and twenty-seven years into their marriage they were still a devoted couple. That morning, Bert knew LaBelle was hurt and angry. She could hear the reporters milling around outside their Georgetown home, waiting to pester Bert with questions when he emerged. Lance was front-page news every day. But LaBelle had been particularly wounded just a few days earlier by a story that resurrected the suicide of her brother Banks David, insinuating that he had taken his own life three years earlier due to the David-Lance family's financial woes. "All that was untrue," LaBelle later wrote in a 1978 memoir. "That article hurt me more than anything else I had read or endured during the long hot summer of allegations." Now she flatly urged Bert not to resign.*

When Lance finally arrived at the White House, he confessed that LaBelle was angry and so upset that he no longer knew what he should

---

* LaBelle was understandably upset. But it was also true that her brother's widow was shocked to discover after his 1974 suicide that Banks David had overdrafts at the Calhoun bank of some $70,000 and loans of $170,000. As president of Calhoun First National Bank, Bert Lance had been overly generous about tolerating overdrafts by his wife's family. LaBelle's other brother, Claude Barker David, and her mother and stepfather also had large overdrafts at the Calhoun bank in the early 1970s.

do. Carter gently said that he believed Lance had made the right decision on the tennis court, and that he should resign. He reminded Bert that a press conference had been scheduled, and, obviously, they needed to have a decision by then. After fifteen minutes, Bert said he understood and left to talk with Clifford and LaBelle.

Carter then had a typically busy day, meeting with the Egyptian foreign minister and lunching with Senator Kennedy to discuss the tax-reform bill and the SALT negotiations. But Bert's fate weighed heavily on his mind. They talked on the phone again in the midmorning and again both before and after lunch. In the midafternoon Bert came back to the Oval Office, this time with LaBelle—who bluntly told Carter that while she understood that the decision had been made, she was nevertheless "adamantly opposed" to her husband's resignation. It was a difficult conversation, but afterward, Carter met with Bert's lawyer, Clifford, and received from him Lance's formal letter of resignation. It was done.

But it was not done. Just before leaving for the press conference, now delayed by two hours, Carter took a phone call from LaBelle, who told the president "in bitter terms" that he had "destroyed Bert" and "betrayed" his "best friend." LaBelle didn't mince her words. "I want to tell you one thing," she told the president. "You can go with the rest of the jackals, and I hope you're happy." It was only a two-minute phone conversation, but emotionally distressing. Carter tried to console LaBelle, "but I was absolutely sure that Bert and I had made the right decision." Jody and Hamilton were furious about LaBelle's pressure on the president. Jody caustically remarked that Carter and Lance could have stuck together, all right, "right down the tube." And indeed, when Carter announced to the assembled press corps that he had accepted Lance's resignation, he nevertheless reiterated that nothing "has shaken my belief in Bert's ability or his integrity."

After the announcement, Lance sent a note to his staff thanking them for their support over the last eight months. "You are a great group," he said. "I am sorry that things didn't work out. . . . Make sure we attain the '81 balanced budget." The damage to the Carter presidency was clear and, as it turned out, lasting. Carter's failure to push Lance out earlier in the summer, when the scandal first became front-page news, led to a steady drip of bad news and problematic comments, the accumulation of which sparked increasing distrust among voters. The president's poll numbers dropped seven points in one month and eventually down to the low fifties—nearly a twenty-point drop from his Gallup approval rating of 70 percent prior to the scandal. His squeaky-clean image had been tarnished. As conservative pundit George Will put it in *Newsweek*, "The Lance affair has reminded Americans that Carter is not a Moses, entrusted by God with new standards of goodness." In the eyes of some, he had been revealed as a politician like any other.

This was unfair. Lancegate was not Watergate. And Bert's questionable banking practices did not touch Carter personally. Indeed, Carter's only crime had been to place loyalty to a friend above the politically opportune. In retrospect, the Lance affair was a petty scandal. If not exactly much ado about nothing, it implicated a small-town banker cutting corners. "Some of the things that they accused him of were accurate but not criminal," Kirbo said. "These were things that bankers regularly do. And some of it was overdrafts, which bankers handle between themselves. He had some serious problems that he couldn't control, but he could straighten out. I understand that. But they had some awfully strong people after Bert, and I just knew that he had to go." To be sure, it was a scandal about money, but one dealing with relatively small sums, not millions of dollars.

Kirbo later ruminated that perhaps the Lance affair just proved that he had been right not to sign up for Washington—and Lance had been wrong to do so. "I understand why he went and why I didn't because he was a bold, confident fellow, as he demonstrated. He just doesn't give up, and he was confident that he could then make enough money and work everything out. And I was pretty sure I'd lose my shirt if I went up there."

The president's domestic policy adviser, Stu Eizenstat, later reflected that Lance "should never have been named to a position requiring Senate confirmation," where his shoddy banking practices and troubled personal finances were bound to be aired in public and used against him and Carter. Instead, Lance should have been provided with an office in the West Wing, where he could have helped Carter, serving as a sounding board. Eizenstat later blamed himself and others in the president's inner circle for not having the "fortitude to tell the president early enough that the banking irregularities of his best friend and most trusted adviser were so serious that he was a political liability and had to go."

Lance was later indicted, and in April 1980, after a sixteen-week trial, a federal district court jury found him innocent on nine charges of misusing bank funds to make loans to his wife, his son, and three friends. The jury was unable to reach a verdict on three other related charges involving perjury. Lance had spent $1.5 million in legal fees, but his long ordeal was over.

Some years after the scandal, Lance got to know *Times* columnist Bill Safire socially. They exchanged Christmas cards and kept in touch. It was a most improbable friendship. But one day Lance asked Safire point-blank why he had been targeted. "You really don't know?" Safire said.

"No," replied Lance. "If I knew, I wouldn't be asking you."

"We didn't want you to become chairman of the Fed."

Such were the ways of Washington, and many of the Georgia boys believed the Washington establishment had orchestrated a campaign of character assassination to bring down one of their own. It was a bitter lesson—and a turning point for the fortunes of the Carter presidency.

Chapter 9
Departures in Foreign Policy

We are now free of that inordinate fear of Communism which once led us to embrace any dictator.

—President Jimmy Carter

Cy Vance, Fritz Mondale, Carter, and Zbigniew Brzezinski
CHARLES BENNETT/ASSOCIATED PRESS

"If you want a magnolia to decorate foreign policy, I'm the wrong person," Patt Derian explained to Deputy Secretary of State Warren Christopher. "I expect to get things done." Patricia Murphy Derian, age forty-seven, was an unlikely choice for a high-ranking appointment to the State Department. But on February 2, 1977, President Carter named this fearless civil rights activist to be the State Department's coordinator for human rights and humanitarian affairs. It was a controversial choice—a woman with no foreign policy credentials. But Derian was destined to become the iconic face of a new brand of foreign policy, one based on the radical notion that human rights and morality should be the guiding principle in America's dealings with the rest of the world. Derian was a twenty-year veteran of the civil rights movement, a white woman with a nursing degree from Virginia who moved in 1959 to

Mississippi—where she learned to stare down racist politicians with her hard blue eyes and wit.

Derian first met Carter during a two-hour meeting at Atlanta's airport in 1974. She was looking for a presidential candidate she could support who might defeat George Wallace in the Mississippi primary. "There was every reason to believe that Wallace would get 80 percent of our delegates," Derian recalled, "and I decided that unless Carter turned out to be a Wallace in a double-knit suit, I would go with him—whether I personally liked him or not. To be perfectly honest, I thought he was going to be soft on race and bad on women." But while chatting, Carter mentioned that he had refused to join the White Citizens' Council when he returned to Georgia from the navy. Derian understood what that meant. She understood the "tyranny of those little towns on people who were nonconformists. . . . It told me he had his principles intact."

Derian went on to become a deputy director of the Carter-Mondale campaign, and after the inauguration, Carter had no hesitation about giving her a high-profile job. Initially, Ham Jordan floated the notion that Derian should become the State Department's chief of protocol, replacing former child movie star Shirley Temple Black. But Derian shot that idea down, quipping, "I don't tap-dance." Carter instead decided to make her the spearpoint of his human rights initiatives, appointing her as the "coordinator" for human rights issues at the State Department. Within six months, he elevated the position to the assistant secretary level. Unusually, he invited her to the White House for her swearing-in ceremony, signaling to the bureaucracy that he had Derian's back. Neither did Carter complain when her staff grew from two to ten. Early on, she decided that she would have to "beat the bureaucracy, force them to deal with me personally." Carter knew Derian would be a disruptive force within the State Department. And he was fine with that. Charlie Clements, an aide to Derian, surmised that the president "wasn't looking so much for diplomacy as moral fiber. Patt had moral fiber in excess."

Derian had to grapple with a host of difficult human rights violations in dozens of countries, from the Philippines to South Korea to Pakistan. She complained that "the NSC [Brzezinski] frequently is an obstacle." Needless to say, veteran diplomats thought she had an "adversarial relationship with much of the building."

Almost from day one, Derian made Argentina a priority. The new military regime in Buenos Aires was waging what later became labeled a "dirty war" against left-wing guerrillas—but many of the victims were civilian members of society. Thousands of people had been "disappeared," never to be found, dead or alive. Derian was shocked to learn from an early-1977 memo that former secretary of state Henry Kissinger had met with the regime's foreign minister in June 1976 and asked, "How long will it take you [the Argentines] to clean up the problem?" When told that they could take care of the terrorists by the end of the year, Kissinger gave his assent.

Derian thought Kissinger had made Washington complicit in the regime's crimes. "It sickened me," she later said, "that with an imperial wave of his hand, an American could sentence people to death on the basis of a cheap whim. As time went on, I saw Kissinger's footprints in a lot of countries." But the problem wasn't just Kissinger. Derian soon realized that many State Department officials believed that human rights policies were "impractical" and merely a "political device and one with a short life." Derian complained that her mission was being undermined and that Washington was "sending a dangerous and double message."

Late in March, Derian flew to Buenos Aires, where she spent a week interviewing a wide range of sources about the country's gross violations of human rights. To her pleasant surprise, she found the American ambassador, Robert C. Hill, a sympathetic ally. Hill greeted her in the embassy and bluntly told her, "I'm going to tell you a secret." And then he confirmed that when then–secretary of state Kissinger had visited Argentina the previous year, he had given "the Argentines the green light" to press their "dirty war" against their left-wing critics. The predictable result was a killing spree. In recent months, hundreds of Argentines had "disappeared" and at least fifteen hundred people had been killed by the regime's militia and police. Among others, Derian interviewed Jacobo Timerman, the editor of *La Opinión*. As an outspoken critic of the regime, Timerman predicted that it wouldn't be long before he was arrested or "disappeared." He was right.

By the time Derian returned to Argentina in August on a second official visit, Timerman was languishing in prison. Derian met with the regime's interior minister and immediately complained about the Timerman case, insisting that she had seen reports that he had been tortured. Timerman was not released and sent into exile until late 1979, but he always credited Derian with saving his life. On the morning of August 10, 1977, Derian arrived at the headquarters of an Argentine naval school of mechanics for what would turn out to be a surreal meeting with its notorious chief, Admiral Emilio Massera. Derian didn't waste much time before she asked about the regime's torturing of political prisoners. Massera replied that the Argentine navy never used torture. At this, Derian replied that she had reports that people were being tortured during interrogations in the very building in which they now sat. She said she had seen a diagram of the naval school: "It's possible that they're torturing people down there even now, while we're talking." It happened to be true, but Massera looked at her grimly and then, with a slight smile, made a show of rubbing his hands together and said, "Ah, you know that story about Pontius Pilate."

The Argentine regime was furious at her visit and tried to bypass her with direct appeals to President Carter. In September 1977 Argentina's dictator, General Jorge Videla, came to Washington and was accorded a meeting in the White House. Carter knew of Videla's cold-blooded reputation. This was a general who had told his army colleagues in October 1975, "If the Argentine situation demands it, all necessary persons must die to achieve the security of the country." But now, as a visiting head of state, Videla assured Carter that he would release most of the four thousand political prisoners by the end of the year.

Carter directly pressed Videla about the whereabouts of the *La Opinión* editor, Timerman, and was assured that his case would soon be resolved. In return, it appears that the State Department quietly agreed to approve export licenses for the sale of submarine periscopes, three Chinook helicopters, and two Lockheed KC-130 tanker aircraft. This attempt at "quiet diplomacy" produced virtually no change in the regime. A year later, few prisoners had been released and the "dirty war" continued unabated. Derian was not surprised. Carter stopped all aid to the junta on September 30, 1978. By then she was routinely receiving anonymous death threats. (By 1983 the regime would "disappear" some thirty thousand political prisoners.)

Late in 1978, Derian married Hodding Carter III, the State Department's on-camera press spokesman. They became one of Washington's high-profile power couples—though Derian was the one who was always getting into hot water. She once debated the academic Jeane Kirkpatrick on CBS television, and when the neoconservative pundit and future United Nations ambassador started talking about the advantages of working with a "moderately repressive autocratic government which is also friendly to the United States," Derian interrupted, "What the hell is moderately repressive—that you only torture half the people?"

Derian's tenure in the State Department was always tumultuous. Her cluttered office was stacked with unpacked boxes, a signal to her staff that she knew she might be fired at any moment. She clashed often with the bureaucracy and threatened to resign on numerous occasions. She had frequent run-ins with Richard Holbrooke, the assistant secretary of state for East Asia. "I thought she was smart as hell," said her principal deputy, Mark Schneider. "Always articulate and passionate." Zbig Brzezinski thought of her as a loose cannon. But the president stood by her, and she would survive—a bellwether of the president's commitment to human rights.

THAT FIRST SPRING, Carter himself made it clear that he wanted "our country to be the focal point for deep concern about human beings all over the world." He made news at a town hall conclave in Clinton, Massachusetts, on March 16. Answering a question about the Middle East, he plainly said, "There has to be a homeland provided for the Palestinian refugees who have suffered for many, many years." The remark stirred plenty of controversy. And then, on May 22, 1977, in his first major foreign policy address, he proclaimed "human rights as a fundamental tenet of our foreign policy." Speaking at Notre Dame, Carter talked about the importance of forging a new relationship with the "newly influential countries in Latin America, Africa, and Asia." No longer, he argued, should U.S. foreign policy be guided by Cold War assumptions:

> Being confident of our own future, we are now free of that inordinate fear of Communism which once led us to embrace any dictator who joined us in our fear.
>
> For too many years we have been willing to adopt the flawed principles and tactics of our adversaries, sometimes abandoning our values for theirs.

We fought fire with fire, never thinking that fire is better fought with water.

This approach failed, with Vietnam the best example of its intellectual and moral poverty.

The speech was an extraordinary departure from postwar orthodoxy. He called for a policy based on "constant decency" and disparaged "secret deals." He called the strategic arms race with the Soviet Union not only "dangerous" but "morally deplorable." But by uttering the phrase "inordinate fear of Communism," Carter was issuing a startling rebuke of Henry Kissinger's Cold War worldview.

The speech also put the country on notice that Carter's foreign policy agenda was loaded with high aspirations. He intended to normalize relations with communist China, cut arms sales, end apartheid in South Africa, and strengthen détente with the Soviet Union. And if this wasn't enough, Carter signaled his determination to tackle the thorny Arab-Israeli conflict. He talked about the need for a "comprehensive peace"—something far more ambitious than Kissinger's step-by-step interim deals. Neither did he avoid mentioning the hot-button "issue of the Palestinian homeland."

Altogether, it was Carter at his most daring, a speech soaring with his personal ideals. It sounded like Carter—passionate, authentic, and bold. Much of the speech was drafted by a new speechwriter, Hendrik "Rick" Hertzberg. A brilliant wordsmith, this thirty-four-year-old future editor of *The New Republic* and *The New Yorker* had been recruited by Carter's chief speechwriter, James Fallows. Both were Harvard men, and both had learned to write at *The Harvard Crimson*. Hertzberg was a pragmatic but idealistic liberal who found himself in sync with Carter's instincts, particularly on human rights as a guiding theme of the administration's foreign policy. Hertzberg was proud of this, his first major effort as Carter's muse. But the phrase "inordinate fear of Communism" had come from a memo written by speechwriter Jerry Doolittle—who had been unhappy with Brzezinski's conventional, hawkish tone. Fallows passed Doolittle's memo to Carter, who liked the phrase and inserted it into the speech without Brzezinski's knowledge. The speechwriters were proud of their end run around Zbig.

The Polish anticommunist in Brzezinski thought the speech naïve. Indeed, he had tried to steer Carter in a more conservative direction with an April 29 memo laying out "Ten Central Objectives." Vice President Mondale had responded with his own memo. Brzezinski's formulations, Mondale objected, "suggest that a major motivation for our espousal of human rights is based on a tactical advantage against the Soviet Union." For Mondale, human rights wasn't just a rhetorical tactical weapon against Moscow. Mondale was siding with Derian—and the president's own instincts.

In the end, the Notre Dame speech "reflected Carter's priorities, not Zbig's," said Jessica Tuchman, one of Brzezinski's aides. "Zbig never would have selected these themes. But Carter cared about these things." Brzezinski understood Derian's cachet with the president—and according to Tuchman, "he was careful to defer to Carter on this. He also knew that Secretary Cy Vance was much closer to Carter's instincts." Brzezinski understood that he had to be prepared to lose many a battle to Vance. "Brzezinski is better informed than anybody Jimmy found," recalled Charlie Kirbo. "Now, he hasn't got the judgment that Vance had, and about ninety-nine percent of the time Jimmy did what Vance recommended."

As a counterweight to Derian's influence, Brzezinski created a new Office of Global Issues within the National Security Council and designated the thirty-year-old Tuchman to be its chief. Tuchman, the daughter of the popular historian Barbara Tuchman, had a doctorate in biophysics, but in 1976 she had decided to take a sabbatical from science to work on Congressman Mo Udall's presidential campaign. Tuchman saw Udall as the smartest liberal candidate in a very crowded field. Udall hired her to conduct "opposition research" on Carter. But during the general campaign she had done a little consulting for Brzezinski, who then hired her onto his NSC staff. She was smart and politically savvy. Because of her background in science, she also handled nonproliferation issues—but human rights took up much of her time in the White House. And more often than not, she disagreed with Brzezinski. "Human rights," Tuchman said, "was always messy. There was just enormous tension between Zbig and Cy. Zbig's definition of a human rights violation was confined to physical torture. But for Cy, human rights violations began at breakfast. He had a much broader definition."

In an effort to adjudicate disputes over human rights issues, Brzezinski persuaded Vance to create a new working group over at the State Department. Any decisions on whether to impose sanctions for human rights violations would have to be debated inside this gatekeeping committee. It became known as the "Christopher Committee," so named after its chairman, Deputy Secretary of State Warren Christopher. Tuchman was designated by Brzezinski to be his representative on the committee. Its meetings were often contentious. "We had arguments all the time," Tuchman recalled. (Tuchman would resign two years later, saying she had "deep disagreements" with Brzezinski over nuclear proliferation and arms sales.) Brzezinski deftly used the Christopher Committee to take human rights considerations off the table in such key areas as military assistance programs and foreign aid. Brzezinski's machinations became a source of mounting frustration for Derian and her allies in the bureaucracy.

Carter's national security adviser often disagreed with his president, both in public and within the privacy of the Oval Office. He saw his mission as one of pushing Carter to use all of America's resources to contain the Russians. "At the time," said Tuchman, "Zbig saw the Soviet Union as any Pole saw the Soviets." Brzezinski saw only one good purpose in pushing human rights, and that was when it was used as a cudgel against the Soviet empire, and he thought human rights purists like Derian could be a nuisance, if not an outright liability. His military aide, Major General William Odom, later captured his boss's view by explaining, "I saw human rights as a brilliant policy. I saw it as the obverse to the Soviets' support of the international class struggle . . . a very pragmatic tactic . . . a way to really beat up morally on the Soviets."

Carter's relationship with Brzezinski was adversarial, both on and off the tennis court. "I liked him personally," Carter recalled. "We played tennis with each other. But we had an ongoing argument because he foot-faulted a lot and I would call him on his foot faults." They also competed intellectually. Carter respected Zbig's mind and thought him always interesting, always entertaining. "I recognized Zbig's strengths and some of his possible weaknesses," Carter later said. "Zbig put together a constant barrage of new ideas and suggestions and plans, and ninety percent of them in that totality would have to be rejected." The two men fundamentally disagreed about almost everything, but oddly, the personal chemistry was right. "We had a good time, most of the time," Brzezinski said in an interview a year before he died at the age of eighty-nine. "We disagreed a lot, and I knew I was getting him furious."

After one particularly contentious debate, Zbig retreated to his office. A few minutes later, Carter's secretary, Susan Clough, walked in and said, "I have a message for you from the president." Clough then ostentatiously placed a letter on his desk. "It was green stationery," Brzezinski recalled, "so I knew it was a letter from the president." Brzezinski ripped open the envelope to find a handwritten note: "Zbig, don't you ever know when to stop?"

Brzezinski was untroubled by this incident and saw it in a flattering light. He was doing his job, giving the president his unvarnished opinions. Unlike Kissinger in his relationship with Nixon, Brzezinski was never obsequious. Carter liked that. If they argued, it was only evidence of how comfortable the president was in the company of his national security adviser. But they made an odd pair, the Southern Baptist from Plains and the brash, aristocratic Pole who was always "immaculately dressed, trim, dapper, and well groomed." Political cartoonists had fun with Brzezinski's angular facial features—his high cheekbones and dagger-sharp nose. The White House press corps soon began referring to him as "Woody Woodpecker," mocking him by humming a woodpecker's telltale laughing warble as he entered a room. Hamilton Jordan only stopped calling him Woody Woodpecker when Brzezinski responded by calling Jordan "Porky Pig." Thereafter, Jordan took to calling him "Dr. Strangelove"—and, oddly enough, Zbig had no objection to that.

Zbig had few friends, but nevertheless most everyone conceded that he was sharp. "Most of the people I talked to in the White House," noted Landon Butler in his diary, "don't have much confidence in Zbig and [his deputy] David Aaron. The suspicion is that they don't think things through, and Zbig's 'get tough' approach is short-sighted and immature." Jim Fallows, the president's chief speechwriter, confided to a colleague that he "didn't like Brzezinski, but at least he . . . keeps coming up with ideas, even if they're bad." Hertzberg noted in his diary that Brzezinski could be "bland, disingenuous and a double-dealer." Like Carter, Brzezinski liked to make the occasional joke, but rarely at his own expense.

In addition to his morning intelligence briefings, Brzezinski religiously drafted a weekly report for the president in which he summarized recent events around the world. The memo always began with a section entitled "Opinion," followed by the bulk of the report, headlined "Fact." Brzezinski used the "Opinion" section to lecture Carter, usually on the theme of how his presidency should take a tougher, more bracing stance versus the Russians. In one such weekly report, Brzezinski complained that too much of the Carter administration's foreign policy was "contractual," focused on "negotiating agreements." They had consequently invested much time in negotiating new arms-control agreements, nuclear nonproliferation treaties, a Panama Canal treaty, and Middle East peace. That was all very well, Brzezinski observed, but it was "gnawing" at him that diplomacy was not enough to shape events. "In some cases," he wrote, "what is needed is a demonstration of force, to establish credibility and determination, and even to infuse fear; in some cases, it requires saying publicly one thing and quietly negotiating something else."

Carter often scribbled marginal notes in his neat handwriting, and on this particular memo, he underlined the phrases "demonstration of force" and "saying publicly one thing" and wrote in the margins, "Like Mayaguez?" and "Lying?" It was a firm rebuke. Kissinger had persuaded President Gerald Ford to make a demonstration of force during the May 1975 *Mayaguez* incident in Cambodia. The disastrous military operation led to the pointless deaths of thirty-six American servicemen. And when Zbig concluded that he would be "developing some ideas" on how to demonstrate U.S. military muscle, Carter tartly scribbled in the margin, "You'll be wasting your time."

On occasion, Brzezinski could be highly manipulative. In the autumn of 1977, he briefed one of the president's speechwriters, Jerome Doolittle, on an upcoming speech dealing with Cuban activities in Africa. Usually, Brzezinski had his own people provide the president with a draft, so Doolittle was surprised that Zbig was going out of his way to involve him early in the process. Zbig handed him a ten-page "fact sheet" that included the allegation that 250 Cuban tank officers were operating within Libya against the Egyptians. Brzezinski wanted this "fact" highlighted in the speech as further evidence of Soviet-backed Cuban aggression. When Doolittle had the temerity to question the source of this allegation, Zbig replied that the intelligence came "from my people."

Doolittle went back to his office, but when he called around to check the allegation, he was quickly told by the State Department that Brzezinski's facts were "utterly groundless." He also called Robert Pastor, a high-ranking member of Brzezinski's own staff, who also dismissed the story. Doolittle concluded that Zbig's fact sheet "was just the CIA emptying out its garbage pail of every bit of raw intelligence they might have had that pointed to greater Cuban involvement in Angola and Africa. . . . Bob agreed that it was CIA work. And he added what might have been obvious to me: that Brz had called us in instead of having Bob or some-body do a draft because he was doing an end run around his own staff, which might have balked at putting this bullshit into the President's mouth."

NOT SURPRISINGLY, THE Soviets were suspicious of Carter's Polish-born national security adviser. In the months ahead, Brzezinski's pres-ence in the White House would only pique Moscow's paranoia. Six days after the inauguration, Carter sent a personal letter to General Secretary Leonid Brezhnev, responding warmly to a highly conciliatory speech the Russian leader had recently given on January 18. With Brzezinski's prompting, Carter also specified that he wished to finish the negotia-tions on a SALT II arms agreement "without delay." President Ford and Secretary of State Kissinger had left office with the SALT II negotiations unsigned but virtually done. Carter's letter indicated he wanted to build on what had been agreed to and "proceed toward additional limitations and reductions in strategic weapons." Brezhnev took this to mean that Carter wished to renegotiate what had already been agreed to at the 1974 Vladivostok negotiations, essentially a cap on strategic delivery vehicles (missiles and bombers) of 2,400 for each side. He was further alarmed by another presidential letter, dated February 14, in which Carter explic-itly stated that he wanted to see "much greater reductions in the size of our respective nuclear arsenals." Worse, from Brezhnev's perspective, was Carter's suggestion that it might be helpful to examine the possibil-ity of "separating the cruise missile and Backfire [bomber] issues from the SALT II."

Brezhnev responded with a long, angry eight-page letter in which he accused Carter of "putting forward deliberately unacceptable proposals." The Russian leader objected that Carter was trying to renegotiate what had already been agreed to at Vladivostok. He pointed out, for example, that Washington had already agreed that the limit placed on the number of missiles equipped with multiple warheads ("multiple independently targetable reentry vehicles," or MIRVs) "was clearly conditioned by achievement of agreement on the whole complex of cruise missiles." The Americans had a clear advantage in new cruise-missile technology, both in numbers and because they had cruise-missile bases geographically near Soviet targets. "Now we are invited," Brezhnev complained, "to leave altogether outside the agreement the whole question of cruise missiles." From the Russian perspective, Carter's backpedaling was one-sided and unconstructive.

Upon receipt of Brezhnev's letter, Cy Vance advised caution. While the Soviet leader's message was "obviously severe in tone . . . I recommend that you not let yourself be drawn into a tone of equal harshness." Brzezinski, however, quietly encouraged Carter to pursue his proposal for deep cuts in the overall number of intercontinental missiles. He further told Carter that Brezhnev's language was "brutal, cynical, sneering and even patronizing." He knew the Soviets were unlikely to accept "deep cuts," but he saw it as a test, and if they rejected Carter's proposals, Washington would score a propaganda victory. Brzezinski was quite cynically playing on Carter's idealism and desire to end the arms race, knowing all along that the "deep cuts" gambit risked scuttling the chances for an early SALT II agreement.

That spring, the Soviet leadership clearly wanted an early SALT II deal—albeit based on what had already been negotiated at Vladivostok. In retrospect, all the president's advisers except Brzezinski agreed that the administration had missed an opportunity to achieve a strategic arms deal. Instead, negotiations dragged out over the summer, and U.S.-Soviet relations became further strained over Carter's high-profile efforts to push the Soviets on human rights. Carter had assured Brezhnev in their early correspondence that he wished to build on détente—but he was also going to talk about human rights. And he did so soon after the inauguration by responding to a letter from the Russian dissident physicist Andrei Sakharov pledging his support for global human rights.

The Soviets were furious at this highly publicized exchange of per-

sonal correspondence and believed it was only a gambit to derail détente. "Surely the Soviets are sophisticated enough," Powell told the
president, "to understand that the domestic flexibility we need to make
progress in other areas is enhanced by our position on human rights."
But the Russians were not sophisticated, only paranoid about this public
interference in their domestic politics. Brzezinski knew this—but chose
only to goad the president into what he knew was provocative behavior.
In March, the negotiations in Moscow collapsed completely; the Soviets
firmly rejected Carter's proposal for "deep cuts." But far from being
alarmed over what others regarded as a diplomatic fiasco, Brzezinski
told the president that they had put the Soviets on the defensive, making
them seem opposed to arms limitations: "The tables have been turned."

In a further escalation, Brzezinski also persuaded Carter to authorize
an ambitious covert operation by the CIA to publicize human rights
abuses in Eastern Europe. Brzezinski just didn't care about SALT. In one
early-morning meeting with Hamilton Jordan and other senior staff,
Zbig was "quite forceful in saying that the Treaty should be delayed." He
considered SALT of "marginal value to our national interest."

Carter later conceded that he had miscalculated by "underestimating
the Soviets' displeasure" over the public nature of his human rights interventions and the "somewhat radical change from the Vladivostok
proposal." He never blamed Brzezinski for taking him down this road.
As a consequence, the SALT II talks would drag out for more than two
years, becoming a domestic political football and an irritant to Soviet-
American relations. But in the end, Carter prevailed. He achieved further limits on the number of strategic launchers and negotiated a
substantially better agreement than Kissinger's earlier framework—but
he never had the time or votes to get the treaty ratified in the Senate.

Many in the administration blamed Brzezinski. Vance's State Department spokesman, Hodding Carter III, later wrote, "Brzezinski, however,
never accepted a defeat as final or a policy as decided if it did not please
him. Like a rat terrier, he would shake himself off after a losing encounter and begin nipping at Vance's ankles, using his press spokesman and
chief deputies as well as himself to tell the world that he had won or that
only he, Zbigniew Brzezinski, hung tough in the national security game
as a foreign policy realist." Hodding thought it a mystery why the president tolerated such a difficult man.

* * *

CARTER EXPENDED FURTHER political capital when he chose early on to tackle the highly contentious issue of the Panama Canal. Renegotiation of the 1903 treaty had been a third rail in American politics ever since the 1964 mass riots in the Canal Zone that killed four American soldiers and twenty Panamanians. Panama had cut diplomatic relations until President Lyndon Johnson had agreed to negotiate a new treaty ceding sovereignty of the Canal Zone back to Panama. Presidents Nixon and Ford had both continued the negotiations despite strong opposition among many Americans. During the 1976 Republican primaries former California governor Ronald Reagan barnstormed the country, saying, "When it comes to the Panama Canal, we built it, we paid for it . . . and we're going to keep it!" The line always garnered applause. In 1975, thirty-eight U.S. senators endorsed a resolution pledging never to alter the 1903 treaty. That was more than enough votes to block the formal ratification of any new treaty.

Carter himself was "only vaguely" aware of the issue until his presidential campaign, when he was routinely asked about it. For the most part, he ducked the issue. But after reading up on the history of how President Teddy Roosevelt had acquired the canal, he concluded it was "obviously unfair." Upon reading David McCullough's bestselling history *The Path Between the Seas: The Creation of the Panama Canal,* he noted in his diary, "It's obvious that we cheated the Panamanians out of their canal. As a matter of fact, no Panamanian ever saw the [1903] treaty at all before it was signed."

Carter was also influenced by intelligence briefings that underscored how vulnerable the Canal Zone was to civil unrest, sabotage, and direct military attacks. In the event of a Panamanian upheaval, he was told, it would take 100,000 U.S. troops to control the zone. Clearly, in the long term, American control was impractical. Abroad, the canal had become an irritating symbol of Yankee imperialism across Latin America. Carter was determined to solve the problem by negotiating a treaty that would both recognize Panamanian sovereignty and phase out American control over a period of years. To this end, he appointed two senior diplomats, Sol Linowitz and Ellsworth Bunker, to negotiate a new treaty. "These were not easy decisions for me to make," he later wrote. "I knew that we were sure to face a terrible political fight in Congress."

That spring and summer Ambassadors Linowitz and Bunker made good progress in their negotiations with Panama's strongman president, Brigadier General Omar Torrijos, a charismatic nationalist who had seized power in a military coup in 1968. By late May, Torrijos had agreed in principle to negotiate not one but two treaties: the first to specify the arrangements for joint operation of the canal until the year 2000, and the second to guarantee thereafter the permanent "neutrality" of the canal. Not incidentally, the second treaty would also permit the United States to defend the "neutral" operations of the canal, ensuring that American shipping would always have passage. This two-treaty strategy was politically quite clever, if only because it allowed Carter to argue that nothing would change in the operation of the canal for another twenty-three years—and even after the year 2000 the United States would have the right to defend the canal.

Even so, Carter knew it was going to be an uphill battle to obtain a two-thirds vote in the Senate. On July 29, 1977, he noted in his diary, "There's a lot of natural opposition to this treaty." In an effort to forestall early opposition, Carter sent telegrams in early August to all senators, urging them "not to speak out against the treaty until they know the details of the agreement." This worked—except for "a few nuts like Strom Thurmond and Jesse Helms."

Carter also reached out to former president Ford and Henry Kissinger and persuaded both of them to issue public statements in support of the treaties. Over a memorable breakfast one morning in late August, Kissinger told Hamilton Jordan and Landon Butler, "After all we've been through, we cannot afford to emasculate another president." And as part of his lobbying campaign, Carter invited virtually all the Latin American heads of state to attend an elaborate treaty-signing ceremony in Washington, DC, on September 7, 1977. It was quite a Washington spectacle. Butler, who organized the affair, called it "an unbelievable show of strength."

General Torrijos was briefly overcome with emotion during his private meeting with Carter that evening. Trying to convey his gratitude, Torrijos suddenly broke down sobbing in his wife's arms. Carter was impressed by this heartfelt display of emotion and convinced that "we were doing the right thing." Torrijos was "a military dictator, but my sense is that he genuinely cares for the poor—a sincere populist."

Despite publicity surrounding the signing extravaganza, a Gallup poll indicated that only 39 percent of the public favored the treaties—and a solid 46 percent were against "giving away" the canal. The president's own standing in the polls still stood at a highly favorable 66 percent. Right-wing Republican operatives like Richard Viguerie predicted that conservatives had the votes in the Senate to defeat the treaties. And even the powerful Senate majority leader, Robert Byrd, privately told Carter that he thought he should "move away from it." That autumn, after visiting the White House for a pro–Panama Canal Treaty event, historian David McCullough wrote to Carter that he was worried: "The opposition has a 'cause,' their response is full of emotion, even passion, while the arguments for the treaties, however intellectually solid, remain for many people largely an abstraction." McCullough urged the president to make his case with more eloquence and passion. "Mr. President, the Panama Canal is a vast, heroic expression of that age-old desire to bridge the divide and bring people closer together. The task now, it seems to me, is to give the country the conviction that this too is what the treaties are all about."

Carter agreed with McCullough's analysis, but he stubbornly insisted he could win this battle. Jordan's deputy, Butler, whose job it was to sell the treaties, was also optimistic: "Frankly, I'm just as sure we'll win this as I was sure Carter would win the election. . . . The politics of the Canal have, so far, fallen into place beautifully. As of now, we've been successful in isolating the right wing. So far, it's just Helms and Thurmond." Butler thought McCullough's letter was superb. "We need to find a way," Butler noted in his diary, "to make the Treaties an expression of our nation's highest ideals. . . . It will be interesting to see if the president heeds it."

Over the next six months, Butler orchestrated a nationwide lobbying campaign, and various surrogates eventually made more than 1,500 appearances in civic venues all over the country. The president sent handwritten notes to such key Republicans as Barry Goldwater, telling the Arizona senator, "I recognize clearly the enormous political pressures which have been building up, but there is no doubt that it is easier for you to withstand them than for most other men, and there is no doubt

that your stature and influence could survive easily an unpopular decision. . . . More simply put, I need your help." Goldwater came around,
and in the end, he voted for ratification. Gradually, the polls turned. Ex-
governor Reagan was still speaking out against the treaties, but conservative pundit and *National Review* editor William F. Buckley, Jr.,
endorsed them.

Improbably, Carter persuaded Hollywood legend John Wayne to
lobby for the treaties. Carter and the politically conservative actor had a
warm exchange of correspondence—and when Torrijos learned of
Wayne's endorsement, he quipped, "He's a helluv'a lot better actor than
Reagan." Wayne's first wife, Josephine, happened to be Panamanian by
birth, and Wayne was a good friend of Torrijos—so it was surprisingly
easy for Carter to persuade the film star to endorse the treaty. Wayne
even wrote his old friend Reagan a firm letter remonstrating with him
for spreading lies about the treaty. "Now I have taken your letter," Wayne
wrote to Reagan, "and I'll show you point by goddamn point in the
treaty where you are misinforming people." Wayne attached a five-page
memo of rebuttal, signed it "Duke," and sent a copy to Carter. The president was delighted and wrote back quickly, "Your letter is great—tough
and factual."

Butler's lobbying efforts included the formation of a "Committee of
Americans for the Canal Treaties," joined by such eminent American
power brokers as Averell Harriman, John J. McCloy, McGeorge Bundy,
and a dozen other members of the foreign policy establishment. Carter's
trade representative Bob Strauss worked to raise hundreds of thousands
of dollars in private monies to fund a media blitz. Strauss volunteered to
host a fundraising dinner at his new Watergate apartment—but then
Times columnist Bill Safire learned that letters had been sent out to the
chief executive officers of several dozen American corporations, soliciting $15,000 contributions in return for a meeting with the president.
Safire called this a "shakedown," and the dinner was hastily canceled.

Butler was furious with Strauss over this public embarrassment. He
believed "Strauss was trying to make himself look good to the business
community by having the president come to his house." Strauss was always looking for a way to "ingratiate himself with the president." Butler
reminded Jordan "that people like Strauss are 'either at your feet or at

your throat,' " and that Mondale had the same opinion of Strauss, calling him an "emotional slob." Hamilton agreed, saying he thought Strauss was "intoxicated" with his press clippings. Butler called Strauss a "fuck-up." But despite such hiccups, Butler remained optimistic that their lob-bying efforts on behalf of the treaties were influencing public opinion.

The Senate vote on the first treaty was finally scheduled for March 16, 1978. Carter spent many hours in the months running up to the vote phoning and cajoling in person the eleven senators who were unde-cided. He persuaded forty-five senators to visit Panama and receive briefings from both U.S. military commanders and Panamanian offi-cials. At one point, Senators Jesse Helms and Robert Dole publicly ac-cused Torrijos of profiting from Panamanian drug dealers. Carter had to share intelligence information to refute these charges. A week prior to the crucial vote, his legislative aide Frank Moore told him that he thought they had only fifty-nine votes for ratification. That meant they needed eight more votes out of the eleven undecided senators. Three days before the vote, Carter wrote in his diary, "It's hard to concentrate on anything except Panama."

Carter had always disdained the wheeling and dealing of legislative politics. And once again, he was astonished at the pettiness of the key senators sitting on the fence. Carter just wanted them to do what they knew was the right thing. But it was never that easy. In this instance, he played the game, and played hard. He kept on his desk a notebook filled with background intelligence on each of the undecided senators. A sen-ator from Oklahoma wanted Carter's promise not to veto an expensive desalinization plant. Senator Dennis DeConcini from Arizona wanted new language in the treaty specifying that the United States could use military force to defend the canal from external threats. Senator Sam Nunn of Georgia wouldn't vote for the treaties unless the other senator from Georgia joined him. Senator James Sasser of Tennessee was in-clined to vote for the treaties, but he was angry at Carter for having ve-toed the Clinch River breeder reactor, a project that would have provided jobs in his state. And the colorful senator from California, S. I. Haya-kawa, at first indicated he would vote for the treaties—but then sent Carter an abusive letter, suggesting that he was having second thoughts. He complained that the president was "soft on foreign affairs and defense." Also, he wanted the president to read his textbook on semantics. Carter did what was necessary, even reading Hayakawa's esoteric book and having him into the Oval Office to discuss foreign policy.

Two days prior to the vote, Carter knew that he was still short of the necessary sixty-seven votes. "This has been one of the worst days of my political life, knowing that we were lost, regaining a little hope. I still haven't given up, but it's going to be an extremely close vote." At midday on March 16, 1978, Carter, Jordan, Powell, and Brzezinski sat in the president's private study next to the Oval Office and listened to the Senate vote. "I had never been more tense in my life as we listened to each vote shouted out on the radio," recalled Carter. By 1:00 P.M., they were "relieved" to hear that the first treaty had garnered the necessary sixty-seven votes—and that afternoon one additional vote was cast for ratification. A month later, the second treaty passed by the same margin. Carter was "exhausted, exhilarated, and thankful." Afterward, Powell boasted to reporters, "This time last year you couldn't have gotten anyone to give you a dollar against a doughnut that we would have gotten any kind of Panama Canal treaty ratified."

Carter believed he had done the right thing, and he felt that passage of the long-overdue treaties had narrowly averted a major national security crisis for both the United States and Panama. General Torrijos publicly admitted that if the Senate had rejected the treaties, he had given orders to have the canal's delicate locks blown up: "We would have started our struggle for national liberation."

The treaties restored essential sovereignty over the canal to Panama and contributed to its democratization in coming years. But Carter understood that the treaties were good for America's own self-worth. The extraordinary Senate debate had reflected a deeper generational reckoning with the American ethos. Opponents of the treaties, argued Senator Frank Church (D-ID) on the floor of the Senate, were on a "sentimental journey back to the era of Teddy Roosevelt, the big stick, and the Great White Fleet." The debate had demonstrated that many Americans still yearned for the stark simplicities of a time when American power and destiny were *manifest*. For these Americans, renouncing the Panama Canal suggested a retreat from manifest destiny and a weakening of American dominance. Carter's appeal, based on both reason and idealism, had prevailed in the Senate over mere sentiment.

A complex postcolonial worldview, he argued, had to take into account that the time had come for America to move on from a unilateralist foreign policy. Carter's vision was certainly prophetic, but neither the prophet nor his message resonated with much of the country. That autumn, he would have reason to ponder the "terrible political costs" of the effort. Five Democratic senators and two Republicans who had voted for ratification lost their seats, in large measure because of their votes on the Panama Canal treaties. One was Georgia senator Herman Talmadge, who had told Carter he "might hold his nose and vote for it." He did so—and was defeated the following November.

PANAMA WAS ONLY one of the dozens of foreign policy issues passing across his *Resolute* desk in the Oval Office. By choice, Carter was simultaneously tackling a host of controversial topics. A decision on whether or not to build a new manned strategic bomber, the B-1, was a case in point. Back in the 1960s, the U.S. Air Force had begun the push to design a new supersonic manned bomber to replace its fleet of B-52 bombers. Rockwell International eventually built four prototypes—each at a cost of $100 million—and by 1977 the air force and the aerospace industry were lobbying Congress to appropriate billions more to build a fleet of the bombers.

Candidate Carter had expressed some skepticism about the B-1. But he now studied the issue with a fresh eye, knowing that many in Congress regarded the program as a job creator. He began poring over briefing papers on the B-1 carefully on June 6, 1977—and gave himself until the end of the month to make a decision. Secretary of Defense Harold Brown and the Joint Chiefs gave him oral briefings, but Carter characteristically read all the papers he could find on the issue, including highly technical engineering reports. He quickly concluded that there was no military justification for building a fleet of B-1s. Technology had made the manned B-1 bomber redundant. The air force's new fleet of cruise missiles could already deliver nuclear weapons more effectively and cheaply than supersonic manned bombers. This fact was publicly known. But still secret was the fact that advanced "stealth" technology would soon make both manned bombers and cruise missiles virtually invisible to enemy radar. Stealth technology remained highly classified, so Carter could not use this argument to explain publicly why the B-1 was unnecessary.

Carter believed that building a B-1 fleet would be "a gross waste of money." On June 24, 1977, Secretary Brown bluntly recommended that the B-1 not be built. Carter took Secretary Brown aside after a morning cabinet meeting and told him that he was now inclined to agree with him. "He seemed to be relieved and somewhat pleased," Carter noted in his diary. Two days later, they met again and discussed how to announce the decision. "It was an easy and logical decision for me, but difficult for the Air Force." That was an understatement. The day before the announcement, the press was reporting that the president was expected to approve production of the full fleet of 244 planes at an overall cost of $100 billion. Senator Barry Goldwater said he would settle for production of only 150 bombers. The House of Representatives voted 243–178 to authorize B-1 production.

Everyone was astounded, therefore, when Carter walked into room 450 of the Old Executive Office Building and opened his tenth press conference by saying, "I think that in toto the B-1, a very expensive weapons system basically conceived in the absence of the cruise missile factor, is not necessary." It was the first time such a weapons system, already developed at a cost of $4 billion and employing thirty thousand aerospace workers, had been scrapped by a president. White House staffers expressed "great surprise and excitement" and applauded the decision. The air force and the powerful aerospace lobby were incensed. Republican congressman Robert K. Dornan of California snidely remarked, "They are breaking open the vodka bottles in Moscow." By contrast, *The New York Times* editorialized that President Carter had proven "himself a statesman by a clean decision to abandon the program." The *Times* columnist Tom Wicker called the decision "the finest moment of his brief Administration."

Congressional conservatives grumbled, but with the support of both Speaker O'Neill and Senate Majority Leader Byrd, Carter was able to sustain his decision. "The adverse reaction was predictable," he noted in his diary, "but less than I anticipated." Carter had no doubt that he had done the right thing.*

---

* In 1981, President Ronald Reagan reversed Carter's decision, and one hundred B-1 bombers were built and delivered by 1988 at a cost of $20 billion. As Carter knew they would be, the B-1s were made redundant by the stealth bomber and have rarely been used in combat.

Despite his years as a naval officer, Carter had fiscally conservative instincts that made him skeptical of Pentagon requests for new and better weaponry. After spending an exhilarating day aboard the 95,000-ton aircraft carrier USS *Eisenhower*, Carter found himself impressed by an "exciting display of professional competence" by its 6,300 crew members. They put on a show for the president, with F-15 fighter jets roaring off the deck and an accompanying nuclear-powered cruiser demonstrating its long-range artillery firepower. Carter enjoyed the spectacle—but noted in his diary that day, "I don't believe we need to build another nuclear carrier, which costs about $2.5 billion and enormous quantities of money to operate." When Congress later tried to add $2.1 billion in a defense authorization bill for an aircraft carrier, Carter decided to veto the entire bill—just to kill the aircraft carrier. Congress then tried unsuccessfully to override his veto. Needless to say, aircraft carriers are always popular in Congress, and Carter's veto was extremely unpopular, even among Democrats. Carter didn't care; indeed, he was proud to note, "We prevailed against an all-out effort to override my veto."

On the other hand, while candidate Carter had sometimes suggested he would cut the defense budget, President Carter actually reversed a post–Vietnam War decline in defense spending. The Pentagon's budget increased annually in real dollars by about 3 percent. His critics on the right nevertheless saddled him with the impression that he was soft on defense.

Taken together, Carter's early record on all these foreign policy issues—human rights, the SALT II treaty, the Panama Canal treaties, and his decision to cancel an expensive weapons program like the B-1 bomber—suggested a president who was unafraid to take on major foreign policy issues, even as these achievements came with considerable political costs. Carter was resolute, and nowhere was this truer than in the Middle East.

Chapter 10
"Israel Trusts No One"

They [the Israelis] prefer land to peace. . . . They think I want
peace at any price.

     —ANWAR SADAT to Jimmy Carter

Anwar Sadat and Carter
KARL SCHUMACHER/GETTY IMAGES

THE PANAMA CANAL treaties and the B-1 bomber cancellation were
victories of substance but somehow politically Pyrrhic. But this did
not dissuade Carter from simultaneously pursuing another equally
thorny foreign policy briar patch—that of Arab-Israeli peace. Brzezinski had persistently tried to steer Carter away from investing too much
time or political capital on the Middle East, as he believed that the
Soviet-American contest was the greater strategic priority. But he was
not ignorant about the Arab-Israeli problem. He had actually partici-

pated in a Brookings Institution study that argued for a comprehensive settlement. The December 1975 report, largely drafted by Brzezinski and William Quandt, later his aide in the NSC, called for a return to the June 1967 borders, full Arab recognition of the Israeli state, and either an independent Palestinian state or a "Palestinian entity federated with Jordan." Both Carter and Vance read the report and thought highly of it. But the resulting controversy surrounding the release of the report only reinforced Brzezinski's instinct to stay away from the issue. Thus, less than three weeks after the inauguration, Quandt told Brzezinski that "PLO Chairman Arafat is seeking ways of establishing a dialogue with the United States. . . . Arafat wants [Edward] Said to discuss with you ways of establishing such a dialogue." But Zbig declined to meet with the prominent Palestinian American and Columbia University professor. If it had leaked, a meeting with Said could have caused a brouhaha.

The president, nevertheless, had an abiding interest in, even a passion for, the troubled region. From his lifelong readings of the scriptures, he possessed more than a passing knowledge of the geography of biblical Palestine. "I was infatuated with the Holy Land," Carter later wrote.

He had first visited Israel in May 1973, while still governor, traveling with Rosalynn and Jody Powell. It was not a superficial trip. Golda Meir was prime minister, and she provided the governor with a secondhand Mercedes station wagon, a driver, and a young guide. The Carters picked their own itinerary and spent nearly a week driving all over the "surprisingly tiny country." They walked around the escarpments of the Golan Heights, lunched with the mayor of Nazareth, swam in the Dead Sea, visited the archaeological ruins of Jericho, and spent three days wandering around the back alleys of Old Jerusalem. They also visited an Israeli military base, received briefings by the Israeli intelligence chief, and held discussions with Prime Minister Meir and General Yitzhak Rabin. The visit made a lasting impression and reinforced Carter's ingrained Judeo-Christian affinity for "this homeland for the Jews." He also deeply believed that the "Jews who had survived the Holocaust deserved their own nation."

As president, Carter wanted to tackle the intractable Arab-Israeli problem precisely because of his concern for Israel. Mondale was surprised to hear Carter say on his very first day in office that Middle East peace was a top concern. He approached the problem analytically, like an engineer, and quickly concluded that all previous negotiations had been designed simply to impose an armistice in the wake of war. Even Kissinger's famous shuttle diplomacy assumed that the most that could be achieved was a step-by-step strategy that might eventually lead to face-to-face negotiations. Carter saw that "the status quo sometimes seemed to suit the major protagonists." He worried that the status quo was not sustainable, particularly over time for the Israelis. He wanted to "resolve the underlying problems"—and that meant addressing the problem of Palestinian rights. It was an ambitious agenda.

During the first few weeks of his administration, Carter spent hours discussing the options, "only to be told by almost every adviser to stay out of the Middle East situation." But Carter ordered the State Department to draw up a peace initiative based on the notion of reconvening all the parties to the conflict on some neutral ground, probably Geneva.

The first step would be an approach to the Israelis. On March 7, 1977, Israeli prime minister Rabin arrived in Washington. The encounter did not go well. "I've put in an awful lot of time studying the Middle Eastern question," Carter noted in his diary that day, "and was hoping that Rabin would give me some outline of what Israel ultimately hopes to achieve in a permanent peace settlement." But Rabin was highly reticent. "It was like talking to a dead fish," Carter later said. He thought him "very timid, stubborn, and also somewhat ill at ease." When Carter took the Israeli upstairs to the residence for a private meeting, Rabin remained stiff and formal. "He didn't unbend at all, nor did he respond."

Rabin was not a garrulous personality, but unknown to Carter at the time, he was under considerable personal stress. He knew Israeli reporters were digging into evidence that he and his wife had maintained dollar accounts in a Washington bank in violation of Israeli currency regulations. A week later, the story broke and Rabin was forced to resign in disgrace. Carter was unimpressed and later noted in his diary that he thought Rabin "one of the most ineffective persons I've ever met." This first encounter with an Israeli leader momentarily caused Carter to doubt whether he should proceed with any major initiative. But his doubts were set aside by his curiosity and eagerness to meet Anwar Sadat, Egypt's impulsive dictator.

*　*　*

THE TWO PRESIDENTS first met on April 4, 1977. "At first, he was a little shy," Carter noted, "or ill at ease, perhaps because he was sick, but it soon became obvious to me that he was a charming and frank and also very strong and courageous leader. . . . I liked Sadat very much." Carter immediately noticed a *zebibah*, a calloused "prayer bump" on Sadat's forehead, not uncommon among Muslims who prayed five times a day, touching their head to the ground. Carter had read the CIA's standard biographical reports on Sadat, but he found himself nevertheless surprised that his "complexion was much darker than I had expected."

They held their first formal meeting in the Cabinet Room from 11:10 A.M. until 12:30 P.M. Mondale, Brzezinski, Vance, Jordan, Powell, and three other American officials sat at the table. Sadat brought his foreign minister, Ismail Fahmi, and four other close aides. But the two presidents did all the talking.

After some polite chatter about how they both came from farming villages, Sadat came right to the point: "On borders, I do not think that you would agree that others should take land by force." But he quickly acknowledged that "minor rectifications of borders on the West Bank . . . This can be done." He acknowledged that the Israelis wanted a real peace with open borders and free trade. But after twenty-nine years of "war and hatred," this would take some time. "This is mostly a psychological problem." Sadat then indicated that he wanted to reconvene the Geneva Convention, suspended since 1973, and negotiate a peace treaty. "What I see is that I will sit at Geneva, and that we will sign a peace agreement that will end the state of belligerency, and we will normalize the situation, and both we and the Israelis will fulfill our obligations under Resolution 242." The latter United Nations resolution, passed in late 1967, expressed the "inadmissibility of the acquisition of territory by war and the need to work for a just and lasting peace in which every State in the area can live in security." It specifically called for the "withdrawal of Israeli armed forces from territories occupied in the recent conflict."

Sadat was being more than frank; he was giving away all his bargaining chips. He volunteered, for instance, that there could be an Israeli-U.S. defense pact to guarantee the peace treaty: "That is okay with me."

As to the "Palestinian question," it was "crucial"—but, he said, "there are lots of alternatives." They needed "some entity, some homeland." In another concession, Sadat offered that "a Palestinian state should have some link to Jordan."

Carter interrupted at this juncture and asked pointedly, "How do the Palestinians respond?"

"In principle, they agree," Sadat said. "But there are differences. I say the link should be established before the peace conference, and they say it can only be established after the state is created. I think I can convince them."

Carter pressed Sadat. "You mean there should be a relationship between a Palestinian state and Jordan?"

Sadat replied yes, a "declared relationship."

Carter then asked whether the Palestinians were ready to recognize Israel's right to exist and to accept Resolution 242. "Israel insists that this be done before Geneva. This now seems irreconcilable. Do you see a solution?"

Sadat replied nonchalantly, "It is easy. Before Geneva, a certain link should be declared between Jordan and the new Palestinian state." It was all a matter of face-saving. But the crucial element was American engagement. "I am urging the United States and the Palestinians to begin a dialogue. This will help them to save face in dealing with Israel. If the U.S. becomes involved in a dialogue, then it is very easy. Israel talks of the Palestinian charter. But the Palestinians have already agreed to come to Geneva with Israel present, and *they will sign a peace agreement at Geneva* [emphasis added]. It is a matter of saving face for both sides."

Sadat then brazenly referred to the highly secret fact that Washington was already talking to the Palestinians. Kissinger and Nixon had opened a back channel to the PLO as early as 1969—and "I know that you have been in touch with [them in] Morocco and Lebanon."

Carter didn't bother to deny it, but merely nodded and said, "I understand."

By this time, Carter had been fully briefed on the CIA's clandestine channel, managed by CIA officer Robert Ames through his friendship with Ali Hassan Salameh—a young Palestinian who as chief of the PLO's Force 17 functioned as Yasir Arafat's intelligence chief. Carter probably was informed of the back channel during the transition, when the CIA sought permission from the outgoing Ford administration to bring Salameh and his girlfriend for a brief, surreptitious visit to America. When Kissinger vetoed the planned trip, CIA Director George H. W. Bush approached the secretary of state designate, Cy Vance, and persuaded him to sign off on the venture. Salameh flew in early 1977 to New York, where he was greeted by a CIA handler and escorted to Washington, DC, for a meeting with Agency officials. At some point, Vance briefed Carter and Brzezinski about the highly sensitive Ames-Salameh back channel. Carter approved the channel in part because he realized that its very existence was encouraging the PLO to move in the direction of a political compromise. On the other hand, Carter was probably nonplussed to be confronted by Sadat with at least the inference that he knew the Americans were talking to the Palestinians.

Sadat's frankness was refreshing. And his optimism about being able to bring the Palestinians to Geneva reinforced the intelligence Carter was getting about the PLO from the back channel. It was all very encouraging and led Carter to believe that a major American initiative was feasible. "Peace in the Middle East should be American," Sadat proclaimed. And when Carter asked if that meant the Americans should offer their own proposals for a comprehensive peace, Sadat nodded vigorously. Everything was possible, Sadat said, "if we can get the land occupied since 1967."

Carter pressed the Egyptian leader and asked him the question that any Israeli would ask: "If this were possible in September or October, could you then immediately open your borders to Israel?"

"This is very difficult," replied Sadat. "It is a psychological problem for us." He then suggested that the withdrawal from the occupied territories could take place in stages over the following year. "But opening borders is impossible for us, in all frankness."

Carter responded with equal bluntness: "In fairness, that should be part of the whole process. We cannot ask the Israelis to withdraw without full peace and open borders." When Sadat insisted that "we are prepared for a real peace agreement with an end to the state of belligerency," Carter pressed again, asking how much time he would need to "open your borders with Israel." He also pressed Sadat about an exchange of ambassadors. He was backing the Egyptian president into a corner. Sadat just could not say how long "normalization" could take. Carter was unrelenting: "Well, this has not been very productive to this point. You don't see any time when it [normalization] could be done."

Sadat replied, "I don't know if in a peace agreement we can add a clause on normalization in five years or so." He was groping, trying to offer Carter something.

But Carter could clearly see that despite all of Sadat's forthrightness, he was unable to give the Israelis what they really wanted: diplomatic recognition, open borders, and trade. As the meeting wound down, Carter turned to Sadat and said, "One final point. It is accurate to say that Israel does not trust us entirely."

"Israel trusts no one entirely," retorted Sadat.

"I can understand why," Carter replied. "She fears for her existence." Even a formal U.S.-Israeli military pact would not calm these existential fears. "The Israelis are looking far ahead into the future. They see normal diplomatic relations and trade as ways of establishing a permanent peace. We have to face that."

No one could say that Carter had not forcefully represented the Israeli position with empathy and understanding. Sadat had listened, and everyone in the room sensed that the two men had acquired a deep respect for each other. It was a poignant beginning of a fateful relationship. Carter always regarded his April 4, 1977, encounter with Sadat as the day when "a shining light burst on the Middle East scene for me . . . a man who would change history." That evening, shortly before 10:00, after a formal working dinner, Carter took Sadat upstairs to the White House residence and they continued their talks in private. For the next hour, the two men "argued without restraint," but in a bantering, lighthearted manner. As it was getting late, Carter decided to "push my luck" and again pressed Sadat about when, if ever, Egypt could exchange ambassadors with Israel.

"Not in my lifetime!" Sadat answered, shaking his head vigorously.

Carter "teased" Sadat, asking if he thought "our successors might be more willing to achieve peace than we were." Finally, the Egyptian haltingly conceded that maybe, "if things go well," diplomatic recognition might happen five years after an agreement. Carter thought this grudging concession was hopeful. Before falling asleep just after midnight, he turned to Rosalynn and confided that it had been "my best day as president."

*　*　*

HEARTENED BY THIS unlikely new friendship, Carter pushed ahead, meeting with Jordan's King Hussein on April 25, Syria's President Hafez al-Assad on May 9 in Geneva, and Crown Prince Fahd of Saudi Arabia on May 24. During a phone conversation with British prime minister James Callaghan, Carter said he was "favorably impressed with the Arab leaders. . . . They may be wonderful con artists but my impression is that they genuinely want to make some progress."

"My own judgment at this time," Carter noted in his diary, "is that the Arab leaders want to settle it and the Israelis don't."

The Israeli part of the equation became even more difficult on May 17, when the leader of the right-wing Likud Party, Menachem Begin, won a landslide election, upending the Israeli political landscape. Carter "had not dreamed" that Begin, a man who he knew had once been declared by Great Britain to be the region's "foremost terrorist," could become prime minister. A few days later, Carter viewed a tape of Begin being interviewed: "It was frightening to watch his adamant position on issues that must be resolved if a Middle Eastern peace settlement is going to be realized." Begin would obviously be a major hurdle, but this did not persuade Carter to set aside his ambitions. The new Israeli leader was extended an invitation to visit Washington in July.

Brzezinski perversely thought Begin's hard-line views presented the Carter administration with a political opportunity to drive a wedge between the new Likud government and the Jewish American community. "Begin, by his extremism," Brzezinski wrote Carter on May 20, "is likely to split both Israeli public opinion and the American Jewish community. A position of moderate firmness on our part will rally to you in time both the Israeli opposition and significant portions of the American Jewish community." Brzezinski was dead wrong.

In preparation for his meetings with Begin, Carter had spent many hours catching up on intelligence reports on the Middle East, reading the history of the Palestinian question, and studying maps of the region. But despite near-record approval ratings in the polls, Carter was already aware that his tentative steps toward orchestrating a comprehensive peace settlement were setting off alarm bells in the Jewish community. So prior to Begin's arrival, he held a series of meetings with leaders from the Jewish American community "to repair my damaged political base among Israel's American friends."

The president's closest political adviser was worried about Begin's impending visit. Hamilton Jordan was specifically apprehensive about the "Jewish lobby." In June, alarmed at the grumblings he was hearing from Jewish American sources, Jordan closeted himself in his office and painstakingly wrote one of his long political memorandums. He excelled at this kind of exercise. Knowing of its political sensitivity, he typed the thirty-five-page memo himself and kept the only copy in his White House office safe.

He began with a Georgian disclaimer: "I would compare our present understanding of the American Jewish lobby (vis-à-vis Israel) to our understanding of the American labor movement four years ago. We are aware of its strength and influence, but don't understand the basis for that strength nor the way that it is used politically. It is something that was not part of our Georgia and Southern political experience and consequently not well understood."

Jordan then offered his boss some statistics: He pointed out that Jews composed less than 3 percent of the U.S. population—but cast almost 5 percent of the votes. They voted predominantly on the Democratic ticket: Carter had received about 72 percent of the Jewish vote. And significantly, Jews registered and voted in larger numbers than any other ethnic group. Indeed, voter turnout among Jewish voters was close to 90 percent. The Jewish voters in New York State were particularly decisive precisely because of their high turnout rate. Jews and African Americans composed about the same percentage of New York's population— but Black turnout was only 35 percent in the 1976 presidential election, whereas Jewish turnout clocked in at a whopping 85 percent. "This means," Jordan wrote, "that for every black vote you received in the [New York] election, you received almost two Jewish votes."

Jewish votes were significant only in those large urban states where Jews were concentrated. But Jordan pointed out that Jewish campaign contributions were "disproportionate nationally and in almost every area of the country." Kansas had a tiny Jewish community, but Republican senator Bob Dole knew that it was "not so small in terms of his campaign contributions." Thus, in 1976, 60 percent of the large donors to the Democratic Party were Jewish, and historically only about 25 percent of campaign contributions to the Republican Party came from the Jewish community.

Jordan was quick to point out that Jewish campaign contributions had to be seen in "the larger context of the Jewish tradition of using one's material wealth for the benefit of others." It was part of the culture, not some anti-Semitic canard. So while the American Red Cross raised about $200 million in 1976, Jordan reported that Jewish charities raised a phenomenal $3.6 billion. Jewish Americans were generous with both their votes and their dollars. And so that naturally meant influence in the political arena.

Jordan then asked how the Jewish community wielded its influence on the issue of Israel. "When people talk about the 'Jewish lobby' as relates to Israel, they are referring to the American Israel Public Affairs Committee (AIPAC)." Formed in 1956, AIPAC was an umbrella organization representing some twenty-eight major Jewish groups, including the American Jewish Congress and the Anti-Defamation League. Jordan explained that AIPAC had "one continuing priority—the welfare of the state of Israel as perceived by the American Jewish community." In the past, AIPAC rarely had any reason to question the wisdom of "policies advocated by the Israeli government." Jordan suggested that Begin's election had resulted in widespread "uncertainty among the Jewish community." For the first time, AIPAC was worrying that American public support for Israel might drop off if Israel's new leaders "prove to be unreasonable."

"I think it is accurate to say," Jordan wrote, "that the American Jewish community is extremely nervous at present." Nervous about Begin, but AIPAC was even more nervous about Carter, a southerner with an unknown pedigree on Israeli issues. Jordan warned Carter that, in sheer political terms, if the Jewish American community publicly opposed his Middle East peace initiative, "you would lack the flexibility and credibility you will need to play a constructive role in bringing the Israelis and Arabs together."

Jordan worried that the Jewish community was already turning against his boss: "It is not so much what you have said, as the fact that the things you have said ('defensible borders,' 'homeland for the Palestinians,' etc.) have been publicly discussed." AIPAC leaders had heard these things before, "but they were always said privately with ample reassurances provided." Now they heard such things said in public by a president with whom they had no personal relationship.

Jordan concluded with an ominous warning: "Although their fears and concerns about you and your attitude toward Israel might be unjustified, they do exist. In the absence of immediate action on our part, I fear that these tentative feelings in the Jewish community about you (as relates to Israel) might solidify, leaving us in an adversary posture with the American Jewish community."

Jordan urged the president to adopt an eight-week lobbying effort to reach out to key Jewish leaders around the country. He wanted Carter himself to cultivate leaders of national Jewish organizations, but also to have such surrogates as Secretary Vance, NSC adviser Brzezinski, Stu Eizenstat, and Bob Lipshutz hold briefing sessions with Jewish leaders and journalists in New York City, Miami, Los Angeles, Chicago, Cleveland, and other cities. Carter agreed. But Jordan's incisive memorandum would prove to be depressingly prescient. Jewish American leaders, if not Jewish voters in general, would become increasingly wary of Carter and particularly his attempts to broker a comprehensive peace. "It was a paradox," wrote the historian Lawrence Wright. "Nothing could be a greater gift to Israel than peace, and nothing was more politically dangerous for an American politician than trying to achieve it."

Carter had ample warning, but he would not be deterred.

ON JULY 19, Carter welcomed Prime Minister Begin and his wife, Aliza, to the White House for a formal dinner. The cooks were instructed to serve a wholly kosher meal. Despite "dire predictions" that they would not get along, Carter found him to be "quite congenial, dedicated, sincere and deeply religious. . . . I think Begin is a very good man." Carter noted in his diary that opinion polls indicated most Israelis were more flexible in their views about relinquishing the West Bank to the Palestinians than was their new prime minister. Carter thought he was the kind of "strong leader" who could be brought around. He was right—and wrong in the long term.

Carter tried in their formal discussions to be quite clear. If they ever reconvened the Geneva peace talks, Carter intended to push for a comprehensive peace based on UN Resolution 242—meaning a withdrawal from the occupied territories "to secure borders" in return for Arab recognition of the Israeli state with open borders and free trade. But Carter insisted that peace also required the creation of a "Palestinian entity"—not an independent state. Begin responded that all this was acceptable, except the Palestinian entity.

Carter then moved on to the difficult question of the growing Israeli settlements in the West Bank. The settlements, he said, were a serious obstacle to peace. Not only were they illegal under international law, but they sent a signal that Israel intended to make the military occupation a permanent fixture. Begin listened in silence, and, according to Carter, he did not argue with the president.

Toward the end of their conversations, Begin lectured Carter at length about the history of the region, citing the Talmud. Much of this was familiar to Carter from his own biblical studies, but Carter thought it was "interesting this time." Later, after the state dinner concluded, Carter took Begin upstairs to the residence, as he had with Sadat, and the two men continued their "frank" discussions in private. Begin promised "to keep an open mind." All in all, Carter thought it had gone well, and he optimistically ordered the State Department to proceed with the plans to reconvene the Geneva talks.

It wasn't going to be easy. Soon after Begin returned to Jerusalem, he declared as permanent several of the larger settlements in the West Bank, effectively annexing parts of the occupied territories. Carter was disappointed, to say the least, but undeterred. At least one prominent Jewish American leader, Arthur Goldberg, the former Supreme Court justice, urged him to "proceed aggressively" toward a Geneva conference. Secretary Vance supported Carter and worked vigorously to make it happen. Vance didn't care that the Soviets were cochairs of the 1973 Geneva Conference, and thus that reconvening Geneva meant giving the Soviets leverage over the peace talks. This was a problem for Brzezinski, who advised against it. But Vance thought any real agreement would require Soviet acquiescence, and he saw no point in evading the issue. Carter agreed.

Part of their calculation was that greater pressure could be exerted on Israel in a multilateral setting like Geneva. Even Brzezinski understood this, telling a British journalist, presumably off the record, at a dinner party that summer that "sooner or later there would have to be a confrontation with Begin over the PLO or the West Bank, even though this would mean a confrontation between Carter and American Jewry."

Throughout that summer, the administration also used back-channel, private diplomacy in an attempt to persuade Yasir Arafat and the PLO to issue at least a qualified endorsement of UN Resolution 242. Any such statement, they believed, would constitute Palestinian recognition of Israel and therefore allow Washington to talk openly with the PLO.

One such back channel already existed through Rosalynn's friendship with Landrum Bolling, a prominent American Quaker leader who traveled frequently to the Middle East. Bolling often saw Arafat in Cairo or Beirut, and afterward he would return to Washington and quietly visit Rosalynn in the White House residence. "I would come with a one-page memo for the president about my meeting with Arafat," recalled Bolling. "Arafat wanted to convince Carter that he was a man of peace. Rosalynn would pass my memo on to her husband later at night. We bypassed all the official channels. Carter would often scribble his answer to the message from Arafat on the memo and have it returned to me. I passed about a dozen messages in this way. And Brzezinski knew that I was bringing these messages from Arafat."

In one such meeting in early September 1977, Bolling urged Arafat to accept Carter's offer to open a dialogue with the PLO—even though the Americans were not willing to promise the creation of a Palestinian state, or even guarantee the PLO a seat at Geneva. But Bolling argued with Arafat that Carter was essentially offering "the 'opening of the gate' to essential PLO participation in the negotiating process and that this could transform the whole situation." Arafat replied that he could not sell "only a promise of a dialogue" to his comrades. He tried, however, to do exactly that in a meeting of the PLO's Central Council on September 20, and reportedly argued so vigorously on behalf of the Carter proposal that he cut his hand while slamming his fist down on a glass table. But he was outvoted, and Bolling returned to Washington and told Brzezinski that the Palestinian leader needed a guarantee that the United States would support the creation of an independent state in return for acceptance of Resolution 242. That was a step too far for the Carter White House.

Nevertheless, after much wrangling over the parameters of the planned Geneva Conference, including whether and how any Palestinian representatives could attend, perhaps as part of the Jordanian delegation, Vance succeeded in persuading the Soviets to issue a joint statement on October 1, 1977, inviting all the state actors to meet in Geneva in the near future. The formal invitation, however, generated enormous controversy, in part because of a passing reference to "the legitimate rights of the Palestinian people." This language, charged a group of Jewish American leaders, was "code-words for Israel's destruction." Carter at first felt bemused by the uproar. After all, there was nothing in the joint U.S.-Soviet communiqué that hadn't been said before. He noted in his diary that "the screams arise immediately" when things are spelled out frankly.

The Israeli government issued a highly negative comment, but so too did various Arab states. American political pundits and prominent Jewish American leaders were highly critical. Rabbi Alexander Schindler, president of the Union of American Hebrew Congregations, was "appalled" by the joint U.S.-Soviet declaration. Brzezinski was equally appalled by the criticism leveled at the administration and him personally. "The Israelis are absolutely shameless in their willingness to whip up [the] troops," noted Butler in his diary. "I've kept good notes on Zbig's thoughts on the subject."

Carter himself "felt particularly embattled at this time." A few days later, he met with the House Jewish Caucus and defended himself, confessing, "I'd rather commit political suicide than hurt Israel." On October 4, he had a long and contentious meeting with Israel's foreign minister, General Moshe Dayan. "He was obviously quite nervous and quite deeply concerned about the Soviet-American statement." Carter insisted that "we were not trying to impose a settlement from outside on Israel." He was extraordinarily blunt, telling Dayan, "Israel was going to find itself isolated, and if I had to defend my position publicly, which I had refrained from doing, it would cause a cleavage that might be serious." He complained that of all the Middle Eastern nations involved in these negotiations, "Israel was by far the most obstinate."

Stunned by this blunt reprimand, Dayan returned to Jerusalem and convinced his government that they had no choice but to attend Geneva. The Jordanians and Egyptians soon indicated they would come as well. But then Syria's Assad backed out, threatening the whole venture. Assad insisted he could not attend unless the PLO had a seat at the table. At this point, even Sadat told Carter he should find some way for a limited PLO presence. With mounting frustration, Carter replied that the

Israelis would never attend under those conditions; the time had come, he insisted, for everyone to stop bargaining and just agree to come to Geneva.

Carter's solution was to urge the Arab states to send to Geneva a unified, collective delegation—sidestepping the contentious issue of Palestinian representation. But Sadat was leery of this, fearing that Egyptian interests—specifically, the return of the Sinai—would be subsumed by Syrian and Palestinian interests. To Carter's dismay, Sadat rejected the idea of a unified delegation.

Any other American politician at this point would have given up. But Carter was relentless, and on October 21 he wrote Sadat a personal appeal, urging him to make a dramatic gesture by publicly endorsing the American peace proposals. "I need your help," Carter implored.

Sadat replied with a handwritten, sealed letter that Carter read on October 31. The Egyptian wrote that "he's going to take bold action to strip away the argument about semantics and get down to the real issues of Geneva. He didn't indicate what he would do."

A few days later, Carter learned what Sadat had in mind—and he was not happy. They talked on the phone on November 2, and Sadat broached the notion of holding a summit conference in East Jerusalem. Sadat said he was intrigued by the idea of a "bold initiative." Carter expressed the opinion that convening all the parties to the Geneva Conference in East Jerusalem would be logistically difficult. In fact, he thought it would "seriously complicate, rather than facilitate, the search for peace in the Middle East." Carter still thought their priority should be the Geneva route. He told Sadat that he was "making intensive efforts" to make Geneva happen. But on the other hand, he was not going to obstruct the Egyptian. When Sadat indicated he'd nevertheless like to meet with Begin, Cy Vance conveyed this intelligence to the Israeli. So Carter was not completely surprised when, on November 9, 1977, Sadat astonished a gathering of the Egyptian parliament by announcing dramatically that he was willing to go to Jerusalem.

Nine days later, on the eve of Sadat's flight to Jerusalem, Carter placed a phone call to Sadat. He gave him his encouragement and said how much he admired what he was doing. Sadat's reply was "overly effusive" in his thanks. "I haven't done anything," Carter noted modestly, "except to convince Sadat and Begin that each of them wanted peace." Notwithstanding his innate Southern Baptist aversion to the sin of pride, Carter knew he had played a not inconsiderable role in precipitating the historic visit. "As you know," Sadat later told him in a handwritten letter, it was Carter's correspondence "which prompted me to undertake the unthinkable visit to Jerusalem."

Begin also credited the American president. In a separate phone call Begin thanked Carter "for what you have done; without you it could not have happened." Carter guardedly pointed out that Sadat's foreign minister had resigned in protest about the impending visit, and pointedly reminded Begin, "There is the need for some tangible contribution for Sadat to take home. He has run high risks. There should be something tangible that he can take as a success." Begin did not respond.

Carter was as excited as Begin—but he was already worrying about the "danger to Sadat's life," and he feared that Sadat's unilateral diplomacy could seriously disrupt the larger Mideast peace negotiations. According to Stu Eizenstat, he was more than a little ambivalent. Eizenstat recalled passing Carter in the hallway one day outside the Oval Office. Carter stopped for a moment and said, "Stu, I think I am going to oppose Sadat's visit. It will be the end of any hope of a comprehensive peace and will result only at best in a bilateral agreement between Egypt and Israel." Eizenstat protested, "Mr. President, you can't do that. Sadat's visit will be historic, and it will be catastrophic if you are seen as opposing the first visit of an Arab combatant to Israel since its creation." Carter grumbled and walked on, clearly annoyed but no doubt resigned to the visit.

Sadat was gambling that his presence in Jerusalem would radically transform Israeli public opinion and ultimately persuade Israeli leaders to trade genuine peace for a complete withdrawal from all the territories occupied in 1967, including the Golan. His vision included the resolution of the Palestinian problem by the creation of a Palestinian entity in the West Bank and Gaza. Carter shared these hopes, but after watching Sadat address the Knesset, he found himself "disappointed with Begin's speech, which was primarily a rehash of what he had always said." Despite Sadat's grand gesture, Begin still seemed determined to hold on to as much land as possible, most particularly the land he called "Judea and Samaria." As a State Department analysis for Secretary Vance put it, many Israelis "still hope that Israel can have its cake and eat it—can have peace without significant territorial concessions on the West Bank and Golan."

Carter noted in his diary, "My concern and prediction is that both Begin and Sadat have an inclination to negotiate privately and to the exclusion of Syria." The very next day Carter noted, "The general reaction on the Mideast visit was that nothing much was accomplished. I'm afraid that our fears concerning their inclinations to deal bilaterally might be confirmed. It's going to be hard to hold Syria." This would all prove to be prophetic. Begin gave Sadat no real concessions, and the unilateral character of Sadat's trip only encouraged Begin to think he did not need to deal with the rest of the Arabs and instead could drive a hard bargain for a separate peace with Egypt. "Although Sadat's visit has been good," Carter noted, "I don't think he can go very far toward resolving the basic problems."

Carter and his advisers still strongly preferred the Geneva option—where they believed all the parties to the conflict would be forced to make real compromises. But by the end of 1977, it was clear that Sadat's mission had effectively sabotaged Geneva, and what remained was a direct dialogue between Israel and Egypt. Carter realized there was no way that he could not be seen as supportive of the venture.

Already, Congressman Ed Koch, who was about to become mayor of New York City, had publicly criticized Carter's evenhandedness, accusing the president of abandoning his commitments "to protect Israel." Koch was a consummate politician, and while he didn't know much about foreign policy or the Arab-Israeli conflict, he knew how to command a stage. On the morning of October 4, Carter flew into New York City to address the United Nations. When the president stepped out of the helicopter at a Wall Street helipad, he was greeted warmly by Mayor Abe Beame. Congressman Koch was also in the receiving line. Koch had just won the Democratic mayoral primary, so he was certain to win the November election.

Koch had decided he would take advantage of this, his first encounter with President Carter, to send a message to Jewish voters. As they were introduced, Koch said, "Mr. President, welcome to New York City." And without missing a beat, he added, "I'm really troubled about your position on Israel, and I have a letter which explains why I think you are wrong." Carter had been warned of Koch's intentions and merely nodded, took the letter, and handed it off to Jody Powell. Instead of pausing to chat with Koch, he turned to others in the crowd of onlookers and made small talk before walking to his limousine for the ride to the United Nations. That was regarded by Koch as a snub. Koch told reporters that he had been scheduled to ride with the president. This was false. But now he stepped forward to the microphone and seized the opportunity to explain to reporters the contents of his letter. He said he had already complained to Brzezinski about his concerns that the president was "catering to Arab demands." Harkening back to the dark days of appeasement in the 1930s, Koch intoned, "We cannot permit another Czechoslovakia."

Such grandstanding earned Koch the headlines he wanted. The next day *The New York Times* put the story on the front page with a photo of Koch handing his letter to the president. The headline read "Koch Mideast Protest Draws Carter Snub." To be sure, Koch's performance was also criticized in some quarters as rude and gauche behavior. One of his opponents in the November election, Mario M. Cuomo, called Koch's treatment of the president "clumsy." Carter himself was clueless, noting in his diary only that Koch had "in a pre-publicized but friendly way handed me a letter about the Mideast, which I accepted and gave to Jody. The news media, as is often the custom, completely distorted the incident, which was very friendly." Later, Tip O'Neill told Carter that "Ed Koch was seriously hurt by the allegation that he had insulted the president." Ironically, Carter felt obliged to reassure the Speaker that he had not felt insulted. Koch, he said, just "wants me to come to New York" for a campaign event, "which I won't do."

This was only the beginning of what would prove to be a long-running soap opera with the flamboyant New York mayor, a man who cultivated his flair for chutzpah. But Koch and Carter spoke a different language. (Carter's media adviser, Jerry Rafshoon, once had to explain to the president the meaning of "a real mensch.") With hindsight, Carter might have earned important political dividends if he had cultivated Koch and campaigned for him in New York. But the personal chemistry wasn't there—and stroking another politician's considerable ego was precisely the kind of thing Carter hated most about his job.

That autumn, just prior to Sadat's trip to Jerusalem, *The New York Times* published a long editorial provocatively entitled "The Jews and Jimmy Carter." The editors began with the proposition that "one of the unsayable things in our political life these days is that most leaders of the American Jewish community are acting as if President Carter is risking Israel's survival for an illusory Middle East settlement." But far from legitimizing these fears, the *Times* editorialists warned that "the spokesmen of American Jews might cease to be taken seriously" if they came to be seen as merely parroting every Israeli position. Such a "siege mentality" ignored reality: "It is a fact of recent history that politically difficult but valuable Israeli concessions have come only in response to American pressure." This was an extraordinary admission and a firm rebuke of Jewish American leaders. But neither was it a full-throated endorsement of the Carter administration's high-risk diplomacy.

On the other side of the political equation, Carter found himself attacked by Arab American leaders. In a brusque exchange with Brzezinski, one such leader, Fouad Moughrabi, suggested that the administration had suffered "a failure of nerve" on the question of Palestinian self-determination. Brzezinski shot back, "Israel is a state. . . . The PLO is not even a government-in-exile, and they ask for too much from a position of weakness." In December 1977, Brzezinski gave an interview to *Paris Match* in which he snidely summed up the administration's attitude: "Bye-bye PLO." Carter had essentially given up on trying to bring the PLO into a public dialogue. The domestic political pressures were too great—and Begin was unbending.

On December 16, the president had a disheartening phone conversation with the Israeli prime minister in which it became clear that Begin intended to offer Sadat mere crumbs. Begin was willing to withdraw only from parts of the Sinai; he would not give up any Israeli settlements in the Sinai. As to the West Bank, he proposed a faux autonomy plan whereby Israel would retain full military control of all the occupied territories. Carter told Begin this was quite frankly wholly "inadequate"—and "may cause the downfall of Sadat." Begin ignored this warning, and as Carter had predicted, the bilateral negotiations on December 25 in Ismailia quickly deadlocked. Sadat had gone to Jerusalem—and now seemingly he had nothing to show for it.

"I am very disappointed with the Israeli attitude," Sadat told Carter in a phone conversation. "They prefer land to peace. . . . They think I want peace at any price."

CARTER ENDED THE year departing on Air Force One for a nine-day tour of Poland, Iran, India, Saudi Arabia, and Egypt. It was a frenetic journey. In Warsaw, he had a long official meeting with Communist Party first secretary Edward Gierek. In an effort to break the ice, Carter told this lifelong communist that he had just come from a visit with the Polish cardinal Stefan Wyszynski, who had described Gierek as a "true Pole and a righteous man." Gierek lightened up at this flattery and remarked that he had recently visited the cardinal. Carter responded that perhaps he should visit the cardinal more often—and even consider becoming a Christian believer. Stunned by this transparent bit of presidential proselytizing, Gierek replied that he had learned to serve his fellow human beings as a communist.

"I told him," Carter noted in his diary, "that it was never too late to become a believer." After this unusual small talk, the two heads of state sat down to several hours of discussions with their respective official delegations. But afterward, Gierek asked if Carter would speak with him in his private office. They met for seventy minutes alone, except for their respective interpreters. Oddly, Gierek again broached the topic of religion. He said he had always espoused atheism, but then he confided that his mother was a believer and had recently visited the Vatican. He asked Carter about his Christian faith. Carter responded like the lay missionary he had once been, explaining his faith to perfect strangers, and concluding with the same query: "I asked him if he would consider accepting Jesus Christ as his personal savior." Gierek said he would like to please his mother, but his official position made it impossible for him to make any public profession of faith. Carter could not know for sure, but he left Poland with the impression that he might have made a covert convert.*

On December 31, the presidential party left Warsaw and flew to Tehran, where Shah Mohammad Reza Pahlavi and Empress Farah hosted a "delightful banquet." King Hussein of Jordan was also present, together with hundreds of other guests. During the exchange of official toasts, Carter praised the shah in effusive terms: "Iran, because of the great leadership of the shah, is an *island of stability* in one of the more troubled areas of the world." Carter was often prone to displays of exagger-

---

* Ten months later, the Polish cardinal Karol Józef Wojtyla was elected as Pope John Paul II, and in June 1979, over Moscow's objections, Gierek gave the Polish pope permission to visit Warsaw. The visit sparked the formation of Lech Walesa's Solidarity movement, which in turn led to the collapse of the communist regime in Eastern Europe just a decade later. Gierek lost his job in September 1980.

ated flattery in such situations, but on this occasion the words for this toast had been written for him by his speechwriter, Jim Fallows. Thirteen months later, the phrase "island of stability" would be quoted with mockery by pundits. But never cited is the fact that Carter's toast also included a pointed quote from the thirteenth-century Persian poet Saʻdī: "If the misery of others leaves you indifferent and with no feeling of sorrow, then you cannot be called a human being."

Privately, Carter had inklings that all was not well in the Persian monarchy. Early the next morning, New Year's Day, Carter drove to the airport with the shah. Glancing out the car window, he was surprised to see a group of angry young men, throwing rocks and shouting "Allahu Akbar." It was an omen.

Few Americans understood anything about Iran, its modern history, or Persian culture. Henry Kissinger blandly asserted in his memoirs that the shah "was for us that rarest of leaders, an unconditional ally." Kissinger knew, of course, that the CIA had installed the shah in a 1953 coup that toppled an elected prime minister and parliament. He didn't care. But of course the average Iranian cared deeply about this sordid history. By 1977, fully one-third of Iran's annual budget was allocated to the military, including billions in arms purchases from the United States. That's what Kissinger meant by an unconditional ally. The Pahlavi regime was transparently awash in corruption and led by an autocrat completely out of touch with his people.

New Year's Eve had not been Carter's first encounter with Pahlavi. The shah had come to the White House just six weeks earlier, on November 15, 1977. It had been an inauspicious visit. As the president and the monarch stood on the South Lawn, trying to make their remarks for the television cameras, they could hear angry demonstrators shouting slogans against the Pahlavi dictatorship. More than a thousand protesters, many of them Iranian students studying in the United States, clashed with police, and a dozen people were injured, including some police. Washington police mounted on horseback unleashed tear gas on the unruly Iranian dissidents—and the wind carried clouds of it across the South Lawn. Tears streamed down the faces of the shah and hundreds of spectators and journalists.

Carter kept to his welcoming remarks and stoically refrained from rubbing his eyes. "It was," he later noted in his diary, "really rough." Afterward, the shah presented Carter with a gift marking America's bicentennial, a Persian handwoven tapestry depicting the classic portrait of George Washington. At the official dinner that evening, Carter managed a weak joke: "One thing I can say about the shah, he knows how to draw a crowd." Unusually, Carter had invited a handful of jazz greats—Dizzy Gillespie, Earl "Fatha" Hines, and Sarah Vaughan—to provide the entertainment. The president of the United States thoroughly enjoyed himself.

In their private conversation, the shah seemed embarrassed by the demonstrations but argued that he was nevertheless proud of his accomplishments. Carter listened and interpreted this to mean that now "he's strong enough to do some overt things on the human rights issue." In a follow-up meeting the next day, Carter took the shah into his private study and bluntly asked him if he could speak frankly. The shah nodded, and so Carter launched into a carefully prepared speech about human rights. A growing number of Iranians, including religious leaders but also a new middle class, were demanding political influence. Couldn't the shah solve these problems through closer consultation with dissidents and an easing of strict police policies?

The shah sat silent for a moment. Carter thought "he was quite embarrassed." But then he replied, "No, there is nothing I can do." He explained that he had to enforce Iranian laws against communism, and that most of these dissidents were in fact communists. The troublemakers, he insisted, "are really just a tiny minority, and have no support among the vast majority of the Iranian people."* Carter gently pressed the issue for a few more minutes, but it soon became obvious that there was nothing he could say that would convince the shah to change his regime's behavior.

Carter knew from his intelligence briefings that there were signs that the "seeds of dissension" within Iran's middle class were taking root. On the other hand, just eight months later, Carter read a CIA assessment that concluded that Iran is not in "even a prerevolutionary situation." Carter didn't know it, but the CIA had long ago agreed to restrict its informants inside Iran to sources approved by SAVAK, the shah's in-

---

* In 1973, the shah had told the Italian journalist Oriana Fallaci that the clerics were "a stupid and reactionary bunch whose brains have not moved . . . for a thousand years."

ternal intelligence service. Because the Agency had no contacts with the opposition, its intelligence was limited.

The shah had, in fact, marginally liberalized his regime in early 1976, appointing a number of technocrats to the cabinet and freeing some political prisoners. He announced that 1977 would be the "year of liberalization." One of his closest advisers, General Hussein Fardust, a known critic of SAVAK, persuaded the shah that the political repression of recent years had backfired. "The human rights situation in Iran has been improving," the CIA reported. "Only government opponents advocating violent overthrow of the regime or who are suspected of terrorist activity are now being arrested." SAVAK was still a feared police agency, and from 1971 to 1978 somewhere between three hundred and four hundred Iranian dissidents were killed by SAVAK or died in detention. International Red Cross inspectors reported in June 1977 that they had counted 3,087 political prisoners. These numbers were bad enough—but they were actually lower than many accounts in the Western press. Martin Woollacott, a *Guardian* reporter living in Iran in the 1970s, later recalled, "SAVAK worked very well in instilling passivity, some fear, and a large degree of acquiescence with a minimum of violence. But the picture of SAVAK as bloodthirsty did not stand up to scrutiny."

The shah's tentative steps toward liberalization were motivated in part by his desire to pave the way for his sixteen-year-old son, Crown Prince Reza, to succeed him. No one knew it back in Washington, but French physicians had diagnosed the shah with a slow-growing but incurable cancer a few years earlier. He knew that he might not have long to live. The shah was certainly surprised by the election of Carter to the presidency, but he had convinced himself that his "liberalization" program—he called it *musharikat* (better translated from the Farsi as "participation")—would meet the new president's expectations for an improvement in human rights.

And while Carter had his doubts, he too convinced himself that the shah was moving in the direction of democratization and liberalization. Both Brzezinski and Secretary Vance encouraged this wishful thinking. Brzezinski told Carter that the shah "clearly seemed to enjoy being a traditional Oriental despot, accustomed to instant and total obedience from his courtiers." He "displayed megalomaniacal tendencies." Brzezinski nevertheless argued that the shah had brought "stability" to the region, while Vance echoed this sentiment, citing the shah's utility in keeping oil prices down. Both men urged Carter to make Iran an exception to the administration's new policy of restricting arms sales to nondemocratic regimes with poor human rights records. Carter went along despite criticism from people like Assistant Secretary of State Patt Derian and liberal pundits, who cited Iran as a glaring and hypocritical exception to his prescription for a foreign policy based on human rights. But Carter had decided that the shah was a "strong ally." If the previous administration had given the shah a virtual blank check, Carter did little to change this policy. Over the next two years, the administration gave a green light to most of the shah's weapons purchases, including, most controversially in the eyes of Congress, the sale of seven AWACS airplanes, equipped with sophisticated early-warning radar technology. Carter also acquiesced in the shah's purchase of several nuclear power plants from European suppliers, nuclear technology that would someday fuel postrevolutionary Iran's covert program to develop nuclear weapons.

All of this was a mistake. But it underscores that, far from placing pressure on the shah's regime, the Carter administration gave the shah what he wanted. As one Iran expert, Barry Rubin, put it, "Complaints after the revolution by the shah and his defenders that Washington forced him to become too soft, and thus encouraged the upheaval, seem, simply, to have no basis in fact."

In reality, neither the Americans nor the Iranians understood each other or what was about to happen. A revolution was brewing and no one in the halls of power realized it. The shah and Carter had nothing in common. Asadollah Alam, the shah's closest friend and palace confidant, snidely noted in his diary that the Georgian was "no more than an ignorant peasant boy." That was a terrible misreading of the tea leaves.

Chapter 11
Washington Distractions

My God, I've been set up for a great big fall!
—HAMILTON JORDAN to Jody Powell

Hamilton Jordan and Jody Powell
ANNIE LEIBOVITZ/ROLLING STONE

BY THE END of 1977, Carter's White House staff was exhausted and distracted. The president had set a hard pace. "The bloom is off the rose with my work," confided Landon Butler to his diary in mid-December. "Ham is more and more difficult to work with—he misses meetings, he's distracted, he doesn't listen, and he makes no attempt whatsoever to lead his staff in any but the most sporadic way." As Jordan's principal deputy, Butler was always juggling his days. He grumbled to himself all the time about the chaos his boss created wherever he went. But Butler also admired Jordan. "He's still capable of fine insights, the kind that can substantially clear the air, but more and more his memos just reflect a firm grasp of the obvious. . . . On the other hand, he's still the person everyone turns to in the crunch. And he's the one who can then discuss the most serious matter with the President."

On December 9, 1977, Jordan submitted another long memorandum to the president, this one analyzing how Carter had divided his time over the preceding year. Hamilton had devoted a month, off and on, to working on the 116-page document. Butler read it quickly and thought it superb: "Its thrust was to argue that the President had spent far too much time in the first year on foreign policy issues, and that he would be in serious political trouble if he didn't pay more attention to domestic problems." Jordan reported that between January and October the president had allocated 62 percent of his time to foreign policy or defense issues—and 38 percent of his time to domestic issues.

Jordan also complained that too many foreign policy decisions were being made without attention to domestic political considerations. "There is not a person who is preoccupied exclusively with the political dimensions of the decision." As a result, "the high quality of your foreign policy decisions will be undermined unnecessarily by domestic political considerations." This was an old story. The distractions and glamour of foreign policy were an occupational hazard of working in the Oval Office. The previous spring Carter had admitted as much during a radio call-in program when he explained that he was working about the same number of hours as he had in the Georgia governor's mansion, "but in addition, it is more interesting because you have all the foreign affairs questions to address."

Carter's work ethic and appetite for the job were widely admired. But Jordan and other aides could see that it came at a cost. After one meeting with Carter in late October 1977, Dr. Peter Bourne noted in his diary, "Carter terribly tired and haggard—I was horrified and could not take my eyes off him." Jordan warned him, "You find it difficult—if not impossible—to say that 'this problem is not important enough to merit my personal attention.' As a result, too many policies, programs and issues receive what I would describe as excessive presidential attention and absorb too much of the precious political and moral capital of your Presidency." Looking ahead to the 1980 election, Jordan wrote, "I feel strongly that we should presume the worst and assume that we will be challenged within our own party and also face strong opposition in the general election. . . . The challenge in the party will come from the left." Jordan was particularly worried about what he saw as a "sharp decline in support among Jews and blacks." This would prove prescient.

Carter was not unsympathetic to his liberal-left constituency. His instincts were always to favor the poor and disadvantaged. And personally, he felt he had a sterling record on civil rights, feminist issues, and labor. Senator Ted Kennedy, the titular leader of the liberal wing of the Democratic Party, had been his most loyal supporter. He had voted with the administration on tax reform, arms control, human rights, the energy bill, and the Panama Canal Treaty. But Kennedy was still a bit miffed that Carter had not offered him a speaking slot at the 1976 Democratic convention. And while Carter's encounters with Kennedy in the White House were still cordial, there was no genuine warmth between the two men.

Kennedy complained that Carter made a pretense of listening. The president would invite Kennedy and other politicians to White House colloquies on various issues. "If you were a guest at one of these gatherings," Kennedy later wrote in his memoirs, "you'd go through the buffet line and eat quickly. And then for the next three hours Jimmy Carter would conduct a seminar on Africa, for instance. He would let you know that he knew every country in Africa and the name of every president of every country in Africa." Kennedy admitted these sessions were "well worth attending." But they were purely "informational." There was no real dialogue. And worse, from Kennedy's perspective, there was no liquor: "He and Rosalynn had removed all the liquor in the White House." This, of course, was not true. Carter drank an occasional bourbon with Kirbo, and he did serve wine at state dinners. But the president thought liquor was out of place at a working White House meeting. And Kennedy thought the president unconscionably stingy. Their relationship was driven by a clash of cultures.

Kennedy later concluded, "He was an outsider, and he was going to run things from an outsider's point of view." Kennedy was worried, particularly about Carter's position on healthcare. The president, he thought, was not taking the initiative. In May 1977, Kennedy told an audience of United Auto Workers, "One hundred and sixteen days after the inauguration, President Carter and his administration have made commendable progress in most areas, but health care has been left behind." Over the next six months, Kennedy's staff worked hard to craft legislation that would satisfy the entire spectrum of the Democratic Party. They persuaded labor union leaders like the AFL-CIO's Lane Kirkland and the UAW's Doug Fraser to compromise on their desire for a single-payer health insurance plan. They reluctantly agreed instead on support for a mandatory and universal plan that nevertheless relied on the existing private insurance companies. Kennedy believed this to be a major concession—but that autumn he was frustrated to learn from Carter's HEW secretary, Joe Califano, that the president wanted more time to study the legislation.

On December 20, 1977, Carter signed into law his reform of the Social Security Act, another piece of tough legislation that included "a substantial tax increase" for anyone earning over $25,000. Republicans called the Social Security Amendments of 1977 the "largest peacetime tax increase in American history," but the bill preserved, literally for decades to come, the fiscal soundness of this popular retirement fund for America's elderly. If Carter had not insisted that Congress act, the Social Security's trust fund would have gone bankrupt by the mid-1980s. He regarded this tax increase as a major political achievement, one that met his standards for fiscal responsibility, but a piece of legislation that benefited the poor. That same evening, he "gave Senator Kennedy his word" that he would introduce yet another major social welfare initiative, a national health insurance bill, in the following year. Kennedy was momentarily reassured that Carter was still committed to a comprehensive healthcare bill—as was Doug Fraser, the United Auto Workers union leader. Fraser also met with Carter the next day, and he too sought a commitment from the president on healthcare.

Labor leaders like Fraser were still suspicious of this southern president. Carter seemed to be doing all the right things, but they still had no personal rapport with the man. Carter actually admired Fraser as "unselfish and also politically competent." But somehow he failed to convey any personal warmth with Fraser—or, for that matter, with George Meany, the AFL-CIO labor boss. Kennedy noted that Carter continued to talk about "universal" and "mandatory" national health insurance but used language that made it seem to be a distant goal, not an immediate priority. Kennedy harbored growing doubts about the president. "I just wasn't sure with Carter."

Senator Hubert Humphrey had no such qualms. Carter had admired the Minnesota liberal ever since he watched him lead the fight over civil rights at the 1948 Democratic convention. The former vice president and liberal Senate workhorse had been helpful to Carter that first year. But Humphrey was now dying of colon cancer. On December 10, 1977, Carter flew into Minneapolis on his way back from a trip to the West Coast, picked up Humphrey and his doctor, and accompanied them to Camp David. It was a special gesture to a dying friend and political ally. He knew that Humphrey had never been allowed by President Johnson to visit Camp David. Carter took delight in rectifying this lapse.

"Hubert seemed to be in good spirits," Carter noted, "although he's getting weaker by the day." Sitting before a warm fire in the presidential cabin, he listened as Humphrey reminisced about his difficult relationship with Johnson; he advised Carter not to be concerned about "daily aberrant criticisms." They watched a couple of movies and took short walks. Carter took Humphrey to church on Sunday and noticed that "he's begun to appreciate the small things: how birds feed and the colors of leaves, the sound of music." All in all, Carter thought it a most enjoyable weekend. Humphrey died a month later.

AT THE END of the year, pundits gave Carter a surprisingly stingy report card on his foreign policy achievements. "It has been a rocky year," editorialized *The New York Times,* "for the man who ran against Washington and then found he had to try to master it." There was no denying Carter's virtues: "decency, simplicity, optimistic energy." But the *Times* editorialists complained about the president's "touching belief that all governmental problems could be solved if only they were worked at." Still, they grudgingly conceded that his freshman year in office was marked by numerous domestic initiatives, including legislation that averted the "collapse of the Social Security system" and making food stamps easier to use for the very poor. He also deserved credit for "giving the highest priority to the creation and enactment of an energy policy in the face of public indifference and Congressional intransigence."

Turning to his record on foreign affairs, the *Times*'s Washington bureau chief, James Reston, wryly observed, "Name any inflammable foreign policy issue, and Mr. Carter has taken it on." In the view of the

Times, the president had tackled too many policy "initiatives" and had ended the year with few concrete achievements.

Carter didn't see it that way. He knew he had played no small role in Sadat's historic visit to Jerusalem. He had negotiated the Panama Canal Treaty and made human rights a central feature of American foreign policy. Domestically, he had tackled energy, civil rights, and Social Security. He had passed a $5 billion student loan program and amnestied Vietnam-era draft evaders. He had canceled the inefficient B-1 bomber, vetoed numerous wasteful water projects, and canceled the expensive breeder reactor program. Unemployment was down 1.5 percent, inflation had fallen to 4 percent, and the nation's gross national product had increased by a robust 5 percent. A record-breaking four million new jobs had been created during his first year in office. He hadn't gotten everything on his agenda, but all in all, he thought "1977 was a good year."

But the press was disposed to be critical. Not even the *Times*'s political humorist, columnist Russell Baker, could give him a break: "Carter offered to rid us of these exhausting and costly entertainments, to dismantle the imperial Presidency which nourished them and to restore the Presidency to the arid, nuts-and-bolts business of governing under republican forms. This is what he has done, and of course it is dull, terribly dull."

Another columnist famous for his humor, Calvin Trillin, created a stir in the spring of 1978 when he claimed to have dredged up a forgotten H. L. Mencken quote from 1928. The Baltimore pundit and satirist had supposedly predicted, "I cheer myself with the thought that someday we will have a president from the deserts of the Deep South. . . . The President's brother, a prime specimen of *Boobus Collumnus Rubericus,* will gather his loutish companions on the porch of the White House to swill beer from the bottle and snigger over whispered barnyard jokes about the darkies. . . . The President's daughter will record these events with her box camera. . . . The incumbent himself, cleansed of his bumpkin ways by some Grady's New South hucksters, will have a charm comparable to that of the leading undertaker of Dothan, Alabama." When Mencken scholars claimed no such scribbling existed in the archives, Trillin deadpanned, "I admit nothing." Trillin, of course, was having fun at the expense of the southerner in the White House.

Sadly, the antics of the president's brother provided satirists in the press with rich material. Billy Carter had spent the first two years of the Carter administration selling his southern good-ol'-boy persona to the highest bidder. He marketed Billy Beer and received speaking fees for his appearances around the country. It was all self-parody, and pretty harmless stuff. But then he accepted a $220,000 loan from Libyan dictator Muammar al-Qaddafi and made several trips to Libya. From all appearances, he seemed to be on the take from the Libyans, and eventually he was forced to register as a foreign lobbyist. When Jewish American organizations criticized his behavior, Billy made matters worse by observing, "There's a hell of a lot more Arabians than there is Jews." Republican Party chairman Bill Brock called these remarks anti-Semitic.

The president, of course, was embarrassed by his brother's behavior, but he knew it was also fueled by alcohol. "He is seriously ill at this point," the president told reporters. "I love him. I know for a fact that he is not anti-Semitic." Billy used to work long hours at the peanut warehouse and then drink some beers with his buddies and go home to have dinner with his family. But when his brother became president, the family business was put into a blind trust. Over Billy's objections, Charlie Kirbo arranged to have the warehouse leased to a third party—leaving Billy embittered toward Kirbo, whom he described as "about the dumbest bastard I ever met." Billy had nothing to do but trade on his name, and drink. The drinking got to be too much. His brother later wrote that Billy "became an apparently hopeless alcoholic while I was president." Finally, in early March 1979, Billy checked himself in to an alcohol rehabilitation center in California. He eventually managed to stop drinking, but the political damage to his brother lingered.

Carter himself was philosophical about the press. He expected the fourth estate to be critical. But he was particularly annoyed by the reporting from *The Washington Post* and *Newsweek*. He thought the *Post's* reporting was "abominable" and *Newsweek* was "the most inaccurate periodical I read."

Jody Powell responded to the critics in the press room by quipping that a more experienced and cynical politician than Carter "would have tried less, gotten less, and been given better marks." By then, Powell and Jordan had made the cover of *Rolling Stone,* shot by celebrity photographer Annie Leibovitz. *Time* magazine had the duo on its cover, featuring a drawing by the caricaturist David Levine—who had them dressed in baggy jean coveralls, holding fishing poles, with a cigarette dangling from Jody's lips. Just two good ol' boys standing in front of the White House. They knew that even favorable publicity made them a target. After *Washington Post* "style" reporter Sally Quinn labeled Jordan the "second-most powerful person in Washington," Hamilton told Jody, "My God, I've been set up for a great big fall!"

Quinn lobbed another snarky hand grenade at the White House in mid-December, this time in a highly entertaining, five-thousand-word spread entitled "Where Did All the Good Times Go?" Her story focused mostly on the by-now-well-worn theme of the divide between Washington society and the "Carter people," who had arrived in town "like an alien tribe" and "stopped serving booze at the White House, cut out dancing, outlawed limousines, and sold the Sequoia." Senator Edward Brooke (R-MA) complained that "when you go to the White House, the place looks physically dirty: People running around in jeans doesn't look right." The president was not playing "the game" of "greeting, glad-handing and backslapping." The Georgians didn't like to socialize: "I think Jody really understands that he needs to get around more," said one anonymous source. "Jack Watson will get out, but Hamilton is just not social. And the President certainly doesn't do anything." Newscaster David Brinkley was quoted as saying, "We don't see them anywhere. I saw Jody one night. He was highly uncommunicative. . . . It's not only silly but bad policy to be standoffish. . . . They need us more than we need them. We were here before they came, and we'll be here after they leave."

In retort, Quinn got the president's personal secretary, Susan Clough, to say for the record, "Most people in Washington find a way of perpetuating their existence here. . . . I find that I am preparing to go."

Quinn quoted the humor columnist Art Buchwald complaining that none of the Georgians came to his annual tennis tournament held on his birthday in October. Why? "Because I just don't know any. . . . I find Carter very hard to satirize because nobody knows him." Quinn portrayed the Georgians as innocents, condescendingly quoting White House counsel Bob Lipshutz as saying, "I do feel more comfortable about Washington parties now that I know which color wine is coming next."

In a curtsy to some modicum of fairness, Quinn quoted the president's media adviser, Jerry Rafshoon: "All the put-downs about grits and down-home barbecues really turned the Carter people off. . . . I'll put Jody Powell up against anybody who went to Harvard. He can discuss anything. Washingtonians were satisfied with LBJ, who had around him some very tacky people. But they were people who'd been around here for a while. Do they think Bobby Baker* has more class than Hamilton Jordan?"

But Quinn's clear theme was that these Carter people would never "meld" with the Washington social scene and, in fact, needed mediators like Bob Strauss, a "slick Texas lawyer, a smooth operator" who was nevertheless "a born-again Washingtonian." Strauss was the only guy who could "soften up a recalcitrant senator, soothe the ruffled feathers of an ambassador, mitigate the disapproval of a journalist."

Slivers of Quinn's story might have been true enough, but most of it was damning caricature. Sally got on the phone with Hamilton's wife, Nancy, who tried to explain their lack of a social life. "We really are friendly," Nancy said. "We like people. But we've all gotten involved. I don't leave my office until 7:30 or 8. Hamilton, 8:30 or 9. It's always been the same working for Jimmy Carter. We don't mean to be offensive. . . . If we do go out to have a pizza with Jody and Nan [Powell] or Frank and Nancy [Moore] it's a big month. . . . But there is no way to get your job done and go out."

By the autumn of 1977, Jody Powell was viewing the press and *The Washington Post*'s reporters in particular with a decidedly jaundiced eye. He told Tim Kraft that he now thought the administration "didn't exactly have a honeymoon with the press. . . . It was more like a one-night stand." When Powell learned that Quinn was doing a story on social life at the White House, he firmly put out the word that "we have nothing to do with her."

He had good reason. A few weeks earlier, Quinn had run a story implying that President Carter had an intimate relationship with his personal secretary, Susan Clough. Jody was incensed. Quinn's story was cleverly written. It began by describing Clough as an attractive thirty-

---

* An aide to then-senator Lyndon B. Johnson, Baker was forced to resign in a scandal involving government contracts and spent eighteen months in prison for tax evasion.

two-year-old woman, "blonde, very pretty and single." Quinn then reported that Clough was "aware" of "the winks and insinuations . . . about her relationship with Carter." But then it became clear that Clough had been ambushed by Quinn when asked directly about an affair: "Her reaction is utter amazement. 'I don't think Jimmy Carter has ever had an affair with anybody but Rosalynn.'" Having grabbed the reader's eyeballs with this tawdry sexual speculation, Quinn's profile proceeded to make it clear that Clough was a charming but quite clueless innocent. Powell was also personally offended by Quinn's sly suggestion that perhaps Clough had obtained her job only because, according to unnamed detractors, "there has been a relationship between her and Powell." Needless to say, Quinn had not gotten Jody to comment. Powell felt burned: "My wife was also less than thrilled." He unsuccessfully tried to persuade Joe Califano to call up his former client at the *Post*: "Surely *you* can call Katharine Graham off the record," growled Powell. Califano demurred, saying that would just draw attention to the story. Powell told one reporter, "I'd like to punch Sally Quinn right in the mouth. Since I can't punch Sally Quinn, maybe I could punch Ben Bradlee and see if she cared." So it was understandable that when, a few weeks later, Quinn let it be known that her upcoming piece would also contain something damaging to Hamilton, Jody decided it best not to engage with a reporter who traded in gossip. Only later would he realize that this had been a mistake.

Quinn published her long essay the week before Christmas 1977. Saving her bombshell for the end of the story, she reported that Jordan had made a rare appearance at a recent dinner party hosted by television personality Barbara Walters. Quinn, who also attended the party, wrote that Hamilton seemed "ill at ease during the cocktail hour, only relaxing when Bob Strauss was around to act as liaison." At dinner, Hamilton was seated next to Madame Ashraf Ghorbal, wife of the Egyptian ambassador, a lovely, matronly woman old enough to be Jordan's grandmother. But according to Quinn, Jordan soon made a vulgar joke: "Fortified with an ample amount of the host's booze, he gazed at the ambassador's wife's ample front, pulled at her elasticized bodice and was prompted to say, loudly enough for several others to hear, 'I've always wanted to see the pyramids.'"

The story ricocheted in newspapers across the country.* The only problem was that no one sitting at Hamilton's table had heard the remark. In fact, everyone denied it. *The New York Times* reported the story the day after Quinn's piece appeared, recounting the whole incident in detail. But the remainder of its story was filled with denials. Egyptian ambassador Ghorbal said that his wife "doesn't remember that she heard anything of the sort" and that "there was nothing to be offended about." Kissinger, who sat at Jordan's table, said he recalled "nothing improper." Vivian Dinitz, the Israeli ambassador's wife, explained that she had been seated next to Jordan, who had been "a model of decorum. . . . I did not hear him say anything like that." ABC newsman Sam Donaldson was at the table but heard nothing of the sort. Art Buchwald was also at the same table but denied hearing Jordan say anything about the pyramids. "It was one of those affairs," Buchwald said, "where nobody seemed to be paying any attention to what anybody else was saying."

Buchwald later told Jody Powell, "That story was crap. I was sitting there, and it didn't happen." The problem was that the story sounded in character even to some of Jordan's friends. Les Francis recalled, "He fucked around. He drank. He was sarcastic and sometimes didn't give a shit." He had a reputation that led some people to believe Quinn's gossip.

When reached for comment by the *Times* reporter, Quinn said she had not seen the incident herself but insisted that two people had talked to her who had witnessed it. She declined, of course, to name her sources. At his daily press briefing, Powell wisecracked, "I'm just hurt that I wasn't invited."

President Carter was annoyed but not surprised by the Quinn story. "I talked to Jody about recent attacks on Hamilton," he noted in his diary. "He and Stu [Eizenstat] had been the only ones left from the Georgia delegation who haven't been seriously roughed up by the news media. Looks like Hamilton's time has come."

Notwithstanding all the denials, *Times* columnist William Safire fea-

---

* Quinn was picking up from an unsourced item in Diana McLellan's gossip column, The Ear, published in the rival *Washington Star*. Without naming Jordan, McLellan had reported that a "White House Biggie" had made the "pyramids" comment after "rudely peeking down Mrs. Ghorbal's modest dress."

tured the story in his column later that week. Safire, of course, had turned his column into a crusade against the Carter administration, most prominently during the Bert Lance affair a few months earlier. As it happened, Safire had also attended the dinner, hosted to honor the Egyptian and Israeli ambassadors in the wake of Sadat's historic visit to Jerusalem the previous month. And even though the dinner was supposed to have been off the record and Safire had been reprimanded by Walters for "note-taking," the columnist could not resist. He began by quoting Buchwald toasting Walters for "bringing together two men who have been ideologically miles apart, who fought each other over the years—Hamilton Jordan and Bill Safire." And then Safire passed on the gossip: "Seems he [Jordan] made a vulgar crack that some at his table took to be insulting to the lady next to him." Safire admitted that because he had been sitting at another table, "I have no lip-smacking details to add." Safire had to know that the story was doubtful, but that didn't stop him from repeating the slur.

Jordan tried to take the incident in stride. The morning after Quinn's bawdy story appeared, he came into the White House and acted nonchalant. His aide Landon Butler noted, "Ham was more relaxed than I had seen him in a long time." But in fact, Jordan was feeling wounded. He had accepted this dinner invitation only because Vice President Mondale had recently urged him to "get out more and let people get to know me." At the time, he had enjoyed the occasion: "There were too many toasts, which made for a very long evening, but otherwise it was uneventful and enjoyable. I was glad to have gone and felt that I had at least begun to pay my dues to social Washington."

When the Quinn story appeared a few weeks later, Jordan was dismayed. Sure, it was a style-section gossip story, and many people thought it amusing. But Jordan knew "nothing remotely like that had ever happened." And despite all the denials of those present, the story took on a life of its own; "the 'pyramids' story just became part of my political biography and was accepted without question." Years later, writing in his memoir, *No Such Thing as a Bad Day*, Jordan confessed, "I put up a brave front, told people that it 'came with the territory,' but I was terribly embarrassed and hurt."

Just two months after the Quinn story, Jordan was the target of another *Washington Post* gossip columnist, Rudy Maxa, who headlined his

February 17, 1978, story "Hamilton Jordan: Carter Aide's Manners Are No Laughing Matter." Citing two unnamed witnesses, Maxa claimed that an inebriated Jordan had accosted a young woman at a Washington bar and spat his drink "over the head" of a woman and down the blouse of another young woman. (Carter kidded Jordan later, saying, "You ought to get out of government and go in the circus if you can do that.")

The story was garbage journalism. But, worried that the press would pick it up and run with it as they had the pyramids story, Jody Powell decided to bat it down. He assigned a White House lawyer to interview the bartender present and get his testimony. According to the bartender, Maxa had the story upside down. It was a vodka-drinking woman who had approached Jordan, not the other way around. And there had been no spitting before the bartender had asked the young woman to pay her bill and leave. A triumphant Powell released a thirty-three-page report refuting the Maxa story. But instead of focusing on the facts, the press decided that the news was Powell's lengthy rebuttal. *The Washington Post* ran a front-page story on Powell's report, basically defending Maxa's reporting and even repeating Quinn's allegation about Jordan and the Egyptian pyramids. What had been initially printed in the gossip pages now was recycled as front-page news. "My overreaction became the issue," Powell later wrote, "rather than the accuracy of the accusations." Powell's forceful denial only seemed to give the story more traction. And despite everything, Maxa and the *Post* defended the veracity of what forever became known as the "amaretto and cream" story.

Ten days later, Jody confided to Jerome Doolittle, one of the speechwriters on Fallows's team, that he had reacted "hard and fast" because "you and I both know that Hamilton's personal life won't stand up under much inspection." On this occasion, Jody thought the White House had a pretty defensible position. "Fighting back hard might cause future gossip writers to back off."

Doolittle already had heard about the bar incident from Jay Beck—one of Hamilton's aides—who was a witness. "Beck said [there were] two women smashed at the end of the bar, kind of making [them]selves obnoxious." Beck had left the scene before the alleged altercation. But Jody told Doolittle what he thought had happened next. The two inebriated women had approached Hamilton and his close friend and former college roommate John Golden, and they began to chat. "Jody said Hamilton kind of liked the girl he was talking to, but John Golden didn't like his. . . . So the repartee got a little sharp, and Golden pinched the ass of the girl in question. She turned around in outrage and faced Hamilton. Thinking it was him, she slapped him." Golden quickly stepped in between the girl and Hamilton, and that was the end of it. "There was no spitting involved," said Jody.

Readers of the *Post*'s style section may have realized that these stories were the worst kind of gossip, but Jordan's image as a boorish southern good ol' boy was now firmly established in popular culture. Quinn's catty tone sent a signal that it was somehow chic to ridicule the Georgians who occupied the White House, including the president. *Time* magazine's Hugh Sidey called it the "yahoo" or "cornpone" syndrome—the notion that the country was being run by a bunch of unsophisticated southern country bumpkins. *Newsweek*'s Meg Greenfield disparaged this notion but nevertheless helped to popularize the image of "barechested, peanut-feeding yahoos" fouling the White House grounds. It was all terribly unfair. But just three or four years after the Watergate scandal, the zealous culture of the Washington press corps was unrelenting. By the spring of 1978, the weekly national staff meeting at *The Washington Post* routinely started out with some editor asking, "Well, what have they screwed up this week?"

Carter speechwriter Jerry Doolittle, after lunching one day with his former colleagues, *Washington Post* editors Larry Stern and Walter Pincus, noted in his diary, "General disillusionment with JC." Part of this disenchantment was only natural; familiarity breeds a degree of cynicism within the press corps. But it was also true that every reporter in town wanted to emulate Bob Woodward and Carl Bernstein—and make a name for themselves uncovering high crimes and misdemeanors. Carter, however, was not an easy target. As press critic Wendy Swanberg put it, "Carter himself was not fun to cover." Writing in *The New York Review of Books*, Garry Wills observed, "There is something about Jimmy Carter that makes journalists want to change the subject." Bert Lance was fun. And so was Hamilton Jordan, once heralded as "Butch Cassidy, philosopher-king of the White House" and now labeled by *Esquire* writer Aaron Latham as the "Slob in the White House."

*   *   *

IT DIDN'T HELP things that Jordan was having a difficult time in his private life. His deputy, Landon Butler, thought him irritable and distracted. "His marriage is on the rocks," Butler noted in his diary, "and that may be a large part of the problem. Rumors appear in the papers. . . . And he looks terrible—his face is puffy, and his eyes red. It's crossed my mind more than once that he may be on drugs." The following month, in January 1978, Jordan separated from his wife, Nancy Konigsmark. He told Butler that he and Nancy had been going to a marriage counselor for three or four months. It might not be the end of their marriage, but "his work was clearly a problem." Carter tried to urge them to find a way to stay together; it was awkward, if only because Nancy remained in the White House as the First Lady's scheduling assistant.

Jordan moved in with Jerry Rafshoon and presidential pollster Pat Caddell, who were sharing a beautiful old Georgetown home at 3419 R Street, once the carriage house of President Ulysses Grant. The two-story nineteenth-century house had an expansive back garden with a lovely swimming pool. Tim Kraft, also recently separated from his wife, moved into the house around the same time. Chip Carter sold Kraft a jukebox that he placed on one of the wraparound porches, much to the annoyance of the neighbors. With three and sometimes four bachelors, all working in the White House, 3419 R Street quickly became a legendary party house. The president knew his aides were young and hard-working and hard-partying. And while he was unhappy to see marriages fall apart, he wasn't naïve or judgmental on a personal level.

Early in 1978, Jordan told a *People* magazine reporter, "I'm the same slob I was during the campaign. I don't take myself seriously . . . but sometimes at night, when I leave and ride by the front of the White House and the lights are on, it is so beautiful, I have some sense of 'Hey, that's where I work, and Jimmy is President now.' But day in and day out, it's a job." The job was all-consuming. In mid-January, Jody Powell joined forces with Eizenstat to urge Jordan to spell out his role as "coordinator." Jordan agreed to write a short memo, and by January 25 the president had signed off on it. "Suffice it to say," Butler noted in his diary, "Ham is now the Chief of Staff—and now I find myself Deputy Chief of Staff."

Chapter 12
Troubles with Liberals

I feel more at home with the conservative Democratic and Republican members of the Congress than I do with the others.

—PRESIDENT JIMMY CARTER, January 19, 1978

Joan Kennedy, Carter, and Senator Ted Kennedy
ASSOCIATED PRESS

PRESIDENT CARTER MAY have thought of himself as a southern liberal, but by 1978 he was getting increasing flak from his liberal base. Jewish liberals, labor union leaders, feminists, big-city mayors, and, most annoyingly, Senator Edward Kennedy—all of them were gradually expressing impatience and frustration with the Georgian sitting in the White House. Politically speaking, Carter should have been spending more time and energy attending to these domestic concerns.

Hamilton Jordan, after all, had just warned the president against spending too much time on foreign policy issues.

But Carter nevertheless invested a good part of early 1978 in the Middle East, trying to keep the Egyptian-Israeli peace talks alive. He and

Anwar Sadat had "no differences." Menachem Begin was another case. Carter believed the Israeli prime minister was "breaking his word of honor to me that no new settlements would be permitted in the West Bank." He sent a sharply worded message to Begin, saying that what he was doing "was an obstacle to peace." During a visit to Washington in early February, Sadat was so discouraged that he was resigned to breaking off talks. Only Carter's personal intervention persuaded him not to pull his Egyptian negotiators out of Jerusalem. The president feared he needed once again to launch a personal intervention to save the situation. On February 3, 1978, Carter found himself pitted against his closest advisers—Fritz Mondale, Cy Vance, and Zbig Brzezinski—all of whom wanted him to back off on his Middle East peace initiatives. Carter refused to budge: "I think we ought to move much more aggressively on the Middle East question." It all came down to the Israeli settlements in the occupied territories. After observing the president at a cabinet meeting, Landon Butler noted in his diary, "The president is damned mad about the Israeli handling of the settlements question."

After Sadat's departure, Carter hosted a dinner for nine Jewish American leaders and briefed them on the talks. "I spelled out the relative flexibility of Sadat's position and the intransigence of Israel." Carter explained that the "illegal settlements" were the primary obstacle. Israel had to recognize that UN Resolution 242 required Israeli withdrawal from the West Bank and Gaza. Sadat was not demanding the creation of a Palestinian state. In return, he was willing to offer Israel full recognition and a real peace with Egypt. Sadat had told Carter that "he did not want Jerusalem to be divided, but there had to be joint sovereignty over one square mile where the religious places were located." Carter thought Sadat was offering a reasonable deal. His conversation with Phil Klutznick, David Blumberg, and the other Jewish leaders at the dinner table that evening focused primarily on the "illegal settlements"—and Carter thought he had nearly all of them on board: "With the exception of Alex Schindler, who always acts like an ass, the rest of them were constructive."

Rabbi Alexander Schindler was the cigar-smoking president of the Union of American Hebrew Congregations, the governing body of Reform Judaism. He was also chairman of the Conference of Presidents of Major American Jewish Organizations and therefore American Jewry's chief spokesman on issues pertaining to American-Israeli relations. A social and political liberal, Schindler had nevertheless embraced Begin when the Likud leader was elected prime minister and made it clear that unity in support of Israel had to be a priority for all Jewish Americans. Rabbi Schindler was a formidable figure. And he came away from this White House dinner with the "feeling that the administration was beginning to orchestrate a campaign against Begin. I didn't want Jimmy Carter to bamboozle the Jewish community the way FDR had."*

Schindler's skepticism was symptomatic of the Jewish community's deep wariness of the Carter administration's Middle East policies. A thoughtful intellectual, this was one rabbi who should have been a Carter ally. But Schindler had been "appalled" by the October 1 U.S.-Soviet communiqué, a transparent attempt, he thought, to force Israel to come to Geneva. Still, after Sadat's trip to Jerusalem, Schindler had accepted an invitation to meet with Sadat at the Egyptian president's Aswan villa. But when they met on January 11, 1978, they argued bitterly. Sadat complained that he had made all the concessions and had received nothing in return. Schindler countered that Begin's critics inside Israel were making the same complaint, that Begin had "given away everything"—and in return, he had received only what was every nation's entitlement: the right to live in peace.

Despite having stood up to Sadat, Schindler had returned to New York and found himself publicly rebuked by Moshe Dayan, the Israeli foreign minister. "We know some Jewish leaders decided to meet with Sadat," Dayan said. "I wouldn't like them to place themselves halfway in between. Remember, it's our future at stake." With these words, Dayan was touching on a sore point. Israeli leaders didn't want Jewish American leaders to second-guess their decisions, particularly on questions pertaining to the defense, and even survival, of the Israeli state. Jewish American leaders were sensitive to the charge that whenever they criticized Israeli behavior—such as the building of settlements in the occupied territories—they could erode public support for Israel among non-Jewish Americans or, even worse, inflame domestic anti-Semitism.

---

* Schindler had in mind Rabbi Stephen Wise's ineffective quiet diplomacy in the face of Franklin Roosevelt's flaccid response to the Jewish community's pleas to open up immigration quotas for Jews fleeing Nazi-conquered Europe. Rabbi Schindler clearly thought his predecessor had been "bamboozled" by the American president.

So just a few weeks after Dayan rebuked him for meeting with Sadat in Aswan, Schindler decided not to accept an invitation to see Sadat at Blair House during his early February 1978 visit to Washington. "We felt we shouldn't intrude," Schindler told *The New York Times*. Philip Klutznick, the chairman of the World Jewish Congress, and seven other Jewish American leaders accepted the invitation that Schindler declined. Klutznick had been more outspoken than most Jewish American leaders in his support for Carter's diplomacy, and on this occasion, he found himself very favorably impressed by Sadat. But even Klutznick was careful with his words: "My feeling is that there are three million Israelis who are living their lives on the front line of this dispute. Unless I'm convinced that Israel is dead wrong on something, absolutely flat-out wrong, I'm going to give them the benefit of the doubt and not go popping off every time I don't like something."

The problem was that men like Klutznick and Schindler were extremely wary of any official attempts to encourage a rift between the Israeli government and the Jewish American community—and, of course, that was exactly what Carter was trying to do when he urged Sadat to meet with Jewish leaders and when he invited them to dine at the White House. Not surprisingly, when Schindler came to the White House on February 8, he felt compelled, in Carter's phrase, to "act like an ass," objecting to the president's characterization of Begin's "intransigence."

This toxic relationship further deteriorated when Rabbi Schindler and other Jewish leaders met later in February with Zbig Brzezinski. Carter's outspoken national security adviser was in a particularly feisty mood. "Zbig is clearly tilted toward Egypt," noted Landon Butler in his diary, "and thinks a little anxiety in the Jewish community is a good thing. He is also absolutely convinced that Begin has reneged on his settlement assurances." Brzezinski had been seething since the autumn with his own resentments about what he regarded as slanderous murmurs that he was anti-Israeli or even an anti-Semite due to his Polish heritage. Zbig decided to confront the allegations head-on. Rabbi Schindler later told *The New York Times* that "the Brzezinski meeting was an absolute unmitigated disaster." Zbig had been "antagonistic, blustering, threatening," and completely "counter-productive." Brzezinski angrily responded in an interview with the *Times,* saying that such attacks were a "subtle kind of pressure," part of a strategy of "intimidation" conducted by Jewish leaders. "If you don't agree with us," they are saying, "we're going to stamp you as an anti-Semite." He claimed he was being singled out to deflect attention from the "indefensibility of the settlements issue in Israel." Self-assured as ever, Brzezinski said, "I've decided to grit my teeth and bear it. What we're doing is in the national interest of the United States and is central to Israel's survival."

This exchange between Brzezinski and Rabbi Schindler was made public on March 10, 1978, a few weeks after the rancorous February meeting and just a day after the resignation of Mark A. Siegel, a thirty-one-year-old White House deputy who served as a liaison with Jewish groups. Siegel had been working as an aide to Jordan when he was assigned the liaison role. It proved to be a contentious position. Like Rabbi Schindler, Siegel had felt blindsided by Carter's attempt the previous October to push Israel into peace negotiations at Geneva. But his decision to resign was probably precipitated by an incident the previous week, when he was booed by an audience at the United Jewish Appeal. Siegel discarded his text and delivered a heartfelt speech "as an American, Jew and committed Zionist" about his commitment to Israel's security. A few days later, he told Jordan he could no longer serve in the liaison role.*

Siegel's was the first resignation in a dispute over policy by a principal aide in the Carter White House. When the president was asked about it at a press conference, he said, "Mark Siegel is a fine young man. . . . But this is an issue that's almost inherently a subject for dispute and disagreement." And then he admitted that explaining his positions on the Middle East "has been a difficult task for me as well as him." It was a gracious response but one that underscored his already strained relations with the Jewish American community.

Stirring the pot, Rabbi Schindler called *The New York Times* to offer his opinion, suggesting that Siegel's resignation "will fan the concern of the American Jewish community that something isn't right, that Israel is not getting a square deal from the Administration. So far, the anger is not at Carter—but there is a big question mark on Carter."

---

* Siegel was already on his way out. Jordan was unhappy with his performance as his liaison to the Democratic National Committee. Instead of firing him, Jordan had decided in February to just ignore him. "Mark is getting the classic Jordan treatment," Butler noted. "Ham will simply see if Mark will self-destruct. . . . Siegel is a walking dead man."

The political pressure on the Carter White House escalated the very next day when a squad of thirteen Palestinian fedayeen landed two Zodiac boats on a beach north of Tel Aviv and commandeered a civilian bus. The terrorists then went on a shooting spree, spraying bullets into passing cars. Thirty-eight Israeli civilians were killed, including thirteen children, and seventy-one people were wounded. It was the single worst terrorist attack in Israel's history. The PLO's Fatah faction publicly claimed responsibility for the attack. But Brzezinski nevertheless told Carter in a top secret memo that the attack "probably had two purposes: 1) to undercut Sadat's peace initiative; and 2) to undercut and discredit Arafat. The operation was planned by Abu Iyad, the number two man in Fatah." Three days later, Prime Minister Begin launched Operation Litani, whereby Israeli forces attacked PLO bases in southern Lebanon. The operation killed an estimated 1,100 people, mostly Palestinian and Lebanese civilians.

Carter issued a statement expressing his outrage over the PLO's "cowardly and senseless attack on a group of civilians." But he also notified the Israelis that his administration would support a UN resolution calling for the withdrawal of their forces in Lebanon. "They're using our equipment," he noted in his diary, "illegally to invade a foreign country, and they overreacted seriously by killing hundreds and hundreds of civilians in Lebanon in their massive attack." Such evenhandedness in the face of bloody events was no doubt rational—but it only raised further questions for those who feared that Israel was not getting a square deal from this president.

Characteristically, Carter himself had no doubts that he was doing the right thing. One of his young Jewish aides, David Rubenstein, knew he was walking into a political minefield. "Ever since 1948," Rubenstein later said in an interview, "the Jewish American community thought it was their job to support Israel ninety-nine percent. You just don't criticize the Israeli government. I don't believe that, by the way. But that was the attitude. And then along comes Menachem Begin, and here you had the president trying to get the Israeli government to do things that they did not want to do—like stop the settlements. Now, I think Carter was right, but many in the Jewish community came to believe that Carter was just anti-Israel." This was a lingering suspicion in 1978, but in some quarters, it was one that would become a hardened certainty in the years to come.

* * *

PALESTINIAN TERRORISM WAS not the only difficult issue on Carter's agenda. That same week the president was dealing with a nationwide coal miners' strike. The coal strike had commenced on December 6, 1977—and by early March the strike was beginning to have deleterious effects on the national economy. "There is a clear possibility of violence," Butler noted. "The coal strike is political dynamite." The union was weak and riven by internal corruption. Coal production had dropped by 60 percent, and hundreds of thousands of coal miners were unemployed. By early February the United Mine Workers of America (UMWA) had negotiated a tentative agreement with the coal mine operators—but on March 5, 1978, the union's members voted two to one against ratification of the agreement. The next day, a frustrated President Carter invoked the Taft-Hartley Act, ordering the miners back to work. But many workers ignored the presidential order—and Carter declined to use federal troops to enforce the injunction. Some called him weak, but by March 19, the strike had ended. The whole affair left Carter with a sour feeling about AFL-CIO labor chief George Meany; he was particularly annoyed that the elderly union leader falsely told reporters on numerous occasions that he had not been consulted by Carter during the coal strike.

Carter's relationship with organized labor was already strained, and the invocation of Taft-Hartley—a blunt instrument despised by union leaders—only confirmed labor's suspicions that this president was unsympathetic toward their agenda. "Carter saw unions as just another interest group," observed Stu Eizenstat. "They did not have a special call on his heartstrings." A luncheon meeting with Meany and other labor leaders quickly descended into open rancor. Meany launched into a diatribe, personally attacking the president for caring more about inflation than wages. Carter muttered to Eizenstat on his way out, "Stu, I will never do this again." The president was visibly angry. Butler noted in his diary, "The president simply doesn't give a damn about labor." Tasked to serve as the White House's liaison to the unions, Butler found the job increasingly frustrating. Neither side understood the other, and Butler found himself caught in the crossfire: "Jimmy Carter doesn't understand these people [union supporters], and simply considers them one of the nuisances of the office."

Carter understood race, but as a southerner he had a blind spot when it came to the culture of trade unions. He left it to Butler to develop a friendly working relationship with labor leaders. And while Butler was sympathetic, the more he dealt with these old union bosses, the more he disliked them. "I have really developed a distaste for the AFL-CIO," he noted. "They are simply incompetent and obstructionist. . . . Meany is an old fart, and he actually has little real power."

If there was a cultural disconnect between labor union leaders and Carter, the president nevertheless spent considerable political capital in 1978 trying to get Congress to pass the Labor Law Reform Act, a top priority of the union movement. The bill would have buttressed the ability of unions to recruit members in nonunion shops and increased the penalties on corporations, particularly in the South, where virulently antiunion companies like the textile giant J.P. Stevens routinely ignored the orders of the National Labor Relations Board. Carter understood the importance of the bill to his labor union constituency, and he did what was expected of him to make it happen. But it was not enough. "The labor law reform breakfast was dull," Butler complained in May, "and the president did a disappointing job. He rambled, he was lifeless, and he probably only confirmed their [labor's] worst fears. He said most of the right things, but he certainly left the impression that his heart wasn't in it—which it isn't."

Over strident opposition from Republicans and southern Democrats, the House passed the legislation, only to see it filibustered in the Senate. The Carter administration worked for months to move the bill through the Senate but failed on six different cloture votes to muster the sixty votes necessary to end the filibuster. It was a terrible defeat for labor unions, and George Meany publicly blamed the president. It was a turning point for the unions but also indicative of the declining percentage of unionized labor in the workforce. By 1977, only 25 percent of the country's workers had a union card, a decline of 10 percent from the 1950s. "The truth is that the AFL-CIO is pitifully weak," Butler noted, "and won't admit it."

IN THE MIDST of this legislative jockeying over labor reform, the Carter White House was also pushing hard for congressional approval of its highly controversial Middle East arms sales package. Butler noted that a

"wave of hysteria seems to be going through the die-hard Jewish lobby."
Carter echoed these views, noting in his own diary on May 11, 1978, that
"the Israeli lobby [AIPAC] is going to be working overtime all weekend."
But four days later, the Senate voted 55–43 to approve the sale of sixty
F-15 fighter jets to Saudi Arabia. Carter had personally lobbied many
undecided senators and guessed that he had changed ten to twelve votes.
He felt vindicated: "Had we lost this vote, my ability to make progress in
Mideast peace would have been almost terminated." Butler thought this
a major political victory. "I think we have done the right thing on the
arms sales package—right for the U.S., and right for Israel." But he admitted to himself that "we are running the risk of setting off a new round
of anti-Semitism, and we will be accused of that ourselves." Still, Butler
couldn't resist crowing, "The president beat the right wing on Panama,
Mr. Meany yesterday, and now he's whipped the Jewish lobby. Is he going
to get a reputation for picking fights?"

EARLY IN 1978, Carter confided to his diary, "I feel more at home with
the conservative Democratic and Republican members of the Congress
than I do with the others, although the liberals vote with me more often."
He had in mind colorful southern conservatives like Democratic senator Russell Long, the son of the legendary Louisiana populist governor Huey P. Long, who had been assassinated in 1935. Long didn't often
vote with the administration, and he had actively opposed Carter's tax-
reform and energy proposals. Early in the administration, Carter had
joked that when he had arrived in Washington, as the first politician
from the Deep South in modern times to lead the federal government,
he soon "found that Russell Long had filled that position for a long
time." Carter thought Long was "always a waste of time," but "entertaining and enjoyable." By contrast, he found most liberal politicians both a
waste of time and "not entertaining." Cultural factors might explain the
president's affinity for southerners, but his instinctive disdain for political wheeling and dealing also contributed to his discomfort with
liberals—who were always demanding more federal programs.

To the consternation of many liberals, Carter seemed to be governing
more as a Teddy Roosevelt Progressive Republican than a Franklin Roosevelt New Deal Democrat. Like the turn-of-the-century Progressives,
Carter was obsessed with ethical stewardship, efficient government, and

making things work on a rational basis. The president shied away from slogans, but when some of his aides suggested he really needed to offer voters some kind of shorthand catchphrase, Carter reluctantly settled on "New Foundations." Speechwriter Rick Hertzberg persuaded him to use the phrase as the touchstone of his 1979 State of the Union speech. "I think it was a good slogan because it was accurate," Hertzberg later said. "The idea of rebuilding the foundation is not putting big new wings on the house but patching up the leaks in the basement and getting a solid foundation. And that was really very much what Carter's approach was about. He was interested in process. . . . And he was interested in bedrock basic values."

After his tour of the South Bronx the previous autumn, Carter wanted to do something to address the urban blight he had seen. But he didn't want to bust the budget, so he proposed in the spring of 1978 a revamped urban program with an increase of $600 million in federal money. Both Mondale and Jordan thought this paltry. "If you propose an urban policy that only contains 600 million new federal dollars," Jordan warned him, "I predict that it will be the single biggest political mistake we have made since being elected." Jordan's memo persuaded the president to spend more on the program.

Ultimately, however, it was the city of New York that benefited most from Carter's urban policies. By the time Carter became president, New York was billions of dollars in debt and standing on the brink of bankruptcy. For too many years the city's politicians had refused to raise municipal taxes to keep pace with the high wages and good benefits earned by unionized municipal workers. Instead, the resulting budget deficits had been paid for with high-interest bonds controlled by such financial titans as David Rockefeller of Chase Manhattan Bank and Walter Wriston of Citicorp. The bonds were coming due, and by 1978, it was clear that the city lacked the revenues to pay off this debt.

On February 2, 1978, the city's mayor, Ed Koch, met with President Carter in the Oval Office. The two men already had a history of bad chemistry. Stu Eizenstat thought the mayor was "pompous, prickly, disrespectful, endlessly demanding," but Carter nevertheless promised Koch that he would do everything he could to prevent the city from declaring bankruptcy. Tough negotiations ensued over the next six months, and on August 8, 1978, Carter signed the New York City Loan

Guarantee Act. The municipal unions were persuaded to make sacrifices, but so too were the bankers, who were required to turn their short-term loans into long-term loans at a lower interest rate. The nation's largest city was saved by a president from the tiny hamlet of Plains, Georgia. But Mayor Koch would make sure that Carter got little political credit for brokering the deal.

Likewise, Carter would garner little praise for building one million new units of public housing, or doubling the Head Start budget, or spending $4 billion on youth employment. Despite these typically Democratic spending programs, the perception persisted that he was a fiscal conservative. This was partly his fault, because he did little to dispel the notion that he was a tightwad. "Spending tended to go up a fair bit for some programs," admitted White House staffer Bert Carp, "because while he [Carter] hated to spend money . . . you could explain to him that he should spend money for this, and, very grudgingly, he would do it."

CARTER'S DOMESTIC POLITICAL problems were always rooted in the economics of the 1970s. The coalition forged by the Democratic Party during the Great Depression was beginning to fall apart under the pressures of stagflation. Roosevelt's New Deal and Johnson's Great Society had been fueled by decades of economic growth partially sustained by real gains in worker productivity. But by the 1970s, Carter inherited an economy with slower growth, higher inflation, and stagnating productivity. Carter's instinct in the face of a growing federal budget deficit was to balance the budget, and that inevitably alienated his liberal constituencies. This became the source of a constant political disconnect.

Carter always thought it a good thing to stand up to what he called political interests: "I wish you could have seen the stricken expression on the faces of those Democratic leaders when I was talking about balancing the budget." That was early in his administration. His attitude at first only perplexed Democrats—and then their annoyance turned to anger and alienation. Mondale was increasingly flummoxed by Carter's apolitical tin ear.

Mondale's aide Richard Moe shared the vice president's New Deal sensibilities. But Moe later realized that larger economic forces were at work: "The world had changed, and it was going to change even more.

But Democrats did not recognize that. That was the great unacknowl-edged fact of the Carter years. Carter, more than any other Democrat, acknowledged the fiscal realities, and congressional Democrats, Mon-dale included, did not."

Stu Eizenstat's young aide David Rubenstein voiced his own frustra-tions, telling speechwriter Jerry Doolittle that "we're going to cook the books somehow to meet JC's $30 billion deficit rhetoric." Carter was still insisting that the administration would meet this wildly optimistic deficit target. But as always, the lion's share of the federal budget was still eaten by the Pentagon, and according to Rubenstein, "no one has really de-cided whether to leave the military budget untouched while everything else is cut." Doolittle came away from lunch in the White House mess with the impression that Rubenstein was "very caustic, no true believer as far as is apparent."

Ironically, just as Carter's liberal base grumbled that he was not push-ing hard enough on their issues, big business marshaled its growing army of corporate lobbyists to push back against the administration's decidedly Naderite approach to federal regulations on consumer protec-tion, labor safety, public health, and the environment. Nader himself was not unaware of the irony, quipping, "The citizens' movement creates jobs. We have been so successful that Washington law firms have hired literally hundreds of additional lawyers in the 1970s to oppose our ac-tivities." The Business Roundtable, a lobbying group founded in 1972 to represent the collective interests of corporate America, now moved de-cisively against the Carter administration's domestic legislative agenda, allocating millions of dollars to lobby Congress.

In late 1977, the Business Roundtable targeted Carter's efforts to enact a consumer-protection bill. Earlier that year, Carter had appointed Es-ther Peterson, a nationally known, dogged advocate for consumer rights, as his White House special assistant for consumer affairs; he told her that he strongly supported the creation of a consumer-protection agency. Nader was ecstatic. "It was a cheap [$15 million a year] but very impor-tant innovation," Nader recalled. "It was an agency that had no regula-tory power but could intervene before other agencies and take them to court for not enforcing the law, for violating their own procedures or not releasing reports. . . . It could've had an enormous leverage effect. The problem was, it was too good of an idea." Corporate lobbyists saw it as a major economic threat, an agency that might well force them to spend millions of dollars to comply with federal regulations. Initially, both Nader and the administration thought they had the votes—but late in the game, the business community persuaded the House of Representatives to delay the scheduled November vote to February 1978. That gave them time to lobby Congress, and the bill was eventually defeated in the House by a healthy margin of 227 to 189. Nader was furious and blamed Carter for not putting "enough White House muscle" behind the effort. Peterson was also outraged that the president's congressional liaison aide, Frank Moore, had failed to inform her that he was delaying the vote on the bill. She almost quit, but Carter persuaded her to remain in the White House. For Nader, however, this was a turning point, and he spent the remainder of Carter's presidency sniping from the outside. Nader was a hard man to please and impatient with any sign of backsliding. But despite Nader's criticisms, it was telling that none of his people abandoned Carter. Pertschuk, Peterson, Claybrook, and many other dedicated veterans of the consumer-rights movement stayed with the administration to the end.

FEMINISTS IN THE Democratic Party were also grumbling that the administration was not doing enough to address their concerns. Former congresswoman Bella Abzug complained that Carter was not lobbying hard enough for passage of the Equal Rights Amendment (ERA). Eleanor Smeal, the president of the National Organization for Women, routinely criticized the president for not appointing more women to high office.

Abzug herself had expected to be offered a cabinet position, but Carter aides, speaking off the record, admitted she was thought to be "too abrasive and aggressive." Midge Costanza, the president's assistant for public liaison, eventually persuaded Carter to name Abzug as the chair of the President's Advisory Committee on Women. Interestingly, Rosalynn Carter had warned that Abzug would be too much trouble. She was right. Abzug badgered the president relentlessly. Carter thought she was "a pain in the neck." Finally, one day she held a press conference on the White House lawn, handing out a press release critical of the administration's efforts, and then marched into the Oval Office for her appointment with the president. She then proceeded to lecture Carter on how his budget priorities were hurting women. She complained that there was money for new weapons systems like the submarine-launched Trident ballistic missile, the stealth bomber, and cruise missiles, but none for national healthcare. "It was a really terrible session," said one unnamed White House aide. "She lit into him in front of nearly forty other people." Carter responded, "I supported you on ERA. I didn't agree with you on abortion, but I let you do your thing. What do my inflation policy and my military policy have to do with women?" Carter thought Abzug's behavior crossed the line, and immediately after the meeting, he had Jordan dismiss her on her way out of the White House. Shocked, Abzug told Jordan that she was being "used as a scapegoat." By then, Costanza herself had quit the White House in frustration, leaving the impression that she had been pushed out. "Costanza was given an impossible job to begin with," wrote the columnist Molly Ivins, "and left to twist slowly in the wind by the President's men." Carter felt bad about Costanza's unhappy departure and quickly appointed Anne Wexler to take over her job. Wexler was a well-connected political operative in the Democratic Party—but not known as a feminist activist in the vein of Costanza or Abzug. Inevitably, Costanza's messy departure and Abzug's controversial firing contributed to an impression that Carter was unsympathetic to feminist concerns.

This was unfair. To be sure, Carter's fiscal conservatism rankled a broad spectrum of his liberal constituency. But the president's record on specific women's issues was actually pretty stellar. He supported the ERA and lobbied for its ratification. And he had appointed many women to important positions in the administration.

This was particularly true in the case of federal judgeships. Only one woman was serving on a federal appellate court when Carter entered the White House. Two years into his term, Carter asked Kirbo to investigate rumors that the Justice Department was dragging its feet on his strong desire to nominate more women and African Americans to the judiciary. Kirbo sat down with White House counsel Bob Lipshutz and Attorney General Griffin Bell to discuss the issue. Lipshutz "made it plain that [Carter] wanted blacks and women to be appointed to the courts and he understood it was his function to see that that was done." Bell said that "he understood what [Carter's] goals were, that he agreed with them." But Bell told Lipshutz he "resented activities indicating that he was not delivering." Bell pointed out that the American Bar Association was routinely evaluating many of Carter's female and minority nominations as unqualified, partly because they often had not published any law review articles. Carter snapped, "How many law review articles did you write before President Kennedy appointed his Georgia campaign chairman [Bell] to the Fifth Circuit?" Bell readily conceded the point, and Carter bluntly warned the ABA that the administration would dispense with their traditional vetting altogether if they did not approve more women and minorities. The ABA got the message.

Carter ended up appointing a total of 262 federal judges, including 56 appeals court judges—and 38 of these appointments, or 15 percent, were women. Among these were Ruth Bader Ginsburg, who was later elevated to the Supreme Court, and Patricia Wald, who became a highly influential appeals court judge. Carter knew Ginsburg was regarded as "excessively liberal . . . She's been a matter of some controversy." Regardless, he made the appointment. To put this in perspective, prior to Carter's presidency, just eight women had ever been appointed to federal judgeships. Similarly, only thirty-one African Americans had ever sat on the federal bench; Carter appointed fifty-seven minorities to the judiciary. These appointments tilted the courts in a liberal direction for a generation.

AT THE END of January 1978, Delaware's thirty-five-year-old senator, Joe Biden, dropped by the White House and tried to warn Carter that he thought "Ted Kennedy is running for president in 1980 and is already lining up support." In addition, Biden conveyed that the Jewish community had a "deep distrust" of the president. Carter was not exactly surprised on either score, but Biden's message was the first concrete report he had that Kennedy was contemplating a challenge. Carter distrusted the Massachusetts senator. Privately, he claimed that there were "no philosophical differences between me and the Senator. He's just an impatiently ambitious man."

Kennedy's sense of entitlement annoyed Carter—who in turn went out of his way not to do the senator any favors. When Kennedy made it known that he sought the appointment of Harvard Law School's Archibald Cox to the federal bench, Kirbo advised against the appointment: "I would think it would be a mistake to appoint Cox as you will have a rash of pressures to appoint people of similar ages." Kennedy took it as a personal affront when Carter declined to appoint his old friend. Carter gave that federal judgeship to the senator's committee counsel, Stephen Breyer, but Kennedy was hardly mollified.

Setting aside their personal chemistry, the two politicians actually shared many liberal aspirations, including the notion that all Americans had a right to healthcare. Democrats had been talking about national healthcare since the Truman administration in the 1940s. In 1973, Ted Kennedy introduced a national healthcare bill that would have fulfilled this dream. A radical piece of legislation, Kennedy's bill would have established a single-payer, nonprofit insurance scheme to cover all Americans. The health insurance companies would have been driven from the market. The bill had the ardent support of Meany's AFL-CIO but also the more liberal United Auto Workers union and a broad coalition of liberal activist groups. But Republican presidents Nixon and Ford had promised to veto it—so it languished.

Carter had endorsed the idea of comprehensive national health insurance during the 1976 presidential campaign. Twenty-six million Americans had no health insurance at all and another 28 million had only minimal coverage. "We have an abominable system in this country," he wrote, "for the delivery of healthcare, with gross inequities toward the poor—particularly the working poor—and profiteering by many hospitals." And once in office, he had instructed his HEW secretary, Joe Califano, to formulate a concrete bill. Califano dithered for much of 1977, knowing the complications.

Frustrated, Kennedy invited Califano to his Virginia home and warned him that he was going to hold Carter to his campaign promise. That autumn Kennedy gave a speech at the UAW's annual convention in which he suggested that healthcare remained the "missing promise" of the Carter administration. In response, Carter told union leaders that he still intended to submit legislation early in 1978. But he warned them that he didn't think he had the votes in Congress to pass a universal health insurance scheme without containing costs, particularly hospital charges. "We can't get this overnight," he told them. "If we demand too much and are not fiscally responsible, the whole thing will be rejected. This needs to be politically feasible." Needless to say, Kennedy and the union leaders chafed at any talk about fiscal responsibility. Kennedy later brusquely told Eizenstat, "I will move it myself if you don't."

In early March 1978, Califano and Treasury Secretary Mike Blumenthal came by the Oval Office and asked Carter to delay any healthcare legislation until the following year. Carter demurred, saying he was "too deep to reverse myself" on his pledge to Senator Kennedy. Five weeks later, Carter had a "heated meeting" with Kennedy, UAW chief Doug Fraser, and the AFL-CIO's Meany. Carter was taken aback by the intensity of the emotions expressed and wondered if Kennedy was "posturing in front of the labor leaders." Finally, in late June 1978, Carter met again with Kennedy—and this time, he told him that while he was still in favor of a comprehensive health insurance program, it would have to be phased in over some years due to budget constraints. Kennedy was furious. Carter later wrote in his 1982 presidential memoirs that he had sought to convince Kennedy that the "best approach was a comprehensive system passed into law and then phased into operation as the federal budget could accommodate the costs." But in his diary, he noted that "it would be years before we could impose it." The president's number crunchers were telling him that Kennedy's comprehensive bill would cost the federal budget $30 billion to $40 billion by 1983. Carter didn't care that most Republicans labeled national health insurance "socialized medicine." But he did care about the federal deficit. "It is ridiculous to think about endorsing a bill like Kennedy's," he told Mondale and Eizenstat. "I am not going to destroy my credibility on inflation and budgetary matters."

The two men had opposing, nearly intractable differences over tactics. Kennedy said he wanted "bold leadership and swift action built around a single piece of legislation." Carter favored an incremental, step-by-step approach—a strategy that Kennedy believed to be "a recipe for failure." On June 26, 1978, Kennedy told the president in a phone conversation, "I don't think you can go to an elderly group and say . . . if hospitals keep their costs down and the economy doesn't go so much into a deficit, then you might be phased in." Kennedy thought there was no political constituency for incrementalism.

Carter saw Kennedy's bill as "an enormously complicated program run entirely by the federal government." As drafted, the Kennedy bill was essentially a watered-down version of the senator's original single-payer plan for universal and mandatory health insurance. It still provided a role for private insurance companies, but the federal government would shoulder the lion's share of the costs. Carter feared it would cost "at least $100 billion—and perhaps twice as much." And politically speaking, Carter didn't think any such bill had a chance of winning congressional approval.

By contrast, Carter wanted to preserve the "existing employer-employee" health insurance relationships. He would have the federal government stipulate basic standards to the private insurance companies. Under his program, private insurers would be required to place a priority on preventive medicine, outpatient care, and complete coverage for infants and children. But the most innovative feature of Carter's eventual proposal was the notion that the federal government would itself offer universal health insurance for "catastrophic" medical issues. Such "catastrophic" insurance would cover emergency or extraordinary medical expenses above a flat ceiling of $2,500 annually for every American family. (For senior citizens and the disabled, out-of-pocket expenses would be limited to $1,250 per person.) The plan would dramatically improve the health coverage of millions of workers and their families, provide basic health coverage to all women and children, and extend fully subsidized comprehensive care to an additional 15.7 million aged and non-aged poor. It wasn't a universal, single-payer system— but Carter believed it would be "a major step toward a fully developed, universal, comprehensive National Health Plan." The White House estimated that some 56 million Americans would receive protection against major illnesses "that they do not have at present."

Carter also knew that his universal "catastrophic" health insurance would be much cheaper than Kennedy's program. (Califano estimated the cost at $15 billion to $27 billion to provide basic benefits for the poor and children, plus catastrophic benefits for all citizens.) And if Kennedy and his labor union allies supported it, the president believed it had "a good chance to succeed."

Stu Eizenstat and Califano lobbied Kennedy over the next few weeks and tried to convince him not only that Carter's program was politically viable but that the catastrophic insurance program was a foot in the door that would pave the way for a truly comprehensive federal health insurance program in the years to come. As a negotiating gambit, Carter and his team proposed building a trigger into the bill whereby the different levels of healthcare benefits would be phased in over time— depending on economic conditions. Interestingly, this idea had come from Mondale, usually the reliable liberal voice in the Carter White House. Kennedy's allies responded that a trigger would be okay, but he could allow the president only the option of *requesting* a delay from Congress. The president alone would not be able to halt the phase-in toward universal and comprehensive health insurance. Carter saw this as fiscally unacceptable. At this point, Kennedy insisted he wanted one comprehensive bill. And while he would talk to Carter on the phone, he refused to come to the White House for a personal meeting. Carter was incensed by this behavior and thought it signaled that Kennedy was done negotiating. In a conference call Kennedy angrily told the president, "You've slid on so many timetables, I fear this will slide more." And he refused to accept Carter's definition of the trigger: "I can't go to the groups [unions] and say we may get benefits if we meet the triggers. The key is one bill with a minimum of standards. Otherwise, opponents can pick it off bit by bit." Afterward, Eizenstat told Carter that "we could not win with a comprehensive bill." He urged the president to reject Kennedy's bill and instead introduce a series of healthcare bills that would expand benefits and coverage incrementally.

The matter came to an abrupt and disastrous confrontation on the morning of July 28, 1978, when Kennedy relented and finally agreed to come to the White House to discuss the healthcare bill. They met in the Cabinet Room. Sitting at the long table were the president's top domestic policy advisers, including Vice President Mondale, Eizenstat, Califano, David Rubenstein, and Joseph Onek—who had worked on the nitty-gritty details of the Carter plan. Onek had previously specialized on health issues for a Nader-inspired public-interest law firm, the Center for Law and Social Policy. He was a public-interest liberal, like many of the people Carter had recruited for the executive wing of the federal government. And he had once served on Kennedy's Senate staff. But now he was on the other side of the table from Kennedy. President Carter began the conversation on a conciliatory note, confessing that he had "slipped on timing." Appealing directly to Kennedy, Carter said, "It will doom health care if we split. I have no other place to turn if I can't turn to you. . . . I would like to leave office with a comprehensive bill in place, but I must emphasize fiscal responsibility if we are to have a chance."

When Carter made it clear that he intended to submit his own bill—

and that he was not going to support Kennedy's more comprehensive bill—Eizenstat leaned over and whispered into Onek's ear, "This is the beginning of Kennedy's presidential campaign." Onek was shocked: "I remember thinking at the time that this was just not possible." But Kennedy made it all too clear that he didn't like the Carter proposal; it was too little and already too late. Carter was unmoved: "We'll just have to hang tough." Kennedy asked the president to delay his press conference announcing the legislation "long enough for him to study the proposal more thoroughly." Carter agreed, and the two men shook hands.

But just a few hours later, Kennedy held his own press conference and blasted the president's "catastrophic" healthcare program. Accompanied by Meany, Kennedy deemed the president's plan "unacceptable" and pledged to "take the issue to the people." Carter thought Kennedy had "betrayed my trust." Clearly, Kennedy had asked for a delay in the administration's announcement only so that he could first denounce it. Carter was deeply annoyed, but he also thought Kennedy's posturing "made us look responsible and conservative with our plan." *The New York Times* editorialized that Carter's approach seemed "a mere downpayment, and a belated one," on his campaign promises—but the newspaper conceded that the president's strategy "appears to have the wiser side of the argument."

It became clear, however, that without Kennedy's support—and the support of the liberal wing of the Democratic Party—Carter's own program would languish. The senator from Massachusetts never even allowed the Carter bill to move out of his Senate health committee. "In effect," Carter later wrote, "he insisted on his own plan or nothing at all." The country got nothing at all.

Carter spent the next two years trying to push both his "catastrophic" health insurance bill and a companion hospital-cost-containment bill through Congress. Had it passed into law, no American would have paid more than $2,500 annually in healthcare costs—and the government would have paid for anything above that amount, defined as catastrophic coverage. Employers would have been required to offer their workers this basic health insurance, equally sharing the monthly premiums with the federal government. Eizenstat estimated that an additional sixteen million citizens would have been covered at a cost of about $18 billion in 1980 dollars.

But without Kennedy's support, the administration could not defeat the powerful medical lobby. The American Medical Association (AMA) contributed an average of $8,000 to each of the 250 House members who voted against these bills. Even a moderate Democratic congressman like Representative Dick Gephardt of Missouri fought Carter on the bill—ostensibly because it wasn't liberal enough.

Some Carter White House aides, like Alicia Smith, were incredulous. Jody Powell was exercised enough to sit down and write Carter a rare memo complaining that Kennedy's approach—a "comprehensive plan now or nothing at all"—had become an "absolute article of faith" over the last thirty years. It was more important, he argued, to provide "badly needed health insurance benefits" at the earliest possible date than to adhere "to some semi-sacred ideological principle." Powell couldn't believe that the Democratic Party's liberal wing was willing to settle for nothing. In the end, the administration couldn't even get passage of a bill to place a cap on hospital costs. "The truth is hospital cost containment didn't have a chance," recalled Onek, "because the hospitals are the strongest lobby in America. . . . Hospitals are like an enormous company with a plant in every [congressional] district. It's often the largest employer in the district. The people on the board of the hospital are the most powerful people in the community. You don't have a prayer."

As Carter had prophesied, Kennedy's own bill went nowhere. Califano quipped that the Kennedy bill had "less of a chance of passing than putting an elephant through a keyhole." Carter finally submitted his own National Health Plan, focused on catastrophic healthcare, in the summer of 1979. "I urge the Congress," Carter said, "not to lose this precious opportunity for progress. The real needs of our people are not served by waiting and hoping for a better tomorrow. That tomorrow will never come unless we act today." The bill would provide free healthcare to infants and pregnant women; employers would be required to subsidize two-thirds of their employees' health insurance, and eventually eighty million more Americans would be insured. Carter's plan would have been a radical step forward.

The Democratic-controlled House and Senate let the bill die. Ironically, three decades later President Barack Obama introduced a universal health insurance bill modeled closely after the Carter bill. Mondale's former aide Richard Moe wrote that Obamacare "bore a striking resemblance to Carter's proposal three decades before." The legislation passed Congress in 2009 with the support of Senator Kennedy, by then diagnosed with fatal brain cancer. In retrospect, Kennedy's refusal to support Carter's incremental, catastrophic national health insurance bill in 1978–79 condemned the country to wait three decades for meaningful healthcare reform. By any measure, this was a tragedy for the country. "The missed opportunity," Eizenstat later wrote, "haunts me to this day."

CARTER'S FRUSTRATION WITH Kennedy's behavior was symptomatic of his dismal relationship with Capitol Hill. The administration's energy bill was once again stalled in Congress, where liberal senators like South Dakota's James Abourezk and Ohio's Howard Metzenbaum made it clear that they would not compromise in their opposition to Carter's efforts to deregulate the price of natural gas. Laboring over yet another energy speech, Jim Fallows told Rafshoon, "The president had to decide whether he wanted to go to war with Congress or not." Carter would eventually pull enough strings on the Hill to prevail, but the legislative battles over healthcare and energy further soured his dealings with liberal Democrats. That August, Senator Tom Eagleton, a moderate Democrat from Missouri, urged him to drop any legislation with a liberal tint and emphasize his "conservative" image. "This, of course," the president noted, "suits me fine."

A few months later, he was interviewed by NBC anchor John Chancellor, who suggested that his fiscal policies just didn't fit with the definition of "the traditional idea of a Democrat that some of us have grown up with." Carter replied, "Well, I can't control how you grew up, John." He then went on to explain that when he was asked during the 1976 campaign, "Are you a liberal or conservative?" he would say, "Well, on fiscal policy, I think I would be characterized as a conservative. On meeting the needs of our people, on having an openness of government, on being compassionate and concerned about human rights, the quality of life, protecting our environment, I would be considered possibly liberal." Carter saw no contradictions. He insisted that the liberal "special interest groups around the country" would be substantially mollified by his fiscal choices. Expenditures on the poor, after all, would substantially increase. The budget numbers would show that what he was doing as president was "completely consistent with the thrust of the Democratic Party historically." But the Democrats on the Hill were not convinced. Most of these legislators still felt they didn't know their own president.

Two years into his presidency, Carter was still discomfited when socializing with any of the powerful egos up on Capitol Hill. One day, Frank Moore persuaded the president to invite two Democratic senators, Fritz Hollings of South Carolina and Lloyd Bentsen of Texas, to play tennis at the White House. At the appointed time, Carter met them on the tennis court, played a quick set—and then said goodbye and walked back to the Oval Office. Hollings and Bentsen clearly had expected to be invited for a drink and a chance to schmooze. But that's not how Carter operated. When Moore later tried gently to point out the awkwardness of leaving the senators so abruptly, Carter snapped, "You told me to play tennis with them. I played tennis with them."

Chapter 13
Troubles with a Speechwriter

He is in trouble now with almost every powerful lobby in Washington: Big Labor, Big Business, Jews, blacks, liberal intellectuals, and farmers—in short, all the powerful constituencies whose opposition he doesn't need if he is to be re-elected in 1980.

—JAMES RESTON, April 5, 1978

Jody Powell, Susan Clough, and James Fallows
WALLY MCNAMEE/GETTY IMAGES

JIM FALLOWS WAS unhappy. At the age of twenty-eight, he had an office in the West Wing and a title as the president's chief speechwriter. But he had never enjoyed writing speeches and always intended to get back to his real passion, magazine journalism. Before coming to the White House, the former *Harvard Crimson* editor had also spent two invigorating years working long hours at the *Washington Monthly,* a low-circulation political opinion journal edited by Charlie Peters. Fallows deeply admired Peters, an idealistic political junkie who had served in the Kennedy administration before founding the *Monthly*. Peters paid his writers and editors practically nothing, but he mentored them to become influential pundits and street-smart investigative reporters. Fallows's predecessor at the *Monthly* was Taylor Branch—later the Pulitzer Prize–winning biographer of Martin Luther King, Jr. "I thought I'd never find someone as good as Taylor," Peters recalled, "but one day one of my people came in and said, 'There's some kid out in the hall waiting to see you.' Jim looked like he was fourteen years old." Peters hired him, and Fallows became one of Peters's most promising rising stars. Coincidentally, Peters's former girlfriend was a Georgia woman who was then Rosalynn Carter's secretary. "So I think that's why one day I got a call from Stu Eizenstat asking about Fallows," Peters said. "This was during the '76 campaign, and they were considering him for a speech-writing slot." Peters encouraged his protégé to take the job. Having been reared in the border states of Kentucky and Tennessee, Peters was impressed with Carter. The Georgia governor seemed to be "getting away with a lot of stuff that was very unusual in the South. He seemed to be authentic, and there was nothing phony about his racial attitudes. I wanted him to be the second coming."

Fallows joined the campaign in late July 1976. But after the election victory, when he got a personal call from Carter asking him to join his White House team, Fallows hesitated. He told the president-elect that he was honored to be asked, but "I'd like to think it over for a day or so." He took the job reluctantly: "Speeches were not something that I was especially fond of." But he knew he was too young and lacked the credentials for a policy job.

Over the next few months, Fallows often felt flummoxed in his responsibilities. As chief speechwriter, he had a staff of only five writers and one researcher. By contrast, Nixon had more than a dozen speechwriters. Fallows frequently found himself being nickel-and-dimed by Hugh Carter, the president's cousin, who was trying to cut White House administrative costs. "We in the speechwriting office are full of sympathy for your in-house economy drive," Fallows wrote sarcastically to Hugh. "We hardly use the air conditioners. . . . We always turn out the lights." He then complained that it was a "tremendous handicap" to have office subscriptions to only *Time, Newsweek, U.S. News & World Report,* and *People*. He begged for permission to subscribe to a dozen other magazines, including the *Washington Monthly, National Review, The Economist,* and *Hustler*—"just kidding, Hugh."

Neither did the California-reared Fallows feel comfortable with the Georgia boys. He never had any substantive conversations with Kirbo, and he thought Frank Moore was pleasant but incompetent. "Jody Powell was much less nice—smart, but he had a mean streak." In retrospect, he compared Jody to President George H. W. Bush's ruthless political operative Lee Atwater. "Hamilton was the nice guy." Jordan was Fallows's frequent tennis partner. Early in the administration, Carter had decided to break with tradition and announced that senior aides in the White House would be allowed access to the tennis court nestled on one corner of the South Lawn. Fallows had been playing serious tennis since high school, and he took advantage of the court's proximity to squeeze in a game whenever he could find a willing partner.

"Hamilton was a decent person," Fallows said. "I liked him. He was a good person. Not like Jody, who could be ever so witty and funny at times, but in a mean way." Fallows's deputy, Hendrik Hertzberg, confirmed that Jim thought Jody could be callous. "I didn't experience that," Hertzberg said. "I liked Jody." In general, Fallows came to believe that the Georgia boys were not able to rise above their irritation with the Georgetown social set. "They were very resentful and insecure about what the Washington establishment thought of them. Katharine Graham and her crowd, well, they were not Carter's kind of people. But by thinking that they were disparaging of the Georgia boys, they made it true, when in fact all those Georgetown hostesses would have been delighted to have the president's chief of staff over for dinner."

Fallows also found it hard to satisfy his only client. Carter had gotten by his entire political life without speechwriters. He had either written his own speeches or just spoken off the cuff. Carter was, in fact, most comfortable and effective when he spoke without a text. "Sometimes in the campaign," Fallows recalled, "we would take recorded transcriptions of what he'd said extemporaneously and stick them into a text. And the paragraph that had flowed so smoothly when he said it off the cuff he stumbled over when he read from a text. He just hates to use texts and hates to practice on his delivery." Most of the time, Carter just preferred talking points, unless it was a formal occasion. Fallows appreciated that the president could be a man of eloquence extemporaneously—but he "has a wooden ear when it comes to working with a text." It was most unfortunate, and it pained his chief speechwriter. One of Fallows's four deputy speechwriters, Jerome Doolittle, had a similar experience with Carter. "His editing," said Doolittle of the president, "almost always made things more awkward." Early in the administration, Doolittle noted in his diary, "Carter doesn't seem to want writers; perhaps to need them, either." Carter knew full well that he wasn't a spellbinder, but he refused to "tamper with his unvarnished, natural style." He'd try on occasion to practice a speech by speaking into a recorder and then listening to how it sounded. But he refused to accept any coaching or speech lessons. Fallows thought this was a mistake—"but it's part of his traits."

Fallows tried hard to make things work; he lobbied for more access to the president, time to discuss upcoming speeches, and time to observe him in cabinet meetings or on official trips. But the president often demurred and made it clear that he thought this would be a waste of his time. Speeches were not a priority. "Carter speeches," Fallows said, "are a much smaller deal for Carter than they were for previous presidents."

The president also didn't want to be bothered with a text until everyone had reached a consensus on what should be said. If it was a foreign policy speech, for instance, Brzezinski had to sign off on it, but also Secretary of State Vance, Jordan, Powell, and often a half dozen other officials. Fallows thought this a "profound mistake," because by the time a consensus was reached, "you get a porridge of a speech." The result was inevitably bland. "But that was what Carter wants," Fallows complained. "They don't want a president," Carter said after giving a dinner speech, "they want Bob Hope." Sometimes, he tried to please, opening one speech with a joke of his own about how he knew that he was their second choice for a speaker—because "they couldn't afford Billy's fee."

Carter was rather demanding of his speechwriters. Five days into the administration, Fallows had to send the new president a few jokes to be included in remarks for the Washington Press Club's Annual Congressional Dinner. Fallows told him the jokes had been written by Doolittle, who had been hired precisely because he had a gruff sense of humor and was known for sprinkling his speeches with one-liners. Carter didn't like them and wrote Jim a stiff note: "Very poor. Next time do more work on it and don't blame Doolittle. . . . At the last minute I had to write my own." In the event, the speech was well received. Carter got a good laugh when he said he had enjoyed his walk down Pennsylvania Avenue until he overheard someone in the crowd say, "There goes Billy's brother."

Twelve of the laugh lines came from Carter himself—and the president used four written by Doolittle. A former *Washington Post* reporter, Doolittle had watched in person as Carter delivered his lines. At the time, he felt good about working in the Carter White House. That night, he walked over the Calvert Street bridge "thinking JC could be a really great president."

In the spring of 1978, the president was scheduled to give a speech in Los Angeles before an audience of the local bar association. Fallows labored over the speech, trying to model it after Carter's famous 1974 Law Day speech, later celebrated by Hunter Thompson in *Rolling Stone*. But the day before the speech, Carter looked over the draft and decided he "hated it." He called Fallows into the Oval Office and told him he was "not satisfied with the speechwriting quality." It was a real dressing-down. Fallows noted that Carter's tone was "not pissed off, but sort of sad." Carter noted in his diary that the "draft I got from Fallows was completely inadequate." Carter thought it "too shrill." Fallows didn't accompany Carter out to Los Angeles—which may explain why he nevertheless thought the president had delivered the speech he had written. Rick Hertzberg heard Carter give the speech and, thinking that Fallows had written it, later told him that it had been "fabulous . . . the best Carter has ever done." Fallows thought it was "my one moment of success, the lawyers' speech." Actually, Carter had completely rewritten the speech, almost on his own, with only a little assistance from Stu Eizenstat.

Fallows may have felt like he was getting mixed signals from Carter. "He's not an intimidating person," Fallows said. "One of his great gifts is his ability to put people at their ease." When the president was mad and intended to chastise, he could be stern. "But it's not like Lyndon Johnson, humiliating someone. You never feel that you're going to be cast out from the tribe because you've made a mistake. Again, I find it a very admirable trait of Carter's, that he understands human frailty." Nevertheless, Fallows chafed at Carter's style, and Carter was not entirely pleased with Jim's work. The young man had not become the president's muse; he was not channeling the southern voice, and he had not found a way to compensate for Carter's weaknesses as a public speaker. The president wasn't going to fire Fallows—but both men seemed uncomfortable with each other. "I kept trying to tell them—not Carter personally, but Hamilton and Jody—that we needed to explain things in a different way," Fallows recalled. He also remembers that he wrote some memos to Jordan, spelling out his criticisms of the administration. But his impression was that they weren't listening. Fallows told Doolittle that he sometimes thought that writing speeches for Carter was a futile exercise: "We exist to construct Potemkin villages which Carter can then knock down." On the other hand, Hamilton Jordan told Fallows in early 1978 that the president had told him that "the smartest thing he's done was to hire Jim as chief speechwriter."

By then, Carter's poll numbers had begun to plummet into the forties and thirties, largely due to the economy's mixed notices of persistent unemployment and rising inflation. Food prices alone rose by a whopping 16 percent in 1978. That May, Rosalynn turned to Jimmy and suggested that perhaps it was time to bring Jerry Rafshoon into the White House. The Atlanta adman had moved his operation to Washington and had been serving as a part-time, informal adviser to the administration. But in May he was brought aboard with a salary of $60,000 to take charge of the White House's messaging. That included supervising Fallows's speechwriting team. Rafshoon would "curb the cacophony," said one press account, and he was also quoted as saying, "We need to get some people out of the speech-writing business and some people in." Fallows liked the irreverent and fast-talking Rafshoon, but he immediately wrote him a note: "This kind of thing does not make our already-difficult life any easier—Your friend, Jim."

By then Fallows was already on his way out. A week earlier, he had written to the president to announce that he intended to resign after the November 1978 midterm elections. He said he found himself "more and more anxious to return to journalism and write for myself once again." He added that he was leaving with "enormous respect for you . . . and high hopes for the Administration's success." Carter replied with a handwritten note, saying that he "would prefer that you continue to work with me, but of course I'll honor your preference." Fallows actually had told fellow speechwriter Doolittle as early as March that he intended to quit. Morale in the speechwriting department was sagging. Doolittle himself was depressed: "The mood toward Carter seemed to be turning worse than poisonous. He's become an object of ridicule and laughter, absolutely the worst thing that can happen."

Fallows left as promised in November, telling friends that he felt "no bitterness." To the contrary, "I feel great personal loyalty to Carter—even as I feel him deficient in some ways. I will vote for him again." But he truly wanted to spend more time with his young son and wife—and he was eager to take up a plum position as Washington editor of *The Atlantic Monthly.*

On his way out, Fallows gave a standard exit interview to a government archivist and said, "If there is a single grievous flaw I find in Carter, it is his complacency about the people he has around him and the ideas that come to him. There's *no passion* in him to find better people, to find better ideas. He is satisfied with those he has." The remark about "no passion" was a harbinger. Fallows was, in fact, leaving with a bagful of criticisms, if not grudges. In mid-December, he dropped by the Old Executive Office Building and saw Doolittle, who was leaving soon to take a job at the Federal Aviation Administration. He told Doolittle that he'd wait until he was gone "before pissing in the punchbowl, so presumably he [Fallows] has revenge on his mind." Doolittle himself left on January 10, 1979, thoroughly unhappy: "Mingled feelings, sad at leaving . . . Penitentiary prisoners must feel something of that. But relieved and glad, too . . . Nothing for me here, not with these people."

Five months later, in the spring of 1979, Fallows published his first essay for *The Atlantic,* entitled "The Passionless Presidency: The Trouble with Jimmy Carter's Administration." The well-written, colorful essay was an insider's critique of the Carter presidency—and it was devastating. Fallows had hesitated, but not for long, about writing such a piece so soon after leaving the White House. His mentor, Peters, urged him to do it. And so too did Bill Moyers and Arthur Schlesinger, Jr. "I thought it would be a useful exercise," Peters recalled. "Jim had complained to me even when he was still in the White House that these people did not know how to govern." Fallows later said he was motivated to "save the Carter presidency from defeat."

Fallows began generously, with fulsome praise for his former boss: "I fully believe him to be a good man. With his moral virtues and his intellectual skills, he is perhaps as admirable a human being as has ever held the job. He is probably smarter, in the College Board sense, than any other President in this century." He had few "quirks." Apart from occasional profanity, Fallows had witnessed nothing in the private Carter at variance with the public Carter. The man was not a hypocrite. He was "patient" and "free of interior demons." Indeed, Fallows confessed, "if I had to choose one politician to sit at the Pearly Gates and pass judgment on my soul, Jimmy Carter would be the one." But that was it. Yes, he believed Carter was a good man. Nothing else remained on the positive side of the ledger.

For Fallows, Carter's deficiencies in the Oval Office were legion. He lacked "sophistication." He was more concerned with discerning the "correct" position on any issue than "with learning how to turn that position into results." He was "arrogant." He "always felt in foreign affairs that if he could only get his adversaries into the room with him, he could win them over." Carter was a "smart man, but not an intellectual." If he chose to, he could be an effective politician—but he didn't want to be one.

Some of Fallows's observations were right on the mark. As president, Carter hated cajoling other politicians. Carter's "skin crawled at the thought of the time-consuming consultations and persuasion that might be required to bring a legislator around." But most of Fallows's criticisms seemed snide and snarky. He observed that while there had been "little abuse of power, it may be because they have so little sense of what power is and how it might be exercised." Carter "thinks in lists, not arguments." Carter, he complained, "believes in fifty things, but no one thing." And this explained why he lacked a passionate vision about where to lead the country.

Clearly, part of Fallows's critique stemmed from his personal political disagreement with the president's particular brand of liberalism. Fallows was an early neoliberal, groomed in particular by his experience with Charlie Peters's *Washington Monthly* to believe in "good governance." Some pundits at the time put Carter in the same camp. But the president was a liberal with a southern populist edge. Carter, Fallows pointed out, despised the Washington mandarins; he was a populist who had plainly said that "too many have had to suffer at the hands of a political and economic elite who have shaped decisions and never had to account for mistakes or suffer from injustice." But for Fallows, this was too simplistic. Carter might be right to rail against the "insularity" of the Georgetown set, but they "happened also to be the people who knew how Washington worked. . . . The insiders were right to scoff at him, for they understood how much he did not know." Fallows thought Carter "needed the insiders' wisdom about the power game if he was to succeed in office." But at the same time, Fallows criticized Hamilton Jordan for showing up at a football game with Redskins owner Edward Bennett Williams, *Washington Post* editor Ben Bradlee, Art Buchwald, and Joe Califano. "Now that Carter's people were sure they'd be accepted," opined Fallows, "they were glad to join the club." The Georgia boys were screwed whether they disdained the "insiders" or tried to hang out with them.

Fallows mocked Carter's arduous efforts at self-improvement—his speed-reading lessons, his carefully timed jogging, his classical music lists—and then complained that the president "complacently resists attempts to challenge his natural style." In the very same breath Fallows confessed his aversion to "the prospect of pop psychology from a journalist"—as if his essay were not exactly that. Near the end of his analysis, Fallows concluded that Carter's "willful ignorance" could be explained only by "a combination of arrogance, complacency, and—dread thought—insecurity at the core of his mind and soul." The twenty-eight-year-old journalist had laid Carter out on the couch and found him "insecure."

The *Atlantic* essay was a vintage piece of New Journalism, personal and biting. One of the more memorable lines in the essay contrasted Ted Kennedy and Carter: "Where Edward Kennedy holds out the promise of the energies he might mobilize and the ideas he might enact, Jimmy Carter tells us that he is a good man. His positions are correct, his values sound. Like Marshal Pétain after the fall of France, he has offered his person to the nation. This is not an inconsiderable gift; his performance in office shows why it's not enough."

Peters worked with Fallows on editing the essay. "I contributed the Marshal Pétain line," Peters boasted. "After Fallows had finished writing the piece, I had a queasy feeling about it. I know Fallows himself worried that it was too harsh. It wounded Carter more than Fallows or I intended. It helped to destroy Jimmy Carter."

Despite everything, what most readers remembered was a minor anecdote that Fallows had used to illustrate Carter's obsessiveness with detail. "The tennis court anecdote was such a small thing," Peters recalled, "but it turned out to be a devastating anecdote." Fallows claimed that during the first six months of his presidency, Carter "would personally review all requests to use the White House tennis court." Fallows recalled sending a note to Carter's secretary, Susan Clough, asking to use the court, usually on Tuesday afternoons and Saturday mornings. "I always provided spaces where he could check Yes or No; Carter would make his decision and send the note back, initialed J." After the *Atlantic* essay was published, Carter told Stu Eizenstat, "He lied, he lied. I don't know if he did it deliberately, but it was a lie."

The truth was complicated. Carter never recalled playing tennis with Fallows. But sometime in the spring of 1977, he had left the Oval Office, donned tennis clothes, and accompanied one of his sons down to the South Lawn. Rackets in hand, they arrived at the court only to see two staffers in the middle of a game. Instead of bumping them, Carter turned around politely and walked back to the Oval Office, where he told Clough that the court was occupied. Clough later said this happened on several occasions. Carter would wander down to the court, and if he saw someone playing, "he'd turn around and go back." The same thing happened to Rosalynn, who had started to take tennis lessons. Finally, Clough sent out word that anyone wanting to use the court should first check with her to see if it was free. She later insisted in a letter to *The New York Times* that "the responsibility for coordinating court requests was mine." Clough explained that "Mr. Fallows' requests were usually sent as part of his cover notes," attached to speech drafts. This would explain why Fallows came away with the impression that Carter himself was managing the court schedule—when, in fact, Fallows had casually circumvented the president's secretary. Clough also later admitted that she sometimes initialed the tennis court schedules, imitating Carter's handwriting. It was all a misunderstanding, but as Eizenstat later wrote, "Fallows' botched account of the president as a detail freak followed Carter not just through the election, but for the rest of his life."

FALLOWS WAS UNDERSTANDABLY nervous when the essay was published, but he nevertheless sent Carter a note with an early copy. "I hope you will be able to see," he wrote, "that this article, while critical, is meant to be constructive." The president passed Fallows's letter to Jody Powell, scribbling on top of it, "We all have to make a living." Carter could be sardonic, but years later he admitted, "I was disappointed. I thought he betrayed me." Powell and Jordan were livid. Jody and Jim had several "angry exchanges" on the phone. "Goddammit, Jim," Jody told him, "this is the kind of thing you send as a letter to the president. You don't publish it." When asked by a *People* magazine reporter to respond, Fallows said, "Jody knows very well that a letter would not make the slightest difference. Carter's failings are the most fundamental public matter." But even several years later, Powell was seething: "I have a hard time speaking in measured tones about Mr. Fallows and his piece."

Jordan was appalled by the essay, but he refrained from calling his former tennis partner until Fallows himself wrote him a note about "the recent controversy over my article." Fallows was unapologetic. "I understand that many people I respect feel it was wrong of me to write that article," he said, "even as I felt it was the right thing to do."

Jordan replied, "I would like to think that you and I can remain friends through all of this and that I can say some things to you that I feel very strongly." Jordan did not question his friend's motives. As a journalist, he conceded that Fallows was no doubt trying to record accurately his "perceptions and observations of a President at work." But the end result was entirely harmful: "Your article had hurt the President among thoughtful people in this city and country."

It was just one article in a monthly magazine. But it was well written and had the cachet of being an insider's revelation. The young Fallows was admired by other up-and-coming journalists, and so the essay became influential, sending a green light to the pundit class to mock the president. The influential *New York Times* columnist James Reston agreed with Jordan: The essay was "more harmful than Fallows intended." An unrepentant Fallows took comfort from a "vital center" liberal curmudgeon: "Some of your old associates may be trying to make you feel badly about alleged betrayal of loyalties," wrote Arthur Schlesinger, Jr. "The higher loyalty, it has always seemed to me, is to truth, public enlightenment and history." Fallows's former colleagues thought otherwise. "That *Atlantic* essay was a knife in the back," said White House staffer Alice Rogoff. "We all liked Jim, but that essay was a violation of every ethical code." Tim Kraft sarcastically quipped, "Fallows is the toast of Georgetown." Landon Butler had even stronger words: "I was appalled by his essay. It was treason, just inexcusable."

Bessie Lillian Gordy, "Miss Lillian," and James Earl Carter, Sr., married in 1923 and raised their first-born son, Jimmy, in the isolated South Georgia hamlet of Archery. They lived in a Sears, Roebuck kit home with no running water or electricity. Jimmy Carter's childhood was steeped in segregation and a culture of white supremacy. And yet, his childhood playmates were mostly African American.

James Earl Carter, Jr.,
age seventeen, 1941.

In 1946, Naval Academy ensign Carter married Rosalynn Smith in Plains, Georgia. "I think I was kin to everybody that Jimmy wasn't," Rosalynn said. "Once we got married, we were kin to everybody in town."

Lt. Carter became a submariner, studied nuclear physics, and served under Captain Hyman G. Rickover (LEFT, with then President Carter), a sharp-tongued officer who ripped through red tape to build the country's fleet of nuclear-powered submarines. "Rickover was not dissimilar from my father," Carter said. "He scared me."

JIMMY CARTER
FOR STATE SENATOR

When his father died in 1953, Carter resigned his Navy commission and returned to Plains to manage the family farm. In 1962, he was narrowly defeated in a race for state senator—until he hired a lawyer, Charles Kirbo, who quickly proved that a critical county ballot box had been stuffed with fraudulent ballots.

Carter and his younger brother Billy built the Carter Peanut Warehouse into a multimillion-dollar business in South Georgia. Carter declined to join the White Citizens Council, prompting a neighbor to place a handwritten sign on the Carter Peanut Warehouse reading COONS AND CARTERS GO TOGETHER. But Carter avoided the civil rights movement until he was elected Georgia's governor in 1970, when he shocked his constituents by announcing that "the time for racial discrimination is over."

Carter and two of his boys, Chip and Jeff (ABOVE), in 1960. Billy Carter (LEFT) sorting peanuts with a Carter Peanut Warehouse worker.

The Carter family—Miss Lillian, Jack, Amy, Jimmy, Rosalynn, Jeff, Annette (Jeff's wife), Chip, and Caron (Chip's wife)—at the Democratic Convention. When Carter told his mother that he was running for president, Miss Lillian responded, "President of *what*?" Carter's consigliere, Charlie Kirbo, told him that an outsider with no connections to Washington stood a good chance of capturing the Democratic nomination. Improbably, by August 1976, the Democratic nominee was being interviewed in a Plains pond by ABC newsman Sam Donaldson. Carter ran as a Southern populist.

Billy Carter in a "Redneck Power" T-shirt, with his softball team.

Carter aides Stuart Eizenstat (foreground, far left) and Hamilton Jordan (just left of the TV) watching election results.

The Carters embracing on Election Night 1976. Carter won 49.9 percent of the popular vote against President Gerald Ford's 47.9 percent. *The New York Times*'s James Wooten observed he was "least acceptable among Northern liberals and Southern conservatives."

Miss Lillian's wit garnered much attention on the campaign trail. When asked by a reporter, "Miss Lillian, aren't you proud of your son?," she answered, "Which one?"

President-elect Carter's close-knit advisers became known as the Georgia boys. Left to right: Stuart Eizenstat, Hamilton Jordan, Jimmy Carter, Richard Moe, Charles Kirbo, Jack Watson, and Landon Butler.

Hamilton Jordan, thirty-two (ABOVE), and Jody Powell, thirty-three (RIGHT), spearheaded Carter's political operations. "That country-boy act is as phony as a three-dollar bill," said one friend. "They're tough cookies." Jordan was a brilliant political strategist. "Hamilton was the poster child for the wild young man," said Alice Rogoff, a young White House staffer. "But in private he was not like that at all. He was the perfect Southern gentleman." Powell's biting humor made him a particularly admired and effective press secretary.

Charlie Kirbo was Carter's personal "wise man"—a slow-talking Southern lawyer who drove a pickup truck to his law office. When asked if Carter listened to anyone, Jerry Rafshoon's wife, Eden, told Gregory Peck, "Why, yes, he listens to Charlie Kirbo, who is very much like Atticus Finch." But Kirbo refused to move to Washington as the president's chief of staff, and instead gave him his advice through numerous memos and phone calls.

President Carter, Amy (age nine), and First Lady Rosalynn Carter in the White House. "There is nothing royal or imperial about them," wrote Sally Quinn in *The Washington Post*. Carter tried hard to "depomp" the presidency. That first winter, he set the thermostat in the White House to 65 degrees Fahrenheit, determined to have the White House set a frugal example for the country. "I couldn't believe it," Rosalynn Carter said.

President Carter, wearing a cardigan, about to give his first speech on the growing energy crisis. Behind him (in the plaid blazer) is his young speechwriter, James Fallows, who resigned two years later and wrote a critical essay about his "passionless presidency." Carter considered it a betrayal.

OMB chief Bert Lance testifying with his lawyer Clark Clifford. White House aide Landon Butler noted that Lance had become "the victim of a press frenzy. . . . But I'm afraid that his defense of himself was probably just as sloppy as his personal banking." Lance was forced to resign.

Gloria Steinem unveiling a *Ms.* magazine cover with a pregnant President Carter—who had earned the ire of feminists for his refusal to use federal funds for abortions.

President Carter forged political alliances with African American leaders like Jesse Jackson (ABOVE) and consumer and environmental activists like Ralph Nader (RIGHT). Carter staffed his administration with both "Nader's Raiders" and African Americans.

Chapter 14
Triumph at Camp David

We are wasting our time with this man!
—Egypt's ANWAR SADAT, September 15, 1978

Menachem Begin, Anwar Sadat, and Carter
DAUGHERTY/ASSOCIATED PRESS

IN THE SPRING of 1978, Ron Nachman, a thirty-six-year-old Israeli-born businessman, and a handful of his Tel Aviv friends drove thirty-seven miles north of Jerusalem, fourteen miles deep into the occupied territories on the West Bank. Parking their vehicles in a wadi, they then hiked up a barren mount known as Jebel Mawat, "the hill of death." By nightfall, they had pitched several tents atop the *jebel*. They called their encampment Ariel, meaning "Lion of God." The new Jewish settlement—located just twenty-one miles west of the River Jordan—had no amenities. But within days, Nachman had hauled up the hill a diesel generator to provide electricity. A tanker truck periodically supplied water. That summer, they replaced the tents with simple homes made from prefabricated concrete blocks. They built a school and an infirmary.

In August 1978, forty Israeli families moved to the settlement. Nachman and his colleagues were all employees of Israel Military Industries, a Tel Aviv small-arms manufacturer best known for its Uzi submachine gun. Nachman was a board member of the arms company. Unlike the fundamentalist religious motivations of the Gush Emunim settlers elsewhere in the West Bank, Nachman's motivations were quite secular and purely nationalist. He believed in the settlement project as a national security imperative. Nachman was garrulous and charming, and his enthusiasm was infectious. In 1972, with the encouragement of General Moshe Dayan, Nachman formed what he called the Tel Aviv Group. Its mission was to populate the West Bank with Jewish settlements. Their goal was not the building of agricultural kibbutzim or small military outposts but modern towns and cities. Nachman envisioned Ariel as Israel's "city of tomorrow."

He had the full backing of the Israeli establishment. On March 29, 1977, a full year before the tents were erected at Ariel, Labor Minister of Defense Shimon Peres authorized the seizure of hundreds of acres of farmlands cultivated for generations by Palestinians from the village of Hares. Peres's order stated that these private holdings were being seized on grounds of military necessity. No compensation was given to the Palestinian landowners. If the Labor government of Prime Minister Yitzhak Rabin had paved the way, the new settlement of Ariel was actually inaugurated by Rabin's Likud successor. Immediately after his stunning upset election, Prime Minister Menachem Begin provocatively paid a visit to the highly controversial Jewish squatter site of Elon Moreh, an illegal outpost northeast of Nablus. "In a few weeks or months," Begin proclaimed to reporters, "there will be many more Elon Morehs!" By August 1978, Ariel was one of many such promising new settlements being promoted by the Begin government. Begin was absolutely committed to the settlement enterprise. When a journalist asked him if he intended to "annex" the West Bank, Begin replied, "We don't use the word 'annexation.' You annex *foreign* land, not your own country."

* * *

THAT AUGUST, JUST as Nachman was welcoming forty families to Ariel, President Carter dispatched personal letters to Begin and Sadat, inviting them both to join him the following month at Camp David. Both leaders quickly accepted this extraordinary invitation from the American president. Carter had been contemplating just such a dramatic step for more than six months. As early as January 23, 1978, he had discussed the idea of a summit with Cy Vance, Zbig Brzezinski, Hamilton Jordan, and Fritz Mondale. All but Jordan were opposed. "I don't think anyone made a convincing argument against the joint summit," Jordan wrote in a handwritten note to the president. "Your instincts are usually good. . . . Everyone agrees that we should not let the thing drag, but everything that is likely to happen (especially settlements) is going to make everything more difficult—including resumption of talks. . . . Sadat is not the problem. Begin is the problem."

Carter's own handwritten notes from that contentious meeting spelled out the dilemma. Just two months after Sadat's extraordinary visit to Jerusalem, the "Sadat-Begin talks have broken down." Carter was confident that "Sadat wants a settlement." But he was "not sure about Begin." The president asked himself, "Should we bring [it] to a head? If so, when should we invite them? Is Camp David best place?" Carter hesitated and instead spent the spring and summer hoping to rejuvenate bilateral peace talks. He blamed the impasse on the Israelis, mostly "because of their insistence on the illegal settlements." The Palestinian terrorist attack on the coastal highway bus, followed that spring by the Israeli invasion of Lebanon, only made things worse.

Eleven days after the coastal highway massacre, Begin came to the White House to discuss the crisis. Carter wanted to talk about the stalled negotiations with Sadat. The president came prepared with a scratch pad of notes: "I then read to Begin and his group my understanding of their position: they're not willing to withdraw politically or militarily from any part of the West Bank; not willing to stop the construction of new settlements or the expansion of existing settlements; not willing to withdraw Israeli settlers from the Sinai, nor if they stay to permit UN or Egyptian protection for them; not willing to acknowledge that UN Resolution 242 applies to the West Bank/Gaza Strip area; and not willing to grant Palestinians a voice in the determination of their own future."

Begin responded limply that "this was a negative way to express their position." But he didn't deny the accuracy of Carter's summary. Privately, Carter was stunned: "For the first time, over their strenuous objections, the true position of the Israeli government was revealed." He began referring to Begin's positions as "the six noes." Carter found himself deeply discouraged by Begin's attitude. The previous evening, he and Rosalynn had spent hours with Begin and his wife, Aliza, talking to them about their early lives. Begin spoke about the murder of his parents and his only brother in the Holocaust. "When the meal was over," Carter later wrote, "I understood some of his attitudes much better." But empathy did nothing to soften Begin's views.

Later that spring, Stu Eizenstat tried to encourage Carter to be more sensitive to Begin's insecurities. Carter trusted Eizenstat implicitly and had encouraged him to cultivate a back channel to the Israelis. But on this occasion, he told Stu, "Begin is solely holding up peace. I have coldness in my heart toward him after our meetings." The very next day, Carter spent thirty minutes alone with Begin and tried to do what Eizenstat had asked. But afterward, he noted in his diary, "He's a small man with limited vision, and my guess is that he will not take the necessary steps to bring peace to Israel."*

By contrast, Carter's correspondence that spring with Sadat revealed a deepening of their trust and friendship. Sadat's eloquent handwritten letters to the president were effusive and deeply personal. The Egyptian demonstrated a remarkable command of written English. "Dear friend," Sadat wrote to Carter on April 24, 1978, "I foresee some testing days ahead. But I firmly believe that you can overcome all difficulties and eliminate various obstacles. The strength of your faith, and the soundness of your judgment can bring us closer to our goals which have been endorsed by the overwhelming majority of people in the four corners of the world. To my mind, no one is more equipped or better qualified to

---

* Ironically, it was on this day that Carter announced his support for the creation of the Holocaust Memorial Museum. He recruited Holocaust survivor and author Elie Wiesel to chair the project's commission, and in 1979 the commission recommended that the museum be built on the Mall. The museum opened its doors on April 26, 1993.

carry out that mission than you, dear friend and brother." On this occasion, Sadat urged Carter to hold to his principles. "I am sure that you know that any softening of your stand will be misinterpreted by Mr. Begin. It would only whet his appetite. . . . Therefore, it would be extremely beneficial if Mr. Begin gets the unmistakable message that your balanced policy remains unchanged." Here, Carter scribbled in the margins, "I agree." Still, the negotiations remained stalled, and no progress had been made since Sadat's trip to Jerusalem.

Finally, in late July 1978, Carter was walking through the woods with Rosalynn at Camp David when he suddenly turned to his wife and said, "It's so beautiful here. I don't believe anyone could stay in this place, close to nature, peaceful and isolated from the world, and still carry a grudge. . . . If I could get Sadat and Begin both here together, we could work out some of the problems between them." Rosalynn encouraged him, and after mulling over the idea for the weekend, Carter confided his decision on Monday, July 31, 1978, at a Camp David breakfast meeting. He instructed Vance to deliver handwritten invitations to the two heads of state. Carter, Rosalynn, and everyone knew it was a gamble. Carter later called it "almost one of desperation."

"Are you willing to be the scapegoat?" Rosalynn asked.

"What else is new?" Carter replied.

Some members of his foreign policy team were opposed to the venture, calling it a "losing proposition." Mondale worried about the political consequences. "If you fail, we're done," he said. "We will sap our stature as national leaders." Brzezinski was similarly pessimistic, noting in his private journal, "the president simply cannot afford to fail, and therefore we must be really ready for a showdown." For Zbig, this meant pressuring the Israelis with the threat that "refusal to accept our proposals will jeopardize the U.S.-Israeli relationship." He thought it a good possibility that Begin would stall at every juncture. "Thus, we have to prepare ourselves for the possibility of massive disappointment, a letdown, and even damage to Presidential prestige. . . . In any case, the die has been cast."

By contrast, Vance was rather supportive, claiming in his memoirs, "It was a daring stroke, which I warmly supported." Vance personally delivered the handwritten invitations. Carter's letter to Sadat was particularly blunt. "During recent weeks little progress has been made," he wrote to Sadat, "and the relationships have deteriorated. A total stale-mate is in prospect. Unless we act boldly and constructively now, those of us who now serve as leaders may not again have such a chance to bring peace to the people of your region." Carter said he wanted to meet "in relative seclusion" with both Sadat and Begin. "I have no strong pref-erence about the location, but Camp David is available."

Sadat quickly accepted the invitation, and so too did Begin. But within a week Carter received disheartening news: "We got word that Israel was planning five new settlements in the West Bank, which is typ-ical, and [I] fired off a quick letter to Begin." The Israeli prime minister sent a "contentious" reply, claiming that he was putting off the new set-tlements until after the Camp David summit. This was not true, since at that very moment forty families were moving into new quarters at the Ariel settlement.

OF THE THREE leaders, Carter had the most to lose politically in such a high-risk summit. Sadat, however, desperately needed a tangible dip-lomatic victory. The unpredictable Egyptian had gone to Jerusalem, defying the Arab street, and had expected to be rewarded with a compre-hensive peace. After nearly eight years in power, the Egyptian *rais* (leader) showed signs of being infected with a touch of grandiosity. He relished the drama of high-stakes politics. In 1973, he had successfully gambled on a daring cross-canal surprise attack on Israeli forces in the October War. And he had astonished the entire world with his bold trip to Jerusalem. But now his Israeli adversary was dismissing the Jerusalem drama as empty showmanship. Begin defiantly told his aides that Sadat would get "nothing for nothing." But if Sadat attended a major summit and got nothing, the humiliation could prove to be deadly. Carter knew this. He quite literally feared for Sadat's life. Carter deeply admired Sadat for his willingness to do the right thing even if it was not politically advisable. In some palpable sense, Carter was motivated to risk his own presidency in order to rescue this Egyptian leader from his near-reckless audacity.

By contrast, Begin had the least to lose from a failed summit—but risked having to pay too much political capital if the summit was a suc-cess. Begin's goal was simple and twofold: to concede very little, and to avoid any public blame if the summit failed, as was likely. Begin had a strong hand.

Brzezinski bluntly summarized the dynamics: "Sadat cannot afford a failure and knows it. Both Sadat and Begin think you cannot afford a failure; but Begin probably believes that a failure at Camp David will hurt you and Sadat, but not him." Begin, in fact, would be happy "to see Sadat discredited and you weakened, thus leaving him with the tolerable status quo, instead of pressures to change his lifelong beliefs concerning 'Judea and Samaria.'"

Carter fully understood that Begin would be maddeningly pedantic—and Sadat would be effusive and emotionally dramatic. These were their working personae. Carter would try to pin them down with sheer relentlessness.

THE PRESIDENT PREPARED for the encounter during a short vacation in the Brinkerhoff Lodge on Jackson Lake in Wyoming. Between hours of fly-fishing for cutthroat trout in the Snake River, Carter pored over briefing books and thought hard about his strategy. The CIA's biographical profiles of Begin and Sadat reminded him that both had used political violence, assassination, and terrorism as political weapons. Both had blood on their hands. Carter already knew both men. He found Begin didactic and unlikable—and Sadat seemed warm and emotionally intelligent. But Carter thought he could transcend their personalities and the unsavory aspects of their political histories. He was determined to go far beyond the "very modest" goal of crafting a declaration of principles for future negotiations. He wanted nothing less than a comprehensive peace treaty to settle the entire Arab-Israeli conflict in all its parts.

By some accounts at the time, the president arrived at Camp David with no strategic plan, ready simply to wing it. This is not accurate. Carter came thoroughly prepared, briefed, and with both a strategy and tactics in his pocket. Late in August, the always steady and methodical Cy Vance sent him a particularly prescient memo on what to expect. "With Sadat, the problem will be to bring him down from the clouds of conceptual generalities," Vance observed. "With Begin, the problem will be his tendency to divert the discussions to side-issues, legalistic details or procedural devices that avoid focusing on the key issues of withdrawal and Palestinian rights." Vance urged Carter to let the two leaders spend the first few days arguing—but to intervene with an American proposal after the Sabbath break on Saturday, September 9. The goal would be to put the Israeli and Egyptian agreements and disagreements in "our language." Vance predicted that Begin's "top priority" would be to achieve a "separate peace agreement with Egypt." Sadat, however, "cannot afford to appear to walk out on the Palestinians." This meant that an agreement could be reached only if Israel agreed to withdraw over some time period from the West Bank and Gaza. "Begin also needs to be persuaded of the importance of a virtual freeze on further settlement activities." Finally, Vance suggested that in order to maintain control over the talks, there should be no press allowed, and Jody Powell would be the sole spokesman to the outside world. In the days ahead, Carter followed Vance's script quite closely.

On the eve of the summit's first day, Carter made a precise list of his goals. The first item on the list was "No more war." Other items included:

- Israel must have security, including military presence on West Bank.
- No independent Palestinian state.
- UN 242 applies—West Bank withdrawal.
- Phased implementation of agreement.
- Jordan/Palestinians have negotiating role.
- Egyptian sovereignty in Sinai.
- Early warning system important.
- Demilitarization of disputed areas.
- Military government [in West Bank] should be terminated.
- United Jerusalem.

There was nothing modest about this list. Every item could be contentious with one party or the other. But taken as a package, Carter's list outlined a comprehensive settlement that most observers might regard as wholly reasonable. Israel would get what it should have desired most—peace and a measure of concrete security with its neighbors. Egypt would get the Sinai back. But it would not be a separate peace just with Egypt. The military government in the West Bank would be dismantled. There would be no independent Palestinian state, and Jerusalem would remain united. But the Palestinians would have some role in future negotiations to arrive at a framework for self-governance within five years. On a separate page, Carter listed some additional principles:

- Inadmissibility of acquisition of territory by war.
- Palestinian Arabs. Voice in determination of our future.
- No new settlements.

DAY ONE: TUESDAY, SEPTEMBER 5, 1978

SADAT STEPPED OUT of a helicopter at Camp David shortly after 2:30 P.M. and greeted Carter with open arms. He kissed Rosalynn warmly on both cheeks and then sat down with Carter on the terrace of Aspen, the presidential cottage. Tapping his jacket pocket, he confided that he had brought with him a comprehensive peace plan. The two men chatted amiably for thirty minutes, and then Sadat announced he was tired from his long journey and needed to sleep.

Two hours later, Begin arrived. They too greeted each other warmly, but Carter thought both of them felt "somewhat ill at ease." Despite his jet lag, Begin insisted he would like to meet with Carter after supper. When the Israeli prime minister remarked that his goal was merely an agreement on general principles, Carter insisted that they aspire to much more than generalities. Later, they met alone in Carter's cabin and talked past each other for two and a half hours. Begin repeated the official Israeli line on settlements, the Sinai, and the Palestinians—giving scant evidence of flexibility. Begin finally left around 11:00 P.M. Carter felt disheartened. "In general," he dictated into his diary, "the conversation was discouraging. He [Begin] simply repeated the old Israeli negotiating points." Falling asleep that first night, he told Rosalynn, "I don't believe he has any intention of going through with a peace treaty."

DAY TWO: WEDNESDAY, SEPTEMBER 6

THE NEXT MORNING, Carter was up at 5:00, as usual. He played tennis with Rosalynn for an hour and then had breakfast with Cy Vance and Zbig Brzezinski. At 10:00 A.M. he met with Sadat and cautioned him that in the forthcoming talks it was important not to put Begin on the defensive. "Unless our proposals were eminently fair to Israel," Carter said, "his ministers and the Israeli people would certainly support him if the peace talks broke down." Sadat responded that he thought Begin was "a very formal man, difficult to approach. . . . He was bitter and inclined to look back in ancient history rather than deal with the present and the future." But then the Egyptian also confided in Carter that he thought "Camp David was inevitably going to be a trap for Begin." Regarding the West Bank, Sadat told Carter a story he had heard about a prominent Austrian Jew named Kahan who had recently asked the Israeli prime minister what he wanted to achieve in the forthcoming negotiations. Begin had placed his hand on the West Bank portion of a map and said, "I want this." Sadat obviously thought this anecdote illustrated Begin's bottom-line intentions.

After further bantering back and forth, Sadat handed Carter a document entitled a "Framework for Peace." As Carter read it, "my heart sank; it was extremely harsh and filled with all the unacceptable Arab rhetoric." Sadat insisted he intended to read the document aloud to Begin at their first face-to-face meeting, scheduled for that afternoon. Carter warned him that if he did so, the meeting would probably be "unpleasant." But then Sadat surprised him by handing him an additional three typewritten pages, spelling out certain "modifications." Taking Carter into his confidence, Sadat revealed just how far he was willing to go at the end of the negotiations.

Conspiratorially, he cautioned Carter that these pages were for the president's eyes only; he had yet to tell his own delegation about these concessions. Carter found himself pleasantly surprised: "I saw for the first time that we might possibly achieve substantial success." Sadat was willing in principle to grant Israel full diplomatic recognition with open borders. The Palestinians would get not a state but a self-governing authority in the West Bank, but Sadat would agree to minor adjustments of the borders. The Israelis would have to withdraw completely from the Sinai, but Sadat was open to the stationing of UN peacekeepers along the border. Astonishingly, Sadat even said that Jerusalem could remain an undivided city.

Despite these confidential concessions, Carter sensed that Sadat basically felt that Begin was "hopeless." Sadat was instead looking to lay the ground at Camp David for some kind of propaganda victory, hoping that "Begin's successors might be forced to accept the Arab position."

Realizing that both the Egyptian and the Israeli were positioning themselves for a failed summit, Carter knew full well that the first direct meeting between the two adversaries might not go well. Shortly before 3:00 P.M., the two men appeared at the Aspen presidential cabin, both wearing coats and ties. Begin wore his perennial black suit, white shirt, and tie. By contrast, Sadat appeared to be "the incarnation of masculine elegance: brushed and combed, carefully dressed in the most expensive of fashions, giving off the aroma of after-shave lotion." Carter sat nervously between them, wearing only casual slacks and a polo shirt, and tried to make small talk. Tactically, he had planned to keep a low profile, hoping that the relaxed setting and the mountain scenery would encourage Sadat and Begin to interact casually and respectfully. It was not to be. Sadat pulled his "Framework for Peace" from his inside pocket and began reading from it, lecturing Begin, and outlining his hard-line demands. Begin stewed for nearly ninety minutes, waiting for Sadat to finish his sermon. When Sadat was finally done, Carter broke the awkward silence by turning to Begin: If the prime minister could just sign on to Sadat's document as written, "it would save us all a lot of time." This broke the tension, and everyone laughed heartily. Begin and Sadat visibly lightened up. At first, Carter wondered why: "I could not understand the reason for the strange hilarity and good will." Gradually, it dawned on Carter that Sadat was merely relieved that Begin had not stormed out of the meeting, and that Begin was actually "relieved" by Sadat's hard-line rhetoric—because it meant that he would not have to make any real concessions. As predicted by Brzezinski and Vance, Begin would be happy with failure. "We adjourned in good spirits," Carter noted, "with Sadat and Begin patting each other on the back."

DAY THREE: THURSDAY, SEPTEMBER 7

IN THE MORNING, Carter spent two hours with Begin, Moshe Dayan, and Defense Minister Ezer Weizman, accompanied by Vance and Brzezinski. Of the three Israelis, Carter respected Dayan, but he actually liked Weizman, whom he regarded as a realist—an Israeli who could provide a counterbalance against Begin's messianic instincts. The feeling was mutual. Weizman shared Carter's frustration with Begin's long-winded speechifying. And the Israeli defense minister admired Carter's "bulldog persistence and his ability to deal with the tiniest of details." But on this occasion the Israelis were in a recalcitrant mood, and Begin kept citing Sadat's hard-line paper as an insurmountable obstacle to any further progress. Carter finally lost patience and became angry, nearly shouting, "What do you actually want for Israel if peace is signed?" He accused Begin of wanting the West Bank over peace and suggested that his proposal for Palestinian autonomy in the West Bank was mere "subterfuge." Begin fumed and said he resented this word. "I don't feel I have your trust," Carter said. "You are as evasive with me as with the Arabs. The time has come to throw away reticence. Tell us what you really need." Carter pressed him hard, suggesting that the "burgeoning of Israeli settlements indicates that you are planning to stay in the West Bank, creating a societal structure on the West Bank, and not [just] a defense system. . . . I don't know if you have the intention to withdraw, if you are willing to forego peace with Egypt to preserve the settlements on the West Bank."

At one point, referring to his own political vulnerabilities, Carter firmly said, "My reelection is not nearly as important to me as the resolution of the Middle Eastern issue." Perhaps he thought this sentiment would put more pressure on Begin. The Israeli remained completely evasive.

Obviously, things were not going well. But at 10:30 A.M. Carter and Begin walked over to the Aspen cabin for another face-to-face meeting with Sadat. This time, Carter decided he would make it clear that he was there merely as the note taker. "I wanted them to address each other directly. While they talked, I took notes without looking up, and they soon refrained from talking to me or attempting to seek my opinion." But the men argued bitterly, their faces often flushed with anger. "Premier Begin," Sadat said, "you want land! . . . Security, yes! Land, no!" Rosalynn was sitting at her desk in her bedroom down the hall from the study and could hear angry, raised voices. After three hours of heated arguments, they finally adjourned for lunch.

Carter was terribly discouraged. After nearly three days, nothing had been accomplished. Carter could detect "no compatibility between the two men." He told Cy, Zbig, Ham, and Jody, "It was mean. They were brutal with each other, personal." Rosalynn noted that when her husband was disturbed, he would get very quiet, and a vein in his temple would pulse visibly. "Tonight, it was pounding," she wrote, "and neither of us could eat much as the sun set on our third day." The Carters hosted an informal buffet dinner and had the U.S. Marine Corps put on a performance of their "silent drill" with flashing bayonets mounted on twirling rifles. After the performance, Rosalynn sat next to a dejected Sadat, who confided to her, "I have given so much and 'that man' acts as though I have done nothing. . . . "'That man' will not let go of the past."

Until then, no members of the press corps had been allowed into Camp David. But that evening dozens of reporters were bused into the grounds and allowed to witness the Marine Corps' silent drill and take photographs of the assembled delegates. No interviews were allowed, but the glum expressions on the faces of Sadat, Begin, and others suggested that things were not going well. Afterward, as Jerry Rafshoon was checking to see that all the reporters were back on the bus to depart, he discovered that Barbara Walters, the famous ABC television interviewer, was missing. Rafshoon went hunting for her and finally found her hiding in the ladies' restroom: "Barbara, will you please come out now?"*

Late that evening, Carter met again with Sadat—but this time he included the Egyptian's three closest advisers, Deputy Prime Minister Hassan Tuhamy, Foreign Minister Mohamed Ibrahim Kamel, and Minister Boutros Boutros-Ghali. "I know you are very discouraged right now," Carter said. He acknowledged that Begin was being obstinate on the relatively simple issue of Israeli settlements in the Sinai. Begin was insisting that he could never agree to dismantle even one Jewish settlement in the Sinai—let alone in the West Bank. Carter told the Egyptians that the U.S. position continued to be that the settlements were illegal and should be removed. He didn't know yet how to resolve this issue, but he insisted that he would find a way forward. "I ask that you give me more time before you leave."

Sadat flatly said he could not compromise on full Egyptian sovereignty over the Sinai. "If sovereignty is to mean anything to Egyptians, all Israelis must leave our territory." He was ready to depart. "Begin haggles over every word and is making his withdrawal conditional on keeping land. Begin is not ready for peace."

---

* Walters told Rafshoon, "You know I had affairs with both Dayan and Weizman."

DAY FOUR: FRIDAY, SEPTEMBER 8

THE NEXT MORNING, Carter learned that both Sadat and Begin were making plans to leave, on the assumption that the summit talks were failing. Carter stalled for time by asking Begin to meet with him at 2:30 P.M. and Sadat at 4:00 P.M. When he met with Begin, the Israeli once again pulled out his copy of Sadat's hard-line position and began listing all the points that were unacceptable. Carter bluntly confided that he knew that Sadat's written positions were not his final offer. Sadat was flexible, and Carter needed the same sort of flexibility from Begin. The Israelis then argued for another thirty minutes about why it was absolutely imperative that the Israeli settlements in the Sinai remain, even though Sadat had already agreed to have 130 kilometers of demilitarized desert between the Egyptian and Israeli borders. Begin ended his lecture with a flourish. "I will never *personally* recommend that the settlements in the Sinai be dismantled. Please, Mr. President, do not make this a United States demand."

Carter didn't say so to Begin, but he made a mental note to himself that the phrase "never personally recommend" left open the possibility that Begin could leave the decision to the Israeli Knesset. Carter thought he saw an opening, and he felt heartened for the first time in three days.

Begin reiterated that the president should not list the removal of Israeli settlements in the Sinai as part of any "proposal to us." It was important, he said, that the whole world understand that there were "no serious differences between Israel and the United States." Carter tartly responded, "Mr. Prime Minister, we cannot avoid addressing the most contentious issues, and this is the one on which the entire Camp David talks have foundered so far. I cannot let Sadat tell me not to discuss Israeli security on the West Bank. I cannot let you tell me not to discuss the Israeli presence on Egyptian territory." Carter firmly explained that he intended to produce the next day a comprehensive American proposal for peace. "It will not surprise either you or Sadat. When it is finished tomorrow, I will present it to you first, and then to the Egyptians. I can see no other possibility for progress." Carter was cornering Begin. As Carter put it in his presidential memoir, "Begin was just now beginning to realize the disadvantage of being the odd man out." As long as Carter had Sadat's agreement on any particular point, Begin could be assigned the blame for any failure in the talks. Begin could survive a failed summit so long as he didn't have to shoulder sole blame for the failure. That Begin ardently wished to avoid this blame gave Carter a certain amount of leverage over the Israeli leader. "I must admit that I capitalized on this situation with both delegations in order to get an agreement; it greatly magnified my own influence."

With the two adversaries incapable of dealing with each other without bitterly arguing, Carter began to implement a new strategy. He would present an American peace plan to each side—but separately. Instead of having Sadat and Begin talk to each other in the same room, he would keep them apart. As it turned out, the two leaders would not meet in formal sessions for the next eight days. Carter had also noticed that Sadat seemed far more flexible and open than his team of advisers, all of whom clearly wanted to restrain Sadat from giving away too much. On the other hand, Begin's advisers—Moshe Dayan, Ezer Weizman, and Aharon Barak—all appeared to be less rigid than their prime minister. Carter concluded that he should meet on his own with Begin's team, excluding Begin, and try to get them to agree to the salient points in the American plan—and then do the same with Sadat alone, but excluding for the most part Sadat's team of advisers.

Carter knew that Begin was perhaps willing to agree to a withdrawal from the Sinai in return for a separate peace treaty with Egypt. But the Israeli wanted to keep the West Bank and ignore the issue of Palestinian self-determination. Sadat was determined to have the whole Sinai back under Egyptian sovereignty, but he was adamant that this had to be linked to an agreement on the West Bank and Palestinian rights: "I will not sign a Sinai agreement before an agreement is also reached on the West Bank." Both parties thus shared a willingness to make a deal on the Sinai—but to make this happen, Carter understood, he had to link it to some sort of compromise on the West Bank, Palestinian autonomy, and a settlement freeze.

The task now was to craft an American proposal and then painstakingly win each party's agreement to the document, paragraph by paragraph. Tactically, he would start with Begin's team and then bring it back to Sadat, "modifying the text only when absolutely necessary." He would do this repeatedly, going back and forth, over the next eight days.

Carter's goal was to avoid settling for a separate peace between just

Egypt and Israel. That, he knew, would leave Sadat isolated and politically defenseless against popular opinion in the Arab street. But he also understood that if he was to be successful this meant he would have to persuade Begin that major Israeli concessions would be rewarded by a genuine and long-term comprehensive peace.

DAY FIVE: SATURDAY, SEPTEMBER 9

CARTER SPENT MOST of the day working on a draft of the American proposal. Vance and Brzezinski assisted him, but they were also helped by Harold Saunders, an assistant secretary of state, and William Quandt, Brzezinski's NSC expert on the Middle East. At some point that day Carter listed on one handwritten page the "Necessary elements of an agreement":

- Inadmissibility of acquisition of territory by war.
- Security for nations involved (Secure, recognized borders).
- Withdrawal of Israel on all fronts from territory occupied (change in borders—satisfy aspirations of Palestinians & security of Israel).
- Terminate belligerency.
- Freedom of navigation.
- Just settlement of refugee problem.
- Legitimate rights of Palestinian people—all aspects.
- Participate in determination of future inhabitants.
- Normal relations.
- Comprehensive settlement thru conclusion of peace treaties.
- Sinai—international borders—airstrips (withdrawal).
- Sovereignty of Egypt—time schedule.
- Remove settlements in Sinai.
- Borders—demilitarized zones / limited armaments zones / UN forces / Early warning / acquisition of arms.
- No force or threat of force to resolve dispute.
- Israeli military government abolished.
- Self-government authority established.
- West Bank/Gaza entity—linked to Jordan.
- Jerusalem—undivided.

- Recognition, no boycott, free movement.
- Returning refugees—safeguards, qualifications.
- Israeli military forces—West Bank/Gaza sovereignty.
- Devolution of authority.
- Limited armaments—Sinai passes.

Carter's list was nothing if not comprehensive. Brzezinski noted in his diary that day how attuned the president was to nuances: "His textual criticisms are as good as those of any expert. In general, his tendency is to make the document tough on the Israelis and more palatable to the Egyptians." Brzezinski feared, in fact, that Carter might be "somewhat too tough." Carter admitted to this inner circle of advisers that he felt close to Sadat. He thought they had much in common. Sadat, he remarked, "is always willing to accommodate [me]. . . . I feel very comfortable with him. My chemistry with him is good. I feel with him the way I feel with Cy Vance."

Vance laughed graciously, and then Brzezinski couldn't resist saying, "Yes, because Cy accommodates you the way Sadat does, isn't that right?"

As everyone laughed nervously, Carter quipped, "Yes, and you're just like Begin."

By that afternoon, Carter's handwritten list of points had morphed into an early master draft of a "Framework for Peace in the Middle East." Carter incorporated two key provisions right from the start:

- Rapid granting of full autonomy to the Palestinians, followed by a five-year transition period for determining the permanent status of the West Bank and Gaza.
- The removal of all Israeli settlements from the Sinai, and a freeze on settlements in other occupied territory until all negotiations were complete.

But controversially, Carter later acknowledged that "we would not include this request [on the removal of all settlements] in the first draft. Otherwise, Prime Minister Begin would have concentrated on it almost to the exclusion of the other issues." Tactically, this may have been wise in the short term, but it only postponed a difficult reckoning.

* * *

WHILE CARTER CRAFTED his comprehensive American proposal, the members of the Egyptian and Israeli delegations went for long walks around Camp David's trails, admiring the autumn leaves. Sadat went for a brisk walk each morning, wearing a track suit. Carter's secretary, Susan Clough, shuttled between the cabins on a bicycle, wearing denim shorts. Guests could snack on sandwiches and drinks at any hour. The camp theater showed various Hollywood films, virtually around the clock. That Saturday evening some of the delegates gathered on Begin's porch to watch him play chess with Brzezinski. The two Polish expatriates, one Catholic and aristocratic, the other a self-styled Jewish revolutionary, could not have been more different. "Poles apart," quipped Yechiel Kadishai, one of Begin's younger aides. Begin made a show of announcing at the start of the match that he had not played chess since September 1940. Brzezinski suspected the claim was a "psychological ploy"—a suspicion confirmed when, toward the end of the match, Begin's wife, Aliza, arrived and exclaimed, "Menachem just loves to play chess!" Both men played aggressively. Brzezinski lost the first game but came back to win the second. Hamilton Jordan whispered to an Israeli spectator, "Do me a favor and make sure Begin wins. Otherwise, Zbig will be unbearable." Begin won the match, three games to one.

DAY SIX: SUNDAY, SEPTEMBER 10

CARTER ATTENDED CHURCH services in Camp David's Hickory Lodge and listened to a sermon by Chaplain Cecil Reed taken from 1 Samuel 17, the story of David and Goliath. After church, the president then invited the delegations for an excursion to the Gettysburg National Military Park. Confined to Camp David for nearly six days, he thought everyone needed an outing. The Civil War site was just twenty miles down the road, but Carter chose to take Sadat and Begin to this once blood-soaked battleground for obvious reasons. He stipulated that there should be no discussion of the peace talks either with each other or with any members of the press. Unbeknownst to Carter, Begin instructed four of his aides to stay behind and prepare a document explaining why the summit had failed—and according to Lawrence Wright's account in *Thirteen Days in September,* he told his legal aide, Aharon Barak, that "then we will go home." Barak began packing his bags.

During the thirty-minute drive to Gettysburg, Carter made a point of sitting between Sadat and Begin, making small talk about the scenery and chatting about Abraham Lincoln and Civil War topics. As a southerner, Carter was steeped in the history of the "War Between the States," and a few months earlier he and Jody Powell had visited Gettysburg in the company of Shelby Foote, the acclaimed Civil War historian. Carter was thus well briefed to talk about this sobering episode in American history. When they arrived, a Park Service ranger guided them through the sites, but Carter frequently interjected his own comments about the battle he had once studied at the Naval Academy. "He did so with great emotion," Dayan later wrote, "and spoke with genuine warmth and praise for General [Robert E.] Lee and his men. He seemed to know every hill and boulder. . . . And when he told the story of how the tattered, bedraggled and barefoot Southern fighters had an additional incentive to capture Gettysburg upon hearing that it had large stores of boots, he seemed to be talking about his own family." Indeed, Carter's own great-grandfather, Littleberry Walker Carter, had fought at Gettysburg.

Carter noticed that Begin expressed little interest in the intricacies of the battle. But when they arrived at the cemetery site where Lincoln had given his short but memorable address, Begin suddenly began reciting Lincoln's words: "Four score and seven years ago our fathers brought forth on this continent, a new nation, conceived in liberty. . . . Now we are engaged in a great civil war. . . ." His voice was at first soft, but as he gained the attention of his audience, the Polish-accented English became firm and distinct. He recited the entire ten-sentence address from memory. Rosalynn was surprised and touched by this display of both intellect and emotion. It infected both Carters with a sliver of hope.

Upon their return from Gettysburg, however, Carter met with Begin, Dayan, Weizman, and Barak and gave them the American proposal. The "discussions quickly became quite heated." Begin immediately objected to the language drawn from UN Resolution 242: "The war of 1967 gives Israel the right to change frontiers," Begin insisted.

"What you say," Carter shot back, "convinces me that Sadat was right—what you want is land."

Begin ended the argument by saying that he did not wish to discuss the document without taking the time to study it carefully. He suggested they adjourn and meet after dinner. The Israeli prime minister, who earlier in the day had signaled to his delegation that they should prepare to leave, obviously now felt a sudden departure would be unwise. Begin did not want to leave knowing that Carter was prepared to blame Israel for the summit's failure. He would have to stay longer.

They reconvened at 9:30 P.M. and argued vigorously until 3:00 A.M. The Israelis began by saying that they wanted to delete all references to UN Resolution 242. Carter interrupted. "This is not the time to beat around the bush. If you disavow UN 242, I would not have called this meeting." Similarly, when Begin defined what he meant by "full autonomy" for the "Palestinian Arabs" on the West Bank, it became clear that he intended to retain an Israeli veto: "Autonomy doesn't mean sovereignty."

"What you want to do," Carter complained, "is make the West Bank part of Israel." Vance added, "The whole idea was to let the people govern themselves. You are retaining a veto."

"No self-respecting Arab would accept this," Carter declared. "This looks like subterfuge."

Carter pushed Begin to be more flexible. Brzezinski noted in his diary that Carter "clearly dominated the proceedings." Even so, Begin kept coming back to his objections concerning the language in UN Resolution 242 that specified "the inadmissibility of the acquisition of territory by war." Begin exclaimed, "We will not accept that!"

"Mr. Prime Minister," Carter responded tartly, "that is not only the view of Sadat, it is also the American view—and you will have to accept it."

"Mr. President," Begin replied, "no threats, please."

Begin even objected to the use of the term "Palestinian people," insisting, "We are also Palestinians."

Privately, Carter was beginning to question Begin's state of mind: "It's becoming clearer and clearer that the rationality of Begin is in doubt."

When they finally adjourned at 3:00 A.M., the president took Dayan aside and asked him to walk with him alone back to his cottage. He told Dayan bluntly that he thought Begin was "unreasonable and an obstacle to progress." He pleaded with Dayan to help him break the logjam. They talked quietly in the premorning darkness, interrupted only by the forest sounds of crickets and toads. But when the one-eyed Israeli general turned away to walk to his cabin, he stumbled into a tree and bloodied his nose. Carter rushed to guide him onto the path, but he felt terrible.

It was nearly 4:00 A.M. when Carter crawled into bed. "What happened?" Rosalynn asked.

"We had to do a song and dance with Begin over every word," he replied. "I'll tell you about it in the morning."

DAY SEVEN: MONDAY, SEPTEMBER 11

THE NEXT MORNING, Brzezinski noted in his diary that Rosalynn had told him that her husband had "described Begin as a psycho, which I think reflects accurately the degree to which Carter was irritated by Begin's performance." Carter told Rosalynn, "Begin was completely unreasonable. If we accomplish anything, it will be a miracle." Carter was physically exhausted and terribly sleep deprived. But over the next two days he shuttled back and forth between the Israeli and Egyptian delegations, negotiating small but sometimes significant changes to the American proposal. "I had become a master," Carter later wrote, "at making insignificant editorial changes to overcome significant objections." He also spent hours studying the maps and geography. One day, Weizman was called to the billiards room, where he was astonished to see the president of the United States on his hands and knees, peering at an enormous map of the Sinai Peninsula spread out on the floor. The map measured fifteen feet by twenty-two feet. Carter wanted to understand the location of every Israeli settlement and every airfield. Weizman had "never seen a man more tenacious."

DAY EIGHT: TUESDAY, SEPTEMBER 12

BEGIN SAID HE wanted to have a private meeting with Carter. The Israeli came to the president's cabin at 8:00 P.M. and began theatrically by announcing, "This is the most serious talk I have ever had in my life, except once when I discussed the future of Israel with [Ze'ev] Jabotinsky [his late mentor in the Irgun, the Zionist paramilitary organization]."

Carter naturally expected Begin to tell him something new and dramatic. Instead, for the next two hours Begin lectured the president about why the language in UN Resolution 242 could not be part of any Camp David accords—and why he could not abandon any of the Israeli settlements in the Sinai. Finally, he pulled from his pocket a brief statement, which he proceeded to read aloud to Carter. It was essentially a draft press release, explaining why the Camp David negotiations had failed. He concluded by saying he wished he could sign the American proposal, but as prime minister, he had to reflect the wishes of the Israeli people. Carter could not restrain himself and responded by citing public-opinion polls in which a substantial majority of the Israeli people favored removing settlements in the Sinai and the West Bank in exchange for peace. Perhaps, Carter said, "my position represent[s] the Israeli people better than" yours.

Incensed, Carter stood up, indicating that it was time for the Israeli to leave. On his way out, he accused Begin "of being willing to give up peace with his only formidable enemy, free trade and diplomatic recognition from Egypt, unimpeded access to international waterways, Arab acceptance of an undivided Jerusalem, permanent security for Israel, and the approbation of the world—all this, just to keep a few illegal settlers on Egyptian land." Begin left, seemingly oblivious to this presidential reprimand.

"It was a fairly heated discussion," Carter noted in his diary, "and unpleasant, and repetitive."

DAY NINE: WEDNESDAY, SEPTEMBER 13

HE WAS CLEARLY disgusted with Begin. But the president was not ready to give up. For the next few days, he went back to his strategy of ignoring Begin and dealing only with Begin's aides. Carter and Vance spent that Wednesday meeting for nearly eleven hours with Begin's attorney general, Aharon Barak, and Sadat's legal aide, Osama al-Baz. They made a lot of progress on minute language. Barak refused to make any concessions on the question of settlements. That, he said, was a topic only Begin could address. But he explained to Carter that he thought the Sinai settlements were such a stickler for Begin precisely because any dismantlement of settlements there could prove to be a precedent for similar concessions in the West Bank. This insight convinced Carter that perhaps the Sinai settlements were not the major obstacle that they seemed. Despite Begin's obstinacy, Carter was coming to the realization that Begin would probably consent to a deal on Sinai, including a removal of the settlements. The real obstacle was any deal on the West Bank.

He went to sleep late again that night, feeling a little more hopeful. Carter rarely had trouble sleeping. But this night was different. He suddenly began worrying about Sadat's personal safety. He had wanted to see Sadat that evening but had been told that the Egyptian president had already gone to bed—unusual for him because he was a night owl. Now Carter, lying in bed, wondered whether Sadat could be attacked by a disgruntled aide. He knew emotions were running high, and while his fears seemed improbable, he could not dismiss them. Finally, at 4:15 A.M., he called Brzezinski and asked him to come immediately. Brzezinski rushed over to the presidential cabin in his pajamas and found the president sitting in the living room with Rosalynn and a Secret Service officer. "Zbig," said Carter, "I am very much concerned for Sadat's life." Brzezinski quickly arranged for guards to monitor access to Sadat's cabin. The incident was all much ado about nothing—but it illustrates Carter's deep affinity for Sadat.

DAY TEN: THURSDAY, SEPTEMBER 14

CARTER WAS RELIEVED the next morning when he looked out the window and saw Sadat starting out on his usual hour-long walk. He rushed out to join him and they chatted pleasantly, partly about the trip to Gettysburg, but also about how long it had taken the American people to recover from the wounds of the Vietnam War. Carter returned from his walk with Sadat feeling upbeat once again. Rosalynn popped into his Aspen cabin study, and as she sat on his lap, he told her, "I think it's all coming together now."

But by the end of that day, everything had come unraveled. Every day at Camp David seemed like a wild roller-coaster ride. "Good heavens," Mondale was heard to mutter, "this is nerve-racking." Sadat may have precipitated matters when he announced that he was prepared to sign the American document—if the Israelis would agree to better language on the status of Jerusalem and Palestinian self-determination. Accordingly, Vance and Brzezinski inserted a reference to having an Arab or Muslim flag in some part of the Old City and provision for direct elections to determine the "final disposition" of the West Bank. After getting Carter's approval on these insertions, Vance and Brzezinski went to see Begin. The Israeli rejected the proposal "in a rather peremptory fashion" and insisted that the new language on Jerusalem was giving him "heart palpitations." Began also announced that he categorically could not sign anything pledging to withdraw all settlements from the Sinai.

When informed of Begin's firm rejection, Sadat was equally adamant that the Sinai settlements had to go. Sadat told Carter that he would sign the American peace proposal alone, turning it into an exclusive document between the United States and Egypt. This would at least leave a record for the world to see that it was Israel that had scuttled the summit. Carter was "clearly very disappointed." Begin's attitude on the Sinai settlements seemed quite inexplicable to the president. But he now sadly told Brzezinski that he thought the summit "would end in failure and no matter what, he would be viewed as the scapegoat by the American Jewish community and much of the press." Zbig tried to cheer him up, and after a game of tennis, a sauna, and a swim, Carter's gloom dispelled a bit and he began to plot a strategy for exiting Camp David "in such a manner as to make it clear that the responsibility for the breakdown rests on the Israelis." To this end, he instructed Vance to once again visit Begin that evening and get "tough" with the prime minister. Vance did as instructed and "had a humdinger of an argument with Begin." They shouted at each other, and Vance left saying that the Israeli position was "unacceptable and unreasonable."

DAY ELEVEN: FRIDAY, SEPTEMBER 15

CARTER AWOKE THE next morning knowing that the summit had failed. But he wanted it to close with some semblance of dignity. To this end, he wrote notes to Sadat and Begin, asking them to summarize their final positions. He intended to write a final document on Saturday that would spell out where they had agreed and where they still disagreed. They would then adjourn on Sunday and issue an official communiqué. Both Sadat and Begin agreed to this plan. In the meantime, with the encouragement of Ezer Weizman, Dayan had a private session with Sadat. Instead of offering any concessions, Dayan merely informed the Egyptian president that the Israelis had decided not to sign any agreements at Camp David. The meeting ended abruptly, with Sadat feeling like the Israelis had played him all along. Sadat impulsively summoned Cy Vance and announced that he intended to leave right away.

Aghast, Vance rushed over to Carter's Aspen study and burst into the room. "Sadat is leaving," he told the president. "He and his aides are already packed. He asked me to order him a helicopter."

Carter was stunned. He felt personally betrayed. He had trusted Sadat and thought he would be the last one to walk out. A subdued and angry Carter asked to be left alone. Staring out the window at Catoctin Mountain, he "prayed fervently for a few minutes that somehow we could find peace." As if girding for battle, he then discarded his T-shirt and jeans and dressed in a suit and tie before walking over to Sadat's cabin. He found the Egyptian president standing on his porch with several aides. Carter nodded to them and then walked abruptly into the cabin. Sadat followed. They sat down and looked at each other in silence. "I didn't say anything for quite a while," Carter later told Brzezinski, "because I didn't know what to say." Finally, Carter said, "I understand you're leaving."

"Yes," Sadat replied.

"Have you really thought about what this means?"

"Yes."

"Let me tell you," Carter said evenly. "It will mean first of all an end to the relationship between the United States and Egypt. . . . It would probably mean the end of my presidency because this whole effort will be discredited. And last but not least, it will mean the end of something very precious to me: my friendship with you."

Sadat looked shaken, and protested, "We are wasting our time with this man!" He then revealed that from his conversation with Dayan he had concluded that any concessions he signed here at Camp David would merely be pocketed by the Israelis—who would then use them as the starting point for future negotiations. He could not, as promised earlier, sign an agreement just between the United States and Egypt. It would only be used against him in future negotiations.

Hearing this, Carter pledged, "I will make it very clear that any promises that he [Sadat] has temporarily made to the Israelis and which the Israelis in the future would try to use as the starting point for any negotiations would be null and void . . . and that we will support him also on the issue of the settlements."*

Sadat thought for a moment, and then said, "If you give me this statement, I will stick with you to the end."

Carter was tremendously relieved. That evening, Fritz Mondale and Carter walked over to Sadat's cabin and together they watched the world heavyweight boxing match between Muhammad Ali and Leon Spinks. Sadat was a fan of Ali's, and so after his victory, Carter placed a congratulatory phone call to Ali, but the boxer didn't phone back until 1:30 A.M., long after Sadat had gone to bed. Ali told Carter he was delighted to know that the president and Sadat had watched the fight.

DAY TWELVE: SATURDAY, SEPTEMBER 16

CARTER ROSE EARLIER than usual on this, the twelfth day of the summit. He assumed that it would end the next day with a joint communiqué explaining why the two parties had failed to come to an agreement. He went for another long walk with Sadat and then met alone with Dayan, who reported that Begin was still unwilling to budge on the removal of the Sinai settlements. But Dayan suggested that when it came to the West Bank, Israel could agree to no new settlements—although he said this could be specified only in a separate exchange of letters between Carter and Begin. He did not want this issue addressed directly in the accords. Carter nevertheless saw this as a major concession. That evening, the president and Secretary Vance met alone with Begin, Dayan, and Barak. It would prove to be the most momentous meeting of the entire thirteen days.

---

* When Carter told this story to Brzezinski four days later, Brzezinski commented, "You know, the implication of this is that you have to be very steadfast on the settlements." Carter replied, "Yes, I hadn't thought of that, but that is true."

They spent an hour going paragraph by paragraph over the document concerning the Sinai. Carter wanted to demonstrate how few differences remained. "I thought the discussion would never end," he later wrote. Begin began shouting at one point, accusing Carter of issuing an "ultimatum" that would lead to "political suicide." But suddenly, Begin revealed his bottom line: He would defer the question of whether the Sinai settlements could be dismantled to the Knesset. A vote would be taken within two weeks, and if the Knesset agreed, the Sinai settlements would be evacuated. Carter deemed this a "breakthrough."

Carter then turned the discussion toward the second document, a "Framework for Peace" that dealt with the contentious issue of Palestinian autonomy in the West Bank. Again Carter went through the document paragraph by paragraph, making minor semantic changes in the language. He thought they had a "surprisingly amicable discussion," and he found both Dayan and Barak "quite forthcoming." But not surprisingly, Begin objected to section 6 of the American proposal, which prohibited new Israeli settlements and even prohibited the expansion of physical facilities in existing settlements. Begin proposed:

- A fixed time (three months) during which no new settlements would be constructed.
- Prohibitions against civilian settlements only.
- The right to build a limited number of new settlements.

Carter firmly rejected all three of these alternatives. Instead, according to an unpublished entry from Carter's diary, Begin agreed, in the presence of his two key aides, Dayan and Barak, to a freeze on West Bank settlements: "On the West Bank settlements, we finally worked out language that was satisfactory, *that no new Israeli settlements would be established after the signing of this framework* [emphasis added]. And that the issue of additional settlements would be resolved by the parties during the negotiations. This would be accomplished with a letter which will be made public from Begin to me."

Oddly, what happened next has been in dispute for more than four decades. It shouldn't be a mystery, because Carter's written record of what was agreed to by Begin is quite clear. As described in a short memo signed by Carter on September 20, "Finally, we agreed on the exact language concerning the settlements, and that the paragraph would be re-moved from the West Bank–Gaza section and included in a letter from Begin to me. I told him it could not be a secret letter and the Prime Minister replied that the text would be made public."

The agreed text stated, "After the signing of this framework and dur-ing the negotiations, no new Israeli settlements will be established in this area. The issue of future Israeli settlements will be decided and agreed among the negotiating parties." Carter's memorandum of this conversation further stipulated: "It was clear and obvious that the 'nego-tiations' applied to the West Bank and Gaza."*

The marathon negotiating session had lasted from 8:00 P.M. until 12:20 A.M. Carter clearly believed he had achieved both an Israeli with-drawal from the Sinai and an agreement that the Palestinians in the West Bank would be allowed over a period of five years to govern them-selves. The two parts—the Sinai withdrawal and the West Bank settle-ments freeze and a promise of autonomy—were linked.

In an entry to a portion of his still-unpublished diary headlined "What Sadat Gets Out of the Framework Agreement," Carter noted, "He will have set in motion a political process in the West Bank and Gaza which virtually assures Palestinian control over the long term. If the Pal-estinian authority is well run and controls terrorism, it will be extremely difficult for Israel to slice away any significant territory after 5 years of Palestinian consolidation. The process, if well conducted, becomes vir-tually irreversible."

No one could say that Carter had brokered a separate peace between just Israel and Egypt. It was a comprehensive peace that addressed the central issue of Palestinian rights. Never before had Israel agreed to "recognize the legitimate rights of the Palestinian peoples and their just requirements. . . . The Palestinians will participate in the determination of their own future."

* Carter's secretary, Susan Clough, sent copies of this September 20, 1978, note to Prime Minister Begin, Secretary Vance, Zbigniew Brzezinski, and Jody Powell—so everyone knew what Carter thought had been agreed to about a settlement freeze. From Carter's perspective, there was no ambiguity. To drive the point home, he even attached a copy of the original typed paragraph 6 with his handwritten edits.

DAY THIRTEEN: SUNDAY, SEPTEMBER 17

EARLY THE NEXT day, Carter again joined Sadat for his morning walk and cheerily boasted, "I got the settlement freeze." He also reassured Sadat that he was quite certain the Knesset would approve the removal of all the Sinai settlements. "Okay," said Sadat, "let's go ahead and sign."

Carter was beginning to feel elated. Perhaps his improbable gamble had paid off. But then Begin once again created a crisis on two issues that Carter thought had been resolved. That afternoon, Barak came back with Begin's promised side letter about a settlement freeze. Carter immediately noticed that the proposed text "differed substantially from that on which we had agreed." Carter told Barak that it was completely unsatisfactory "and read to him the text on which we had agreed, which was still lying on my desk. He did not disagree with the agreed text."

A greatly annoyed president told Barak, "Go back and get the right letter. I want you to write that as long as the negotiations go on with the Palestinians there will not be settlements." Barak did not argue with Carter—who later wrote in his memoirs, "Barak confirmed that my language was accurate." Nevertheless, the clock was ticking, and Carter was by then focused on organizing a signing ceremony. He imprudently agreed to receive the corrected language in this critical side letter the next day, after the accords were already signed. This was clearly a mistake; Carter should have known by now that Begin was perfectly capable of breaking his word. "That man," as Sadat routinely called him, had no intention of freezing the West Bank settlements for more than three months. Indeed, he was committed to making them an integral part of Israel. Begin certainly betrayed the spirit of Camp David—but according to Carter and Vance, he also broke the letter of what had been agreed to on Saturday night, September 16. "My notes are clear," Carter later wrote in his memoir, "that the settlement freeze would continue until all negotiations were completed—and Cy Vance confirms my interpretation of what we decided."

Vance actually asked one of his deputies, Harold Saunders, to draft a letter with the correct language on a settlement freeze and hand it directly to Begin for his signature. Furthermore, Carter attached a note to the side letters specifying, "This is the exact language to be used. Do not use any other language on or off the record." In the event, Begin signed two of the three side letters—but he never returned the agreed-upon letter concerning the West Bank settlements. Vance's explanation for why Begin was able to pull off this piece of subterfuge is quite straight-forward: Begin precipitated not one crisis on that Sunday but three. He had earlier agreed to three side letters, dealing with the settlement freeze in the West Bank but also the status of Jerusalem and the role of the Knesset to vote on the dismantlement of the Sinai settlements. But on Sunday afternoon Begin suddenly found language in all three side letters that he now deemed objectionable.

Begin's objection on the Sinai settlements was highly tendentious: He wanted the letter to say that peace negotiations *would* commence after the Knesset voted on the Sinai settlements—while Carter insisted that negotiations on a peace treaty "would *not* commence until *after* the Knesset had voted." With Barak's intercession, Carter managed to prevail on this relatively minor issue, and Begin eventually signed the side letter.

But Begin went into an absolute rage when Vance gave him the side letter on the status of Jerusalem. The letter merely reiterated Washington's long-standing view that East Jerusalem was deemed to be occupied territory under international law. Begin announced that he would not sign at all if any kind of letter on Jerusalem was attached to the accords. Carter hastily convened a meeting with Dayan, Weizman, Barak, Israeli ambassador Simcha Dinitz, Mondale, Vance, Brzezinski, and Jordan. It turned into "a very unpleasant session," but Barak—who usually was the most reasonable of the Israelis—said the situation was hopeless. Just the same, Carter proposed editing the offending letter. Instead of quoting any of the official statements on Jerusalem, the letter would simply report that the U.S. position on Jerusalem was unchanged.

Carter still thought Begin would not yield on the issue—and he was now fully prepared to return to Washington and acknowledge that the summit had failed. And yet despite everything, the president had not completely given up. He suspected that an emotionally distraught Begin was simply looking for an excuse to walk away. But he nevertheless decided to walk over to Birch Cabin and convey to Begin the gist of the new language on the Jerusalem side letter. At the last moment, Susan Clough handed him a sheaf of photographs taken at Camp David over the previous thirteen days. She reminded him that Begin had asked for the photographs as souvenirs for his grandchildren. Clough had taken the initiative of calling someone to ascertain the names of all the grandchildren. Carter dreaded the meeting with Begin but took a moment to autograph the photographs with the name of each child. At 3:26 P.M., he found Begin sitting on the porch of his cabin. The Israeli seemed particularly reserved.

"Mr. Prime Minister," Carter greeted him, "I brought you the photographs you asked for."

"Thank you, Mr. President," replied Begin coolly. But then he looked at the top photograph and saw the inscription to one of his granddaughters: "To Ayelet." He glanced at the other inscriptions, and his eyes began to tear up.

"I wanted to be able to say," Carter said, " 'This is when your grandfather and I brought peace to the Middle East.' "

Obviously moved, Begin invited Carter into his cabin, and the two men sat down and chatted quietly. Carter briefly thought Begin would finally spare him any melodrama. But Begin couldn't resist telling a long-winded story of a tenth-century rabbi who had taken three days to consider a difficult, even impossible, request. "I am not like the Rabbi of Mainz," Begin said. "I don't need three days to consider the matter. I tell you here and now that Jerusalem is the eternal capital of the Jewish people." Unless Carter withdrew his letter on Jerusalem, the summit would end in complete failure. Carter gently reported that he had rewritten the Jerusalem letter and submitted it to Dayan and Barak. Perhaps, he said, Begin could read it and reconsider his decision. Carter calmly explained that he could not completely withdraw the letter, if only because that would mean breaking his promise to Sadat.

The meeting ended, and Carter walked back to Aspen Lodge feeling very dejected. He found Sadat waiting for him, dressed and ready to go back to Washington for the expected signing ceremony. Carter sadly announced that Begin was now refusing to sign anything. The summit was a failure.

At that moment, the phone rang. It was 3:57 P.M., and Carter heard Begin say, "I will accept the letter you have drafted on Jerusalem."

Carter could hardly believe it. At this point, he was prepared to see Begin change his mind again or raise some other objection. But over the next hour and a half Carter, Vance, and others met to review all the last-minute textual changes in the accords. Around 5:30 P.M., Vance turned to Carter and said, "That's it. I think we have it."

Brzezinski noted in his diary later that Carter looked "rather tired, with a wistful smile on his face, but not particularly elated." No one cheered, but there was a palpable sense of relief. Just then the skies suddenly darkened, and a violent thunderstorm hit Camp David. "The lightning seemed almost to be striking us," Brzezinski wrote. "One had a sense of something momentous taking place."

It was Carter's personal triumph, a formidable achievement. But somehow the accords were missing one critical document. Only later, in fact the very next day, did it become clear that Begin was withholding the side letter on the West Bank settlement freeze. Carter still thought this issue had been resolved, because Barak had promised to hand over a letter with the correct language. It never happened. "Because of the Jerusalem issue," Vance later explained, "which consumed much of [Sunday], we were unable to get the settlement letter signed at Camp David." Vance fully expected Begin to sign the letter the next morning—but that would be after the Framework for Peace had been signed Sunday evening. In retrospect, perhaps Begin's histrionics over Jerusalem and even the Sinai settlements were a last-minute diversion, designed to buy time and divert attention from the far more critical issue of a settlement freeze in the West Bank.

THUNDERCLOUDS WERE STILL sweeping across Catoctin Mountain Park as Carter planned a hasty exit from Camp David. Begin and Sadat initialed the two-part accords, but Carter wanted to announce to the world what had been achieved with a signing ceremony in the White House's East Room that very evening. All three men met in front of Aspen Lodge, and after embracing, they motored over to the Camp David helipad, where they boarded Marine One and at 9:37 P.M. helicoptered off into the storm toward Washington. As the thunderstorm buffeted the helicopter, Susan Clough nervously thought to herself that it would be "a darn shame after two tough weeks and at last a great triumph if they should crash." By 10:31 P.M. the three leaders were seated at a small table in the East Room. They signed the accords, and then Carter briefly summarized the two documents. The first, he said, dealt with "the need to solve the Palestinian problem in all its aspects." And the second, he explained, restored full Egyptian sovereignty to the Sinai and outlined a peace treaty between Egypt and Israel that would be signed within three months. A subdued Sadat read a short statement in which he said, "Let us pledge to make the spirit of Camp David a new chapter in the history of our nations." Begin quipped that the Camp David summit should be renamed "the Jimmy Carter conference.... I think he worked harder than our forefathers did in Egypt building the pyramids." After the ceremony, a clearly elated Begin told an old friend, "I have just signed the greatest document in Jewish history!"

Shortly after noon the next day, Monday, September 18, Carter called King Hussein of Jordan and briefed him on the accords. "The Israelis," he told Hussein, "recognize that the legitimate rights of the Palestinians have to be honored and that there *will be no new settlements in the West Bank or Gaza Strip during the time of the negotiations* [emphasis added] and any additional settlements would be as determined by the negotiations themselves." From Hussein's perspective, this was the crucial issue—the fate of the West Bank.

But later that afternoon Carter noted in his diary, "It became obvious that Begin was making an ass of himself with his public statements.... They should have left a nursemaid with him—either Dayan or Barak or Weizman." The prime minister had told an Israeli reporter that he would continue building settlements and that Israeli troops would remain in the West Bank indefinitely. Carter was also furious that morning when he learned that Begin had sent over the requested side letter on a settlement freeze—and it contained the same language that Carter had rejected earlier.

That evening the president addressed a joint session of Congress, and with Begin and Sadat sitting in the balcony, he pointedly said, "After the signing of this framework last night, and during the negotiations concerning the establishment of Palestinian self-government, no new Israeli settlements will be established in this area." It was as firm a public rebuke of the Israeli prime minister as anyone could make. The next day, before departing the country, Begin came by the Oval Office, and once again Carter told him that his public statements were jeopardizing everything they had negotiated. Begin made a noncommittal reply. But Carter noted in his diary, "He's trying to welsh on the deal." Two days later, Carter again complained that Begin was publicly "denying the agreement we had worked out Saturday night, on which I have a complete record and a perfect memory."

Carter's notes and his memory were confirmed by no less a source than Moshe Dayan, who on September 20 asked an American diplomat to tell the president and Vance that he, Weizman, and Barak were "extremely upset over Begin's public disagreement with the President over the duration of a settlements freeze." Dayan said "he was certain that he, Weizman, and Barak 'and others in the Cabinet' can prevail on Begin to agree to a formulation covering cessation of settlement activity which will be acceptable to us. In retrospect, Dayan observed, it had been a serious error 'to leave Begin on his own' in Washington and New York. He (Dayan) should have stayed on, for if he had this unfortunate situation would never have arisen."

Decades later, Carter told Lawrence Wright, the Pulitzer Prize-winning author of *The Looming Tower* and *Thirteen Days in September,* "Begin promised me and Sadat very clearly that he would stop all settlement building. When he got back to civilization, he began to lie. He began to say that he only meant they would stop settlement building during the time of negotiation." On the other hand, Aharon Barak, one of the three Israelis in the room at the time, told Wright many decades later that after reviewing his own notes, he believed that Begin "didn't agree to more than three months." Barak's version, of course, is completely contradicted by Carter and Vance and their own contemporaneous notes—and the president's very categorical description of what Begin agreed to in his September 20, 1978, note, a copy of which was sent to Begin. The Israeli prime minister never backed down and never acknowledged that he had indeed acquiesced to a settlement freeze. Instead, he continued to make inflammatory statements in public and complained in private to Carter about the criticism he was receiving from his old Irgun colleagues. In a "Personal for the President's Eyes Only" letter Begin said he was writing "man to man" to explain that he was under a great deal of pressure. "I hear very often the argument that we must understand the delicate situation of President Sadat vis-à-vis the Arab world. . . . What about my situation, my difficulties?" His former Irgun colleagues, he wrote, were now in "revolt" against their former commander. "Some young people dabbed on the walls of Ze'ev

Jabotinsky House the words: 'Begin—traitor.' I have to live with all these phenomena." In Begin's mind, his trauma trumped any Arab narrative. He was the victim, not Sadat.

Carter seems to have decided that wisdom lay in not answering this plaintive note. But in a phone conversation two weeks later he gently urged Begin to be "as flexible as possible." In response, Begin again complained about the "Begin traitor" graffiti he was seeing on the walls of Jerusalem. Carter ignored this and lodged his own complaint: "It is very difficult to negotiate over and over with the Israeli government on the same issues once we thought it had been concluded."

"No sir," Begin shot back, "we don't negotiate over and over."

Afterward, Carter noted in his diary that Begin was "very abusive." Privately, the president believed the peace accords were "apparently coming apart."

The two leaders were talking past each other. But from Carter's perspective, Israeli envoys like Weizman, Dayan, and Barak had indeed made commitments, only to have Begin claim that they "had no authority to speak for Israel." Carter had also received a report "quoting Dayan saying they did not intend to carry out the West Bank portion of the agreements"—an implicit acknowledgment that Dayan, for one, understood that the Israelis had indeed agreed at Camp David to a five-year settlement freeze. By then, a frustrated Dayan was telling Carter that "he couldn't negotiate for Israel anymore."

The very public dispute over the West Bank settlements was certainly ominous, but it did nothing to quell the initial acclaim for what Carter had seemed to achieve at Camp David. *The Washington Star* reported, "President Carter's emergence as the peacemaker in the Middle East is a political as well as a diplomatic triumph that makes Americans feel good about themselves and their president, stifles temporarily at least criticism within his own party. . . . It has made many American Jewish leaders euphoric and is a giant step in retrieving the president's political standing with the Jewish community." James Reston quoted Henry Kissinger as saying it was a "tremendous achievement." William F. Buckley wrote, "We all owe a great debt to President Carter." Art Buchwald quipped, "The thing that made this so successful is that we were all prepared for failure."

Richard L. Strout, writing in his venerable TRB column for *The New*

Republic, used the occasion to give voice to what many pundits thought about this president: "So now, what do we say about Jimmy Carter? He is the despised kid at school who stepped up to bat and clouted one over the fence, bases loaded. He is so easy to underestimate. Enemies don't hate him; they patronize him. He is soft-spoken, a poor speaker, almost unctuous; America has never had a president quite like him, perhaps. . . . The post-Summit agreement may collapse. Those polls may sink again. But how hard he is trying."

Two days after the signing of the accords, Carter and Mondale met with seven leaders of major American Jewish organizations in the Roosevelt Room of the White House. Carter later recalled the meeting as "delightful, full of fun and good cheer." But he also noted the "extreme strain" between his administration and the Jewish community in the United States. "I pointed out in a nice way that controversies I had put on the table that caused the strain had been the source of ultimate success." Carter appealed to these key Jewish leaders "to restrain Begin, who is acting in a completely irresponsible manner." For the moment, they were supportive, but over the next few months they certainly did nothing to restrain Begin. Carter's political isolation from the Jewish American community would only become more apparent as he felt compelled to criticize Begin's behavior.*

Sadat too would become more politically isolated throughout the Arab world. Carter had hoped that the Arab monarchs in Saudi Arabia, Jordan, and Morocco would come aboard, but they all condemned the accords. Sadat's own foreign minister and longtime friend, Mohamed Ibrahim Kamel, resigned his post even before leaving Camp David, telling Vance, "You will live to regret this agreement, which will weaken Sadat and may even topple him. . . . No Arab will accept this agreement, which will remain unimplemented. All that will happen is that it will

---

* Carter's White House liaison to the Jewish American community, Edward Sanders, wrote to him to say that he had learned that two prominent Jewish American leaders, Ted Mann and Richard Maass, were "taking steps to inform Prime Minister Begin of their unhappiness with his public utterances since the end of the Camp David summit." Sanders advised Carter that there now existed "a great amount of goodwill for you." But he nevertheless warned that "quiet private diplomacy should be the order of the day. . . . Any action from the White House which is perceived as being anti-Begin will put that goodwill in jeopardy."

allow Begin a free hand in the West Bank and Gaza with a view to their annexation." Kamel's gloomy predictions would prove to be more or less on the mark.

But at the time, most pundits in America celebrated the accords. "The process is underway, the baby is being born," wrote I. F. Stone in *The New York Review of Books.* "And for that we must be grateful first of all to President Carter. It is his triumph." Begin, asserted Stone, might be "a tactless and arrogant man." Stone was quick to acknowledge that Begin was already talking "recklessly, of keeping troops on the West Bank forever, of not relinquishing sovereignty, of suspending new settlements on the West Bank only for three months or less. This is nonsense, and he must know it." Stone rightly saw there was reason for optimism if one looked at the accords with rational eyes as an evolving peace process. "The agreements cannot be read with legal, myopic eyes; they are dynamic triggers of change. It is not so many years since Golda Meir, no rightist but a Labor Socialist Zionist, resolutely and mercilessly refused even to admit that there was such a thing as a Palestinian people. *Begin has admitted they are there.*"

Izzy Stone was wrong. Begin did not want a peace with the Palestinians.* He wanted a separate peace with Egypt, taking the only major Arab military power off the battlefield. But in the West Bank, he wanted the land. In this sense, Camp David may have been Carter's greatest diplomatic triumph, but it was Begin's greatest subterfuge. Within weeks of Camp David, Begin announced that his government intended to build eighteen to twenty new settlements in the West Bank over the next five years. Carter was furious. "There is no other explanation," the president noted in the margins of a State Department cable that suggested that Israel was merely taking the time "to create new settlements which would become inalterable facts." He later concluded in his memoirs,

---

* That autumn, Begin authorized Mossad to assassinate Ali Hassan Salameh, the PLO's intelligence chief. Salameh was targeted in part because the Israelis believed him to be involved in the 1972 Munich attack. But they also knew he happened to be the PLO's back channel to the CIA. He was known to be urging Arafat to abandon the "armed struggle" and seek a negotiated two-state solution. Salameh was killed by a Mossad car bomb on January 22, 1979—sending an unequivocal message to the Palestinians that they could expect no deals from the former Irgun chief who had blown up the King David Hotel in 1946.

"Begin wanted to keep two things, the peace with Egypt—and the West Bank." The Israeli prime minister got both. He was a formidable negotiator, clever and relentless in advancing what he perceived as his country's national security interests. While Carter understandably thought he had secured Begin's pledge on the settlement freeze, he failed to get Begin's signature on the relevant letter. This would prove to be a fundamental mistake.

Three months after the signing of the Camp David Accords, Begin went out of his way to announce the authorization of another batch of West Bank settlements. Stu Eizenstat happened to be in the Oval Office when Carter heard the news. The president rarely displayed any real anger, but on this occasion, he bitterly complained that Begin had lied to him. That's how Carter saw it: Begin had lied. Eizenstat fully understood why the Israeli settlements were an obstacle to peace. And yet he told Carter that he thought the Israeli prime minister was an honorable man: "I do not believe he would have consciously misled you." Eizenstat ventured to argue that given Begin's views, he never would have agreed to a long-term settlement freeze. Carter looked at Eizenstat and then sat down at the *Resolute* desk, reached into a drawer, and pulled out a document. "These are my notes from my meeting with Begin," he said. "Here you can see 'five-year settlement freeze.'"

"Mr. President," Eizenstat replied lamely, "there must be an honest disagreement."

Carter would always believe otherwise.

THAT AUTUMN OF 1978, Ron Nachman and his fellow settlers continued to build their sleek new settlement, dubbed Ariel. Only a large urban settlement, Nachman argued, could create the facts on the ground necessary to make Israel's claim to the West Bank a reality. Funded by Begin's Likud government and tax-deductible U.S. donations raised from Nachman's frequent fundraising trips to America, Ariel eventually became a modern suburban town of twenty thousand people wedged between the Palestinian urban centers of Salfit and Nablus. Today, it is one of the largest settlements in the West Bank—and one of the most remote. Most of its settlers are either Russian or American immigrants. Ariel soon boasted a municipal swimming pool, an industrial zone, schools, and eventually Nachman's crowning achievement—Ariel University, with its fourteen thousand students. In the spring of 1981, Begin visited Ariel and proudly announced that the Jewish population in the West Bank had risen from 5,000 to 24,000 under his tenure. Ariel and other settlements clearly violated the spirit of Camp David. But they also were planting the seeds for a prolonged occupation that would alter the fundamental identity of the Israeli state. As Carter feared, the settlements would poison his greatest diplomatic triumph.

Chapter 15
"A Weird Period for Liberals"

Now the president seems to pull his presidency out of certain disaster.

—LANDON BUTLER, March 18, 1979

Hamilton Jordan and Carter
KEYSTONE/GETTY IMAGES

IN THE WAKE of Camp David, the president was gratified to receive a thirteen-point bump in his poll numbers, from a miserable 38 percent approval in June to a respectable 51 percent approval rating in late September. Carter was eager to use this political capital to advance a string of legislative initiatives. On October 13, 1978, he signed a civil service reform bill—a sweeping revision of the federal bureaucracy that rewarded civil servants for their competence, not just their longevity on the job, and allowed for the dismissal of employees who were doing lousy work. The same day the House approved his natural gas deregulation bill by a margin of two votes. On October 20, he signed a bill extending the deadline for approval of the Equal Rights Amendment. "The women are very happy and enthusiastic," Carter noted in his diary. "Fifteen states have not ratified it; still three to go before we have the requisite thirty-eight." On October 24 he signed the final airline-deregulation bill, and two days later he signed the Ethics in Government Act, requiring full financial disclosure from all high-ranking civil servants, judges, and members of Congress. "The next step," Carter noted, "should be public financing of congressional races."

On October 27 he signed the Humphrey-Hawkins Full Employment Act—a symbolic law that in its first draft had committed the federal government to use federal dollars to create temporary jobs during an economic downturn, while also combating inflation by controlling the supply of money. Carter had expressed skepticism about the bill during the '76 campaign—but he had come around to endorsing, somewhat tepidly, a virtually toothless version of the original bill. Full employment became merely a "goal." Conservatives nevertheless scorned the bill's underlying Keynesian approach to running the economy, and liberals, particularly African American congressmen, expressed bitter disappointment that the administration had backed away from a real federal jobs program. *Newsweek* reported that Humphrey-Hawkins was "so watered down as to be almost meaningless," and *The New York Times* editorialized that the vapid bill "would play a cruel hoax on the hard-core unemployed, holding before them the hope—but not the reality—of a job." Once again, the president had managed to alienate both the Left and the Right, and his congressional allies.

Carter's relationship with Speaker O'Neill reached a nadir in August, just prior to the Camp David summit. One of O'Neill's college friends, Bob Griffin, was fired as deputy director of the General Services Administration. Griffin wasn't getting along with his boss, Jay Solomon, who demanded his dismissal. From the White House's perspective, it was a relatively minor personnel issue. Unfortunately, O'Neill had phoned Frank Moore, the president's congressional liaison, and Moore had acknowledged that there was a problem and that the president was likely to back Solomon. But Moore also tried to reassure O'Neill that a decision was not imminent. Moore then advised Carter to postpone any decision on Griffin's status. But the president's communications director, Jerry Rafshoon, urged Carter to follow through and approve Griffin's firing. O'Neill only learned that his college buddy had been fired by reading about it in *The Washington Post*. The Speaker was livid and announced to his staff that Moore was henceforth banned from his office. "He didn't tell me the truth," O'Neill said. Carter was taken aback, and in a move to placate the Speaker, he offered Griffin another job in the Office of the U.S. Trade Representative. Moore wrote O'Neill an apology and eventually it all blew over. But Moore told the president that the Speaker "still doesn't feel like there is any warmth on the part of the White House and that people here just don't like him—but doesn't feel that I am in that group now." Their relationship would always be cool.

Moore thought the problem was that "you [Carter] simply do not enjoy the level of respect to which you are legitimately entitled." He thought "the modern Congress is like the proverbial, stubborn jackass—you have to hit it between the eyes with a 2 x 4 to get its attention." Moore's advice was to have Carter deploy a rare presidential veto against his own Democratic-controlled Congress. On October 3, Carter shocked his own party by vetoing a $10.2 billion public-works bill that contained another slew of water projects that he deemed wasteful, inflationary, and harmful to the environment.

Speaker O'Neill and Senate Majority Leader Byrd were appalled. O'Neill thought he had the votes to override the veto. "Tip is working hard on all members," Moore reported to the president. But Carter went to work and made sixty phone calls to various members of Congress and managed to sustain the veto by a hefty margin of fifty-three votes. He was getting his way, but there was a lot of grumbling from his own party. He knew the public-works veto had "cast a pall over everybody." He knew it was bad politics for a sitting Democratic president to veto public-works projects that could have created thousands of jobs across the country. After the veto was sustained, Speaker O'Neill came by the White House fully expecting the president to ask for his resignation. "Do you want me to throw in the towel?" Carter scoffed and reassured the Speaker that it was just a political scuffle.

On November 7, 1978, Democrats lost three seats in the Senate and fifteen in the House but still retained a 58–41 majority in the Senate and a resounding margin of 277–158 in the House. Relatively speaking, Carter thought the midterm election results were encouraging for his domestic legislative agenda. Most sitting presidents lose some seats during a midterm election. Carter's challenges, however, came not from the

Republican Party minority but from liberal Democrats to his left. Two days after the election, Carter signed five major bills constituting a much-watered-down version of his energy package. He was unhappy that Congress had refused to include a windfall-profits tax on oil, designed to encourage conservation. But many liberal Democrats and environmentalists criticized the bill for deregulating natural gas prices and promoting both coal and nuclear energy. Some saw it as a gift to the oil companies.

With inflation running at an alarming 8 percent, Carter had instructed his budget director, Jim McIntyre, to propose some anti-inflationary budget cuts for the forthcoming fiscal year federal budget. Included were some severe cuts in healthcare programs. HEW Secretary Joe Califano leaked the preliminary budget numbers just prior to a first-ever midterm convention of the Democratic Party, scheduled for early December 1978 in Memphis. Democratic Party leaders, including the president, had hoped that the unprecedented event would help to galvanize voters, but it became, perhaps inevitably, an echo chamber for various grievances within the party.

The mini convention attracted 5,000 grassroots party activists, including some 1,600 party delegates. Carter addressed them for twenty-five minutes on the evening of Friday, December 9, and described Democrats as "practical dreamers" who have returned "compassion and competence" to government. But he warned the delegates, "It is an illusion to believe we can preserve a commitment to compassionate, progressive government if we fail to bring inflation under control." He received a decidedly lackluster response from the delegates. It really wasn't the message they wanted to hear.

On Saturday morning he placed a wreath on the balcony of the Lorraine Motel, the site of Martin Luther King, Jr.'s assassination a decade earlier. He then flew back to Washington that afternoon, leaving Stu Eizenstat and Califano to joust with Senator Edward Kennedy on a healthcare panel moderated by the governor-elect of Arkansas, Bill Clinton. Not surprisingly, Kennedy used the occasion to highlight his criticisms of the Carter administration's budget cuts. "There could be few more divisive issues for America and for our party," Kennedy declared, "than a Democratic policy of drastic slashes at the expense of the elderly, the poor, the black, the cities and the unemployed." With a rhetorical flourish, Kennedy told the now-cheering crowd, "Sometimes, a party must sail against the wind. We cannot afford to drift or lie at anchor. We cannot heed the call of those who say it is time to furl the sail."

Listening to the speech, Hamilton Jordan turned to Pat Caddell and muttered, "The son of a bitch is going to run."

Carter felt he was being politically sandwiched between traditional liberal party dogma and a national electorate that was trending conservative. Many of the midterm convention delegates expressed unhappiness with Carter's fiscal priorities. Carol Bellamy, president of the New York City Council, asked why the administration was proposing a 3 percent rise in the defense budget (above inflation) while simultaneously slashing social spending. The Defense Department, she said, should "share equally" in any reductions.

Carter had campaigned for the presidency on a platform that pledged to cut waste in the defense budget. But like all presidents before him and since, he had found it difficult to control Pentagon spending. He had gone out of his way to eliminate boondoggles like the B-1 bomber and the neutron bomb. He regularly but quite ineffectually complained to Secretary of Defense Harold Brown that the Pentagon was not "following my guidelines re zero-based budgeting." (Carter was a big fan of zero-based budgeting, on the theory that examining the expenditure of every dollar on an annual basis would reveal opportunities for savings.) On the other hand, he approved funding for the MX missile, the Trident submarine, and cruise missiles. Brzezinski, Brown, and other members of his national security team argued that these modern weapons systems were essential. Cold War assumptions, defense lobbyists, and Congress itself made it very hard to control a rising defense budget, let alone cut it. Zero-based budgeting was not going to make a difference in a defense budget running to $123 billion, or nearly 5 percent of the national gross domestic product.

Yet if Carter had wanted to cut the defense budget when he took office, he eventually came to feel differently and ultimately reversed himself. After briefings from the Joint Chiefs, Carter looked at the numbers and concluded that, when measured in constant dollars, the defense budget had declined by 35 percent over the past eight years, unsurprising since the Vietnam War had been winding down during these years.

But Carter also accepted intelligence estimates that the Soviet Union had been increasing its defense expenditures by about 4 percent annually. He should have known that estimating Soviet defense spending was an extremely uncertain, often spurious exercise. Defense hawks like Paul Nitze from the Committee on the Present Danger routinely inflated Soviet defense expenditures in rubles in order to justify higher Pentagon budgets. In any case, Carter was convinced by the Pentagon that it was time "to rebuild our long-neglected military forces." By 1978, he was committed to 3 percent annual increases in the defense budget. Defense spending was rising to nearly 30 percent of all federal expenditures. Many congressional liberals thought such expenditures were wrongheaded and unnecessary.

The left wing of the Democratic Party viewed Carter with growing suspicion, if not outright hostility. Congressman Ronald V. Dellums (D-CA), an outspoken radical leftist from Berkeley, said, "If there is any purpose to this meeting, it is to challenge the right-wing analysis of American problems today that President Carter has embraced." Carter had nearly as strong views about these left liberals.

A few weeks earlier, he had visited Minnesota on a campaign trip to help local Democrats and encountered Congressman Don Fraser, a liberal Democrat who had instigated the whole idea of having a midterm Democratic convention. (Fraser would lose his bid for a U.S. Senate seat that autumn.) Carter was put off by Fraser's politics. The congressman reminded him of those Democrats back in 1968 who had supported Eugene McCarthy and then failed to turn out to vote for Hubert Humphrey—and thus put Richard Nixon in the White House.

"This is one group of Democrats with whom I feel uncomfortable," Carter noted. "They have a commitment to political suicide in order to prove some far-left philosophical point. It is really disgusting." Congressman John Conyers, Jr. (D-MI), attacked Carter's anti-inflation message, telling a gathering of African American delegates at the midterm convention that the president would be defeated in 1980 if he didn't change course. "He owes us the presidency," Conyers said. "If you like your president and want to keep him, you'd better knock some sense into his head about a program of full employment, housing and national health insurance."

Carter just didn't understand left liberals like Congressmen Conyers, Fraser, and Dellums. This was unfortunate, because these politicians were utterly decent men and devoted to the same populist instincts as the president. If the president had spent any time socializing with them, he no doubt would have been able to build some common ground. But nearly two years into his presidency, Carter had planted seeds of suspicion throughout the winning coalition that had carried him into the White House. It wasn't only liberals. All the key elements of the Democratic coalition were unhappy, largely because the president seemed unwilling to spend federal dollars on their issues. "I'm discouraged at the differences I have with the Democratic Congress about their pressures to spend more money on defense, water projects, public works, transportation, education, health, labor—almost across the board," noted the president in his diary. But Carter nevertheless thought most Americans wanted a smaller and leaner government. "Public opinion will be on our side."

Carter was not an economist. He had always been a budgetary tightwad. But his fiscally conservative instincts did not fully explain his troubles with liberals in his own party. His ambivalence toward his own liberal base within the Democratic Party was heightened that autumn when he had to decide whether to veto a tax-cut bill. The bill in question had started out as a tax-reform measure. But by the time Congress and various corporate lobbyists had finished with it, the bill had become riddled with loopholes and exemptions. Politicians across the political spectrum were suddenly under pressure from a tax revolt symbolized by the passage in California of Proposition 13—a state law that imposed a drastically low ceiling on property taxes. Democratic legislators like Congressman Al Ullman (D-OR) had restored many of the business deductions that Carter wanted cut, including the infamous "three-martini" business lunch deduction.

Carter angrily told reporters that he could not "tolerate a plan that provides huge tax windfalls for millionaires and two bits for the average American." He pushed hard for the repeal of a lower tax rate on capital gains—but the Democratic Congress voted to support a Republican provision to lower the capital gains tax on investments. It was a giveaway to wealthy special interests. Worse, it included a major tax cut that would add billions to the federal deficit. After getting up one morning at 5:00 to study the bill, Carter decided it offered very little reform and an inexcusably generous tax cut. "I am hoping I can veto the tax bill," he told

Eizenstat and his treasury secretary, Mike Blumenthal, "and use this as an example of my anti-inflationary program. Tax reform is so screwed up." His advisers pushed back, arguing that the economy needed a second stimulus. They also warned him about the political optics of a Democratic president vetoing a tax cut passed by a Democratic Congress just before a midterm election. Carter hesitated but finally caved in to the pressure from his own White House advisers. He signed the tax bill on November 6, 1978, and afterward he told Eizenstat, "I have always depended on your advice, but you disappointed me on the tax bill." In retrospect, Eizenstat came to understand that Carter's instincts were correct. "I deserved the rebuke," he wrote in his account of the Carter presidency.

As Carter feared, the tax cut only stoked inflation at a time when the economy was beginning to stagnate. Pundits soon coined a new word—"stagflation"—to describe a phenomenon economists had never encountered. "It's a weird period for liberals," said Michael Harrington, a left-leaning author and founder of the Democratic Socialist Organizing Committee. "The problem is the conventional liberal wisdom of the past doesn't work anymore. This is like 1931. Just as the conventional wisdom of the 1920s was totally shattered by the depression, the conventional wisdom of the 1960s has been shattered by inflation." Rising unemployment and a recession had never before been accompanied by inflationary pressures on prices. Conventional economic theory, as postulated by John Maynard Keynes, offered no policy solution to correct an economic downturn characterized by rampant inflation. Normally, Keynes would have prescribed greater federal spending in an economic downturn—and less such spending to dampen inflationary pressures. Carter and his economic advisers wanted to stimulate the economy in order to create more investment and more jobs, but they did not wish to spend too many federal dollars, for fear that this would stimulate inflation. They were caught in a unique policy conundrum.

Carter was certainly right to be concerned that inflation hurt working-class and poor citizens more than the middle class. "Inflation has hit us hardest not in the luxuries but in the essentials—food, energy, health and housing," the president said in one speech early in his administration. "You see it every time you go shopping." On October 24, 1978, he addressed the nation again on the topic and announced that inflation was now "our most serious domestic problem." He explained that over the past twenty-one months, "we have created six million new jobs for American workers." The unemployment rate had been reduced by 25 percent. These were both very good numbers. But inflation had increased from 6.5 percent to 8 percent. When asked for the solution, the president, perhaps too candidly, flatly admitted, "I do not have all the answers. Nobody does." But then he went on to emphasize the role of government spending in fueling inflation. "The federal deficit is too high," he said. "Our people are simply sick and tired of wasteful federal spending and the inflation it brings with it." Sounding very much like a Republican, Carter pledged to cut the budget deficit, "slash Federal hiring," and "remove needless regulation." He talked about "hard choices" and a "time of national austerity." No wonder AFL-CIO labor chief George Meany called Carter "the most conservative president since Calvin Coolidge."

Actually, it was not so clear that government deficits were the major cause of inflation in the 1970s. In the spring of 1977, Labor Secretary Ray Marshall flatly told Carter, "Budget deficits do not cause inflation." Marshall pointed out that the fiscal deficit in 1974 was only $5 billion and yet the inflation rate was 9 percent. Two years later, the deficit had spiked to $66 billion and the inflation rate had fallen to only 5 percent. Carter was nevertheless making strenuous efforts to keep the federal budget in fiscal year 1978 to about $500 billion, with a projected deficit of only about $25 billion. (By contrast, the federal deficits under the Republican administrations of Ronald Reagan and George H. W. Bush ballooned dramatically—but inflation in the 1980s declined.)

In mid-October, Carter decided to appoint Alfred E. Kahn as his inflation czar. The Cornell professor of economics had previously served Carter as chairman of the Civil Aeronautics Board, where he had successfully managed the administration's deregulation of the airline industry. Kahn didn't want the new position. Carter insisted on his appointment and wrote him a handwritten note the day after his inflation speech, giving him his marching orders: "Please present to me as soon as possible your ideas for implementing our anti-inflation plans. I want all major employers and unions to sign up." Kahn protested that he knew nothing about inflation, and besides, "I am very independent, and I say what I believe. I will accumulate a series of enemies."

Kahn was also smart enough to know that there were no easy answers. Both he and the president were firmly opposed to mandatory wage and price controls. Those had been tried by President Nixon with dismal results. The only alternative was trying to persuade major corporations and labor unions to abide by a voluntary set of wage and price targets—and Kahn knew that was like trying to herd cats. Essentially, all he had was the power of persuasion. During his first month, Kahn appeared on TV news shows like *Meet the Press, Issues and Answers,* and the *NBC Nightly News.* He gave twenty-one speeches and numerous press interviews and testified before Senate and House committees. He cajoled union leaders to keep wage demands on a reasonable track and Fortune 500 CEOs to keep prices down. But in the coming months, the consumer price index continued to tick upward.

The owlish-looking Cornell economist was often flamboyant and always blunt-speaking. After Kahn predicted a "very serious depression" if inflation was not tamped down, Eizenstat privately advised him not to use the word "depression." At his next press conference, Kahn candidly admitted that he had been instructed to be careful with his language. Henceforth, he said, he would refer to an economic downturn as a "banana." Reporters laughed. And they laughed again when Kahn altered the euphemism to "kumquat" after the chairman of United Fruit Company complained that he was giving bananas a bad name.

Kahn's efforts had a quixotic flavor. He was keenly aware of the psychological perceptions that drove the inflationary cycle. Inflation could be driven in part by short-term consumer expectations. One day, Kahn arranged for the president to meet with CEOs from the food industry and lobby them to keep their prices down. Shortly afterward, McDonald's cut the price of cheeseburgers due to a drop in the wholesale price of beef. Kahn jumped on this little victory and urged Carter to "have lunch with Amy at McDonald's sometime soon." The publicity would reward the fast-food chain for battling inflation. Unfortunately, the next day a chagrined Kahn had to admit that he had done some research and discovered that beef prices were again inching upward and McDonald's was contemplating a price increase. Kahn said he would know whether this was going to happen in a week, but in the meantime, "will you be willing not to eat at McDonald's?" Carter wryly scrawled a reply on the memo: "Fred: I'm willing to a) eat or b) not eat, depending on further advice from my mentor."

Kahn admired Carter's tenaciousness and thought "he was really very good on economics." But he believed the president had "a couple of blind spots" in his understanding of the dynamics of inflation. "He thought middlemen were the source of inflation in food," Kahn later said. "It takes one to know one, maybe, since he ran a peanut warehouse." Carter's instinct as a southern populist was to blame the middlemen. Kahn thought this a bit naïve. "You know, if you bust a few people, you can make the standards work better. There was some of that naïveté."

By the spring of 1979, Kahn was desperately trying to think of stronger measures. He understood that OPEC-driven oil prices explained a big part of inflation. It was no accident, he observed, that the "two waves of double-digit inflation" were both instigated by oil price hikes. Higher oil prices meant higher transportation costs and higher production costs. Kahn asked the president to consider oil import duties, import quotas, or even gasoline rationing. He knew "people hated rationing," so he urged Carter to impose a "huge gasoline tax." But there was no support for this in Congress. Nothing was working. Kahn tried quitting, but Carter talked him out of it. "I can't figure out," he wryly told a reporter in late 1979, "why the president doesn't fire me. Actually, I do know—nobody would be foolish enough to take this job."

CARTER MAY HAVE felt that inflation was his biggest domestic priority, but his diary notations that autumn of 1978 dealt with Cuba, Nicaragua, SALT, China, and a host of other foreign policy questions. In mid-December, the president was excited to learn that communist China's leader, Deng Xiaoping, had agreed to Washington's terms for normalization of diplomatic relations. Carter credited Brzezinski for initiating this breakthrough during a trip to China the previous spring. Zbig had been particularly impressed by the diminutive Chinese leader, so much so that upon his return Carter told him that he had been "seduced." When the good news came in December that they finally had a deal, Carter called Brzezinski. On a whim, he teasingly asked if Zbig had heard that the Chinese had canceled the agreement. "He almost fainted before I could tell him I was joking."

China was a momentous diplomatic achievement, finishing what Kissinger had only started with his secret trip to China in July 1971. But

Carter was still spending an inordinate amount of his time on the thorny Middle East. The Camp David Accords were meant to be quickly followed up by a formal Egyptian-Israeli peace treaty and concrete steps to evolving some form of Palestinian autonomy in the West Bank. Carter had hoped to see a peace treaty signed by November 7—the day of the congressional midterm elections. The next day he again turned to foreign policy, meeting with Vance, Brzezinski, Jordan, and Mondale to discuss the Middle East. "It is obvious that the negotiations are going backwards," Carter noted in his diary. Brzezinski questioned whether it was wise tactically to be pushing so hard for an Egyptian-Israeli peace treaty. Once Begin had a peace treaty, he would have little incentive to compromise on the West Bank. Brzezinski argued the Israelis essentially wanted a separate peace with Egypt, American aid, and "finally a free hand in the West Bank."

When Carter remarked that Brzezinski's assessment was perhaps overly simplistic, Zbig snapped sarcastically, "Thank you." The president looked at Brzezinski for a moment and then said rather sadly, "Yes, but I agree with you."

The president was undecided. He vacillated that autumn between telling the Israelis and the Egyptians that he was giving up and, alternatively, making yet another push to get the two parties to honor their Camp David commitments. In early December he told Vance, "I would be willing to lose my election because I will alienate the Jewish community." But he thought they needed to exert more pressure on the Israelis. "If there is a breakdown, we will have to go with Sadat." Negotiations nevertheless dragged on into the new year with no results. "Stu," said the president one day, "what can I do about Israel?"

Finally, in late February 1979, Carter met again in the Oval Office with Mondale, Vance, Jordan, and Brzezinski to prepare for Begin's scheduled arrival in Washington on March 1. This time, Rosalynn was a witness, sitting quietly against the wall. She was visibly disturbed when Brzezinski forcefully stated that he thought the Israelis "would prefer Carter not to be reelected and that this objective was influencing their current tactics." Without disputing this, Mondale nevertheless argued that pressing Begin would be "politically counterproductive." The president, he said, should take a passive and neutral stance—and just let things "go on their own." Brzezinski was appalled by Mondale's attitude but thought the vice president's advice would prevail. The next day, Carter privately told Brzezinski that he was reluctant to become more involved, if only because every time he did so, the American press portrayed him as "anti-Israeli." Clearly, Carter seemed inclined to give up and let the Camp David Accords collapse.

Ironically, Begin's behavior the next day changed Carter's mind. The Israeli stepped off the plane and immediately "made some very combative comments." He seemed "extremely nervous" and complained that he had "suffered personally from the Camp David concessions he had made." He announced that he "refused to let us force him" into signing any other "worthless document." In a formal meeting the following day, Begin put on a similar performance, saying at one point that Sadat "still wants to destroy Israel." Carter thought him "sullen and moody" and "completely inflexible." The meetings with Begin went so badly that Carter later told Brzezinski, "If he hadn't been my guest I would have asked him to get the hell out." But the sum result of these exchanges "made Carter's adrenaline flow" and persuaded him once again that only a "bold stroke" could break the impasse.

That evening Carter put on a winter coat and sat alone on the Truman Balcony, wondering what to do. Finally, he decided that he would fly to Cairo first, get Sadat's agreement on a treaty, and then go to Israel. "If we're not successful," he noted in his diary, "just describe what we proposed and what they've given up, and let the whole thing shift to the UN." Only Brzezinski and Jordan encouraged the president to make the trip. Mondale, Vance, and Jody Powell all thought it a "risky enterprise." Powell was particularly "timid." Mondale thought "the whole thing was doomed to failure." Speaker O'Neill noted in his diary that it was a "terrific political gamble. If he comes back empty-handed, he had better go back to Plains." Carter knew he "was way out on a limb." But he had made up his mind.

On March 8, 1979, he arrived in Cairo and quickly got Sadat's "carte blanche" for the coming negotiations with the Israelis. The next day they took the train to Alexandria, and hundreds of thousands of Egyptians cheered them from the railroad sidings. Carter had never seen such large crowds. "I told Sadat this was one time a politician didn't have to exaggerate the numbers."

On Saturday, March 10, Carter and his presidential entourage flew into Tel Aviv and drove to Begin's Jerusalem residence. The Israeli prime minister had sent Carter an encouraging message—but now his mood had suddenly darkened. Begin abruptly told Carter that he could not sign any agreement. "I couldn't believe it," Carter noted. "I stood up and asked him if he thought it was necessary for me to stay any longer." The two men then argued standing up for forty-five minutes. At one point, Carter angrily asked him if he really wanted a peace treaty, because it seemed as if "he did with apparent relish everything he could do to obstruct it." Begin marched up to the president, and, looking him in the eye from a foot away, he said he wanted peace "as much as anything else in the world." Carter left shortly before midnight: "I have rarely been so disgusted in all my life," he noted in his diary. "I was convinced he would do everything possible to stop a treaty, rather than face the full autonomy he had promised in the West Bank/Gaza."

Begin's mood was still icy and negative the next day when he invited Carter to a cabinet meeting. "He asked me first to preside and then rudely interrupted," Carter noted. "It was a fruitless session." To be sure, the parties had in hand a draft text for a peace treaty between Egypt and Israel. They also had a draft note that would be attached to the treaty, addressing the commitments made in the Camp David Accords to implement "full autonomy" in the West Bank and Gaza. But even on this already-agreed-upon issue, Begin strongly objected to setting a firm date for holding elections. He would agree only to the "goal of completing the negotiations within one year so that elections will be held as expeditiously as possible." Begin was wearing the president down.

That evening, just as the sun set, Brzezinski visited the president in his King David Hotel suite. Carter was lounging on a sofa and he and Rosalynn were clearly dispirited. When Jordan walked in, Carter made "some rather earthy comments about Begin personally." Hamilton sarcastically asked if he was speaking "on the record." Zbig laughed and pointed to what he imagined were listening devices in the ceiling and said, "The remark is already on the record."

On Monday, Carter addressed the Knesset, and "there was quite a buzz when I said the people were ready for peace, but the leaders had not yet shown the courage to take a chance." Carter's strategy to bypass Begin and appeal directly to the Israeli people had an effect on the obstinate Israeli prime minister. That evening, Vance and Dayan spent hours

together and hammered out language to address the remaining disagreements in the peace treaty. Carter was scheduled to leave Tuesday,
and that morning he was to meet at 9:00 with Begin over breakfast.
Unusually, Carter and Rosalynn were running late, so they had Jordan
and Rafshoon greet the Begins outside the president's suite. Chatting
pleasantly, Begin suddenly said mischievously, "I've always liked the
King David Hotel." Rafshoon and Jordan nodded politely in agreement.
"You know," Begin added, "I blew it up once, using explosives in milk
canisters." Not sure what to say, they stared at the prime minister—who
grinned and said, "Don't worry, I'm not going to do it again."

A moment later, Carter joined them and suggested he and Begin
should breakfast alone. Before sitting down, they stood at the window
and admired the panoramic view of Old Jerusalem. Carter then pressed
Begin, promising him that Sadat would sell Israel oil pumped from the
Sinai oil fields developed by the Israelis—and if these deliveries were
interrupted, the United States would fill the gap. The only other major
sticking point in the treaty was language about Palestinian autonomy.
By then, Carter was well aware of Begin's negotiating technique: "refusing to budge until failure seemed inevitable." Carter was virtually walking out the door when, almost as an afterthought, he returned to the
sticky topic of political autonomy for the West Bank. "I pressed him
hard," Carter later wrote in his memoirs. But Begin only vaguely hinted
that perhaps he could ease some of the political restrictions on Palestinians in the West Bank—symbolic of his earlier commitment to the establishment of a "self-governing authority" over a transitional five-year
period. It was a vague promise, but it was something. As the meeting
broke up, Carter told Begin that he would convey the peace treaty to
Sadat that very afternoon. The president had high hopes that he had
achieved the final breakthrough.

The two leaders and their wives then entered an elevator with two
security guards and descended—only to have the elevator suddenly stop
six feet above the King David lobby. For the next twenty minutes the
hotel's employees tried to get the elevator unstuck, but they finally had
to pry the door open with a crowbar. The two couples then awkwardly
climbed down a ladder to make their escape, witnessed by dozens of
reporters and spectators. It was a bad omen.

That afternoon, Carter flew into Cairo, and upon seeing Sadat on the tarmac, he blurted out, "I feel like I am coming home!" It was such a relief to be out of Jerusalem. Carter still had to pin down Sadat's approval of all the concessions he had made in Jerusalem. Brzezinski marveled at his performance as he briefed Sadat on the talks: "Carter, though playing a weak hand, did one of the best selling jobs of his career." The president began by telling Sadat that for the first two days Begin had behaved terribly: "He was unpleasant, [and] interrupted me. But then the moderates began to convince him to be more constructive. Begin now waits to hear your position." Carter focused on the Sinai and Washington's willingness to give the Israelis guarantees on oil supplies. He made it seem as if the Israelis had made some concessions, and he glossed over the issue of Palestinian autonomy. He pressed Sadat to accept the negotiated treaty: "This will enable us to say to the world that there is a U.S.-Egyptian agreement, and the Israelis will have to accept it or reject it." After only a few minutes of private conversation, Sadat puffed on his pipe and then accepted a press release drafted by Brzezinski, changing only one word, from "beginning" to "cornerstone."

Carter then phoned Begin, who seemed almost surprised by Sadat's acquiescence. The Israeli prime minister had every reason to exult. He had been tough and unyielding on the core issues. He had been compelled to restore the entire Sinai to Egyptian sovereignty, but in return he had won a peace treaty with Israel's most formidable military adversary, including full diplomatic recognition. Begin and Sadat both signed the letter attached to the treaty that pledged themselves to the election of a self-governing authority for the Palestinians in the West Bank and Gaza within five years. In theory, therefore, it was not a separate peace just between Israel and Egypt. But in practice, the "goal" of full autonomy for the Palestinians quickly became a dead letter. The Egyptian-Israeli peace treaty ushered in a cold peace and ultimately allowed the Palestinian issue to fester.

Critics on all sides have debated whether Carter could have achieved a truly comprehensive peace. In 1986, Brzezinski's chief Middle East aide, William B. Quandt, wrote an account of Camp David and the peace treaty negotiations in which he complained, "Carter had no stomach for confrontation with Israel." By then, Quandt had become bitterly disillusioned. The reality, however, was that Begin never had any intention of loosening his grip on the occupied territories. Carter had, in fact, repeatedly confronted the Israelis, both in private and publicly, at great political risk. "The last two weeks," Landon Butler noted in his diary, "have been a blur—now the president seems to pull his presidency out of certain disaster." Ironically, Carter's standing in the polls declined after the signing of the peace treaty on March 26, 1979. Six months after the emotional highs of the Camp David drama, most Americans were worn out with the contentious Arab-Israeli issue.

Carter had once again personally triumphed. The Camp David Accords and the Egyptian-Israeli peace treaty were towering achievements compared to the meager results of Henry Kissinger's Middle East shuttle diplomacy just a few years earlier. Indeed, Carter overcame far more difficult diplomatic hurdles than Kissinger's much-heralded strategic opening to communist China—where, after all, both Nixon and Mao were eager for a deal. By contrast, Carter improbably persuaded two embittered adversaries to change course. Nothing would have happened without the highly personal intervention of the American president. He had risked his presidency to do what was right. Nevertheless, Carter would not reap any lasting political benefits from his achievement.

At the time, however, there was a palpable sense of a historic turning point. On March 26, 1979, Begin and Sadat signed the peace treaty on the White House lawn, and that evening Carter hosted a celebration under a large green-striped tent. "It was a remarkable evening," Brzezinski wrote in his diary. "Not only was there joy, but a real sense of reconciliation." Brzezinski sat at a table with a number of celebrities, including Henry Kissinger, Muhammad Ali, and Ezer Weizman—whose son Sha'ul had been severely wounded during the October 1973 war. In the course of the evening, Weizman was brought to tears by the sight of Sadat embracing Weizman's disabled son. Sadat made a toast and provocatively predicted that the peace treaty would someday lead to Palestinian statehood. Begin surprised everyone by responding graciously—and just ignoring the mention of the Palestinians. "There was electricity in the air," Brzezinski noted, "a sense of joy, people mixing, shaking hands, patting each other on the back. And for Carter, of course, it was a spectacular and historic triumph."

Chapter 16
An Ayatollah's Revolution

Zbig—After we make joint decisions, deploring them for the record doesn't help me.

—PRESIDENT CARTER to Zbigniew Brzezinski, January 12, 1979

Ayatollah Khomeini
GILBERT UZAN/GETTY IMAGES

WHILE CARTER HAD focused his energies on the Israeli-Egyptian peace treaty, a revolution had been brewing in Iran. Back in January 1978, Iranian police had opened fire on a marching crowd of protesters in the religious city of Qom, killing at least six students. In keeping with Shi'a Islamic practice, these deaths were memorialized by a religious ceremony forty days later—and this observance occasioned another round of protests that led to further clashes and six more deaths in the city of Tabriz. A forty-day cycle of violence ensued throughout the year. Initially, these incidents were mostly ignored by the press and the Carter administration. National security adviser Zbigniew Brzezinski had on his staff only one aide with experience in Iran. Gary Sick, a forty-three-year-old active-duty U.S. Navy captain, had served in the Persian Gulf and later acquired a doctorate in Middle East studies from Colum-

bia University. As early as February 1978, Sick wrote to Brzezinski, telling his boss what he did not want to hear—that the "truly massive riots
in Tabriz" appeared not to be orchestrated by communists but "were the
work of what may be the true threat to the shah's regime—the reactionary Muslim right wing which finds his modernization program too liberal and moving too fast away from the traditional values of Iranian
society." Brzezinski paid no attention, and like most members of the
American foreign policy establishment, he assumed that the Pahlavi regime was firmly ensconced. The shah was Washington's key ally in the
region; he'd been famously restored to power in a 1953 coup organized by
the CIA, and more recently, the Nixon administration had favored him
with billions of dollars of high-end arms sales. Brzezinski firmly believed that "successful revolutions were historical rarities," and he
couldn't imagine that the shah couldn't handle a few hundred rioters.

President Carter himself shared this assumption. Nevertheless, that
spring and summer the demonstrations in Iran escalated, culminating
in early September with a general strike. The government responded by
imposing martial law. But on September 8, 1978, some twenty thousand
protesters defied the government by gathering in Tehran's Jaleh Square.
Army soldiers opened fire on the crowd, killing at least eighty-eight civilians and wounding many more. The Jaleh Square massacre only in-
flamed revolutionary passions. At that moment, Carter was hosting
Sadat and Begin at Camp David. But he managed to take time away
from those negotiations to place a call to the shah.

They spoke for all of five minutes. The shah insisted that he was determined to end the "diabolical" demonstrations, and Carter nevertheless
politely encouraged him to continue his liberal political reforms while
restoring law and order. The White House press office publicized the
news that the president had phoned the shah, a fact that convinced many
Iranians that Carter was willing to ignore the Jaleh Square massacre.

Not surprisingly, the anti-shah demonstrations spread across the
country that autumn, and Iranian students in America began their own
protests. "Chip was attacked yesterday," Carter noted in his diary on October 14, 1978, "on a Texas college campus by Iranian students." Campus
police and Secret Service agents had to rescue his son. "The Iranian students are getting out of hand in some cases," Carter noted. "They are
helping the shah more than they hurt him."

But the Iranian crisis continued to spiral out of control. By November 2, the shah was expressing doubts about whether his regime could survive. Strikes in the oil fields had caused oil revenues to decline by two-thirds by the end of October. With the economy collapsing, Tehran's elite were fleeing abroad, taking their capital with them. The shah told Carter that he was contemplating whether he should abdicate. "We encouraged him to hang firm and count on our backing," Carter wrote. Four days later, the president reiterated that he would support whatever action the shah took, including setting up a purely military government. "He is not a strong leader," Carter noted, "but very doubtful and unsure of himself." Carter was unaware that the shah was quietly battling lymphoma, a fact the monarch had kept from his family and palace courtiers. This intelligence lacuna about the shah's medical condition was indicative of how little Washington understood Iranian society. By 1978, the Pahlavi regime was rapidly unraveling—and Washington's policy makers were oblivious. Ironically, just one month prior to the Jaleh Square massacre, the CIA had assured the White House that "Iran is not in a revolutionary or even a 'pre-revolutionary' situation."

Brzezinski believed all this wrongheaded intelligence and used his influence to convince an ambivalent president that the Pahlavi regime should and would survive. Carter should have followed his own instincts. He was ambivalent about the shah precisely because he knew from the reports of Patt Derian, his assistant secretary of state for human rights, that the monarch was no paragon of human rights. Brzezinski nevertheless convinced Carter that geopolitical considerations trumped Derian's criticisms of the regime's human rights record. This was the first of the administration's many mistakes. When Derian blocked the sale of tear gas to the regime in March 1978, Brzezinski quickly had the decision reversed. As the crisis worsened in the streets of Tehran that autumn, Brzezinski doubled down on his own instincts and helped to shape a policy that placed the Carter administration on the losing side of a revolution. That would prove to stoke anti-American emotions in postrevolutionary Iran.

Brzezinski's views were also colored by the pressure he was already receiving from some of the shah's influential supporters in New York. Former vice president Nelson Rockefeller, for instance, phoned Brzezinski that autumn to complain that the administration was doing nothing to help the regime. Brzezinski was also painfully aware that Henry Kissinger was telling anyone who would listen that the administration was bungling the Iranian crisis. Early in December 1978, James E. Akins, a former ambassador to Saudi Arabia, was sitting in the upstairs dining room of a Pan Am 747 flight into Washington when he overheard Kissinger holding forth to his fellow passengers, loudly denouncing the "evils of the Carter administration."

Akins had been fired in 1975 by Kissinger. There was no love lost between the two men, but Akins was nevertheless astonished to hear Kissinger complain so openly about the "amateurishness and the incompetence of the Carter administration." Not aware of Akins's presence, Kissinger described Carter as the "weakest" president "since before the First World War." He said Carter's human rights policies were a "disaster." Under Carter, "we had stopped putting pressure on our enemies and were concentrating on our friends. He mentioned specifically Iran, the Philippines, South Korea and Brazil as friendly governments which were weakened by this 'naïve' approach." When his rapt listeners asked about Brzezinski, Kissinger archly described his successor as "someone who knows everything and understands nothing." Akins quickly relayed to Brzezinski a memo conveying every word of the overheard conversation. Carter had personally always treated Kissinger with kid gloves, while, in return, the former secretary of state was always "poisoning the well."

Brzezinski, for his part, cared very much what men like Kissinger thought of him. They were rivals, dating back to their Harvard years. He was well aware that Kissinger had close ties to the Rockefeller brothers and such other highly influential members of the old foreign policy establishment as John J. McCloy. And he knew these men were becoming highly critical of the Carter administration's handling of the Iranian crisis. Not incidentally, Chase Manhattan Bank was quite literally the shah's personal banker. Each year Chase handled some $2 billion in Iranian transactions. And throughout the 1970s the Iranian government usually had at least $6 billion on deposit at various Chase bank branches throughout the world. As one financial analyst explained, "Iran became the crown jewel of Chase's international banking portfolio." By 1979, Chase had on its ledgers more than $1.7 billion in syndicated Iranian loans—the equivalent of $5.8 billion in 2021 dollars.

Chase itself held more than $500 million in outstanding loans to the Pahlavi regime.

David Rockefeller was worried about his bank's exposure, admitting to his colleagues that the "risks were too high relating to the CMB position in Iran." Rockefeller told a private meeting of his Chase Manhattan Bank employees that he was convinced that communists were directing the street demonstrations in Tehran. McCloy's old friend Robert Bowie—who was then serving as deputy director of the CIA—had recently returned from Iran convinced that left-wing guerrilla groups and the communist Tudeh Party were directing the revolution. McCloy had known the shah for two decades, and as a token of their friendship, each Christmas the shah sent the McCloys five pounds of fine beluga caviar. Not surprisingly, the influential chairman of the Council on Foreign Relations strongly believed that the Carter administration should do something to help the shah in his troubles.

McCloy, Kissinger, and both David and Nelson Rockefeller made their unhappiness known to Brzezinski and other members of the Carter administration. Operating through the Council on Foreign Relations and their own networks of contacts within the government, this private foreign policy establishment began buttonholing administration officials and providing background briefings for the press. The Pahlavi regime, they argued, was still an "oasis" of stability. The shah's opponents were extremists who could be handled with strong police action. And if the shah was displaying any lack of will, it was probably because he was receiving mixed signals from the U.S. embassy in Tehran. For Brzezinski, an Iran without the shah was unthinkable, and any analysis that failed to conform to this "shared view" was unsound. This groupthink became a critical factor in the coming months as the crisis unfolded, and Brzezinski unreservedly pushed the establishment's view of what should be done.

"I'M INCREASINGLY CONCERNED about Iran," Carter wrote in early December. By then, it was clearly very late in the game. That week, Ambassador Akins returned from the region and sent the White House a candid assessment of the Iranian situation. "Our reporting from Iran," Akins wrote to Brzezinski, "was frequently colored by what we all hoped to be true: that the shah would continue in power indefinitely." All of this intelligence was just flat wrong. Akins believed "the shah's power has already been usurped." The regime was falling apart from "the extraordinary corruption of the shah's twin sister, his other sisters and brothers, his nieces and nephews and his mother-in-law." Akins knew that Brzezinski was strongly inclined to believe that the Carter administration should intervene militarily, perhaps by supporting an army coup, to rescue the shah. "I cannot see how this would be successful," Akins wrote. "We certainly could not keep any action secret." And an ineffectual American intervention "would only ensure that the successor government would be even more anti-American than we must expect it to be."

Akins's observations were both astute and dispassionate. But his advice would be ignored. Brzezinski ardently believed that the president should signal his support for the shah "without reservation" and urged the Iranian monarch to take "decisive action" to restore order. Zbig simply assumed that the Soviet Union and local Iranian communists must be orchestrating the street protests. As evidence, he gave President Carter a *New Republic* article written by Robert Moss, an Australian reporter who had made a reputation for himself as a "professional anticommunist polemicist." It was flimsy reporting from a highly biased source. Brzezinski had no real understanding of Iran's internal politics, but he articulated, as usual, a forceful position. The shah was pro-Western and anti-Soviet, so Brzezinski thought the monarch should be supported absolutely.

The president himself was disconcerted to realize that as the crisis escalated his advisers were sharply divided. The State Department—pushed by another seasoned diplomat, Henry Precht, the country director for Iranian affairs—believed that the shah's regime was unraveling. Precht had served as a political officer in the U.S. embassy for four years (1972–76), and by 1978 he was arguing that Washington had to prepare itself realistically for a post-Pahlavi revolutionary government. Precht had opened up a back channel to Dr. Ibrahim Yazdi, an Iranian American medical doctor living in Texas who was helping to organize anti-shah protests in the United States. Yazdi supported the Ayatollah Ruhollah Khomeini, the Shi'a cleric who was inspiring the revolution with his taped sermons from exile in Iraq and later France. Precht and other Foreign Service officers like him were hopeful that if the Pahlavi regime collapsed, it would be replaced by a coalition of secular-oriented followers of the Mosaddegh-era National Front. But even Precht later conceded that he "did not have a real sense of Khomeini. . . . My impression at the time was that Ayatollah Khomeini wanted to set up a secular government . . . and the clerics would be in the background." This vague perception of Khomeini's intentions would prove to be terribly misguided. But at the time, the ayatollah himself was projecting an image that suggested he would be only a spiritual figurehead of the new regime. "Dictatorship," he said in one of his taped sermons, "is the greatest sin in Islam." He allowed Western-educated men like Dr. Yazdi and the French-trained Abol Hassan Bani-Sadr to serve as his spokesmen. And it was also quite demonstrably true that the anti-shah protests that autumn had the support of millions of Iranians. Neither was there any precedent within Shi'a tradition for anyone to predict popular support for a theocratic dictatorship of revolutionary clerics. That decidedly illiberal outcome became a reality much later, many months after the shah's downfall.

Ultimately, it was clear that the Carter administration had no feel for what was happening in Iran. As things deteriorated in the streets of Tehran, Brzezinski recruited George Ball, a blunt-speaking, highly opinionated former under secretary of state, to head a special task force on Iran. Ball spent two exhausting weeks reviewing the documents and interviewing everyone who claimed to know anything about Iran and then wrote an incisive report: "We made the shah what he has become. We nurtured his love for grandiose geopolitical schemes and supplied him with the hardware to indulge his fantasies. . . . His regime is coming apart under the pressures of imported modernization." Ball concluded that Carter should force the shah to relinquish much of his power and make his government more representative. Ball thought the shah's position was probably untenable, but perhaps he could survive as a constitutional monarch if he could be persuaded to transfer power to a "council of notables" that would in turn hold elections. Brzezinski was appalled by this recommendation and, citing what happened to the short-lived Kerensky government during the Russian Revolution, argued that this would only pave the way for the opposition to seize power. The Pole in Brzezinski was always thinking of Russia.

Ball was nevertheless allowed to present his report to President Carter on the afternoon of December 14, 1978. As usual, Carter was fully briefed and had read the report. And while he agreed with Ball's analysis, he said he was not prepared to "tell another head of state what to do." Carter instead mentioned that he intended to send Brzezinski to Iran. Zbig's presence, he suggested, might bolster the shah's courage. Ball replied "with all due respect" that sending Brzezinski "is the worst idea I have ever heard." This evidently gave Carter pause, and later Ball said he thought his only achievement had been to persuade the president not to send Zbig to Tehran.

Ball also made a point of privately reporting to Secretary Vance that Brzezinski was going behind Vance's back and conducting discussions with the shah's ambassador, Ardeshir Zahedi, without the knowledge of anyone in the State Department's hierarchy. Vance was outraged and believed any such back-channel messages "contributed to the shah's confusion about where he stood and to his inability to decide what to do." Vance immediately confronted Brzezinski, who categorically denied the accusation. Vance said he didn't believe him and insisted that they see the president together right away. The president listened to Vance's complaint. According to Vance, Carter asked Zbig "if this was true." Zbig denied it. Carter said he would review the relevant communications—and that was the end of it. That evening, he noted in his diary that Vance had come to see him about "problems between NSC and State." But it was his impression that "I think the air was cleared." Vance didn't think so and described it as "a painful experience."

Carter had already sent mixed messages. A week earlier, when asked by reporters if he thought the shah would survive, he had candidly replied, "I don't know. I hope so. . . . We personally prefer that the shah maintain a major role in the government, but that is a decision for the Iranian people to make." And then on December 12, he told the press, "I fully expect the shah to maintain power in Iran. . . . The shah has our support and he also has our confidence." On the other hand, in response to criticism that perhaps Carter administration pressure to liberalize had uncorked revolutionary sentiments, the State Department's human rights czar, Patt Derian, bluntly told a reporter in late December, "I think that what's happening in Iran now is an expression of the people's will, and that it would be pretty easy to try to write it off as something that we had generated and somehow sparked."

By late December it was clear that events on the ground in Iran were making the shah's position untenable. Gary Sick told Brzezinski that a new government of national salvation, a government that included the opposition, had to be formed by the first week of January. Otherwise, Sick predicted, "the shah and his dynasty are going to be swept away." Brzezinski refused to believe it and simply ignored Sick's assessment. The shah indicated that the choice was coming down to a face-saving coalition government of some sort—which really meant surrender—or an "iron fist" military government. Secretary of State Cy Vance was opposed to a military crackdown, but Brzezinski thought the "iron fist" should remain on the table as a possible option.

But the shah himself said he "did not have the heart" for a bloody crackdown, and if the military tried this option, he would leave the country. The despot was remarkably ambivalent and at times clearly distraught. By then, the shah was popping ten milligrams of Valium per day, plus six milligrams of chlorambucil as chemotherapy to treat his lymphoma. A French doctor who examined him in late December wrote, "The patient was almost unrecognizable, visibly suffering from apparently dreadful tension." Carter, however, had no idea that the shah was in such poor physical and mental health.

On New Year's Day 1979, the shah's newly designated prime minister, Shapour Bakhtiar, addressed the Iranian people on nationwide radio and television and pledged to form a truly social democratic government. Bakhtiar had served decades earlier in Mosaddegh's cabinet, but he had no ties to the Khomeini clerics behind the street demonstrations. The shah and the Carter administration were just hoping that Bakhtiar could stabilize the situation and forestall a complete collapse of the army.

On January 3, 1979, the U.S. ambassador stationed in Tehran, William H. Sullivan, sent a message to the White House, recommending that Carter "advise the shah to abdicate." A tough, experienced career diplomat, Sullivan had a reputation for speaking his mind without reservation. Once, in the Philippines, when First Lady Imelda Marcos remarked that she didn't know what else she could do to help the poor, Sullivan snapped, "Try feeding them cake."

With his shock of thick white hair and a dignified, ramrod bearing, Sullivan looked the part of an ambassador. Confident and articulate, he expected people to take his views seriously, and when they didn't, he could be abrasive. That autumn, Brzezinski found himself on the receiv-

ing end of a string of increasingly caustic cables from Sullivan. Not surprisingly, Brzezinski used the cables to convince the president that
Sullivan was out of line. Matters came to a head in late December when
Carter discovered that his ambassador was taking initiatives without authorization from his bosses in the State Department. Earlier that autumn, Sullivan had opened up back-channel talks with Khomeini's
people in Tehran—and now he urged Carter to send an envoy for direct
talks with Khomeini, who remained in his Paris exile. When Carter
balked at this, Sullivan was incensed. The strong-willed ambassador was
entirely confident in his own judgment that the Pahlavi regime was finished and that it was imperative that the United States reach out to Khomeini in order to negotiate a less bloody transition. Sullivan also thought
it was in Washington's interest to build bridges to the people who were
about to take power in Tehran.

By then, Carter so distrusted the advice he was getting from Sullivan
that he was persuaded by the Pentagon to dispatch to Tehran a high-
ranking military officer, General Robert Huyser, ostensibly to report on
the military situation but actually to serve as a check on the ambassador.
General Huyser arrived in Tehran on January 4—the same day President Carter traveled to the French Caribbean archipelago of Guadeloupe for a long-scheduled summit with German, French, and British
leaders. It was terrible timing, but Carter now had to manage the Iranian
crisis over the next few days while juggling meetings with Helmut
Schmidt, Valéry Giscard d'Estaing, and James Callaghan about global
trade, nuclear weapons, Vietnam's recent invasion of Cambodia, and a
host of other foreign policy issues.

The day Carter arrived in Guadeloupe he received another message
from Sullivan, reporting that a group of Iranian generals were plotting a
coup. Sullivan suggested that "the shah was involved in this arrangement, was knowledgeable about it." Sullivan obviously opposed this
coup plotting, as did Secretary Vance. But Carter instructed Sullivan to
see the shah as soon as possible and report back on his attitude toward a
possible coup. Carter later explained, "Cy wanted us to stay away from
both the military and the shah, in favor of Bakhtiar. My own belief was
that the shah, the military leaders and Bakhtiar were all acting in concert. At the time, I thought the shah and the military would prevail."

The next day, Sullivan met with the shah. According to Carter's diary notes—finally declassified in 2008—the monarch confirmed the coup rumors. The shah insisted that these rumors "should help strengthen Bakhtiar." Sullivan reported, "The shah wants us to cooperate with a coup under those circumstances. . . . The shah says that the coup group is representative and strong enough." The shah still planned to leave the country. "Sullivan's assessment," Carter noted, "is that if the shah leaves, Bakhtiar has a chance. If the shah stays in Iran, Bakhtiar has no chance. Sullivan's advice is that we should support the military provided they support Bakhtiar."

Clearly, Carter was inching across the line, evolving dramatically from a once-strong disinclination to intervene in the internal affairs of Iran. But facing the prospect of further chaos, the president was signaling that he could tolerate a coup. Brzezinski was encouraging him in this direction. (Brzezinski had bluntly told Carter on January 3, "We should have encouraged the military to stage a coup." Carter had responded, "We couldn't do this.") But when Vance had learned of the coup rumors, he had immediately cabled General Huyser, instructing him to delay any meetings with Iranian generals. Vance then called the president in Guadeloupe and asked for further instructions. Carter consulted with Brzezinski, who had accompanied the president to the summit, and soon afterward the president instructed Vance to approve Huyser's meetings with the generals. There could be no doubt of the president's intentions. He wanted Huyser to explore the coup option.

In a separate track, Ambassador Sullivan had arranged his own plot. Sullivan viewed Bakhtiar as only an interim act, a means to get the shah to abdicate. Sullivan's goal was to negotiate a smooth, relatively bloodless transition to a revolutionary regime dominated by moderate leaders from the old National Front government. Sullivan thought of these men as "social democrats."

To this end, Sullivan had promised in his backdoor negotiations with moderate opposition leaders like Mehdi Bazargan that he could arrange for the departure of more than a hundred top military officers identified as loyal to the Pahlavi regime. Sullivan promised that these senior officers would leave on the same plane with the shah, and that they could be replaced by officers chosen by the revolution. In return, the opposition leaders like Bazargan—who was already being talked about as a future prime minister if Khomeini returned—would pledge that there would be no further retributions carried out against the military. "Sullivan's plan," Gary Sick later wrote in his history of the revolution, *All Fall Down,* "was to endow these men with real power by engineering an accommodation between themselves and the military. . . . If this worked, the transition to power could be accomplished with a minimum of bloodshed, and a relatively liberal leadership would acquire the strength, through its association with the army, to moderate the excesses of Khomeini and his immediate entourage."

Sullivan's gambit was a quite brazen piece of unauthorized diplomacy. It might be brilliant or entirely foolish. Astonishingly, no one back in Washington had any idea of what he was doing. Sullivan kept Carter in the dark about his potential deal with the opposition and only renewed his request that the administration open direct talks with Khomeini by sending an official envoy to meet with the ayatollah in Paris. Carter received the request upon his return from Guadeloupe on January 10. After discussions with Brzezinski, Mondale, Vance, and others, the president rejected Sullivan's request for a direct meeting with Khomeini. Carter was still disinclined to do anything that might have the appearance of undermining the Bakhtiar government. He sent a message to Sullivan saying only that the French government could be used as a conduit to the ayatollah. Furthermore, Carter said that he was extending General Huyser's mission in Tehran and had authorized the general to sound out his contacts in the Iranian army about a possible military government.

Sullivan received this cable in the middle of the night and rashly replied with an angry cable of his own. The president's refusal to open direct contact with Khomeini was "insane" and "incomprehensible." He characterized it as a "gross and perhaps irretrievable mistake." Carter was deeply offended when Brzezinski showed him Sullivan's "unbelievable cable." Carter confided in his diary that he wanted to recall Sullivan, "but Cy said he was just hot-tempered, and we decided to leave him there for now."

General Huyser remained in Iran for a full month, reporting almost daily on his contacts with the army.* He stayed in Ambassador Sullivan's residence and the two men amicably agreed to disagree. As Carter noted in his diary, "Sullivan thought we ought to permit Khomeini to take over, and that it would lead to democracy; Huyser thinks it would lead to communism. Sullivan thinks the military is very weak; Huyser thinks it's strong." Events would soon show both Sullivan and Huyser to be wrong.

Brzezinski, in the meantime, continued to promote the idea of a military coup. "My own simple view was that we support a military action to end the unrest," Brzezinski said years later, "and then follow it up with reforms." But the shah told Zbig that "he did not want to bequeath a bloodied throne to his son." The shah decided he was going to leave the country, ostensibly for an extended holiday, but clearly, he felt he had no choice but to vacate the throne. Brzezinski was disappointed. "I *acquiesced* [emphasis added] to the shah's departure largely because I feel that he had become an impediment to any decisive action." The shah's departure was not a question Zbig could decide. The regime was no longer in control of the streets, and the army was slowly melting away due to hundreds of desertions every day.

But Brzezinski, quite unrealistically, thought an army coup could still happen. On January 12 he wrote to the president that he disagreed with the State Department's Iran experts. "We are giving up on the shah only after being forced reluctantly to conclude that he is incapable of decisive action." Zbig was pressing Carter on "the need for a coup." Obviously irritated, Carter scribbled in the margins, "Zbig—After we make joint decisions, deploring them for the record doesn't help me."

Time was running out. On January 16, 1979, the shah, his wife, and a half dozen bodyguards and personal valets climbed into a helicopter outside the palace and flew to the capital's international airport, where they boarded a Boeing jet. Prime Minister Bakhtiar walked aboard the aircraft to say goodbye. "You now have all the power and authority," the

---

* Huyser later told David Rockefeller over lunch at the Knickerbocker Club that he had indeed tried to stiffen the resolve of the Iranian generals, urging them at one point to order their troops to shoot to kill protesters in the streets of Tehran. "I got stern and noisy with the army," he said, according to minutes of the luncheon. But the top general, he complained, was "gutless."

shah told him. "I leave the country in your hands and with God." The shah then walked to the cockpit and started the jet engines. He had decided that he would personally pilot the aircraft out of Iranian airspace. "He was worried," recalled the shah's longtime bodyguard, Colonel Kiumars Jahanbini, "they might conspire to take him somewhere other than the planned destination." Carter had been told that the deposed monarch's first destination would be Aswan, Egypt—but that after a short visit there as a guest of Anwar Sadat he would fly on to California. But four days later, Carter was informed that the shah had decided to move his family to Morocco. "This suits me fine," Carter noted, "although Brzezinski was somewhat disturbed. I think the shah's presence in a Moslem country is better for Bakhtiar. . . . And I believe the taint of the shah being in our country is not good for either us or him."

The shah left behind a country on the verge of civil war. Throngs of people spontaneously poured into the streets to celebrate the end of the thirty-eight-year reign. Police and military were absent, and a carnival air of benign anarchy settled over the capital. Groups of bearded young men chanted slogans, calling for the return of Ayatollah Khomeini from his Paris exile. Carter understood that Khomeini's return probably spelled the end of Bakhtiar's civilian government. Desperate to forestall this, Carter actually called France's president, Valéry Giscard d'Estaing, and asked if he could somehow keep the ayatollah from returning to Iran. The French president thought this unlikely. Bakhtiar told Carter he was contemplating arresting Khomeini if he returned. But this too was clearly impractical.

On January 18, Brzezinski once again made an argument for an army coup, this time in a private seven-page memo to Carter. The president read it and merely commented that it was "sensitive." Carter was feeling caught between Zbig's desire for an "iron fist" and the far more cautionary advice he was receiving from Cy Vance and the State Department. On the morning of January 19 Vance and Mondale argued that if Bakhtiar's civilian government was going to survive, it would soon have to "broaden" its political base—and that meant bringing into a coalition government some of Khomeini's people. Carter responded by trying to thread the needle: "We never agreed among ourselves to a coalition government. . . . We will back the military in their support of Bakhtiar but we don't want it to slide any further to the left." The president's comment again betrayed a lack of good intelligence on the ground, because things were decidedly not sliding to the left. And in a nod to Zbig's views, Carter added, "The threat of a military coup is the best way to prevent Khomeini from sliding into power."

None of this was based on any realistic understanding of what was happening in the streets of Tehran. The people were in control of the streets, not the army. Carter and Brzezinski were wrong to think they could at this late stage keep Khomeini out of power. And Vance and Mondale were wrong to think that the ayatollah would confine his role to being merely a spiritual figurehead of a postrevolutionary democratic government. Khomeini himself had cleverly signaled that he would be a benign titular figure and that in a postrevolutionary Iran, "we will sell our oil to whoever purchases it at a just price." The ayatollah's messengers were clearly trying to influence Washington not to instigate a coup.

But Brzezinski would not let go of the idea of using military force. On January 23 he told Hamilton Jordan that "military coups are not necessarily bad—that in Brazil and elsewhere they have been both popular and successful." Ham replied, "The best thing that could happen would be a successful coup—[and] the worst thing that could happen would be an unsuccessful coup." Zbig agreed. "Nothing could be worse than a half-assed coup." At this late stage, however, a coup d'état was just a fantasy.

One only had to see what happened when, on February 1, 1979, the seventy-eight-year-old ayatollah flew into Tehran and was wildly cheered by hundreds of thousands of Iranians. "Khomeini returned to Iran with a minimum of violence," Carter noted in his diary. "The military are keeping their powder dry." Brzezinski downplayed the popularity of political Islam, writing to the president the very next day, "We should be careful not to over-generalize from the Iranian case. Islamic revivalist movements are not sweeping the Middle East and are not likely to be the wave of the future." Zbig was still placing his bets on the Bakhtiar regime, and unbelievably, he still saw the real threat to American interests in Iran coming from the communists, not the clerics. There was zero evidence that the Tudeh Party communists had any influence over the anti-shah masses in the streets. But Brzezinski's ideology and worldview told him otherwise.

Within days there was ample evidence that the Bakhtiar government was crumbling. But Carter nevertheless put out a public statement endorsing Bakhtiar, on the assumption that such a statement would bolster Bakhtiar's confidence and improve army morale. The president was being poorly advised. Just hours later, the evening news networks carried reports from unnamed State Department officials asserting that they expected Bakhtiar to survive only a few more days. Carter was enraged by these leaks and called in a group of midlevel Foreign Service officers and angrily rebuked them. "I laid down the law to them as strong as ever in my life." He promised that if there was another round of leaks, he would "direct Cy to discharge the leaders who were responsible, even though some innocent people may be punished." Carter rarely displayed anger. But this time he was visibly incensed. "I told them again either to be loyal or resign. Then I got up and left." It was not the president's finest hour, and inevitably, news of the presidential reprimand quickly leaked.

The very next day, Carter met with Kissinger privately. The former secretary of state flatly reported that "the shah feels betrayed." Kissinger criticized the performance of Ambassador Sullivan, and then he advised Carter, "We have only two options: either a military coup or [Iran becomes] another Libya," meaning presumably a pariah regime like that of Libya's strongman, Muammar al-Qaddafi. In a time of revolution, Kissinger lectured the president, "force was absolutely necessary; compromise was permissible only before or after the crisis." Carter listened politely to this highly contentious advice—not knowing what Kissinger had said publicly about him behind his back on a crowded Pan Am 747. But he was certainly emotionally attuned enough to sense that Kissinger was being his unctuous self. Carter knew he had to tolerate Kissinger. And, of course, Kissinger's hard-line instincts mirrored the relentless advice he was also receiving from Brzezinski.*

Four days later, on Sunday, February 11, 1979, while Carter was skiing at Camp David for the weekend, Brzezinski convened an emergency meeting of the NSC's Special Coordinating Committee (SCC). The Iranian army had attempted to impose a curfew the previous evening, but it was widely flouted by angry demonstrators. Shooting broke out be-

---

* At the same time, Kissinger was privately telling David Rockefeller that he thought the most likely outcome was "a sort of Bonapartist counter-revolution that rallies the pro-Western elements together with what was left of the army."

tween troops of the Imperial Guard and low-ranking army soldiers. Fragmentary reports from Tehran were confusing, but they painted a picture of chaos and uncertainty. A late-night meeting of Iranian generals ended inconclusively. The Iranian army chief of staff, General Gharabaghi, was unreachable, and soon reports reached Washington that the army had withdrawn to its barracks and declared its "neutrality." As the president's men discussed what they should do in this situation, Brzezinski found himself "playing a lonely hand." He alone argued that it was not too late to explore whether "Option C" (the code name for a coup) could be launched to restore order and replace the Bakhtiar government with a military regime. Brzezinski and Under Secretary of Defense Charles Duncan called General Huyser in Germany and asked him if he was willing to go back to Iran immediately and "conduct a military takeover." Huyser thought that this was "no longer feasible." He bluntly told Brzezinski that he would go back only if he had unlimited funds and "10,000 of the best U.S. troops." Almost as an afterthought, Huyser said he'd also want the "undivided" support of the American people. Brzezinski was stunned. "There was a long pause," Huyser later wrote in his memoirs, "so I answered the question for them. I said I didn't think the people I was talking to were ready for that type of action, nor did I believe the American people would give their support." No doubt Huyser was thinking of the American experience in Vietnam, where he had flown B-52 combat missions.

Discouraged, Brzezinski nevertheless placed phone calls to Ambassador Sullivan and General Philip Gast—the ranking American general on the ground—to solicit their advice on "Option C." Within minutes, Under Secretary of State David Newsom was on the phone with Sullivan, asking him about the viability of a coup d'état. At that very moment, Sullivan was frantically trying to reach Ibrahim Yazdi, one of Khomeini's aides, to get him to intercede and rescue twenty-six American military officers besieged in a bunker. Sullivan was livid when he heard Newsom's question.

"Tell Brzezinski to fuck off," Sullivan yelled.

"That's not a very helpful comment," responded the mild-mannered under secretary.

"You want it translated into Polish?" Sullivan replied, and then he slammed the phone down.

By the end of the day, the Iranian military chain of command had virtually wilted away. Bakhtiar fled to Paris, and Khomeini's designated prime minister, Mehdi Bazargan, replaced him. The revolution was triumphant. Khomeini retreated to the holy city of Qom, and for a time the Bazargan government—a coalition of old National Front politicians and a younger generation of moderate Islamic nationalists—gradually restored a thin veneer of order.

Carter was deeply discouraged. The next morning, February 12, he held a press conference and fielded questions on a host of pressing issues. "The President looked tired," Landon Butler noted, "and his answers were lackluster. It must be terribly frustrating to have so many major issues—Iran, the Middle East, inflation—he's strung out with no clear indication of their outcome. Nothing seems to be going right for him. My guess is that he is in one of the low parts of his presidency. . . . He hasn't found his voice."

Three days later, on February 14, 1979, the U.S. embassy was briefly overrun by armed militant groups. Ambassador Sullivan and the entire embassy staff were taken hostage. But Bazargan and his newly appointed foreign minister, Ibrahim Yazdi, quickly interceded and got them released.* Sullivan believed his views had been vindicated; Brzezinski's repeated attempts to trigger a coup had proven ludicrous. But that was not how President Carter saw it. Carter never would have committed American military forces to save the Pahlavi regime. But he had been convinced by Brzezinski that it would be wrong if the United States were to turn its back on the shah. And he was deeply angered when his own ambassador repeatedly ignored White House directives to send strong messages of support to the shah.

Brzezinski, however, was unrepentant. On February 20, 1979, after hearing about the first executions by firing squad of four prominent generals, Brzezinski noted in his journal, "A depressing story of chaos and confusion. The more I hear of what is going on, the more depressed I am over the fact that I did not succeed in getting the U.S. government to approve and, if necessary, to initiate an Iranian military coup."

---

* A few weeks later, Sullivan cabled Washington, "It is possible to say that some event, such as a visit by the shah to the United States, could provide the excuse which would trigger another assault [on the embassy]."

Brzezinski was convinced in his heart that something could have been done to save the Pahlavi regime. He abhorred the very idea of revolution, if only because for him it conjured images of Bolsheviks, and he was instinctively reminded of what they had done to his ancestral homeland. Another Pole saw things differently. Ryszard Kapuscinski was a foreign correspondent for the Polish Press Agency when he visited Iran to witness its unfolding revolution. He saw it emerge from the bottom up, and later he explained the shah's downfall as something akin to fate: "The shah was reproached for being irresolute. Politicians, they say, ought to be resolute. But resolute about what? The shah was resolute about retaining his throne, and to this end he explored every possibility. He tried shooting and he tried democratizing, he locked people up and he released them, he fired some and promoted others, he threatened and then he commended. All in vain. People simply did not want the shah anymore; they did not want that kind of authority."

A foreign correspondent like Kapuscinski, armed with a measure of empathy and an ability to listen, could fly into a very foreign culture and quickly acquire a feeling for what people were thinking and dreaming. Brzezinski had no such sensibilities.

"It was difficult to know from afar why and how the President placed so much value on Brzezinski," remarked the State Department's official spokesman, Hodding Carter III. "A second-rate thinker in a field infested with poseurs and careerists, he has never let consistency get in the way of self-promotion or old theories impede new policy acrobatics." The scion of a legendary Mississippi newspaper family, Hodding had taken a strong disliking to the national security adviser, partly because of his sharp elbows but largely because he disagreed with Brzezinski's Eurocentric view of the world. Hodding's wife, Patt Derian, the assistant secretary of state for human rights, couldn't agree more.

THE CARTER ADMINISTRATION'S public support for the shah until the bitter end exacerbated relations with the new revolutionary government. It convinced Khomeini that Carter was somehow an evil actor. Khomeini himself would prove to be uncompromising in his hostility to Americans in general, but his personal animosity for Carter in particular would drive events. To make matters worse, the fate of the shah quickly became a bone of contention. The Bazargan government issued a warrant for the shah's arrest and insisted that the monarch had stashed many billions of dollars abroad. That was probably an exaggeration, but according to an investigation by *The New York Times,* the shah and his private foundation certainly controlled $2 billion to $4 billion worth of assets that had been transferred out of Iran during the years prior to the revolution.

More than two months later, when it was clear he had worn out his welcome in Morocco, the shah sought refuge in America. But by then, Carter thought his presence on American soil unadvisable. "I authorized Vance to notify the shah that he could not come to our country because of threats to Americans still in Iran." Vance called Kissinger and David Rockefeller and asked if either of them would be willing to tell the shah that it would be best if he postponed any visit to America. Both men indignantly refused and began to make their own calls around the world in search of a haven for their old friend. Hours before the Pahlavi party was virtually pushed onto a plane in Morocco, Rockefeller arranged for temporary sanctuary in the Bahamas. He sent his late brother Nelson's public relations man, Robert Armao, to greet the shah. Armao would thereafter serve as the deposed monarch's spokesman, accompanying him throughout his journeys in exile. Rockefeller's personal assistant at Chase Manhattan Bank, Joseph V. Reed, Jr., was assigned to handle the shah's finances and the logistics of his security needs. And later, when the shah's health deteriorated further, Rockefeller dispatched a close personal friend, Dr. Benjamin Kean, to supervise his medical care.

With the shah temporarily ensconced in a beachfront villa in the Bahamas, Rockefeller and Kissinger turned their attention back to Washington, where they were determined to persuade the Carter administration to allow the shah permanent U.S. asylum. To this end, they organized a "special project," code-named "Project Alpha." Rockefeller dipped into his private funds to pay Chase Manhattan Bank employees and lawyers from John J. McCloy's law firm, Milbank, Tweed, Hadley & McCloy, for the time they spent working on Project Alpha. McCloy and other Milbank, Tweed lawyers charged the hours they spent on the project to their daily log sheets. Thousands of dollars were spent on phone, travel, and legal expenses over the next year. At one point, they paid an academic specialist on the Middle East $40,000 to write a short book intended to answer the shah's critics.

Frequent strategy meetings were held at One Chase Plaza, and the always exuberant Reed kept everyone informed of the latest developments through a flurry of "personal and confidential" memos. The shah was given his own code name—"the Eagle"—and Reed referred to Rockefeller, Kissinger, and McCloy as "the Triumpherate." It was a remarkable lobbying effort, something only a Rockefeller could have mounted.

Carter had no idea of the scope of this privately orchestrated effort to interfere with his conduct of U.S. foreign policy. Neither did Brzezinski, who expressed genuine surprise and "outrage" when he learned about Project Alpha decades later. It was perfectly brazen and quite effective.

Over the next seven months, Project Alpha pestered numerous members of the Carter administration to provide asylum for "the Eagle." Kissinger fired the first volley. On April 7, 1979, he called Brzezinski and berated him "in rather sharp terms" for the administration's stance. As much as Zbig disliked being lectured by Kissinger, he happened to agree with Kissinger's belief that Carter's emphasis on human rights and liberalization was "naïve." He also agreed that the shah should be offered sanctuary. Brzezinski encouraged Kissinger to call Carter directly. Kissinger did this right away and reminded the president that he had an appointment to see Rockefeller in two days. He told Carter that he would support whatever Rockefeller had to say about the shah's predicament. "I said," Kissinger recalled, "I felt very strongly about this." Two days later, Brzezinski reported to Carter his conversation with Kissinger and irritated the president by saying that asylum was a question of principle: "We simply had to stand by those who had been our friends."

Carter heard the same sentiments from Rockefeller when the Chase chairman visited the White House on April 9, 1979. The president sat "stiff and formal" as he listened to Rockefeller tell him that a "great power such as ours should not submit to blackmail." Rockefeller left with the "impression that the president didn't want to hear about it."

Carter was certainly annoyed by the lecture. That night he dictated for his diary, "The main purpose of this visit, apparently, is to try to induce me to let the shah come into our country. Rockefeller, Kissinger and Brzezinski seem to be adopting this as a joint project." Carter felt there were good reasons to keep the shah out. "Circumstances had changed since I had offered the shah a haven. Now many Americans would be threatened and there was no urgent need for the shah to come here." As he told Ham Jordan, "It makes no sense to bring him here and destroy whatever slim chance we have of rebuilding a relationship with Iran. It boils down to a choice between the shah's preferences as to where he lives and the interests of our country."

Kissinger and his Project Alpha partners, however, were not about to accept Carter's definition of the national interest. After learning from Rockefeller that the president had been unmoved by their private appeals, Kissinger decided to go public. That same evening, he told a Harvard Business School dinner in Manhattan that "a man who for 37 years was a friend of the United States should not be treated like a *Flying Dutchman* looking for a port of call." It was an all-too-apt metaphor—though not the one Kissinger intended, since the foolish captain of the mythical *Flying Dutchman* was condemned to his eternal wanderings at sea for high crimes against man and God. But Kissinger had made his point, and the press picked up on the phrase and broadcast it widely. The conservative columnist George Will snidely observed in his April 19 column: "It is sad that an Administration that knows so much about morality has so little dignity."

This was only the beginning of a well-orchestrated and persistent revolt by a private foreign policy establishment against the Carter administration's treatment of the shah. On the same day Will's critical column appeared, Rosalynn Carter noted in her diary, "We can't get away from Iran. Many people—Kissinger, David Rockefeller, Howard Baker, John McCloy, Gerald Ford—all are after Jimmy to bring the shah to the United States, but Jimmy says it's been too long, and anti-American and anti-shah sentiments have escalated so that he doesn't want to. Jimmy said he explained to all of them that the Iranians might kidnap our Americans who are still there."

McCloy in particular was relentless, badgering Brzezinski by phone and writing letters to Vance, Deputy Secretary of State Warren Christopher, Under Secretary of State David Newsom, and United Nations ambassador Donald McHenry. McCloy even invited to lunch Brzezinski's NSC aide Gary Sick. What McCloy had to say about the shah's "good deeds" was all very familiar, but Sick was flattered that the old man had bothered to "track me down to make a point."

The president himself knew that he needed the cooperation of McCloy on a host of issues. McCloy was a powerful counterbalance to the anti-SALT testimony of Paul Nitze and other members of the neo-conservative Committee on the Present Danger who opposed the treaty. Unfortunately, Carter's relations with McCloy had never been very good. They came from two very different worlds. Reflecting the personal dislike that Germany's Helmut Schmidt felt for Carter, McCloy had gotten the impression that the Carter administration was jeopardizing the special relationship between Germany and the United States that he had cultivated as high commissioner to occupied Germany in the late 1940s.

Carter tried to make amends by inviting McCloy to a private lunch on June 12, 1979. They met first in the Oval Office, where McCloy presented the president with a gift, an antique hunting rifle. Carter then escorted his eighty-four-year-old, slightly stooped guest outside, where the two men sat down at a small round table on the terrace and lunched alone. They spent an hour talking, and once again McCloy made his pitch for providing the shah with sanctuary. Carter listened politely. Afterward, he scrawled a short note to McCloy. "Enjoyed having lunch with you today." Carter had little patience for coddling the rich and powerful, but with McCloy he obviously felt he had to try to placate the old man everyone knew as the "chairman" of the establishment.

By the midsummer of 1979, the campaign was beginning to have an effect on the White House. After a final push from Kissinger, Vice President Mondale told Carter that he had changed his mind and now supported asylum for the shah. In a late July meeting, Brzezinski and Mondale so annoyed the president with their arguments that he finally cut them off by saying, "Fuck the shah. I'm not going to welcome him when he has other places to go where he'll be safe." He complained to Brzezinski that "Kissinger, Rockefeller and McCloy had been waging a constant campaign on the subject." Prophetically, he said he did not want the shah "here playing tennis while Americans in Tehran were being kidnapped or even killed."

Carter was right to be skeptical. The Iranian revolution was an unmitigated disaster for his administration. The president had been ill-served by nearly all his advisers, most particularly his national security adviser. Ironically, it was not until two months after the shah's departure that the CIA finally translated and published Ayatollah Khomeini's seventy-four-page blueprint for a harsh, fundamentalist Islamic republic, written by him in exile nine years earlier. The document in Farsi had been circulating for years in Tehran's bazaars and religious schools, but no one had bothered to take it seriously. Everyone had underestimated the fierce cleric, including his supporters in the old National Front, university students, journalists, and other intellectuals. But in the next few years the revolution would send to the gallows or firing squads more than twelve thousand Iranians.

Chapter 17

Tilting Against American Exceptionalism

Too many of us now tend to worship self-indulgence and consumption. . . . This is not a message of happiness or reassurance, but it is the truth and it is a warning.

—President Jimmy Carter, July 15, 1979

Carter and Patrick Caddell
ALAMY

"I ENJOYED MY FIFTIETH news conference today," Carter noted in his diary on May 29, 1979, "although there's a blackbird-type movement among the press to say how despondent the White House is these days."

It had been a challenging spring. The economy was weakened by both rising unemployment and double-digit inflation. And then there had been a partial meltdown of a nuclear energy reactor at Three Mile Island in Dauphin County, Pennsylvania. The accident was caused by a series of human errors, compounded by a stuck valve and a flawed design in a valve indicator light. The reactor was shut down, but not before the plant released significant amounts of radiation.

The crisis began at 4:37 A.M. on Wednesday, March 28, 1979, but the president didn't become directly involved until Friday morning, March 30, when he spoke on the phone with Joseph Hendrie, chairman of the Nuclear Regulatory Commission. Carter advised the Pennsylvania governor to evacuate children and pregnant women from the immediate vicinity of the plant.

But two days into the event, Carter was informed that the reactor core had sustained more damage than initially thought, and engineers were struggling to determine how to vent a large radioactive gas bubble from the reactor's containment vessel. Carter, of course, felt that his navy training in nuclear engineering gave him an understanding of the technical issues. He kept detailed diary notes about what he was told by the experts and soon concluded that the situation was stable. It was certainly the worst nuclear accident in U.S. history, but he found himself annoyed at *The Washington Post*'s "irresponsible scare tactics designed to terrify the public and, not incidentally, sell newspapers."

By Sunday, April 1, media coverage of the accident had nevertheless created a sense of panic in the general public—which prompted Carter to stage a public visit to the site. He decided to have Rosalynn accompany him on the trip "to show our confidence." After attending Sunday church services, the Carters flew in a helicopter to an airport a few miles from the accident and then were driven to the reactor. They were photographed walking through the control room, "primarily to demonstrate the safety of it." The engineer in Carter was unworried about the radioactivity and later noted in his diary, "We were getting about one-third as much radioactivity in the control room, one hundred feet away from the reactor, for instance, as a passenger in an airplane at an altitude of thirty-five thousand feet."

Notwithstanding such confidence, some were not so sure. Jessica Tuchman Mathews, a thirty-two-year-old aide on the National Security Council, thought it was "very courageous" of the president to risk a visit. Mathews had a doctorate in biochemistry from Caltech and thought the accident was "very scary." She recalled sitting in a White House meeting early in the crisis and being asked whether she thought it was advisable to order a general evacuation. "I voted against a general evacuation. I remember thinking it was the first time what I said actually mattered. If there was an explosion and no evacuation, well, that would have been a disaster. And yet if we ordered an evacuation of millions of people, well, inevitably in that kind of panicky situation, many people would have been hurt. The price of being wrong was high in either direction." In the event, 140,000 people fled in a voluntary evacuation from a twenty-mile radius.

The crisis receded after a few days, and on April 5 Carter gave yet another speech on the nation's energy problems, suggesting that the nuclear accident highlighted the need to lift federal controls on the price of oil: "Although this accident is of immediate concern, the fundamental cause of our nation's energy crisis is petroleum—oil and gas. We are dangerously dependent on uncertain and expensive sources of foreign oil. . . . Just ten years ago we imported hardly any oil. Today we buy about half the oil we use from foreign countries. . . . There is no single answer. We must produce more; we must conserve more, and now we must join together in a great national effort to use American technology to give us energy security in the years ahead."

Congress wasn't listening—and neither were most voters. To be sure, most Americans were angry to see that the major oil companies had jacked up gasoline prices, citing temporary interruptions in oil supplies due to the Iranian revolution. Iranian oil production declined by 4.7 million barrels per day, or about 7 percent of global production. But the Saudis and other producers stepped up production, so global supplies declined by only about 5 percent overall. Oil prices, however, rocketed from $13 per barrel in mid-1979 to $34 per barrel a year later.

Carter's decision to issue an executive order to gradually decontrol crude oil prices was seen by liberals as rewarding the oil companies with the opportunity to raise prices even higher. The president argued that this was the only way for market forces to kick in and provide the incentive for the production of more oil globally. But of course, in the short term, decontrol meant even higher prices at the pump—and greater inflationary pressures on the economy.

By late April, furious commuters in California and many other states found themselves having to idle their cars in long lines at gasoline stations, waiting hours to fill up their tanks. The president had been warning Americans for two years about the growing energy crisis, but he was not winning any popularity contests by being right. Sixty percent of Americans still thought their president was honest, and 67 percent believed him to be competent. In February 1979 his overall popularity stood at 42 percent. But by late that spring, a CBS/*New York Times* poll showed that this number had plunged to an abysmal 33 percent. Americans were not doubting Carter's personal integrity, but they were now clearly skeptical about his presidency.

Carter viewed these discouraging numbers with a certain detachment, if not equanimity. Rosalynn was more disturbed than he was about falling poll numbers. They did not shake his natural self-confidence, but they piqued his curiosity. "We were in deep shit [and] headed for a very, very precipitous decline," recalled Patrick Caddell, the president's private pollster, who was still in Boston running his private polling firm, Cambridge Survey Research. Caddell spent about a week each month in Washington, hanging out in the White House, dispensing his political insights. Carter's campaign speechwriter, Patrick Anderson, thought of Caddell as "big and fleshy, fast-talking and self-serving . . . a world-class bullshit artist."

Gregarious and slightly edgy, Caddell, age twenty-nine, exuded a certain charm. Born in South Carolina, he had graduated from Harvard, and soon afterward he became George McGovern's chief pollster during the 1972 presidential campaign. He favored pinstripe suits and French cuffs but somehow always managed to look slightly disheveled. "Swarthy and slightly oafish," wrote reporter Kandy Stroud, "he looks like Eeyore from *Winnie the Pooh*." He later would grow a full black beard, with a distinctive white streak running through it, to cover a receding chin. Caddell was a contrarian who had one big idea: Elections could be won by attacking the so-called establishment—a message that appealed to alienated voters in the 1970s. Ironically, he began his political journey as a McGovernite, but by the end of his life he was flogging the same populist, antiestablishment brand to Donald Trump and right-wing Republicans.

Caddell was a mercurial personality, and Carter had his ups and downs with the young wunderkind. Pat was not one of the Georgia boys, but he was one of the few outsiders who socialized regularly with them. Still, his status was uncertain. Early in the administration, Caddell had warned the president about the dangers of getting bogged down in substance and the need for "style" and symbolism. This was not a message to Carter's liking. "Carter got mad at me," Caddell said. "He wouldn't talk to me for a long time." But with his slide in the polls in late 1978 and early 1979, Carter began listening again. "This is my pollster," he said to Anwar Sadat, introducing Caddell to the Egyptian president at the March 1979 Egyptian-Israeli peace treaty signing ceremony. "He's the person who brings me the bad news—but he always tells the truth, and I love him anyway."

Caddell also had a back door into the White House via his personal friendship with Rosalynn. "While we would go home to our wives," Rafshoon recalled, "Pat would be on the phone calling Rosalynn, saying, 'It's all falling apart.'" On April 9, Caddell managed to have a two-hour breakfast with Rosalynn in which he convinced her that it wasn't just long gasoline lines that were making the American people pessimistic about the country's future. It was, Caddell argued, an existential crisis that was festering deep inside the American soul. Two weeks later, on April 23, Caddell submitted a 107-page memorandum entitled "Of Crisis and Opportunity." Caddell painted a bleak psychological portrait of a nation still scarred by the Kennedy and King assassinations, the Vietnam War and Watergate. It was, he wrote, "a crisis of confidence marked by a dwindling faith in the future."

Caddell warned that the president was in danger of losing his bid for a second term. To win, he had to "reshape the structure, nature and purpose of the United States in fundamental ways of which your predecessors could only dream." Carter needed to reach for "higher levels of motivation and morality." Citing the sociologist Christopher Lasch, the British economist John Maynard Keynes, and the presidential historian James MacGregor Burns, Caddell urged Carter to become a transformational president. "And that is your opportunity, Mr. President . . . a transforming leader, evolving into a great President who leaves an imprint as great as Washington's, Lincoln's, Wilson's, Kennedy's, or Roosevelt's."

It was heady stuff. Eizenstat was dismayed when he read the memo. He thought it "hyperbolic" and "historically reckless." Ham Jordan also thought Caddell's pop psychoanalysis of the nation "goofy stuff," and he predicted that Carter would dismiss it as well. It would be "the end of Pat, because he's really gone too far."

The Carters, however, met with Caddell and Powell for more than an hour on the morning of April 28, 1979, and discussed the "basic deep-seated and growing concerns among the American people about the future, and what I as president might do about it." Carter found himself open to some of Caddell's philosophical arguments, perhaps because they resonated with his own religiosity. Over the next few weeks he began reading some of the books Caddell cited. Years later, Jordan would tell Stu Eizenstat that Caddell was "almost a Rasputin, he was kind of in Carter's head and Rosalynn's head."

That spring, it became clear that Caddell's memo had stimulated Carter to revisit some of the antiestablishment themes of his '76 campaign. On Sunday evening, May 20, the Carters sat on the Truman Balcony, sipping drinks with Caddell, Rafshoon, Jordan, and Powell. Caddell had been plying the president with articles, books, and memos on the country's collective state of mind—and not surprisingly, he found Carter that evening in a "foul mood about everything, particularly about politics, about Washington, about the elites." Rafshoon was also feeding Carter much the same line, telling him that he should run for reelection in 1980 as "an experienced outsider." Carter observed that he'd have to "try to tie these two apparently contradictory terms together."

Around this time, Brandt Ayers, the publisher of Alabama's *Anniston Star,* dropped by the White House. A liberal southerner, Ayers had known the Carters for a decade and had been elated at the election of a man from the Deep South. But Ayers was now worried and depressed. "The people are down on the country and themselves," he bluntly told Pat Caddell, "and they don't see any leadership from the White House. What the hell is wrong with you folks?"

Caddell agreed and told him he should talk to Rosalynn. A few minutes later Ayers was escorted by Jerry Rafshoon to the Map Room, where he greeted the First Lady. When Ayers obliquely referred to the administration's troubles, Rosalynn brusquely interrupted. "Brandy, what can we do? Jimmy doesn't know." It was an awkward admission and Ayers was taken aback. After a moment of hesitation, he suggested that maybe they should host a series of dinner parties with various experts "who're not afraid to tell the president—with the bark off." Rosalynn nodded.

Ten days later, Caddell persuaded Carter to extend dinner invitations to a select group of intellectuals to discuss the country's sour mood. "We had a strange private dinner," Carter noted on May 30, 1979, "to assess the depth of despair, hopelessness, discouragement, and fear among the

American people, to see if it was inevitable and what I as president should both know and do." Rosalynn participated in this four-hour dinner discussion, along with Jody Powell and Caddell. It was an intimate affair, held upstairs in the private quarters of the White House. Sitting at the dinner table were professors Daniel Bell and Christopher Lasch; journalists Bill Moyers, Charlie Peters, and Haynes Johnson; and John Gardner, the founding chairman of Common Cause, the liberal, grassroots watchdog group. The one outlier among the group was the young civil rights activist the Reverend Jesse L. Jackson. Otherwise, these men were all pragmatic intellectuals, certainly politically liberal, but highly skeptical of this southern president.

Bell was best known for his 1960 book *The End of Ideology*. A Harvard sociologist, Bell was a skeptic who, he boasted, specialized in "generalizations." In 1976, he had published *The Cultural Contradictions of Capitalism,* a book that provocatively argued that capitalism's very success in producing material abundance might also destroy the Protestant work ethic. Similarly, Lasch had recently published an equally provocative book, *The Culture of Narcissism: American Life in an Age of Diminishing Expectations,* which had become a national bestseller that spring. Lasch's critique suggested that postwar American society had incubated a self-indulgent "pathological narcissism," which in turn had undermined the country's sense of community and family. Carter was attracted to both Bell's and Lasch's critiques of American society; their ideas sat well with his own personal and religious values that spoke to frugality and community. That evening, however, he found them "too erudite for their comments to be practical." Moyers echoed Bell and Lasch by talking about the country's loss of a sense of community. Oddly, Carter found Moyers "a little too preachy" and Reverend Jackson to be "the most level-headed and constructive." He thought Peters, the gruff-spoken editor of the *Washington Monthly,* was "negative."

Peters thought the dinner was "very interesting. . . . No one was trying to show off." Carter was unaware of Peters's role in editing Jim Fallows's highly critical essay about his presidency in *The Atlantic,* published earlier that month. "It was clear that night," Peters recalled, "that the administration was at a crisis point. Carter was clearly unpopular. They were asking us, What's wrong with the country? I said you had to shock the country into making sacrifices. I suggested reform of Social Security.

I told Carter that maybe he should consider rationing of gasoline. But I could see when I said this that Carter's jaw clenched up, and that was a sign that he didn't like my ideas." Peters came away from the dinner feeling that these Carter folks still didn't know how to govern. Later that summer, Peters and Caddell unsuccessfully tried to persuade Carter to make Moyers his chief of staff.

Still, everyone at this most unusual dinner was impressed that Carter should even entertain a freewheeling discussion of his presidency. Bell sent a cordial note afterward to Powell, thanking him for a remarkable evening. "What I found most refreshing was the openness and candor of the discussion," Bell wrote. "I feel, however, that we learned more about the President than we were able to give to him. That is fine, for it adds some humility to the judgments one has about the President." Carter had surprised these intellectuals by his introspection; he was clearly much more complicated than the man they knew from his portrayal in the press.

But not everyone in the Carter White House thought such intellectual soul-searching was helpful. Rosalynn called Eizenstat on June 2 to say that she thought "the situation is desperate. . . . We need to get a chief of staff." Gas lines in California were then running as long as five hundred cars, and for the first time ever the price of gasoline topped a dollar a gallon. (A year earlier it had been sixty-five cents.)

With these headlines in mind, Rosalynn confided to Eizenstat, "We need to get rid of [Energy Secretary] Schlesinger." She knew Schlesinger was seen as somewhat aloof and ineffective—and if energy issues had become a problem, it made sense to blame the energy czar. Rosalynn's political instincts told her that people were unhappy for very down-to-earth, practical reasons—perfectly illustrated when a few days later OPEC announced a 50 percent increase in oil prices.

Mondale was also unhappy with Carter's reaction to the energy crisis. His liberal instincts told him the president should be reaching out to the labor unions and other traditional Democratic interest groups. He wanted the president to take some kind of executive action to lower gasoline prices and deal with the gas lines. "Mondale could see his own political future going down the tubes," recalled Eizenstat. Feeling stymied, the usually buoyant and cheerful vice president decided to take a lower profile, cutting back on his office hours. Some of Mondale's aides found him despondent and fatalistic. Handed a copy of Caddell's long-winded psychological profile of the country's mood, Mondale reacted with astonishment that anyone could take such sophomoric navel-gazing seriously. He angrily told Eizenstat that he thought it was a "bunch of crap" and "crazy." He confided to several close aides that he was thinking of resigning, or perhaps just announcing that he would not seek to run on the ticket again.

Frustrated but not sure what to do, Mondale suddenly left Washington on May 27 for an unscheduled vacation in Minnesota's northern wilderness lake country. He spent an entire week in the woods, occasionally using his special satellite phone to chat with old friends, seeking their counsel. Listening to her despondent husband, Joan finally told him on May 29, "It'll be better if you quit." But after spending a week in the woods, Mondale calmed down and decided, for the moment, that he was ready to go back to work.

He returned to a chaotic White House in crisis. The president was scheduled that month to make two whirlwind visits abroad, the first to Vienna, where he would meet with Soviet leaders and sign the SALT II treaty, and the second to Japan for an annual meeting of the G7—the seven largest global economies—where Carter anticipated some contentious negotiations over trade issues. Signing the SALT II treaty was a major accomplishment, a serious and long-awaited step toward ratcheting down the nuclear arms race. But it was so long in coming that Carter got little credit when it finally happened. He also got some harsh criticism from neoconservative Republicans, but also from his old adversary Senator Scoop Jackson, who nastily compared this "accommodation with a totalitarian superpower" to the appeasement of Adolf Hitler in the 1930s.

Carter knew he faced an uphill battle to win Senate ratification of the SALT II treaty, so it was no coincidence that he decided to announce that same June that he was approving the highly controversial development of some two hundred mobile MX missiles, an experimental missile with ten warheads that could be moved about on railroad tracks, ostensibly to evade detection by Soviet satellites. In retrospect, the MX should be seen as one of the Cold War's more ludicrous schemes, a desperate attempt to shore up the mad logic of nuclear deterrence. But at the time, Brzezinski, Harold Brown, and even Cy Vance urged him to

approve the new weapon system, arguing that this might mollify hawkish senators and persuade them to ratify SALT II. But the MX came
with an estimated price tag of $30 billion. Not surprisingly, Senator Ted
Kennedy and many other liberal Democrats denounced the MX as both
redundant and an extravagance. They were right. Eventually, only fifty
MX missiles were deployed in 1987, and instead of circling vast tracts of
the Nevada desert as proposed, they were installed in old missile silos
in Wyoming and thus never became mobile. The scaled-back program
still cost at least $20 billion. In the end, Carter was nevertheless talked
into grudgingly approving the development of this outlandish weapon
system by his defense and national security advisers—but he was profoundly unhappy with the decision, noting in his diary that month
that he was sickened by "the gross waste of money going into nuclear
weapons." He told Stu Eizenstat that the MX expenditures were "a total
waste. . . . I am almost physically nauseated by the NSC deferring to the
Joint Chiefs of Staff, and then they sit back and critique my decisions."

He may have been nauseated, but he had still felt compelled to give
the generals what they wanted.

That same June of 1979, Carter attracted more criticism from liberals
by unveiling his newly revised catastrophic health insurance bill. The
legislation was endorsed by many congressional Democratic leaders—
but, as expected, Senator Kennedy denounced it as too little and not
universal enough. Carter complained, "Kennedy, continuing his irresponsible and abusive attitude, immediately condemned our health
plan. He couldn't get five votes for his, and I told Stu and Joe Califano to
fight it out with him through the public news media." Kennedy's opposition angered Carter deeply: "It's really time to do something about
health care, catastrophic illness, the problem with the poor not having
health care at all." But Kennedy's opposition proved fatal to any legislation, and Carter later lamented, "We lost a good chance to provide comprehensive national health care, and another thirty years would pass
before such an opportunity came again."

At the end of that same day, on June 12, 1979, Carter met with Rosalynn and his closest advisers—including Mondale, Jordan, Powell,
Rafshoon, Moore, Kraft, and Eizenstat—to talk about the political environment. Led by Rosalynn, everyone urged Carter to appoint Jordan
as his chief of staff, and this time the president tentatively agreed, and

Jordan acquiesced. But the appointment would not be announced until later in July. Carter bluntly acknowledged that things were tough, and "very likely to get worse in the future." But he said he was undeterred and confident that he would prevail in 1980. A week later, at a breakfast meeting with congressional leaders, someone asked what he would do if Kennedy decided to run. Carter snapped, "I'll whip his ass."

The comment immediately leaked to the press, and over lunch, Mondale told Carter he thought the remark was "ill advised." But Carter was unrepentant and later heard from White House staffers that "it was the best thing for morale since the Willie Nelson concert."

Morale, in fact, was pretty abysmal. Late that June, while the president was conducting urgent negotiations abroad, a nationwide truckers' strike disrupted the economy. Truckers were angry about the fuel price hikes. Carter responded with a colorful piece of political theater. On June 20, 1979, he dragged reporters up to the White House roof for a ceremony to inaugurate the installation of thirty-two solar water-heating panels. In a reference to the gasoline shortage, Carter acknowledged that "some few Americans have reached a state of panic." But he insisted that "America was not built on timidity or panic." He announced that he was committed to spending more than $1 billion "to stimulate solar and other renewable forms of energy," in the expectation that within two decades 20 percent of the nation's energy would be generated by solar power.

"In the year 2000," he told the crowd of reporters, "this solar water heater behind me, which is being dedicated today, will still be here supplying cheap, efficient energy." But then he added, "A generation from now, this solar heater can either be a curiosity, a museum piece, an example of a road not taken, or it can be just a small part of one of the greatest and most exciting adventures ever undertaken by the American people." Carter often indulged himself with a bit of hyperbole, but the $28,000 solar panels would indeed become a metaphor for his administration. They were a novelty—and way ahead of their time.

A few days later, the president flew off to Tokyo for the G7 summit of economic powers, hoping to persuade the international community to take collective action on energy prices. The negotiations, however, were disagreeable. "Our luncheon was bitter and unpleasant," Carter noted. German chancellor Helmut Schmidt "got personally abusive toward me." The prickly chancellor had previously criticized Carter over various issues, including Carter's unilateral decision in 1978 to cancel the deployment of neutron bombs in Western Europe. But policy disagreements aside, the two men just didn't like each other.

"All the news from home was bad," Carter noted, "with the truckers' strike, long gas lines, and the apparent stalemate in our summit." OPEC had jacked up the price of oil by 60 percent since December. Flying back aboard Air Force One from the Tokyo G7 summit, Carter had intended to stop over in Hawaii for a brief vacation with Rosalynn, but he canceled this excursion after receiving two urgent messages, one from Caddell, who melodramatically told him to "come back right away or not come back at all."

The other, more thoughtful, missive came from Eizenstat, who wrote, referring to the gasoline shortages, "I do not need to detail for you the political damage we are suffering from all of this. It is perhaps sufficient to say that nothing which has occurred in the Administration to date— not the Soviet agreement on the Middle East, not the Lance matter, not the Panama Canal treaties, not the defeat of several major domestic legislative proposals, not the sparring with Kennedy, and not even double-digit inflation—have added so much water to our ship." Nothing else, Eizenstat warned, had so angered the American people as having to wait in long lines to buy gasoline at more than a dollar a gallon. Eizenstat was himself struggling to fill his gas tank. "I couldn't get any damn gas for my car, and that was a real crisis. I mean, I couldn't get to work to chair my five o'clock energy meetings."

Eizenstat urged the president to return from Tokyo, rest up for a long weekend at Camp David, and then be prepared to be seen working every day to deal with the energy crisis. Another presidential speech should be devoted to energy, making the case for the administration's proposal for a windfall-profits tax on the oil companies, the proceeds of which would be used to fund federal programs on solar, wind, and other renewable energy sources. Moreover, Eizenstat argued, an enemy had to be blamed for the energy crisis, and that enemy was OPEC, the foreign cartel that had just caused prices to rise so dramatically. This gave Carter the opportunity "to shift the cause for inflation and energy problems to OPEC, to gain credibility with the American people, to offer hope of an eventual solution, to regain our political losses."

The other Georgia boys—Powell, Rafshoon, and Jordan—endorsed Eizenstat's prescription, and together they all persuaded Carter to schedule a major presidential address on the energy crisis for July 5. But as soon as a draft speech was prepared, the president's aides began arguing about it. Eizenstat, Mondale, and Schlesinger wanted the speech to be entirely prescriptive, telling the American people what the administration was going to do to end the gas lines. Caddell, however, sought to address what he insisted was the larger issue—the public's loss of confidence. Without telling anyone else, Caddell sent Carter his critique of the speech draft—plus a revised and updated version of his 107-page "Crisis and Opportunity" memo. Carter read both documents carefully early on the morning of Wednesday, July 4, at Camp David. He thought the revised memo "one of the most brilliant analyses of sociological and political interrelationships I have ever seen." He called Rosalynn to his side, and the more of it they read together, "the more I became excited." They both realized that Caddell was taking them down a lonely, uncharted road: "I think we two are the only ones that are reasonably sold on his premises."

Caddell thought it would be a mistake to confine the speech, now scheduled for Friday evening, just two days hence, to energy issues.

Carter read the speech draft without enthusiasm, and, still jet-lagged from the trip to Japan, he went to bed, leaving his copy on the coffee table. At 4:00 A.M. Rosalynn awoke and, finding herself incapable of getting back to sleep, picked up the speech and read a page or two. She was not impressed, and when Jimmy asked her what she thought, she replied, "Nobody wants to hear it. They've heard about new energy programs ever since you've been in office, and prices are still going up." Jimmy agreed and surprised her by saying, "I decided last night to cancel it." He just didn't think people would really listen to yet another speech on energy. He also agreed with Caddell that "the problems of the nation are much broader and deeper."

Not only did Carter decide to cancel the Friday speech, but in a moment that can only be described as an epiphany, he decided to stay at Camp David and invite some of the best thinkers in the country to advise him on the state of the nation. Carter's diary indicates that it might have been Rosalynn who prompted this Camp David domestic summit. It was, he noted, "*our idea* to have people come to Camp David." Carter "felt a remarkable sense of relief and renewed confidence" after he canceled the energy speech. He loved Camp David's rural surroundings, and of course, it had been the scene of his greatest foreign policy triumph. So perhaps he was thinking that another summit in Catoctin Mountain Park could produce a similar domestic triumph.

None of his aides agreed. That afternoon at 3:00 the president had a conference call with Mondale, Rafshoon, Jordan, and deputy press secretary Rex Granum. When he announced he wasn't going to do the energy speech, they all argued with him that it was scheduled, and he had to do it. Carter was adamant. He was in a petulant mood. Instead, he asked them all to come up the next day to Camp David, where he would explain what he had in mind.

Rafshoon immediately called Eizenstat and told him of the president's decision. A shocked Eizenstat called Mondale, who told him, "Carter is very tired and in a funky mood. . . . I don't understand him." The president was indeed jet-lagged from his foreign travels. But more than halfway through his first term, the job was taking its usual toll. Always of slight build, he had actually lost weight during the previous two years. One reporter, Elizabeth Drew, wrote that "his body seems shrunken, somewhat stringy." It was, in fact, the body of a fifty-four-year-old man who was still often jogging twenty miles a week. On occasion, he could run five miles in just thirty-eight minutes—7.6 minutes per mile—a very good pace for a man in his fifties.

The next afternoon, July 5, Mondale, Eizenstat, Powell, Jordan, Rafshoon, and Phil Wise, the president's appointments secretary, arrived in Camp David via helicopter. They immediately met with the Carters in what Eizenstat later called "a showdown with Caddell." A four o'clock meeting went on until late that evening and turned into a heated debate. Eizenstat later called it "the most ferocious, almost violent, meeting" he attended during the entire four years. Carter explained that he now felt that "the sense of despair" was such that "the people don't listen to us." No one was ready to listen—and so he was going to try a dramatic change of course. Carter's diary noted that "Stu and Fritz were adamantly against what we proposed, and everyone else reluctantly agreed." Eizenstat urged calm, telling the president, "Don't panic and overreact."

But it was Caddell's meeting, and he forcefully argued that the country had still not recovered from the multiple upheavals of the 1960s. He cited his polling to show that "people had been thru trauma [and] had not faced it." Caddell flatly said what they were dealing with was "not a political phenomenon." It was a "loss of values" and now a "search" for values. "This is why Jimmy [was] elected," and now the president "must climb out of the transactional pit" by creating a cathartic moment and then resolving it with a "breakthrough" speech that got "back to the old JC." The polling numbers "had gone to hell" during the previous three weeks, and there were "not enough fingers for all the dike holes."

Mondale was incensed. Staring directly at Caddell, he said his memo "was the craziest goddamn thing I've ever read." He didn't believe the American people were selfish or self-absorbed: "There is not a psychiatric problem with America, but real problems with coping economically. The worker making $22,000 a year was slipping." Turning to Carter, Mondale said, "Mr. President, we got elected on the ground that we wanted a government as good as the people; now as I hear it, we want to tell them we need a people as good as the government; I don't think that is going to sell." Mondale argued that Caddell's paper had exaggerated the problems, and "things [are] not too bad." He advised the president to "get tough with the Cabinet" and "use a whip," and above all, "focus on domestic affairs," because "people see you as preoccupied with foreign affairs." Carter listened and took careful notes but finally indicated that he found Caddell's memo highly persuasive. "I've read it, and I'm going to do it all." Fritz shot back, "You're very tired and this is affecting your thinking."

With everyone's nerves on edge, Carter took Mondale on a walk outside "to get him cooled down." He thought Fritz was quite distraught. "I told him that my mind was set, that I had to have his support. . . . Fritz was extremely fearful about the consequences of what we were planning to do." By the end of the evening, Carter was compiling a long list of people he wanted to invite to an ad hoc Camp David summit. The names included governors and other politicians but also people from a broad variety of academic and intellectual disciplines.

Mondale thought the whole idea of a freewheeling domestic summit was unnecessary and politically risky, if only because the media would hyperventilate about who was invited and what was being said. But Carter was determined. Before adjourning late that night, the president also initiated a "frank discussion" about the cabinet. Everyone,

including Fritz, Ham, Jody, and Stu, recommended that it was time
to do a housecleaning. Some thought that Califano, Blumenthal, and
Schlesinger should be fired, if only because they were not team players.
Mondale vigorously defended Califano. Surprisingly, Carter defended
all three cabinet secretaries, despite his complaints about them in previous months.

In the meantime, Powell released a terse statement, merely announcing that the president "has decided to cancel the speech." He refused to
elaborate. Taking his cues from Caddell's memo, Carter thought the
abrupt cancellation would get people to pay attention. Caddell wanted
more drama and suspense around the president's actions—and now he
was getting it.

The next day, the dollar plunged on currency markets, and the price
of gold climbed to record levels. "An air of mystery continued to surround the sudden and unexplained cancellation of the speech," reported
The New York Times. The White House press office had no information
on when the president might return from his mountain retreat, but he
was reported to have gone fishing in a nearby trout stream in the morning and then retreated to his desk in the afternoon. Reporters were mysteriously informed that the president "will be consulting with a number
of individuals whose judgment he respects, both in and outside government." A frustrated Senate Republican leader, Howard H. Baker, Jr.,
complained that the president must "end the vacillation and get on with
a coherent energy program." Critics said the president's absence from
the White House and his ominous silence were evidence of indecisive-
ness.

Over the next six days, the mystery of what was going on at Camp
David only deepened. The press was able to report on who came to the
mountain retreat and who left—but little of what was said inside these
meetings was known. Terence Smith of *The New York Times* wrote that
"the discussions, expected to continue well into next week, have reportedly been broadened beyond the specific issue of energy and include
such politically sensitive questions as inflation, unemployment and the
economic projections for the rest of the year."

Eight Democratic governors were present on Friday evening for nearly
six hours. A dispirited Mondale had left that afternoon, determined not
to subject himself to what he thought of as a pointless exercise. Back

in his White House office, Mondale called in his chief of staff, Richard Moe, and vented his frustrations to him about the whole exercise and in particular Caddell's role in it. Mondale was so worried and angry that he ordered Moe to go up to Camp David himself and monitor the situation. Moe packed a bag and went up right away. As he walked into a senior staff meeting, he was startled to hear Jordan, Rafshoon, Caddell, and Powell discussing a plan to request resignation letters from all cabinet secretaries. Moe thought this extremely unwise and blurted out that Nixon had tried that and it hadn't worked out very well, referring to the Saturday Night Massacre of October 1973. "It brought the conversation to a halt," Moe recalled. "The cabin went silent. After a while small talk ensued and eventually one-by-one they left the cabin. Clearly, I had walked into a conversation they were not eager to continue."

On Saturday, a collection of establishment "wise men" came to the mountaintop, including Clark Clifford, Sol Linowitz, and John Gardner. Energy experts came on Sunday, economists on Monday morning, and civil rights leaders that evening. Tuesday was reserved for congressional leaders and Wednesday for labor union leaders like Lane Kirkland and Doug Fraser, and a group of mayors.

Carter dressed casually and led the conversations, most often in the Aspen Lodge living room. Clifford found the setting entirely too informal. The former secretary of defense and powerful Washington lobbyist, whose influence dated back to the Truman presidency, archly observed that the president was "still running against Washington [and] had a lack of understanding of what takes place within the Beltway." Clifford later told Eizenstat that it had been "as unusual a weekend as I have ever spent." He thought the whole scene unseemly: "The president of the United States was sitting on the floor with a big pad of yellow paper, taking notes while people sat around him, five or six of us, and told him what he was doing wrong." This meeting reconvened after dinner at 9:00 P.M. and didn't break up until 1:00 A.M. It was intense and exhausting, but Carter actually seemed to be energized by the criticism.

Charlie Kirbo was present for the entire week. As usual, Kirbo mostly just listened. He particularly enjoyed the evening session with the civil rights leaders. "We sat on the floor . . . and he [Carter] just told everybody, 'Now I want you to tell me how you feel about the government, and I don't want you to pull any punches. You just say whatever you want to say about it.' This Black man, Jackson from Chicago . . . He was never at a loss for words. [Carter said,] 'I might not pay any attention to you, and I might.' So, we just talked on and on and on. I really enjoyed it and learned a lot."

Other participants thought the whole scene was a circus. Ham Jordan began referring to it as the "Caddell Summit." Landon Butler was present when the eight governors were invited to give their "candid assessment" of the president's job performance. They were each allowed three minutes to speak. Jack Watson tapped on a glass when their time was up. "Some of them gave good advice," Butler noted, "others gave poor advice. The president sat through it all." Eizenstat thought Bill Clinton, the thirty-two-year-old first-term governor of Arkansas, gave some constructive advice: "Mr. President, don't just preach sacrifice but liberation—and that it is an exciting time to be alive. Say your program will unleash a burst of energy." Butler got impatient after an hour and left for a walk. "Camp David is serene and lovely. But the tension among the people here is incredible—Dick Moe [Mondale's chief of staff] is a nervous wreck, and everyone else can hardly talk."

Carter was usually impatient in face-to-face meetings; he was always telling his aides that he could absorb more information from reams of memos than from any long-winded meeting. But for ten exhausting days, he forced himself to sit through one interminable session after another, often filled with personal criticism of him or his cabinet secretaries. After one particularly grueling session, Jordan warned him against allowing the meetings to "degenerate into a bitch session about you." Carter ignored this advice. The encounters were often tough and sometimes colorful. The morning of Tuesday, July 10, he listened with growing irritation as two well-known economists, John Kenneth Galbraith and Lawrence Klein, debated energy policy. Klein extolled the merits of a wholesale decontrol of petroleum prices. Galbraith countered with an argument for a nationwide program to ration gasoline, as had been done by President Roosevelt during World War II. Carter thought the meeting "a waste of time."

But another session that Tuesday provided the president with an epiphany. That evening, he met with nine religious leaders, including such prominent figures as Terence Cardinal Cooke, Notre Dame president Theodore Hesburgh, and Rabbi Marc H. Tanenbaum, the national director for interreligious affairs at the American Jewish Committee. Added at the last minute was Robert Bellah, a prominent Berkeley sociologist of religion. The president's aides quickly dubbed them the "God squad." Carter welcomed them all and confided that he was feeling "lonely" and discouraged. Trying to be supportive, Rabbi Tanenbaum remarked on how pleasant it was to be at Camp David, the scene ten months earlier of Carter's greatest diplomatic triumph. Perhaps the energy crisis called for similar presidential leadership. "We have passed from an era of superabundance," Tanenbaum observed, "to an era of growing scarcity of resources." The rabbi criticized the nation's "unrestrained consumerism" and "mindless self-indulgence." He then asked, "How do we achieve personal happiness that does not depend on the endless accumulation of goods?"

The gasoline shortages were so jarring to the nation's psyche precisely because Americans had come to believe that they were entitled to abundance. This line of thought appealed to Carter's sensibilities. As the historian Kevin Mattson later observed, the president was "moving away from his inner technocrat to his inner moralist." Carter wanted larger answers. But how does one speak truth about the stark reality of "growing scarcity" to a people who think of themselves as "chosen" and endowed with a manifest destiny? That was the political dilemma.

Bellah jumped into the discussion at this point to suggest that the way to square this particular political circle was to speak about what the Puritans had called the *covenant*. By invoking the communal notion of shared values, perhaps the president could persuade citizens to transcend mere self-interest. But it was tricky. Bellah knew that by invoking such ideals one could also awaken jingoistic sentiments. The Puritan notion of America as a shining "city on a hill" also inspired crass nationalism. American exceptionalism was a dangerous thing. Bellah warned Carter that he shouldn't "just give a speech that said OPEC was at fault." Carter astonished Bellah by candidly admitting, "It would be rather self-righteous to blame it all on OPEC. Americans don't like it when a foreign country can interfere in our life, but we've been interfering in OPEC countries' and most other countries' lives rather heavily for a long time." Bellah urged Carter not to worry about the politics. He just needed to come down from the mountain with hard truths.

Carter was inspired by this intellectual exchange. He noted in his diary, "The best meeting may have been with the religious leaders. They made very moving and deep analyses of the problems of our nation and helped shape my Sunday night speech more than anyone else." His speechwriter, Rick Hertzberg, thirty-six, who had silently watched the exchange between Carter and his "God squad," was similarly impressed. The next day Carter dispatched Hertzberg to draft an entirely new speech, now scheduled for the evening of July 15. Carter and Hertzberg thought they now had the right message—and it was not going to be just another boring speech on energy.

In the meantime, out of the president's earshot, many of his closest aides were deeply worried about the administration's prospects. White House senior staff, including the Georgia boys, were themselves not quite sure what might happen. "The polls, I think," noted Butler, "are taking their toll. Everyone is pointing their finger at everyone else." Jordan claimed that the president was even "dissatisfied with Stu [Eizenstat]— that he gets no new ideas, and that Stu simply prides himself on being the hardest working man in Washington." Jordan intimated that he was going to be "elevated to a far higher position than he had thought before" and that when the summit was over, there would be a major reorganization. Butler noted in his diary, "He said the president had said Ham should be a junior president." Butler didn't believe it and thought Ham was actually just getting "kicked upstairs, that Kirbo wants a strong man in to actually run the White House, and that there is not much future for me." Butler argued that they should replace the president's White House counsel, Bob Lipshutz, with a "strong person" who could do policy planning and properly organize the staff. (In fact, this is what would happen a few weeks later when Lipshutz was replaced by Lloyd Cutler, a high-powered corporate lawyer and Washington fixer.) But at the time, Butler sensed that Jordan himself felt threatened: "He is insecure, tormented and a little confused. He's a genius in many ways, a child in many others."

AFTER TEN DAYS, on July 14, 1979, Carter came down from Catoctin Mountain Park and spent the next day editing the speech that would ultimately become a turning point in his presidency. The following evening at 10:00, he sat down in the Oval Office and addressed the nation over live television. He spoke for thirty-three minutes, dressed in a dark blue suit and a striped gray-and-blue tie. His tone was somber, even angry at times, like a prophet. He spoke with hands that repeatedly turned into fists that shook and all but pounded the *Resolute* desk. His eyes were humorless and intense. He began with the barest hint of a soft smile, saying, "Good evening. This is a special night for me. Three years ago, I accepted the nomination of my party to run for president of the United States. I promised you a president who is not isolated from the people, *who feels your pain.*"

He then explained that ten days earlier he had canceled a scheduled speech on energy and instead invited to Camp David people from "every segment of our society." He reported that it had been "an extraordinary ten days," and then he quoted what a "southern governor" had told him: "Mr. President, you are not leading this nation—you're just managing the government. . . . Don't talk to us about politics or the mechanics of government, but about an understanding of the common good. . . . We're in trouble. Talk to us about blood and sweat and tears. If you lead, Mr. President, we will follow." The unnamed southern governor was actually the newly elected governor of Arkansas, Bill Clinton. Carter quoted a number of other common citizens and experts talking about the current gasoline shortages, including Jesse Jackson (without naming him) as saying, "Our neck is stretched over the fence and OPEC has a knife."

But quickly switching gears, Carter bluntly said that "after listening to the American people I have been reminded again that all the legislation in the world *can't fix what's wrong with America.*" The real but invisible threat to America was a fundamental crisis of confidence. Americans had always believed in the march of progress. "We've always had a faith that the days of our children would be better than our own," he said. "Our people are losing that faith. . . . In a nation that was once proud of hard work, strong families, close-knit communities, and our faith in God, too many of us now tend to worship self-indulgence and consumption." Taking a page straight from Christopher Lasch's *The Culture of Narcissism,* Carter observed, "Human identity is no longer defined by what one does, but by what one owns. But we've discovered that owning things and consuming things does not satisfy our longing for meaning. We've learned that piling up material goods cannot fill the emptiness of lives which have no confidence or purpose."

The speech had turned into a sermon about America's failings. "This is not a message of happiness or reassurance," Carter said, "but it is the truth and it is a warning."

The president then echoed Caddell's analysis by explaining that this loss of faith and purpose began with the assassinations of the Kennedy brothers and Martin Luther King, Jr., and the traumas of Vietnam and Watergate: "We were taught that our armies were always invincible, and our causes were always just, only to suffer the agony of Vietnam. We respected the presidency as a place of honor until the shock of Watergate." Americans, he insisted, had not recovered: "These wounds are still very deep. They have never been healed."

To make matters worse, when Americans turned to their government for redress, they found "a Congress twisted and pulled in every direction by hundreds of well-financed and powerful special interests." Washington was paralyzed by false claims, evasiveness, and "every extreme position defended to the last vote, almost to the last breath by one unyielding group or another."

This was indeed the old Jimmy Carter speaking, the southern populist railing against special interests and well-paid lobbyists. "You don't like it," he said angrily, "and neither do I."

Carter then devoted the last ten minutes to a few concrete answers. "First of all, we must face the truth," he preached, "and then we can change our course." It would require "restoring" faith in ourselves and the nation. But beating the energy crisis would be "the immediate test of our ability to unite this nation." He then pledged to use his presidential authority to set import quotas on oil. From now on, he said, the country would import no more foreign oil than arrived in 1977. He called for a massive federal investment to develop domestic sources of energy, "especially coal, our most abundant energy source." But he also pledged to submit legislation to create a national solar energy bank, with the goal of having solar power account for 20 percent of the nation's energy by the year 2000.*

All of this, of course, would cost a lot of money, so Carter called upon Congress to immediately pass his proposed windfall-profits tax on the oil companies. He proposed another law, requiring utilities to switch

---

* By 2020, nearly 20 percent of America's electrical generation came from renewable sources—but only 3 percent came from solar power.

from oil-fired power stations to coal-fired stations. (At this point, Carter was clearly less worried about coal-induced pollution than rising oil imports from the Middle East.) He proposed an "energy mobilization board" modeled after Roosevelt's War Production Board. He asked for $10 billion to rebuild the country's mass transit systems. Finally, he called for a "bold conservation program" requiring every citizen to conserve energy.

He talked about "a rebirth of the American spirit." And in closing, he said, "I will do my best, but I will not do it alone. Let your voice be heard. Whenever you have a chance, say something good about our country."

As the camera faded, ABC newscaster Frank Reynolds came on looking somewhat disconcerted. He characterized the speech as "remarkable" and "almost a sermon." Sixty-five million Americans had tuned in to the speech, and most were impressed by the president's sincerity and the passion. Thousands called the White House phone line to register their approval. *Newsweek* reported that Carter's polling numbers jumped by 11 percent overnight. A Gallup poll registered an unprecedented seventeen-point jump. Telephone calls and mail poured into the White House with overwhelmingly favorable comments. The very skeptical Eizenstat later admitted it "went over spectacularly well."

It sounded authentic, if only because Carter had clearly spoken from the heart. "Jimmy Carter got his voice back tonight," wrote David Broder in his *Washington Post* column. "He believed what he said." But it was a strange speech coming from a president in the midst of a gasoline shortage. People who liked it were acknowledging their unease about the direction the country had taken since the turbulent 1960s. It was hard to deny that Americans had become disillusioned, hardened, and cynical.

On the other hand, in the context of the daily energy crisis, it seemed a bit off that Carter appeared to be blaming ordinary American consumers for "self-indulgence and overconsumption." This was not his intention, of course, but by trying to talk about both the practicalities of the gasoline shortages and the coarsening of the nation's "spirit"—two very different phenomena—Carter was inadvertently opening himself up to criticism from the pundit class that he was blaming the country for his administration's inability to manage the price of oil. It was a no-win. Carter never used the word "malaise" in the speech. But Caddell passed to several journalists a copy of his long memo, where he had used the word to describe the country's mood. Within days pundits began labeling it just that—the *malaise speech.*

The New York Times was quick to criticize the speech, in an editorial headlined "Riding Casually to War." The president had defined the problem "boldly and correctly," but the plan to impose limits on oil imports was hardly a call for sacrifice. "Why this timidity?" asked the *Times* editorialists. "After twelve extraordinary days of deliberation, he proposes not a war on energy or even the moral equivalent of war. His plan is accommodation to dependence."

This was perhaps unfair. After all, Carter had proposed the next day in a speech in Kansas City that Congress appropriate $140 billion—to be funded by a windfall-profits tax on the oil companies—that would pay for new investments in solar, wind, and other energy sources, including coal. This money, he said, would "give the American people the financial weapon to win the energy war." Newspapers across the country featured the Kansas City speech on their front pages, often with a photo of the president with his shirtsleeves rolled up and waving a closed fist for emphasis. He looked forceful and presidential—and for a brief moment, many Americans thought, Well, maybe he could solve this energy crisis. But in the same speech, Carter came back again to Caddell's themes, reiterating the need to "bring us all together from the *battlefield of self-ishness* to a table of common purpose." The president was proposing concrete initiatives, but the whole package was too complicated and negative.

Carter's political advisers inside the White House knew this, and some had urged him to speak with less nuance. Eizenstat had told him to blame OPEC and take radical steps against the oil cartel. And his energy czar, James Schlesinger, had urged him to consider "a dramatic proposal" to decontrol gasoline prices completely. Prices would no doubt skyrocket—but the gasoline lines would disappear, ostensibly because many Americans would decide they could not afford to drive as many miles as they had before the crisis.

Carter had rejected both Eizenstat's and Schlesinger's proposals. Blaming OPEC might play well politically for a short time, but it would not diminish the long lines at gas stations around the country. And while eliminating price controls on gasoline would almost certainly end the gas station lines, it would do so by hurting the working poor, many of whom commuted long distances to low-paying jobs. "I cannot quarrel," Alfred Kahn told the president, "with your rejection of immediate decontrol."

Adopting decontrol would have constituted a major break with the Democratic Party's traditional liberal approach to such issues. Carter couldn't do it. Instead, he gravitated toward Caddell's "crisis of confidence" themes. As such, Caddell's approach allowed Carter an escape from his dilemma. Most of his political advisers were unhappy with this strategy. Jerry Rafshoon had predicted that a speech based on Caddell's themes would be "counterproductive to what we're trying to do. It could even be a disaster." Greg Schneiders, who was by then working with Rafshoon, agreed. "It's an interesting academic treatise," Schneiders said, but he argued that most Americans would be put off by the philosophizing: "More likely, the reaction would be 'bullshit.' He kept us waiting and watching for ten days to produce this? What's he going to do about the problems? People don't want to hear Jimmy Carter *talk* about our problems and they certainly don't want to hear him whine about them."

In the end, Rafshoon and Schneiders were probably right. The optics of the speech were wrong. Nevertheless, in the immediate aftermath of the speech, all of the president's doubting aides felt pleasantly surprised that it seemed to have worked. When Carter rose from his Oval Office desk and walked over to the Roosevelt Room, he was greeted by Eizenstat, Jordan, and others with a standing ovation. Their euphoria would not last long.

Chapter 18
"You Should Fire People"

I was the fool who came up with that idea.
—GERALD RAFSHOON

Paul Volcker, Carter, and G. William Miller
ASSOCIATED PRESS

EARLY ON THE morning of Tuesday, July 17, 1979, Carter unexpectedly showed up at the regular meeting of senior White House staff in the Roosevelt Room. Stu Eizenstat was shocked by what happened next. The president sat down and, speaking in what Eizenstat thought were "uncharacteristically blunt" terms, observed, "We have defects that need to be resolved." At Camp David, he said, he had "heard a lot of criticism of the White House staff: that we lack cohesion, that there is too much fragmentation, that there is excessive sniping at the cabinet." He acknowledged that he had also heard criticism of his own management style: He was too deeply involved in minor details. Consequently, he had decided to appoint Ham Jordan as chief of staff, "with extraordinary power over you. . . . Ham will not be a peer of yours as before. You will carry out Ham's orders, and if he believes someone should be replaced, he'll talk with you; and if he says you're gone or your assistants are gone then you are." Eizenstat was stunned and later wrote in his biography, *President Carter,* "In all the years I had worked closely with him, I had never heard such a sharp tone."

Carter then surprised everyone by saying, almost as an afterthought, "I may ask all of the cabinet for pro forma resignations." He left quickly, before anyone had a moment to register their concerns. Mondale's chief of staff, Richard Moe, was sitting next to the president, and he too was startled by the announcement. He recalled overhearing a discussion of cabinet resignations when he walked into a senior staff meeting ten days earlier at Camp David—and he felt annoyed that he and Mondale had not been consulted. Moe quickly went to find Jordan and encountered him outside his office in the West Wing. He bluntly told Jordan that it was a "mistake," and one that would shake the country's confidence. Jordan responded strongly, and the two men exchanged the "harshest words" of their friendship. Jordan made it clear that the decision was done.

Not more than forty minutes later, the president met with his cabinet, accompanied by Jordan. Everyone noticed that Ham was wearing a blue suit and tie instead of his usual khakis. Carter announced Ham's elevation as chief of staff and said something about dismissing cabinet officers who had been "disloyal." There is some confusion about what was said next. The president's diary entry for that day painted a benign picture: "They [the cabinet members] reached a consensus that all would resign orally, since they served at my pleasure anyway, and all seemed pleased with this arrangement." This was somewhat disingenuous. Everyone else in the room thought they heard Carter asking for written letters of resignation. Secretary Vance may have said something about how every cabinet member serves at the pleasure of the president—so there was no need for everyone to offer their resignations. The president, he said, should simply ask for the resignations of those he wished to fire. Ham Jordan later claimed that Vance had volunteered, "Maybe we should offer our resignations, so you'll be in the posture of just accepting some resignations, like you're just starting all over again."

In any case, Eizenstat reported that Carter left the cabinet meeting only after asking for and receiving everyone's resignations. It was a stunning development. HEW Secretary Joe Califano turned to Treasury Secretary Michael Blumenthal and remarked, "All hell's going to break loose." Actually, Carter had for days if not weeks determined that he wanted to replace just a handful of his cabinet officers. Eizenstat had noted in one of his yellow legal pads that in their July 5 Camp David meeting Rosalynn Carter had quietly but firmly told her husband, "You should fire people who are disloyal or no good."

Rosalynn had in mind Califano, who she thought was lobbying against the administration's efforts to establish a new Department of Education. Califano had also annoyed Rosalynn by seeming to be unresponsive to her suggestions about mental health policy. The president himself was fed up with Califano. The final straw may have been an "eyes only" letter from the U.S. ambassador in Sweden, reporting that Califano was "sashaying around the world (China, Scandinavia, Switzerland)" using an Air Force plane for a party of twenty-three aides, press, and his two sons. The ambassador complained that "his demands are both pretentious and excessive." Jordan shared a copy of the letter with Kirbo, who promptly sent it to Carter with a note saying, "I thought we were past Joe but this shakes me up." Carter agreed, and he also knew that Jordan and Powell suspected Califano had leaked numerous stories over the past few years to his former employer, *Washington Post* publisher Katharine Graham. Califano might be effective, but he was disloyal.

Carter nevertheless did not relish the idea of firing anyone. His media adviser, Jerry Rafshoon, knew this. And so too did Jordan. But it was Rafshoon who came up with the gimmick of a symbolic mass resignation. "I was the fool who came up with that idea," Rafshoon confessed many years later. "I threw the idea at him." He told Jordan that he thought they needed to do "something dramatic." He also felt that a mass resignation was "the only way you could get Jimmy Carter to fire somebody." Jordan seized on Rafshoon's idea and passed it on to the president. "We were trying to get him to fire Califano and Blumenthal," recalled Rafshoon. Jordan, Powell, and Rafshoon all had it in for Califano, whom they regarded as arrogant and disloyal. But they also wanted Blumenthal and Schlesinger out. The energy secretary in particular had become a lightning rod for criticism of the administration's energy policies.

That afternoon, Eizenstat met with the president, Jordan, and Powell.

Carter said he had already accepted Schlesinger's resignation. In fact, the energy secretary had tried to resign earlier but had been rebuffed. Schlesinger wanted to leave. He knew he was unpopular, both inside the White House and among congressional liberals. He was done.

But Califano was a different story. Eizenstat warned Carter that if he accepted Califano's resignation, "he'll cut you up with his Washington connections."

"I am being cut up anyway," Carter responded.

Eizenstat also defended Blumenthal. But the straitlaced treasury secretary had not made any friends in the White House. And he had annoyed the president with his conservative views on tax reform, particularly on the question of capital gains taxation. Jordan, Powell, Rafshoon, and even Fritz Mondale thought it was time for Blumenthal to step aside, together with Califano and Schlesinger. Carter agreed, but he nevertheless "dreaded this duty." That evening he called Kirbo at 10:01 and chatted for seven minutes. Kirbo always had a way of reassuring his old friend.

The next day the president fired a handful of cabinet officers. He met with Califano for twenty minutes in the late afternoon of July 18 and told him the news. Califano was shocked at his firing. He thought the president still needed his services.

That same evening, Carter spoke on the phone with Schlesinger—who was actually relieved to be on his way out. Similarly, Blumenthal took his dismissal with equanimity. Carter also accepted Attorney General Griffin Bell's resignation; Judge Bell had already told the president of his firm desire to leave office by the summer of 1979. Bell was only unhappy that his departure now had the appearance of a firing. Carter felt a "slight distrust" about Bell's loyalty to him. Bell was Rosalynn's cousin. But despite this family connection, they had occasional policy disagreements, sparring, for instance, about judicial selections pertaining to Carter's commitment to women and Black appointments.

Another issue arose from the formulation of the administration's amicus brief requested by the Supreme Court in *Regents of the University of California v. Bakke,* a seminal case on the constitutionality of affirmative action. Back in September 1977, Bell had circulated an early draft of an amicus curiae brief in support of Allan Bakke, a Caucasian man whose application for medical school had been rejected by the University of

California at Davis. Bakke had filed suit, charging discrimination. The draft, considered a working document, was prepared by Solicitor General Wade McCree, a former judge on the Sixth Circuit, and Drew Days, who was head of the DOJ's Civil Rights Division. Early in his career, Day had served with the NAACP's Legal Defense Fund, and later he became President Clinton's solicitor general. Stuart Eizenstat and Hamilton Jordan jumped on the political implications of Bell's brief, arguing that African Americans would perceive it as an abandonment of affirmative action if Bakke won.

Initially, Bell reasoned that the Justice Department could support Bakke's particular suit under the facts stipulated by the university regents and still favor affirmative action as a policy matter. Jordan alerted Carter to the issue with a strongly worded memo—and after reading the draft brief, Carter told Eizenstat that "it was not well done." Carter wholly grasped the legal and political dilemmas: "We can't go with quotas, and decisions have to be based on the merits of the students." On the other hand, he believed "race could be a factor, but not the exclusive factor."

When Bell was alerted to the White House's concerns, he pointed out that he had delegated the writing of the amicus brief to Wade McCree, his solicitor general and the "best black lawyer in America," and Drew S. Days III, the first Black to head the Civil Rights Division. Not surprisingly, this early draft of the amicus brief leaked, and the Carter White House got an earful of criticism from members of the Congressional Black Caucus. Carter had to call Bell into the Oval Office and explain that his administration's position was to support affirmative action—but without any explicit quotas. Bell readily agreed to continue to work on the brief with McCree and Days. Bell called both men, whose nearby offices were on the same floor of the Justice Department, and told them, "I want the two of you to go into the room with one assistant each, close the door, and I want you to come out with a brief, and don't let anyone interrupt you; don't take any calls."

McCree and Days emerged with a strong brief that both Carter and Bell thought would stand up to time. They were right. But the whole affair had left Carter uneasy about Bell's political judgment. The *Bakke* brief controversy blew over that autumn, and in June 1978 the Supreme Court upheld the administration's position in a landmark decision.

Bakke got to go to medical school, but affirmative action programs survived. Carter considered it a victory for the administration and for the principle of affirmative action.

In any case, by the summer of 1979, Bell was eager to resign. He thought he had achieved Carter's main goal for the Justice Department—to restore the morale and professionalism at the Justice Department that had been shaken by the Watergate scandal.

Carter was undecided on only one more cabinet officer—Transportation Secretary Brock Adams. Jordan had found Adams less than an enthusiastic supporter of the president's position on airline deregulation and automobile fuel standards—and he was annoyed that the secretary refused to allow the White House to vet his deputy. When Carter nevertheless asked Adams to remain, the secretary hesitated and then insisted that he had to be able to appoint his own deputy. Carter sighed and told Adams he should resign.

It was done. Five cabinet members were gone—Bell, Schlesinger, Adams, Blumenthal, and Califano. But only the last three were leaving unhappily. Carter immediately focused on their replacements. Bell was quickly superseded by his deputy, Benjamin Civiletti.

Oddly enough, for a brief moment, Carter seriously considered appointing David Rockefeller as his treasury secretary. He had the banker fly down from New York on July 18, and they met upstairs in the private residence for nearly forty-five minutes that morning. It was an awkward encounter. Carter had been annoyed with the Chase Manhattan Bank chairman all spring due to his pestering him about giving the shah of Iran asylum. Despite this, Carter realized from his Trilateral Commission days that recruiting a Rockefeller to his cabinet had a certain cachet. But when he began sounding out the banker about the treasury position, Rockefeller interrupted with a string of questions. It was "as though he was interviewing me for a job," Carter noted with irritation. The two men ended the meeting without coming to a decision. But soon afterward, Carter told Ham Jordan to call Rockefeller and tell him that "it would be better for him not to serve in the Treasury Department." So that was the end of that outreach. The whole exchange did nothing to smooth over their relationship.

That same morning of July 19, 1979, *The New York Times* ran a front-page story reporting that Jordan had been named chief of staff. Just below was another article headlined "Edgy Capital Sifting Rumors on Shake-up." People were bewildered by the reported cabinet purge. "It's unprecedented and couldn't come at a worse time," Senator Henry Jackson told reporters. The *Times* quoted one unnamed White House official as saying, "Armageddon happened yesterday. He really did it." Another official told the *Times,* "The whole thing is unbelievable. It boggles the mind. At least Nixon did it after an election." Indeed, Nixon had asked for the resignations of his entire cabinet the day after he won reelection in November 1972. So actually, what Carter had done wasn't unprecedented. Cabinet changes in any administration are common, not atypical. Nevertheless, the manner in which these five resignations were announced caused a media storm. Lesley Stahl of CBS News labeled the firings a "slaughterhouse, a purge."

The reaction from Congress was also critical. "Everyone around here is very, very disgusted," said Congressman Benjamin Rosenthal, a New York Democrat. "I'm genuinely worried about the stability of the country. What he wants—team players—is a legitimate element, but the destruction of confidence in our Government is hardly worth it." *Time* magazine observed, "The President basked in the applause" of his July 15 speech "for a day and then, on Tuesday morning, he set in motion his astounding purge, undoing much of the good he had done himself." Indeed, by the end of July, a Lou Harris/ABC News poll placed Carter's approval rating at 25 percent—exactly where it had been prior to his mountain retreat.

Carter later admitted in his memoirs, "I handled the Cabinet changes very poorly." Jordan told Eizenstat that the mass resignations were a "bad idea." Rafshoon agreed, telling Eizenstat, "It was really a case of everybody being tired and panicked."

THE CAMP DAVID domestic summit was an extraordinary affair in presidential introspection. No other president before or since has subjected himself to such a self-critical exercise. It could only have happened with this president's peculiar blend of intellectual curiosity, self-confidence, and religiosity. Camp David was his odd way of compensating for his greatest sin—an overweening pride and confidence in his own intelligence. Ironically, the president came down from the mountain with even greater self-confidence and a steely determination to enforce his will and command loyalty from his political team.

In retrospect, the July cabinet changes marred what had been achieved in an intellectual sense at Camp David. But it is also true that the cabinet firings were blown all out of proportion. There wasn't exactly a "mass firing," just a long-anticipated cabinet shuffle. Only Califano made a public stink about his removal. But in doing so he underscored his partisan political loyalty to Senator Kennedy, whom everyone expected to challenge Carter. Califano insisted that when the president fired him, he had also praised him for doing a "superb" job. This stirred the pot, and by the end of the week Jody Powell was calling Califano a liar. In the end, it was all petty politics. Carter and his Georgia boys knew they were the outsiders in the nation's capital. The president was still routinely referring to Washington as an "island." But they were also proud of their status as outliers— and even argued that their greatest achievements had so far come from ignoring the advice they received from Washington's establishment. Powell summed it up pretty adroitly for *The New Yorker*'s Elizabeth Drew: "There's no doubt that we needed and still need advice from people more experienced in the comings and goings and ins and outs of Washington than we are; on the other hand, if you look at the positive things this Administration will be remembered for, most times their advice was not to do them." Powell was thinking of the Camp David Accords, the Panama Canal Treaty, and the human rights focus on foreign policy. But in retrospect, he could also have listed the administration's struggle to deregulate natural gas and develop alternative energy sources.

But at the time, none of this mattered. Both the "malaise" speech and the cabinet firings became deeply woven into a negative narrative. "The past two weeks will be remembered," wrote the editors of the neoliberal *New Republic*, "as the period when President Jimmy Carter packed it in, put the finishing touches on a failed presidency."

The "malaise" speech was certainly a marker, perhaps a turning point, in the Carter presidency, but the critics were way too premature with their obituaries. Carter was far from done.

IT WAS NOT understood at the time, but the most significant consequence of the cabinet firings was the elevation of Paul Volcker to head

the Federal Reserve. Miffed by David Rockefeller's insouciance, an attitude Carter thought arrogant, the president quickly offered the Treasury
post to G. William Miller, a former Textron executive. Miller agreed to
leave his post as chair of the Federal Reserve to take the Treasury post.
But that meant Carter now had to find someone to replace Miller at the
Fed. Inflation was then running at 13 percent, and Carter thought he had
to make a Fed appointment that would send a strong message to the
markets.

Not having a suitable candidate in mind, Carter and Jordan asked
Mondale's chief of staff, Richard Moe, to make some exploratory calls.
Moe quickly got on the phone, soliciting names from a long list of bankers, businessmen, and economists. "I remember spending a whole weekend at the White House making phone calls," Moe recalled. "It's amazing
how quickly you can get people on the phone when you're using the
White House operator." Fifty-two-year-old Paul Volcker quickly rose to
the top of almost everyone's list. A Princeton graduate, Volcker had
written his senior thesis on the Federal Reserve's failure to curb inflation
during World War II. He went on to a banking career, and in 1975 he had
been appointed president of the Federal Reserve Bank of New York,
where he established a reputation for being a fiscal conservative. Moe
was impressed by Volcker's credentials. "But two or three people advised
me," he recalled, "that we should really know that Volcker was not a
team player." Moe nevertheless sent Carter a memo on Sunday night,
reporting that Volcker seemed to be a favorite on most everyone's list.

On Monday, the president instructed Miller to call Volcker and arrange for the banker to be in the Oval Office on Tuesday at 2:30 P.M.
Volcker agreed to take the air shuttle the next day. Literally five minutes
before the scheduled appointment, Moe ran into Miller and mentioned
that he was worried about Volcker not being a team player. Miller asked
him if Moe had put this in his memo to Carter. When Moe said no,
Miller hastily walked Moe into the president's private office, and they
quickly conveyed their concerns to the president. Carter asked if there
was another candidate. Moe mentioned Alden W. "Tom" Clausen, the
president of Bank of America. There was no time for further discussion,
because at that moment Volcker walked into the Oval Office, accompanied by Miller. The six-foot-seven-inch banker towered over the presi-

dent. Clutching an unlit cigar, Volcker spread his large frame across the couch. "Volcker was sitting," Carter later recalled to Eizenstat, "almost lying down in the couch, which was not the normal posture for any visitor to a president. . . . He acted like he was in his own living room, and he was entertaining a janitor rather than talking to the president of the United States."

On the plane down from New York, Volcker had scribbled down three points on the back of an old prescription note: First, he felt strongly about the Fed's independence; second, he thought inflation had to be quashed "head-on." And third, "I would advocate tighter policies than Miller."

Volcker wasted no time making his points. "Mr. President, let me tell you now, I think we need to do some things with the economy that are not going to be popular at all." He would not accept the Fed position if the White House intended to interfere with his actions.

Carter replied, "I need to get somebody in here who will take care of the economy—let me take care of the politics." The president thought Volcker seemed "intelligent, highly trained, very experienced." Carter was also pleasantly surprised to learn that he was a Democrat. Still, the meeting ended after twenty-five minutes without the president offering him the job. Volcker left thinking he had talked too much. That night, he told his two closest friends over dinner, "I just blew any chance of becoming Fed chair."

There was considerable dissension inside the White House over the impending nomination. Bert Lance passed a message through Jerry Rafshoon: "I want you to tell him [Carter] something from me. He should not appoint Paul Volcker. If he appoints Volcker, he will be mortgaging his reelection to the Federal Reserve."

Mondale was also opposed to Volcker. The vice president feared that Volcker's predilection for tough monetary policies would cause an unnecessary recession. Carter was impressed by Volcker's bluntness. But the large man's gruff demeanor must have also given him pause, because late that afternoon Carter called Tom Clausen and got him on the phone from his Bank of America headquarters in San Francisco. Carter asked the banker if he'd be interested in becoming the new Fed chairman. Clausen replied, "Well, let me ask my wife." He then actually put the president on hold. When he came back on the line a minute later, Clausen said, "No, it's not good timing." Nonplussed, Carter hung up and told Moe and Miller that he was ready to offer the job to Volcker.

The following morning, Carter was roused by his usual wake-up call at 5:30. He was in the Oval Office thirty-five minutes later and spent the next hour and a half alone, reading memos and the newspapers. He waited until 7:38 A.M. before placing a call to Volcker in New York and offering him the Fed chairmanship. Volcker was still in bed, barely awake, but he managed to collect his thoughts and accept. The nomination was announced that day, July 25, and after a quick Senate confirmation hearing, Volcker was sworn in on August 6. Ten days later, Volcker's Federal Reserve raised the Treasury's discount rate by half a percentage point, to an unprecedented 10.5 percent. This was only the beginning of Volcker's attack on inflation.

On September 18, 1979, the Fed voted yet again to raise the discount rate. But when the markets still failed to respond, Carter himself asked Volcker, "Isn't there any way you can control the quantity of money supply without raising interest rates so much?" Volcker was not a Milton Friedman monetarist—he did not believe that the supply of money in circulation was the only factor in dictating prices—but the president's comment got him thinking that perhaps a little "practical monetarism" would reset the market's inflationary expectations.

Just three weeks later, on October 6, Volcker struck again. The Fed increased the discount rate by a full percentage point, to 12 percent. But the real news was that for the first time the Fed announced that it was also imposing strict limits on the quantity of money. Commercial banks would be required to set aside more of their deposits as reserves—and the Treasury would simply be printing fewer greenbacks. Very quickly the prime lending rate rose to an astonishing 21.5 percent, and mortgage interest rates ballooned to 18 percent.

Initially, such punishing interest rates and a throttling down on the money supply failed to quash the inflation beast. Volcker was unmoved, and despite the political costs, Carter refused to criticize his Fed chief or make any move to restrain his harsh medicine. Many in Carter's inner circle complained about the political damage being done to the president by Volcker's actions. Eizenstat thought Volcker's strategy of focusing on the money supply and letting interest rates fluctuate was a huge mistake: "We had to live with that for the rest of the term." Nearly a year later, on the eve of the 1980 election, Volcker told the president that he was about to raise the discount rate once again. Out on the campaign trail, Carter allowed himself a mild criticism of the Fed's policies as "ill-advised." But privately, Carter noted in his diary, "This will hurt us politically, but I think it's the right thing to do." It would also cost the nation some 2.4 million manufacturing jobs.

Volcker's policies would eventually break the inflationary cycle of psychological expectations, but it would take three or even four years—time Carter did not have. "I always give him a lot of credit in my mind," Volcker later told Eizenstat. "I may be the only person in the United States who appreciates that he sat there as much as he did and took a lot of guff on monetary policy." Hiring Volcker was an act of presidential courage—but no one recognized it at the time.

Chapter 19
Foreign Policy Imbroglios

I have concluded that we should attempt to achieve normalization of our relations with Cuba.

—PRESIDENT JIMMY CARTER

Patt Derian
RICARDO CEPPI/GETTY IMAGES

L IKE ALL MEN who have occupied the Oval Office, Carter was learning that presidential power has its limits. This was true on the foreign policy ledger as well as in domestic affairs. And while his advisers kept telling him to pay more attention to domestic issues, like most presidents, he found himself filling his calendar with foreign affairs. These issues seemed more pressing, and there was at least an illusion that he could exercise consequential power. But in reality, presidents are just as much victims of events abroad as they are at home. Things happened and Carter often found himself reacting in the moment, trying to juggle events.

Early in his administration, Carter inherited a tangled investigation of an act of terrorism carried out by Chilean secret police just a mile from the White House. On September 21, 1976, just six weeks prior to Carter's election, Orlando Letelier, once the foreign minister of Chile, was driving to his office at the Institute for Policy Studies, a left-wing think tank in downtown Washington, DC. Sitting in the passenger seat was Ronni Karpen Moffitt, a twenty-five-year-old fundraising coordinator for the institute. Her husband, Michael Moffitt, an economist, was sitting in the backseat.

Cruising past the Chilean embassy, Letelier was easing the car into Sheridan Circle when Michael Moffitt heard a hissing sound, "like a hot wire being placed in cold water." He then saw a flash of light over his wife's head and heard the deafening roar of an explosion. The car was lifted into the air and came crashing down to the curbside in front of the Romanian embassy. When Michael crawled out of the burning car, he saw Ronni stumbling away, so he turned to find Letelier. "There was a huge hole in the car," Moffitt later told John Dinges and Saul Landau, the authors of a book about the assassination. "Orlando was turned around, facing the back of the car. . . . He was moving his head back and forth." Moffitt tried to pull him from the wreckage. "I looked down and I could see bare flesh, the bottom half of his body blown off." Letelier died before he could be transported to a hospital. Ronni Moffitt drowned in her own blood, her carotid artery severed by shrapnel.

The Justice Department quickly assigned an assistant U.S. attorney, Eugene M. Propper, to investigate what was obviously an assassination of a prominent Chilean dissident. Letelier had served not only as foreign minister but also as the Chilean ambassador to the United States during the presidential term of Salvador Allende, an outspoken socialist who had been elected president in 1970. Allende was ousted in a coup by General Augusto Pinochet on September 11, 1973. Letelier was imprisoned on Dawson Island for a full year, but due to his prominence, he was released and expelled in September 1974. Five months later, he landed in Washington, where he became a prominent and articulate critic of the Pinochet regime.

President Carter had fully backed the Justice Department investigation into the Sheridan Circle murders. Not surprisingly, the Pinochet regime did everything it could to stonewall the investigation. But by

March 1978, Justice Department investigators were able to identify two
agents of the Chilean Directorate of National Intelligence (DINA) as
prime suspects. One such DINA agent, Michael Townley, was actually
an American citizen married to a Chilean.

Carter's ambassador in Chile, George Landau, bluntly told the Chileans that normal diplomatic relations depended on Townley's extradition. Negotiations ensued and on April 8, 1978, Townley found himself
in handcuffs on a plane bound for America. He quickly made a plea
deal, and in exchange for telling all he knew about the Letelier assassination, he was promised a sentence of no more than ten years in prison.
Townley confessed that he had personally slid under Letelier's car and
affixed a powerful plastic explosive beneath the driver's seat. He also
named the man who had ordered the mission, DINA chief Manuel Contreras. And he implicated a handful of anti-Castro Cuban exiles who
had assisted him in the assassination. A year later, Townley and two of
his Cuban American accomplices were convicted of the murders. Townley received a ten-year sentence—though he was later paroled after serving only sixty-two months in prison and then released under the federal
witness protection program and given a new identity.

But while Townley was still in prison, the Carter administration demanded the extradition of Chile's intelligence chief, Contreras. In response, General Pinochet's government insisted that the Chilean courts
would handle the case. Predictably, on October 1, 1979, the Chilean Supreme Court formally denied Washington's request for the extradition
of Contreras and two other Chilean army officers.

The decision precipitated a fierce debate inside the Carter administration about how to respond to this blatant defiance. Assistant Secretary of State Patt Derian suggested recalling the U.S. ambassador and
imposing stiff economic sanctions. Brzezinski's NSC aide, Robert Pastor, opposed such retaliatory measures, asking, "By what right can the
U.S. State Department judge another government's laws and court?" Assistant Secretary of State for Inter-American Affairs Viron P. Vaky similarly argued that the United States could not accuse the Chilean
government of having committed an act of terrorism in Washington.
Derian thought this was ridiculous, since the American courts had already convicted Townley and his accomplices of the murders. Townley
was employed by the Chilean intelligence service, so "the secret police of

Chile were responsible for the assassination.... We therefore not only can but should make that assertion." Derian was furious and warned Secretary of State Vance that the Pinochet regime would realize that "we were not serious" if Washington failed to impose sanctions.

In the end, Derian got her way, but only symbolically. Carter made it clear that he "did not wish to break relations." But on November 30, 1979, the president ordered a reduction in the size of the U.S. embassy in Chile, the termination of military sales, a "phasing down" of the U.S. military mission, and a suspension of Export-Import Bank financing. The State Department issued a statement calling Letelier's assassination an "egregious act of international terrorism" and insisted that the Chilean military regime had, "in effect, condoned this act of international terrorism." Such plainspoken language was a rare occurrence in diplomatic circles, but it did nothing to change Pinochet's behavior. *The Washington Post* reported that the Carter administration's sanctions amounted to "little more than a wrist slap."

Liberals thought Carter's response to Chile's defiance was tepid, but he was also taking heat from Republican critics for imposing any sanctions at all on a right-wing, anticommunist regime. Months later, Congressman Henry Hyde (R-IL) came to the Oval Office to complain that U.S. efforts to persuade the Chilean government to put on trial the Letelier assassins was like "the U.S. putting J. Edgar Hoover on trial ... and we shouldn't have expected the Chileans to do it either." Carter remonstrated that the "assassination of Letelier and an innocent American person was a terrible and unconscionable act, which took place in the streets of Washington, our capital." Hyde was unconvinced and said that he could not "believe that Pinochet approved such" an assassination.

In fact, CIA officers had briefed Carter's aide Robert Pastor in late 1978 and told him that they had concluded that Pinochet had personally ordered the assassination. Pinochet viewed Letelier as a major threat. The Chilean dictator thought the articulate dissident was using his platform in a Washington think tank to delegitimize Pinochet's regime. And perhaps he thought the assurances of support he had received from Henry Kissinger in 1976 meant that the Americans would not seriously investigate the assassination of a Chilean dissident just miles from the White House. Pinochet clearly miscalculated. What he had ordered was an outrage that could not be ignored. Bob Pastor must have conveyed this critical intelligence to Carter—but the president nevertheless decided he could not use this information to publicly accuse another head of state of murder.

In retrospect, Carter never got the credit he deserved for solving the crime and imposing sanctions on Chile. His Justice Department successfully demanded the extradition of key suspects and convicted them in a U.S. court. He could have also taken the radical step of releasing the CIA's intelligence implicating Pinochet personally in this act of terrorism on American soil—and that might very well have accelerated Chile's return to democracy. But this was an imponderable. Patt Derian and her community of human rights activists clearly thought Carter could have done more. And Washington's national security establishment thought he had already gone too far in pressing the case. Once again, Carter had managed to alienate both the Left and the Right.*

PINOCHET'S CHILE WAS not the only dictatorship in Latin America. In the mid-1970s, nearly all of Central and South America was ruled by autocrats. A decade later, a dozen of these regimes had transitioned to some degree of democratic rule. Carter's human rights diplomacy certainly played a role in this trend toward popularly elected regimes. But it was a difficult road—and none more so than in Nicaragua. This Central American country of a little more than three million people had been ruled by the Somoza family dynasty since 1937. The Somozas owned much of the country's wealth, and corruption was rampant.

By 1977, Anastasio Somoza Debayle had exercised dictatorial powers for a decade, relying heavily on his control of the National Guard— a military institution financed and trained by the United States. Needless to say, Carter viewed Somoza's abysmal human rights record with distaste. When in early 1978 Somoza's thugs assassinated the country's leading newspaper editor, Pedro Joaquín Chamorro, riots and a general strike virtually shut down the country for two days. In response to months of repression, the Carter administration eventually cut off aid to

---

* In 1987 the CIA reassessed the Letelier assassination and presented "what we regard as convincing evidence that President Pinochet personally ordered his intelligence chief to carry out the murders." The CIA report also confirmed that "Pinochet decided to stonewall on the US investigation to hide his involvement."

Somoza's National Guard in February 1979, pressured the suspension of World Bank loans, and urged the dictator to hold elections or at least bring into his government moderate elements of the opposition. Somoza refused. An armed insurgency spearheaded by the left-wing Sandinista National Liberation Front made rapid gains in the countryside.

By the early summer of 1979, the Sandinistas controlled most of the country outside the capital city of Managua. Carter's State Department and CIA knew that the Sandinistas were receiving arms and financial support from Castro's Cuba as well as Panama's left-wing military strongman, General Omar Torrijos. By mid-June 1979, State Department advisers were telling the president that "the question was not if Somoza will fall, but when and under what circumstances." David Newsom, under secretary for political affairs, remarked that "Somoza has alienated so many people that he has given anti-Communism a bad name."

Resigned to the reality of a Sandinista victory, Carter's advisers—led by Brzezinski—nevertheless argued that perhaps renewed aid to the National Guard could bolster moderate political forces inside the revolutionary regime. Brzezinski specifically recommended talking to another Nicaraguan general about "creating an alternative to Somoza." Brzezinski wanted to tell this general that if Somoza "agrees to step down, we will assure sufficient support to the National Guard to guarantee stability during this transitional process." This was the same advice Brzezinski had given Carter six months earlier during the Iranian revolution. Brzezinski knew little about Nicaragua. The United States had aligned itself for decades with the reactionary Somoza regime, and now it was entirely too late in the game for Washington to have much influence over the outcome.

Carter must have sensed the unreality of the advice he was being offered, because instead of authorizing the aid, he wrote in the margins of the Brzezinski memo, "Ok, but before we provide support to the National Guard, the transitional governing group who controls the Guard must be determined by me to be legitimized by adequate support from OAS [Organization of American States] members or by Nicaraguan people."

The president was not going to be snookered into supporting what could have amounted to a military coup. Secretary Cyrus Vance nevertheless was authorized to meet with an exiled Nicaraguan general; they discussed his possible participation in a post-Somoza provisional government. But by June 28, the U.S. ambassador in Nicaragua had secured Somoza's agreement that he was prepared to resign and was reporting that bringing the exiled general [Julio Gutiérrez] "into play looks like too much of a long shot at this point. Besides, I learned here that his reputation among opposition groups is not repeat not good. I think a more fruitful course of action would be to encourage the contacts between FSLN (Sandinista National Liberation Front) elements and the Guardia Nacional elements to begin the negotiations of a cease-fire." Even this gambit proved unrealistic.

Nevertheless, Brzezinski refused to dismiss the possibility of a non-Sandinista "executive committee" taking Somoza's place. His State Department counterparts thought he was simply ignoring the facts on the ground. As late as July 10, Brzezinski and his national security team were urging a delay of Somoza's early departure "on the grounds that the U.S. would be seen as the 'midwife' of a radical regime in Central America." Deputy Secretary of State Warren Christopher countered that Washington "would be blamed for leaving Somoza in power and prolonging the bloodshed, while some credit could be won by precipitating his departure." As usual, the State Department's position proved to be more realistic. Somoza finally fled the country on July 17, making way for the Sandinista junta to assume power on July 20 in a ceremony attended in downtown Managua by a jubilant crowd of 75,000 people. One member of the Sandinista junta, Daniel Ortega, gave a speech reminding the crowd that the Yankees had installed the Somozas in power, supported them for decades, and now had finally played a role in forcing the last Somoza to leave. Ortega suggested it was now time for Nicaragua to be left alone to govern itself.

Carter agreed in principle, but, pushed by his advisers, he also took the precaution of signing a presidential finding authorizing a covert CIA program to "assist democratic elements in Nicaragua to resist efforts of Cuban supported and other Marxist groups to consolidate power." Simultaneously, Carter authorized humanitarian aid to the revolutionary regime, hoping to keep the door open to a working relationship with the Sandinistas.

The revolutionaries clearly had the overwhelming support of the Nicaraguan people. Therefore, there was nothing the Carter administration could have done to prevent a Sandinista victory. But his critics on the right would nevertheless blame the president in the years ahead for facilitating the rise of a left-wing regime. Jeane J. Kirkpatrick, a Georgetown University professor, skewered the Carter administration in a widely read *Commentary* essay in November 1979 for turning Nicaragua into a second Cuba. In both Iran and Nicaragua, Kirkpatrick argued, "the Carter administration not only failed to prevent the undesired outcome, it actively collaborated in the replacement of moderate autocrats friendly to American interests with less friendly autocrats of extremist persuasion." The charge was ahistorical and simplistic in the extreme, but it nevertheless resonated in neoconservative political circles.

CARTER'S NEOCONSERVATIVE CRITICS would have been further outraged if they had known the full extent of his secret diplomacy with Cuba's Fidel Castro. Less than two months after taking office, Carter signed a presidential directive informing Secretary of State Cy Vance and other officials, "I have concluded that we should attempt to achieve normalization of our relations with Cuba."

Carter was by no means naïve about the authoritarian nature of Castro's regime. But he thought that after nearly seventeen years of economic embargo, perhaps it was time to try some diplomacy. Ending the regime's trade and cultural isolation, he reasoned, might lead to internal liberalization. By the end of March 1977, high-level negotiations were taking place in New York and Havana hotel rooms, shrouded in secrecy. "The second round of talks with the Cubans broke the ice," reported Assistant Secretary of State Terence Todman. In September 1977 both countries agreed to open "interest sections" in their respective capitals—a step short of full diplomatic missions. Negotiations continued fitfully throughout the next few years. Both parties made progress on a host of relatively minor issues—the release of Americans sitting in Cuban prisons, fishing boundaries, and Cuba's agreement to talk in principle about compensation for nationalized U.S. properties worth some $2 billion. (The administration was angling for a settlement worth $600 million.)

Carter exchanged correspondence with Castro, and in early 1978, he sent Paul Austin, chairman of Coca-Cola, as his personal emissary to Havana. Carter told Castro that Austin was a "trusted friend and advisor." In a direct appeal, Carter wrote to Castro, "As you know, I have hoped it would be possible for you and me to move towards full normalization of relations. . . . Mr. Austin has my complete confidence." Austin made a number of highly secret trips into Havana over the next two years, but events had a way of interfering with this private diplomacy.

As negotiations dragged out, a constant sticking point was Cuba's military expedition of nearly twenty thousand Cuban troops and civilian advisers stationed in Angola. Brzezinski argued vociferously that the U.S. economic embargo on Cuba could not be lifted until the Cubans ended their African adventures. State Department spokesman Hodding Carter told the press that given the Cuban intervention in Africa, "it appears we have gone as far as we can at this time." The Cubans exacerbated the situation over the next few months by deploying several thousand troops to support the Marxist regime in Ethiopia in its dispute with Somalia, led at the time by another corrupt military dictator, Mohamed Siad Barre. The Somali dictator had himself provoked the crisis by invading the Ogaden region of Ethiopia, prompting the Soviets to intervene with aid and Cuban troops. This development alarmed Brzezinski, who saw the Cubans as proxies for a growing Soviet threat to East Africa.

Brzezinski wanted Carter to authorize a show of force, specifically by sending an aircraft carrier to the Horn of Africa. Both Secretary Vance and Secretary of Defense Harold Brown opposed this escalation. Vance observed, "We are getting sucked in. The Somalis brought this on themselves. They are no great friends of ours. . . . For us to put our prestige on the line and to take military steps is a risk we should not take." Carter sided with Vance and Brown and refused to send the aircraft carrier. And Brzezinski complained in his private journal, "Everyone otherwise was against me. . . . All of them seem to be badly bitten by the Vietnam bug and as a consequence are fearful of taking the kind of action which is necessary to convey our determination."

Brzezinski was even willing to threaten the Soviets by linking the pending SALT II treaty negotiations to the behavior of the Cuban proxies in Ethiopia. Vance angrily protested that Brzezinski's talk about linking the two issues was undermining congressional support for the SALT II treaty, a goal Vance considered far more important than a minor border war between two impoverished authoritarian regimes in the Horn of

Africa. "We will end up losing SALT," he told Brzezinski, "and that will be the worst thing that could happen. If we do not get a SALT treaty in the President's first four years, that will be a blemish on his record forever." Zbig shot back, "It will be a blemish on his record also if the treaty gets rejected by the Senate."

Relations between Vance and Brzezinski were obviously getting frayed. Zbig always enjoyed a heated argument, but now he noticed for the first time that Cy was getting red in the face and raising his voice with growing impatience. "I could sense," Brzezinski later wrote, "that personal tension was entering our relationship." But Brzezinski was unrepentant. And while he lost this argument with Vance, he continued to badger the president to link passage of the SALT treaty with Soviet behavior in Angola, Zaire, Yemen, and eventually Afghanistan. SALT was never ratified—and Brzezinski would later proudly quip that "SALT lies buried in the sands of the Ogaden."

In retrospect, the linkage doomed SALT, and this was a foolish mistake. At the time, Carter sensed that his headstrong national security adviser had a myopic view of problems like the Nicaraguan revolution, Angola, and other African crises. Brzezinski judged everything through the prism of what he regarded as an unending Cold War with the Soviet Union. Carter did his best to resist Brzezinski's hawkish views, but he never considered firing him. One Sunday he saw Zbig on *Meet the Press* being "abusive against the Soviets—excessively so—and I chastised him about it. He was quite upset."

The president nearly always agreed with Vance's more measured views. Vance was certainly less entertaining, but Carter understood he possessed a gravitas that balanced Brzezinski's conventional Cold War instincts. "Zbig is too competitive and incisive," he noted in his diary in February 1979. "Cy is too easy on his subordinates, and the news media aggravate the inevitable differences." But Carter also knew he was contributing to the institutional rivalry: "I hardly know the desk officers in State but work very closely with the NSC people."

Brzezinski's animosity toward Castro's Cuba also undermined Carter's early efforts to normalize relations with the communist regime. By 1978, Carter's overtures to Castro were faltering due to the administration's insistence that Cuba had to bring home its military expeditions from Angola and East Africa. Carter persisted, however, and in early 1980

Brzezinski's deputy, Robert Pastor, flew to Havana for highly secret meetings with the Cuban dictator. Pastor met with Castro for eleven straight hours of "candid" and "cordial" talks. Castro confessed his "embarrassment" at the Soviet invasion of Afghanistan and clearly expressed his desire for some kind of accommodation with the United States. Castro said that he "sees Cuba as the victim of our rivalry with the Soviets rather than as a contributing factor." When pressed about withdrawing Cuban troops from Africa, Castro said he had reduced his forces in Ethiopia by 30 percent, but that "it is easier to go in than get out." When Carter was later shown a "sensitive eyes only" memo on the negotiations, he scribbled in the margins, "Extraordinarily frank and helpful."

And then everything changed when, on March 28, 1980, a group of angry Cubans hijacked a bus in Havana and stormed the Peruvian embassy, killing a guard in the process. The Cuban hijackers then demanded political asylum. Soon some 10,000 other Cubans flooded the Peruvian embassy grounds, also demanding asylum. When the Carter administration offered to take in 3,500 of these Cubans, Castro responded by brazenly announcing that anyone who wished to leave his communist "paradise" could do so by boat from the harbor in Mariel, a small town twenty-five miles west of Havana. Suddenly, hundreds of boats from South Florida manned by anti-Castro Cuban Americans began showing up in Mariel, offering to ferry Cuban refugees to Florida. Castro encouraged the exodus of all these dissidents—and it had been a long-standing U.S. policy to accept any Cuban refugees who reached the Florida coast. Carter was sympathetic to the plight of these refugees, but at the same time he felt compelled to try to persuade Castro to stop the exodus. Castro rebuffed him. Between April and October 1980 an estimated 125,000 Cubans reached Florida shores, including thousands of criminals whom Castro released from Cuban prisons. Carter was unwilling to turn away refugees, and yet the chaotic nature of the boat lift was itself a humanitarian crisis.

In May 1980, he felt compelled to order the U.S. Coast Guard to impose a blockade, and gradually, over the summer, the exodus declined to several thousand a month. Most of the refugees settled in South Florida, but many were farmed out to immigration processing centers in Arkansas, Pennsylvania, and Wisconsin. Not surprisingly, the arrival of so many destitute Spanish-speaking refugees was highly unpopular. For most Americans, Carter appeared helpless and inept in managing the crisis—and most Cuban Americans in the critical electoral state of Florida criticized him for imposing a blockade to stem the exodus. Needless to say, the Mariel boat-lift crisis put a damper on Carter's diplomatic outreach to Castro's regime. Events beyond his control had taken charge and scuttled an innovative foreign policy initiative. Carter was annoyed, and despite everything, he remained determined to change the Cuba-U.S. relationship. As late as September 1980, even in the midst of a highly charged reelection campaign, he sent Austin, Coca-Cola's chairman, back to Havana. On his own initiative, and without Carter's approval, Austin went so far as to suggest to Castro that he and Carter should have a "face to face summit meeting" before Christmas. It was not to be.

CARTER FACED A similar quandary over another refugee crisis—this time in Southeast Asia, involving the Vietnamese "boat people." Small numbers of refugees had trickled out of Vietnam ever since the fall of Saigon in April 1975. But the numbers of Vietnamese smuggling themselves out on small boats began to surge in late 1978. Dealing with this refugee exodus was complicated by the fact that Washington still did not have diplomatic relations with its former enemy. Early in his administration, Carter had signaled his desire to heal the wounds of the long Vietnam War by normalizing diplomatic relations with the Hanoi regime. To this end, he sent Assistant Secretary of State Richard Holbrooke to Paris to negotiate with Hanoi's envoys. To Holbrooke's frustration, the negotiations broke down when the Vietnamese insisted that the Americans needed to provide $5 billion in postwar reconstruction aid to Vietnam—as promised in a secret side letter to the 1973 Paris Accords, signed by President Nixon. When Holbrooke indicated that the $5 billion would never be approved by Congress, the Vietnamese promptly released Nixon's secret letter to the public. This, of course, was embarrassing. Holbrooke's mission ended in failure, and Carter was sorely disappointed.

Not Brzezinski, however, who later wrote Carter a memo saying, "I cannot help suspecting that guilt feelings over the Vietnamese war have something to do with the evident desire of Cy [Vance] and Holbrooke to move on this issue rapidly." Carter sent the memo back with a handwritten note in the margins: "I don't have guilt feelings & I want to move re VNam." Clearly, the president was again annoyed with Brzezinski. But the national security adviser was pushing on the president another one of his geopolitical strategic arguments. Brzezinski's priority now was the push for normalization of diplomatic relations with China—not Vietnam. "You need to choose," he told Carter, "Vietnam or China, and China is incomparably more important to us." Carter disagreed and argued that normalization with both countries were not incompatible goals. "Zbig, you have a tendency to exalt the PRC [People's Republic of China] issue." Brzezinski thought the Vietnamese were in the pockets of the Soviets. And to his mind, events soon proved him correct. In late December 1978, the Vietnamese launched a full-scale invasion of neighboring Cambodia, quickly dislodging the genocidal Khmer Rouge regime from Phnom Penh. One might think this was a good development. Carter had called the Khmer Rouge the "worst violator of human rights in the world today." News of the regime's brutal repression had trickled out, but now we know that Pol Pot and his Khmer Rouge comrades had orchestrated the methodical killing of 1.5 million to 2 million people between 1975 and 1979. Only the Vietnamese invasion brought an end to these "killing fields."

But in Brzezinski's view, Vietnam's unilateral invasion of its neighbor violated international law, and that was all that mattered. Brzezinski was also motivated by geopolitical reasons to tilt against Vietnam and in favor of the Chinese. He persuaded the Carter administration to adopt a narrow, highly legalistic position condemning Vietnamese aggression. This position just happened to accord with China's own view of the invasion. The Chinese continued to send arms and supplies to the remnants of Pol Pot's forces, hiding in the jungles of western Cambodia near the border with Thailand. And then, on February 16, 1979, the Chinese dispatched 170,000 troops to invade northern Vietnam. Carter himself voiced the view that "the Soviet-backed . . . Vietnamese invasion of Cambodia gave the Chinese little choice but to invade Vietnam." How the president could convince himself of this simplistic view is a mystery. Earlier, in fact, he had bluntly warned Chinese leader Deng Xiaoping that an invasion by Chinese forces of Vietnam would be a mistake. Perhaps he was not paying enough attention—or rather, he was completely absorbed by events elsewhere, specifically the Iranian revolution.

In any case, the administration's position on Vietnam and Cambodia became frozen. Washington would insist that the Vietnamese had to withdraw their troops from Cambodia, even though the resulting vacuum would surely give the detestable Khmer Rouge an opportunity to return. Brzezinski drove the policy over objections from Assistant Secretaries Patt Derian and Richard Holbrooke in the State Department. The absolute low point came in September 1979, when the administration voted to give Cambodia's seat in the United Nations to representatives of Pol Pot. Holbrooke was distressed, calling it the "single most difficult thing" he'd ever been asked to do in his diplomatic career. "It ran counter to my private views," he wrote. "But, as a public official, I had to swallow hard." Even Vance went along, acknowledging that most of America's allies in Southeast Asia wanted to censure Vietnam for its aggression.

Carter himself never really explained the muddled decision, only later admitting that "the situation in Cambodia was both disturbing and confusing to us." But the decision to seat the Khmer Rouge at the United Nations smelled of hypocrisy, an embarrassing exception to the president's commitment to human rights and a capitulation to realpolitik. Derian called the decision to seat Pol Pot's representative "incomprehensible." Derian and Holbrooke had fought frequently, and sometimes their arguments turned into shouting matches. Holbrooke's willingness to fall into line with the administration's official position on the Pol Pot UN vote only made their working relationship worse.

On the other hand, Derian was pleased when the administration found a way to step up and respond to the flood of boat people coming out of Southeast Asia in the spring and summer of 1979. Tens of thousands of such refugees were fleeing Vietnam and Cambodia each month, often in small, unseaworthy boats. Many were drowning at sea. Both Derian and Holbrooke pushed the administration to rescue these people. "Are you telling me," Vice President Mondale angrily queried a U.S. admiral, "that we have thousands of people drowning in the open sea, and we have the Seventh Fleet right there, and we can't help them?" Carter made it happen and also agreed to accept many thousands of these refugees into the United States.

He knew this would be politically unpopular. In an effort to build support for a humanitarian response, he sent Rosalynn, accompanied by Holbrooke, on a highly publicized visit to refugee camps in Thailand. "Rosalynn Carter walked through the hospital and orphanage tents of a camp for 30,000 Cambodian refugees today," reported *The New York Times,* "knelt next to the mats on which the sick lie in the sand and declared at the end of her visit, 'It's like nothing I've ever seen.'" She picked up a four-month-old baby boy who weighed only four pounds. He "looked like a tiny monkey." She cuddled for a moment a little girl—who literally expired as Mrs. Carter was walking out of the camp a few minutes later. It was a heartrending experience. Four months later, President Carter signed the Refugee Act of 1980, a signal reform of U.S. immigration laws, to allow a special quota of fifty thousand refugees each year to become American citizens. Over the next decade a million and a half Indo-Chinese refugees were admitted to the country. Many of them had served in the South Vietnamese army and been sentenced as collaborators to "reeducation" camps. Given America's long and bloody legacy from the Vietnam War, providing them sanctuary was the right thing to do—though certainly not a popular decision with many voters.

ON SATURDAY, SEPTEMBER 22, 1979, the president dictated an unusually cryptic one-sentence note in his daily diary: "There was an indication of a nuclear explosion in the region of South Africa—either South Africa, Israel using a ship at sea, or nothing." The note quite accurately reflected the extreme complexity of the intelligence he had received that day. At 6:53 the previous evening (Washington time), a U.S. intelligence Vela satellite—specifically designed to detect nuclear explosions—had logged a highly suspicious double flash of light in the Indian Ocean some 1,400 miles southwest of South Africa. Brzezinski briefed the president for ten minutes the next morning on the alarming but still inconclusive intelligence. He told Carter that the satellite stationed over the South Atlantic Ocean had detected the signature of a nuclear explosion—an initial brief, intense flash of light, followed by a longer flash. The satellite data suggested that a small nuclear device of only two to three kilotons had been detonated. The ten-year-old array of Vela satellites had been deployed to enable the United States to monitor compliance with the 1963 Atmospheric Test Ban Treaty. Vela had successfully detected "every known atmospheric nuclear explosion" over the past decade—a total of forty-one French and Chinese nuclear tests. It was a highly reliable system. This particular event, however, had taken place in one of the most isolated parts of the planet, in midnight darkness on the open seas, halfway between Antarctica and South Africa. In other words, if it was a nuclear event, the perpetrators had obviously hoped to escape detection. Brzezinski told Carter that immediate suspicion had fallen on the apartheid regime in South Africa, but that it might have been an Israeli test of a low-yield nuclear weapon, carried out with the assistance of the South Africans. Both men were well aware of intelligence from the autumn of 1977 suggesting the existence of an "Israeli–South African relationship involving the transfer of technology, equipment, nuclear materials." That Israel could be involved was certainly not out of the question.

Carter instructed Brzezinski to share the information "in strictest confidence" with the two top leaders of the respective congressional intelligence committees, but he added a handwritten warning: "Do not let any allegation leak to public until we are sure of facts. . . . Keep me informed." He and Brzezinski spoke again on the phone later that morning and again in the afternoon. And that evening, they continued their discussions when the Carters, including eleven-year-old Amy, had dinner at the Brzezinski home across the Potomac River in McLean, Virginia. They spent three hours with the Brzezinskis and then motored back to the White House, accompanied by twelve-year-old Mika Brzezinski, who had arranged a sleepover with Amy. It was a rare night out for the Carters.

The next morning, members of the Special Coordinating Committee met in the White House Situation Room and tentatively concluded that "a nuclear explosion (1-3 KT) probably occurred early Saturday morning (South Africa time) in the south Atlantic. . . . South Africa is the most likely candidate." The news circulated to a very few top officials in the State Department, but no one knew what should be done with the intelligence. Hodding Carter III, the assistant secretary of state for public affairs, later told investigative reporter Seymour Hersh, "There was sheer panic. It was very much 'Oh, shit. Oh, dear. What do we do with this?'"

Carter quickly authorized an investigation by a CIA panel of three respected scientists: Harold M. Agnew, former director of the Los Alamos National Laboratory; Richard L. Garwin, a designer of the hydrogen bomb and an IBM scientist at the Watson Laboratory; and Stephen

Lukasik, chief scientist at the RAND Corporation. Their highly classified report concluded on October 10, 1979, that the Vela signals "were consistent with detection of a nuclear explosion in the atmosphere." One of the scientists, Garwin, wrote on October 19, 1979, that he would "bet 2 to 1 in favor" of the incident being a nuclear test. But this was not the certainty some Carter administration officials wanted to hear.

Over the next month the administration began to backpedal on this clear conclusion. "We were in the worst possible position," one government official later told Hersh. The Vela sighting "could only be a nuclear event. Our capturing it fortuitously was an embarrassment, a big political problem, and there were a lot of people who wanted to obscure the event."

Brzezinski and other officials feared that the news was likely to leak—and if they had to confirm that an illegal nuclear test had been carried out, well, that would put them in the awkward position of sanctioning the perpetrators. Brzezinski chaired another meeting in the White House Situation Room and listened silently as various aides debated heatedly about what should be done. "The meeting was going nowhere," recalled NSC staffer Jerry Oplinger. Finally, the president's science adviser, Frank Press, suggested that they set up "an unbiased outside study." Oplinger later told Hersh that Press kept asking, "What do we do if it leaks out that we've concluded it was a test? He [Press] did not want that panel to conclude that there had been a nuclear explosion."

Predictably, news of the Vela incident leaked to the media on October 26, 1979, but by then the White House was ready with an announcement that a high-level panel of scientists led by MIT professor Jack Ruina would investigate the incident. But Press made sure that Ruina's mandate was narrowly focused: to evaluate whether the Vela satellite's data could have resulted from natural phenomena. In other words, they wanted the panel to conclude that it had been a false alarm. And indeed, in January 1980, the Ruina panel put out a preliminary suggestion that perhaps the Vela satellite had merely picked up "the possible reflection of sunlight from a small meteoroid or a piece of space debris passing near the satellite." The Ruina panel's report eventually concluded the following spring that the Vela data "was probably not from a nuclear event." One of the panel members, the famous physicist Wolfgang Panofsky, admitted that this was a "scotch verdict," meaning it was not proven one way or another.

Brzezinski himself later confirmed that he had thought it was politically convenient to muddy the waters: "We knew something happened. We didn't know precisely what happened. We had our suspicions. For political reasons, I think. It wasn't pursued to the very end because it wasn't clear. Suppose we find out, what do we do then?"

And when he was asked, "If it's the Israelis, it becomes even more awkward?" he replied, "Well, that's what I had in mind. Yeah."

Debate over the controversy had become quite heated within the intelligence community. If the Vela incident was a nuclear test, and if it was determined that Israel was responsible, well, that would exacerbate the administration's already difficult relationship with the Israelis. Years later, Leonard Weiss, a mathematician and nonproliferation expert who served as a top aide to Senator John Glenn (D-OH), told the Israeli American historian Avner Cohen that a high-ranking State Department official told him "that if I continue to say that the Vela event was a nuclear test, my reputation would be destroyed." Clearly, the established wisdom was veering toward the convenient conclusion that Vela had detected a nonnuclear event.

Carter himself had reason to believe otherwise, and on February 27, 1980, he noted in his diary, "We have a growing belief among our scientists that the Israelis did indeed conduct a nuclear test explosion in the ocean near the southern end of South Africa." He had been given strong evidence from specific intercept intelligence that the Israelis were responsible. The president also had intelligence from the National Security Agency that a small flotilla of Israeli naval vessels had been in the South Atlantic. Further confirmation had come from his old Naval Academy classmate Admiral Stansfield Turner, who reported that most CIA analysts believed Vela had indeed detected a low-yield nuclear test. That same month, *CBS Evening News* aired a report by one of its correspondents, Dan Raviv, who claimed that he had Israeli sources who confirmed that it had been an Israeli test. The Israeli government accused Raviv of breaking military censorship laws and stripped him of his press credentials.

Further evidence of a nuclear event emerged a few months later when the U.S. Naval Research Laboratory analyzed hydro-acoustic data determined to be "unique to nuclear shots in a maritime environment." Dr. Jack Vorona, the Defense Intelligence Agency's head of science and technology, calculated that the probability of Vela generating data similar to a nuclear "footprint" from lightning or other natural causes was virtually nil. He also cited evidence gathered from the site itself, showing that a deep hole had been discovered in the shallow ocean floor. Dr. Vorona thought the evidence of a nuclear event was definitive, and he flatly asserted that the White House panel's report was a "white wash, due to political considerations."

Carter seems to have been unaware of these dissenting views, but regardless of the Ruina panel's official conclusion, he nevertheless believed Vela had indeed detected a nuclear test. At the time, of course, all the intelligence reports about the incident were highly classified. But he believed the Israelis were responsible—a conclusion that decades later reflects the prevailing view among most scientists and historians. The legendary investigative reporter Seymour Hersh reported in his 1991 book *The Samson Option* that former Israeli government officials told him that the Vela incident was, in fact, the testing of a low-yield nuclear device. As Leonard Weiss wrote in the *Bulletin of the Atomic Scientists* in 2015, "more and more information revealed in various publications over the years strongly supports the premise that a mysterious double flash detected by a US satellite in 1979 was indeed a nuclear test performed by Israel with South African cooperation, in violation of the Limited Test Ban Treaty. The US government, however, found it expedient to brush important evidence under the carpet and pretend the test did not occur."

Carter was in a quandary. If the White House confirmed the initial scientific judgment that it had been an Israeli test, his administration would be under enormous pressure to censure the Israelis. Alternatively, if the administration announced that there had been a surreptitious atmospheric test—but that it could not detect the source—this admission would undermine support for the SALT II treaty. Like all nuclear arms limitation treaties, SALT was supposed to be verifiable. The administration preferred to just sidestep the whole issue, and that was best done by having the Ruina panel issue an inconclusive report, claiming that they could not determine if it had been a nuclear event, let alone whether the Israelis and South Africans had collaborated on the clandestine test. It was an evasion.

When pressed by the Carter White House, the Israeli government had always officially denied that it possessed nuclear weapons. This too was an evasion, and Carter knew it. The Israelis had always intimated to the Americans that they would not publicly test a nuclear device because they did not wish to be the first to introduce nuclear weapons in the Middle East. But now they had crossed that dangerous threshold by actually testing a nuclear weapon. Carter had probable cause to conclude that the Vela satellite had caught the Israelis in yet another lie. But he had already spent considerable political capital pressuring the Israeli prime minister to sign the peace treaty with Egypt. And given the muddled nature of the intelligence his own administration had generated about the Vela incident, Carter knew he could not publicly accuse the Israelis of carrying out a surreptitious test. This annoyed the president, but there was little he could do.

Chapter 20
Much Ado About Nothing

Andy [Young] was not penitent at all, saying he had done what he thought was right.

—JIMMY CARTER, diary, August 15, 1979

Ambassador Andrew Young,
Andrew "Bo" Young, and Carter
GETTY IMAGES

CARTER'S PRESIDENCY, so far, had endured only one relatively minor scandal—the Bert Lance affair—but neither was it a Teflon presidency. Carter missed Lance. He had been a genuine friend and a useful sounding board. Charlie Kirbo still served the same function but from a distance. Hamilton Jordan and Jody Powell were always close, but they were young men, still in their early thirties. The president's spe-

cial assistant for health issues, Dr. Peter Bourne, was something different. At thirty-nine years of age, Bourne was slightly older in years and
far more mature intellectually than the other Georgia boys. He dressed
in stylish three-piece suits and spoke in precise, wholly grammatical
sentences. "Peter was not Jody's and Ham's sort of guy," observed Patrick
Anderson, Carter's speechwriter during the 1976 campaign. "They were
tough-talking South Georgia shitkickers and he [Peter] was a tweedy
intellectual with a flaky English accent. Moreover, his wife, Mary King,
was the kind of hard-charging feminist they considered a royal pain in
the ass." Carter liked Bourne—and Rosalynn thought of him as a friend
but also a mentor. She admired the psychiatrist's work with drug addicts
and had come to rely on him for her work on mental health issues.

"We had a pleasant evening with Peter Bourne and Mary," Carter
noted in his diary on March 10, 1978. Unusually, they had dinner that
evening at the Bourne home, together with one other couple, Mr. and
Mrs. Thomas E. Bryant, the executive director of the President's Commission on Mental Health. "This is the first time since we've been in
Washington that Rosalynn and I have been out together for supper with
friends." This was, of course, a remarkable admission, but Carter was
probably the most private and socially reticent man ever to occupy the
White House. By the spring of 1978 he had turned down more than one
dinner invitation from *Washington Post* publisher Katharine Graham—
but he would dine out at the residence of his psychiatrist friend. Back in
the summer of 1976, Carter had told a reporter for *The Washington Post*
that Bourne was "about the closest friend I have in the world." This was
probably Carter being overly effusive, but the sentiment was genuine.
He felt at ease around Bourne, who reportedly was "one of the few people who can go into the Oval Office at any time."

So it was most unfortunate when, a few months later, Powell was
forced to announce that Dr. Bourne was being placed on a leave of absence. Bourne quickly acknowledged to the press that he had written a
perfectly legal prescription for fifteen Quaalude pills for his personal
assistant, Ellen Metsky, who had come to him complaining of sleep dep-
rivation. "I wrote a real prescription to and for use by a real person with
a real medical problem. The prescription was written for a resident of
the District of Columbia, where I am licensed to practice." But he also
admitted that he had made out the prescription to a "Sarah Brown," a

fictitious person, in order to protect Metsky's confidentiality. Legally, this was a gray zone, but officials at the American Medical Association deemed it unprofessional conduct. Carter didn't ask for his friend's resignation. "But when I got up this morning," Bourne told a *Post* reporter, "and looked at the papers, I knew what I had to do. This was really a very trivial issue. But it created a burden for the president. The best thing I can do is resign."

The "Quaalude affair" was on its face a minor issue. Local authorities later decided not to charge Bourne with any crime. But *The Washington Post* editorialized that Bourne's actions represented an "unaccountable lapse of judgment," particularly for a White House official advising the president on drug abuse. His departure, however, was also a blow to the administration's liberal tack on drug policy.

Carter had campaigned on a platform that included a tough position on opium eradication in neighboring Mexico. But he also favored decriminalization of marijuana. Bourne had aggressively advocated both positions, winning enemies within the Drug Enforcement Agency and among conservatives opposed to any liberalization of marijuana laws. His critics were delighted with his downfall, and particularly so on the issue of a questionable prescription for Quaaludes. In the larger scheme of Carter's presidency, the Bourne affair was a hiccup, a momentary political embarrassment. And despite the headlines, the Carters continued to see their old friends. Later that December, they had Peter and Mary over for drinks and watched a film in the White House theater. They viewed *Elmer Gantry* (1960), based on Sinclair Lewis's tragic satirical novel about a con man feigning piousness as an evangelical preacher.

Shortly after Bourne resigned on July 20, 1978, various divisions within the White House convened all-staff meetings to discuss the problem of drug use. Jody Powell met with his press office staff, including interns, in a large, first-floor corner room of the Old Executive Office Building. Powell was determined to convey a tough warning. He sternly announced that he didn't care who smoked pot, but it was illegal, and if you smoked weed, well, you could not work in the Carter White House. As he was finishing, Powell heard a murmur of giggles on the right side of the room, and so he walked over to the laughter and confronted a group of interns sitting on the floor: "What's so funny?" In response, one intern pointed to David A. Kaplan, a recent graduate of Cornell University soon headed to law school, and said, "Well, David here has never smoked grass." Most of those in the room snickered. Kaplan explained it wasn't a moral thing—he just couldn't stand the smell. Powell paused and then said, "You've *never* smoked pot? You should be fired for *that* reason!" The room erupted in laughter.

A FAR MORE serious crisis for the Carter administration erupted on August 14, 1979, when news outlets reported that UN ambassador Andrew Young had met with a member of the Palestine Liberation Organization. Carter was out jogging with Rosalynn on the south grounds of the White House when he was interrupted by Cy Vance, Warren Christopher, Jordan, and Powell. Vance was clearly upset and announced that Young had lied to him and would have to resign. The implication was that if Young didn't resign, then Vance would. Vance had threatened his resignation more than once, usually over his conflicts with Brzezinski. But this time he seemed to mean it. Carter was disturbed by the news and quickly grasped that his good friend had "gotten himself into serious trouble."

Andy Young was one of the president's closest political allies, a key bridge to the African American community, and despite numerous controversies—he had, for instance, characterized Richard Nixon, Gerald Ford, and Henry Kissinger as "racists"—he had nevertheless become the living symbol of the administration's commitment to place human rights at the center of its foreign policy. But he was brash and unusually candid even when he knew his opinions were out of step with the foreign policy establishment. Speaking about Africa and the apartheid regime in Rhodesia, he had once said that the British "practically invented racism." He had called for an end to the U.S. embargo of Castro's Cuba, labeling it a failed policy. He had said that the United States shared heavy responsibility for the hundreds of thousands of "boat people"—refugees from Vietnam—because of the war. And he had called for establishing diplomatic relations with communist Vietnam, despite Hanoi's recent invasion of Pol Pot's Cambodia.

History would suggest that Young's instincts on all these issues were correct—but such views were regarded in Washington at the time as beyond the pale. Carter always backed his UN ambassador. Needless to say, Young had made a few enemies inside the Carter administration.

Zbig Brzezinski, for instance, thought Andy Young "really wasn't a heavy hitter." Young was at the United Nations, Brzezinski said, because "Carter wanted him there because of color."

Late that summer, just before Ambassador Young was scheduled to begin a monthlong term as a rotating president of the Security Council, he learned about a resolution being circulated by various Arab nations to grant formal recognition of the PLO as a government-in-exile. To be sure, the Carter administration had been trying to persuade the PLO to amend its charter, acknowledging the legitimacy of the Israeli state. This in turn might lead to further negotiations, building on the Camp David Accords. But Ambassador Young knew that if submitted, any UN resolution recognizing the PLO would have to be vetoed, and that would be diplomatically embarrassing. With the full knowledge of the State Department, Young tried to persuade the Arab delegations to withdraw their resolution.

It was with this purpose in mind that Young had lunch in his official Waldorf Towers apartment on July 25, 1979, with four Arab ambassadors. Young argued that a U.S. veto would only strengthen the "rejectionists"—those hard-liners inside the PLO and elsewhere in the Arab world who opposed a political solution and favored armed struggle against Israel. Kuwait's ambassador, Abdullah Bishara, conceded this might be true, but nevertheless they could not postpone the UN resolution on Palestine without the acquiescence of the PLO. Bishara then invited Young to drop by his Beekman Place townhouse that very evening so he might make his case directly to the PLO's UN observer, Zehdi Labib Terzi, a suave and dignified Greek Orthodox Palestinian born in Jerusalem. There is some confusion about what happened next. According to Stu Eizenstat, Bishara's oral invitation was made in the presence of other State Department officials in the room. If so, Young presumed that his colleagues in Washington were aware of the invitation.

On the other hand, Young himself later explained to an Israeli reporter that he told Bishara, "Well, I wish you'd try [to convince Terzi] but I will stop by your house and, if you do not have any luck, maybe, you know, I will." Young acknowledged that he was "not in any way instructed by my government to do it." He admitted, "In fact, my government knew nothing about it. I informed them later, but in informing them I informed them that it was an inadvertent meeting."

In any case, Young accepted the invitation to appear at Bishara's residence, knowing that the PLO representative would be present. He took his five-year-old son with him that evening, knowing that Bishara had a son about the same age. Perhaps Young felt that his son's presence would make the encounter seem all the more casual and unofficial.

He knew, of course, that any such contact with a member of the PLO violated a 1975 pledge made by then secretary of state Henry Kissinger to the Israelis that no American diplomats would negotiate with the Palestinian organization. Candidate Carter had reiterated the pledge during the 1976 campaign—even though he thought the ban "absolutely ridiculous." In practice, both Kissinger and Carter as president were fully aware that the CIA had maintained a clandestine back channel to the PLO since 1969. Moreover, Israel's intelligence agency, Mossad, was also aware of this back channel, conducted by the CIA's veteran Arabist, Robert Ames, through Ali Hassan Salameh, the chief of the PLO's Force 17 intelligence group. The back channel had been used to exchange useful operational intelligence, but Ames had also used his relationship with Salameh to influence Yasir Arafat to begin thinking about a political compromise to the thorny Palestinian-Israeli conflict. Ambassador Young probably had no need to know any of the details about the Ames-Salameh back channel, but he was certainly aware that as a practical matter U.S. intelligence would have cultivated contacts within the PLO. Young also knew from his experience in the civil rights movement that "not talking to the enemy is the worst possible thing."

In point of fact, everyone knew of Young's attitude. He had made this clear from day one. Immediately after he was sworn in as UN ambassador, Young had made the rounds, and when introduced to the Egyptian ambassador, he candidly said that he hoped he'd get a chance to meet with some representatives of the Palestinians. "I mean, he said it on the first day," recalled Young's chief assistant, Stoney Cooks. "He went there with this in mind, that, 'I have got to tear down these barriers.'" Cooks reported that a full year before Young met with Terzi, he had dined with a high-ranking PLO diplomatic emissary. After this encounter in the summer of 1978, Young asked Cooks if he should inform the State Department. Cooks told him to write a memorandum of conversation about the meeting and hand it to Philip Habib, the under secretary of state for political affairs. Habib read it and approved the contact, but he told Young not to send the memo to Washington. It would be better, he indicated, if such contacts were conducted under the radar, unofficially. "Andy was trying to find a handle," recalled Cooks, "for essentially moving the PLO question from no contact, to some contact, to some relationships, to some method of moving the situation."

Habib and many others in the State Department thought this was only common sense. "Of course we were talking to the PLO," said Ambassador Donald McHenry, the number-three diplomat at the time in the UN mission. "I knew it, Vance knew, Carter knew it. The problem was that Kissinger had made a ridiculous promise to the Israelis." Young's allies in the department included Bill Maynes, assistant secretary of state for international organization affairs; Dick Moose, the assistant secretary for African affairs; and Anthony Lake, the director of policy planning. "Andy had grown up in the civil rights tradition," said Maynes, "where you talk to anybody who would talk to you, and the idea that we wouldn't talk to the PLO seemed to him preposterous."

Maynes actually played a critical role in the unfolding events because he happened to be the only high-ranking officer in the UN ambassador's office on the Saturday morning when the first news report broke about Young's meeting with the PLO's Terzi. After talking on the phone with Young, Maynes churned out a memo of press guidance, downplaying the meeting, implying that Ambassador Young had unexpectedly run into Terzi at the Kuwaiti ambassador's home. "Bill read me the press guidance," Cooks recalled. "I am certain that Bill gave this press guidance to Andy." According to Cooks, Young never personally told Secretary Vance or any other State Department official anything about the Terzi meeting. But Maynes sent the press-guidance memo he had written to Washington, and later the State Department spokesman flatly told inquiring reporters, "Ambassador Young has had no secret meeting with Mr. Terzi. . . . He [Young] went out for a walk with his son and they dropped in on the Kuwaiti ambassador. During their talk Mr. Terzi arrived unexpectedly."

As far as Vance or Tony Lake or other officials were concerned, Young had personally characterized the meeting as inadvertent. That was on Saturday. But by Sunday night the Israeli media had lit up with reports about the Young-Terzi meeting. The next morning, Young saw how awkwardly the State Department spokesman had handled the growing controversy, and decided he was going to have to take things into his own hands.

That Monday evening, Young went to see the Israeli ambassador to the UN, Yehuda Zvi Blum. Young "came clean" with the Israeli, explaining that he had met with Terzi only in his capacity as incoming president of the Security Council—and only for the purpose of persuading the Arab states to withdraw their resolution condemning the Israeli settlements in the West Bank. Young knew, of course, that Blum would quickly inform his superiors in Tel Aviv, but he hoped that his explanation would both be persuasive and remain confidential. Perhaps inevitably, the gist of Young's message to Blum leaked to the press the very next day. "Tuesday all hell breaks loose," recalled Cooks. The State Department's official statement—based on Maynes's press guidance from Saturday—had to be completely reversed. Young's meeting with Terzi had been planned and was not an inadvertent event.

Secretary Vance and Policy Director Lake felt like they had been lied to by Young. Vance also felt that Young's unpredictable tendency to speak off the cuff on numerous occasions had made him a liability. But if Young had lied about the nature of his meeting with Terzi, well, that was grounds for dismissal. Maynes might have been able to explain what had happened, but he had flown off to China on an official trip and was then out of the loop. And Andy Young never even tried to blame Maynes for the misleading press-guidance memo. Cooks insisted, "Andy was actually covering for Bill." That may have been true, but on paper Young had presumably acquiesced to the waffling press guidance drafted by Maynes. And this made it seem to Vance and others in the State Department that Young had lied to Maynes, who had then retold Andy's misleading characterization of the Terzi meeting. Vance felt Young had lied, and that was the end of it. But Wolf Blitzer, then the Washington correspondent for *The Jerusalem Post,* probably got the story right when he reported that Young had told Maynes the "truth about the exact nature of the meeting but the State Department decided to cover it up."

In any case, that's not how Vance saw it, and Young quickly decided Tuesday evening that he had to resign. "The sharks are out," he told McHenry, "and not only do they smell blood, they see it."

Carter reluctantly accepted the resignation, but he later called it "one of the most heart-wrenching decisions I had to make as president." That evening, Carter called Eizenstat to talk about the crisis. The president was clearly agitated, telling Eizenstat, "Andy must go, and the question is how to do it with a minimum of trouble to Andy, to the administration and to black-Jewish relations." Eizenstat argued with him, suggesting that the problem could be resolved with a verbal reprimand, leaving Young in place at the United Nations. But Carter was not convinced, saying that this was the "eighth or tenth time Andy has caused problems." And besides, "Cy is making it a choice between Andy and himself."

One of Carter's long-standing supporters, Jesse Hill, a prominent African American businessman from Atlanta, called him at the White House shortly after midnight and tried to talk him out of firing Young. Hill even flew in to Washington the next day and met with Carter in the second-floor residence. Also present were Andy Young and Jesse Jackson. There is no record of this meeting, but it must have been emotionally difficult for everyone. That same morning, Eizenstat once again tried to persuade Carter to relent, but the president was adamant: "I love Andy like a brother, and I want to guide him. But he has embarrassed us too many times in the past. . . . Plus, he lied to the State Department."

Not since Bert Lance's resignation two years earlier had the president sustained such a personal blow to his administration. Standing at the press podium, Jody Powell actually wept when he had to read aloud Carter's letter accepting Young's resignation. The president strongly felt the prohibition against any contacts with the PLO was "preposterous," and he told both Vance and Brzezinski not to make any further such promises to the Israelis: "If the Israelis couldn't trust us, they could find another 'trustworthy' partner."

Still, Carter had been led to believe that Young had flat-out lied to Vance: "He would have retained his position if he had been truthful to the secretary of state." Carter noted in his diary that "Andy was not penitent at all, saying he had done what he thought was right." Indeed, speaking at a press conference, Young told reporters, "I really don't feel a bit sorry for a thing I have done." The president was clearly anguished that a longtime friend—and his closest political ally in the African American community—was being sacrificed for politics. Carter hated to be pressured, and yet, in this instance, he caved. The decision was both regrettable and out of character for a president who disdained doing anything that was politically correct. Years later, he would write, "I have never been sure that this was the right decision."

One aspect of the whole affair, however, remains a mystery: Who originally leaked the fact of Young's meeting with the PLO's UN observer? Most speculation at the time focused on Ambassador Blum, the assumption being that the Israelis wanted Young fired because they saw him as too overtly sympathetic to Palestinian concerns. *Time* magazine, for instance, reported that Young's conversation with Terzi had been recorded by an Israeli listening device planted in the Kuwaiti ambassador's home. Stu Eizenstat wrote in his account that "much evidence points to the Israelis."

But there is another scenario. "There was an intercept," said one high-ranking diplomat. The FBI routinely conducts electronic surveillance of foreign missions at the United Nations, so when Young encountered the PLO's Terzi at the Beekman Place residence of the Kuwaiti ambassador, the FBI quickly captured a record of the conversation and sent it to Washington. "Someone got hold of this intelligence intercept," said this diplomat, "and used it against Andy."

Suspicion naturally fell on Zbig Brzezinski, but when asked about the leak, the national security adviser claimed ignorance. Young himself pointed out that while the State Department had publicly claimed to be in the dark about his July 26 encounter with Terzi, they actually had a detailed, nearly verbatim transcript of the conversation within four days of the meeting. "I don't know how they got it," Young told the press shortly after his resignation, "but I have seen such a report." State Department spokesman Tom Reston denied this, but *The Washington Post* confirmed that Young had been given access to a July 30, 1979, intelligence report that contained such information. Clearly, this was the classified document that some high-ranking official had leaked. Young said he had seen the July 30 intelligence report only on August 15, the day after he resigned. He said he had not planned to say anything about it, but "when folks at the State Department started putting out the word that I had to resign because I had lied, that got to be too much." It is hard not to conclude that Young had been torpedoed by his enemies inside the administration—not by the Israelis.

Young was not just any diplomat, and his resignation had far-reaching political ramifications. "You would think it was over when Andy resigned, but it wasn't," said Ambassador McHenry. "African Americans criticized the president for abandoning Andy under Jewish pressure—and Jewish Americans complained that the whole incident underscored the administration's critical outlook on Israel." When the news first broke of Young's encounter with Terzi, the *New York Daily News* published a headline screaming, "Jews Demand Firing Young."

This was somewhat of an exaggeration. Just a few Jewish leaders called for Young's dismissal. *The Washington Post* reported that Rabbi Joseph Sternstein, president of the conservative American Zionist Federation, had wired President Carter, "Only the dismissal of Ambassador Young can restore confidence in your administration." And Bertram Gold, executive vice president of the American Jewish Committee, issued a formal statement saying that if Young "indeed did talk with the PLO on his own, he should be fired."

But these public sentiments were the exception. Most Jewish American leaders were more circumspect, precisely because they understood, as one unnamed Jewish leader told *Commentary* magazine, that Andy Young was an iconic civil rights leader, "and we realized the significance of that." Theodore Mann, chairman of the Conference of Presidents of Major American Jewish Organizations, called Young's meeting with the PLO envoy a "deplorable act"—but he did not go on to call for his dismissal. On the other hand, Black leaders knew full well that most Jewish Americans were alarmed at the notion of an American ambassador talking to the PLO and applauded Young's resignation. "The perception on the street," said the Reverend Wyatt Tee Walker, an official from the Southern Christian Leadership Conference, "is that the Jews did this to Andy Young."

Jesse Jackson angrily told reporters that he blamed Young's forced departure on a "capitulation" to pressure from "our former allies, the American Jewish community." Vernon Jordan, president of the National Urban League, pointedly asked why President Carter had accepted Young's resignation when the American ambassador to Austria, Milton A. Wolf, had not even been reprimanded for having had a similar unauthorized meeting several months earlier with a PLO official in Vienna.

Young himself stoked the controversy by calling the Begin government in Israel "stubborn and intransigent" and said it was time for a "redefinition of our relationship with the state of Israel." In the same breath,

Young called for "increased dialogue" between African Americans and Jewish Americans. But both Blacks and Jews were too angry and suspicious of each other for any genuine dialogue. "There are some who attribute—and we think rightly so—the exit of Young to Jewish pressure," editorialized *The Afro-American*. "And rumors have it that it was the Israelis who 'bugged' the meeting of Andy with the PLO representative. Be that as it may, the truth is the Jews have been acting like spoiled children in their responses to all these events." Black leaders felt betrayed and patronized.

The circumstances of Young's firing also prompted some Black leaders to voice sympathy for the Palestinians—and of course, such expressions further alarmed Jewish Americans. Jackson announced he would accept an invitation to visit Yasir Arafat in Beirut. And the Reverend Joseph Lowery, the president of the Southern Christian Leadership Conference, went out of his way to meet with the PLO's Terzi and endorsed Palestinian rights of self-determination in "their own homeland." That was not all. African American leaders met in New York in late August and asserted that it was time to reassess the Black-Jewish relationship. Notwithstanding their alliance during the civil rights struggle, Blacks were unhappy with the Jewish community's growing antipathy toward affirmative action. Neither were Black leaders any longer going to turn a blind eye to Israel's opportunistic relationship with the hated apartheid regime in South Africa. Jewish leaders responded with a joint statement asserting that "we cannot work with those who, in failing to differentiate between the Palestinian Arabs and the Palestine Liberation Organization, give support to terrorism." The Young affair had unloosed a slew of long-festering grievances.

While African American and Jewish American leaders traded barbed sentiments, Carter happened to be on a working vacation, floating down the Mississippi River aboard the *Delta Queen*. And to the annoyance of Jewish American leaders, he seemed oblivious to their urgent appeals that he release a statement denying that they were responsible for Young's resignation. "The Young affair has been a painful experience for many of us," said Hyman Bookbinder, the Washington representative of the American Jewish Committee. Bookbinder complained about some of the "outrageous" things being said by Black leaders: "Some of it is out-and-out anti-Semitism." By September, Jewish leaders were turning their anger on President Carter, arguing that his silence was allowing Blacks to foster the perception that Jews were to blame for Young's departure. Rabbi Alexander Schindler uncharitably told a reporter that Carter's silence was "a pure and simple exploitation of anti-Semitism for political purposes." Another unnamed Jewish leader told *The Washington Post*, "I was sure the president would get the blame off our backs. But he must have decided he could not risk the political backlash of the blacks."

By the end of September, the punditocracy was piling on, criticizing the administration for allegedly being silent. The conservative *New York Times* columnist William Safire attacked Carter's secretary of state, Cy Vance, for being too "lawyerly" in his response to questions about why Young was fired. Vance had replied, "It was not the result of actions by the Jewish community"—absolving Jewish Americans, Safire argued, but not the Israelis. Safire seemed to think that if Vance and the president had answered "truthfully," then "much of the animosity that has developed between black leaders and Jews since that time would have been nipped in the bud." Safire was being both naïve and tendentious. Three days before Safire published his column, the president had, in fact, categorically declared that no "American Jewish leaders or anyone else" had lobbied him to fire Young. This was not quite the case, but Carter said it anyway to reassure rattled Jewish leaders that he was not blaming them for the brouhaha.

Safire's attack nevertheless resonated with Jewish Americans and traditional supporters of Israel. The message was that the Carter administration was enabling "evil" by saying nothing. Needless to say, this was a grossly unfair but also politically lethal piece of punditry. The whole affair was a political disaster for the Carter administration, alienating two core constituencies and making it even more difficult for the president to pursue his high-risk efforts to end the Palestinian-Israeli conflict.

Andy Young had provided the Carter presidency with much-needed ballast against the foreign policy establishment. He thought outside the box. He didn't accept Brzezinski's knee-jerk Cold War shibboleths. He had opposed Brzezinski's lobbying to give the deposed shah asylum. Arguably, the Carter administration would soon make some critical mistakes that would not have occurred had Young remained in his post as UN ambassador.

* * *

SOMETIMES A SMALL, even ridiculous incident changes the optics of a presidency in a large way. Late one afternoon in the spring of 1979, Carter was sitting with Jody Powell and a few other aides on the Truman Balcony, overlooking the South Lawn. Sipping lemonade, Carter related how he had just returned from a weekend visit to Plains, where he had spent an hour on April 20 trout fishing from a rowboat on Miss Lillian's pond. Carter was alone—though a White House photographer stood on the bluff overlooking the pond, and Secret Service agents hovered nearby at the Pond House. Around 6:00 P.M., Carter said, he suddenly noticed a large animal swimming toward his rowboat. As it got closer, Carter took his oar and splashed water toward the creature, and it turned away. He thought nothing of the incident, but upon docking his boat, a Secret Service officer asked, "What was that animal that was trying to get into the boat with you?" Carter replied, "It was a rabbit."

Hearing this, Powell laughed, incredulous. Later, Carter admitted, "All my Georgia friends said rabbits don't swim." A week or two later, Carter happened to learn that the White House photographer had taken a photograph of the incident. "When we looked at the photograph," Carter said, "I knew it was a rabbit, but it was hard to tell in the photograph. So, I had him blow the photograph up. It was plainly a rabbit." Feeling vindicated, the president showed the evidence to a still-skeptical Powell and a few other doubters—who in turn presented Carter with an enlarged photo of the rabbit with an inscription saying, "Brzezinski will go to any extreme to deliver a message to the president."

Jody thought the whole story hilarious. Several months later, he was having a drink with Brooks Jackson, a White House correspondent for the Associated Press, when he embellished the story a little bit. Jackson then filed a story on the AP wire that was carried by newspapers all over the country. "A 'killer rabbit' attacked President Carter on a recent trip to Plains, Ga.," Jackson wrote, "penetrating Secret Service security and forcing the Chief Executive to beat back the beast with a canoe paddle. . . . It was hissing menacingly, its teeth flashing and nostrils flared." The *Los Angeles Times*'s Washington correspondent, Eleanor Randolph, followed up with a story headlined "Carter Has a Hare-

Raising Experience on Plains Trip." Randolph's account had the president "parrying and thrusting his oar at the 'banzai bunny.'" Deputy White House press secretary Rex Granum refused Randolph's request for the rabbit photo, saying that "there are certain stories about the President that must forever remain shrouded in mystery."

Carter naturally made light of the story. He was in Plains when the story broke in *The Washington Post* on the front page, with the headline "Bunny Goes Bugs: Rabbit Attacks President." As he walked out of his home at 7:00 A.M., Sam Donaldson and a bevy of other reporters asked him some serious questions about Cuba, the SALT II talks, and the recent nomination of Donald McHenry to replace Andy Young as UN ambassador. But then a reporter, probably Donaldson, asked, "Oh, by the way, rabbits. Are you going fishing today, sir?" When Carter allowed that he might, he was asked, "Can you give us your version of what happened? Would you like to clear your good name?"

As everyone laughed, Carter explained, "It was just a fairly robust-looking rabbit who was swimming without difficulty, and he was apparently disturbed by some predator, maybe dogs or a fox. He jumped in the far side of the pond. . . . I thought it was a beaver or otter. . . . But as he got closer to me I saw that it was not either one of those kind of animals. So I had a paddle in the boat, and when the rabbit got close enough to the boat for me to recognize it and saw that it was going to attempt to climb in the boat with me, I thought that would be an unpleasant situation for me and the rabbit."

REPORTER: "One of you would have to get out?"
THE PRESIDENT: "Yes." *(Laughter.)*
REPORTER: "Did you do him in?"
THE PRESIDENT: "I never did hit the rabbit. I just splashed water toward him, and he finally veered his course and went over to the bank and climbed up."
REPORTER: "We have a Freedom of Information Act [request] to get that picture, by the way. We have filed suit." *(Laughter.)*

Carter replied good-naturedly, saying that the photo taken by the White House photographer from the pond shoreline was very clear. He acknowledged that many people "doubted my veracity . . . that a rabbit was swimming. But rabbits swim and that one was swimming without any difficulty at all."

The reporter replied: "I hope you catch more fish than rabbits the next time."

That same afternoon in Washington, Senator Robert Dole (R-KS) said Carter should apologize for "bashing a bunny in the head with a paddle." In a sly reference to Carter's *Playboy* magazine interview, Dole pointed out that "this isn't the first time President Carter has gotten into trouble with bunnies. It seems to me he had a problem back in the fall of 1976, as well." Obviously, politicians and journalists were having fun with the story on a very slow news day.

Four days later, Jody Powell was asked again about the photo of the rabbit, and he demurred, saying that if they released the photo, "the rabbit controversy" would only receive more press coverage than SALT or the debate over a windfall-profits tax. Jokingly, he said he was afraid it could also pit "the NSC against State, State against the CIA, Domestic Policy versus Commerce and other agencies over whether it was a *ribbit* or a possum." Jody then ended the exchange with reporters, saying that he "has not more doubts about the existence of the rabbit than . . . about the existence of *rooster pepper sausage*."*

It was all in good fun—but the "killer rabbit" story had an unexpected life of its own. It circulated widely and became part of the currency with which to ridicule the Carter presidency. It became a metaphor for critics who thought of Carter as hapless and enfeebled. Powell sorely regretted that he had leaked the story. "It was a nightmare," he later wrote. By August 1979, Powell thought, "If the president had been set upon by a pack of wild dogs, a good portion of the press would have sided with the dogs and declared that he had provoked the attack." Powell was only half joking.

---

* A year earlier, various members of the Washington press corps had published comical, tongue-in-cheek reports that Judge Bell and Charlie Kirbo had smuggled several pounds of "rooster pepper sausage" past the Secret Service and into the White House. Rumors had it that the rare, spicy South Georgian concoction was an aphrodisiac. Powell dismissed the story as a spoof: "Judge Bell and Squire Kirbo are putting on not only the rest of the country, but the president too."

* * *

A FAR MORE serious story broke that same month concerning Carter's newly anointed chief of staff, Hamilton Jordan. The Carters had decided to spend a full week, August 17–24, vacationing on the Mississippi River aboard the *Delta Queen,* a steam-powered paddleboat. Amy accompanied them. Every morning, Carter managed to jog four or five miles on shore. He and Rosalynn got in a little fishing and read a lot. In the evenings when the steamboat docked, Carter would make a speech to several thousand spectators gathered on the shoreline. "All of us enjoyed the trip—remarkably beautiful, in northern places looking like European rivers, with high bluffs, mountains in the background. I spent a lot of time in the pilothouse learning about the Mississippi River, while reading *Life on the Mississippi* by Samuel Clemens."

But on August 23, the president's idyllic journey downriver was interrupted by a phone call from the new attorney general, Benjamin Civiletti, informing him that the Justice Department had received an allegation that three White House aides—Hamilton Jordan, Jody Powell, and Tim Kraft—had been seen snorting cocaine at Studio 54, a New York discotheque that was all the rage in 1978. Andy Warhol, Michael Jackson, and scores of other celebrities were regulars. "It was the most magical club that ever existed," said one patron. "If you got in, you were a star, not just a person."

Powell happened to be with the Carters aboard the *Delta Queen,* and he soon told the president that he had never once visited Studio 54. Back in the White House the next day, Jordan admitted that he had visited the discotheque once but said he had never snorted cocaine. Kraft also denied the story. Jordan offered to resign, but Carter would have none of it. Carter knew the allegations came from the owners of Studio 54, Steve Rubell and Ian Schrager, both of whom were under indictment and attempting to plea-bargain their way out of jail. "I'll stay aloof," Carter noted in his diary, "and let the lawyers handle it." The allegations by two celebrity discotheque owners facing tax-evasion charges might appear to be flimsy. But politically, the optics of a cocaine allegation were not good. It might have seemed unsubstantiated, but the Justice Department was compelled by vaguely worded standards in the Ethics in Government Act of 1978 to investigate the matter. Carter himself had personally supported this law, designed to address the abuses of the Watergate affair. Now, by law, the president was forced to stand back and allow his Justice Department to investigate. Naturally, the charges became front-page news in *The New York Times* and *The Washington Post*. Only later did it become apparent that the story had been leaked to the *Times* by a lawyer for Rubell—none other than the notoriously unscrupulous Roy Cohn.

As a young man, Cohn had worked for the late senator Joseph McCarthy, but by the 1970s he was known in New York legal circles as a much-feared legal adversary whose clients included organized crime figures and the young real estate developer Donald Trump. According to his friend Roger Stone, Cohn "did not like Jimmy Carter" and had no qualms about informing the Justice Department that his client Rubell would testify against Jordan in exchange for immunity on the tax-evasion charges. Cohn also offered up a taped statement from a "Johnny C"—a twenty-eight-year-old drug dealer. John Conaghan, aka Johnny C, was himself arrested a month later for selling Quaaludes and cocaine as he was about to enter Studio 54. Interviewed on television, Conaghan conceded he was not "100 percent sure" that he could identify Jordan. But Rubell nevertheless insisted, "I saw him [Jordan] take a hit in each nostril. He tried to pick up some girls and he succeeded."

For a moment, when Jordan realized that Cohn was behind the story, he thought the attorney general would quickly dismiss the allegations from such obviously unreliable and shady sources. "Maybe this will be a three-day story and blow over," he told Powell.

"Are you kidding?" Jody scoffed. "The president's top aides, a president who is a born-again Christian, Studio 54, drugs. . . . They will have to deal with it. Batten down the hatches because we are going to have a bumpy few days here."

Jordan told reporters that he had visited the disco for less than an hour in late 1978 with Tim Kraft and another Carter administration official, Evan Dobelle, age thirty-three. Ironically, Dobelle had been chief of protocol at the White House, but by the summer of 1979 he was chief of the campaign committee to reelect Carter, working closely with Jordan. "We walked around," Jordan said. "I remember going there, sort of as a spectator sport. I did not request the use of any drugs." Kraft and Dobelle corroborated Jordan's account. "Everybody knows Hamilton has a weakness for women and booze," commented White House poll-ster Patrick Caddell, "but he doesn't do drugs."

The Ethics in Government Act of 1978 gave Attorney General Civi-letti ninety days to mount a preliminary investigation of any charges leveled at a high-ranking government official. He could then dismiss the charges as without merit—or otherwise appoint a special prosecutor. Civiletti quickly determined that Jody Powell had never set foot in Stu-dio 54, and despite a flurry of lurid press reports, Civiletti was about to conclude that there was no credence to any of the allegations against Jor-dan when *The Washington Post* broke a second story claiming that Jor-dan had also snorted cocaine at a Los Angeles dinner party in October 1977. "The person who made the latest charge," the *Post* reported, "did not claim to see the White House aide use cocaine, but named another person who allegedly did, the sources said." This was obviously thin stuff. Two days later, *The New York Times* piled on with another story on the California incident—but careful readers of the report would learn that the new accuser, like Rubell and Schrager, was also under criminal indictment and was in the market for a plea deal.

Civiletti, who was on the verge of dropping the charges, now felt the new wave of publicity compelled him to appoint a special prosecutor. He named a hard-nosed trial lawyer, Arthur H. Christy, as special pros-ecutor on November 29, 1979, and the case dragged on. Christy later said that he wanted to dismiss the charges in the first week but thought this would be impolitic. According to Bob Woodward, Christy became so frustrated with one unreliable witness that he grabbed him by the necktie, slammed him against the wall, and called him out as a liar. Six months later, after nineteen sessions and thirty-three witnesses, a fed-eral grand jury voted 24–0 not to bring an indictment against Jordan. Christy told a few reporters on background that Jordan had been "set up" by Roy Cohn. By then, Jordan had spent $175,000 in legal fees defend-ing himself. He later tried to get his legal fees reimbursed, but the courts turned him down. His White House salary at the time was $56,000.

Unbeknownst to the special prosecutor, there was another connec-tion between the Carter White House and Studio 54. Rumors had been circulating that one of the president's sons had visited the disco. When the story initially broke in late August, Chip Carter went to see his father and confessed that he had visited the hip discotheque in the company of not Jordan but a low-ranking White House aide. Chip volunteered to both his father and Jordan that they could deflect the charges away from Jordan by telling the press that he was the one in the disco. Chip thought he was proposing to do the honorable thing; he was expendable, and Jordan was not. Needless to say, both the president and Jordan ignored Chip's offer.

The Studio 54 episode was a travesty, both for justice and for the Carter White House—not to speak of Ham Jordan's reputation. Some chalked it up to an overzealous post-Watergate press corps. *Washington Star* gossip columnist Diana McLellan thought Jordan had made himself the enemy of the press corps, if only "because he was bathed in the sallow afterglow of thousands of unanswered calls." But if Jordan's cultivated bad-boy behavior had made him a target, this did not excuse the press for its behavior toward his boss, the president. Gossip journalism masked as investigative reporting became a major phenomenon during the Carter presidency and inevitably distracted the president from the nation's business.

Chapter 21
Fateful Decisions

To hell with Henry Kissinger.
—PRESIDENT JIMMY CARTER

CIA Director Stansfield Turner, Defense Secretary Harold Brown,
Vice President Walter Mondale, National Security Adviser Zbigniew
Brzezinski, President Carter, and Secretary of State Cyrus Vance
BETTMANN/GETTY IMAGES

BY THE AUTUMN of 1979, the Carter administration found itself on the defensive on numerous fronts. The nation's gross domestic product was actually growing at a healthy 3.16 percent rate. But unemployment was up to nearly 6 percent and inflation was running at 12 percent. Carter's standings in national polls dropped to a new low. Most Americans still thought their president honest and well-meaning. But he did not inspire confidence. In a June CBS News/*New York Times* poll 66 percent agreed with the notion that the country needed someone "who would step on some toes and bend some rules to get things done." Frustrated voters were beginning to look elsewhere for leadership. Among registered Democrats, 52 percent said they would vote for Senator Ted Kennedy if he ran—and only 23 percent expressed a preference for Carter. By September, Carter's approval rating had sunk to a pathetic 19 percent. Hamilton Jordan knew what these numbers meant. Kennedy was probably going to challenge Carter for the 1980 Democratic nomination. And indeed, on September 7 Kennedy came to the White House, and during the course of a private one-hour lunch in the second-floor residence, he told Carter that he intended to run. Carter was not surprised, but neither was he any less confident about his own prospects as a sitting president. His consigliere, Charlie Kirbo, shared his confidence. "It's true that Jimmy Carter is an unusual president. He does not conduct himself like a movie star. . . . It may be that Jimmy Carter's critics have simply confused glamor with leadership."

Arthur Schlesinger, Jr., noted in his diary earlier that year that he thought Carter would do what Lyndon Johnson had done in March 1968 and just announce that he was not running. Schlesinger convinced himself that Carter "must be aware, since he is an intelligent man, that he is miscast in his job." Schlesinger was wrong, but sorely disaffected.

Carter had always thought that Kennedy's charismatic personality harbored existential flaws, a weakness that made the senator vulnerable to attack. When Jordan's deputy, Landon Butler, heard that Kennedy intended to run, he wrote a memo to Jordan, pointing out that both Kennedy and Carter were scheduled to be on the same platform in Boston the following month. "The President's speech at the Kennedy Library could well be a pivotal point. We must make plans, now, to ensure that this speech is among the best the President has ever given." Rick Hertzberg soon got to work on it.

The day after his lunch with Kennedy, Carter awoke at 5:30 A.M. and went out for a two-hour jog with his White House physician, Dr. William Lukash. The twelve-mile run "convinced me that I do not want to be a marathoner." The following Saturday, however, he participated in the ten-thousand-meter Catoctin Mountain Park Run, an annual event that was held just a short distance from Camp David.

The president was one of 980 runners who entered the hilly race. He'd been jogging nearly daily around the White House, but this was his first competitive race since the Naval Academy. It was a hot and steamy day, and Carter "made a serious tactical mistake" when he tried to cut four minutes off his previous best time of fifty minutes. "I overexerted and had to drop out of the race." Twenty minutes into the race, Carter was struggling up a steep hill when Dr. Lukash noticed him getting pale and wobbly. The doctor advised him to drop out, but Carter at first refused, until finally he collapsed into the arms of Secret Service agents, who helped him to the roadside. They drove him quickly back to Aspen Lodge, where Dr. Lukash had the president stripped and covered with cold towels. He then injected nearly a quart of salt water through a vein in his left arm. As a precaution, they then administered an electrocardiogram. The exam showed no heart abnormalities. He was fine, just dehydrated. Two hours later, he attended a ceremony where he presented the winners of the race with their medals.

The next morning, however, a photo of Carter looking like death incarnate was splashed on the front pages of newspapers across the country. *The New York Times* reported, "President Carter, wobbling, moaning and pale with exhaustion, dropped out of a 6.2-mile foot race today." Pundits naturally saw it as a metaphor. The *Times* editorialized the next day, "A weakened America will be led for the next 14 months by an alarmingly weak president. Congress knows it. The Russians know it. The Israelis and Arabs know it. The oil companies and labor unions know it. Does Jimmy Carter understand the fact and know how to deal with it? The signs are not encouraging." The *Times* would go on to acknowledge that Carter had not caused inflation or stagnation or the oil crisis. But they nevertheless blamed him, as did many Americans, for being weak.

In his defense, Carter joked that he was just an "evangelist on running." Dr. Lukash said the president was actually in very good shape, and Carter himself told reporters, "I feel great. I pressed myself too much. But they had to drag me off. I didn't want to stop."

A chain-smoking Jody Powell was not amused. "If you get in it," he had told the president, "then you'd darn well better finish." He understood the optics were terrible.

REPUBLICANS BLAMED CARTER for a sluggish economy, but they also charged that Carter was a weak foreign policy president, a politician who had given away too many American prerogatives. In Republican eyes, he had given away the Panama Canal, pressured the Israelis on the West Bank settlements, and undermined anticommunist allies like the shah's Iran and Somoza's Nicaragua. He had also pursued détente with the Soviet Union, and in the view of neoconservatives, he had negotiated a weak SALT II treaty. Undeterred, Carter had made SALT II ratification his number one foreign policy priority. This in turn made the administration even more vulnerable to pressure from the Kissinger-McCloy-Rockefeller campaign to give the Pahlavi monarch asylum in America.

At the end of July 1979, Kissinger made the linkage explicit when he bluntly told Brzezinski that his continued support for SALT II was dependent upon a "more forthcoming attitude on our part regarding the shah." Carter was thoroughly annoyed by this linkage. Kissinger was just a private citizen, but his voice still influenced the media and, by extension, public opinion. At a breakfast meeting on July 27, 1979, Carter told a gathering of his foreign policy advisers that Kissinger, Rockefeller, and McCloy were literally waging a campaign on behalf of the shah and that "Zbig bugged me on it every day." Brzezinski bristled at this and interrupted sharply, "No, sir."

"Well," replied Carter, "not every day, but very often."

Though he could see that the president was irritated, Brzezinski wouldn't let the matter drop, arguing that the United States could not allow itself to be influenced by "threats from a third-rate regime." At this, both Carter and Vance became quite angry and pushed back against the notion that they were succumbing to threats. Both men thought the national security adviser was way out of line. Nevertheless, according to Zbig, his persistence had paid off, because the president agreed that Vance should explore in a very tentative manner any contingency plans for bringing the shah into the country.

ADDING TO THE political pressure was yet another foreign policy crisis in September 1979 in which the administration again needed McCloy's assistance. Reports leaked that the intelligence community had "discovered" a Soviet combat brigade stationed in Cuba. Conservatives alleged that such a force was a violation of the agreement reached during the October 1962 missile crisis, whereby the Soviets agreed not to introduce offensive weaponry into Cuba in exchange for a pledge by the United States not to invade the island. The "news," of course, was old news, and anyone familiar with the 1962 negotiations knew that the Soviets had maintained a small combat brigade in Cuba for years. Nevertheless, there was considerable furor, both in the press and in Congress, alleging a new Soviet threat in Cuba.

President Carter quickly determined that the Soviets had stationed approximately the same number of troops in Cuba for seventeen years. He noted in his diary that the Soviet brigade was not a violation of any previous understandings—but he recognized that "politically it's devastating to SALT." Trying to calm the waters, he went on national television on September 7 and emphasized that the Russian soldiers had been there for some years. But inexplicably, perhaps wanting to appear tough, he also said "this status quo is not acceptable." These words neatly boxed him into a hard-line position. Brzezinski then took advantage of this public relations mistake to fan the crisis further, insisting that the president could not back down. This put Brzezinski on a collision course with both the president and the secretary of state.

Vance calmly went about ascertaining what the facts were. On the afternoon of September 10, 1979, he had the Soviet ambassador, Anatoly Dobrynin, drop by the State Department for an unpublicized visit. Dobrynin took the private elevator to the seventh floor and walked into Secretary Vance's paneled office. Vance bluntly asked him, "Anatoly, were those troops there during the Kennedy administration? During the Johnson administration? During the Nixon administration? During the Ford administration?"

"Yes, exactly," replied Dobrynin.

"Then what is all this about?" asked Vance.

Dobrynin shrugged and said, "I should ask you what it is all about."

But while Vance tried to find some diplomatic way for the president to extract himself from what amounted to a fake crisis, Brzezinski warned Carter, "A cosmetic outcome will not wash." He advised him to use the crisis to announce a budget increase in defense spending and the deployment of additional troops to Guantánamo Bay, and to issue a tough statement condemning Soviet interventions in Africa and elsewhere.

But on September 23, Vance brought the Senate Democratic leader,

Robert Byrd, into the Oval Office shortly after 9:00 P.M. In the presence of both the president and Brzezinski, Byrd frankly said the Soviet brigade in Cuba was a "phony" issue. Byrd said it was "inappropriate for a mighty nation to go into a delirium over about 2,300 Soviet troops that had neither airlift nor sealift capability to leave Cuba." The administration, he said, would just have to cool its rhetoric and find a way to save the SALT II treaty. Carter got the message, and over Brzezinski's strident objections he decided to make a public show of calling together a panel of establishment "wise men" to advise him on the matter. Jack McCloy, Henry Kissinger, George W. Ball, McGeorge Bundy, Clark Clifford, Averell Harriman, and other establishment luminaries quickly rendered a judgment. McCloy's opinion, however, was essential, since only he and the late Adlai Stevenson had conducted the phase of the negotiations with the Soviets in 1962 that had addressed the question of what kind of Soviet military personnel would be allowed to remain in Cuba after the withdrawal of the missiles. After scrutinizing the evidence during a CIA briefing, McCloy flatly said the Soviet combat brigade was not a violation of the 1962 "understanding." On Saturday, September 29, 1979, the "wise men" met with Carter and firmly told him that he had to defuse the crisis.

It was all about nothing. Clifford said he was "appalled" to learn that the Soviet brigade had been in Cuba since 1962. He called it a "false issue" and said the "brigade has a right to be in Cuba." George Ball remarked that the U.S. "cannot be frightened by 2500 troops!" Mac Bundy found it "unbelievable" that the affair had been so blown out of proportion. Brzezinski was accused of using his hard-line rhetoric "to revive the Cold War."

McCloy and the other "wise men" were paraded before reporters at a White House luncheon, and in off-the-record comments to the press they made it clear that there was no crisis. Carter now had the political cover he needed to extract himself from the controversy. Pushed by Kirbo—who thought it would be wrong to allow the Soviet-brigade controversy to derail SALT II ratification—the president gave a televised speech on October 1 that attempted to settle the matter. He reassured the American people that there was "no reason for a return to the Cold War." Carter thought it went well. Afterward, he walked over to the Roosevelt Room, where some fifty friends and White House aides had gathered to celebrate both the speech and his fifty-fifth birthday with a champagne party.

Though invited, an angry Brzezinski made a point of not attending. He later wrote in his memoirs that "this was the only time that I ever thought seriously of the possibility of resigning." He sulked for three days and then finally went to see the president in the Oval Office at 8:00 A.M. on October 4. Still fuming, Zbig lectured Carter, using language he later characterized as "the most disagreeable comments I ever made to the president in the course of our years." They argued for twenty-five minutes. Zbig complained bitterly about "Soviet adventurism." Finally, for the first time in decades, the United States had warned the Soviets that there would be "negative consequences" for their behavior in Iran, the Middle East, Vietnam, Africa—and, most recently, Cuba—"and then we did nothing about it." This was dangerous, he argued, because it could encourage the Russians to miscalculate in a future crisis.

Carter had listened to this litany of complaints from his national security adviser on frequent occasions. But this time, looking "quite furious," Carter snapped that he "had no intention of going to war over the Soviet brigade in Cuba." Unbelievably, Brzezinski argued with him, responding that he was not advocating war but just insisting that they had to "lay it on the line more explicitly in regard to Soviet adventurism around the world." It is astonishing that Carter didn't dismiss his obstreperous adviser. "Maybe he thought of firing me," Brzezinski later mused. "He never indicated that to me." That Carter didn't do so is evidence of the president's patience and tolerance for Brzezinski's willingness to speak his mind.

Brzezinski himself later tried to explain this in his memoirs by suggesting that he and Carter shared "a surprising affinity between Poland and the South, two people bred on a history that overcame defeat, on a code of chivalry and honor that proudly compensated for backwardness." One day Zbig read to the president a passage from William Styron's 1979 novel *Sophie's Choice,* in which the southern novelist explored this theme: "Despoiled and exploited like the South, and like it, a poverty-ridden, agrarian, feudal society, Poland has shared with the Old South one bulwark against its immemorial humiliation, and that is pride." This seems like an overly complex explanation. But Brzezinski "thought that in a strange way it conveyed something about the relationship between the two of us." Perhaps, but the truth may simply be that Carter hated the prospect of having to fire such a close adviser.

In any case, over time it would become clear that Brzezinski's unflagging persistence was having its effect. He was wearing the president down.

So too was Jack McCloy. During the Soviet-brigade-in-Cuba nonsense, this Republican stalwart and unofficial chairman of the foreign policy establishment had helped Carter once again on a bipartisan foreign policy issue—just as he had earlier on the fight over the Panama Canal Treaty and the issue, touchy for some Republicans, of normalization of diplomatic relations with China. Not surprisingly, by the autumn of 1979, the Carter administration was finding it harder to resist McCloy's entreaties. The shah himself made it clear how he felt in early September when he told two Rockefeller associates visiting him in his Mexican refuge, "I ask President Carter directly why I am not welcome in the United States. . . . I cannot accept this insult. . . . I cannot ignore the fact that I have been mistreated by President Carter."

That September, Cy Vance went up to New York to attend an off-the-record meeting of the Council on Foreign Relations, where he defended the administration's decision not to provide the shah asylum. McCloy was not impressed, and in private even Vance was beginning to have second thoughts. Then, on October 6, David Rockefeller's assistant, Joseph Reed, called the State Department and revealed that the shah was seriously ill and might need medical treatment in the United States. Reed was told that a "substantial medical case" would have to be made before the administration could change course. Ten days later, Reed passed on more detailed information about the shah's health. The deposed monarch, he revealed, had been battling cancer for more than seven years and now needed immediate treatment in a New York medical facility.

Upon hearing this news, Vance changed his mind and told the president on October 19 that, as a matter of "common decency," the shah should be admitted to the United States. Hamilton Jordan also found domestic political reasons to reverse course. "Mr. President," Jordan argued, "if the shah dies in Mexico can you imagine the field day Kissinger will have with that? He'll say that first you caused the shah's downfall and now you've killed him."

"To hell with Henry Kissinger," Carter snapped. "I am the president of this country." Carter was still resisting a decision his gut was telling him might lead to untoward complications. The president turned to everyone in the room and asked, "What are you guys going to advise me to do if they overrun our embassy and take our people hostage?"

ON THE MORNING of October 20, 1979, President Carter and Rosalynn flew up to Boston to attend a long-scheduled dedication of the newly built John F. Kennedy Presidential Library. For Carter, it was like walking into enemy territory. Greeted by Senator Ted Kennedy, Carter found himself surrounded by members of the Kennedy clan, including Caroline and John F. Kennedy, Jr., and the murdered president's widow, Jacqueline Kennedy Onassis. Carter kissed the senator's wife, Joan, on the cheek, but as he drew close to Mrs. Onassis, "she flinched away ostentatiously." A *Boston Globe* reporter wrote that Mrs. Onassis "seemed startled at first, then her smile dropped into an expression of displeasure, then annoyance."

It was all very awkward, particularly since everyone assumed Senator Kennedy would soon announce that he was challenging Carter for the Democratic nomination in 1980. Carter had brought along a prepared text, drafted by speechwriter Rick Hertzberg, but, sensing the mood of the crowd of six thousand people assembled for the historic occasion, Carter decided to begin with a sly joke. "I never met him," Carter said of JFK, "but I know that John Kennedy loved politics. He loved laughter. And when the two came together, he loved that best of all." Carter then reminded his audience that a reporter had once asked President Kennedy at a March 1962 press conference "whether you could recommend this job to others." Kennedy had replied, "I would not recommend it to others—at least for a while." At this moment, Ted Kennedy, who had been looking down, absorbed in studying his own speech notes, straightened up in his chair and looked at Carter. The president then delivered his punch line, grinning at Ted, "As you can see, President Kennedy's wit and also his wisdom is certainly as relevant today as it was then." Even Ted had to laugh.

Carter then delivered an unusually poignant speech, speaking at one point of that day on November 22, 1963, when he heard that the president had been shot. He had stepped outside his peanut warehouse and knelt on the steps and prayed. "In a few minutes, I learned that he had not lived. My president. I wept openly, for the first time in more than ten years, for the first time since the day that my own father died."

Carter then went on to explain that "change is the law of life," and the world of 1980 would be as different from 1960 as that year was from 1940. "Our means of improving the world," he warned, "must also be different." After a decade of high inflation and growing oil imports, "our economic cup no longer overflows." And in a pointed challenge to the Kennedy sitting on the dais, Carter argued, "Because of inflation, fiscal restraint has become a matter of simple public duty. We can no longer rely on a rising economic tide to lift the boats of the poorest in our society. . . . We have a keener appreciation of limits now: the limits of government; limits on the use of military power abroad; the limits on manipulating without harm to ourselves a delicate and balanced natural environment."

It was as good a speech as Carter had ever given, or at least as good as his famous Law Day speech back in 1974, and also delivered, ironically, in the presence of Ted Kennedy. Even some of his most acerbic critics in the press, columnists David Broder and Mary McGrory, gave it rave reviews. It marked the opening of his unofficial campaign for reelection as president.

That Saturday afternoon, the Carters returned to the White House, and late that evening he spoke on the phone with Brzezinski, telling him that he had finally decided to permit the shah to go to New York for medical treatment. He had reluctantly decided that he could no longer deny medical treatment to a man who was "diagnosed as fatally ill with cancer." Still worried about the security of the embassy, he emphasized that Zbig should take care to "inform our embassy in Tehran that this would occur." Vance and the State Department had suggested that the administration should first try to get the Bazargan government in Tehran to acquiesce to the shah's visit. But Carter thought this smacked of trying to get their "permission" and rejected this gambit. Instead, the Bazargan government was merely to be informed of the decision.

The shah flew into New York on October 22, 1979, whereupon Rockefeller's aide, Joseph Reed, circulated a memo to McCloy and other members of Project Alpha congratulating them: "Our 'mission impossible' is completed. . . . My applause is like thunder."

Rockefeller, McCloy, and Kissinger had in fact used the pretext of the shah's allegedly dire medical condition to bamboozle the president into making a decision he did not think wise. They played on his humanitarian instincts. "I was told the shah was desperately ill," Carter later said in an interview. "I was told that New York was the only medical facility that was capable of possibly saving his life." Neither of these things was true.

It would take decades for the facts to emerge, but we now know that the shah, while long diagnosed with lymphocytic leukemia—a slow-moving cancer—actually received poor medical treatment at the hands of Rockefeller's high-priced doctors in New York. He was misdiagnosed with malaria, he survived a botched operation to remove some gallstones, and worse, his doctors failed to remove an enlarged spleen. When months later his spleen was finally removed in an operation in Cairo, the doctor accidentally nicked his pancreas. He developed an abscess that was not treated with intravenous antibiotics. He ultimately died not from cancer but from a series of medical mishaps, ironically initiated by the team of celebrity New York doctors chosen for him by Rockefeller. The shah had been secretly diagnosed with lymphocytic leukemia six years earlier; like most such patients, he was living with the condition, not dying from it. Needless to say, Rockefeller and his Project Alpha cohorts did not bother to convey this information to the president.

LESS THAN TWO weeks later, on Sunday, November 4, Hamilton Jordan received a phone call at 4:30 A.M. from the duty officer in the White House Situation Room. The voice on the other end of the line told him, "We want to advise you that the American embassy in Tehran has been overrun by demonstrators and the American personnel are believed to be held in captivity."

"My God," responded Jordan groggily. "Are there any injuries? Was anyone killed?"

"Not that we know of, Mr. Jordan—but we really don't have complete information."

Carter himself had received a similar call from Secretary Vance. The president was at Camp David that weekend, and he later recalled his visceral emotional reaction: "I could picture the revolutionaries keeping the 72 hostages, or whatever the number was at the time, in the compound, and assassinating one of them every morning at sunrise until the shah was returned to Iran or until we agreed to some other act in response to their blackmail. It's still a very vivid memory to me."

That morning Carter's appointments secretary, Phil Wise, called Jordan and asked if he thought it advisable for the president to rush back to Washington. Jordan replied, no, he thought all the embassy personnel would be released in a few hours, just as had happened the previous February when the embassy was temporarily overrun by Iranian protesters. Hamilton went for a jog and then over breakfast told his companions, "They'll be released before tonight."

Jordan had something else weighing heavily on his mind that day. That evening CBS News was scheduled to broadcast a special one-hour interview of Ted Kennedy by one of its senior correspondents, Roger Mudd. The network had promoted the show heavily, and Jordan knew from several reporter friends that the highly anticipated interview might well be a political embarrassment for the senator. Mudd had taped the interview during two sessions with Kennedy over several weeks. The veteran journalist was a skilled interviewer, and oddly enough, Kennedy had not subjected himself to extensive questioning in years. Mudd asked him tough questions about everything from the shaky status of his marriage to details about the 1969 Chappaquiddick accident in which Mary Jo Kopechne had died. Kennedy seemed wholly unprepared, answering with stumbling hesitations and half sentences. And when Mudd asked him directly why he wanted to be president, Kennedy rambled incoherently.

Jordan was stunned when he saw the interview and only frustrated that millions of Americans that evening happened to be tuned in to a different network, airing Steven Spielberg's blockbuster film *Jaws.* "The biggest political story of the year," Jordan thought, "and everybody's going to be watching mechanical sharks eating swimmers instead of Roger Mudd eating Ted Kennedy. I wanted everyone to see what I saw: the Kennedy legend reduced to a bumbling, inarticulate man."

Carter had the same reaction to Kennedy's performance. "I thought [it] was devastating," he noted. "It showed him not able to answer a simple question about what he would do if elected or why he should be president." Like Jordan, the president was "disturbed" by the hostage taking in Tehran, but he fully expected the embassy personnel would be released quickly. The next day, however, he recorded his growing irritation with "the idiot Khomeini."

Brzezinski had received a similar call at 5:10 A.M. that Sunday, and like the president, he had no expectation that the incident would last longer than a day or two. When he was told that Carter had already been informed of the embassy storming, Zbig decided not to disturb him further. Carter called him shortly after 8:00 A.M. and they spoke again at 9:20 A.M. On both occasions they chatted for only three or four minutes. Zbig told him that he thought no military action was possible. The situation was too fluid, and they would just have to wait for Iranian authorities to intervene. Carter spent most of that Sunday making nearly forty phone calls to various mayors, congressmen, and Democratic Party officials to talk about his reelection campaign. Late that evening, after watching the CBS special report on Kennedy, he and Rosalynn went down to the White House theater and viewed the 1943 war drama *Sahara,* starring Humphrey Bogart in the role of an American tank commander lost in the Libyan desert. It was a relaxing diversion from an unexceptional day in the life of the president. He had no idea that this day would be the first of 444 days of unrelenting crisis.

No ONE IN the Carter White house had any firm idea of what had happened in Tehran. The president knew only that the embassy had been overrun by a mob of hundreds of angry Iranian students and that an unknown number of Americans were being held hostage somewhere on the expansive grounds of the U.S. embassy compound. *The New York Times* initially reported that "about 90 Americans had been seized." In its prerevolutionary heyday, the embassy compound had housed the offices of more than a thousand American citizens. It was days before the administration learned that the actual number of hostages seized on November 4 was sixty-six. Carter had no intelligence on who had planned and executed the seizure.

It was, in fact, a stunt organized by a handful of Iranian students; the Imam Khomeini had not been consulted and had no knowledge of their plans. But within a day, it became clear from news accounts that Khomeini had given his blessing to the action, if only because he could use the resulting crisis as a means to consolidate his personal power. On November 6, Prime Minister Mehdi Bazargan and his American-educated foreign minister, Ibrahim Yazdi, resigned to make way for a more hardline government. That same day Carter decided to send two private emissaries, former attorney general Ramsey Clark and William Miller, the staff director for the Senate Select Committee on Intelligence, to negotiate with the Revolutionary Council. They got as far as Turkey before Khomeini refused to allow them into the country. This caused Carter to begin to think about "punitive" actions. But he felt constrained, not only for the safety of the sixty-six hostages but because he knew there were still some 570 other Americans living in Iran. Any kind of military response might well result in the taking of additional hostages—or loss of life. Carter was spending "every spare moment, trying to decide what to do." But he noted in his diary that it was "almost impossible to deal with a crazy man [Khomeini], except that he does have religious beliefs." Carter hoped his religious beliefs would prevent him from murdering the hostages. "I believe that's our ultimate hope for a successful resolution of this problem."

Brzezinski, of course, was quick to request contingency plans for a military mission to rescue the hostages. Carter gave his acquiescence to what he thought was only prudent contingency planning. But Zbig immediately began meeting secretly in his office two or three times a week to plan a rescue mission. Included in these meetings were Defense Secretary Harold Brown, CIA Director Stansfield Turner, General David Jones (the chairman of the Joint Chiefs of Staff), and various other military officers. Carter must have been aware of these meetings, but he had little notion of how deeply his national security adviser was inserting himself into planning what became a large-scale, highly ambitious covert military operation.

At this stage of the crisis, Carter was focused on the diplomatic game. He even refused, for instance, to allow an aircraft carrier to be diverted into the Persian Gulf, fearing that even this move would escalate the crisis and endanger the hostages. On the other hand, Carter told his advisers that once the hostages were released, he was strongly inclined to punish Iran militarily. But in the meantime, the president would use diplomatic pressure and economic sanctions. During that first week of the crisis Carter had authorized the CIA to use its Beirut "back channel" to urge the PLO's Yasir Arafat to use his influence with Khomeini.

Not surprisingly, Brzezinski was frustrated by the president's measured responses. He thought Carter was being too patient. Zbig also thought Cy Vance was giving the president the impression that nothing could be done. This was generally true. On November 12, for instance, just a week into the crisis, the State Department's intelligence division handed Vance a memo concluding that "the detention of the hostages could continue for some months." Vance was being advised that there was "almost no prospect" that diplomatic initiatives or economic pressures or even military action could have any successful results in the short term. Only time would solve the mess. Vance thought this unhappy analysis was nevertheless correct. Brzezinski thought it weakminded. After huddling with Jody Powell and Hamilton Jordan, Zbig noted in his diary, "We all agreed that for political reasons, as well as for substantive reasons, the President should be tough on the Iranian issue. Ham is bringing Kirbo up here because he thinks that Kirbo will stiffen the President's back and cancel the weak advice likely to be given by Vance." Kirbo, however, proved to be cautious in his advice and urged Carter to pursue the diplomatic track.

Carter met regularly, often several times a week, with a rump version of the National Security Council called the Special Coordinating Committee. It was informally chaired by Brzezinski and attended by Vice President Mondale; the secretaries of state, defense, and treasury; the attorney general; the CIA director; the chairman of the Joint Chiefs; and both Jody Powell and Hamilton Jordan. At one of these early meetings, on the morning of November 9, Carter listened as his aides argued about whether the shah should be asked to leave. Mondale and Vance strongly thought the shah's early departure for any other asylum venue, perhaps Mexico, would facilitate the release of the hostages. A dismayed Brzezinski spoke up to say that this would be giving in to the demands of a "student mob in Tehran." Carter sided with Brzezinski. In the middle of the meeting, however, he was called to the phone to speak with Rosalynn, who was visiting refugee camps in Thailand. While the president was out of the room, Ham Jordan, knowing of the First Lady's hawkish political instincts, quipped, "When he comes back, he will probably declare war on Iran."

At noon that same day, Carter traveled the few blocks over to the State Department and took an emotional meeting with relatives of the hostages. Zbig thought it a bad idea, and he deliberately avoided such meetings so as not to be "swayed by emotions." Carter thought it was the right thing to do and felt gratified by the warmth and support he received from the families.

Early on the morning of November 14 Treasury Secretary William Miller phoned the president and informed him that the new Iranian government was trying to withdraw its funds from American banks. It was 5:40 A.M., but Carter was already in the Oval Office. "I told him," Carter noted in his diary, "to impound all Iranian assets until we could ascertain what Iran owes us in every possible form."

The president thought he was acting in the interest of the nation. Carter didn't realize it, but by freezing Iranian assets he was acting to the benefit of Chase Manhattan Bank. He had been badly misinformed about what was taking place. In the months after the revolution, Khomeini's regime had gradually transferred some $6 billion out of its Chase accounts. These were oil-revenue funds deposited over the years by the shah to Chase Manhattan, his favorite banking partner. By the autumn of 1979, it became apparent that Chase would soon not have enough Iranian funds on deposit to cover the bank's outstanding loans to the former Pahlavi regime. Chase was the lead syndicator of a $500 million loan made to the shah prior to his downfall. Chase bankers were now worried that the revolutionary regime might have legal grounds to repudiate this loan. When the loan was authorized in 1977, Chase's own Iranian lawyers had warned the bank that the shah had not bothered to get the parliament's approval, as required under Article 25 of the Iranian constitution. Technically, the loan was unconstitutional. If Tehran were to repudiate the loan, Chase would have to answer to its partner banks in the syndicate. Chase was highly exposed.

The chairman of Chase Manhattan Bank, of course, was David Rockefeller—and Chase's legal counsel were none other than the lawyers from John McCloy's firm, Milbank, Tweed, Hadley & McCloy. In the aftermath of the Iranian revolution, Milbank, Tweed lawyers had consulted with the Treasury Department about preparing contingency plans for freezing Iranian assets. These discussions had started as early as February 1979. But they took on a new urgency when the embassy was seized on November 4. The very next day Chase received a telex from the Iranian government authorizing a payment of $4.05 million interest due on the $500 million loan. Chase was instructed to take the payment, due on November 15, from one of Iran's accounts in its London branch. Chase did not acknowledge these instructions and instead reached out to Treasury Department officials and urged them to order a freeze of Iranian assets. The Chase bankers clearly saw the hostage crisis as a timely excuse to execute a freeze order. Iran's acting foreign affairs minister, Abol Hassan Bani-Sadr, only helped Chase's case for a freeze when he announced early on the morning of November 14 that his country was going to withdraw its deposits from all American banks. Bani-Sadr's announcement had precipitated Miller's call to Carter early on the morning of November 14.

But now Chase bank officers went a step further. Since Carter's freeze order on November 14 took effect one day prior to the day on which Iran's $4.05 million interest payment was due, the payment was not taken from Chase's London branch, as instructed by the Iranians on November 5. Chase then boldly declared Iran's $500 million loan in default. Moving with deliberate haste—and even before receiving the required Treasury Department authorization—Chase seized all of Iran's Chase accounts and used those monies to "offset" any outstanding Iranian loans. "When the dust had cleared," wrote financial analyst Mark Hulbert, "Chase had no loans to Iran left on its books."

The decision to freeze Iranian assets in all American banks—both in the United States and abroad—seemed at the time to be a plausible response to the taking of hostages. But in retrospect, it might well have prolonged the crisis, adding a difficult financial complication to the eventual negotiations. The fate of the hostages would now be contingent on untangling billions of dollars owed Iran and her creditors.

A WEEK AFTER the freeze order, on November 20, Carter ordered the deployment of U.S. military assets into the region, beefing up strike forces stationed on the island of Diego Garcia in the Indian Ocean. Two weeks into the crisis, he now agreed to allow the USS *Kitty Hawk* aircraft carrier—equipped with large helicopters—to sail from Subic Bay in the Philippines to the Persian Gulf. Clearly, everyone meeting in the White House was now worried that the hostages might be held for a long time.

On November 17, Khomeini had announced the release of thirteen African American and female hostages who, he explained, "were not

American spies." Secretary Vance believed their release was the direct result of Arafat's intercession. But in garbled interviews with reporters, the ayatollah also was reported to have said that "if the shah is not returned, the hostages could be tried" or "will be tried." Worried that the hostages might actually be tried for espionage, Carter gathered his key advisers on November 23, the day after Thanksgiving, at Camp David. Attending this critical meeting were Mondale, Brown, Vance, Brzezinski, Jones, Turner, Jordan, and Powell. Their task was to draft a credible public threat that if the hostages were tried for espionage, serious consequences would follow.

Earlier, both Brzezinski and Eizenstat had argued the merits of a naval blockade of Kharg Island, the port from which Iran exported most of its oil. Brzezinski told Eizenstat that he thought it would be a "terrible mistake" not to use military force. Powell objected to any military muscle: "If we seize Kharg Island, then what? We have Kharg Island, and they have the hostages." Vice President Mondale had also weighed in, telling Carter that all his advisers favored some kind of military action to block Iran's oil exports. "I know that," Carter replied, "and I am not going to have it on my conscience that it would kill the hostages." But that was earlier in the crisis; now Carter was persuaded that if Khomeini staged a show trial of the hostages, he would "mine the entrances to all the Iranian ports."

When Vance expressed some hesitation about whether this would be a wise course, Carter firmly instructed him "to notify Khomeini through sure channels that any trials of our hostages would result in severe restrictions on Iranian commerce, that no negotiations through the UN would be conducted, and that any harm to our hostages would result in direct retaliatory action." This warning was indeed conveyed through diplomatic channels—and Khomeini never again spoke about an espionage trial. The implied threat of a mining operation or naval blockade had worked.

Carter was obviously under a lot of pressure, and sometimes he let it show. Thursday, November 29, was a particularly bleak day, cold and gray. The president met for fifteen minutes that morning with his new attorney general, Benjamin Civiletti, who conveyed the unhappy news that he felt compelled to appoint a special prosecutor in the Studio 54 case involving Hamilton Jordan. "He gave a ridiculous reason," Carter noted in his diary. Civiletti conceded there was not enough evidence to warrant an indictment—but he nevertheless needed to have a special prosecutor investigate "whether the accusers were guilty of perjury."

Carter was angry that his friend and chief of staff was going to be dragged into a nasty and expensive litigation—all for nothing. That afternoon, perhaps to vent his anger, Carter jogged eight miles in freezing-cold weather along the C&O Canal through Georgetown. He was accompanied only by his physician, Rear Admiral William Lukash, and an air force aide. Carter had told the Secret Service to meet him at Fletcher's Boathouse—but when they arrived, the Secret Service cars were nowhere to be seen. "I stood there about ten minutes, while I fumed, and then ran back into town," he noted in his diary. "I was really furious, and my hands almost froze."

That evening he received more frustrating news. The issue was the shah. Some days earlier, Brzezinski had shown up at 7:00 A.M. for his regular intelligence briefing of the president—only to find Secretary Vance huddled alone with Carter. Such one-on-one meetings were most unusual, and Zbig naturally thought Vance was making an end run around him. He was right. Vance had convinced Carter that the shah had outstayed his welcome and it was time to find him a refuge outside the United States. Mexico's President José López Portillo had agreed to give him asylum. Carter thought the problem was solved, but suddenly, at 6:30 on the evening of November 29—less than an hour after his freezing jog—Vance called the president "with the unbelievable news" that López Portillo had reversed himself and announced that the shah was no longer welcome. Carter was furious all over again.

A new refuge for the shah was back on the table. But no one wanted the toxic former monarch, except perhaps Egypt's Sadat. By December 2, the Egyptian had said he would reluctantly take him in if he had to leave the United States. Carter was in a quandary: "The situation is that I want him [the shah] to go to Egypt, but don't want to hurt Sadat. Sadat wants him to stay in the United States but doesn't want to hurt me. It is a decision for me to make."

Later that evening Carter had what Brzezinski called "a most disagreeable conversation" with his outspoken national security adviser. Zbig had called the president, who was up at Camp David that Sunday evening, to say that he thought it would be a very bad idea to let Sadat offer the shah asylum. Zbig thought, quite correctly, that it would be "dangerous for Egyptian stability" to have the shah in Cairo. The implication was that the shah should remain in America. Thoroughly irritated, Carter exploded at Zbig over the phone and accused him of "conspiring with Kissinger and Rockefeller to get the shah permanently into the country." According to Brzezinski's notes, the president said that he thought Cy Vance "was sitting on his ass and doing nothing." Clearly outraged at being sandbagged, Carter hung up on his national security adviser. Late that night, he noted in his diary, "Zbig and Cy have not done anything to prepare an alternative place for the shah to go. Zbig has been too much a part of the David Rockefeller community and has always wanted the shah to stay in this country."

Carter was justifiably irritated by both Rockefeller and Kissinger; he knew Kissinger was privately telling everyone that he thought Carter was mishandling the hostage crisis. "There is no way to keep anything secret in Washington," Carter later wrote. When an infuriated Cy Vance complained to Carter about Kissinger, the president felt obliged to invite the former secretary of state to the White House "to work out our differences." Kissinger tried to claim that his published criticisms concerning Iran had all been taken from interviews given prior to the embassy seizure. He promised in the future to avoid such comments, and he reassured Carter that he would use his influence to help the administration persuade the Senate to ratify the SALT II treaty. Carter pretended to be mollified, but he knew better: "Things were better for a few days—and then reverted."

As it became evident that there would be no early resolution to the hostage crisis, George Ball went on *Meet the Press* and bluntly complained that "had it not been for Mr. Kissinger and a few others making themselves enormously obnoxious for the administration, trying to force the shah into this country, maybe we wouldn't even have done it, even for reasons of compassion." Needless to say, Kissinger never accepted responsibility for what he had done.

In the event, Carter found a temporary home for the shah and his family entourage at Lackland Air Force Base, near San Antonio, Texas. This at least got the shah out of New York City and away from the glare of publicity. But Vance had convinced Carter that the shah's physical presence on American soil was a certain impediment to all their diplomatic efforts to obtain the release of the hostages, so the president was relieved when Ham Jordan persuaded General Omar Torrijos to invite the shah to move into an island villa off the coast of Panama. On December 15, the day of the shah's departure for Panama, Carter rose early and decided to phone the shah: "I gave him my best wishes and told him he would like Panama." The deposed monarch would never return to America.

A MONTH INTO the hostage crisis, political pressure grew on the president to act. On December 4, Carter walked into the East Room of the White House and, with Vice President Mondale at his side, formally declared that he was seeking reelection. It was a subdued affair, attended only by his family and a small audience of White House staffers and administration officials.

"I have made some mistakes," he said, "and I have learned from them. I have fought some bitter fights against selfish special interests, and I expect to go on leading the fight for the common good of our people. I carry some scars and carry them with pride." Inflation was running at more than 13 percent; unemployment was ticking up and the economy seemed headed for a mild recession. Carter was nevertheless defiant and resolute: "I intend to win." But he also indicated that, until the hostages were released, he would be running his campaign from inside the White House.

The press quickly dubbed this his "Rose Garden" campaign strategy. Oddly enough, the president's political fortunes had flipped dramatically in the month since the embassy seizure. Carter noted that the polls were "surprisingly good for me." He still trailed Kennedy, but his own approval rating in the latest Gallup poll had jumped from 30 percent to 61 percent in one month. The American people were rallying to their president in a time of crisis.

The next day, Carter met with a hundred members of Congress and talked mostly about Iran. They pressed him to take stronger action, presumably to use military force in some fashion against the ayatollah. Brzezinski also weighed in again, telling the president that "time was not working to our advantage." A few days earlier, Defense Secretary Brown had gently resurrected the idea of mining Iranian ports. Brown conceded that mining harbors was still an act of war, but "a bloodless act of war, like invading an embassy and taking hostages." Brown thought they could hold off on military action for another ten or fifteen days—or perhaps even three weeks: "But even then, I do not think we can delay facing up to at least the mildest military action for more than about a month from now." Carter scribbled in the margins of this memo, "Zbig-Harold, I agree completely." But when Brzezinski and Mondale attempted to push for an imminent decision to mine the harbors, Carter demurred. In Carter's mind, the military option was receding.

On December 7, he paid another visit to the State Department, where he met again with the relatives of the hostages. Afterward, in comments to a group of State Department employees, Carter flatly stated, "I am not going to take any military action that would cause bloodshed or arouse the unstable captors of our hostages to attack or punish them." The remark was quickly leaked to *The New York Times*. If the Ayatollah Khomeini was paying attention, he presumably now knew that Carter would not use the military option. Stu Eizenstat thought this was a "serious mistake." Khomeini should have been kept guessing. But in Carter's mind, he never ruled out a military option, particularly a naval blockade or mining of harbors. He later insisted, "I never placed the hostages' lives first." Instead, he had two goals: protecting the honor of the nation and protecting the hostages. He was just fortunate, he thought, that he never had to choose one over the other. According to the polls, most Americans agreed that military force should not be used if it might endanger the lives of the hostages. So for the time being, presidential restraint and patience were good politics.

Brzezinski, however, was still impatient to have his president be seen as tough. Privately, he thought Carter's reluctance to use force was subtle evidence that at heart he was simply a pacifist.

ON FRIDAY MORNING, December 21, 1979, Carter signed a presidential finding authorizing a CIA covert program to maintain contact with anti-Khomeini dissidents in Iran. He knew such contacts were unlikely to move Iran toward a democratic, civil society—but he thought the effort should be made. That same morning, Brzezinski handed him a troubling intelligence report suggesting that the Soviets were augmenting the number of military "advisers" they had stationed in Afghanistan. Carter was worried enough about the report to take note of it in his diary.

That afternoon, Carter, Rosalynn, and Amy took the helicopter to Camp David, planning to spend the entire Christmas week hanging out in Catoctin Mountain Park. Aspen Lodge had truly become their preferred home. Its rustic atmosphere and simplicity reminded them of their simple one-story ranch home in Plains. Three years into his presidency, Carter had actually spent close to one-quarter of his days at Camp David. They were relieved to get out of Washington. It seemed like a "sad time" to be in the city. The hostages had now been held for nearly six weeks—and there seemed nothing festive about this Christmas season. On Secretary Vance's suggestion, Carter had decided not to light up the traditional Christmas tree erected just south of the White House. It would be left darkened, a depressing symbol of the times. "It's relatively lonely at Camp David," Carter noted. "Just Rosalynn, Amy and I. This is the first time in twenty-six years that we haven't been with our folks for Christmas—since the year my daddy died. I told all the senior staff at the White House and the Filipino stewards to bring their families up for Christmas Day."

On Christmas Eve, the Carters watched *Chapter Two,* a romantic comedy based on Neil Simon's Broadway play. The next morning, Amy awoke them at 5:30, eager to open her Christmas presents. Carter talked on the phone with his mother in Plains and otherwise spent the day quietly keeping to himself. That evening, the president, Rosalynn, and Amy walked over to Laurel Lodge, where they had Christmas dinner with thirty-nine family members of the military support staff at Camp David. He was called away in the middle of the dinner to take a phone call from Brzezinski, who gravely informed him that it looked like a full-scale Soviet invasion of Afghanistan was under way. Carter took in the news calmly and afterward watched *The Black Stallion,* an adventure film produced by Francis Ford Coppola. Watching movies was one thing the presidential family did a lot. The next evening, they saw *Going in Style,* a caper comedy starring George Burns, Art Carney, and Lee Strasberg.

By then, Carter was reading intelligence and newspaper reports about the burgeoning crisis in Afghanistan. It was clear that a violent coup had led to the ouster and summary execution of the impoverished country's president, Hafizullah Amin, an Afghan Marxist who had himself seized power only three months earlier. Carter was alarmed by reports that the coup had actually been carried out by thousands of Soviet troops, who seized Kabul's radio station and assaulted the presidential palace. "They [the Soviets] have had 215 flights," he noted in his diary, "moving 8,000 or 10,000 people in—an extremely serious development."

Early on the evening of December 27, Charlie Kirbo arrived at Camp David, and together with Rosalynn they watched yet another film, *Advise & Consent,* the 1962 classic political drama starring Henry Fonda. Afterward, Carter decided that they would have to cut short their holiday vacation and return to the White House the next morning. He felt certain that the dramatic Soviet intervention in Afghanistan was a game changer. The next day he used the dedicated White House–Kremlin hotline to send "the sharpest message I have ever sent to [Leonid] Brezhnev, telling him that the invasion of Afghanistan would seriously and adversely affect the relationship between our two countries."

Carter was already well briefed about the intricacies of Afghanistan's convoluted internal politics.* The Afghan monarchy had been overthrown in July 1973 by the deposed king's cousin, Mohammed Daoud Khan, and a republic was proclaimed. But in April 1978, Khan was assassinated during a coup by a minuscule Afghan Communist Party led by Nur Mohammad Taraki. The communist-led coup came as a complete surprise to Moscow. The American-educated Taraki considered himself a secular Marxist, but not surprisingly, his attempts to reform the country's feudal economy met strong resistance from conservative tribal and religious leaders.

The Russians were actually very reluctant to become involved. Politburo documents show that Taraki's regime requested Soviet troops in March 1979—and the Kremlin refused to intervene. Soviet prime minister Alexei Kosygin told the Afghan president on March 20, 1979, "The entry of our troops in Afghanistan would outrage the international community, triggering a string of extremely negative consequences in many different areas." But in September 1979, Taraki was himself overthrown and executed by Hafizullah Amin, a rival leader of a hard-line

---

* Through the centuries, Afghanistan had served as a veritable quagmire for numerous foreign invaders. In 1839, a British expeditionary force of 16,500 troops had famously occupied Kabul—only to be forced to retreat three years later. On their way out, the British force was ambushed by Afghan tribesmen—and only one British officer was allowed to escape to report on the massacre.

faction within the Communist Party. Amin cracked down on both his left-wing comrades and the conservative tribal leaders, imprisoning thousands and executing hundreds of political enemies. Amin's ostensible Russian allies soon judged that his ruthless tactics and rigid ideology were making him too many Afghan enemies.

In mid-December, the Soviet politburo came to the conclusion that Amin was creating the conditions for a reactionary, Iranian-style Islamist backlash. Amin was a disaster and had to go, and in his place, Brezhnev's inner circle of apparatchiks decided they would place in power a more moderate and sensible Afghan communist, former deputy prime minister Babrak Karmal. Thus, when Soviet troops were airlifted into Kabul on Christmas morning, ironically, they did so in order to depose a ruthless communist in favor of a "moderate" communist who might have more credibility in Afghan society. The Kremlin justified its "intervention" by saying they had come to "put down the rebellion of conservative Muslim tribesmen." This was actually true. This was not just disingenuous Soviet propaganda.

Carter knew that this too was true, because six months earlier Brzezinski had persuaded him to authorize a covert CIA program to fund this rebellion and to supply nonlethal aid to these conservative Muslim tribesmen, otherwise known as the mujahideen. Back on April 4, 1979, CIA Director Stansfield Turner had come to the White House with a team of experts to give the president a major briefing on Afghanistan. Carter was handed "detailed maps showing the spread of dissident strength." Two days later, Brzezinski "pushed a decision" through the Special Coordinating Committee to aid the mujahideen. Brzezinski wanted to exacerbate the rivalry between the two Afghan Communist Party factions. "It was in our interest," Brzezinski later explained, "to make their lives more difficult, [both] towards each other, [and] towards the Soviets."

Early in May 1979, Brzezinski warned Carter that the growing Soviet presence in Afghanistan could also facilitate the separatist movement in neighboring Baluchistan. He ominously warned that an independent Baluchistan would give the Soviets "access to the Indian Ocean while dismembering Pakistan." Brzezinski had a fondness for thinking grand strategic thoughts. The reality was that the tribesmen of Baluchistan had been in open revolt against the Pakistani army's repressive occupation of the province for years. The Soviets had not inspired this rebellion and had no influence over the Baluch. But for Brzezinski, the Kremlin's support of a puppet regime in Afghanistan inevitably raised the specter of Russian historical ambitions for a southern seaport.

These arguments nevertheless persuaded Carter to send the appropriate congressional intelligence oversight committees a formal "finding" on July 3, 1979, authorizing $500,000 in cash, communications gear, and other nonlethal supplies for the Afghan insurgents. Brzezinski later said that he wrote a note to the president on that same day, predicting "that in my opinion this aid was going to induce a Soviet military intervention." In August, the CIA broadened this covert assistance, funneling Soviet-made arms taken from Egyptian arms stores to Pakistan, where the weapons were smuggled into Afghanistan. This aid was critical to escalating the mujahideen's military attacks on the Kabul regime, so much so that by November 3 Brzezinski again warned Carter that the Soviets might well intervene militarily. On December 17—just eight days before the Soviet invasion—CIA Director Turner was able to report to the Special Coordinating Committee that "most of the countryside is now in rebel hands, but no major cities are expected to fall unless there are significant defections from the Army." Turner went on to predict accurately, "We believe the Soviets have made a political decision to keep a pro-Soviet regime in power and to use military force to that end if necessary."

The Soviet invasion on Christmas Day should therefore not have come as a surprise to the Carter White House. Brzezinski saw it as a confirmation of his worldview.* Privately, Zbig noted in his diary, "Had we been tougher sooner, had we drawn the line more clearly, had we engaged in the kind of consultations that I had so many times advocated, maybe the Soviets would not have engaged in this act of miscalculation." He felt vindicated. Some historians have argued that the aid provided to the mujahideen in the summer and autumn of 1979

---

* The fact that American covert aid to the mujahideen preceded the Soviet invasion by six months was revealed by Brzezinski himself in his 1983 memoir, *Power and Principle*. Betty Glad and many other historians have since documented Carter's covert program to aid the Afghan rebels.

was actually designed to provoke a Russian intervention. By one account, Brzezinski, upon hearing of the invasion, exclaimed to William Odom, his military adviser on the NSC, "They have taken the bait!" Years later, Brzezinski told a French journalist that "this secret operation was an excellent idea. It succeeded in drawing the Russians into the Afghan trap." On the other hand, on December 26, 1979, just a day after the invasion, Brzezinski told the president, "We should not be too optimistic about Afghanistan becoming a Soviet Vietnam." Zbig certainly hoped that Afghanistan might become a quagmire for the Soviets, but he was realistic enough at the time to warn Carter that the poorly led and poorly organized Afghan mujahideen could not be compared to the highly motivated and well-supplied Vietcong. In 2010, Brzezinski told his French biographer, Justin Vaïsse, "We didn't really trap them, but we knew what they were doing, and they knew what we were doing.... When we started to give them [the mujahideen] money, I told Carter that I think they'll [the Soviets] go in, and they'll probably use that as an excuse in part, but that they're going in anyway, because they are taking over the regime."

Carter was nevertheless genuinely shocked when the Russians invaded. "There goes SALT II," he exclaimed to Rosalynn. He had worked hard for Senate confirmation of this critical arms-control treaty, and now this seemed like an "impossible task."

Hamilton Jordan called Carter from Georgia and asked if he should return immediately to Washington. "No," Carter replied, "unless you can get the Soviets out of Afghanistan."

Jordan remarked, "As if we didn't already have our hands full with the hostages."

"This is more serious, Hamilton," said the president. "Capturing those Americans was an inhumane act committed by a bunch of radicals and condoned by a crazy old man. But this is deliberate aggression that calls into question détente and the way we have been doing business with the Soviets for the past decade."

In retrospect, Carter's assessment was too simple. Historians have found good evidence from the Soviet politburo minutes that paints a different picture of their intentions and expectations. Brezhnev and his aging comrades foolishly thought their military intervention in a country on their southern border would be short-lived and the disruption to détente only temporary. They had no understanding of what a quagmire Afghanistan would become, and they were completely unprepared for Carter's angry and forceful response. But far from being a sign of strength, the decision to embark on the Afghan adventure was evidence of decay and profound weakness at the very heart of the Soviet Union.

Chapter 22
An Unhappy Spring

The President looked as if someone had stabbed him.
—ZBIGNIEW BRZEZINSKI, April 24, 1980

Zbigniew Brzezinski and Carter in the Oval Office
GETTY IMAGES

CARTER HAD RESISTED Brzezinski's anti-Soviet entreaties for nearly three years, repeatedly rejecting his advice and tending nearly always to side with his secretary of state's views. All that would change; the president would now tilt decisively toward Brzezinski. To be sure, Cy Vance was upset by the Soviet invasion—but he thought the Kremlin's decision to intervene was driven by internal developments inside Afghanistan, and that, far from proving the Russian intent to project power, the Afghan invasion was merely a foolish and costly anomaly. "Dear Cy," wrote Thomas J. Watson, Jr., the American ambassador in Moscow, "Afghanistan was an unfortunate aberration. . . . It is also proving to be a very bad decision for the Soviets." Vance agreed, and Brzezinski, of course, strongly disagreed, seeing the invasion as a confirmation of Soviet expansionism. Zbig insisted to Carter that the invasion proved that the Soviets were becoming "more assertive," while the United States was becoming "more acquiescent."

On the last day of 1979, Carter taped a television interview with ABC News anchorman Frank Reynolds and confessed, "My opinion of the Russians has changed most drastically in the last week, [more] than even the previous two and one-half years." The statement was a faux pas, if only because it made him seem, perhaps unfairly, indecisive and naïve about the Soviets. On the other hand, his opinion really had changed, and henceforth, he would become more willing to listen to the advice he received from his hard-line national security adviser.

Literally within hours of the Soviet invasion, Brzezinski was telling the president that the Afghanistan resistance would require additional funds and military arms. Covert operations based in Pakistan and targeting the Soviet puppet regime in Kabul had to be ramped up. He also proposed economic sanctions against the Soviet Union, including a technology export ban and a grain embargo. Carter would soon endorse all these sanctions. The grain embargo was somewhat of a surprise, since it risked alienating voters in the upcoming Iowa caucuses. But Carter approved it at a lively cabinet meeting on January 4, 1980. "Perhaps it was just my imagination," Butler noted, "but I thought Zbig looked somewhat full of himself, and that Cy appeared mildly shaken." Vance registered his dissent by warning everyone that "no one should believe for a minute that the Soviets would withdraw their troops anytime soon." More controversially, on January 20, 1980, Carter announced that American athletes would be forced to boycott the Summer Olympics in Moscow unless the Soviets withdrew from Afghanistan.

With the exception of Brzezinski—who supported any and all measures against the Russians—Carter's advisers were divided among themselves. Mondale supported an Olympic boycott, but he opposed a grain embargo, knowing how unpopular this would be with Midwest farmers. Secretary of Agriculture Bob Bergland fought Brzezinski over the grain embargo, arguing that it would have no effect on the Russians because they would simply buy their grain from Argentina. (Bergland was right.) Vance opposed the Olympic boycott and favored some trade sanctions— but argued that Russian behavior in Afghanistan need not scuttle the administration's efforts to ratify SALT II. Nuclear arms controls were more important, Vance thought, than Afghanistan. But Carter wasn't listening to the more dovish and nuanced advice he usually got from his reserved secretary of state.

On January 23, 1980, Carter gave his fourth State of the Union message and dramatically asserted, "The implications of the Soviet invasion of Afghanistan could pose the most serious threat to world peace since the Second World War." Vance was appalled by such heated rhetoric. Carter insisted, however, that the Soviet threat required an unprecedented U.S. military guarantee to protect Washington's regional allies in the Middle East. "An attempt by any outside force to gain control of the Persian Gulf region will be regarded as an assault on the vital interests of the United States," Carter warned. "It will be repelled by the use of any means necessary, including military force." Harkening back to President Harry Truman's 1946 pronouncements at the beginning of the Cold War, the press quickly dubbed this proclamation the "Carter Doctrine."

It would have been more accurate to call it the "Brzezinski Doctrine." Brzezinski had written the initial draft of the speech, and just hours before Carter went up to Capitol Hill to give the speech, Vance and another White House aide cut out Zbig's reference to a "regional security framework." Vance saw this language as opening the door to bloated and wasteful defense expenditures with the Saudis, the Egyptians, the Turks, and the Pakistanis. Brzezinski found out about this end run, however, and managed to persuade Jody Powell to pencil the language back into the speech. Vance had lost another skirmish in his bureaucratic warfare with Brzezinski. But history would prove Vance correct; Brzezinski's "Carter Doctrine" never amounted to much more than a cover for wasteful arms exports.

In the wake of Afghanistan, the Carter administration also increased spending on defense—which had already been growing at an average of nearly 3 percent annually. Even more troubling from the perspective of many liberals was Carter's decision to embrace a new posture on nuclear weapons strategy. Partly this was in response to the Soviet deployment of medium-range SS-20 missiles on mobile launchers inside the Soviet Union. The United States and the North Atlantic Treaty Organization (NATO) responded by deploying more accurate medium-range Pershing II missiles in Western Europe. When Germany's tough-minded chancellor, Helmut Schmidt, proposed a freeze on these deployments, Carter turned him down. And later in the summer of 1980, Carter secretly signed Presidential Directive 59 (PD-59), a sweeping new nuclear strategy developed by Brzezinski. The new war-fighting doctrine embraced the notion that the United States had to be prepared to fight a "limited" nuclear war, targeting the Soviet Union's political leadership and military assets.

Brzezinski convinced Carter that the previous doctrine of assured mutual destruction no longer had sufficient credibility to deter a nuclear exchange. The threat of massive retaliation against whole cities in the Soviet Union, Brzezinski argued, was no longer a credible threat. Only by making the possible use of tactical nuclear battlefield weapons a real option could one restore genuine nuclear deterrence—and make a nuclear war less likely. All nuclear warfare "strategy" is by definition tinged with the madness that afflicted the characters in Stanley Kubrick's 1964 black comedy *Dr. Strangelove*. But the "countervailing strategy" of PD-59 was particularly convoluted. Carter signed PD-59 in secret: "I changed targeting of nuclear weapons to permit more flexibility in case we are attacked—letting me destroy Soviet military and command control and communication centers instead of all their major urban centers." Not long afterward news of the new strategy leaked to the press. In the ensuing controversy, it emerged that Brzezinski had kept the State Department in the dark. Everyone in the administration was unhappy, and no one was more uncomfortable with the optics of PD-59 than the president, who had come into office committed to making the country less reliant on nuclear weapons.

BRZEZINSKI NOW APPEARED to be unleashed. And as the president tilted in Zbig's hard-line direction, some inside Carter's inner circle were disturbed by Brzezinski's new influence and prominence. "He's a genuine hawk," Butler noted in his diary on January 3, 1980, after listening to Zbig energetically compare the Afghan crisis to the 1948 crisis over Greece that compelled President Harry Truman to proclaim his famous Truman Doctrine. Brzezinski "clearly wants to see punitive U.S. actions against the U.S.S.R." Averell Harriman—one of the deans of Washington's foreign policy establishment—warned his friend Senator Edmund Muskie (D-ME) that the Carter administration "had come off track, particularly because of Zbig's advice. . . . Brzezinski was with the President all day and was giving him a lot of distorted judgments."

Around the same time, Charlie Kirbo counseled Carter in a private memo, "I must say that I find people are generally somewhat frightened by Brzezinski and I do not believe he is a good man to have out front, particularly on television." Kirbo thought Zbig "just kicked up dust everywhere he went. . . . It really turned off a lot of people." And on Afghanistan, Kirbo thought that the administration had perhaps overreacted, since "the Russians were already aware they had made a mistake by seizing Afghanistan." Carter himself seemed to be aware of this, noting in his diary, "We have evidence that the Politburo is split on the advisability of the Afghan invasion."

Ironically, historians now understand that seventy-three-year-old General Secretary Brezhnev was literally senile when he made the decision to invade Afghanistan. "The scary part," noted Anatoly Chernyaev, a member of the Kremlin's inner circle, "is that the final, sole decision was made by someone who is completely senile. . . . It was a terrifying sight." Chernyaev wrote this in his diary on January 28, 1980. The Soviet apparatchiks knew what a disastrous mistake had been made—and yet many of Carter's advisers were clueless about the disarray within the Kremlin.

Kirbo was no foreign policy maven, but his instincts were right on the mark. Afghanistan was quicksand to any foreign army, and the Russians were no different. They quickly became bogged down in an endless guerrilla war, fanned in part by American arms to the rebels. The conflict would drag on for nine years, killing hundreds of thousands of Afghan civilians. The Soviets lost more than fourteen thousand troops. Millions of Afghans fled as refugees to Pakistan. The war certainly contributed to the Soviet Union's internal political collapse in 1991—but America's erstwhile mujahideen allies morphed into the Taliban, a regime that later hosted Osama bin Laden and al-Qaeda. Afghanistan was thus a disaster for everyone, including the Americans, who themselves invaded Afghanistan in 2001 and became bogged down in their own endless insurgency.

Brzezinski, however, never had any qualms. In 1998, he told a journalist from *Le Nouvel Observateur,* "For almost ten years, Moscow had to carry on a war that was unsustainable for the regime, a conflict that brought about the demoralization and finally the breakup of the Soviet empire." And when he was asked if he had any regrets about funding a collection of Islamic fundamentalists, some of whom later became al-Qaeda terrorists, Zbig replied forcefully, "What is more important in world history? The Taliban or the collapse of the Soviet empire? Some agitated Moslems or the liberation of Central Europe and the end of the cold war?" For Brzezinski, it was always about the Russians. He insisted that the Afghan crisis—and America's tough response—accelerated the collapse of the Soviet system and thus helped America "win" the Cold War. His critics dismissed this view as simplistic. No less an authority than George Kennan, the eminent diplomat, argued that Brzezinski's confrontational policies in the wake of the Afghan invasion actually had the effect of strengthening the hard-liners inside the Kremlin's politburo. "Thus the general effect of Cold War extremism," Kennan wrote in 1992, "was to delay rather than hasten the great change that overtook the Soviet Union at the end of the 1980s." Cy Vance generally agreed with Kennan, but after Christmas 1979, Cy no longer had the ear of the president.

THE CARTER ADMINISTRATION's calculations over the Iran hostage crisis also changed dramatically after the Soviet invasion of Afghanistan. The idea of using military force against the Iranians became less attractive psychologically. Brzezinski now did not want to use the American military against a Muslim country at a time when he thought it urgent to inspire Muslims everywhere to resist the Soviets. America's priority, he argued, should be to sustain a viable "low-level . . . insurgency" and "to keep the Islamic states mobilized against the Soviets in Afghanistan."

In early February 1980, Brzezinski visited Pakistan and Saudi Arabia as part of an effort to persuade the Saudis to funnel aid to Afghan rebels based in Pakistan. At one point, he visited a Pakistani military observation post on the Khyber Pass, near the Afghan border, and was photographed inspecting a Chinese-made machine gun. Handing the rifle back to the Pakistani sentry, he asked if the weapon was in working order. The guard aimed the gun toward the sky and fired off several rounds, but as he did so, the rifle slipped and nearly fired into Brzezinski and the group of Pakistani and American officials. It was a comic scene, flirting with near tragedy. But a photo of Brzezinski holding a machine gun on the Khyber Pass was published in newspapers around the world, a colorful symbol of the Carter administration's new bellicose stance against Soviet aggression.

CARTER FELT THE Soviets, and Brezhnev in particular, had betrayed his goodwill and trust. At the same time, he was grappling every day with the Iranians, who seemed in no hurry at all to negotiate an end to the hostage crisis. On the other hand, the president was adeptly using both of these foreign policy crises to enhance his own political standing at home. Americans naturally tended to rally around a president facing down foreign adversaries. And Carter knew how to press his advantage as the incumbent in the White House. With the Iranians, Carter's steady patience in the face of the crazed ayatollah was evidence that he was placing the safety of the hostages above partisan politics. And at the same time, his forceful condemnations of Soviet aggression in Afghanistan made him seem tough. The combination of patience and toughness made him seem presidential.

A month after Senator Kennedy jumped into the race for the Democratic nomination, the polls had flipped; Carter was leading Kennedy 48 percent to 40 percent. An enormously frustrated Kennedy thought Carter had mishandled both Iran and Afghanistan—but was now benefiting politically from the consequences of these very same mistakes. Tired of repeating his assigned talking points about how "we're all united as Americans," Kennedy finally told a reporter that the shah had led "one of the most violent regimes in the history of mankind." He was corrupt and had stolen "umpteen billions of dollars from his country." Carter, he said, never should have given this human rights abuser political asylum. Privately, of course, Carter agreed. But Kennedy's comments were seen by the pundits as giving aid and comfort to the enemy.

The backlash was fierce. President Gerald Ford's former CIA director, George H. W. Bush—who was running for the Republican presidential nomination—charged that Kennedy's comments "might endanger the lives of the hostages." The *New York Post*'s front page blared, "Teddy: The Toast of Tehran." Within a day, Kennedy tried to defend himself, saying, "We all support our country's efforts to end the crisis in Iran. But [that] . . . does not and cannot mean that this nation must condone the shah and the record of his regime." His defense seemed churlish.

The Kennedy and Carter campaigns faced their first contest in the

Carter loved classical music, but in the 1960s he became a fan of Bob Dylan (left, during their first meeting in the Governor's mansion). "First thing he did was quote my songs back to me," Dylan recalled. "He put my mind at ease by not talking down to me."

Carter singing "Salt Peanuts" with Dizzy Gillespie (ABOVE RIGHT) on the South Lawn of the White House. Willie Nelson (BELOW RIGHT) became a long-standing friend and supporter, spending the night in the Lincoln Bedroom, and, unknown to Carter at the time, smoking weed on the White House roof with Chip Carter. "I like them very much," Carter wrote in his diary of the Nelsons. "They are at ease with us, and vice versa."

Senator Edward Kennedy thought President Carter "was an outsider, and he was going to run things from an outsider's point of view." Carter insisted that there were "no philosophical differences between me and the Senator. He's just an impatiently ambitious man."

Senator Joe Biden warned Carter in early 1978 that he thought "Ted Kennedy is running for president in 1980 and is already lining up support."

Carter nominated Justice Ruth Bader Ginsburg to the appellate court—knowing that she was regarded as "excessively liberal. . . . She's been a matter of some controversy."

As part of his commitment to renewable energy, Carter installed solar panels on the White House roof only to have President Reagan remove them a few years later.

The Carters and Pennsylvania governor Dick Thornburgh being briefed inside the damaged Three Mile Island nuclear reactor.

Carter jogging at Camp David, shortly before he collapsed from dehydration. Pundits saw it as a metaphor for a weakened administration. Similarly, the press ridiculed President Carter with the story of a "killer rabbit" (BELOW) "penetrating Secret Service security and forcing the Chief Executive to beat back the beast with a canoe paddle."

President Carter had strained relations with New York mayor Ed Koch. "I don't believe," Carter said, "I ever met a man so completely wrapped up in himself." Carter appointed Bella Abzug to a White House commission on women—but he fired the outspoken feminist after concluding that she was "a pain in the neck."

President Carter appointed Joseph Califano to the cabinet as HEW secretary but fired him in 1979 for insubordination and leaking to his friends at *The Washington Post*.

Carter being interviewed in January 1979 by NBC News anchorman John Chancellor. Media wizard Jerry Rafshoon looks on.

Israeli Prime Minister Menachem Begin, President Carter, and Egyptian President Anwar Sadat at Camp David. The thirteen-day summit was a personal diplomatic triumph for Carter—but within days he concluded that Begin had lied over the issue of freezing the West Bank settlements. "These are my notes from my meeting with Begin," Carter told Stu Eizenstat. "Here you can see '5-year settlement freeze.'"

Begin won the chess match against National Security Adviser Zbigniew Brzezinski, three games to one.

Hamilton Jordan, Zbigniew Brzezinski, Cyrus Vance, and Carter, lounging at Camp David. Carter later noted in his diary that Begin was "trying to welsh on the deal."

Zbigniew Brzezinski at the Khyber Pass with machine gun in hand. Carter enjoyed Brzezinski's company and wit but rejected nearly all his hawkish, Cold Warrior views. After one spirited argument, Carter wrote him a note: "Zbig, don't you ever know when to stop?"

Leonid Brezhnev, general secretary of the Soviet Union, kissing President Carter at the SALT II arms control signing ceremony in Vienna, Austria.

The Shah of Iran, wiping his eyes from a cloud of tear gas on the White House South Lawn.

David Rockefeller and Henry Kissinger launched Project Alpha in 1979, a Rockefeller-funded lobbying campaign to pressure Carter to give the deposed Shah asylum in America— precipitating the Iran hostage crisis.

US CAN NOT DO ANYTHING

Iranian students occupied the U.S. Embassy in Tehran and initially held sixty-six American diplomats hostage. Prodded by Brzezinski, Carter finally gambled on a risky helicopter rescue mission that ended disastrously at Desert One (BELOW). When he learned the news, "The President looked as if someone had stabbed him." Secretary of State Cyrus Vance resigned, blaming Brzezinski: "He is evil, a liar, dangerous."

Poor whites and minorities flocked to Carter in his 1980 bid for reelection, but he lost many white middle-class and wealthy voters to the ex–California governor and former B-movie actor Ronald Reagan. The campaign was overshadowed by the 444-day hostage crisis. The hostages were finally released just minutes after Reagan took the oath of office. Carter (LEFT) with former hostage Chargé d'affaires Bruce Laingen.

Former President Carter greeting a child while on an election-monitoring visit to Nepal in 2008.

Iowa caucuses, scheduled for January 21. Carter, of course, had made Iowa his springboard to a national campaign in 1976. But this time, he remained in the White House or, on weekends, at Camp David, making dozens of phone calls to his supporters. Practically unnoticed by the national press, Carter's political operatives fanned out across the state. Rosalynn and other family members became his surrogates. The president's decision to embargo grain sales to the Soviet Union was certainly not popular in the farm state. But Carter explained the embargo as a sacrifice necessary for national security, and many Iowans seemed to buy it.

Neither was the Carter campaign afraid to go on the offensive, hammering away at all the doubts about Kennedy's personal character and integrity raised by Roger Mudd's November 4 interview with the senator. The president's old Georgia friend John Pope told Iowans, "Ted Kennedy leads a cheater's life—cheats on his wife, cheats in college." Carter himself echoed these harsh attacks in a television ad: "I don't think there's any way you can separate the responsibility of being a husband or a father or a basic human being from that of being a good president." These frontal attacks on Kennedy, combined with the Carter campaign's grassroots ground organization, proved to be decisive. Carter trounced Kennedy in the Iowa caucuses, 59 percent to 31 percent. A generation of Kennedy family charisma had vanished overnight. "I could not believe it," Kennedy later wrote in his memoirs.

Hamilton Jordan's deputy, Landon Butler, had concluded even before the Iowa results that the "President's hand is hot." Butler thought, "Kennedy is a goner. His campaign has no credibility that I can see. He's like George Wallace: he was popular when he was sending them a message, but when he actually ran, he was not taken seriously." Butler predicted that the former governor of California, Ronald Reagan, would be the Republican nominee—and he was fine with that, thinking that Reagan was too extreme to appeal to most voters.

Carter himself was feeling equally confident, noting in his diary, "Rumors are that Kennedy will get out of the campaign." He was wrong. The prospect of defeat somehow liberated Kennedy from the weighty baggage of his political legacy, and he now unleashed a less scripted campaign, accusing Carter of bringing the country "Republican inflation . . . Republican interest rates . . . and Republican economics." Columnist

Mary McGrory wrote of this new, unfettered Kennedy, "He has been freed from the shadow of his brothers. . . . The man who could not shake Chappaquiddick is being reborn as the conscience of his party." Kennedy may have found his mission, but on February 26, Carter again defeated him, this time in the New Hampshire primary by a margin of 49 percent to 38 percent. The following month Carter swept to victory in three southern primaries, and then again decisively defeated Kennedy in Illinois 65 percent to 30 percent. The president and all his campaign staff, including Jordan and Tim Kraft, were convinced that Kennedy would concede the nomination no later than March 25, when they expected to sweep the delegate-rich New York and Connecticut primaries. "If we beat Kennedy there," Gerald Rafshoon said, "that will be the nail in his coffin."

But they hit a bump in the road on March 1, when the president's United Nations ambassador, Donald F. McHenry, voted in favor of a resolution denouncing the Israeli settlements in the West Bank and Gaza. Carter had told McHenry to vote for the resolution—so long as a paragraph concerning Jerusalem was cut from the proposed language. McHenry carried out these instructions to the letter and got the paragraph cut. This delayed the vote by one day. The resolution was still highly controversial, marking the first time the United States had refused to abstain on a UN resolution condemning Israeli settlements. Carter wanted to rebuke Prime Minister Begin for a recent decision to authorize a settlement in the heart of the West Bank city of Hebron.

The United Nations resolution passed on March 1, and the next day it was front-page news in *The New York Times* and elsewhere. Israel filed a formal protest, and Jewish American leaders expressed their strong disapproval. They pointed out that the resolution still mentioned Jerusalem in the preamble, and the phrasing might be interpreted as questioning Israeli stewardship over the city's holy sites. By Monday morning, March 3, the furor in New York was such that Vice President Mondale and Ham Jordan came to the Oval Office and informed Carter that "the Israelis and American Jews were extremely upset about the U.N. vote on the settlements in Jerusalem." Carter protested that it was his understanding that Jerusalem was not even mentioned. They showed him a copy of the resolution, where Jerusalem was mentioned six times.

"I couldn't believe it," Carter noted. "I called Cy [Vance] in Chicago.

He said he thought 'Jerusalem' had been deleted." In the event, later that afternoon the White House issued a statement saying that McHenry's vote had been cast in error. Carter acknowledged that "it's embarrassing to admit a mistake," but he hoped that by doing so the political fallout would blow over.

On March 8, just two weeks prior to the primary, Carter invited New York mayor Ed Koch to have lunch in the White House. Carter knew the mayor was unhappy about the UN resolution, and he wanted to mollify him. The lunch was an embarrassment, at least from Carter's perspective. Carter began by saying, "If you don't mind, Ed, I would like to say a prayer over lunch." Koch said, "Fine," and after the prayer he launched into a lengthy lecture. "Mr. President, you have to understand that the Jews for two thousand years have had people sell them out." Koch went on in this vein for many minutes, cataloging the historical grievances of the Jews. And then he accused Andy Young, Don McHenry, and even Cy Vance of being biased: "They are pro-Arab. They are not for Israel." Koch described McHenry as "smarter than Young because he doesn't go as public as Young." But McHenry, he said, "is just as vicious on the subject of Israel as Young was."

Carter noted in his diary that Koch had talked "about the distrust of American Jews toward me." Jewish voters, he said, were reluctant to see him win a second term because "once you are elected you may get worse on this issue." Koch bluntly predicted that most Jews were going to vote Republican in November. The mayor, of course, had always burnished his reputation for brashness, but his performance on this occasion gave new definition to "chutzpah."

After Koch finally left, Carter sat in silence for a long moment, and then Jody Powell overheard him mutter to himself, "I don't believe I ever met a man so completely wrapped up in himself." Powell couldn't agree more. He thought Koch was a "political ingrate" whose "practiced buffoonery" reminded him of none other than their old Georgia nemesis Lester Maddox. Carter and Koch were not made for each other's company.

Koch had thoroughly enjoyed himself, and when he got back to Manhattan, he gave an interview in which he charged that the president was surrounded by a "Gang of Five" pro-Arab advisers, naming as "anti-Israeli" UN ambassador Don McHenry, former UN ambassador Andy

Young, Zbig Brzezinski, Cy Vance, and Assistant Secretary of State Harold Saunders. An angry Vance told reporters that Koch's description of him was "absolute baloney." Both McHenry and Vance called the mayor and remonstrated. Koch was unrepentant. McHenry was deeply offended by the mayor's behavior. "Ed Koch was a bastard," McHenry said. "He once called me up and swore at me, using really foul language. I made a point after that to never meet with him, and I once refused to shake his hand." Carter thought Koch's comments were "disgraceful" and noted, "Koch is almost acting like a fanatic this last couple of days."

The contretemps over Koch and the UN resolution had lasting repercussions. Polling in the weeks leading up to the New York primary showed Carter winning the crucial race by twenty points. Kennedy himself fully expected to lose, and his speechwriter, Bob Shrum—who had once worked for Carter for all of ten days in the 1976 campaign—was instructed to prepare a short withdrawal statement. It would not be needed. Carter was hosting a congressional buffet dinner in the White House on the evening of March 25 when Rosalynn took a phone call from Pat Caddell. The pollster had bad news. The president was losing the New York primary by an eighteen-point margin. Seventy-five percent of Jewish voters had flocked to Kennedy. "It's the U.N. vote in the Jewish community," Caddell told Jordan. "We're getting wiped out. . . . It's a protest vote."

Carter was terribly disappointed, but Jordan assured him that Kennedy would have to win more than 60 percent of the delegates in the remaining primaries if he intended to take the nomination. Jordan thought this was a near mathematical impossibility. Carter was nearly assured of capturing the 1,666 delegates necessary to secure the nomination, but his team was painfully aware that a long, drawn-out fight could leave the Democrats divided and weakened in the autumn campaign against whomever the Republicans nominated. And, indeed, over the next few weeks voters returned a mixed verdict. Carter won Wisconsin, Kansas, and Louisiana, but Kennedy then won Arizona, Vermont, and Pennsylvania. The Carter campaign was still gathering delegates, marching inevitably toward the magic number—but it was not able to force Kennedy out of the race. Part of the problem was simply that Carter himself was not out on the road, meeting voters. The president was absorbed and even distracted by the Iranian crisis. And so too was his chief campaign strategist, Hamilton Jordan, who was himself deeply involved in secret negotiations over the hostages.

As Jordan's aide, Landon Butler, put it, "There seems to be two White Houses: one that is taking care of business as usual, and one which is working on Iran/Afghanistan." Jordan was supposed to be managing the president's campaign to defeat Kennedy—but he was quietly skipping many of those meetings in favor of a series of clandestine encounters.

ON CHRISTMAS DAY 1979, two Paris-based lawyers, Héctor Villalón, an Argentinian, and Christian Bourget, a French human rights activist, arrived in Panama with a message for the Panamanian strongman Omar Torrijos. They explained that they were in touch with revolutionary Iran's new foreign minister, Sadegh Ghotbzadeh, who was prepared to open a back channel to the White House. According to Villalón and Bourget, Ghotbzadeh wished to arrange a secret meeting with Hamilton Jordan. Ghotbzadeh, the two lawyers explained, wanted to find a way to end the hostage crisis, but he distrusted the State Department, believing it to be too influenced by Kissinger and David Rockefeller. The Panamanians passed the message on to the White House, and in mid-January Jordan flew to a U.S. Air Force base south of Miami, where he was introduced to Villalón and Bourget. Jordan liked the two lawyers, and six days later he resumed discussions with them in a London hotel room. At one point, Bourget picked up the phone and placed a direct call to Ghotbzadeh in Tehran, proving that he had access to the foreign minister. They explained to Jordan that Ghotbzadeh led a moderate faction of the Iranian regime.

As a young man, Ghotbzadeh had studied at Georgetown University, so he was familiar with the West. And yet he was also a genuine revolutionary with a long history of anti-Pahlavi activism; he had become a close aide to Ayatollah Khomeini during his exile in Paris. Ghotbzadeh wanted to see the Islamic republican model survive, and to that end he believed the hostage crisis had become a distraction from the business of governing. At the same time, Ghotbzadeh was painfully aware that any public dealings with the Americans could undermine his own political standing. As foreign minister, he had decided to use Villalón and Bourget as clandestine intermediaries, deniable cutouts to the Americans.

The two lawyers told Jordan that Ghotbzadeh had outlined for them a scenario that would lead to a resolution of the hostage crisis: The Carter administration would quietly acquiesce in the formation of a United Nations commission that would go to Tehran and investigate Iran's historical grievances against the United States. But publicly the White House would criticize the UN commission—thus elevating its credibility inside Iran. According to Ghotbzadeh, the commission would hold public hearings in Iran and with great fanfare publicize the results of its investigations. But having aired Iranian grievances, the commission would then pronounce the holding of hostages "un-Islamic." Khomeini would then have the suitable political cover to order the release of the hostages. It was not a wholly improbable game plan.

Jordan reported back to Carter and was given a green light to pursue the idea. On February 8, 1980, Jordan flew to Zurich for another meeting with Villalón and Bourget. To his surprise, this time the two lawyers said that Ghotbzadeh wanted to meet with Jordan personally. They would arrange the encounter to take place on February 17 in Paris. Jordan thought this was very good news, and back in Washington, he spent hours with Vance and Brzezinski, with Carter being briefed for the meetings. Everyone was worried, however, that news of the negotiations would somehow leak, particularly if Jordan was spotted flying to Europe.

As a precaution, Jordan decided he had to fly incognito and in disguise. To this end, he called CIA Director Stan Turner and asked if an Agency officer who specialized in disguises could drop by the White House. That afternoon at 4:00 Jordan met with a CIA officer in the White House's empty barbershop.

"What is your objective, Mr. Jordan?" asked the CIA officer.

When Jordan explained that he needed to travel and walk in and out of a hotel without being recognized, the CIA man opened a briefcase and proceeded to "dress" Jordan in a graying wig, a glue-on mustache, and gold-rimmed, tinted eyeglasses. He told Jordan to practice walking more slowly, like an older man. When he was done, the CIA man pulled out a Polaroid camera, snapped several photos of Jordan, and handed one to him. "What do you think?"

Jordan was astonished. He said he didn't think his own mother would recognize him. The CIA man placed the disguise accessories in a small green case and handed it to Jordan. He then turned off the light and departed, leaving Jordan standing in the darkened barbershop. Jordan felt "like a make-believe 007." When he got back to his office, he hid the Polaroid shot in his safe.

Three days later, Jordan found himself on the supersonic Concorde, jetting to Paris. Wearing his disguise, he took a taxi to Villalón's spacious Paris apartment. And then, shortly after midnight on February 17, 1980, Jordan was introduced to Ghotbzadeh. They sat down at a candlelit mahogany table set with exquisite chinaware and crystal wine goblets. "I appreciate the great risk you have taken in coming here and meeting with me," Jordan said.

"It is a risk that I take freely in the cause of peace," replied Ghotbzadeh. "But also, I must trust you never to reveal my identity."

"You have my word," Jordan said. "But what would happen?"

"Well, my friend," Ghotbzadeh said with a laugh, "first I would lose my job and then I would lose my neck!"

The two men then settled down to a long, meandering discussion. Ghotbzadeh subjected Jordan to a history lesson, cataloging America's complicity in the shah's crimes against the Iranian people. Jordan listened patiently until he finally interrupted, "How do we resolve this crisis peacefully, honorably, and quickly?"

Ghotbzadeh replied, "All you have to do is kill the shah."

"You're kidding," said a shocked Jordan.

"I am very serious, Mr. Jordan. The shah is in Panama now. . . . Perhaps the CIA can give him an injection or do something to make it look like a natural death."

Jordan told him this was impossible. After more such banter back and forth, Ghotbzadeh finally came back to the "scenario" proposed by Villalón and Bourget and assured Jordan that he could tell President Carter that "my government will abide by every detail of the scenario drawn up by you and the French lawyers."

"What about the Ayatollah Khomeini?" asked Jordan. "Has the scenario been approved by him?"

On this critical point, Ghotbzadeh explained that the plan had indeed been explained to the imam—who had seemed to acquiesce in it by virtue of his silence: "If he had objected to our proposal, he would have said so."

After three hours together, Jordan gave Ghotbzadeh his private home and office phone numbers and told him to feel free to call him at any time. They shook hands and the foreign minister departed.

Jordan called Carter within the hour, but because he was using an unsecure, open phone line, he had to be intentionally vague. "Mr. Carter," said Jordan, "I just wanted you to know that the meeting took place and was satisfactory from our perspective."

"Any startling news?" asked Carter.

"No, but I think everything is on track."

Unfortunately, everything was not on track. Over the next few weeks both parties—the Carter White House and Ghotbzadeh's colleagues in Tehran—tried to play the roles assigned to them in the "scenario." For a time, Carter had real hopes that the hostages could be released in a matter of weeks. But in the end, the ayatollah refused to play his assigned role; Khomeini never issued the public statements that would have set the "scenario" in motion.

In mid-February Carter made a conscious decision not to initiate a hostage rescue mission planned by the Pentagon. Brzezinski had been pushing for just such a military contingency since the beginning of the crisis, meeting often with a secret military committee charged with planning a rescue. Carter knew it to be a highly complicated and risky mission. Jordan's secret diplomacy posed far better odds of success than a military operation. Late in February, Brzezinski again pressed the president, asking him this time to approve a reconnaissance flight into Iran to inspect possible landing sites for a rescue mission. Carter refused. Ten days later, Brzezinski renewed his request, and again Carter declined to approve the flight, on the grounds that diplomacy still had a chance.

Over the next six weeks, Carter experienced a roller-coaster ride of heightened expectations followed by dashed hopes. At one point, the frustrated president noted in the margins of one of Jordan's memos, "Ham, they are crazy. J." On another day, after Jordan excitedly announced that he thought the hostages were finally going to be transferred from the students to the control of the Iranian government,

Carter looked up from his paperwork and replied, "Really? I'll believe it when it happens."

In late March, when Jordan once again reported on "a fresh incentive to get the scenario back on track," Carter glared at his young aide and said, "The scenario? It's beginning to seem like a deal that we made with ourselves. Everybody's on board except the one person who can free the hostages—Khomeini!"

On March 21, 1980, the Carters helicoptered up to Camp David with Secretary Vance and his wife, Gay Vance. The two couples watched a movie together, *Watch on the Rhine*. The president was trying to patch things up with Vance: "I know he's had a difficult week." The next morning, Carter met for five grueling hours with Vance, Defense Secretary Brown, Admiral Turner, General Jones, Brzezinski, and Brzezinski's deputy, David Aaron. The men argued over the details of the Pentagon's highly intricate plan for a helicopter mission to rescue the hostages.

Vance expressed his strong objections to a rescue mission—or any military force—so long as the hostages were unharmed. He argued that Khomeini was clearly using the hostage crisis to consolidate his Islamic theocracy. Vance thought the ayatollah would free the hostages only when he felt he had defeated his weakened secular political opponents and when they no longer had any political value—and he was confident that this day would arrive within months if not sooner. He urged patience: "We should allow them to slowly unravel from an outrageous position."

His arguments seemed to prevail. Vance left the meeting believing that a presidential decision to use military force was not imminent. All the talk about a rescue mission was only contingency planning. At least so Vance thought.

Carter nevertheless authorized heightened surveillance of the embassy in Tehran by a team of covert CIA operatives. He also reluctantly agreed to let the CIA fly a small reconnaissance Otter aircraft to an isolated desert staging spot in the Iranian desert. The three-man crew would inspect the desert floor and determine if it was indeed firm enough to bear the weight of the C-130 aircraft that would be used in any rescue mission. Even these tentative steps involved significant risk, but Carter nevertheless assured himself that he was not letting "any momentum build up for the rescue itself." And why? Well, as he noted in his diary that evening, he knew that any rescue mission "would undoubtedly result in substantial loss of life on both sides." But Carter felt he was running out of diplomatic options. Brzezinski was pressing him to act, but so too was Rosalynn. "Mine the harbors," she told him. "Do something; mine the harbors!" But he had responded, "And have them take one hostage every day? Line them up before a firing squad and kill them?"

Rosalynn was deeply frustrated and confided in her diary that her husband, "in my opinion, is the hostage to this situation."

It was agonizing. By April, Carter felt he had no good options.

Finally, on April 3, 1980, Jordan had to tell the president that the latest news out of Tehran was not good: The Revolutionary Council had met earlier that day and announced that the Americans had failed to meet the conditions for a transfer of the hostages. Worse, it seemed that the new Iranian president, Abol Hassan Bani-Sadr, had decided to wash his hands of the matter. Carter was disheartened but not surprised. He stood up and walked over to the window that overlooked the Rose Garden and muttered quietly, "I don't know what we do now. I really don't."

The previous day, Carter had been told that the CIA's reconnaissance mission of the potential landing site, designated "Desert One," had been carried out without a hitch. The three-man crew had reported that the site seemed ideal. The rescue plan was ready to be executed and awaited only the president's decision.

Operation Eagle Claw was an extremely complicated plan. It called for eight RH-53 Sea Stallion heavy helicopters to take off from an aircraft carrier in the Persian Gulf and fly six hundred miles to Desert One, where they would be met by six C-130 cargo planes carrying 135 troops from the Delta Force hostage-rescue team, fuel for the helicopters, and other supplies. The helicopters would be quickly refueled and then fly that same night to a remote mountain landing site known as Desert Two—just fifty miles outside Tehran.

The Delta Force troops would then be met by a handful of CIA operatives smuggled into Iran who had previously purchased a number of heavy trucks. After hiding out for the daylight hours, the Americans would then drive in darkness into the heart of crowded downtown Tehran. One team would pick up the three U.S. diplomats detained at the Foreign Ministry building, while the bulk of the Delta Force troops would be driven to the U.S. embassy, arriving around 11:00 P.M. After scaling the wall of the embassy compound, the American troops would then have precious minutes to find the fifty-three hostages, overpower or kill their guards, and then herd the hostages aboard the helicopters timed to land in an adjoining soccer field just at the appropriate moment. Flying overhead throughout the operation would be two C-130 gunships, prepared to disperse any Iranian crowds with their Gatling guns, firing seventeen thousand rounds per minute. If everything had gone well up to this point, the helicopters would fly to yet another isolated desert airstrip at Manzariyeh, just sixty miles southwest of Tehran. There the Delta Force troops and all the hostages would board C-141 Starlifter cargo planes and fly out of Iranian airspace.

The entire operation can only be described as a desperate gamble, a high-risk mission with no margin for ill luck. It would be a miracle if none of the hostages were killed—and in all likelihood many Iranians would be killed. Indeed, a CIA report dated March 16 predicted that perhaps 45 percent of the Delta Force would be lost during the assault on the embassy compound—and perhaps 60 percent of the hostages would be killed. CIA Director Turner was given a copy of this report—but there is no evidence that Turner showed it to Carter.

Despite these heavy odds, Brzezinski was all for it. On April 10, 1980, he gave the president a memorandum entitled "Getting the Hostages Free," in which he argued that the negotiating track had hit a dead end. "In short, unless something is done to change the nature of the game, we must resign ourselves to the continued imprisonment of the hostages through the summer or even later. . . . We have to think beyond the fate of the fifty Americans and consider the deleterious effects of a protracted stalemate, growing public frustration, and international humiliation of the U.S." Not only did Zbig want Carter to endorse the risky helicopter rescue mission, he also urged him to approve a simultaneous "retaliatory" air strike on Iranian targets. Zbig sensed that his president's patience was finally wearing thin—and he was soon proven correct.

At 11:30 A.M. on Friday, April 11, 1980, Carter walked into the Cabinet Room for a luncheon meeting with Jordan, Powell, Brzezinski, Mondale, Secretary Brown, CIA Director Turner, and Deputy Secretary of State Warren Christopher. Carter knew that Vance was on a brief vacation in Florida, so Christopher was standing in on his behalf. Also present for this momentous meeting was General David C. Jones, chairman of the Joint Chiefs of Staff. "Gentlemen," Carter announced, "I want you to know that I am seriously considering an attempt to rescue the hostages." Carter brought with him a long list of questions about the proposed rescue mission. He asked Brown and General Jones to outline the plan. The general spread out a big map of Iran on the table and, using a pointer, explained the intricacies of the mission. The meeting went on for nearly two hours. At one point, Jordan leaned over to Christopher and whispered, "What do you think?"

"I'm not sure," Christopher replied. "Does Cy know about this?"

When Jordan assured him that Vance knew about the contingency plan, Christopher whispered back, "No, no—does he realize how far along the president is in his thinking about this?"

Vance did not know, and he wasn't there to hold back the tide. Brzezinski weighed in forcefully with an emphatic endorsement, praising both the plan and the Delta team that would execute it. Turner was a little more cautious. And both Jordan and Powell gave a backhanded endorsement, saying it was "our best option." Christopher abstained, saying he hadn't discussed the plan with Vance and didn't feel he could speak on his behalf.

By Jordan's account, Carter ended the meeting by saying that he would merely "explore the rescue option." But it was clear to everyone that the president had virtually decided "that it was time for us to bring our hostages home." That evening, he dictated a cryptic entry in his diary, noting that "at this meeting we made the basic decisions about the order of priority of our options."

Vance was "stunned and angry" when he returned late on Monday afternoon, April 14, and learned from Christopher what had happened in his absence. He immediately called Carter and made an appointment to see him the next day. Shortly after noon on Tuesday, Vance spent twenty minutes alone with the president and voiced his "strong objections" to the rescue mission. Carter listened and offered to let Vance present his views to another meeting of the National Security Council.

Shortly before 1:00 P.M., they walked into the Cabinet Room for another luncheon meeting with Secretary Brown, CIA Director Turner, General Jones, Warren Christopher, Jordan, Powell, Brzezinski, and

W. Graham Claytor, Jr., the deputy secretary of defense. Carter began the session by announcing, "Cy has some concerns about the rescue mission." Vance made his case, saying that he had "serious doubts that the mission will work." The Delta team would have to move undetected all the way into the center of a city of five million. "I cannot imagine that all this could be accomplished without harming some of the hostages or rescuers." And even supposing that everything went according to plan, Vance asked, couldn't the Iranians take hostage any number of the several hundred Americans living in Tehran, many of them teachers or small-business owners, Americans married to Iranians, and working journalists? "We'll be back where we are now."

According to Jordan's account, the president stared hard at Vance and then asked, "Are there any reactions to Cy's comments?"

Jordan recalled everyone sitting in awkward silence, fidgeting. No one spoke up in defense of the secretary. Finally, Carter interrupted the silence: "Let me respond, Cy." After four months of planning, he said, the Joint Chiefs thought they had a plan that would succeed. And as to the several hundred Americans living in Tehran, "we are not responsible for private citizens in Iran who have refused time and again to follow our advice to leave!"

"But they are Americans, Mr. President!"

Carter was not impressed. Brzezinski weighed in, suggesting that "we needed to lance the boil with a rescue mission." The only alternative to a finite rescue mission was a naval blockade, and such an open-ended military action, Zbig argued, would push the Iranians into the arms of the Soviets. No one challenged Zbig's assumption that a regime dominated by ultraconservative, fundamentalist mullahs could so easily abandon its anticommunist beliefs and embrace the Soviet heathens. But as always with Brzezinski, what mattered was to never leave an opening for the Russians to expand their empire. Zbig's concerns were misplaced and irrelevant. Carter nevertheless had clearly run out of patience and had decided to send the Delta Force: "I will stick with the decisions I made." Vance looked down at his yellow legal pad, his arguments made—and ignored. The president's mind was made up—but quite uncharacteristically, it was not a measured decision. He was acting against the advice of the man whose judgment he most trusted.

*   *   *

ON THE EVENING of April 16, 1980, Carter spent two and a half hours being briefed on Operation Eagle Claw in the White House Situation Room. When he was introduced to Delta Force's commander, Colonel Charlie A. Beckwith, Carter immediately picked up on the colonel's southern accent and asked if he was from Georgia. "Even better, Mr. President," replied the colonel. "I'm from Schley County."

"Really," the president said, "you're my neighbor. Who are your folks?"

The fifty-one-year-old Beckwith was a veteran of both the Korean and Vietnam wars. Known as "Chargin' Charlie" in the Green Berets, Beckwith was a plainspoken, can-do sort of officer. He famously kept a sign on his desk at Fort Bragg reading "Kill 'em all. Let God sort 'em out." When Carter asked him what critical aspect of the mission worried him most, Beckwith replied, "The helicopters, sir. They're not made for long-distance, heavy-duty flying at low altitudes with full loads. That's why we've added two extra choppers to give us a wide margin of safety. Our experts believe we could lose a helicopter."

Carter seemed pleased with Beckwith's candor. How many choppers should be sent was indeed a critical question. But it was just one of many. During one of the recent planning meetings a general had whispered to David Aaron that he thought they should revisit the issue. Aaron passed this message on to Zbig—who later claimed in his memoirs that "we decided to increase the number of helicopters to eight." But clearly, by April 11, Beckwith was already telling the president that the mission needed a minimum of six choppers—and they were sending eight.* What he meant was that he thought he needed a minimum of six choppers flying from Desert One to Tehran—because he figured there were good odds that he would lose two or even three choppers during the Tehran portion of the mission. Beckwith later told Jordan that in a

---

* A Pentagon review board, led by Admiral James L. Holloway III, concluded that "an unconstrained planner would have more than likely required at least 10 helicopters, 11 under the most likely case, and up to 12 using peacetime historical data." But Brzezinski strongly felt that a larger armada of helicopters would have increased the risk that the Iranians would detect the mission. In any case, he later wrote in his memoirs, "Personally I never had any political or moral regrets about the rescue mission."

worst-case scenario, "we could have gotten out with three and made it to the desert for the flight out."

As the meeting broke up, Jordan pulled Vance aside and asked, "Do you feel any better about this after hearing their plans?"

"Yes, Ham," replied Vance. "I feel a little better. But generals will rarely tell you they can't do something. I just don't believe it. This is a damn complex operation, and I haven't forgotten the old saying from my Pentagon days that in the military anything that can go wrong will go wrong. I'm just opposed to the idea of a military operation as long as there is a chance of negotiating the release."

Ham privately felt "disgusted" with Cy. He understood that Vance's "unrelenting opposition" to the mission was putting the president in an awkward position politically. Brzezinski had confided in Ham earlier that day that "Cy is the ultimate example of a good man who has been traumatized by his Vietnam experience." The snide put-down captured Zbig's disdainful attitude.

Vance may have been entirely isolated, but he was convinced that the president was making a serious mistake, both for the hostages and for the country. On April 17, the day after the briefing with Colonel Beckwith, Vance told Carter that he would have to resign if the mission went forward. Carter gently argued with him. "Vance has been extremely despondent lately," Carter noted in his diary. "I called Cy in for an extended discussion. For the third or fourth time, he indicated that he might resign. This happens every time we get into a real crunch and have to make a difficult decision, but after he goes through a phase of uncertainty and disapproval, then he joins in with adequate support for me."

Both men respected each other, and until recently they had shared the same instincts and judgments. But ever since the Soviet invasion of Afghanistan, Vance sensed that Carter had stopped listening to him and was tilting toward Brzezinski's unmeasured and impetuous prescriptions. They had disagreed over Afghanistan, but also over the flap concerning the UN vote on condemning Israeli settlements. Vance had also been perturbed when, in March, Carter had refused him permission to meet with the Soviet foreign minister, Andrei Gromyko, to discuss Afghanistan. Vance took this as another sign that his advice was being routinely ignored.

And now Cy felt that the president was being pushed into a rash gamble to rescue the hostages. Vance didn't think the mission could rescue any hostages without substantial casualties—and the use of military force would only make the situation worse. He no longer felt effective. "I sensed in my bones," Brzezinski later wrote, "that he was ready to quit. He looked worn out, his temper would flare up, his eyes were puffy, and he projected genuine unhappiness." On April 21, Zbig confided to Carter that he thought Vance would resign. That same morning, the president had an extraordinarily awkward meeting with Vance. Also present were Brzezinski and Secretary Brown. Carter directly asked Vance to meet later that week with three Methodist bishops who were seeking an appointment to urge the president not to use military force against the Iranians. Vance felt such a meeting would place him in a highly dubious position. He would have to falsely reassure the bishops that military force was not in the cards, or else he would have to sit in silence. Vance refused, saying he could not do it. Carter was stunned. "I stood up, and the three men left." The president thought this was a "very serious moment—the first time I, as President, had ever had anyone directly refuse to obey an official order of mine." That evening at 6:00, Vance came by the Map Room in the White House and, with great sorrow, handed the president a resignation letter. They conversed awkwardly for sixteen minutes. Carter went out of his way to say that he thought there was "no serious difference between us on major issues of foreign policy." But he would not try to talk Vance out of resigning.

He was annoyed by Vance's "irrevocable" decision but also saddened: "My heart went out to Cy Vance, who was deeply troubled and heavily burdened." They agreed that they would not make Vance's resignation public until after the rescue mission—whatever the outcome. Both men knew they were at a terrible reckoning.

CARTER WOULD LATER describe Thursday, April 24, 1980, as one of the "worst" days of his life. Determined not to tip off the press about the impending rescue mission, the president tried to keep a regular schedule. He met with Brzezinski at 8:00 A.M. for fifteen minutes. At 8:25 A.M. he met with his domestic policy adviser, Stu Eizenstat, and afterward he discussed regulatory reform with a group of congressmen in the Cabinet Room. At 9:30 A.M. he saw Shimon Peres, then chairman of Israel's opposition Labor Party, for thirty minutes and discussed the Middle East. At 10:35 A.M. he huddled with Brzezinski, Powell, and Jordan to discuss the operation, just as six C-130 transport planes and eight RH-53 helicopters were breaching Iranian airspace. That's all they knew. Shortly after 11:00 A.M. the president had to meet with a group of businessmen representing metal-products industries to discuss inflation. Twelve minutes later, Carter returned to the Oval Office, where he sat down with Mondale and informed him that Cy Vance had tendered his resignation. At 11:44 A.M. Carter placed a phone call to Charlie Kirbo in Atlanta. The two old friends chatted for four minutes. Carter then called Ham Jordan into the Oval Office and told him, "I got a disturbing call that a couple of our helicopters are down."

"Do you have any details?" Jordan asked.

"No, but Harold [Brown] may have something more to tell us at lunch. That's not the reason I wanted to see you." After pausing for a moment, Carter said, "Cy is going to resign. I don't want you to tell anyone about it. I just told Mondale, but no one else knows. Think about what we can do."

At 12:00 noon they walked into the Cabinet Room to meet with Secretary Brown, Mondale, Vance, Brzezinski, and Powell. While eating sandwiches, Brown informed them that "two helicopters may be down short of the landing site." Radio silence was being maintained, so it was another three hours before they had confirmation that one chopper had been forced to land in a bad sandstorm and another had turned back when a safety light warned the pilot of a malfunction.* By 4:21 P.M. Carter had learned that the six remaining helicopters had landed at Desert One and were being refueled from the C-130s. General Jones was reporting that everything was ready for the next stage of the operation. Soon the remaining six helicopters would fly off to Desert Two, the final staging site in the mountains above Tehran.

But then, at 4:45 P.M., Secretary Brown phoned Brzezinski in the Oval Office to report, "I think we have an abort situation. One helicopter at Desert One has a hydraulic problem. We thus have less than the mini-

---

* In fact, a special investigation later by Chief of Naval Operations James L. Holloway III criticized the decisions of the two pilots to abort their flights. Both helicopters were probably technically capable of flying for many more hours.

mum six to go." Brzezinski argued with Brown, questioning him sharply on why they couldn't go ahead with only five choppers. Zbig insisted that they needed to obtain the opinion of the Delta Force commander on the ground, Colonel Beckwith. If he was prepared to proceed with five choppers, Brzezinski would "back him all the way." While Brown agreed to get Beckwith's personal recommendation, Brzezinski went to inform Carter.

When told the bad news, the president muttered, "Damn, damn."

In the meantime, Colonel Beckwith, standing in the darkened desert, sand swirling around him from the roar of the C-130 engines, was asked if he would consider proceeding with only five helicopters. Beckwith replied, "Give me a couple of seconds to think it over." He then answered, "There's just no way." He still believed they would lose two more helicopters to mechanical failure during the next stage of the operation—and that would leave only three to fly out the fifty-three hostages and ninety-five Delta Force commandos. It wasn't enough.

At 4:56 P.M., Carter placed a phone call to Secretary Brown to get the latest from Desert One. Brzezinski knelt by his desk, taking notes as they spoke. Zbig whispered to Carter, "You should get the opinion of the commander in the field. His attitude should be taken into account." Carter asked the question and was told by Brown that Beckwith felt it necessary to abort. Zbig heard Carter say, "Let's go with his recommendation." The president hung up the phone, looked at Zbig, and then cradled his head, with his arms resting on the desk. He had been utterly defeated by a chain of mundane mishaps—a nasty sandstorm, a faulty warning light, a mechanical hydraulic failure. "I felt extraordinarily sad for him," Brzezinski wrote in his memoirs. "Neither of us said anything."

It only got worse. A few minutes later, Carter and Brzezinski were joined by Jordan, Powell, and Mondale. Jordan was stunned to learn that the mission had been aborted. "What did Beckwith think?" he asked Carter. Jordan was disappointed to learn that even the brash colonel had recommended an abort. Vance and Brown arrived, and everyone crowded into the president's private study adjacent to the Oval Office. Carter was sitting coatless, his shirtsleeves rolled up. He sat slouching in his chair, clearly depressed. Vance joined Mondale on the couch and listened as Carter explained why the mission had been canceled. "At least there were no American casualties," Carter said, "and no innocent

Iranians hurt." Vance felt "a sense of relief." The mission had gone awry, as Cy had predicted, but at least it had been bloodless. And then suddenly, the red phone on the president's desk rang. Carter straightened up in his chair and reached for the phone.

"David?"

"Yes, sir," replied General Jones. "The news is not as good as I indicated to you a few minutes ago. An RH-53 [helicopter] getting . . . trying to get out of Desert One ran into a C-130. The only report we have is there's some burns and injuries to people, our people."

"This was on the ground?" asked Carter.

"On the ground, is the report," replied Jones. "On the ground there at Desert One. Still sketchy report and some burns and injuries and people. We have no idea how many or how serious. We will try to get that as soon as we can."

"Uh-huh," Carter said calmly. "Okay, thank you David."

In a steady voice, the president then turned to his aides and explained that one of the choppers, while attempting to refuel, had crashed into a C-130 loaded with Delta Force members. General Jones thought there were casualties. Twenty minutes later Jones called back to say that "all Americans who are alive are off the ground."

A stunned Carter replied, "All Americans what?"

Jones then explained that he was being told that "there are some who evidently were fatalities. . . . They made a decision on the spot to take everybody out in the 130's and to leave the helicopters there because of the risk of losing people."

"Right," replied the president.

Jones then flatly reported that at least one of the helicopter pilots "is believed missing and presumed dead. . . . There may have been some trapped in there. And they haven't been able to make an exact counting."

Upon hearing this terrible news, Carter sighed deeply and said calmly, "I understand."

"We will try to get an account as soon as we can on . . . " said Jones.

"That's unbelievable, isn't it?" said Carter.

"Yes, sir," replied Jones.

"Okay," said Carter. "I'll be sitting here by the phone."

A short time later, Carter was told that five air force men had been burned alive in the cockpit of the C-130, and three members of the helicopter crew were also incinerated. Also killed was an Iranian agent who had been serving as a translator on the mission.

"The President looked as if someone had stabbed him," Brzezinski later wrote. "Pain was evident all over his face." But he nevertheless remained calm and in control of his emotions. Vance broke the awful silence, saying quietly, "Mr. President, I'm very, very sorry."

Soon the men adjourned to the Cabinet Room, where they began discussing a public announcement. Carter asked to see a copy of President John F. Kennedy's famous televised statement taking responsibility for the 1961 Bay of Pigs fiasco. At one point that evening, Jordan suddenly felt dizzy and excused himself, walking out to the South Lawn. He was sickened at the realization that people had died. Finding the night air humid and stifling, Jordan felt a sudden wave of nausea. He ran back into the Oval Office. "I ducked into the President's private bathroom and vomited my guts out."

Later that night, after it was clear that the Delta Force C-130s had exited Iranian airspace, a chain-smoking Jody Powell told Carter he had to think about what to tell the American people the next morning. Why had they launched this rescue attempt at this moment? What was the rationale? Carter nodded and then turned to Vance and said half ironically, half bitterly, "Cy, perhaps you can draft a statement for me presenting the rationale for the mission." It was Carter's way of acknowledging that Vance had been right. But at the same time, he was really angry with Vance, knowing that he was deserting him at a moment of crisis.

For his part, Vance blamed Brzezinski for badgering the president into green-lighting the doomed rescue mission. Indeed, Vance blamed Brzezinski for everything that had gone wrong over the past three years. At the end of 1980, he blurted out to Richard Holbrooke, "I still cannot understand how the president was so taken in by Zbig. He is evil, a liar, dangerous."

THE RESCUE MISSION had been an unmitigated debacle. Just two days later, one of Brzezinski's intellectual rivals, Harvard professor Stanley Hoffmann, opined in *The New York Times,* "The rescue operation is a disaster from every conceivable point of view . . . incompetent, devious and incoherent." Michael Metrinko, a political officer who spent much of his time as a hostage in solitary confinement, later flatly concluded that the rescue attempt was "one of the most stupidly planned, botched-up military-political escapades of the season—unworkable, unwinnable, and if they had succeeded, we would have been dead. So I'm really glad that it ended in Tabas [the nearest town to Desert One]."

Stu Eizenstat had not known anything in advance about the mission, but when he was awakened at home by a phone call with the news from the White House Operations Center, he turned to his wife, Fran, and remarked dejectedly that for all practical purposes "the election was over." The president didn't get much sleep that night, but he was awakened at 5:30 the next morning, and by 7:00 A.M. he was broadcasting live on national radio and television a brief statement, taking full responsibility for what had happened. Kirbo thought this was a colossal mistake. "I almost cried," he later said, when he saw Carter on television that morning. Charlie would have had the secretary of defense make the announcement. But he knew "Carter had a policy about not making somebody else say the bad things."

Twenty minutes later, the president received a phone call from Henry Kissinger, who "made a superb statement to me of full support and admiration." Carter asked him "to call the networks." Kissinger did so, but characteristically, his comments offered the beleaguered president a decidedly backhanded compliment. As Arthur Schlesinger observed in *The New York Times* the next day, "One of the few voices of approval yesterday came from Henry A. Kissinger, who seems to argue that our adversaries will behave with more circumspection if they think that the President is crazy." Carter studiously ignored the irony of being defended in this manner by a man who bore significant responsibility for igniting the hostage crisis six months earlier with his unctuous lobbying on behalf of the shah. The president would have to take what support he could get from any quarter.

"I AM STILL haunted by memories of that day," Carter wrote two years later. In hindsight, he sometimes wondered if it had been a mistake to focus so much presidential attention on the fate of the hostages. Publicity had inflated their value to the revolutionary regime in Tehran. "I think the issue would have died down a lot more if I had decided to ignore the fate of the hostages or if I had decided just to stop any statements on the subject. . . . But if that had happened, what would the

Iranians have done to the hostages to revive the issue? That was always a concern to me." For Carter, the hostage crisis underscored the limits of power. "There are limits, even on our nation's great strength," he reflected. "It's the same kind of impotence that a powerful person feels when his child is kidnapped." This was an analogy, however apt, that most Americans did not want to hear.

Chapter 23
Whipping Kennedy's Ass

Deep down, I suspect he'd rather see Reagan elected than me.
—PRESIDENT JIMMY CARTER

Carter shaking hands with Kennedy at the 1980 convention
BOSTON GLOBE/GETTY IMAGES

ODDLY ENOUGH, MANY Americans applauded the audacity of the failed rescue attempt. Pat Caddell's polling registered an uptick in the president's favorability ratings. Carter himself remarked at an April 29 press conference, "There is a deeper failure than that of incomplete success. That is the failure to attempt a worthy effort, a failure to try." And having gambled and failed, both Carter and many voters seemed willing to move on. Two days after the rescue mission, Carter selected Maine senator Edmund Muskie to replace Vance as secretary of state. The president also quickly decided to reverse his pledge not to go out on the campaign trail until the hostages were released. Fritz Mondale bluntly told him that the "Rose Garden" strategy had worked for the first couple of months. People were initially sympathetic to the notion that the president should remain in the White House and concentrate on the hostage crisis. But now, Mondale said, "they just aren't buying that anymore." He heard the same advice from Senate Majority Leader Robert Byrd, who said, "The Ayatollah Khomeini doesn't just have fifty-three hostages. He also has the President hostage." Carter reluctantly agreed, and then awkwardly told reporters on April 30 that he had decided to end his self-imposed isolation in the White House because the problems confronting the country were now "manageable enough" to permit him to get on the campaign trail. Watching the president on the White House closed-circuit television, Jordan winced and groaned, "We'll catch hell for that." Carter acknowledged the error a few minutes later in the Oval Office: "Poor choice of words, huh?"

"I'm afraid so, Mr. President," said Jordan.

"At least I'm free," Carter replied.

That same day, Bert Lance was finally found not guilty of nine bank fraud charges. Carter was relieved for his old friend. This was about the only good news he had received in months. Newspaper headlines announced that the economy seemed headed into what the president claimed would be a "mild and short" recession. Many economists disagreed, predicting a deep slump. Unemployment was running at 7 percent, the highest rate in three years. Despite the bad economic news, the Carter reelection campaign was continuing to rack up delegates in the race against Kennedy. "The gig is up for Ted Kennedy," noted Landon Butler on May 5.

Butler was wrong. On June 3, Kennedy handily won both the California and New Jersey primaries, giving him a total of 1,220 delegates. But by then the president had amassed 1,988 committed delegates, far more than the 1,666 needed to secure the nomination. Kennedy was clearly defeated, but he still wasn't giving up. The senator told the veteran political journalist Elizabeth Drew, "It isn't just a campaign, it's a cause."

Late in the afternoon of June 5, Kennedy walked into the Oval Office for a meeting with the president. Carter naturally was hoping to hear the senator say he was bowing out. Instead, Kennedy spent nearly an hour fumbling around, explaining somewhat incoherently that he and Carter "still had issues dividing us." Kennedy insisted that he was "representing the concerns of millions of Americans." Carter listened patiently until Kennedy finally left after fifty minutes. Shortly afterward a curious Jordan strode into the Oval Office and asked, "What happened?"

"Nothing good," snapped Carter. "He was nervous and kept rambling on about wanting to debate me, and that I should change my policies and stimulate the economy. . . . Finally, I said, 'Ted, are you going to get out or not?' He said that he wouldn't and that was that." Carter was clearly annoyed. He told Jordan that Kennedy had even volunteered that he could not agree to support the Carter-Mondale ticket "even if we had such a debate." Carter thought Kennedy would "fight us right through the convention. . . . Deep down, I suspect he'd rather see Reagan elected than me."

Kennedy insisted to reporters after emerging from the White House that he had "more than a prayer" of becoming the Democratic nominee. His only path to the nomination now, however, was a decidedly undemocratic scheme. Driven by his animosity for Carter, Kennedy began listening only to his inner circle, the older generation of men who had run his brothers' campaigns. They told him to pressure the delegates to change the rules at the August convention, making it possible for delegates committed to one candidate by the primaries to nevertheless change their vote in an "open convention." This would be ignoring the will of millions of primary voters. But Kennedy had talked himself into thinking that Carter's fiscal conservativsm was hurting blue-collar working people and that his stand against this Democratic president was a matter of bedrock principle.

Ham Jordan thought Kennedy was now on a "kamikaze mission." A few days prior to the California primary, Jordan had met privately in his apartment with a member of Kennedy's inner circle. The Kennedy aide told him confidentially that he was worried about the senator's political future. "Some of the people the Senator is listening to now don't care about the party or about him. They're convinced that Carter is such a bad man that he has to be defeated even if it means a Reagan presidency."

"Is that what you think?" Jordan asked.

"No," answered the Kennedy man. "I don't think the president is a bad man. But I do think he's been a poor president."

They then discussed whether there was some way to ease Kennedy gracefully out of the race. Perhaps Carter could finally agree to a debate, giving Kennedy the platform he wanted to air his differences with the administration. Jordan knew this sitting president would never agree to alter his policy positions or "debate" a rival he had already defeated. "It'll never happen."

That summer the Democrats were irrevocably divided. "I've lost all respect for Kennedy," Butler noted in his diary. "He has raised no serious issues—he's simply tried to undermine the President and cast aspersions on his motives and his competency." Bitterness reigned on both sides. "It's been a long, tough, tedious, divisive primary season," Carter noted sadly. The liberal wing of the party harbored a deep-seated distrust of a president who seemed to have gone out of his way to alienate such core constituencies as organized labor, feminists, and Jews. "Carter was a moderately conservative Democrat," Stu Eizenstat later wrote, "heading a party dominated by outspoken liberal interest groups." Everyone in the president's inner circle knew that uniting the party would be difficult. And it didn't help matters that the campaign seemed rudderless.

"Ham is taking less and less interest in day-to-day affairs," Butler complained. "That means almost zero. . . . Ham is more distracted and inconsistent than I've ever seen him—he's told me on two occasions that he plans to leave after the Fall elections." Butler thought Jordan was almost bored with his job, and he worried that the presidential reelection campaign was "incredibly disorganized." But Butler thought the chaos of the campaign extended into the White House. "Ham has been all but completely out of touch for weeks. . . . The White House is more leaderless than ever, with only the President to preside over the operation."

Finally, on June 4—the day after the disappointing New York primary—Pat Caddell and Jerry Rafshoon sat down with Jordan. Rafshoon told him, "Pat and I have been thinking about this for a while. We think you should leave the White House and work full time on the campaign." Jordan argued with them half-heartedly, but soon he found himself pounding out a memo to the president: "Quite frankly, Mr. President, I am worn out emotionally and intellectually and have no desire to continue working at the White House." He added that his White House salary was not enough to pay his "huge legal bill" from the Studio 54 investigation. After reading the memo, Carter consulted with Kirbo and Rosalynn and then gave Jordan the green light to move over to the campaign. "We are going to have a tough damn time in the fall the way Kennedy is behaving," Carter told him, "and the way the economy looks."

A week later Jordan presided over a meeting at the Hay-Adams Hotel, just a block from the White House, where he listened to a group of veteran California Democrats brief the campaign on Carter's presumptive

Republican opponent, former California governor Ronald Reagan. Carter had told Jordan the previous autumn, "I expect to be running against Reagan." Many Democrats thought Reagan was probably their weakest opponent. Kirbo, however, thought Reagan could be a formidable opponent. "He is right effective," Kirbo told Carter in July, "but manages to say nothing specific." One of Kirbo's law partners derisively described Reagan as "a geriatric marvel who appears to have extended his life span by periodically soaking himself in an elixir consisting of equal parts Grecian Formula 44 and Wild Root Cream Oil."

For some seasoned Democrats, Reagan was a sick joke. But Jesse Unruh, the former Speaker of the California House who had been defeated by Reagan for the governorship, warned Jordan, "Hamilton, don't make the same mistake that every person in this room has made at one time or another and underestimate Ronald Reagan. You may think he's too old or too much of a right-winger or just a grade-B movie actor. He's all of those things, but above everything else Ronald Reagan is an excellent communicator. You can argue with him or debate and think you've got him cornered, then he'll say something folksy, shrug his shoulders, and he's gone."

Jordan dutifully reported back to Carter in a long campaign memo, "People tend to underestimate Reagan. While he may not have a first-class mind or be a deep thinker, he is not dumb. . . . They say that he just has an uncanny ability to say things in a way that appeals to a broad spectrum of the voters. True, it is almost always simplistic and sometimes wrong, but people hear him and believe him. For this reason, our California friends predict that he will do well in any debate setting." As usual, Jordan was his most perceptive when in campaign mode. His political instincts were right on the mark.

Two weeks later, after spending a few days on Maryland's Eastern Shore, sleeping late and reading several books on presidential campaigns, Jordan wrote an "eyes only" memo to Carter. "The Kennedy challenge hurt us very badly," he wrote, "not only within the Democratic Party but with the electorate as a whole." Jordan was particularly distressed that the polls were showing that a significant number of voters thought there was little difference between "you and Ronald Reagan." He warned that any personal attacks on Reagan might backfire due to the former actor's folksy demeanor. Their reelection strategy, therefore, should focus on spelling out "the differences" between the candidates, particularly on foreign policy issues. But it wouldn't be enough to just "run on our record." The problem there was that many of the president's proudest accomplishments—energy conservation, the Panama Canal treaties, the Camp David peace treaties, SALT II, China normalization— were "all political losers." Carter indeed had a record to run on; he had tackled a great many tough issues. But in doing so he had angered many voters across the political spectrum.

ON JULY 14, 1980, Republican delegates gathered in Detroit to nominate Ronald Reagan as their candidate. The next day *The New York Times* ran a front-page story revealing that the president's brother, Billy Carter, had formally registered with the Justice Department as a foreign agent of the government of Libya. Billy disclosed that he had been paid more than $220,000. He also acknowledged taking two all-expenses-paid trips to Libya in the autumns of 1978 and 1979. Plus, he'd accepted as gifts four gold bracelets, a $2,000 saddle, a suit of clothes, and a ceremonial sword. Billy said the payments were for work on a "propaganda campaign" to promote Libyan dictator Muammar al-Qaddafi's foreign policy objectives. The Justice Department had considered filing civil charges against Billy Carter for failing to register as a lobbyist under the Foreign Agents Registration Act—which is why Billy had belatedly registered.

The embarrassing story had been brewing for months, and President Carter felt compelled to release a statement condemning his brother's work on behalf of Qaddafi: "I do not believe it is appropriate for a close relative of the president to undertake any assignment on behalf of a foreign government." Everyone knew, however, that the president had no control over his flamboyant younger brother. Billy had finally stopped drinking by the summer of 1980, but he was still an irrepressible character. He was only five years old when Jimmy left Plains for a career in the navy—and when Jimmy returned, "I hardly knew him [Billy] eleven years later." Still, over the years they had worked together in the family peanut warehouse business, and Carter clearly loved his brother's "colorful personality." But they disagreed about just about everything in politics.

Billy's association with the Libyans first came to notice in 1978 when he led a highly publicized delegation of Georgian businessmen to Libya.

The president heard of the trip only when his secretary, Susan Clough, told him she had heard Billy was on his way to Libya. And then, in January 1979, Billy hosted a delegation of Libyans visiting Atlanta. Obviously, Billy posed something of a public relations embarrassment even before the news broke that he had been taking large sums of money from the Libyans. The president was forced on this occasion to explain his relationship with Billy to NBC News anchor John Chancellor: "Billy and I have very strong differences of opinion on many issues. He expresses those differences much more frequently than do I. . . . And I hope the people of the United States realize that I have no control over Billy, [and] he has no control over me." When Jimmy heard that his brother was planning a second trip to Libya in August 1979, he spoke directly to him and tried to persuade him to cancel the trip. Billy went anyway.

The story was then given new life when, on July 23, 1980, the press reported that Zbig Brzezinski had briefly used Billy Carter as an intermediary to see if the Libyans could do anything to help get the hostages out of Iran. It later turned out that using Billy had been Rosalynn's idea. Rosalynn told Jimmy that she had talked with Billy, "who thought he could be useful." The president explored the idea with Brzezinski. On November 17, 1979, Billy happened to drop by the White House and had lunch with Jimmy and Rosalynn. The president later admitted, "I told him and Zbig to get together to discuss what message we might pass along to the Libyans." Carter must have realized that having Billy involved in passing such a message could only enhance his brother's standing with the Libyans. The president later acknowledged that this "may have been bad judgment but I was the one that made the judgment." He decided to take the risk simply because his priority at the time was to use whatever diplomatic gambits he could to get the hostages released. Nothing came of this Libyan back channel.

But the story was too good to be dropped. The Senate Judiciary Committee opened an investigation into what the press was now calling "Billygate." The president swiftly announced that the White House would fully cooperate with any inquiries and waive any claims to executive privilege. In early August, Carter had to spend an afternoon and an evening trying to determine the facts. "It was tedious and aggravating," he noted in his diary, "because there was no substance to [the] whole affair. . . . The irresponsible press has made every effort to prolong the whole thing into another Watergate." Finally, on the evening of August 4, Carter spent an hour fielding questions about all aspects of the case. He thought the press conference went well. He was very persuasive, and the story would eventually die down. "All in all," Carter noted, "it's been a very unpleasant experience."

BILLYGATE HAD TAKEN its toll. Ten days before the Democratic convention opened in New York City, a Louis Harris/ABC News poll gave Carter a 77 percent disapproval rating. Jordan was shocked and asked Pat Caddell to explain why Carter should have a worse rating than even Richard Nixon at the height of Watergate. "You know," Caddell responded, "it's not like our ratings have been good or anything, but the president's approval rating has hung around thirty-five percent. But in the last ten days, our polls show that his approval rating has dropped twelve percent. That's an unbelievable drop! This damn Billy Carter stuff is killing us."

But it was also all about the economy, which that January fell into a recession. In 1980 average gross weekly earnings actually fell and unemployment was over 7 percent. Working-class Americans were hurting.

Jordan feared a full-fledged revolt by Carter delegates. The influential *New York Times* columnist James Reston floated the idea that Carter could unify the party only by throwing the convention open. Three days later, Senator Robert Byrd told a reporter that Carter would have "a stronger mandate" if he beat Kennedy in an open convention. Carter's lieutenants knew they controlled hundreds more delegates than the Kennedy forces, but there were signs of unease among Carter delegates, particularly inside the New York and Illinois delegations. A public defection of just a handful of delegates could easily trigger a full-scale stampede.

Thomas E. Donilon—then a twenty-five-year-old Carter aide in charge of keeping tabs on the delegates—later told veteran political reporter and author Jon Ward, "We absolutely felt we could lose the convention." Kennedy himself was hopeful that "the right chemistry develops" to upend the convention. The crucial battle would come on Monday, August 11, the very first evening of the convention, when a vote would be taken on whether to change the rules and permit an open convention. Everyone seemed worried except the president, who was relaxing at Camp David. "I have a lot of problems on my shoulders," he noted in his diary shortly before the convention. "But strangely enough, I feel better as they pile up. My main concern is propping up the people around me who tend to panic." Despite everything, he felt confident. Told the day before the convention opened that the Kennedy forces were threatening a filibuster, Carter instructed Jordan to warn Kennedy, "We'll either take it out of his time or postpone his speech until after the business of the evening."

Carter and his inner circle were in campaign mode—and that meant they could be ruthless and tough-minded. Jordan, Powell, Rafshoon, and Bob Strauss were keeping tabs on the delegates from within a command-center trailer positioned just off the convention floor. Strauss was in his element, a phone at each ear, alternately cajoling and threatening wavering delegates. "Look at him," laughed Powell. "Strauss is like a pig in shit." At one point that afternoon, Jordan heard a rumor that the entire Maine delegation were going to change their votes to draft former Maine senator and now secretary of state Ed Muskie. Jordan quickly called Carter, who within minutes got Muskie on the phone. Muskie swiftly snuffed the move. That evening, there were heated debates on the rules question, but in the end the Carter machine trounced the Kennedy forces 1,936 votes to 1,390.

Soon afterward, at 9:46 P.M., Kennedy called Carter at Camp David and said that he would withdraw his name as a candidate. Carter pressed him, specifically asking if he intended now to endorse him—and join him onstage Thursday evening when Carter would formally accept the nomination. Kennedy stiffly said that would depend on "how we worked out details of the platform." Carter quickly pointed out that they really couldn't expect to resolve all their policy differences in the next three days. Kennedy conceded this was true, but he offered no way out of further bickering over the platform. The phone conversation lasted less than four minutes, and Carter found himself surprised that Kennedy "seemed to be in a good mood." Kennedy had conceded—but he was still acting like a man not ready to end his ideological challenge and unite the party. Afterward, Jordan asked Carter if Kennedy had pledged his support. "I didn't press him, Ham," the president said. "It was an uncomfortable call for him. I'm not sure what he'll do Thursday or in the fall."

The next evening Kennedy was allowed his one moment in the spotlight, and he seized the opportunity to have his rhetorical revenge against the man who had humiliated him. Carter had decided to give Kennedy a prime-time speaking slot at the convention. In return, the Kennedy campaign had agreed not to delay the convention schedule with obstructionist procedural tactics. Still, it was a gamble. Carter's men knew the speech might easily sway many of their own delegates to vote for Kennedy's platform planks—specifically, a $12 billion spending measure designed to stimulate the economy, an idea President Carter opposed because he thought it would only stimulate inflation. This was predictable. Carter would stubbornly ignore the politics of doing what other politicians in his predicament would have gladly done—spend some taxpayer money on a popular bill.

Emotions were running high late on Tuesday, August 12, a few hours before Kennedy was scheduled to speak, when Kennedy's floor manager, Harold Ickes, decided to invoke an arcane rule to temporarily close down the proceedings. Ickes's move had no rational purpose; he acted out of spite, later telling the author Jon Ward, "We just said, 'Fuck 'em.' This had turned into a real grudge match. I mean, we weren't thinking about the country. We weren't even thinking about the general election. It was, 'Fuck 'em.'"

Seeing what Ickes had done, Tom Donilon, Carter's floor manager—and later President Barack Obama's national security adviser—ripped off his headset and ran toward the stage. There he saw another Carter aide physically confronting Ickes on the stairs. "What the fuck are you doing?" Donilon shouted. "You can't do this!"

Ickes turned to him and said, "Go fuck yourself. I'm shutting this convention down, Tom."

The standoff lasted for a few tense minutes, until finally Kennedy himself phoned Ickes and asked what was going on. Ickes explained he had shut down the proceedings on a technicality. When Kennedy asked how long he expected this to last, Ickes replied, "For two hours." By Jon Ward's account in his 2019 book *Camelot's End: Kennedy vs. Carter and the Fight That Broke the Democratic Party,* Kennedy took a long moment and then said, "Harold, I think it's time we got on with the convention."

Kennedy's speech that evening was an emotional stem-winder. He was as eloquent as a Kennedy could be for a lost cause. "I have come here tonight not to argue as a candidate but to affirm a cause." He spoke of Franklin Roosevelt's New Deal legacy, he talked about the old liberal values of fairness and compassion, and he made a pitch for national health insurance. "There were hard hours on our journey," Kennedy said about his campaign, "and often we sailed against the wind." He mentioned Carter only once, congratulating him on his victory. But he did not endorse him. Instead, he ended on a heart-tugging plea for his cause: "And someday, long after this convention, long after the signs come down, and the crowds stop cheering, and the bands stop playing, may it be said of our campaign that we kept the faith." Referring to his martyred brothers, he quoted their favorite line from a Tennyson poem: "To strive, to seek, to find and not to yield." And then he ended with a promise: "For me, a few hours ago, this campaign came to an end. For all those whose cares have been our concern, the work goes on, the cause endures, the hope still lives and the dream shall never die."

It was not a concession speech. As Kennedy turned away from the podium, a spooky silence reigned across the convention hall for a few seconds, and then the teary-eyed crowd erupted with riotous applause and cheers. The crowd went wild for nearly thirty minutes as Speaker Tip O'Neill banged his gavel, trying to restore order. Sitting in the Carter command trailer, Bob Strauss shook his head and muttered, "Great speech, great speech." Against all reason, Ham Jordan felt himself moved emotionally. Watching it on television from the White House, even Carter called it "a stirring and emotional speech." Jordan later observed, "We may have won the nomination, but Ted Kennedy had won their hearts." And when order was finally restored and the convention moved to vote on the three critical economic planks in the platform, it quickly became clear that the Carter forces would lose on all three. So instead of a roll-call vote, Carter's team agreed to a voice vote—and Speaker O'Neill unilaterally ruled that the Kennedy planks for a $12 billion stimulus plan and a jobs bill had won, while he simply ignored the roars from the crowd to declare that the plank in favor of wage and price controls had lost. It was a humiliating defeat for a sitting president who had just been renominated by his party. Worse was to come.

Two nights later, on Thursday evening, August 14, Carter was formally nominated and came to the podium for his acceptance speech—only to have the teleprompter malfunction. "I was amazed and disconcerted because I couldn't see the teleprompter at all—just a word here and there. . . . I had to make the entire speech either from memory or from glancing down at my written text." This may explain a comical gaffe when he somehow referred to the late Vice President Hubert Humphrey as "Hubert Horatio Hornblower." Later, he appealed for party unity, saying, "Ted, your party needs, and I need, your idealism and dedication working for us." All in all, it was a decidedly lackluster speech, particularly in contrast to Kennedy's spellbinder two nights earlier. As he ended the speech, Jordan saw an aide tugging without success on a cord to release thousands of balloons onto the convention floor. Just a dribble of balloons floated down to the floor. "That's not a good omen," Jordan thought to himself. "We can't get the balloons out any better than we can get the hostages out."

As the convention delegates cheered the president, Vice President Mondale and his wife, Joan, joined the Carters onstage and waved to the crowd. Standing at the podium, Bob Strauss invited various Democratic politicians and Carter administration figures up to celebrate. Embarrassingly, when Strauss introduced Zbig Brzezinski, the delegates reacted spontaneously with audible boos. Zbig was not popular among grassroots liberals. Jordan winced but wondered where the hell was Kennedy—who of course was expected to join the president onstage in a show of unity. More than that, everyone expected to see Carter and Kennedy standing together with arms upraised, symbolically burying their enmity.

But Kennedy was nowhere to be seen. Carter, Mondale, and other luminaries had to dance awkwardly around the stage for nearly twenty minutes before Kennedy finally bounded up the steps. He slowly made his way over to the president and stiffly shook his hand, and as Carter patted him on his shoulder, Kennedy rudely turned away to shake hands with others. Carter was left to stare as the senator walked around the stage, obviously avoiding him. This pathetic, even comical, ballet went on for minutes, and Carter tried to guide the senator toward the microphone at the podium, but Kennedy studiously ignored him. Finally, Kennedy walked up to Carter, again shook his hand, and abruptly turned around, waved to the crowd, and walked offstage to thunderous applause. When hundreds of delegates began chanting, "We want Teddy!," the senator bounded back on the stage to acknowledge the applause, as if it were a curtain call in a theater. Carter himself was left with nothing to do but politely clap his hands and smile wanly. And then Kennedy left once again—without grabbing the president's hand and lifting it into the air. Kennedy had dissed the president.*

"I think," observed ABC-TV commentator Ted Koppel, "it almost would have been better from Carter's point of view if he had not come." The senator's behavior was noted by both the press and millions of television viewers. But only a few knew he had been drinking. "He was loaded," insisted a young Carter White House aide, Elaine Kamarck. Kennedy's aide Bob Shrum denied this. But later that evening, Carter himself dictated a note for his diary and reported that Kennedy "seemed to have had a few drinks, which I would have probably done myself. He was fairly cool and reserved. I thought it [Kennedy's appearance] was adequate, but the press made a big deal of it."

After it was all over, the Carter people were stunned by Kennedy's conduct. Why? Why would the Kennedy crowd persist in defeat, knowing that their displays of rancor would only further weaken a Democratic president in the face of the Reagan challenge from the right? Well, Kennedy partisans hated to see all the romantic notions of the Kennedy mystique coming to an end. Camelot was dying, and most ignobly, at the hands of these crude Georgia boys. And on the other side of the equation, the Georgia boys could not fathom the animosity. They felt their man was not only a liberal and a populist but a politician of integrity and intelligence who had accomplished much in his few years in the White House. For the Georgians, Kennedy's behavior at the convention was all about ego. As Jody Powell later said, "We neglected to take into account one of the obvious facets of Kennedy's character, an almost childlike self-centeredness."

The optics on television were emasculating for Carter. In reality, Carter and his Georgia boys had engineered a miraculous comeback. No one had thought they had a chance against Kennedy a year earlier— but they had defeated him decisively, destroying the myth of inevitabil-

---

* Kennedy knew full well what was expected of him—and before leaving his hotel room that evening, his aide Bob Shrum had made him practice the raised, clasped hands more than once. And as they arrived at Madison Square Garden, Shrum told him, "Don't forget."

ity about Camelot. But on television, it didn't seem like it. Watching the spectacle from his home in Georgia, Bert Lance moaned, "That's the worst thing that I have ever seen Jimmy Carter do, because it portrays a weakness that he's got to stand there and wait around." Lance knew Carter never stood for anyone being late. It was "completely out of character for him." Carter was still the tough, confident political animal he had always been, but many voters watching the convention thought him somehow weak.

The other reality was that Kennedy's prolonged challenge had weakened the Carter campaign forces. Kirbo later reflected, "If he had gotten out when people always get out in the past, when you've got more than enough votes to nominate you, they would have supported Jimmy. If our people had been rested up, we would have had several million dollars more money. But we had to continue to run, and then we had to fight in the convention. And we unwisely agreed to some planks in there that really hurt us—to satisfy the Kennedy people, and then gave him half a million dollars of our money that satisfied his staff, and then didn't get a bit of help out of it."

Watching the podium dance that night from the convention floor was Paul Corbin, a longtime Kennedy family retainer. Corbin had been working for the Kennedys ever since he first encountered Bobby Kennedy back in the mid-1950s. A former labor organizer and once a member of the Communist Party, Corbin was the kind of loyal political operative who harbored no ethical qualms about doing whatever was necessary to win. He was now seething with resentment against the Carter campaign. As he stormed out of the convention hall, a reporter from *Reader's Digest* asked him what his plans were now that Kennedy was out of the race. Corbin yelled defiantly, "I'm going to go work for Reagan!"

Chapter 24
The October Surprise

Casey said the Iranians should hold the hostages until after the election.

—JAMSHID HASHEMI

Ed Meese, Ronald Reagan, and Bill Casey
GETTY IMAGES

By THE LATE summer of 1980, Washington's political class under-stood that President Carter's reelection chances might well hinge on a last-minute resolution of the hostage crisis. Ex-governor Ronald Reagan and his vice presidential nominee, former CIA director George H. W. Bush, were sixteen points ahead in the polls, but Republican campaign strategists feared that this substantial lead could collapse in the wake of a sudden and dramatic release of the hostages. Reagan's campaign man-ager, William J. Casey, had a name for this nightmare scenario. He called it an "October surprise."

Bill Casey, sixty-seven, was managing the Reagan campaign from his corner office on the fifty-third floor of the Pan Am Building in Midtown Manhattan. A partner of the law firm Rogers & Wells, Casey had forged an unusual legal career over four decades. A devout, even fervent Catholic, Casey had grown up in Queens, the son of a civil servant. He went to Fordham University, a Jesuit university, and later got a law degree. But when America entered World War II, Casey joined the Office of Strategic Services (OSS), the precursor of the CIA. He finagled his way to London, from where he ended up running OSS agents whose job was to infiltrate Nazi Europe and aid the French Resistance. Casey learned in the OSS how to cut corners. General Eisenhower had forbidden the recruitment of prisoners of war—but Casey invented a loophole by labeling them "volunteers." His years in the OSS gave him a lifelong passion for intrigue, spy craft, and skullduggery.

After the war, Casey returned to the law, inventing tax shelters for his corporate clients and dabbling in various venture capital schemes. Politically ambitious, he persuaded President Nixon to appoint him chairman of the Securities and Exchange Commission. By 1980, Casey was worth more than $10 million, but along the way he acquired a reputation for ruthlessness and a disdain for moral complexities. Former CIA director Richard Helms called him a "conniver." John Bross, another old CIA hand, thought Casey was "capable of great kindness and great ruthlessness." Yet another legendary clandestine CIA officer, Clair George, said, "I liked Casey. He was nuts."

There was nothing subtle about Casey. He told a *New York Times* reporter that spring that he thought Carter was willing to use the hostages as a political football. He cited the fact that on the morning of the Wisconsin primary the president had appeared on a news show to announce a "positive step" in the hostage crisis—and yet, while nothing developed, Carter won the primary against Kennedy. "We expect Carter will try everything to get elected—so we'll be ready for everything."

"This campaign is ours," said one Reagan aide after the Republican convention, "but it's ours to throw away too.... If [Carter] does something with the hostages, or pulls something else out of the hat, as only an incumbent president can, we're in big trouble." Casey soon put in motion a media strategy to inoculate the electorate, planting the suspicion that the president was "playing politics" with the hostages. If the hostages were suddenly released, he wanted voters to think that perhaps Carter had paid too high a price. Casey's aide, Richard Allen, explained, "If we could do all that in advance it would automatically discount anything that happened. We could say, 'See, right here we predicted it.'" It was a classic bit of psychological warfare.

Not surprisingly, Casey had help from David Rockefeller's Project Alpha operation. Rockefeller was, after all, a lifelong Republican and now did what he could to derail Carter's reelection bid. According to records found by *The New York Times*'s David D. Kirkpatrick, the Chase public relations team coordinated with the Reagan campaign to sow rumors about "possible payoffs" to win the release of the hostages. "I had given my all," wrote Rockefeller's aide, Joseph Reed, in a letter to his family in late 1980, to blocking any effort by the Carter administration "to pull off the long-suspected 'October Surprise.'"

At the same time, Casey sent a private message to the Iranians that they could get a better deal from a Reagan presidency. Casey knew from reading the newspapers that the PLO's Yasir Arafat had brokered the release in mid-November 1979 of thirteen of the hostages who were women or African Americans. Arafat had garnered plenty of favorable media coverage for his efforts and was indeed still using his Iranian contacts to broker a resolution of the crisis. Assuming that Arafat still had influence with Ayatollah Khomeini, Casey decided it would be advantageous to reach out to anyone who had a back channel to Arafat.

One such individual was Jack Shaw, a forty-one-year-old businessman who was helping Casey to raise funds for the campaign. A former vice president of Booz Allen Hamilton, Shaw had done business in Saudi Arabia, and that summer Casey reportedly asked Shaw if he could use his contacts to send a message to Arafat.

Shaw subsequently had lunch in Washington with Mustafa Zein, a Lebanese businessman who had access to Arafat. According to Zein, Shaw asked him if Arafat was still trying to secure the freedom of the remaining hostages. When Zein confirmed this, Shaw bluntly asked if Arafat could be persuaded to delay his efforts until after the election. Shaw argued that the "Palestinian interest lay with a strong president like Reagan, who would push for a just and lasting peace in the Middle East." Zein first checked out Shaw's bona fides with John Shaheen, another businessman who had befriended Casey when the two men worked together in the OSS. "Shaheen confirmed to me," Zein said, "after speaking directly with Casey, that Jack Shaw was representing

Casey." In August, Zein flew to Beirut and passed the message on to Arafat.

The PLO chief received a similar message from yet another old friend of Reagan's who contacted Bassam Abu Sharif, an adviser to Arafat. According to Abu Sharif, this unnamed Reagan friend "said he wanted the PLO to use its influence to delay the release of the American hostages . . . until after the election." Abu Sharif claimed that Arafat rejected both overtures, and sixteen years later this was confirmed by Arafat himself, who on January 22, 1996, told Carter during a visit to Gaza, "Mr. President, there is something I want to tell you. You should know that in 1980 the Republicans approached me with an arms deal if I could arrange to keep the hostages in Iran until after the election. I want you to know that I turned them down."

Casey was dabbling in off-the-books private diplomacy. Sending messages to the Iranians through intermediaries like the PLO was a gray area—not exactly kosher. Taking a meeting with a representative of the Ayatollah Khomeini to discuss the hostage crisis would fall into an entirely different category of behavior. Indeed, it could be deemed a blatant violation of the 1799 Logan Act prohibiting private citizens from negotiating disputes with foreign powers.

THE CASEY STORY is a disturbing and enduring mystery. President Carter at the time knew nothing of Casey's backdoor diplomacy, and in the years since, he has remained studiously agnostic. And yet numerous journalistic investigations, several books, and one major congressional investigation make it hard not to conclude that whatever happened in the summer of 1980 also planted the seeds for the Iran-Contra scandal of 1986. As such, it is a story that just won't go away.

Casey was a busy man in the summer of 1980. But a little more than a week after the Republican National Convention anointed Reagan as the party's presidential candidate, Casey flew to London on a personal trip. He had accepted an invitation to present a paper to the 1980 Anglo-American Conference on the History of the Second World War. The conference began on Monday, July 28, and Casey was scheduled to give his speech at 9:30 A.M. on Tuesday, July 29. The previous Thursday, July 24, Casey was photographed in Washington, DC, accepting a check for

$24.9 million in public campaign funds from the Federal Election Commission. The following day, Friday, July 25, he flew on the Eastern Air Lines shuttle to New York City.

But his whereabouts from the rest of that day through the weekend of July 26–27 are unaccounted for by any travel records. We know for certain only that when the London conference opened on Monday morning, July 28, Casey was absent. Another presenter, the presidential historian Robert Dallek, recalled wanting to "strut my stuff" in front of Reagan's campaign manager. But when Dallek scoped the room, Casey was clearly absent. According to an attendance chart kept by one of the conference organizers, Casey "came at 4:00 PM," indicating that he had arrived at the tail end of the afternoon session on Russia. Professor Dallek and others recalled that Casey attended the formal reception that evening at 6:15 and later went out to dinner.

The next morning, Dallek had breakfast with Casey, who then gave his talk on the OSS's contribution to the war effort from 9:30 A.M. to 11:00 A.M. Casey then had lunch at the conference and attended that afternoon's session before he left for the airport, probably catching the British Airways Concorde flight for Washington, DC, at 6:30 P.M. If so, he arrived that same evening, July 29, in Washington. And in any case, Casey's calendar for July 30 has a notation that he had dinner with George H. W. Bush at 6:45 P.M. at the aptly named Alibi Club—an exclusive men's club founded in 1884. Casey presumably briefed the vice presidential candidate on his European trip.

On the surface, Casey's twenty-four-hour appearance at this World War II conference in London was merely an enjoyable trip down memory lane. He even had a few minutes to stop by his favorite London bookshop, Hatchards, a venerable bookseller founded in 1797, where he bought four books, including a volume entitled *Master of Deception*. But numerous investigators nevertheless wondered in retrospect whether his attendance at the London conference was a cover for a highly covert side trip to Madrid, Spain.

The mystery focuses on Casey's whereabouts on Saturday, July 26, and Sunday, July 27. According to the testimony of an Iranian businessman, Casey spent at least part of that weekend in Madrid. Jamshid Hashemi told investigators from the House October Surprise Task Force in 1992 that he and his brother Cyrus orchestrated two meetings that weekend between Casey and a representative of the Islamic Republic of Iran, Ayatollah Mehdi Karrubi.

The Hashemi brothers had credible connections to both the Khomeini regime and the CIA. Both Cyrus, born in 1942, and Jamshid, born in 1936, had been critics of the Pahlavi regime. Fearing arrest by the shah's secret police, the Hashemi brothers fled Iran in the wake of Khomeini's exile in 1963. With London as their base of exile, they built on their private fortune, trading commodities. They supported the 1979 revolution, and cultivated their contacts with the new regime, partly through their cousin Akbar Hashemi Rafsanjani, an aide to Ayatollah Khomeini. Jamshid was soon rewarded with a prominent job in the Ministry of Information, directing the regime's national radio network. Cyrus, however, moved to Stamford, Connecticut, where he set up an import-export company dealing in commodities like rice and sugar, machinery parts, and Persian carpets.

Cyrus had all the appearances of a cosmopolitan globe-trotting businessman. When he traveled to Europe, he usually took the supersonic Concorde and stayed in the fanciest hotels. And when the American embassy was stormed in November 1979, Cyrus told his American friends that he wanted to help broker an end to the hostage crisis. Former attorney general Elliot Richardson told Robert Parry, the late investigative reporter, that he first met Cyrus Hashemi in late 1979. "He was elegantly turned out by a Bond Street tailor. He was very personable, unassuming, soft-spoken, intelligent, gracious in manner. . . . He lived on a very opulent scale, not ostentatiously so, more Oxfordian than blatantly nouveau riche." Richardson was impressed and soon put him in touch with Carter administration officials.

Hashemi also used his American lawyer, Stan Pottinger, a partner at Milbank, Tweed, Hadley & McCloy, to communicate on a regular basis with Harold Saunders, the assistant secretary of state for Near East affairs. Saunders described Hashemi to Secretary Vance as "a friend of many of the revolutionary elite." On December 5, 1979, Saunders reported to Secretary Vance that "Hashemi appears to be in contact with key individuals in Tehran and is pressing urgently for a resolution of the crisis within the next two weeks. He hopes to arrange a meeting with

Khomeini's nephew and an American representative (possibly [Ramsey] Clark) in London."

Another Saunders memo three days later reported that Hashemi "has contacts with a lawyer married to Khomeini's niece and another Iranian who is a near relative of Khomeini." State Department documents make it clear that the Hashemi brothers were well known by Carter administration officials, who hoped that they could broker real negotiations with the revolutionary regime in Tehran. Pottinger later described Hashemi as "a liberal, secular man—a thoughtful and serious person." Pottinger thought he genuinely loved America and believed the hostage crisis was harmful to both Iranian and American national interests.

In late 1979, Jamshid flew to London from Tehran at his brother's request and met with John Shaheen, Casey's old OSS buddy. (Cyrus knew Shaheen because they both had worked on a project to build an oil refinery in Newfoundland.) And then on New Year's Day 1980, Jamshid flew into Washington, where Cyrus had arranged for him to meet with Charles Cogan, chief of the CIA's Near East and South Asia clandestine division. They met at a hotel in Washington on January 5, 1980.

On the agenda was the Carter administration's desire to open up some further back channels to anyone with contacts in Tehran. The Hashemi brothers were a natural target. But the Carter White House had also approved a covert operation to influence the upcoming presidential election in Iran, scheduled for January 25, 1980. The leading candidate was the French-educated Abol Hassan Bani-Sadr, a left-wing academic. Bani-Sadr's main opponent in the election was thought to be retired admiral Ahmad Madani, an Iranian naval officer who had fallen out with the shah in 1973. Khomeini had briefly appointed him as minister of defense for two months in the spring of 1979, but he was regarded by the clerics as not sufficiently religious. Perhaps for the same reason, the CIA decided he was a preferable presidential candidate over Bani-Sadr.

The Hashemi brothers were old friends and supporters of Admiral Madani and convinced the CIA that they could funnel funds into the admiral's presidential campaign. Time was short, but the CIA's Cogan gave the Hashemi brothers $500,000 for Madani's campaign. It was too late; Madani won only 17 percent of the vote. Cogan quickly asked for an accounting of his funds and was told by the brothers that they had managed to spend less than $100,000. Cyrus returned $290,000 of the funds. The operation had failed, but the Hashemi brothers nevertheless remained on good terms with the CIA.

Sometime in March 1980 Jamshid Hashemi was staying at the Mayflower Hotel in downtown Washington when he heard a knock on the door. He was not expecting visitors, but when he opened the door, two men introduced themselves. Roy Furmark explained that he was a businessman who had met Cyrus in the Bahamas in 1979. The other man was none other than Bill Casey. Jamshid was startled and a little alarmed when Casey explained that he wanted to talk about the American hostages. "Casey wanted to discuss political matters," Jamshid later explained. "I cut him short. I said, 'I don't know who you are.'" He then called his brother Cyrus, who explained that his mysterious visitor was Reagan's campaign manager. Cyrus then asked to talk to Casey over the phone, and the two men agreed to meet in New York.

Obviously, Cyrus was playing both sides of the street, dealing with both the Carter administration and, through Casey, the Reagan campaign. On March 21, 1980, at a family gathering in his Wilton, Connecticut, home to celebrate the Iranian New Year (Nowruz), Cyrus told his brother that since the Republicans might well win the upcoming November election, it would be useful to have a relationship with Casey. He explained that his friend John Shaheen was an old friend of Casey's and it couldn't hurt to keep in touch with the Reagan campaign manager.

In early May, Cyrus called his lawyer in Washington, Stan Pottinger, and claimed that he had persuaded Reza Pasandideh, a nephew of Ayatollah Khomeini's, to agree in principle to fly to Madrid for a meeting with a Carter administration envoy. Gary Sick, Brzezinski's aide for Iranian affairs, later wrote that this meeting in fact happened, on Wednesday, July 2, 1980. Cyrus and the American envoy flew from London that day, met Pasandideh in Madrid's Ritz Hotel, and flew back to London on the same day. (It was a two-hour flight each way.) While the meeting didn't result in any dramatic breakthrough, the Carter White House regarded it as a promising channel of communication. And as Sick later wrote in his investigative book *October Surprise*, "It demonstrated beyond any doubt that the Hashemis were capable of organizing a clandestine meeting between Iranian clerics and Americans." Three weeks later, the Hashemis would produce a second act in Madrid, this time starring Bill Casey.

ON FRIDAY, JULY 25—the same day that Bill Casey flew from Washington, DC, to New York City—Jamshid Hashemi checked in to the luxurious Plaza Hotel in downtown Madrid under the thinly disguised alias "Abdululi Hashemi." Traveling with Jamshid was another Iranian, Hassan Karrubi, a colleague from the Iranian Ministry of Information. Karrubi's brother, the Hojjat al-Islam Mehdi Karrubi, arrived around the same time but apparently stayed in the residence of the Iranian ambassador to Spain. Jamshid Hashemi had worked with Mehdi Karrubi, age forty-three, when both men served on a postrevolutionary committee to monitor the country's radio stations. Jamshid knew he was regarded as a trusted member of Khomeini's inner circle. Karrubi was also known to be aligned politically with Ayatollah Mohammad Beheshti, another powerful cleric in the regime.

"Cyrus asked me to bring Ayatollah Mehdi Karrubi out of Iran for a meeting in Spain," Jamshid later told investigators. Sometime after Casey met Jamshid at the Mayflower Hotel in March, Casey had asked Cyrus to meet with an Iranian official who could speak with authority about the hostages—and the Hashemi brothers regarded Karrubi as the perfect envoy for this purpose. (Interestingly, Cyrus had also passed on Karrubi's name to the Carter administration.) Madrid was chosen not only because they had already had a similar meeting there on July 2 but also because Spain did not require visas from Iranians and there were direct nonstop flights from Tehran to Madrid.

According to Jamshid's deposition with congressional investigators in 1992, two meetings were held between Casey and the Ayatollah Karrubi in a lavish suite at Madrid's Hotel Ritz. Jamshid said he and his brother Cyrus hosted the meetings and served as translators. The first meeting has to have occurred late on the morning of Saturday, July 26, soon after Casey's arrival in Madrid. Mehdi Karrubi, dressed in robes and a turban, began by lecturing Casey on the unhappy history of U.S.-Iranian relations under the shah. Casey allegedly responded by asserting that relations with Iran were "good when Republicans were in control of the White House." Casey then predicted that Reagan would triumph in the November election and that if the hostages were released, the new

Reagan administration would promptly return Iran's frozen assets and hand over military equipment previously purchased by the shah. After three hours, the men adjourned and agreed to meet again the next day, Sunday, July 27.

Karrubi reportedly began the Sunday meeting by pointedly asking Casey what he wanted. Casey replied by asking if Karrubi had the authority to "conclude a deal on behalf of Khomeini, and whether he could give assurances that the hostages would be well treated." Jamshid later told Ted Koppel on ABC's *Nightline,* "Casey said the Iranians should hold the hostages until after the election . . . and the new Reagan administration would feel favorably towards Iran, releasing military equipment and the frozen Iranian assets." Karrubi replied that he would have to return to Tehran and seek instructions from Khomeini.

According to Jamshid's sworn testimony to the 1992 October Surprise Task Force, a third meeting occurred between Casey and Karrubi sometime between August 8 and August 12 in Madrid. Karrubi allegedly told Casey that Khomeini had approved the deal: The hostages would be "treated as guests" and released only on the day of Reagan's inauguration. Iran expected in return that Casey and his colleagues would help the Iranians to obtain certain arms supplies.

All these shocking allegations emerged only twelve to thirteen years after the fact. Jamshid Hashemi's testimony became central to the 1991–92 congressional investigations into the "October surprise." His story—and those of other players—also spawned two major books, one by Brzezinski's aide Gary Sick (*October Surprise*) and another a year later by investigative reporter Robert Parry (*Trick or Treason*). By then, Jamshid's brother Cyrus had died, quite suddenly in 1985, apparently from a rare leukemia. (Jamshid thought his brother had been poisoned.) Casey himself was felled by a brain tumor in 1987, soon after he was implicated in the Iran-Contra scandal. Indeed, the "October surprise" revelations began to trickle out only when investigators dug into the origins of the Iran-Contra scandal, whereby it became clear that the Reagan administration's scheme to deliver weapons to Iran had its origins in Casey's 1980 negotiations with Karrubi.

The 1991 congressional investigation was itself politically contentious. By then, former CIA director George H. W. Bush was president, and his own White House counsel fought bitterly to fend off congressional subpoenas from the House's October Surprise Task Force, chaired by Congressman Lee Hamilton (D-IN). The body of evidence to corroborate Jamshid Hashemi's allegations was decidedly complex.

The tax records of the Plaza Hotel left no doubt that Jamshid was in Madrid over the weekend of July 26–27. On the other hand, telephone records indicated that Cyrus Hashemi was at his Connecticut home that weekend, not in Madrid. And the task force's investigators found what they called "overwhelming evidence" that Casey was in California that weekend, attending a gathering of fellow Bohemian Club members at their Bohemian Grove encampment. Similarly, they concluded that there was "no credible evidence of any link between any sales or transmittals of U.S. arms, spare parts or other assistance to Iran with the release of American hostages in Iran." In the end, the task force was able to release a bipartisan report on January 23, 1993, that essentially exonerated Casey. Congressman Hamilton wrote an opinion piece in *The New York Times* entitled "Case Closed."

The "October surprise" was characterized as some loony conspiracy story. But within months, Robert Parry's *Trick or Treason* was published, and he effectively demolished Casey's Bohemian Grove alibi. Parry was able to find receipts that proved that Casey attended the Bohemian Grove encampment in early August, not late July. Oddly, the "October surprise" task force investigators had to admit that Casey's 1980 passport had disappeared, and though they had found Casey's calendar diaries, the pages for the critical dates of July 26–27, 1980, were missing.

Upon closer inspection, it also became clear that within weeks of Reagan's inauguration, the new administration had acquiesced in the Israeli sale of a relatively small order of 106 mm recoilless rifles to the Islamic Republic. An Israeli government report stated that Secretary of State Al Haig "had not responded negatively to Israeli contacts with the Iranians and to the possibility of the supply of military equipment to Iran." Altogether, Israeli sales of military equipment to Iran during the first two years of the Reagan administration totaled just over $180 million.

And then in 1986 the Iran-Contra scandal broke. *The Washington Post*'s Bob Woodward and Walter Pincus reported that "then–Secretary of State Alexander M. Haig, Jr., gave his permission in 1981 for Israel to ship U.S.-made military spare parts and fighter plane tires to Iran, nearly four years before similar shipments set in motion the controversy now besetting the Reagan administration." The *Post* was at least insinuating that perhaps the 1986 arms-for-hostages deal had originated with the "October surprise" of 1980. Nevertheless, these further revelations seemed only to muddy the waters in the public debate. With President Bush's defeat at the polls in late 1992, the public was ready to move on.

Nearly two decades later, Parry found entirely new evidence in the archives of the George H. W. Bush Presidential Library. Dated November 4, 1991, the memorandum in question was written by President Bush's deputy White House counsel, Chester Paul Beach, Jr., and it described the State Department's efforts to collect documents in response to the House task force's subpoenas for "material relevant to the October Surprise allegations." Beach had just had a meeting with his counterpart at the State Department, a lawyer named Ed Williamson. "In this regard," Beach noted, "Ed mentioned only a cable from the Madrid embassy indicating that Bill Casey was in town, for purposes unknown."

The cable is damning evidence that Bill Casey did indeed make that side trip from London to Madrid in late July 1980. And shockingly, the Bush White House deputy counsel knew of this evidence—but it was never turned over to Congressman Lee Hamilton and his October Surprise Task Force.

Now we know why. Two days later, on November 6, 1991, Beach's boss, White House counsel C. Boyden Gray, convened a meeting to discuss how they should handle the new evidence. Gray said the "October surprise" investigation was "of special interest to the President." It was essential, he told his staff, that there be "no Surprises to the White House. . . . This is partisan." The Madrid cable was never turned over to Hamilton's task force. When Parry eventually shared the Beach memo with Hamilton, the congressman expressed his dismay: "If the White House knew that Casey was there, they certainly should have shared it with us."

Obviously, Republican operatives close to Reagan, Casey, and Bush worked hard to bury the story. But it kept getting resurrected. Many years later, in September 2019, Stu Eizenstat pressed James Baker about Casey's alleged trip to Madrid. Baker—who served as Reagan's first chief of staff—replied, "Would I be surprised if Casey did it? There is nothing about Casey that would surprise me. He is a piece of work."

There the story rests, like a beached whale, dead and stinking. The implications for the Carter presidency were devastating. The Republican Party's campaign chairman was negotiating with a foreign power to prolong the hostage crisis and thereby tip the scales in the November election against a sitting president. By any definition, this was an act of treason. But Republican operatives and Casey himself probably regarded it as mere hardball politics. And after all, it had been done before, in the 1968 election, when another Republican presidential candidate had passed private messages to the South Vietnamese president, Nguyen Van Thieu, telling him to stall on the peace talks. Richard Nixon always denied these allegations of a 1968 "October surprise" gambit, but we now know from the private diary of his chief of staff, H. R. Haldeman, that Nixon was lying.

Chapter 25
The Defeat

So what if Reagan wins? Nothing will change since he and Carter are both enemies of Islam.

—AYATOLLAH KHOMEINI

Carter and Ronald Reagan at the Al Smith Foundation dinner at the Waldorf-Astoria, October 1980
NEW YORK POST/GETTY IMAGES

BY THE AUTUMN of 1980, President Carter understood his reelection was by no means a certainty. Tim Kraft, the campaign aide responsible for orchestrating his win of the Iowa caucuses in 1976, told him bluntly that he was once again the underdog. "I think we are in tough shape," Kraft wrote, "and you are going to have to get out there and fight for it." Carter admitted privately that many Americans were of the opinion that "I am not a strong leader and have [an] inadequate vision for the future." The Democratic Party's traditional coalition was fractured. Liberals thought he was not liberal enough, feminists thought he wasn't a reliable ally, and many blue-collar voters blamed his administration for stagflation. White voters, particularly white male southerners, were disaffected, many of them uncomfortable with Carter's support for affirmative action and women's rights.

By contrast, Republicans seemed fully united behind Ronald Reagan's starkly conservative message. Reagan brazenly launched his autumn campaign at a fairground near Philadelphia, Mississippi, just down the road from where the Ku Klux Klan murdered three civil rights activists in 1964. "I believe in states' rights," Reagan said. This wasn't just a racial dog whistle; it was an explicit appeal to the racism of southern white voters, a challenge to Carter's southern base. Carter was appalled and noted in his diary that the Klan had endorsed Reagan and proclaimed that the Republican Party platform "could have been written by a Klansman." Carter warned that if elected, Reagan would be divisive, turning Americans against one another, "black from white, Jew from Christian, North from South, rural from urban." But his attacks on Reagan struck many voters as churlish.

Reagan was prone to outrageous gaffes, but at the same time his folksy demeanor deflected people from thinking the worst of the man. At a Labor Day rally in New Jersey, people laughed when he joked, "A recession is when your neighbor loses his job. A depression is when you lose yours. And recovery is when Jimmy Carter loses his!"

There was also a wild card named John Anderson, a Republican congressman from Illinois who was suddenly running a strong media campaign for president as an independent. With Anderson polling at an astonishing 15 percent, Carter found himself trailing Reagan by six points. "Most of Anderson's supporters," Carter noted in his diary, "steal the Democratic liberals who are disaffected with me. They don't yet recognize their incompatibility with Anderson's record and his basic philosophy because it's so chameleon-like." Anderson was becoming yet another obstacle to Carter's reelection, precisely because he was attracting mostly young, educated liberals.

Anderson's soft constituency in the polls included a significant number of Jewish voters. And though Jewish Americans constituted a tiny sliver of the electorate, Carter's campaign staffers recognized that they could easily determine the outcome in New York, Pennsylvania, and Florida—states Carter would absolutely need to carry in a close election. In 1976, he had won an unsurprising 72 percent of the Jewish vote. But in early September, Carter spent a contentious hour arguing with a group of Jewish American leaders. Howard Squadron, the chairman of the Conference of Presidents of Major American Jewish Organizations, emerged from the meeting and told reporters, "In the past, one could judge the Jewish community to be fairly definitely in the Democratic column. In this election, it's still up in the air."

Squadron and his colleagues challenged the president's Middle East policies, criticizing in particular the administration's recent decision to abstain on a 14–0 vote in the United Nations Security Council on a resolution condemning Israel's unilateral claim of a united Jerusalem as its capital. Carter vigorously defended the abstention, arguing that it was necessary for Washington to be neutral on such questions in order to enhance the prospect of future peace negotiations. Two years after the Camp David Peace Accords, Jewish leaders still harbored doubts about Carter's stance on Israel.

The very next day, Carter was disappointed to learn that the League of Women Voters had invited Congressman Anderson to take part in what was planned as the first of several presidential debates. Anderson and Reagan promptly accepted the invitation, but Carter declined, saying he would agree only to a two-man debate with Reagan. Anderson's candidacy, he said, was "primarily a creation of the press." He pointed out that Anderson had not won a single primary or caucus, and he clearly was going to draw votes that otherwise would have gone to the Democrats.

This was particularly true in New York State, with its forty-one electoral votes. That same week, the Republican congressman had mysteriously managed to get the endorsement of the Liberal Party, guaranteeing Anderson a line on the state's presidential ballot.

Carter would have been shocked had he learned that it was none other than Roy Cohn—the same sleazy lawyer behind Hamilton Jordan's Studio 54 troubles—who had greased the wheels. Cohn arranged for Reagan's Northeast campaign manager, Roger Stone, to deliver a suitcase filled with $125,000 in cash to a lawyer representing the Liberal Party. "I take the suitcase to the law office," Stone recounted years later to a reporter. "Two days later they have a convention. Liberals decide they're endorsing John Anderson for president. It's a three-way race now in New York State."

Anderson was bad news, but Carter was also still deeply annoyed with Ted Kennedy. After several weeks of often petty negotiations, the senator had agreed to make some half dozen campaign appearances on behalf of Carter—but only in return for Carter's helping the Kennedy campaign to retire the $1.7 million debt left over from his failed challenge. Carter and Kennedy aides insisted the negotiations were "cordial" and "satisfactory," but everyone in the Carter camp thought this was an extraordinarily bitter pill. The poisonous atmosphere left over from the primary months lingered well into the autumn campaign.

LIBERALS WERE DISAFFECTED—but so too were southern evangelicals, a slice of the electorate that Carter had won overwhelmingly in 1976. In June 1979, the Reverend Jerry Falwell, the television host of the *Old-Time Gospel Hour,* founded a right-wing evangelical movement he named the "Moral Majority." That was the same year in which the Southern Baptist Convention was taken over by sharply conservative fundamentalists. Carter was "dismayed" by this turn of events. He thought the Baptist Church was being dominated by "those who believe that Christianity gives its adherents material benefits." And they were pushing aside Baptist leaders who believed in "ministering to the poor, the despised and the homeless."

For his part, Falwell sharply criticized Carter for his hands-off stance on abortion rights and his strong support for the Equal Rights Amendment (ERA). He accused Carter of using the traditional Southern Baptist doctrine on the separation of church and state to hide his actual liberal views on these hot-button social issues. In the year and a half leading up to the 1980 election, Falwell had barnstormed the country, particularly the South and the Midwest, telling evangelicals, "I am absolutely convinced that the vast majority of all Americans believe in decency, the family, the home, Bible morality, and all that we have long considered holy and sacred. However, this great 'Moral Majority' has been silent too long."

Falwell's politics were no doubt motivated in part by racial bias. His sermons in the 1950s had blatantly argued that segregation of the races was sanctioned by the Bible and that communists were fomenting integration—and besides, "the true Negro . . . does not want integration." Like many evangelicals, Falwell was incensed when the Internal

Revenue Service decided in 1978 to deny tax-exempt status to all-white private "Christian" schools. Carter, of course, supported the IRS ruling and really didn't care about the political consequences of alienating supporters of this thinly disguised segregation.

Nevertheless, sensing that his support among evangelicals was slipping away, Carter invited seven prominent preachers, including television evangelists Jim Bakker, Rex Humbard, and Oral Roberts, to a White House breakfast on January 22, 1980. Reverend Falwell took the opportunity to ask the president, "Is it fair to say that your definition of a family would not include the marriage of homosexual men or lesbians?" A tape recorder openly placed on the table by Falwell himself recorded the conversation, but Carter apparently only nodded in response to Falwell—who then responded effusively, "Thank you, thank you very much."

Afterward, Carter noted in his diary that these evangelical leaders were "really right-wing: against ERA, for requiring prayer in school, against abortion (so am I)." Carter nevertheless came away from this encounter thinking that despite the disagreements, "they are basically supportive of what I'm trying to do." He was wrong. In fact, Falwell and all of these televangelists, including Billy Graham, were determined to see that he remained a one-term president.

Soon after this White House breakfast, Falwell told an "I Love America" rally in Anchorage, Alaska, that he had asked the president, "Sir, why do you have known practicing homosexuals on your senior staff here at the White House?" Falwell claimed Carter had replied, "Well, I am president of all the American people, and I believe I should represent everyone." To which Falwell claimed he had replied, "Why don't you have some murderers and bank robbers and so forth to represent?" The crowds cheered. *The New York Times* eventually ran a story in August headlined "White House Says Minister Misquoted Carter Remarks." Falwell responded by claiming that the transcript from his own tape recording was "incomplete" and that the president was merely attempting to "discredit evangelical ministers who disagree with him on many social and political issues." Carter was disgusted and replied plainly, "He [Falwell] just lied about it."

That same day, August 7, 1980, Carter held a courtesy meeting in the Oval Office with Bailey Smith, the newly inaugurated president of the

Southern Baptist Convention, who told him, "We are praying for you, Mr. President, that you will abandon secular humanism as your religion." Perplexed, Carter replied that he had never used the phrase and wasn't familiar with what it meant. That evening, he asked Rosalynn, "What is a secular humanist?" She said she didn't know. Jerry Falwell nevertheless spent the rest of the autumn campaign pinning the label on Carter, associating his presidency with "abortion, pornography, the drug epidemic, the breakdown of the traditional family in America, the establishment of homosexuality as an accepted alternate life-style and other immoral cancers which are causing the U.S. to rot from within." The Moral Majority spent $10 million that autumn on radio and television advertising, labeling Carter a "traitor to the South and no longer a Christian."

Carter was genuinely shocked by such vitriol. "My religious beliefs are very precious to me," he told a Memphis audience late in the campaign. "But until this year, I have never had anybody question the sincerity of my belief in God and my commitment of my life as a Christian believing in Jesus Christ as my savior."

On September 26, 1980, the Carters went to Camp David and watched that evening a special televised investigation by Bill Moyers on Falwell's Moral Majority. Carter was annoyed by the report: "Although he [Moyers] condemned it in the last four minutes, I thought he gave the religious nuts fifty minutes of uninterrupted bragging on themselves. It is a disquieting movement." Disturbingly, opinion polls indicated this once rock-solid Carter constituency was now supporting Reagan by a margin of two to one. Falwell's political ally Paul Weyrich, a conservative religious activist, later explained, "What galvanized the Christian community was not abortion, school prayer, or the ERA. . . . What changed their mind was Jimmy Carter's intervention against the Christian schools, trying to deny them tax-exempt status on the basis of so-called de facto segregation." In other words, it really was all about latent racism.

HANGING OVER THE entire autumn campaign season was one overriding issue—the hostages. Carter was still spending an inordinate amount of time on the Iran crisis. If Reagan and his campaign manager, Bill Casey, feared an "October surprise" release of the hostages, Carter naturally was hoping for the same. In the wake of the shah's death in Cairo on July 27, 1980, the Iranians began signaling that perhaps they were finally ready for serious negotiations. On September 9, 1980, the White House received an indirect message, passed through the West German foreign minister, that an Iranian official named Sadegh Tabatabaei, a high-level functionary in the prime minister's office, wanted to meet with American envoys in West Germany. The German-educated Tabatabaei was thought to be a credible intermediary, if only because his sister was married to Ayatollah Khomeini's son Ahmad. Carter was suddenly optimistic that perhaps a breakthrough was imminent. Tabatabaei signaled that Khomeini was now willing to limit his demands to the unfreezing of Iranian financial assets, an American pledge not to interfere in Iranian affairs—and a return of the late shah's fortune.

Under a shroud of extreme secrecy, Deputy Secretary of State Warren Christopher flew to Bonn on September 17 and met with Tabatabaei in a West German foreign ministry guesthouse. Christopher was surprised by the Iranian's cosmopolitan appearance. The handsome, thirty-seven-year-old Tabatabaei was wearing gray flannel pants and a tweed blazer. Their talks went well. "The biggest hang-up," Carter noted in his diary, "is going to be on the shah's assets." But Christopher offered vague assurances that Washington would "help overcome banking secrecy" to facilitate the Iranian effort to ferret out the locations of Pahlavi family assets. He also pledged that if the hostages were released, the United States would not launch any punishing military attacks on Iran. And finally, Christopher assured Tabatabaei that approximately $6 billion in frozen Iranian assets would be released. (This included an estimated $240 million in military equipment that Iran had already paid for prior to the revolution.) Carter was relieved, believing that "this was the first time we were certain we were in direct contact with the ayatollah."

Unfortunately, five days later, just as Tabatabaei was scheduled to return to Tehran, Iraq's dictator, Saddam Hussein, launched a surprise invasion of southern Iran. Ayatollah Khomeini suddenly had to turn his attention to marshaling Iran's defenses. "Iran was losing," Carter observed just two days after the outbreak of the war, "which should make them more eager than Iraq to accept a cease-fire." This should be true, responded Defense Secretary Harold Brown, "except they are crazy." Indeed, the war would last eight years, killing an estimated one million Iraqis and Iranians.

The outbreak of a bloody ground war quickly reordered the ayatollah's priorities. Khomeini may have decided that the hostage crisis had run its course, having given him the time to consolidate power against his secular political rivals. Many Iran observers inside the Carter administration certainly hoped the ayatollah would now find a way to end the hostage crisis—and soon. On October 9 Carter received an encouraging message from Tabatabaei that "the American proposal has fallen on fertile ground." Tehran seemed to be signaling that a deal might be rapidly sanctioned by the Iranian assembly. Two days later, Carter tried to sweeten the negotiations by approving a message to the Iranians signaling that he would agree to ship an inventory of spare parts they had bought and paid for prior to the revolution—contingent, of course, on the release of the hostages.

That same October week, Secretary of State Ed Muskie received from Yasir Arafat a verbatim transcript of a very recent conversation the PLO chairman had shared with the newly elected speaker of the Iranian parliament, Akbar Hashemi Rafsanjani. According to Arafat, Rafsanjani told him flatly, "The Imam [Khomeini] has taken a decision to resolve the issue of the hostages. . . . The U.S. had agreed to our terms. But the latest events [the war] have forced us to postpone all this." When Arafat had then asked if that meant there would be no solution, Rafsanjani said, "Not necessarily." He explained that a special committee had been formed to handle the problem—but Khomeini specifically wanted to know "what the Palestinian terms are for the resolution of the issue of the hostages."

Arafat replied, "There are no Palestinian terms. . . ."

RAFSANJANI: "The imam has ordered me to include something for Palestine."
ARAFAT: "My advice to you is: If you want to resolve the hostage issue, do not include any terms for Palestine, because our terms are different. . . . We do not ask for anything for Palestine."
RAFSANJANI: "What if the imam insists?"
ARAFAT: "This is the imam's concern, not ours. Do I understand from this that the hostages issue is on the way to resolution?"
RAFSANJANI: "Yes, in spite of the war."

Time was short—the November 4 election was less than a month away—but clearly this tantalizing exchange suggested that the Iranian regime might be very close to resolving the hostage crisis. The problem was that there was no one "regime" but many factions inside the Islamic Republic. Rafsanjani's conversation with Arafat is evidence that the speaker of the Iranian parliament was aware of the secret Tabatabaei-Christopher talks in Bonn. But that did not mean that the "regime" was speaking with one voice. There were factions within the parliament opposed to any deal with President Carter. Iran's beleaguered president, Abol Hassan Bani-Sadr, certainly favored a release of the hostages—but he had not been informed of Tabatabaei's Bonn mission. The highly influential Ayatollah Mohammad Beheshti was aware of Tabatabaei's talks with Christopher. But Beheshti was playing a complicated game. Bani-Sadr later wrote in his memoirs that "it became increasingly obvious to me that Beheshti wanted to solve the hostage problem on someone else's behalf. That someone could only be Ronald Reagan." In retrospect, it may be that Khomeini and Beheshti sanctioned the Tabatabaei-Christopher talks as a means of pinning down the terms for a release of the hostages—but they were not committed to releasing the hostages prior to the election. After all, if they were also aware of the July promises made by Bill Casey in Madrid, well, they might have had reason to wait until after the November election.

Bani-Sadr claimed that he warned Khomeini that Reagan's militancy posed a danger to the Islamic Republic: "We should not contribute to Reagan's election." But Khomeini replied, "So what if Reagan wins? Nothing will change since he and Carter are both enemies of Islam."

Khomeini announced that he was ready to let the Iranian parliament (*majlis*) decide the fate of the hostages—but in reality, he was letting the clock run out. Early in October the Iranian parliament created a seven-member commission to study the issue, with the expectation that the crisis would be resolved within a matter of days or weeks.

As late as October 24, Carter managed to be hopeful, noting in his diary, "The Iranians are still making favorable noises. I think they are playing with us to some degree, relishing the publicity as they've always done." He knew they were "confused internally," but nevertheless he thought they were not sending any negative signals. At a White House breakfast with his foreign policy advisers that day, he expressed the hope that the hostages might be released in a few days—and even said that he'd like to send Cy Vance to greet the freed hostages in Germany. It was an optimistic thought.

Two days later, the Iranian *majlis* held a formal debate on the hostages—but hard-liners opposed to a settlement absented themselves, leaving the *majlis* with less than the necessary two-thirds quorum. This led to another weeklong delay before a vote could be taken. Surprisingly, the Carter White House had an inside account of the *majlis*'s deliberations from none other than Cyrus Hashemi—the same source who allegedly set up Bill Casey's clandestine meeting in Madrid with a representative of the Ayatollah Khomeini. On October 21 and 22 Hashemi reported to Harold Saunders, the State Department's assistant secretary for the Near East, that he had talked on the phone with the new speaker of the parliament, Akbar Hashemi Rafsanjani. Saunders immediately sent a memo about this conversation to Secretary of State Ed Muskie, identifying Hashemi as "an Iranian banker in New York who is an adviser to the Iranian Parliament's hostage commission."

Hashemi claimed that Rafsanjani had met with Khomeini the previous day and that the ayatollah was in a stubborn mood. Told that the Americans were willing to meet Iran's conditions for a release of the hostages, Khomeini "got angry and said he did not want to do anything that would help with the reelection of the President. . . . He did not wish to release the hostages before November 4." On the other hand, the very next day Khomeini "was reported to be much calmer." When Ayatollah Beheshti talked about the impending release of the hostages, Khomeini did not object. Rafsanjani told Hashemi that Khomeini was clearly "less adamant" and "would not veto [it] if the Majlis says yes."

In retrospect, Hashemi's information proved to be right on the mark: Khomeini clearly was ready to green-light the hostage release, but he did not want a deal to be announced until after the November 4 election. Hashemi was in a position to know why. He was the only player in contact with all the other actors, including the Carter administration, the Iranian *majlis*—and, allegedly, Ronald Reagan's campaign manager, Bill Casey. Hashemi was playing all sides.

TWO WEEKS BEFORE the November 4 election, the League of Women Voters caved to Carter's terms and agreed to exclude Anderson from a debate scheduled for October 28 in Cleveland, Ohio. Their rationale was that Anderson's polling numbers for his independent bid had faded. By this time, Rafshoon and Pat Caddell had serious qualms about a one-on-one debate with Reagan, particularly one taking place so close to the election. Charlie Kirbo was also opposed to a debate so late in the game. But Carter felt confident that he could take on Reagan. On the eve of the debate he also felt buoyed by a Gallup poll that showed him outpacing Reagan by 45 percent to 42 percent.

On October 25, 1980—just three days prior to the Carter-Reagan debate—Paul Corbin walked into the Reagan-Bush campaign headquarters in Arlington, Virginia. Not many of his friends knew it, but the veteran Kennedy political operative was now on the payroll of the Reagan campaign. That rainy Saturday morning at 9:35, he signed in with the receptionist and went to see Bill Casey—who handed him a paycheck for $1,500. Later that same day, Casey dropped by the campaign office of James Baker, Reagan's senior adviser. According to Baker, Casey told him, "Here is something you might give to your debate prep team." Baker thumbed through the three binders and then sent them to David Gergen's debate preparation team. Within hours, a slew of people in the Reagan campaign knew they had in their possession the Carter debate-briefing books. This included Congressman David Stockman, who was playing the part of Carter in Reagan's debate practice sessions.

There is little doubt that Corbin had orchestrated the theft. Then-congressman Dick Cheney later phoned Baker to tell him that Corbin had confessed to a member of his staff, Tim Wyngaard, that he had received the briefing books from someone in the Carter White House and passed them on to Casey. Corbin still had connections inside the administration; he was friends with Landon Butler's assistant, Laurie Lucey, the daughter of former Wisconsin governor Pat Lucey—whom Carter had appointed as his ambassador to Mexico. Lucey, however, was a Kennedy man, and he had quit his ambassadorial post in the autumn of 1979 to join Kennedy's campaign. (He later accepted an invitation to be John Anderson's running mate.) His daughter had quit her White House job around the same time, but Bob Dunn, another longtime Lucey aide, had then become an assistant to the White House appointments secretary, Phil Wise. Both Laurie Lucey and Dunn later denied that they had anything to do with filching the briefing books. To compound the mystery,

Jerry Rafshoon recalled seeing Corbin himself in the White House one day later in the campaign and thought it strange that the Kennedy man was there. Congressional investigators later speculated that a copy of the briefing books had been lifted from Brzezinski's office. "The papers were left on his desk," said Congressman Donald J. Albosta, "and this one night they . . . disappeared, and they became gone."

Years later, Baker confessed to Stu Eizenstat that he "probably shouldn't have passed it [the briefing books] on—but I did." But he also insisted that the material "didn't help us a damn bit [and] wasn't worth shit." Eizenstat disagreed. And so did Carter, who told the author Craig Shirley, "I don't think there's any doubt that it made some difference."

Carter's performance in the October 28 debate was decidedly lackluster, and Reagan clearly seemed to anticipate the president's lines of attack. When Carter criticized Reagan for opposing national health insurance, Reagan brushed him off with a wave of his hand, saying, "There you go again." It was just about the only memorable moment in their encounter—except possibly for Carter's reference to Amy. In response to a question about the SALT II treaty, Carter ineptly tried to personalize the issue by saying, "I had a discussion with my daughter Amy the other day. . . ." He had asked thirteen-year-old Amy what she thought the most important issue was in this election, and she had replied, "The control of nuclear arms." The pundits later had fun ribbing Carter for citing Amy.

Reagan used his avuncular acting skills to dispel the fears of many undecided voters that he might become a loose cannon as commander in chief. "Are you better off than you were four years ago?" Reagan asked in his closing statement. And many Americans concluded not. Carter knew that Reagan had "made a better impression on the TV audience than I did." He was annoyed and complained that the former actor "has his memorized tapes. He pushes a button, and they come out."

In the days after the debate, Caddell's polling numbers registered a significant shift toward Reagan. "When people realized that they could get rid of Carter," said Rick Hertzberg, "and still not destroy the world, they went ahead and did it."

CARTER STILL RADIATED self-confidence. When he turned fifty-six on October 1, 1980, he reflected, "If I'm re-elected, I'll be sixty when I go out of office—a good retirement age." Throughout October he campaigned relentlessly, visiting dozens of cities in Michigan, New York, Wisconsin, Illinois, Tennessee, North Carolina, Florida, Missouri, South Carolina, Ohio, Mississippi, Texas, and other states. "My hands are getting scratched up on the back," he noted, "because the crowd gets emotional and a lot of people weep. It's kind of a high-pitched shrill sound that comes out of the crowds now. . . . There's a lot more intensity of interest than in weeks gone by." Carter sometimes found himself energized by the crowds. But he had never been a rabble-rouser on the campaign stump, and this was still his major handicap. Facing one of his most enthusiastic crowds in Houston, Texas, on October 31, Carter gave another lackluster speech: Eizenstat was present and noted in his diary that the president "absolutely silenced them; he rambled; no coherence." Eizenstat thought all the worrying about the hostages, the long nights in the Oval Office, and the long days on the campaign trail had taken their toll: "He had aged perceptibly."

Saturday, November 1, 1980, would be yet another long day. It began with the president rising before dawn in Houston. By 6:17 A.M. he was driven from the Warwick Hotel to the Hermann Park Golf Course, where he went jogging for nearly thirty minutes. Returning to the Warwick, he chatted for a few minutes on the phone with Rosalynn. By 8:29 A.M. he was flying to Brownsville, for another campaign event. Late that morning, he flew to San Antonio, where he spoke at the Alamo, and then flew that afternoon to Abilene. By 4:34 P.M. he was flying to another Carter-Mondale rally in Fort Worth. Two hours later he was on Air Force One, bound for Milwaukee, Wisconsin, where he addressed a campaign rally for twenty minutes and then gave a short interview to a reporter from the *Milwaukee Sentinel*. He then hopped back aboard Air Force One and flew to Chicago, arriving at 10:27 P.M. He checked in to a private suite at the Hyatt Regency hotel, and by 10:57 he was talking on the phone with Rosalynn.

Just before collapsing into bed, he was told that the Iranian *majlis* was about to convene and the expectation was that this time they would muster a quorum. He fell asleep at midnight—only to be awakened by a White House operator at 2:30 A.M. His secretary, Susan Clough, had more messages for him about Iran. Deputy Secretary of State Warren Christopher called at 3:47 A.M. to report that the *majlis* had apparently met and voted to approve the four points negotiated with Tabatabaei.

Christopher told him that Tehran would soon transmit a formal offer to release the hostages. This initially struck Carter as extremely encouraging news.* Within twenty minutes he phoned his closest adviser, Rosalynn, and they very briefly discussed the matter. Carter said he had decided to rush back to the White House. "Why don't you stay?" Rosalynn responded. "Why do you have to come back?" The politically astute First Lady was already thinking about how it would appear to voters if the president suddenly interrupted his campaign trip. Expectations had been built up more than once and then nothing had happened. It would look like Carter was desperately trying to influence the election. Carter merely responded, "I cannot pass up a chance." He thought he needed to be in the Oval Office to handle all the details.

Eizenstat and other members of the presidential party were soon roused and told they had to rush back to Chicago's O'Hare Airport to board Air Force One. By 5:23 A.M., Air Force One was in the air. Eizenstat was upset. He thought the dramatic rush back to Washington was a mistake. He felt so strongly about this that he went into the president's private cabin and pointed out that many Americans might think that he was pausing his campaign for merely "political purposes." Carter replied, "That's a good point, and that's my feeling." The president understood the optics, but he really could not resist trying once again to get a deal. It was an old story; he just wanted to get the thing done, and damn the politics.

On the flight back Eizenstat scribbled on an Air Force One notepad, "1. The American people resent Iran interfering in our election." Voters would not want to see their president giving the Iranians better terms just because it was on the eve of the election. At this point, Eizenstat thought, it would be better to resolve the hostage crisis after the election.

By the time they landed at 7:35 A.M. at Andrews Air Force Base outside Washington and helicoptered back to the White House, everyone was tired and disheveled. Carter walked into the Oval Office at 7:58 A.M., and fifteen minutes later he was in the Cabinet Room, presiding

---

* Simultaneously, Cyrus Hashemi was reporting to the State Department that on late Thursday night, October 30, Ayatollah Khomeini had "overruled everybody" and told his aides "to proceed with the release of the hostages." Based on such reports, perhaps Carter had reason to be hopeful.

over an hour-and-a-half-long meeting with his top aides to discuss the Iranian terms. Carter quickly realized that the breakthrough he had been hoping for was still elusive. The Iranian message still contained clearly unacceptable language, such as a reference to the need to "confiscate the shah's property." The meeting broke up shortly before 10:00 A.M., but they reconvened at 2:00 P.M. Everyone was in a desultory mood. Eizenstat later wrote that he had never attended a meeting as "grim and portentous as this." The Iranians were demanding a response to their terms by Monday, the day before the election. Carter acknowledged that he had to make it clear to the American people that "we won't be pushed around." On the other hand, he mused that the Iranian *majlis's* term sheet had used "abusive language for domestic consumption, but their terms weren't unreasonable." He thought he should respond in the same manner. Rafshoon, Jordan, and Powell thought this too mild. Rafshoon argued he should "just tell them to go to hell. Really get out there and tell them we're not going to be pushed around anymore." Carter insisted that such language might endanger the safety of the hostages. According to Eizenstat's account, Rafshoon interrupted coarsely, "I'd tell them to go fuck themselves."

"Will that get the hostages out?" Carter asked.

Jordan said no, "but the American people want to hear it."

"Oh yeah," Carter replied, "what if they decide to take the hostages out in the courtyard and shoot them? And maybe shoot one every hour? I'm not going to let that happen."

Carter was still where he had been at the very start of the hostage crisis, some 364 days earlier—heavily invested in their personal safety. He would sacrifice his presidency to avoid the slightest risk of miscalculation. As the meeting ended, Carter walked back to the Oval Office. He spent the rest of the afternoon with Charlie Kirbo. And then he calmly went to the press briefing room at 6:21 P.M., and, interrupting a Redskins football game, he spent four minutes on national television explaining that the Iranian parliament's proposal appeared to be constructive. *The New York Times* headline the next morning blared, "U.S. Gets Iran Terms on Hostages; Carter Calls Them 'Positive Basis' for Achieving Captives' Freedom." The *Times* story reported, "With only two days to go before the election, the Administration seemed closer than it had ever been to freeing the hostages, but it was uncertain whether this would happen." Elsewhere in the story, however, Carter was quoted as saying, "I wish that I could predict when the hostages will return," but "I cannot." Clearly, the negotiations were not over.

Americans had heard this disheartening mixed message before—and football fans found themselves deeply exasperated that their game had been interrupted for nothing.

That evening Carter retired early, falling into bed at 8:45 P.M., utterly exhausted. He had been virtually without sleep for forty hours.

THE NEXT MORNING, November 3, the White House signal board operator awakened him with a phone call, as requested, at 5:00. Over the next hour, he had phone conversations with Ed Muskie, Warren Christopher, Jody Powell, and Ham Jordan. By 5:50 A.M. he was in the Oval Office, talking on the phone with the ubiquitous Kirbo. Another phone call to Rosalynn—who was out of town campaigning—was followed by meetings with Powell, Rafshoon, Kirbo, Jordan, Jack Watson, and his pollster, Pat Caddell. Astonishingly, as bad as the whole year had been—the failed helicopter mission, the long, drawn-out Kennedy challenge, the Billy Carter affair—the president could tell himself that he had somehow clawed his way back in the polls to well within the pollsters' 5 percent margin of error. Indeed, the final preelection poll by *The New York Times* and CBS News gave Reagan 44 percent to Carter's 43 percent, with Anderson at 8 percent. Reagan still seemed to have the edge in the Electoral College, but most pundits thought the election would be very close. Any news at all from Tehran therefore might have a significant effect on the outcome. "You just assume it has some impact," Caddell told *The New York Times*. "You hope that people react that the president's patience paid off." Bill Brock, the Republican national chairman, felt in his gut that the latest hint of possible settlement of the hostage crisis "helps the president just a bit." So despite everything, Carter had hopes.

By 9:03 A.M. Carter was walking across the South Lawn to board a Marine helicopter to Andrews Air Force Base. The rest of the president's day was spent in the air, flying to Akron, Ohio; St. Louis and Springfield, Missouri; Detroit; Portland, Oregon; and Seattle—giving speeches at campaign rallies, before finally flying back to Georgia. It was one of those roller-coaster kinds of days. Eizenstat was on Air Force One and jotted down in his notebook that he could feel "the heavy hand of defeat in the air." And yet he thought Carter gave inspiring speeches in Portland and Seattle before enthusiastic crowds: "He handled it like a true champion. I felt proud of him."

But while the president was flying back to Georgia in the early-morning hours of Election Day, Pat Caddell called Hamilton Jordan in Washington with the latest polling numbers. "The sky has fallen in," Caddell told Jordan around 2:00 A.M. "We are getting murdered. All the people that have been waiting and holding out for some reason to vote Democratic have left us. I've never seen anything like it in polling. Here we are neck and neck with Reagan up until the very end and everything breaks against us. It's the hostage thing." Caddell estimated it was going to be a Reagan landslide by eight to ten points. Jordan was shocked, but he decided Carter had to know and so told Caddell to call him on Air Force One.

Oddly, Carter was in a good mood when the call from Caddell came through. "What's happening, Patrick?" he said lightly. "Mr. President," replied Caddell, "I am afraid that it's gone." He flatly reported that the undecided votes were swinging decisively to Reagan. They were down in the polls by at least seven points. The news spread quickly through Air Force One, and when Carter emerged from his cabin, Eizenstat gave him a tearful hug and said, "Mr. President, we have let you down." Carter took the news calmly and told Powell and others standing around not to inform Rosalynn. He wanted to do that himself.

The First Lady had arrived back in Plains around 2:00 A.M. from her own campaign tour of Wisconsin, Missouri, Illinois, and Alabama. But she too had sensed defeat, and seeing her son Jack in the living room, she blurted out to him, "We're going to lose."

"I know, Mom," replied Jack. "I came back home tonight so you wouldn't be all by yourself."

Carter's helicopter from Robins Air Force Base in Georgia landed in Plains at 7:41 A.M. and Rosalynn was there to greet him. Locking eyes, they knew right away that each understood that they had lost. During the motorcade to vote at the Plains School, Rosalynn asked, "How bad is it?"

Gesturing with a thumb down, Carter said, "It's gone. . . . It's all over."

After voting, Carter gave a short speech at the Plains depot platform, and before flying back to Washington, he visited his mother. By noon, the Carters were back in the White House, awaiting the election news. Exhausted, they retreated to their bedroom and tried to nap. In the midafternoon the president spoke with his pollster for two minutes on the phone; Caddell confirmed that the exit polls indicated that "we were not doing well." Around the same time, Rosalynn received a call from Tim Kraft, who told her that he didn't believe Caddell's numbers. He was still optimistic. Momentarily uplifted, Rosalynn ran into the bathroom, where Carter was changing his clothes, to tell him this encouraging news. Carter looked at her, sat down on the edge of the tub, and said, "Pat knows."

"I know he does," Rosalynn sighed. She then sat down on his lap and wept. "We clung together as the realization sank in further."

Early that evening they had dinner with their son Jack and his wife, Judy. Joining them were Judy's mother, Edna Langford, Emily Dolvin— the president's aunt—and Charlie Kirbo, with his wife and three of his daughters. Charlie was there at the beginning, and he would be there for the end of the Carter presidency. By 7:30 P.M. the networks had called the election for Reagan—and at 9:50 P.M. Carter conceded, even before the polls had closed on the West Coast. "I promised you four years ago that I would never lie to you," he told campaign workers gathered in the ballroom of Washington's Sheraton Hotel. "So I can't stand here tonight and say it doesn't hurt."

Carter had lost in a landslide in the Electoral College, winning only forty-nine electoral votes in six states plus the District of Columbia. Reagan won with 50.7 percent of the popular vote; Carter received 41 percent and John Anderson took 6.6 percent. Carter was convinced that Anderson's votes had come mostly from die-hard Kennedy supporters. It may have looked like a landslide—but actually nearly 50 percent of eligible voters didn't bother to cast a ballot. This meant Reagan was elected president with votes representing barely a quarter of the electorate.

Still, it was a humiliating drubbing. Carter wasn't terribly surprised, but he later wrote in his memoirs that the results "hurt me deeply." Two-thirds of Jerry Falwell's Moral Majority evangelicals had voted for Reagan. Carter won the Jewish vote with only a plurality of 45 percent, down from 72 percent in 1976. He was particularly bitter that "the Jews didn't even give me a majority," while Hispanics and African Americans voted for him by an overwhelming majority—"better than 80 percent."

When Al Moses, the president's liaison to the Jewish community, suggested that "the Jewish community eventually would see the great contribution I made to Israel," Carter responded, "That may or may not be true, but it certainly was not indicated by the outcome of the election."

Carter won Georgia, but otherwise the "New South" had turned its back on the only southern president in almost 140 years. Reagan took 61 percent of the votes from the former Confederacy. He captured white voters by 56 percent to Carter's 36 percent. On the other hand, Carter won 83 percent of African American voters, while Reagan took only 14 percent of the Black vote. That was the stark racial divide. The class divide was equally glaring: Reagan won a large majority of voters earning more than $15,000 annually—while Carter won the majority of the poor, but they constituted only 27 percent of those who voted. Carter narrowly won a plurality of union household members, by a margin of 48 to 45 percent. If they managed to vote, poor whites and minorities flocked to Carter, but he lost the middle class and the rich.

The pundits would say that the nation had turned its back on Jimmy Carter—but really the numbers showed that it was the white middle class who gave up on this president.

Chapter 26
White House Twilight

I hope that history will show that I have never flinched in dealing with issues that some of my predecessors have postponed.
— PRESIDENT JIMMY CARTER

Hamilton Jordan, Rick Hertzberg, and Carter toasting the hostages
JIMMY CARTER PRESIDENTIAL LIBRARY AND MUSEUM

CARTER FINALLY RETIRED at 12:30 A.M. after telling the White
House operator to give him a wake-up call at 7:30 A.M.—not his
usual 5:30 A.M. An hour after waking, he was in the Oval Office, meeting
with Kirbo. The two old friends chatted for twenty-five minutes about
the election. It had been a very tough year, and by that morning it was
clear that the Democrats had lost thirty-four seats in the House and lost
control of the Senate for the first time since 1954. Carter faced what had
happened with quiet resignation. Later that morning, he invited into the
Oval Office members of the White House press corps and took questions for forty-five minutes. The session began on a light note when an
unnamed reporter asked jovially if it was true that Jody was driving him
in his aging blue Volkswagen next week to Iowa—as if the defeated president were intending to launch another relentless campaign. Everyone

laughed, and then Carter said, "I know you all have been through a hard time these last thirty-six or forty-eight hours campaigning. I slept late this morning and feel good."

Helen Thomas of United Press International then asked when he first knew he was going to lose. "Monday night," Carter replied. "Saturday evening, we thought that we were well ahead in the polls, two or three points. Pat's polls have always been unbelievably accurate. Monday night Pat sent word that we had dropped precipitously."

"How will history judge you?" asked another reporter.

"I don't know yet," Carter replied. He expressed regret that he wouldn't have a second term. But he then cited his Middle East peace efforts, the Panama Canal Treaty, normalization with China, and the fact that the country had not gone to war as evidence that, at least in the arena of international affairs, historians would give him high marks. "But I hope that history will show that I have never flinched in dealing with issues that some of my predecessors have postponed."

At one point, a reporter asked if he felt like a "great load has been lifted off your shoulders."

"Well," he replied with a grin, "I've still got the full load for the next two and a half months."

Already that morning he had met with Brzezinski, Secretary of State Muskie, and Deputy Secretary Warren Christopher about the latest news from Iran. The hostage crisis would continue to consume his hours. But Carter also had at least one more major piece of legislation he wanted to enact before leaving office, an issue close to the hearts of environmentalists.

BACK IN NOVEMBER 1979, Carter had written to the great landscape photographer Ansel Adams, "All of us consider the protection of Alaskan lands the top environmental issue of our time." Adams and other prominent conservationists had been sounding the alarm on preserving this last chunk of America's wilderness, arguing that Alaska's vast and largely untouched wilderness needed to be protected from unrestricted oil and gas exploration. In 1971, Congress had enacted legislation that protected 80 million acres, and an additional 45 million acres were quarantined until December 18, 1978—unless Congress acted to bar oil and gas development prior to that date. In anticipation of this looming deadline, legislation had been introduced in 1977 to make the moratorium permanent. But while popular with national environmentalists, the proposed conservation measures were vigorously opposed by Alaska's business interests. Both Alaska senators, one Democrat and one Republican, were blocking the Carter administration's conservation efforts. Without their support, Carter feared the moratorium would end in late December, opening much of the wilderness to commercial exploitation.

As the deadline approached, Carter's interior secretary, Cecil Andrus, sent him a memo in late November 1978, suggesting a radical solution. If Congress would not act, why not use the 1906 Antiquities Act, an obscure and little-used law that gave the president the unilateral power to designate buildings or lands as national monuments? Stu Eizenstat supported the gambit, and on December 1, 1978, Carter formally designated 56 million acres of Alaskan wilderness as a national monument.

The Alaskan political establishment was flabbergasted. A crowd in Fairbanks burned Carter in effigy, and some Alaskans defied the president's order by illegally entering the designated "monuments" to hunt and fish. Despite its unpopularity, Carter warned that his sequestration order would stand until Congress agreed to pass its own legislation to preserve the land. There the matter stood for the next two years.

Carter stubbornly held his ground. In late June 1980 he visited the state briefly on his way to a state funeral in Japan and got in a few hours of trout fishing. Demonstrators protested his presence. The Jaycees at the state fair staged an event, charging throngs of contestants a dollar to throw an empty Coke bottle at a photograph of either President Carter or Ayatollah Khomeini. More players chose to throw the bottle at Carter's image than the ayatollah's. The president was that unpopular. But Carter didn't care. He knew his use of the Antiquities Act had changed the political dynamics. Alaska's Republican senator, Ted Stevens, gradually entered into negotiations with the White House, conceding that some kind of compromise was better than the current impasse. Carter didn't oppose development of Alaska's oil and gas resources, but he would not accept a bill that jeopardized the Arctic National Wildlife Refuge—the calving grounds and migratory route for one of the world's last great caribou herds. He was also determined to preserve the wilderness areas in Misty Fjords and Admiralty Island.

Carter studied the problem with his typical attention to detail. He loved inspecting maps. And for obvious reasons, by the end of his presidency he was thoroughly familiar with the maps of Israel, Palestine, the Sinai desert, and the environs of the captured American embassy in Tehran. But he had also become an expert on Alaska's geography.

At one point in their wrangling over the Alaska land act, Senator Stevens met with President Carter in the Oval Office. Stevens mentioned one obscure area that he believed should be excluded from the proposed wilderness refuge. "Well, let's check that," the president responded. Carter then retrieved a huge map and rolled it out on the floor of the Oval Office. Stevens was astonished to see the president down on his hands and knees, inspecting the area in question. "No, I don't think you are right," Carter observed. "You see, this little watershed here doesn't actually go into that one. It comes over here." The senator had to concede the point, and on the car ride back to Capitol Hill he turned to his aide and remarked, "He knows more about Alaska than I do!"

Carter was still negotiating with Senator Stevens and other legislators after the November 1980 election. "Everybody told us we were crazy," Frank Moore recalled. But Carter prevailed, and on December 2, 1980, this lame-duck president signed the Alaska National Interest Lands Conservation Act, creating more than 157 million acres of protected wilderness areas and national parks. The complicated piece of legislation he signed that day was nearly six inches thick. But he proudly noted that it set aside "for conservation an area of land larger than the state of California." The bill nearly doubled the size of the nation's Wild and Scenic Rivers System and tripled the size of its Wilderness Preservation System. But in a nod to the energy industry, it also permitted oil and gas exploration in 100 percent of Alaska's offshore areas and 95 percent of the state's other lands. It was a grand compromise, but one that Carter ardently believed would give generations of Americans the opportunity to see much of Alaska's "splendid beauty undiminished and its majesty untarnished." He would leave office believing that this piece of legislation—preserving the "crown jewels" of the Alaskan wilderness—marked one of his truly lasting achievements as president.

CARTER WAS A man who always had to be doing something—building something, reading something, or catching a fish. He and Rosalynn spent much of the first week after the election up at Camp David. One day he spent hours in the carpentry shop making four very complicated little fly-line drying reels, keeping one for himself and giving the others away to his fishing friends. On the morning of November 8, he fished and went hunting, shooting some quail and pheasants. He relished these little pleasures. But that afternoon he also made some working phone calls, discussing with Warren Christopher the wording of the White House's formal response to Iran's latest position on the hostage situation. Christopher was bound for Algiers, where the Algerian government had agreed to host conclusive negotiations.

With the election over, it was quite evident that the Iranians were now ready to release the hostages. Indeed, the Algerian government agreed to serve as the intermediary between the United States and Iran only because the broad outlines of a deal were clearly on the table. The Iranian *majlis*'s conditions for the release of the hostages were fairly straightforward.

In response, President Carter was ready to sign a formal declaration pledging not to interfere in the internal affairs of Iran. He was also prepared to convey a signed presidential order unblocking all Iranian financial assets frozen in U.S. banks, including $2.5 billion in Iranian assets held by the Federal Reserve Bank of New York and approximately $3 billion of Iranian assets on deposit with U.S. banks abroad. Both Iran and the United States would agree to set up a claims-settlement procedure that would quickly arbitrate all further claims by private American companies. The U.S. government would also pledge to refrain from pursuing any other legal claims stemming from the seizure of the U.S. embassy in Tehran. In other words, the hostages would not be able to sue the Iranian government. Carter was prepared to respond to the Iranian insistence that the United States return any assets of the late shah by issuing a presidential order prohibiting any of the late shah's assets to be transferred out of the United States. The Americans were not going to confiscate the late monarch's assets in the United States—but Carter was willing to make an effort to compile information from government sources that would help to identify any such properties owned by the shah in the United States. Finally, the Carter administration would publicly release all these presidential orders only after the Algerian government was able to confirm that all fifty-two American hostages had safely departed Iran.

Carter was enormously impatient and frustrated, if only because he felt that such a deal could have happened months earlier, and certainly prior to the election. But the Iranians were not done haggling. Carter's response was conveyed by the Algerians to the Iranians on November 12 in Algiers. The Iranians were not satisfied. They wanted further details on the location and size of frozen Iranian assets—and they still wanted a return of the shah's assets. Brzezinski characterized the Iranian message as "insulting" and urged Carter to reject it outright. Brzezinski even suggested that the White House should signal that it was willing to send military aid to Iran's mortal enemy, Saddam Hussein's Iraq, if the Iranians were not more forthcoming. Carter disagreed and instructed Christopher "to prepare a positive response to the Iranians that they could use for propaganda purposes—and have an addendum of the caveats through which we could deal with our legitimate claims against Iran."

Carter understood that the internal power struggle raging within the revolutionary regime required him to react on a psychological level to Iranian demands. Sometime after the November election, Hamilton Jordan handed him an "eyes only" memo with an extraordinary suggestion. "My greatest fear," Jordan explained, "is that once we have gone as far as we can substantively on the Iranian demands, the hardliners will find a good reason to continue to thwart the efforts of the moderates to free the hostages." Jordan thought the president would then have to orchestrate some kind of "face-saving gesture for the hardliners" to get them to relent. They would need to "be creative in a public relations sense" if they had any hope of seeing the release of the hostages "before you leave office."

Jordan had a novel idea. "This may sound crazy," but he volunteered himself as a high-value hostage. He would go to Iran or Algiers and take the place of the fifty-two hostages "if that would break the current logjam." He thought this was the kind of "illogical and creative approach we are going to have to take to the situation." Jordan said he was "completely serious. . . . I am young and in good health and have no dependents." He said it would be "a great honor to render such a service to my country." No written record exists of Carter's response, but he must have been touched by Jordan's offer. Needless to say, Jordan did not fly off to Tehran.

Throughout November and December, the Iranians dragged out the talks in Algiers. "We still don't have any sure word as to who is in charge of the hostages," Carter complained in late November. "They're all liars, so there's no way to tell what the facts might be." Not surprisingly, most of the haggling had to do with money. Unfreezing the frozen Iranian assets turned out to be a highly complicated and contentious affair involving not only the governments of Iran and the United States but also dozens of private bankers. Over time, it had become clear that the fate of the hostages was intimately tied up with the demands of the American and European bankers to be repaid with interest on their Iranian loans. One lawyer involved in the negotiations later said, "It was obvious that there would be no hostage release without a financial settlement." John J. McCloy and David Rockefeller—who had played such a key role in instigating the hostage crisis by lobbying the president to provide the shah with American asylum—now were deeply involved in the Algiers negotiations, in effect prolonging the hostage ordeal in order to protect Chase Bank's financial interests. One of McCloy's senior Milbank, Tweed partners, Francis D. Logan, who sat on the law firm's ten-member governing Firm Committee, was one of a handful of American lawyers who made secret trips to London and Algiers to negotiate the deal.

Carter was painfully aware of the bankers' obstructive role. At one point, he told White House counsel Lloyd Cutler "to push the American banks hard, that I did not want them to hold up the hostage release because they were squabbling over who was going to get the money that Iran agreed to forgo."

The issue came down to whether the banks were willing to pay Iran a reasonable market interest rate on the frozen funds they had kept locked up for fourteen months. Some of the European banks were holding out to pay the lowest possible interest rates. "The Bank of America and one small one," Carter noted in his diary, "are trying to cheat the Iranians." In the end, the bankers would walk away with a very generous settlement; the Iranians paid the private banks $3.7 billion. Indeed, when the American bankers learned the final terms of the deal, they "nearly fell off their chairs." Wall Street's lawyers—and none more so than the legal team at Milbank, Tweed—earned millions of dollars in legal fees. The hostage crisis, in the words of one reporter, was nothing less than a "bonanza for the bar." Chase Bank's chairman, David Rockefeller, privately acknowledged that it "worked out very well, far better than we had feared."

* * *

IRONICALLY, ONE OF the intermediaries who kept popping up during these frustrating negotiations was none other than Cyrus Hashemi, the Iranian businessman. Hashemi was intimately involved in the negotiations with the Iranians over the final details for the unfreezing of Iranian assets and the release of the hostages. Hashemi was in frequent contact with Harold Saunders at the State Department. And his personal lawyer, Stan Pottinger—the well-connected former Justice Department official—was also used as a conduit to the administration. "Pottinger has briefed us on the most recent exchanges Cyrus Hashemi has had with Tehran," Saunders reported on November 19. "Hashemi believes progress has been made." But a full month later, on December 19, the Iranians conveyed through the Algerians their "final response," demanding that the United States deposit $25 billion in an escrow account to cover all their claims. Carter thought this "obviously ridiculous and unacceptable." Once again, the negotiations seemed stuck at a complete impasse.

Around this time, Gary Sick, Brzezinski's adviser on Iran, ran into Richard V. Allen, Reagan's designated national security adviser. Allen had temporarily moved into a suite in the Old Executive Office Building, next door to the White House. Seeing Sick in the hallway, Allen had one question: "Will the hostages be released before the inauguration?" Sick hesitated and then answered somewhat tentatively, "Yes."

Carter's people had seen relatively little of the Reagan transition team. And what little they saw left them unimpressed. Inexplicably, Reagan's transition team refused to be briefed on the hostage negotiations. Carter himself met with Reagan alone in the Oval Office on November 20. They had a polite conversation, Reagan making only a few stiff remarks, all of which, Carter thought, were pabulum from his basic stump speech. Carter did most of the talking, touching on everything from the aid to Afghanistan's rebels to the impending passage of a Superfund bill to handle the storage of toxic waste. He advised Reagan to set aside at least a day or two to be briefed on the president's procedures for deploying nuclear weapons. Reagan just listened without asking any questions.

At one point, Carter noticed that Reagan was not taking any notes, and since he was covering a great many complicated issues, he wondered how the president-elect could possibly absorb all this information. He asked him if he needed a pad of paper to take notes, but Reagan politely declined. But when Carter mentioned the current political crisis in South Korea, where the military junta was threatening to execute the dissident leader, Kim Dae Jung, Reagan volunteered that he was "very envious" of the way the South Korean regime was able to handle protesters—by closing universities and drafting demonstrators into the army. Reagan said he wished he had such authority. Stunned by this insensitive remark, Carter was silently appalled. On his way out of the Oval Office, Reagan paused and asked if he could have a copy of the notes Carter had used to brief him. Carter quickly obliged.

He thought Reagan "affable" and "a decent man"—though "remarkably old" in his attitudes. "His life seems to be governed by a few anecdotes and vignettes that he has memorized," Carter noted for his diary. "He doesn't seem to listen when anybody talks to him." As to Reagan's team of advisers, Carter thought of them as "the group of jerks that are coming in to replace us." Feelings were raw on all sides. Washington society still had no sympathy for the departing Georgians. One evening in December 1980, the president's aide Landon Butler attended a dinner party at the Georgetown home of Polly and Clayton Fritchey, good friends of Katharine Graham's. "Polly was complaining about the Carter presidency," Butler recalled, "and I responded by listing all his accomplishments—despite the Nov defeat. Polly looked at me coolly and said, 'Yes, but they were so tacky.'"

THE CARTERS SPENT Christmas Day 1980 at their modest ranch home in Plains. That morning, they exchanged gifts. Carter gave Rosalynn a small television set, since they no longer had a working set in Plains. Rosalynn gave him a book on woodworking, a hobby he planned to focus on in retirement. Later that day, they visited Miss Lillian at the nearby Pond House and saw Rosalynn's mother, Allie, for Christmas lunch. They also spent time with Carter's sister Gloria and brother Billy. "I enjoyed being with them," Carter noted. Just before Christmas, Kirbo had sat down with Carter and conveyed to him some bad news about the Carter Peanut Warehouse. While it had been in a blind trust for four years, Kirbo said, the warehouse had accumulated about $1 million in debt. To make matters worse, the Carter farmlands had sustained three annual crop failures in a row. Unless a buyer was found for the warehouse business, the Carters were facing bankruptcy.

With this grim news on his mind, Carter flew with Rosalynn back to Camp David on December 26, and they tried to distract themselves with the pleasures of the mountain retreat. The next afternoon, Carter was cross-country skiing on one of Camp David's nature trails when his right ski hit a rock. He fell and broke his left collarbone. In considerable pain, the president was helicoptered to the Bethesda Naval Hospital, where doctors placed him in a restraining strap and prescribed a little codeine. An hour later, he was back at Camp David, and he spent the last days of 1980 sleeping and reading.

On December 31, he and Rosalynn helicoptered back to the White House, and that evening they attended a New Year's Eve party at the home of Jody and Nan Powell "to see the end of 1980," Carter noted in his diary, "with no regrets." At midnight, Carter placed a phone call to his old friend Willie Nelson—but, not surprisingly, Willie was unavailable, and instead he spoke briefly to Willie's manager. Carter and Rosalynn finally got back to the White House at 12:40 A.M. His broken collarbone was still giving him considerable pain. All in all, it had been a truly very bad year.

THE NEXT MORNING, the Carters flew to New Orleans to attend the Sugar Bowl. For the first time, the University of Georgia team won a national championship, beating Notre Dame 17–10. In the crowds of people, Carter tried to protect his shoulder from being jostled, but Georgia's Heisman Trophy–winning running back, Herschel Walker, shook hands so hard that the president later felt sore all over again. Back in the White House, Carter collapsed in his bed by 10:45 P.M.

But the next morning at 7:35, Carter chaired a foreign policy breakfast for an hour and a half, discussing the Iran situation. Present were Mondale, Brzezinski, Warren Christopher, Lloyd Cutler, and Deputy Secretary of Defense Graham Claytor. Carter was tired and extremely frustrated. He told everyone that they needed to prepare for a breakdown in the negotiations. He thought Ayatollah Khomeini might even put the hostages on trial. In that event, Carter was prepared to ask Congress for a declaration of war. He thought they might then need to impose a naval blockade or perhaps mine the Iranian harbors. Carter was venting. While the Iranians seemed to be in no hurry, Carter noted just four days later that the new Iranian response was "very close to an acceptance." And by January 10, Christopher was reporting from Algiers that all the signals from Tehran seemed positive. In fact, Carter complained that only "a few greedy bankers" were complicating the final stage of negotiations. By January 17, Algerian commercial aircraft were standing by in Algiers, ready to fly into Tehran to pick up the hostages.

In the midst of the Iranian saga, Israel's ambassador, Ephraim "Eppie" Evron, came to say goodbye. Carter was pleased that Evron was "almost emotional" in his effusive praise for what the president had done for Israel over the previous four years. But afterward Carter noted in his diary, "I don't see how they can continue as an occupying power depriving the Palestinians of basic human rights, and I don't see how they can absorb three million more Arabs into Israel without letting the Jews become a minority in their own country. Begin showed courage in giving up the Sinai. He did it to keep the West Bank." The latter was a bitter fact, almost an admission that Begin had played him during the Camp David talks. And yet the president was right, even prophetic, to pose the existential question. By hanging on to the West Bank, the Israeli prime minister had planted the seeds for a prolonged occupation and a seemingly endless conflict.

ON JANUARY 14, 1981, Carter gave a nationally televised farewell address. The speech was drafted by Rick Hertzberg, and it voiced all of Carter's most liberal instincts. It focused on three issues: "the threat of nuclear destruction, our stewardship of the physical resources of our planet, and the pre-eminence of the basic rights of human beings." He spoke with a strange, unprompted passion about what had happened thirty-five years earlier to Hiroshima—and warned Americans that the "risk of a nuclear conflagration . . . is becoming greater." The survivors of a nuclear war, he warned, "would live in despair amid the poisoned ruins of a civilization that had committed suicide." As if this apocalyptic vision were not fearsome enough, he shifted to warning about the "growing dangers to our simple and most precious possessions: the air we breathe, the water we drink, and the land which sustains us." Finally, he spoke of the "battle for human rights," which at home included "adequate medical care for all Americans," a job for "all those able to work," and an end to racial discrimination. The speech was pure fire and brimstone, a sermon from a Carter unleashed. When

Rosalynn read a draft, she exclaimed, "Why, Jimmy! These are the reasons you lost." He didn't care. A few days later he wrote to Hertzberg, "Not bad for a tenth draft."

CARTER WAS DETERMINED in his last hours as president to exert "every ounce of my strength" to liberating the hostages. He, Rosalynn, and Amy spent their last day at Camp David on Saturday, January 17, as he waited to sign the final set of documents for the hostage-release deal. He talked on the phone with Warren Christopher in Algiers, who told him that it had been tough, but he thought they'd have an agreement the next day. And indeed, by noon on Sunday, January 18, Carter had signed the necessary documents. After packing up their belongings, Jimmy and Rosalynn took one last walk around Camp David, pausing to snap a few photographs of the rustic camp where they had spent so many enjoyable hours away from Washington. And then they flew back to the White House, where Carter holed himself up in the Oval Office for most of the next forty-eight hours.

He had invited the Powells, the Rafshoons, the Mondales, and the Kirbos to be his guests in the White House. But aside from a few scattered minutes lying down on the couch, Carter did not sleep. He was obsessed with every bit of news he could gather on the hostage deal. Shortly after midnight, in the early-morning hours of Monday, January 19, he was informed that two planes had left Ankara, Turkey, bound for Tehran to pick up the hostages. At 2:00 A.M. he heard that the Iranians had finally signed all the necessary documents. At 5:30 A.M. he stretched out on the couch for a few minutes but then suddenly awoke with an uneasy feeling. Worried, he called Deputy Treasury Secretary Robert Carswell and was alarmed to learn that Iran's Bank Markazi had failed to transmit the technical instructions for transferring the $12 billion in frozen assets into their accounts. Worse, it emerged that the Bank Markazi officials objected to some of the details and were now refusing to issue the necessary orders. In response, Carter told Christopher to remind the Algerians that his presidential authority expired in less than twenty-four hours. Turning to Hamilton Jordan, Carter exclaimed, "They're going to screw around and have to renegotiate this thing with Reagan."

No one was sure if the Iranians were delaying over substance or trivia—or whether they just had a schedule timed to Reagan's inauguration. Part of the problem may have just been the cumbersome work of having to translate each telex message back and forth among three languages—English, French, and Farsi. It was not until 2:23 A.M. on Tuesday, January 20, that Treasury Secretary Bill Miller called Carter to say, "It looks good!" But a half hour later, he called to say that the text was garbled with typos and errors. Another delay occurred at 3:40 A.M. when Carswell reported that the U.S. federal attorneys in Algiers were refusing to sign the agreement. One of the attorneys became so agitated that he fainted. Impatiently, Carter ordered the attorneys: "Have them sign the agreement." Not until 6:35 A.M. did Christopher call to say that the last tranche of $7.977 billion had been transferred into an escrow account for the Iranians at the Bank of England.

Told that the hostages had boarded two planes and were sitting on a runway, awaiting permission to take off, Carter asked Phil Wise to place a call to Governor Reagan, who was staying across the street in Blair House. Carter wanted to give him the good news—but a few minutes later, Wise returned to say that the call had been intercepted by Reagan's aides, who reported that the president-elect was sleeping and "was not to be disturbed."

"You're kidding," Carter said incredulously.

"No, sir, I'm not."

In the midst of all this drama, Rosalynn came into the Oval Office at 7:35 A.M. and reminded Jimmy that he had forgotten to shave. She handed him a razor and told him he also needed a haircut. The White House barber was summoned, and Carter had his haircut while he talked on the phone.

At 8:28 A.M. Carter was told that the planes with the hostages were "now at the end of the runway." And there they sat for the next three and a half hours.

And so Carter anxiously waited for any news. Finally, at 10:45 A.M., Rosalynn called the Oval Office and said, "Jimmy, the Reagans will be here in fifteen minutes. You have to put on your morning clothes and greet them."

Carter, of course, did not own any formal wear, but he left for the residence upstairs, muttering, "Well, I better go put on my monkey suit."

When he got upstairs, "I looked in the mirror, as I put on the rented clothes, and wondered if I had aged so much as president or whether I was just exhausted."

Four years earlier, his first visitor in the Oval Office had been Max Cleland, a Vietnam veteran and triple amputee. Now his last visitor would also be Cleland. The administrator of Veterans Affairs rolled his wheelchair into the Oval Office, bearing a gift for the departing president. Cleland presented Carter with a plaque engraved with a Thomas Jefferson quote:

> *I have the consolation to reflect*
> *That during the period of my*
> *Administration not a drop*
> *Of the blood of a single citizen*
> *Was shed by the sword of war.*

Carter would always cherish this gesture from a grievously wounded war veteran. But then he had to turn and walk out of the Oval Office for the last time to greet President-elect Reagan at the front portico of the White House. As they drove together up Pennsylvania Avenue to the inaugural platform beneath the Capitol, Reagan "seemed somewhat disconcerted that no one was in the reviewing stands." He also remarked critically on the number of banners displayed in support of the Equal Rights Amendment. Reagan's concerns seemed shallow and even petty. But Carter kept his thoughts to himself.

BACK IN THE White House, Hamilton Jordan was hunkered downstairs in the Situation Room, waiting for any news. Jordan was hoping to learn that the hostage planes had taken off from Tehran prior to Reagan's inauguration. Standing on the inaugural platform, Carter had asked the Secret Service to keep him informed on the status of the hostages. Jordan had two phone lines open in the Situation Room, one to Warren Christopher, who was sitting in the CIA station in Algiers, and the other to Phil Wise, who was standing near Carter. Jordan waited as long as possible. He was still there when Reagan took the oath of office at noon. Finally, at 12:25 P.M.—after Reagan had been sworn in as president— Jordan's secretary, Eleanor Connor, yelled at him that Reagan's aides were pouring through the South Gate. Jordan and Connor were hastily escorted off the premises by a Marine guard. As they were hustled out of the Situation Room, Jordan was stunned to see that the pictures of Carter on the walls had already been replaced with photos of Reagan— on horseback! "Reagan really did get elected, didn't he?" Jordan remarked to Rafshoon, who was also on his way out the door.

Around the same time, the Secret Service watched silently as a disheveled Jody Powell pushed his aging blue Volkswagen off the White House grounds and into the street. The fifteen-year-old engine had refused to start. It was a metaphor. The Georgia boys were done. But contrary to the conventional wisdom offered by the Washington punditocracy, they left behind a consequential presidential legacy. Jimmy Carter had changed the country.

Part 3

THE POST-PRESIDENCY

Carter made the wooden cross at the Maranatha
Baptist Church in Plains, Georgia.

Chapter 27
Keeping Faith

I'd like for the last guinea worm to die before I do.

—EX-PRESIDENT JIMMY CARTER

Rosalynn and Jimmy Carter working for Habitat for Humanity
NEWSDAY/GETTY IMAGES

Ex-president Jimmy Carter was still standing on the inaugural platform when a Secret Service agent informed him that an Algerian jetliner carrying all fifty-two hostages had taken off from Tehran, bound for Algiers. Carter was ecstatic. He called it "one of the happiest moments of my life." He and Rosalynn were then driven with Fritz and Joan Mondale to Andrews Air Force Base, where they boarded what had been Air Force One for a flight home to Georgia. As they climbed the stairs to the plane and turned to wave to the crowd, Rosalynn and thirteen-year-old Amy were seen sobbing, tears running down their faces. Their "involuntary" departure from the White House was emotionally wrenching. Seeing that Amy was upset at having to leave two girlfriends who had come to say goodbye, Carter invited them to join them. "Come on, everybody," he said. "This is a time to be happy. Get on board." The plane was full, so the children and their mothers crowded into the presidential suite for takeoff. During the flight down to Georgia, Phil Wise, Carter's longtime personal aide, walked through the press section of the plane playfully yelling, "We're free, we're free, thank God Almighty, we're free at last."

Carter knew he had one more duty to perform. The newly inaugurated president had offered him the use of an Air Force plane to fly to Germany the next day to greet the newly freed hostages. Carter was eager to make the trip.

Back in Plains late that afternoon, the Carters were greeted by a crowd of three thousand Georgians lining Main Street in a steady winter drizzle. Carter's voice quavered with emotion as he thanked the crowd and spoke about the hostages. "It is impossible for me to realize—or any of us—how they feel on that plane because they recognize that they are hostages no more, that they are prisoners no more, and they are coming back to the land we all love." When he was finished speaking, he asked for a moment of silence to honor the eight men who had died in the failed rescue mission—and then, according to the historian Douglas Brinkley, "a country-western band launched into a dirge-like version of 'Dixie,' a song suppressed during Carter's campaign and presidency because of its identification with the Confederacy." The Carters delighted everyone by dancing a slow polka to the tune of "Dixie."

The crowd lingered over a potluck supper of casserole while the Carters eventually walked the several blocks to their home at 209 Woodland Drive. That evening, their eldest son Jack, Jody Powell, Ham Jordan, and Frank Moore, on behalf of all the White House staff, presented the former president with a homecoming gift: a fine collection of carpentry tools bought from Sears, Roebuck for his woodworking shop in the garage. Carter was touched. It was exactly what he wanted—encouragement to divert himself with some creative manual labor.

That night, in anticipation of the flight to Germany the next day, he didn't get much sleep. By 5:30 A.M. he was climbing aboard a helicopter for the ride to Robins Air Force Base in Georgia, where he boarded a plane bound for Rhein-Main Air Base in Frankfurt. On the flight over, Carter nervously prepared for his meeting with the former hostages, studying photographs of each one and taking notes on their individual backgrounds. He knew it would be an emotional moment for him and all of the hostages. He had to be prepared for some tough questions, and perhaps even some anger.

Upon landing in Germany at nine o'clock in the morning, he was hastily briefed by a doctor who had already seen the hostages. Carter was warned that the hostages were traumatized by their rough treatment during 444 days of captivity: "I was going to be facing some hostility among the hostages." A few minutes later, he entered, with "some degree of trepidation," a small dining room. He saw the hostages standing stiffly in front of their chairs. It was an awkward moment. But the ex-president walked over to the nearest former hostage and they spontaneously embraced. Carter then greeted each former hostage, trying to say something personal about their family or service. "Some of them kissed me on the cheek," he noted. "I was relieved and pleased." After a few minutes, Carter gave an off-the-cuff speech, saying how proud all Americans were of their heroism. He talked for some fifty minutes, offering a candid and detailed account of his diplomatic efforts to obtain their release. He bluntly explained that his concern for their lives was the same concern that the embassy marines had felt at the start of the siege: "We could very well have killed a lot of Iranians, but it would have resulted in deaths among the Americans."

When he asked for questions, the first query concerned the failed rescue mission. Carter explained what had happened, and how eight men had died in the Iranian desert. The second question, predictably, focused on why the shah had been allowed into America, precipitating the assault on the U.S. embassy. Carter did his best to explain—and he was not further challenged. All in all, he thought the encounter had been a friendly one. Photographs were taken, with Carter posing with most of the former hostages—and then he made his farewells and departed for the Frankfurt airport. On the flight back, Lloyd Cutler opened a fine bottle of champagne and Carter toasted to the freedom of the hostages. They arrived back in Plains just before sunrise on January 22— not even twenty-four hours after they had left Georgia.

THE NEXT DAY, Carter and his son Chip got to work installing wooden plank flooring in the attic of the Plains house on Woodland Drive. The

Carters were intent on living in the twenty-year-old house, but space had to be made in the attic for the storage of papers and clothes from the White House. Their simple ranch house, bounded by eleven acres of oak and hickory trees, had four small bedrooms. Rosalynn used one bedroom as her office and turned another into a dressing room. Amy occupied one bedroom—though she later went off to boarding school in Atlanta. Because the ex-presidential couple always traveled in a car driven by the Secret Service, they had no need for a personal car; so they remodeled the garage into a woodworking shop for Jimmy. Eventually, a small guest apartment was built atop the garage. Life in Plains would be most ordinary.

It was a radical readjustment, even for a couple who had called Plains their home for most of their lives. For one thing, they knew they stood on the edge of bankruptcy. "What so many people don't know is how distressed financially we were," Carter later explained to *The Washington Post*'s Paul Hendrickson. "We didn't know what we'd do. First, we'd lost the election, and that was a shock. Then the trustee [Charlie Kirbo] of our estate came and told us he had some more bad news for us."

Kirbo soon fixed things for his good friend, arranging the sale of the peanut warehouse business for $1.5 million to the Illinois agribusiness corporation Archer-Daniels-Midland (ADM). They closed on the ADM deal on March 6, 1981, allowing Carter to pay off "all our debts—a great relief to me." He and Rosalynn were able to hold on to two thousand acres of farmland producing peanuts, cotton, corn, and soybeans—but their most reliable source of income came from eighteen hundred acres of pine timber. "No one could accuse me of becoming rich in the White House," he remarked.

By then, Carter had already decided that his new vocation was to be an author. On the same day he sold the peanut warehouse, Bantam offered him a $900,000 book advance, half to be paid on delivery of the written presidential memoir. "*Keeping Faith* was written to redeem our family finances," Carter said. He churned out two to three thousand words each day on a state-of-the-art computer word processor that cost him a hefty $10,000. "It's expensive," the frugal Carter complained, but "maybe worth the money."

Emory University in Atlanta eventually paid him to teach on a regular basis, also supplementing his $69,630 federal pension as an ex-president. *Keeping Faith* was published in November 1982 and sold well enough to earn Carter another book contract. Two years later, Rosalynn published *First Lady from Plains,* a candid autobiography that spent eighteen weeks on the *New York Times* bestseller list. The Carters were once again financially secure.

By the early spring of 1981, Carter had settled into a routine, waking as usual an hour before sunrise, working on his memoir for several hours, and then having breakfast with Rosalynn and Amy. After seeing Amy off to school, he would spend a few more morning hours on his word processor. In the afternoons, he often spent time in his wood shop, building furniture, or out inspecting his farmlands. He still enjoyed a daily jog, though in Plains he rarely ran more than two or three miles. He had run many more miles when he was living in the White House. "I guess I was almost a fanatic with running," he told a reporter. Was it to handle the stress? "Yes," he replied. "I suppose that was part of it."

In the 1990s, he returned to a hobby he had first dabbled in during his navy years—oil painting. "I realized many years ago that I do not have any special talent as an artist or craftsman," he confessed. "But with a lot of study and practice I have become fairly proficient." He sold some of his paintings at Carter Center auctions for $50,000 and on occasion as much as $1 million. In 2018, he published a small coffee-table book that reproduced more than fifty of his favorite oil-on-canvas paintings, many of them scenes from his life in Plains.

CARTER HAD TO be working, whether it was on his word processor or in the wood shop, where he handcrafted fine wooden furniture, including rocking chairs, tables, and bed frames. He also had to think about raising money for his presidential library and museum. The federally funded National Archives and Records Administration would finance the archival operations of any such presidential library, but the building of the library and museum had to be privately funded. And the more he thought about it, the more he disliked the whole notion of a traditional presidential museum. "I don't want a monument to me," he insisted to Rosalynn. One night in January 1982, Rosalynn woke up in the middle of the night and was startled to see Jimmy sitting up in bed, wide awake. This was most unusual. When she asked him if he was sick, he replied, "I know what we can do at the library. We can develop a place to help people who want to resolve disputes." He was thinking of Camp David and his mediations with Sadat and Begin. Conflict resolution would become his mission. The idea excited and motivated him. Raising money for a museum glorifying his presidency sounded distasteful and decidedly selfish to this ex-president. Fundraising for a conflict-resolution center that would allow him to use his prestige to broker an end to civil wars and monitor free elections around the world sounded like a less selfish endeavor. "There is life after the White House!" wrote Rosalynn.

Over the next ten years the Carters raised $150 million to finance the start-up of a presidential library and museum and the Carter Center, all to be built on a stretch of parkland adjacent to downtown Atlanta. Early donors included Edgar Bronfman, Anne Cox Chambers, Averell Harriman, Ted Turner, and Ryoichi Sasakawa, a right-wing, billionaire Japanese philanthropist who had made his fortune after World War II in gambling concessions. More controversially, Carter also accepted millions of dollars from another billionaire, Agha Hasan Abedi, the Pakistani chairman of the Bank of Credit and Commerce International (BCCI), who in 1991 would become embroiled in a global banking scandal. "I never felt deceived or betrayed," Carter told ABC News. "But I have obviously been shocked and disturbed at what has been revealed." He admitted to the historian Douglas Brinkley that Abedi "may have snookered me."

Over the years, Carter formed other, more long-lasting partnerships. By 1990, the Carter Center had an annual budget of $17.5 million and a staff of 110 working on human rights projects, preventive healthcare, election monitoring, and conflict resolution in the Middle East, Latin America, and Africa. Thirty years later, the center's annual cash budget had grown to $100 million, much of it coming from the Gates Foundation, the MacArthur Foundation, and the Ford Foundation.

The Carters continued to live in their simple ranch house in Plains, but they spent three or four days a month in Atlanta, sleeping in a studio apartment at the Carter Center that was equipped with a fold-down Murphy bed. Carter and Rosalynn personally wrote letters to various heads of state, urging them to release numerous individuals they considered to be prisoners of conscience. The Carter Center took on long-term, challenging projects like attempting to wipe out Guinea worm disease and river blindness in Africa and the Amazon. "We don't go into areas where others can or are doing the work," Carter explained. "We fill vacuums." And he wasn't afraid of controversy. Over the years, he traveled with Carter Center teams to monitor more than 110 elections in particularly dicey political arenas like Haiti, Nepal, Nicaragua, the West Bank, Gaza, and Panama. When in 1989 he famously caught General Manuel Noriega's election officials stuffing ballot boxes in Panama, Carter stunned everyone by jumping up on the platform in an election hall and yelling in Spanish, "Are you honest people, or are you thieves?" In 1990, he was responsible for persuading Nicaragua's Sandinista strongman Daniel Ortega to accept his surprising defeat at the polls that year. "I can tell you from my own experience," he told Ortega, "that losing is not the end of the world." Hearing this, Rosalynn piped up, "I thought it was the end of the world!" Ortega laughed, but in the end he agreed to recognize the ballot-box results.

THERE WERE MANY such adventures, some triumphs and some failures. Carter was indefatigable. "He's a pure Calvinist," observed Andy Young, "the kind of man who's got to wake up every morning with a full schedule. . . . He makes me feel guilty for serving on corporate boards because he's shunned all that." Carter became close friends with Ted Turner, the wealthy founder of CNN, the pioneering all-news cable network headquartered in Atlanta. They shared a love for baseball and fly-fishing. Turner thought his new friend was "extremely competent, a fabulous fly-fisherman, a crack shot [who] possessed an uncanny intelligence." Americans got used to seeing this ex-president, dressed in blue jeans with a carpenter's belt, hammering nails into two-by-fours for a house under construction by a team of volunteers for Habitat for Humanity. He and Rosalynn turned this Habitat gig into a weeklong ritual every year.*

Carter traveled frequently all over the world. On October 6, 1981, he was shocked and saddened to learn of the assassination of his friend Anwar Sadat. The Egyptian president had been killed by machine-gun fire while sitting in a reviewing stand in Cairo. The assassins, members

---

* In July 1994, the Carters learned that the Albany, Georgia, home of his childhood nanny, Annie Mae Hollis, then seventy-seven years old, had been washed away in a flood. Annie Mae had nearly drowned. Carter and other Habitat volunteers built her a small new house on the same lot.

of the Egyptian Islamic Jihad, hated Sadat for what he had done at Camp David. Both Carters flew on Air Force One to Cairo for the state funeral, accompanied by Gerald Ford, Henry Kissinger, and Richard Nixon. Initially, it was an awkward reunion for the three ex-presidents, but by the end of the journey Carter and Ford formed an enduring and warm friendship. Somewhat later, Ford asked Carter if he could promise to deliver a eulogy at his funeral. Carter did so on January 2, 2007, telling the mourners that he and Ford were both amused by a *New Yorker* cartoon in which a young boy looks up at his father and says, "Daddy, when I grow up I want to be a former president."

In Egypt again some years later, he made a point of visiting Sadat's widow, Jehan, who, after an elaborate Egyptian dinner one evening, turned to Carter and explained that she had recently found a note written by Sadat shortly before his October 1981 assassination. Awkwardly clearing her throat, Jehan pulled out the note and read: "Jimmy Carter is my very best friend on earth. He is the most honorable man I know. Brilliant and deeply religious, he has all the marvelous attributes that made him inept in dealing with the scoundrels who run the world." Stunned for a moment, Carter then smiled and replied, "Well, maybe, but I'll never change."

Some people had forgotten that this soft-spoken politician could be tough and relentless. Carter was incensed when in October 1981 *The Washington Post's* gossip columnist, Diana McClellan, ran an item in her Ear column alleging that Carter had "bugged" Blair House, where the Reagans had stayed during the transition. McClellan reported that "at least one tattler in the Carter tribe has described listening to the tape itself."

Upon reading the gossip item, Carter angrily phoned his lawyer and old friend Terrence Adamson, who had worked under Attorney General Griffin Bell in the Justice Department. Carter said he wanted a public apology from the *Post* editors. If not, he was going to sue them for libel. Adamson duly wrote the *Post's* publisher, Katharine Graham, but the newspaper declined to offer any such apology. The *Post's* editor, Benjamin Bradlee, asked one reporter, "How do you make a public apology? Run up and down Pennsylvania Avenue bare-bottomed, shouting, 'I'm sorry'?" Upon seeing this statement in the press, Adamson quickly went on CNN and needled Bradlee: "I would like to present that proposal to my client." Bradlee's flippant remark further angered Carter.

Things got worse when Bradlee published a curiously backhanded editorial in which the *Post* acknowledged that it was "utterly impossible to believe" McClellan's rumor—but the paper did not apologize for publishing the "accurately sourced" item. The editorial argued that it may have been an unfounded rumor, but the fact that the "story was circulating" about town was legitimate news. Carter remained incredulous. "The editorial simply acknowledged that the story was false, that they knew it was false when they published it, but that they felt they had a right to publish reports they know to be untrue." Jody Powell piled on, telling a reporter from *The New York Times* that the *Post*'s editorial "may be more embarrassing and revealing than the sight of Mr. Bradlee running naked down Pennsylvania Avenue."

Carter pressed his case in the court of public opinion and clearly delighted in making the *Post* and Ben Bradlee squirm. It was, after all, *The Washington Post*—and often Bradlee's wife, Sally Quinn—whose breezy lampooning of Bert Lance, Hamilton Jordan, and the other Georgia boys had contributed so much to the public perception of the Carter administration as weak and ineffectual. This Georgian ex-president was not going to let Bradlee off the hook.

Bradlee found himself forced to fact-check McClellan's Ear story, and he soon learned that she had picked up the item from a freelance writer, Dotson Rader, who often wrote for *Parade* magazine. But Rader told Bradlee that he had advised McClellan not to publish the story. And when pressed, Rader explained that his sources had spoken of a "tape," not a "bugging." The distinction was important because it was possible a reporter could have gone into Blair House and tape-recorded a conversation. But using the word "bugging" clearly implied that a listening device had been planted to eavesdrop on the Reagans.

In the event, Bradlee realized there was no evidence of either a tape or a listening device. Reluctantly, the *Post* instructed its lawyer, Edward Bennett Williams, to work out the terms of a written retraction and apology with Carter's lawyer. The next day, the *Post* published a front-page story quoting from a letter sent by Bradlee to Carter: "We now believe the story [our source] told us to be wrong and that there was no 'bugging' of Blair House during your Administration." Carter accepted the apology and said he would not file a libel suit. It had been a minor kerfuffle—but Carter felt vindicated and relished his public reprimanding of the celebrated *Post* editor.

IN THE MID-1980S, as the AIDS virus became a national epidemic, Carter angrily blamed President Reagan for ignoring a plague that was disproportionally killing homosexuals, African Americans, and drug addicts. "What did Christ do with lepers?" he said. "He had love for them. Even if we condemn what causes AIDS, we should have compassion for the victims. God gave us freedom to decide what we believe, to eliminate our natural prejudices." (He had always supported civil rights for gays, but his views on gay marriage evolved, as did most Americans'.)

But the health initiative most closely associated with the Carter Center was the ex-president's campaign to eliminate dracunculiasis—otherwise known as Guinea worm disease. Carter first heard about this scourge in 1986 from his old friend Dr. Peter Bourne, who was then serving as an assistant secretary general in the United Nations. Carter knew that smallpox had been eradicated globally during the 1970s—so he asked Bourne what other diseases might be eliminated by a similar public health campaign. Bourne replied that Guinea worm disease was easily treated, but the political will was lacking to mount a global campaign. Bourne briefed Carter on the parasitic disease, which at the time was maiming some 3.5 million people each year in Africa and the Indian subcontinent. People became infected simply by drinking dirty water contaminated by Guinea worm larvae. A larva spent as much as a year in the human body, eventually emerging through the skin as a full-grown worm measuring two to three feet in length. Victims often became incapacitated. "There were dozens of different health problems we could have tackled," Carter said, "but eradicating guinea worm was something tangible."

After raising millions of dollars from private individuals and corporations, Carter put together an ambitious program to identify each and every case of the disease. Villagers then had to be taught to avoid the contaminated water. It was an enormously complicated public health undertaking, stretching across much of Central Africa and Pakistan. By 1993, Carter's efforts had eradicated Guinea worm disease in Pakistan. The parasite persisted, however, in parts of Africa for many more years.

In 1995, the Carters toured villages in Nigeria and met with victims of the disease. "All had worms emerging from their bodies," Rosalynn noted in her diary. "I will never forget the eyes of one little boy with two worms coming out between his knuckles. His hand was swollen as though it would burst, and he kept lifting it to me, as though I could make the hurting go away." The Carters never gave up, and by 2018, the number of human cases had fallen to a mere twenty-eight individuals. And a year later there were fewer than a dozen cases, mostly in Chad.

Just a year after Carter tackled the Guinea worm–eradication program, he became aware of another public health issue widespread in Africa—onchocerciasis, or river blindness. This ancient affliction was caused by yet another parasitic worm, this one transmitted to humans through the bites of blackflies. The resulting worms often gestate for years under the human skin, causing a terrible skin rash, weight loss, and, after a dozen years, lesions in the eyes that lead to total blindness. But in the autumn of 1987, Dr. Roy Vagelos, the chairman of Merck, a large pharmaceutical company, announced that it had developed a pill that could both prevent river blindness and arrest its development in those already infected. A single pill of Mectizan—the same medicine used to prevent heartworm in dogs—was effective if taken annually.

Ironically, Merck had a cure for a disease that afflicted millions of people so poor that they could not afford the miraculous pill, however cheap it might be. Merck's Vagelos concluded that the right thing to do was to give away Mectizan to those who needed it in villages all over Africa and Latin America. To this end, he offered to donate $80 million worth of Mectizan tablets if the Carter Center could figure out how to distribute the pills.

Carter jumped at the chance to help some eighteen million Africans living with the onchocerciasis worm, hundreds of thousands of whom were in danger of becoming completely blind. As described by Brinkley in his biography of Carter's postpresidential years, *The Unfinished Presidency*, Carter used his status as an ex-president to prod African leaders to organize the complex distribution of the magic pills. He was untiring. Carter himself would meet with the relevant heads of state, the health ministers, the finance ministers, and the education ministers. He would persuade them to form distribution teams, often financed by World Bank funds.

He was the catalyst. "That's the only way to really reach every village with *mectizan*," he said. Between 1988 and 1995, the Carter Center helped to distribute some 29 million Mectizan tablets. In 1998, upon the discovery that the same basic medicine could also address elephantiasis, or "big foot disease," the program was expanded. By 2017, Merck was providing the medicine for 100 million treatments annually. Carter was hopeful that both river blindness and elephantiasis were on a trajectory to elimination.

CARTER HAD ALWAYS operated as a guarded politician. As a state senator and governor in Georgia and as president, he sometimes had to parse his words, calculating what to say to each audience. If he wanted to, he could be quite astute at this game. But as an ex-president he soon realized that he could go anywhere and say just about anything he wished without worrying about the political consequences. He was free now of circumspection. And he was determined to use this freedom to fashion his own rules for life as an ex-president. He became quite unguarded in his opinions. When Mayor Ed Koch refused Habitat for Humanity's plea to donate abandoned real estate on New York's Lower East Side for a Habitat project, Carter called the mayor a "jerk."

NOT SURPRISINGLY, CARTER did not shy away from controversy with the Israelis by speaking his mind about the Palestinians. In February 1983, he and former president Gerald Ford co-authored a *Reader's Digest* essay in which they said that Israel's continued expansion of settlements in the West Bank "has caused both of us deep disappointment and a sense of grave concern that is shared by many other stalwart supporters of Israel." A month later, he bluntly told an elite audience of policy makers at the Council on Foreign Relations, "Israel is the problem toward peace." He was particularly concerned, even at this early stage, about Israel's expansion of Jewish settlements in the West Bank. When *New York Times* columnist A. M. Rosenthal accused the ex-president of bias for his criticism of Israeli human rights abuses against Palestinians in 1990, Carter responded forcefully. "I know that when any statement is made that is critical of Israel . . . it's going to be condemned. I don't have any apology to make. I am concerned about the genuine belief that I am biased, but a lot of the accusations about bias are deliberately designed to prevent further criticism of Israel's policies. And I don't choose to be intimidated."

Just four days later, on April 4, 1990, Carter arrived in Paris, where he met PLO chairman Yasir Arafat for the first time. The meeting had been arranged by Mary King, the wife of Carter's longtime aide Dr. Peter Bourne. Arafat and the Carters spent two hours together, cordially discussing how to advance the prospects for peace. Arafat complained that the Reagan administration had reneged repeatedly on its promises—to which Rosalynn interrupted, "You don't have to convince us." Everyone laughed, and then she apologized: "I think my husband asked me to take notes so I can't take part in the conversation." Carter then added, "Yes, but she tells me what to say before we come to the meeting." At one point, Rosalynn teared up, showing her distress at what she had seen at a Palestinian orphanage in the West Bank. In response, both Arafat and Carter began to cry. They then clasped hands and Carter led them in prayer. Arafat was stunned by this emotional display. "His face was flushed," recalled King later to historian Douglas Brinkley. "He had been thrown off balance. I could tell that Arafat had been deeply moved."

The highly unusual encounter was a classic example of Carter's conflict-resolution strategy. He had complete confidence in his ability to ferret out the humanity in the most hardened and cynical leader. It was his strength, even if his critics would call it naïve. In this instance, Carter emerged from his meeting with Arafat, regarded by many as a "celebrity terrorist," to praise the PLO chairman for having "done everything possible in these last months to promote the peace process." He flatly declared that peace between the Palestinians and Israelis was "inevitable."

The Israelis, of course, were horrified. They condemned the encounter. Carter didn't care what they thought. Instead of backing off, he stayed in touch with Arafat, advising him even to the point of writing him a draft position paper. He worked doggedly to persuade the Palestinian leader to choose negotiations and peace over confrontation. He was undeterred when Arafat embraced Iraq's Saddam Hussein after the Iraqi invasion of Kuwait. And in retrospect, Carter's ongoing relationship with Arafat probably provided a critical psychological impetus to preparing the way for the Oslo breakthroughs for a far-reaching settlement in 1993.

Carter had heavily invested himself in the peace process over many decades. In 1996, he and a Carter Center team of observers monitored the first presidential election in Gaza and the West Bank. Carter visited with Arafat in Gaza City—and came away with high hopes that the Oslo process toward a genuine peace was irreversible. Not surprisingly, he felt a growing frustration when the process began to fall apart during the second intifada, which began in September 2000.

In 2006, Carter published his twenty-first book, entitled *Palestine: Peace Not Apartheid*. The highly provocative title created a huge controversy even as the book splashed onto bestseller lists and sold several hundred thousand copies in hardcover. To no avail, Stu Eizenstat and other advisers had tried frantically to convince Carter not to use the word "apartheid" in the title. Carter's longtime aide on Middle East issues at the Carter Center, Ken Stein, resigned in protest.* Fourteen other members of the Center's Board of Councilors also submitted their resignations. Carter was unrepentant and publicly defended his book. He admitted that he had chosen "that title knowing that it would be provocative." But he also confessed, "I've been hurt, and so has my family, by some of the reaction. . . . This is the first time that I've ever been called a liar, and a bigot, and an anti-Semite."

At one point in his book tour he declined to accept lawyer Alan Dershowitz's challenge to a debate at Brandeis University. (Dershowitz had called the book's title "indecent.") While he received a standing ovation from Brandeis students, the "apartheid" in the book title undoubtedly marked a negative turning point in Carter's troubled relationship with the Jewish American community. When his critics labeled the ex-president an anti-Semite, it was not only unfair but preposterous. The controversy was all about Israel, not Jews.

In the years since leaving the White House, Carter's impatience with the Israeli leadership had become more pronounced. He was particularly appalled by Prime Minister Ariel Sharon's decision to build a wall through the occupied West Bank. He argued in his 2007 book that "Israeli leaders have embarked on a series of unilateral decisions. . . . Uti-

---

* Carter had always insisted that Stein should share his unvarnished opinions. After working closely together on Carter's 1985 book on the Middle East, *The Blood of Abraham,* Stein later recalled, "When I disagreed too strenuously, Carter impishly smiled and with his blue eyes twinkling, said, 'Remember, Ken, only one of us was president of the United States.'"

lizing their political and military dominance, they are imposing a system of partial withdrawal, encapsulation, and apartheid on the Muslim and Christian citizens of the occupied territories." When questioned, he repeatedly said that the apartheid he was describing in the West Bank "was not based on racism." But if in 2007 some critics thought it was too early to use the word "apartheid," within a decade such a prominent Israeli leader as former prime minister Ehud Barak would be warning that the country was on a "slippery slope toward apartheid." Carter now seemed eerily prescient.

AMERICA'S MOST PERIPATETIC ex-president confessed that he sometimes felt compelled to practice what he called "pariah diplomacy." He was not afraid to go solo. After Iraq's August 1990 invasion of Kuwait, Carter opposed President George H. W. Bush's march to war, going so far as to send a private letter to allied leaders, urging them not to support the U.S. position in the Security Council. He argued that Saddam Hussein was not about to invade Saudi Arabia and that the crisis could be resolved by intra-Arab diplomacy. Secretary of Defense Dick Cheney was outraged when he learned of Carter's letter: "Writing it was just plain wrong. For him to go behind our backs and ask world leaders to denounce our war policy was reprehensible, totally inappropriate for a former president." Carter was unapologetic and felt vindicated when it became apparent that the 1991 Gulf War had quite unintentionally planted the seeds for the 9/11 attacks. Dispatching American soldiers to the Arabian Peninsula led directly to the formation of al-Qaeda and Osama bin Laden's challenge to the house of Saud. Carter believed military interventions always carried bloody unintended consequences.

Carter had a similar blowup with President Bill Clinton in 1994 when he accepted an invitation from North Korea's dictator, Kim Il Sung, to talk about that rogue communist country's nuclear program. "Carter is someone," said Aaron David Miller, a State Department official at the time, "who believes that when you have a problem with someone, you go talk to them." Carter also believed that the Clinton administration's strategy of ramping up sanctions and quietly threatening force would not work to end the North Korean regime's production of plutonium. So he flew off to North Korea, hoping a little private diplomacy could change the dynamics. Clinton only reluctantly authorized his national security adviser, Anthony Lake, to brief Carter prior to this trip, emphasizing that no new offers should be made to the North Korean dictator. Inevitably, Carter went off script in his negotiations with Kim Il Sung. The two men had a cordial conversation and soon made a deal: The North Koreans would agree to a temporary freeze on plutonium production and allow for international inspections, and in return the United States would help to replace the offending gas-graphite reactors with light-water reactors, unsuitable for the production of bomb-grade plutonium.

Carter immediately called the White House to report on his breakthrough diplomacy. Clinton and his foreign policy team were actually in deliberations about sending an additional ten thousand American troops to South Korea—a major escalation—when Carter called. Minutes later, they were astonished to see the ex-president announcing the news in a live CNN interview. Clinton felt blindsided. "We were amazed to discover," Carter later noted in his diary, "that our actions in North Korea had been met by criticism and partial rejection in Washington." Clinton's people were skeptical that Kim Il Sung had any credibility. Bush's former secretary of state Lawrence Eagleburger said he was "horrified" that Carter was "taking the word of this murderer who runs North Korea." But contrary to the skeptics, North Korea and the United States signed a pact later that autumn along the lines negotiated by Carter. By then, Kim Il Sung had suddenly died of a heart attack—but the agreement held up for a number of years. Whatever his critics thought, it was hard not to concede that Carter's personal diplomacy had averted a war on the Korean Peninsula in the 1990s.

HIS REAL JOB in these years was as an author. He was an unusually disciplined writer, churning out manuscripts, initially on a first-generation word processor. Over the next forty years, he published more than thirty books, some weighty volumes on politics or history and some lighter meditations on religion, ethics, and the virtues of the outdoors. Many became bestsellers, including even a small volume of poetry. In 2010, he published *White House Diary,* a five-hundred-plus-page annotated version of about 20 percent of his presidential diary. He even wrote a charming children's book, *The Little Baby Snoogle-Fleejer,* illustrated beautifully by Amy Carter—who by then had become an artist and art teacher at an elementary school in Georgia. He published one novel, set in the South during the Revolutionary War. But some of his best books were slices of memoir: a book about his mother, an account of his first political campaign, and a lyrical and quite evocative memoir of his childhood in Plains: *An Hour Before Daylight: Memories of a Rural Boyhood*—which became a finalist for the 2002 Pulitzer Prize.

One book jeopardized the tranquility of his marriage. Peter Osnos, his editor at Random House, had persuaded the Carters to collaborate on a book that would share their personal prescriptions for happiness, wellness, and longevity. Ironically, it turned out that after forty-one years of marriage, they learned that they could not write a paragraph together. "I write very rapidly," Carter explained, "and Rosalynn treated my chapters as rough drafts. She writes slowly and carefully, and considers the resulting sentences as though they have come down from Mount Sinai, carved into stone." When they stopped talking to each other, they decided it was time to quit and return the publisher's advance. Osnos flew down to Plains and came up with a Solomonic solution: They would write alternate paragraphs, not editing each other—and each paragraph's author was identified by a *J* or an *R. Everything to Gain: Making the Most of the Rest of Your Life* was published in 1987—and Jimmy avowed, "Our marriage survived."

Like any married couple, the Carters have had their differences. Rosalynn was not only strong-willed and opinionated but equally stubborn in her own way. "We've had some heated and extended arguments," she wrote in 1987. Many of their spats stemmed from Jimmy's obsession with punctuality. He described her as "adequately punctual, except as measured by my perhaps unreasonable standards." Then one day in August 1984 Carter was working in his study when he suddenly realized it was Rosie's birthday and he had forgotten to buy her anything. Inspired, he sat down and wrote her a note: "Happy Birthday! As proof of my love, I will never again make an unpleasant comment about tardiness." He signed the note and presented it to her with a kiss.

No one was particularly surprised when, in 2002, Carter was awarded the Nobel Peace Prize. The Norwegian committee cited Carter's "decades of untiring effort to find peaceful solutions to international conflicts, to advance democracy and human rights and to promote economic and social development." Israel's prime minister at the time, Ariel Sharon, graciously said, "If only for his efforts to achieve the peace agreement with Egypt, and the fact that his agreement is still holding, he deserves the peace prize."

IN MAY 2015, Carter suddenly began feeling ill while on a trip to Guyana, where he was monitoring an election. Back in Atlanta, his doctors at Emory University identified a tumor growing on his liver. Carter delayed any surgery until he could complete a scheduled book tour for his newly published memoir, *A Full Life: Reflections at Ninety*. Finally, on August 3, 2015, surgeons removed one-tenth of his diseased liver.

The news was good—and then suddenly worse. As Carter explained on August 20 at a nationally televised press conference, "At first, I felt that it was confined to my liver and the operation had completely removed it, so I was quite relieved." That same afternoon an MRI of his head and neck revealed four spots of melanoma in his brain. "I just thought I had a few weeks left," Carter said, "but I was surprisingly at ease. I've had a wonderful life, I've had thousands of friends, and I've had an exciting and adventurous and gratifying existence." He explained that he had agreed to undergo stereotactic radiation, using tightly focused beams of radiation on each of the four spots of melanoma in his brain. And he would be taking injections of pembrolizumab (Keytruda), a new drug recently approved by the Federal Drug Administration that had demonstrated promising results in the treatment of some forms of melanoma. But after this dramatic and emotional news conference, well, most Americans thought he was saying his final farewell.

Carter was clearly at peace with himself. I saw the press conference on live television. Just weeks earlier, I had signed a contract to write this biography. So the event was particularly poignant for this biographer. Wearing a simple blazer and blue jeans, he confessed that he was still hoping to fly off to Kathmandu, Nepal, in November to work on a long-scheduled Habitat for Humanity project in that impoverished South Asian nation. "Now I feel that it's in the hands of God," he said.

It was surreal—the former president calmly talking without notes or a prepared text about his imminent death, and at the same time candidly addressing his feelings about his life, his presidency, his triumphs, and his regrets. As to the latter, he highlighted his efforts to bring peace to the Middle East and mournfully noted that "the prospects are more dismal than any time I remember in the last fifty years. . . . The government of Israel has no desire for a two-state solution." Nor did he avoid the painful topic of the Iran hostage crisis that so bedeviled his presidency. "I wish I had sent one more helicopter to get the hostages, and we would've rescued them," he said, "and I would've been reelected." And, smiling broadly, he quipped, "I'd like for the last guinea worm to die before I do."

After speaking for eight minutes, he calmly answered questions for another thirty minutes before walking off the Carter Center stage and waving goodbye. It was as if he had given his own eulogy. But as it turned out, it was not his time to leave. His doctors prevailed, and the new drugs to treat his particular melanoma proved to be astonishingly successful. By early 2016, a CAT scan of his brain could detect no evidence of the melanoma. He had survived.

Epilogue

President Jimmy Carter, January 5, 1981
YOUSUF KARSH

Pundits wryly joked that Carter was the only ex-president to have used his presidency as a "stepping-stone" to higher achievements. I was one of those pundits, writing in 1990 a cover story in *The Nation* magazine with the headline "Citizen Carter: The Very Model of an Ex-President." Rosalynn Carter told me she was unhappy with the essay. While praising his postpresidential good works, I had described him as a "conservative/populist Democrat from the New South" who as president had been unable to lead the Democratic coalition or govern. At the time, the Carters disliked the implication that if his ex-presidency was admirable, his presidency had nevertheless been a failure. Thirty years later, they felt the same way. Carter thought he had worked hard to be not only an ethical president but an effective one. He had spent long hours in the Oval Office, trying to do his best. He had enjoyed the job and relished grappling with the flood of paper that had crossed the *Resolute* desk. "Obviously, it's the most intensive, educational process imaginable," he later said. "You have such a large number of things to learn about simultaneously, you can either avoid the learning process, or you can jump into it with enthusiasm. I did the latter. . . . I was exhilarated by it and gratified by it. . . . I still look on it as one of the most pleasant and gratifying experiences of my life. There was never a time that I was there that I was in despair or felt hopeless, frustrated, or, I have to say with an element of humility, that I felt inadequate. I never felt that somebody else could be doing a better job at particular times than I was. And I always did my best."

Even in defeat, he had no regrets, and in retrospect, he liked to quote Mondale, who had told him, "We obeyed the law, we told the truth, and we kept the peace." Carter liked to add, "We championed human rights." On one level, this might seem a low bar by which to judge a presidency. But few of Jimmy Carter's predecessors or successors in the White House could boast that they had not lied, broken the law, or taken the country to war. By this standard, Carter's presidency was exceptional, even stellar. Bert Lance's banking shenanigans made unfortunate headlines, but in retrospect, they seem positively quaint in the history of presidential scandals. Likewise, the Studio 54 allegations against Hamilton Jordan damaged the Carter White House in the court of public opinion. But Jordan was fully exonerated of charges that turned out to have been manufactured by Roy Cohn, perhaps the nation's most notorious and unscrupulous lawyer.

Historically, Carter's four years in the White House were bookended by Nixon's Watergate affair and Reagan's Iran-Contra scandal. By comparison, Carter's administration was legally and ethically pristine. But this president also took pride in what his administration accomplished, not just that he managed to avoid scandal and the spilling of American blood in combat. And indeed, the record of these achievements is not to be lightly dismissed.

Both the domestic and foreign policy ledgers are lengthy and fulsome. Carter, not Reagan, began the deregulation of the American economy. Deregulation of the airlines, trucking, and railroads introduced more competition in these critical sectors. For the first time, middle-class Americans began to fly in large numbers. Craft beers became ubiquitous. Deregulation of natural gas brought similar economic efficiencies to the energy sectors. Carter's energy policies resulted in a decline in foreign oil imports—and stimulated the growth of solar, wind, and other renewable energy. At the same time, Carter strengthened consumer regulations in terms of auto safety and pharmaceuticals. Passenger airbags and mandatory safety belts saved the lives of upwards of nine thousand Americans annually. Carter's tougher environmental regulations gave the country cleaner water and cleaner air to breathe. America's wilderness preserves dramatically expanded, most notably in Alaska. And against all odds, Carter's war against double-digit inflation was actually won when he made the politically damaging decision to appoint Volcker as chairman of the Federal Reserve—and refused to interfere when Volcker squeezed the money supply and jacked up interest rates. President Carter can also take credit for transforming the judiciary, appointing scores of African Americans, Hispanics, and women to the federal bench.

In the field of foreign policy, Carter's accomplishments are remarkable. He secured Senate ratification of the Panama Canal Treaty, normalized relations with China, negotiated a SALT II arms-control agreement with the Soviet Union, and personally brokered the Camp David Accords, effectively taking Egypt off the battlefield for Israel and creating a road map for Palestinian self-determination. Carter's investment in brokering an Arab-Israeli peace settlement probably hurt his efforts to win reelection, but the issue was too close to his heart for him to be deterred from trying. Human rights were not just a priority. Human rights became the cornerstone of Carter's entire foreign policy. Early in his administration Carter had shocked the pundits by proclaiming, "Being confident of our own future, we are now free of that inordinate fear of communism which once led us to embrace any dictator who joined us in our fear." This allowed him to forge working relationships with rising nationalist forces in Latin America, Africa, and Asia.

The emphasis on human rights also planted the seeds for the crum-

bling of the Iron Curtain in Eastern Europe and the eventual collapse of
the Soviet Union itself. Carter's focus on democratic human rights undoubtedly helped to accelerate the dissolution of the Soviet system. Diplomacy and American "soft power" played a role. American rock and
roll, for instance, did its part to subvert communism during these years.
The Soviet Union did not collapse, as some pundits still seem to believe,
under the pressure of Reagan's defense expenditures but largely due to
the forces of political liberalization nurtured by Mikhail Gorbachev.
Human rights as a policy issue was a key factor. None of Carter's successors, whether Democrat or Republican, could walk back his human
rights policies. It remained a touchstone of American foreign relations—
until the inauguration of Donald Trump as president in 2017.

CARTER'S FAILURES WERE also consequential. On the domestic ledger,
most notable was his political failure to enact national health insurance.
He would always blame Ted Kennedy for this missed opportunity. But
Carter himself must share some blame for his failure to forge a compromise with the liberals. This fight demoralized the Democratic Party and
left it in shambles just as Ronald Reagan mounted his challenge to the
liberal order.

In terms of foreign policy, Iran and the interminable hostage crisis
must be counted as Carter's most damaging defeat. In retrospect, he
should have trusted his first instincts and refused to allow the deposed
Pahlavi monarch asylum in America. He should have firmly resisted the
shortsighted counsel from Henry Kissinger, David Rockefeller, and his
own national security adviser.

Zbigniew Brzezinski's wit and intellect energized the Carter White
House, but his hawkish and ideologically driven Cold War views were
never in sync with this president. Carter often disagreed with Brzezinski's instincts and policy prescriptions on Iran and a host of other foreign policy issues, but he never seriously considered firing his voluble
adviser. He was too loyal to this friend. If Iran was a foreign policy disaster, Brzezinski contributed heavily to these unhappy events. When
the Tehran embassy was overrun, ideally Carter should have found a
way to either quickly end the siege or deescalate the publicity value of
the hostages to the revolutionary regime. Either way, there were no easy

solutions, but Brzezinski's hard-line views, if anything, merely boxed the president into a long period of impossible choices, one of which—the high-risk helicopter rescue mission—was a military and political disaster. Carter never acknowledged this and, somewhat lamely, often suggested that one more helicopter might have made a difference in the impossibly complicated operation.

In the end, Carter's presidency was hijacked by the Iranian revolution. The hostages, nevertheless, all came home—and in large measure this can be attributed to Carter's patient diplomacy. But patient diplomacy probably cost him a second term.

That electoral defeat is also shadowed by the apparent willingness of the Republican nominee's campaign manager to do everything he could to avoid an "October surprise" release of the hostages. Though not conclusive, the evidence strongly suggests that Bill Casey did go to Madrid in the summer of 1980 and did meet with an Iranian envoy. If so, Casey muddied the waters of negotiation and probably contributed to a delay in the release of the hostages until the day Ronald Reagan was inaugurated. Casey got away with his possibly treasonous caper—and helped to scuttle Carter's second-term presidency.

Casey also played a role in the theft of Carter's 1980 debate briefing binders. And then there was Roger Stone delivering a briefcase full of cash to ensure that the Liberal Party of New York State endorsed John Anderson. Carter was the target of more than one dirty trick.

ON THE OTHER hand, what is historically significant about the Carter era is the undeniable fact that those years were a tipping point. One kind of liberalism, rooted in the social compact of Franklin Roosevelt's New Deal, finally gave way in the late 1970s to a harsher world. After Carter came a far more conservative era, a crueler social compact, based on Reagan's tax cuts for the wealthy and an unregulated neoliberal globalization that accelerated the deindustrialization of America. The oil embargo of 1973 and subsequent energy price hikes instigated a period of significant inflation—and then an unprecedented period of stagflation. But otherwise, globalization of the world economy was a relentless, inexorable force. Carter's normalization of relations with Deng Xiaoping's China, for instance, was an inevitable product of these economic forces, not their cause. Similarly, Carter did not cause the Iranian revolution or the Soviet invasion of Afghanistan—but these events marked a major historical turning point.

Unfortunately, the winding down of the Cold War in the late 1970s and '80s took place at the same time as the rise of xenophobic and religious fundamentalism in much of the developing world. The year 1979, for instance, saw not only the rise of the Islamic Republic in Iran but also the siege of Mecca by Saudi jihadists—which in turn inspired the young Saudi zealot Osama bin Laden, who later founded al-Qaeda in the 1990s. America and the world experienced highly disruptive change in the 1970s. In this sense, Carter, more than most modern presidents, was a victim of events. And this fact has always colored the American public's view of his "failed" presidency. Such historical forces would have vexed any president, but for someone like Carter, who was neither a dogmatist nor an indefatigable proponent of American exceptionalism, they proved especially tricky to navigate with a public that above all things craved moral clarity when it came to America's role in the world.

Americans as a people have drenched themselves with a sense of destiny, a sense of exceptionalism—and they do not like to see themselves as victims of historical forces beyond their control. Neither do they like to be told that there are limits, either material or aspirational, to the American dream. Carter insisted that there were constraints. He did so most famously in his July 1979 so-called malaise speech, where he bluntly rejected the notion that the American character, as the Harvard historian Arthur M. Schlesinger, Sr., wrote, "is bottomed upon the profound conviction that nothing in the world is beyond its power to accomplish."

Carter was a southern liberal—and that meant his instincts were always pragmatic. He was a realist but a political outlier. He challenged us to question the myths of American innocence and American exceptionalism, and he did so as a liberal southerner who took his intellectual cues, oddly enough, from William Faulkner, the Mississippi novelist, and Reinhold Niebuhr, the elite northern Protestant theologian, a realist and skeptic who once wrote that "power cannot be wielded without guilt" and that "the disavowal of the responsibilities of power can involve an individual or nation in even more grievous guilt." Both Faulkner and Niebuhr saw the world with all its sinfulness. Carter deeply admired both writers and shared their dark worldview intellectually and spiritually. As a Southern Baptist Christian, he believed in "the fallibility of human beings and the basic weakness of mankind." He thus saw a world that desperately needed fixing. His policy prescriptions, however, were ideologically ambiguous at a time when the country wanted easy solutions.

As a politician, he presented himself to voters with a grinning, seemingly optimistic visage. Over time, particularly in the White House, where he methodically tackled some of the most divisive issues in all their complexities, his very folksiness and wide smile became disconcerting. They didn't fit the inner Niebuhrian.

In retrospect, it should be no surprise that Carter brought to the presidency certain southern sensibilities. As C. Vann Woodward, the widely read historian of the South, wrote, part of this outlook included the southerner's "chastening experience of being on the losing side of a war." A southern white heritage included a painful awareness of the possibilities of defeat and failure. Many such descendants of the defeated Confederacy possessed a natural skepticism for the innocent and liberal notion that no human problem was too difficult to overcome. History had taught them that this was a delusion. The engineer in Carter was by nature a problem solver. Only a dogged pragmatic idealist could have come from nowhere to win the presidency in 1976. But he quite sensibly rejected any reflexive notions of American exceptionalism. He preached that there were limits to American power and limits to what we could inflict on the environment—and limits to our unilateralism.

CITING FAULKNER IN an interview early in his presidency, Carter described "the buildup in the South of a special consciousness brought about by the self-condemnation resulting from slavery, the humiliation following the War Between the States and the hope, sometimes expressed timidly, for redemption. I think in many ways now that those former dark moods in the South of recrimination against self and others and alienation from the rest of the nation—I think they've been alleviated." In 1977, Carter obviously hoped his presidency would provide his native South with a measure of redemption. But four years later, his own southerners turned against him, accusing him of having betrayed his own heritage by being way too liberal. Carter did what he thought was right and alienated the evangelical voters, the right-to-lifers, the anti-feminists, and a host of other conservative constituencies. He alienated many white Americans who harbored feelings that the civil rights movement had gone too far. Affirmative action had gone too far. African Americans had gained too much at the expense of "ordinary" Americans. If the New South proved to be not that new or liberal, the rest of the country proved to be just as conservative on a host of issues. Perhaps Carter was too much of a Georgian Yankee for the New South—and too much of a populist southerner for the North. In either case, his presidency was ahead of his times. Carter's rise to power had offered hope for reconciliation between North and South—and hope for a healing of the racial divide. His loss signaled that the country was reverting to a new era of harsh partisanship, political division, and extremism. It was a tragic narrative of defeat familiar to any southerner.

Acknowledgments

B IOGRAPHY IS ALWAYS a long road. I first began thinking about this book in 1990. After more than ten years, I had finally submitted my first book, *The Chairman*, a biography of John J. McCloy, the powerful Wall Street lawyer who for much of the twentieth century came to epitomize the American foreign policy establishment. At the end of his long career McCloy played a critical role in the 1979–80 Iran hostage crisis. Writing about those events sparked my curiosity about the one-term presidency of Jimmy Carter. It occurred to me that perhaps I could write a biography of this southern president. When I mentioned the idea to my mentor, Victor Navasky, the editor of *The Nation* magazine, he suggested that I explore the notion by writing an article for him about what Carter was doing with his ex-presidency. I always follow Victor's advice, but the resulting cover story, "Citizen Carter: The Very Model of an Ex-President," nevertheless convinced me that it was too early to tackle a Carter biography, largely because most of his two million pages of presidential papers were still classified.

But having spent a little time in Atlanta and Plains, Georgia, I also suspected that this northerner was the wrong person to write about this very southern president. The South seemed to me to be a foreign land, and to write about Carter I would have had to approach the topic as a foreign correspondent, move to Georgia, learn the language, and immerse myself in this alien culture. In any case, I backed off the project.

Many books and twenty-five years later, I came back to Carter. I was still a tourist in the South, but I had not lost my fascination with this enigmatic president. Biography is always an arduous quest for understanding the world, and I was still curious to learn about what happened during this critical tipping point in the late 1970s. I was also better prepared as a historian to tackle this large, momentous presidential story.

Since 1990, I have written biographies that delve deeply into the Vietnam War, Watergate, nuclear weapons, and the Arab-Israeli conflict—and clearly, part of my fascination with Carter is that his own political odyssey is also associated with all of these issues.

President Carter was in his early nineties when I began this project—and though he remained a very busy man, directing the Carter Center's many humanitarian projects, he nevertheless made time to see me for the occasional interview. During our very first interview I complained that I couldn't find anywhere in his presidential papers the private memoranda sent to him over the years by his lawyer and political adviser Charles Kirbo. Expressing surprise at this news, President Carter said he would look into the matter. Three days later, his longtime personal assistant and historian, Dr. Steven Hochman, called me to say that they had found the papers stored in cardboard boxes in Kirbo's widow's attic. Some months later I was given permission to read these voluminous letters and memos, written to Carter from 1962 all the way through his presidential term. These "unprocessed" Kirbo papers will soon be accessible to scholars via the Carter Library—and they represent an invaluable and original thread in the narrative of this biography.

I also want to thank President Carter for the greatest gift he could give to a biographer—his diaries. As president, Carter dictated his thoughts about the day nearly every evening. His secretary Susan Clough then transcribed the diary and returned the tape to him each day, to be reused again and again. We thus have no audio of Carter's diary, but there are more than five thousand pages of transcriptions. In 2010, President Carter published about 20 percent of these in his book *White House Diary*. It is an extraordinarily candid and insightful diary. I requested but was denied access to the remainder of the unpublished diary, on grounds that it had not gone through a full declassification and privacy review. President Carter has made arrangements for the full diary to be transferred to the Carter Library. Someday, historians will have the benefit of seeing the full diary—but regrettably, it will be too late for this biography.

MANY FRIENDS AND colleagues encouraged me to embrace this project. Victor Navasky may have started me on the quest in 1990, but he has been an inspiration for decades. I am also grateful to Gail Ross and

Howard Yoon, stellar literary agents who have patiently represented me for three decades. They have helped me craft all my book proposals.

I will always be astonished that my dear friend Martin J. Sherwin trusted me to join him as a co-author on his long-awaited biography of J. Robert Oppenheimer. That book won the 2006 Pulitzer Prize, which has opened so many doors and, indeed, made it possible for me to tackle a presidential biography.

Another presidential biographer, Robert Dallek, encouraged me over many lunches at his favorite Irish pub. His wife, Geri, came up with the title for his JFK biography—*An Unfinished Life*—which inspired my own version of that phrase as a subtitle for this book.

The National Archives is an underappreciated (and underfunded) national treasure, and so too is the Jimmy Carter Presidential Library and Museum in Atlanta. Altogether, I spent nearly five months in the Carter archives, copying more than twenty thousand pages of Carter presidential documents. I could not have been so productive without the expert assistance of such professional archivists as Sara Mitchell, Mary Ann McSweeney, Aisha Johnson-Jones, Dave Stanhope, Brittany Parris, Keith Schuler, and the Carter Library director, Dr. Meredith Evans. I particularly want to thank Sara Mitchell for helping me at the last minute, and in the middle of the 2020 pandemic, to obtain access to a number of Carter photographs.

I thank my good friend Kathy Lichtenberg for allowing me to occupy her lovely cabin retreat on a lake near Atlanta during my work in the Carter Library. I am also grateful that my old friend Mercedes Arnold— the mother of my late college classmate Daniel Wright—agreed to spend many hours in the Carter Library, digging through the archival boxes. Thanks also to Dr. Glenn Speer, who used his relentless talents as a detective to help me solve more than one research mystery.

The journalist and historian Jonathan Alter graciously shared his insights and occasionally some documents even as he was working on his own biography of Carter. He published *His Very Best: Jimmy Carter, a Life* last year, so this book is also a beneficiary of his work. I mourn the sudden passing of yet another Carter biographer, Professor Leo Ribuffo, whose own manuscript, we can hope, will someday be edited for publication. I also benefited from the work of previous Carter biographers, including, most notably, Randall Ballmer, Dr. Peter Bourne, Stuart E.

Eizenstat, E. Stanly Godbold, Jr., Burton and Scott Kaufman, William Lee Miller, Nancy Mitchell, Kenneth E. Morris, and Julian E. Zelizer.

I imposed on many friends and colleagues to read my draft manuscript. The Pulitzer Prize–winning historian Lawrence Wright reviewed my chapter on the Camp David negotiations, and I benefited heavily from his own book on the subject, *Thirteen Days in September.*

Historians Eric Alterman, David Nasaw, and Martin Sherwin read the entire manuscript and helped me immeasurably to shape the narrative.

Carter's personal lawyer, Terry Adamson, read the entire manuscript and prevented me from making too many mistakes. He was always there to answer queries and introduce me to other Carter sources. He also facilitated my access to the Kirbo papers. He is a southern gentleman and, at least to this Yankee, he represents the best of the South.

President Carter's personal assistant for more than three decades is Dr. Steven Hochman, a historian of eighteenth-century America. Steve took time away from his demanding job to read the manuscript, and he corrected many errors. I will always be grateful for his assistance and charming openness.

Richard Moe—who served as Vice President Mondale's chief of staff—also read the entire manuscript. I benefited from his comments and thank him for his encouragement over these past five years. After we beat this pandemic I hope we can resume our lunches at La Tomate on Connecticut Avenue.

Ken Ackerman graciously lent me his files on the Bert Lance investigation.

Tim Kraft gave me his handwritten notebooks—not exactly diary notations, but useful nonetheless.

This book would lack much of its color and intimacy if I had not been able to quote from the personal diary of Landon Butler, who served as a presidential assistant during the Carter White House years, working with Hamilton Jordan. Butler was my fly on the wall, preserving his thoughtful observations in a diary for the benefit of all historians. Everyone should keep a diary—but few of us do. Butler also read the entire manuscript.

About halfway through this project, I had a phone interview with Carter speechwriter Jerome Doolittle. We talked for nearly an hour, but

I felt that I hadn't learned anything terribly new. As we were about to hang up, I asked Jerry if he had any old correspondence tucked away in his closets or attic. He suddenly piped up and said, "Well, I have a diary." It was neatly typed, covering the first two years of the Carter administration. Doolittle gave me the diary and has allowed me to quote generously from its contents.

The Doolittle and Butler diaries are two examples among many other archival sources that allowed me to write this narrative with a certain measure of authenticity.

I also quote from a handful of diary excerpts published in Zbigniew Brzezinski's memoir, *Power and Principle*. When I interviewed Brzezinski I asked him about obtaining access to his full diary, but he pointedly declined, saying that his full diary would be published—but only after Carter's death. After Brzezinski died in 2017 my inquiry to the family about the diary was met, regrettably, with silence. This biography is not the first to chronicle Carter's life, nor will it be the last. But future biographers will certainly be eager to incorporate such primary sources into their works.

Dr. Avner Cohen—an authority on the history of Israel and nuclear weapons—provided me with critical insights into the mysterious Vela story.

Professor Abbas Milani of Stanford University read my chapters about the Iranian revolution and the hostage crisis, and reassured me with his insights about this complicated history.

The journalist and historian John Dinges read what I wrote about the Carter administration's investigation into the assassination of Orlando Letelier.

Michael Schwartz and Emily Medine—close friends over many decades—provided encouragement and a refuge at their mountain home in Hidden Valley, Pennsylvania. More important, they gave me the benefit of their expertise on coal, solar, and other energy issues as they read my narrative about Carter's attempts to deal with the energy crisis of the 1970s.

Gerald Rafshoon, the president's good friend and adviser on "communications," is a biographer's dream. Jerry is a storyteller who knows how to paint on a large canvas. He always has at hand the most telling anecdote to make you understand the point of it all. He is gregarious and charmingly self-deprecating. Anyway, it was fun to spend time with Mr. Rafshoon and I want to say that I learned a lot in his presence.

I also want to thank many other fine people from Carter's inner circle of friends and former aides, including Jay Beck, Kathy Cade, Story Evans, Rex Granum, Phil Wise, Les Francis, Jim Free, Joel McCleary, David Rubenstein, Nan Powell, Paul Sullivan, and Alicia Smith. I attended four of the Carter Center's annual retreats, where I encountered many of these former Carter officials. It was remarkable to see how all these talented and ambitious people were still very much friends four decades after their White House years.

Adam A. Marshall, staff attorney for the Reporters Committee for Freedom of the Press, agreed to represent me pro bono in a lawsuit we filed against the State Department. Marshall compelled the State Department to make a thorough search for a document I knew existed pertaining to the "October surprise" mystery. The document in question was never found. But I am grateful for the committee's efforts on my behalf.

Precisely because biography is such a long journey over time, biographers must impose on their friends to listen to numerous stories about what they have unearthed. In my case, this includes such old friends as Marie Arana, Jonathan Yardley, Joseph Kanon, Robin Straus, Aviva Kempner, Andrew Meier, Caleb Rossiter, Maya Latynski, Arthur Samuelson, Michele de Nevers, Branko Milanovic, Stephen Frietch, Nancy Nickerson, Gar Alperovitz, Henry and Arlene Opatut, Charles Glass, Don Wilson, Keith and Shakun Leslie, Laura Parker, Jeff Stein, Adam Zagorin, Nilgun Tolek, Nina Shapiro, and Helma Goldmark. My three sisters—Christina, Nancy, and Shelly—always humored me even when I repeated myself.

Shortly after I embarked on this project, I received a phone call from David Nasaw, the biographer of Joseph Kennedy, Andrew Carnegie, and William Randolph Hearst. Nasaw wanted to know if I might be interested in a job—a "real job," as my wife would say, a job with a salary. I said no, and then I began to reconsider. Nasaw was talking about the directorship of the Leon Levy Center for Biography, a wholly unique, boutique institution housed at the Graduate Center of the City University of New York. Generously funded by Shelby White and the Leon Levy Foundation, the center's sole mission is to promote the art and craft of biography. Each year, it awards four fellowships to working biographers (plus a fifth devoted to science biographies, funded by the Alfred P. Sloan Foundation) and provides them with a quiet working space. Since 2007, some fifty biographers have received this fellowship—and so far twenty-five very fine biographies have been published. This was no ordinary job, but a chance to promote my own vocation.

I knew I had a job: writing this biography. But I couldn't resist the opportunity to lead this invaluable institution. Besides, Navasky told me to do it, and as I explained earlier, I always do what he says.

In any case, I am glad I took the job. I have learned from my fellow biographers how to improve my own craft. And over the past four years I have subjected many of the Leon Levy Fellows to my stories about Carter. And not a few have been forced to read my draft chapters—including Eleanor Randolph (who covered the Carter campaign and White House as a reporter), David Greenberg, Channing Joseph, Matthew McKnight, Abigail Santamaria, Laura Snyder, Rebecca Donner, Stephen Heyman, Jennifer Homans, Samanth Subramanian, Justin Gifford, Bruce Weber, and Lindsay Whalen.

I am very grateful to Shelby White, who brought me into this global community of fellow biographers and gave me the excuse to meet and often interview such giants in the field as Robert Caro, David Blight, Ruth Franklin, Taylor Branch, the late Edmund Morris, the late James Atlas, Nancy Greenspan, Tom Segev, Judith Thurman, Paul Hendrickson, Seymour Hersh, Stacy Schiff, Claire Tomalin, George Packer, Rick Perlstein, Michael Massing, Mary Dearborn, David Garrow, William Dalrymple, Fredrik Logevall, Carla Kaplan, Blake Bailey, Gary Giddins, Ben MacIntyre, Lawrence Weschler, Sam Roberts, Geoffrey Ward, and many other fine biographers.

I have also been most fortunate to have as my colleague Thad Ziolkowski, the Biography Center's associate director, whose literary sensibilities have always compensated for my lack thereof. I have also been enriched by my fellow biographers at the New York University Biography Seminar and Biographers International Organization (BIO). All in all, it has been a wonderful adventure.

Every biographer needs an editor—and in Kevin Doughten I found a discerning intellect. Kevin understands that no biography is ever "complete." When I finally submitted this work, he challenged me to rewrite critical sections, particularly its bookends, to explain to my readers more about my own opinions and conclusions. I will forever be grateful for his astute editing of a long and complicated manuscript. Thanks as well to David Drake, Annsley Rosner, Gillian Blake, Lydia Morgan, Mark Birkey, Richard Elman, Emily Hotaling, Dyana Messina, Sally Franklin, Allison Fox, Chris Brand, Hilary C. Roberts, Simon Sullivan, and the rest of the team at Crown Books.

This book is dedicated, once again, to my wife, Susan Goldmark. She is a most formidable intellect and a meticulous line editor. After a rewarding career at the World Bank—where her ample salary subsidized this struggling biographer over many years—she finally had time to accompany me into the archives. There she learned just how hard is the biographer's daily regimen, plowing through folder after folder, box after archival box. I am forever grateful for her presence and gentle impatience.

Our son clearly decided from an early age not to tread where his father walked; biography was not his thing. I dedicated a previous book to Joshua, writing that my young son would "invent his own identities." And he did, as an artist and budding industrial designer. And now he and his partner, Valeria, will live their own biographies.

January 4, 2021
Washington, DC

Bibliography

BOOKS

Abramson, Rudy. *Spanning the Century: The Life of W. Averell Harriman, 1891–1986*. New York: William Morrow, 1992.

Alam, Asadollah. *The Shah and I: The Confidential Diary of Iran's Royal Court, 1968–77*. Edited by Alinagh Alikhani. London: I.B. Tauris, 1991.

Allman, Gregg, with Alan Light. *My Cross to Bear*. New York: William Morrow, 2012.

Alter, Jonathan. *His Very Best: Jimmy Carter, a Life*. New York: Simon & Schuster, 2020.

Alterman, Eric. *Sound & Fury: The Washington Punditocracy and the Collapse of American Politics*. New York: HarperCollins, 1992.

Alterman, Eric, and Kevin Mattson. *The Cause: The Fight for American Liberalism from Franklin Roosevelt to Barack Obama*. New York: Viking, 2012.

Anderson, Patrick. *Electing Jimmy Carter: The Campaign of 1976*. Baton Rouge: Louisiana State University Press, 1994.

Anderson, William. *The Wild Man from Sugar Creek: The Political Career of Eugene Talmadge*. Baton Rouge: Louisiana State University Press, 1976.

Anziska, Seth. *Preventing Palestine: A Political History from Camp David to Oslo*. Princeton, N.J.: Princeton University Press, 2018.

Auchmutey, Jim. *The Class of '65: A Student, a Divided Town and the Long Road to Forgiveness*. New York: PublicAffairs, 2015.

Ayers, H. Brandt. *In Love with Defeat: The Making of a Southern Liberal*. Montgomery, Ala.: NewSouth Books, 2013.

Ball, George. *The Past Has Another Pattern*. New York: W.W. Norton, 1982.

Balmer, Randall. *Redeemer: The Life of Jimmy Carter*. New York: Basic Books, 2014.

Bani-Sadr, Abol Hassan. *My Turn to Speak: Iran, the Revolution and Secret Deals with the U.S.* Lincoln, Neb.: Potomac Books, 1991.

Bill, James A. *The Eagle and the Lion: The Tragedy of American-Iranian Relations*. New Haven, Conn.: Yale University Press, 1988.

Bingham, June. *Courage to Change: An Introduction to the Life and Thought of Reinhold Niebuhr*. New York: Charles Scribner's Sons, 1961.

Bird, Kai. *The Chairman: Making of the American Establishment*. New York: Simon & Schuster, 1992.

———. *The Good Spy: The Life and Death of Robert Ames*. New York: Crown, 2014.

Bollier, David. "Chapter 3: The Office of Citizen." In *Citizen Action and Other Big Ideas*. Washington, D.C.: Center for Study of Responsive Law, 1991. Available at https://nader.org/2004/01/06/chapter-3-the-office-of-citizen/.

Bourne, Peter G. *Jimmy Carter: A Comprehensive Biography from Plains to Post-presidency*. New York: Scribner, 1997.

Bowden, Mark. *Guests of the Ayatollah: The Iran Hostage Crisis; The First Battle in America's War with Militant Islam*. New York: Grove Press, 2007.

Branch, Taylor. *Parting the Waters: America in the King Years, 1954–63*. New York: Simon & Schuster, 1988.

Brinkley, Douglas. *The Unfinished Presidency: Jimmy Carter's Journey Beyond the White House*. New York: Viking, 1998.

Brower, Kate Andersen. *The Residence: Inside the Private World of the White House*. New York: HarperCollins, 2015.

Brzezinski, Zbigniew. *Power and Principle: Memoirs of the National Security Adviser, 1977–1981*. New York: Farrar, Straus and Giroux, 1983.

Califano, Joseph A., Jr. *Governing America: An Insider's Report from the White House and the Cabinet*. New York: Simon & Schuster, 1981.

———. *Inside: A Public and Private Life*. New York: PublicAffairs, 2004.

Canellos, Peter S., ed. *Last Lion: The Fall and Rise of Ted Kennedy*. New York: Simon & Schuster, 2009.

Carter, Dan T. *The Politics of Rage: George Wallace, the Origins of the New Conservatism, and the Transformation of American Politics*. New York: Simon & Schuster, 1995.

Carter, Hugh, as told to Frances Spatz Leighton. *Cousin Beedie and Cousin Hot: My Life with the Carter Family of Plains, Georgia*. New York: Prentice-Hall, 1978.

Carter, Jimmy. *Always a Reckoning and Other Poems*. New York: Times Books, 1995.

———. *The Blood of Abraham: Insights into the Middle East*. Boston: Houghton Mifflin, 1985.

———. *A Call to Action: Women, Religion, Violence, and Power*. New York: Simon & Schuster, 2014.

———. *Faith: A Journey for All*. New York: Simon & Schuster, 2014.

———. *A Full Life*. New York: Simon & Schuster, 2015.

————. *An Hour Before Daylight: Memories of a Rural Boyhood.* New York: Simon & Schuster, 2001.

————. *Keeping Faith: Memoirs of a President.* New York: Bantam Books, 1982.

————. *Living Faith.* New York: Times Books/Broadway Books, 1998.

————. *Paintings of Jimmy Carter.* Macon, Ga.: Mercer University Press, 2017.

————. *Palestine: Peace Not Apartheid.* New York: Simon & Schuster, 2006.

————. *The Personal Beliefs of Jimmy Carter: Winner of the 2002 Nobel Peace Prize.* New York: Broadway Books, 2002.

————. *A Remarkable Mother.* New York: Simon & Schuster, 2008.

————. *Sharing Good Times.* New York: Simon & Schuster, 2004.

————. *Turning Point: A Candidate, a State, and a Nation Come of Age.* New York: Times Books, 1992.

————. *White House Diary.* New York: Farrar, Straus and Giroux, 2010.

————. *Why Not the Best?* Nashville: Broadman Press, 1975.

Carter, Jimmy, and Rosalynn Carter. *Everything to Gain: Making the Best of the Rest of Your Life.* New York: Random House, 1987.

Carter, Rosalynn. *First Lady from Plains.* Boston: Houghton Mifflin, 1984.

Cash, W. J. *The Mind of the South.* New York: Vintage Books, 1991.

Chernyaev, A. S. *The Diary of Anatoly S. Chernyaev.* Washington, D.C.: National Security Archive, 1980.

Clifford, Clark, with Richard Holbrooke. *Counsel to the President: A Memoir.* New York: Random House, 1991.

Cooper, Andrew Scott. *The Fall of Heaven: The Pahlavis and the Final Days of Imperial Iran.* New York: Henry Holt, 2016.

Cowie, Jefferson. *Stayin' Alive: The 1970s and the Last Days of the Working Class.* New York: New Press, 2012.

Dayan, Moshe. *Breakthrough: A Personal Account of the Egypt-Israel Peace Negotiations.* New York: Random House, 1981.

Dinges, John, and Saul Landau. *Assassination on Embassy Row.* New York: Pantheon Books, 1980.

Eizenstat, Stuart E. *President Carter: The White House Years.* New York: Thomas Dunne Books, 2018.

Farrell, John A. *Richard Nixon: The Life.* New York: Doubleday, 2017.

————. *Tip O'Neill and the Democratic Century: A Biography.* Boston: Little, Brown, 2001.

Faulkner, William. *Absalom, Absalom!* 1936. Repr., New York: Modern Library, 1993.

————. *Requiem for a Nun.* 1951. Repr., New York: Vintage, 2012.

Fitzgerald, Frances. *The Evangelicals: The Struggle to Shape America.* New York: Simon & Schuster, 2017.

Follett, Ken. *On Wings of Eagles.* New York: William Morrow, 1983.

Frank, Thomas. *The People, No: A Brief History of Anti-populism.* New York: Metropolitan Books, 2020.

Gates, Robert. *From the Shadows: The Ultimate Insider's Story of Five Presidents and How They Won the Cold War.* New York: Simon & Schuster, 1996.

Gati, Charles, ed. *Zbig: The Strategy and Statecraft of Zbigniew Brzezinski.* Baltimore: Johns Hopkins University Press, 2013.

Gillon, Steven M. *The Democrats' Dilemma: Walter F. Mondale and the Liberal Legacy.* New York: Columbia University Press, 1992.

Glad, Betty. *Jimmy Carter: In Search of the Great White House.* New York: W.W. Norton, 1980.

———. *An Outsider in the White House: Jimmy Carter, His Advisors, and the Making of American Foreign Policy.* Ithaca, N.Y.: Cornell University Press, 2009.

Godbold, E. Stanly, Jr. *Jimmy & Rosalynn Carter: The Georgia Years, 1924–74.* New York: Oxford University Press, 2010.

Goldberg, J. J. *Jewish Power: Inside the American Jewish Establishment.* Boston: Addison-Wesley, 1996.

Goldstein, Joel K. *The White House Vice Presidency: The Path to Significance, Mondale to Biden.* Lawrence: University Press of Kansas, 2016.

Graham, Katharine. *Personal History.* New York: Vintage, 1998.

Greider, William. *Secrets of the Temple: How the Federal Reserve Runs the Country.* New York: Simon & Schuster, 1989.

Guest, Iain. *Behind the Disappearances: Argentina's Dirty War Against Human Rights and the United Nations.* Philadelphia: University of Pennsylvania Press, 2000.

Herken, Gregg. *The Georgetown Set: Friends and Rivals in Cold War Washington.* New York: Random House, 2014.

Hersh, Seymour M. *The Price of Power: Kissinger in the Nixon White House.* New York: Summit, 1983.

———. *The Samson Option: Israel's Nuclear Arsenal and American Foreign Policy.* New York: Random House, 1991.

Hodgson, Godfrey. *All Things to All Men.* New York: Simon & Schuster, 1980.

Hoffman, Paul. *Lions of the Eighties: The Inside Story of the Powerhouse Law Firms.* New York: Doubleday, 1982.

Holzer, Harold. *The Presidents vs. the Press.* New York: Dutton, 2020.

Hulbert, Mark. *Interlock: The Untold Story of American Banks, Oil Interests, the Shah's Money, Debts, and the Outstanding Connections Between Them.* New York: Richardson & Snyder, 1982.

Huyser, General Robert E. *Mission to Tehran.* Southwold, U.K.: Bookthrift, 1990.

Jacobs, Meg. *Panic at the Pump: The Energy Crisis and the Transformation of American Politics in the 1970s.* New York: Hill and Wang, 2016.

Jordan, Hamilton. *A Boy from Georgia: Coming of Age in the Segregated South.* Edited by Kathleen Jordan. Athens: University of Georgia Press, 2015.

——. *Crisis: The Last Year of the Carter Presidency.* New York: J.P. Putnam's Sons, 1982.

——. *No Such Thing as a Bad Day: A Memoir.* Atlanta: Long Street Press, 2001.

Kamel, Mohamed Ibrahim. *The Camp David Accords: A Testimony by Sadat's Foreign Minister.* New York: Routledge & Kegan, 1987.

Kapusciniski, Ryszard. *Shah of Shahs.* New York: Harcourt, 1985.

Kaufman, Burton I., and Scott Kaufman. *The Presidency of James Earl Carter, Jr.* 2nd ed. Lawrence: University Press of Kansas, 2006.

Keefer, Edward C. *Harold Brown: Offsetting the Soviet Military Challenge, 1977–1981.* Washington D.C.: U.S. Department of Defense Historical Office, 2017.

Kendall, Joshua. *First Dads: Parenting and Politics from George Washington to Barack Obama.* New York: Grand Central, 2016.

Kennedy, Edward M. *True Compass: A Memoir.* New York: Twelve, 2009.

Kissinger, Henry. *White House Years.* Boston: Little Brown, 1979.

K'Meyer, Tracy Elaine. *Interracialism and Christian Community in the Postwar South: The Story of Koinonia Farm.* Charlottesville: University of Virginia Press, 1997.

Lance, Bert, with Bill Gilbert. *The Truth of the Matter: My Life In and Out of Politics.* New York: Summit Books, 1991.

Lance, LaBelle. *This Too Shall Pass.* New York: Bantam Books, 1978.

Lasch, Christopher. *The Culture of Narcissism: American Life in an Age of Diminishing Expectations.* New York: W.W. Norton, 1978.

Lee, Dallas. *The Cotton Patch Evidence: The Story of Clarence Jordan and the Koinonia Farm Experiment (1942–1970).* New York: HarperCollins, 1971.

Lemov, Michael R. *Car Safety Wars: One Hundred Years of Technology, Politics, and Death.* Madison and Teaneck, N.J.: Fairleigh Dickinson University Press, 2015.

Lewis, Finlay. *Mondale: Portrait of a Modern Politician.* New York: Harper & Row, 1984.

Marton, Kati. *Hidden Power: Presidential Marriages That Shaped Our History.* New York: Pantheon Books, 2001.

Massing, Michael. *The Fix: Solving the Nation's Drug Problem.* New York: Simon & Schuster, 1998.

Mattingly, Doreen J. *A Feminist in the White House: Midge Costanza, the Carter Years and America's Culture Wars.* New York: Oxford University Press, 2016.

Mattson, Kevin. *"What the Heck Are You Up To, Mr. President?": Jimmy Carter, America's "Malaise" and the Speech That Should Have Changed the Country.* New York: Bloomsbury, 2009.

Mazlish, Bruce, and Edwin Diamond. *Jimmy Carter: An Interpretive Biography.* New York: Simon & Schuster, 1979.

McAndrews, Lawrence J. *The Presidents and the Poor: America Battles Poverty 1964–2017.* Lawrence: University Press of Kansas, 2018.

McCullough, David G. *The Path Between the Seas: The Creation of the Panama Canal, 1870–1914.* New York: Simon & Schuster, 1977.

McFadden, Robert, Joseph B. Treaster, and Maurice Carroll. *No Hiding Place: The New York Times Inside Report on the Hostage Crisis.* New York: Times Books, 1981.

McGarr, Kathryn J. *The Whole Damn Deal: Robert Strauss and the Art of Politics.* New York: PublicAffairs, 2011.

McLellan, David S. *Cyrus Vance.* Totowa, N.J.: Rowman & Allanheld, 1985.

McLellan, Diana. *Ear on Washington.* New York: Arbor House, 1982.

Milani, Abbas. *The Shah.* New York: St. Martin's Press, 2011.

Miller, William Lee. *Yankee from Georgia: The Emergence of Jimmy Carter.* New York: Times Books, 1978.

Mitchell, Nancy. *Jimmy Carter in Africa: Race and the Cold War.* Stanford, Calif.: Stanford University Press, 2016.

Mondale, Walter F., and Dave Hage. *The Good Fight: A Life in Liberal Politics.* New York: Scribner, 2010.

Morris, Kenneth E. *Jimmy Carter, American Moralist.* Athens: University of Georgia Press, 1996.

Morris, Willie. *North Toward Home.* New York: Vintage, 2000.

———. *Terrains of the Heart: And Other Essays on Home.* Oxford, Miss.: Yoknapatawpha Press, 1981.

Niebuhr, Reinhold. *Reinhold Niebuhr: Major Works on Religion and Politics.* Edited by Elizabeth Sifton. New York: Library of America, 2015.

Norton, Howard, and Bob Slosser. *The Miracle of Jimmy Carter.* Plainfield, N.J.: Logos International, 1976.

October Surprise Task Force. *Joint Report of the Task Force to Investigate Certain Allegations Concerning the Holding of American Hostages by Iran in 1980.* Washington, D.C.: U.S. Government Printing Office, 1993.

Packer, George. *Our Man: Richard Holbrooke and the End of the American Century.* New York: Knopf, 2019.

Padgett, Dorothy. *Jimmy Carter: Elected President with Pocket Change and Peanuts.* Macon, Ga.: Mercer University Press, 2016.

Parry, Robert. *Trick or Treason: The 1980 October Surprise Mystery.* New York: Sheridan Square, 1993.

Perlstein, Rick. *Reaganland.* New York: Simon & Schuster, 2020.

Persico, Joseph E. *Casey: The Lives and Secrets of William J. Casey, from the OSS to the CIA.* New York: Viking Penguin, 1990.

Powell, Jody. *The Other Side of the Story.* New York: Morrow, 1984.

Quandt, William B. *Camp David: Peacemaking and Politics.* Washington, D.C.: Brookings, 1986.

Rabhan, David. *Conscious Coma: Ten Years in an Iranian Prison.* Saint John, N.B., Canada: Xlibris, 2018.

Ribuffo, Leo P. *Right, Center, Left.* New Brunswick, N.J.: Rutgers University Press, 1992.

Rubin, Ron. *A Jewish Professor's Political Punditry.* Syracuse, N.Y.: Syracuse University Press, 2013.

Ryan, Paul B. *The Iranian Rescue Mission: Why It Failed.* Annapolis, Md.: Naval Institute Press, 1985.

Sandbrook, Dominic. *Mad as Hell: The Crisis of the 1970s and the Rise of the Populist Right.* New York: Alfred A. Knopf, 2011.

Schlesinger, Andrew, and Stephen Schlesinger, eds. *The Letters of Arthur Schlesinger, Jr.* New York: Random House, 2013.

Schlesinger, Arthur M., Jr. *Journals: 1952–2000.* New York: Penguin Press, 2007.

Schlesinger, Robert. *White House Ghosts.* New York: Simon & Schuster, 2008.

Schmidli, William Michael. *The Fate of Freedom Elsewhere: Human Rights and U.S. Cold War Policy Toward Argentina.* Ithaca, N.Y.: Cornell University Press, 2017.

Schneller, Robert J., Jr. *Breaking the Color Barrier: The U.S. Naval Academy's First Black Midshipmen and the Struggle for Racial Equality.* New York: New York University Press, 2007.

Schwartz, Thomas A. *Henry Kissinger and American Power: A Political Biography.* New York: Hill and Wang, 2020.

Shapiro, Ira. *The Last Great Senate: Courage and Statesmanship in Times of Crisis.* New York: PublicAffairs, 2012.

Shawcross, William. *The Shah's Last Ride: The Fate of an Ally.* New York: Simon & Schuster, 1988.

Shirley, Craig. *Rendezvous with Destiny: Ronald Reagan and the Campaign That Changed America.* Wilmington, Del.: Intercollegiate Studies Institute, 2009.

Sick, Gary. *All Fall Down: America's Tragic Encounter with Iran.* New York: Random House, 1985.

———. *October Surprise: America's Hostages in Iran and the Election of Ronald Reagan.* New York: Crown, 1991.

Sklar, Holly, ed. *Trilateralism: The Trilateral Commission and Elite Planning for World Management.* Boston: South End Press, 1980.

Smith, Gaddis. *Morality, Reason and Power.* New York: Hill and Wang, 1986.

Sorensen, Ted. *Counselor: A Life at the Edge of History.* New York: HarperCollins, 2008.

Stein, Judith. *Pivotal Decade: How the United States Traded Factories for Finance in the Seventies.* New Haven, Conn.: Yale University Press, 2010.

Stewart, James B. *The Partners: Inside America's Most Powerful Law Firms.* New York: Simon & Schuster, 1983.

Stroud, Kandy. *How Jimmy Won: The Victory Campaign from Plains to the White House.* New York: William Morrow, 1977.

Strout, Richard L. *TRB: Views and Perspectives on the Presidency.* New York: Macmillan, 1979.

Sullivan, William H. *Mission to Iran.* New York: W.W. Norton, 1981.

———. *Obbligato: Notes on a Foreign Service Career.* New York: W.W. Norton, 1980.

Temko, Ned. *To Win or to Die: A Personal Portrait of Menachem Begin.* New York: William Morrow, 1987.

Thompson, Hunter S. *The Great Shark Hunt: Strange Tales from a Strange Time.* New York: Simon & Schuster, 2003.

Turner, Stansfield. *Secrecy and Democracy: The CIA in Transition.* Boston: Houghton Mifflin, 1985.

Vaïsse, Justin. *Zbigniew Brzezinski: America's Grand Strategist.* Cambridge, Mass.: Harvard University Press, 2018.

Vance, Cyrus. *Hard Choices: Critical Years in America's Foreign Policy.* New York: Simon & Schuster, 1983.

Vidal, Gore. *Palimpsest: A Memoir.* New York: Random House, 1995.

Volcker, Paul A., with Christine Harper. *Keeping At It: The Quest for Sound Money and Good Government.* New York: PublicAffairs, 2018.

von Hoffman, Nicholas. *Citizen Cohn: The Life and Times of Roy Cohn.* New York: Doubleday, 1988.

Ward, Jon. *Camelot's End: Kennedy Versus Carter and the Fight That Broke the Democratic Party.* New York: Twelve, 2019.

Weizman, Ezcr. *The Battle for Peace.* New York: Bantam Books, 1981.

Wexler, Laura. *Fire in a Canebrake: The Last Mass Lynching in America.* New York: Scribner, 2004.

Whipple, Chris. *The Gatekeepers: How the White House Chiefs of Staff Define Every Presidency.* New York: Broadway Books, 2018.

———. *The Spy Masters: How the CIA Directors Shape History and the Future.* New York: Scribner, 2020.

Wilkie, Curtis. *Dixie: A Personal Odyssey Through Historic Events That Shaped the Modern South.* New York: Scribner, 2002.

Wills, Garry. *Under God: Religion and American Politics.* New York, Simon & Schuster, 1990.

Witcover, Jules. *Marathon: The Pursuit of the Presidency, 1972–1976.* New York: Viking Press, 1977.

Woodward, Bob. *Veil: The Secret Wars of the CIA, 1981–1987.* New York: Simon & Schuster, 1987.

Woodward, C. Vann. *The Burden of Southern History.* Baton Rouge: Louisiana State University Press, 2008.

Wooten, James. *Dasher: The Roots and the Rising of Jimmy Carter.* New York: Summit Books, 1978.

Wright, Lawrence. *Thirteen Days in September: Carter, Begin and Sadat at Camp David.* New York: Alfred A. Knopf, 2014.

Yaqub, Salim. *Imperfect Strangers: Americans, Arabs, and U.S.-Middle East Relations in the 1970s.* Ithaca, N.Y.: Cornell University Press, 2016.

Young, Andrew. *An Easy Burden: The Civil Rights Movement and the Transformation of America.* New York: HarperCollins, 1996.

Zelizer, Julian E. *Jimmy Carter.* New York: Times Books, 2010.

ARTICLES, ESSAYS, AND REPORTS

Adamson, Terry. "Hardworking Bell Leaves a Legacy to Be Appreciated." *Journal of Southern Legal History* 18, nos. 1 and 2 (2010).

AJC Staff. "Hundreds More Were Lynched in the South Than Previously Known: Report." AJC.com, June 14, 2017. https://www.ajc.com/news/local/hundreds-more-were-lynched-the-south-than-previously-known-report/gOEGtsSud4utD6Uiqkx1LN/.

Altman, Lawrence K., M.D. "The Shah's Health: A Political Gamble." *New York Times,* May 17, 1981.

Andersen, Martin Edwin. "Kissinger and the 'Dirty War.'" *The Nation,* October 31, 1987.

Auletta, Ken. "The Waiting-for-Jimmy Blues." *New York,* July 12, 1976.

Bell, Griffin, III. "Citizen Lawyer." *Journal of Southern Legal History* 18, nos. 1 and 2 (2010).

Bird, Kai. "Citizen Carter: The Very Model of an Ex-President." *The Nation,* November 12, 1990.

Bluestein, Greg. "Ex-governor Investigated in 1946 Lynchings." NBCNews.com, June 15, 2007. http://www.nbcnews.com/id/19251476/ns/us_news-life/t/ex-governor-investigated-lynchings/#.Xp4QFlNKhBx.

Bond, Julian. "Why I Don't Support Jimmy Carter." *The Nation,* April 17, 1976.

Brill, Steven. "How a Legal Ploy Backfired." *American Lawyer,* reprinted in *Washington Post,* November 4, 1979.

———. "Jimmy Carter's Pathetic Lies." *Harper's,* March 1976.

Brinkley, Douglas. "Out of the Loop." *New York Times,* December 29, 2002.

———. "What It Takes." *New Yorker,* October 21, 1996.

Brookings Middle East Study Group. "Toward Peace in the Middle East, December 1975." Washington, D.C.: Brookings Institution Press, 1975.

Burr, William, and Avner Cohen, eds. "New Evidence on 22 September 1979 Vela Event." National Security Archive, Briefing Book #570, December 6, 2016. https://nsarchive.gwu.edu/briefing-book/nuclear-vault/2016-12-06/vela-incident-south-atlantic-mystery-flash-september-1979.

Carter, Hodding, III. "Life Inside the Carter State Department." *Playboy,* February 1981.

Clymer, Kenton. "Jimmy Carter, Human Rights, and Cambodia." *Diplomatic History,* April 2003.

Cochran, Jeff. "When Jimmy Carter Met Bob Dylan." *Like the Dew: A Journal of Southern Culture & Politics,* February 8, 2010.

Cogan, Charles. "Partners in Time: The CIA and Afghanistan Since 1979." *World Policy Journal,* Summer 1993.

Conaway, James. "Willie Morris in the Land of Faulkner." *Washington Post,* December 28, 1982.

Crawford, Clare. "A Story of Love and Rehabilitation: The Ex-Con in the White House." *People,* March 14, 1977.

Dawidoff, Nicholas. "The Riddle of Jimmy Carter." *Rolling Stone,* February 2, 2011.

Drew, Elizabeth. "Phase: In Search of a Definition." *New Yorker,* August 27, 1979.

Epps, Garret. "The Myth of Hamilton Jordan." *Washington Post Magazine,* December 17, 1978.

Fallows, James. "History vs. Loyalty." *Washington Monthly,* June 1999.

———. "The Passionless Presidency." *The Atlantic,* May 1979.

Friedman, Robert I. "The Settlers." *New York Review of Books,* June 15, 1989.

Gati, Charles. "The World According to Zbig." *Politico,* November 27, 2013.

Gershman, Carl. "The Andrew Young Affair." *Commentary,* November 1979.

Giddins, Gary. "Jazz at Jimmy's." *Village Voice,* June 26, 1978.

Goldman, Peter. "Sizing Up Carter." *Newsweek,* September 13, 1976.

Gross, Samantha. "What Iran's 1979 Revolution Meant for US and Global Oil Markets." Brookings.edu, March 5, 2019. https://www.brookings.edu/blog/order-from-chaos/2019/03/05/what-irans-1979-revolution-meant-for-us-and-global-oil-markets/.

Hendrickson, Paul. "Jimmy Carter, Casting Back." *Washington Post,* May 22, 1988.

Herbers, John. "Aftermath of the Andrew Young Affair: Blacks, Jews and Carter—All Could Suffer Greatly." *New York Times,* September 6, 1979.

Holland, J. William. "The Great Gamble: Jimmy Carter and the 1979 Energy Crisis." *Prologue,* Spring 1990.

Inscoe, John C. "Georgia in 1860." *New Georgia Encyclopedia,* September 9, 2010. https://www.georgiaencyclopedia.org/articles/history-archaeology /georgia-1860.

Jackson, Brooks. "Killer Rabbit Attacks Carter in Canoe—Loses." *Los Angeles Times,* August 29, 1979.

Jauvert, Vincent. "Les révélations d'un ancien conseiller de Carter." *Le Nouvel Observateur,* January 15–21, 1998. Translation available at https://dgibbs .faculty.arizona.edu/brzezinski_interview.

Kifner, John. "Putting the Hostages' Lives First." *New York Times,* May 17, 1981.

Kirkpatrick, David D. "Bank's Secret Campaign to Win Entry to U.S. for Shah of Iran." *New York Times,* December 29, 2019.

Kirkpatrick, Jeane J. "Dictatorships and Double Standards." *Commentary,* November 1979.

Klein, Joe. "Hamilton Jordan and Jody Powell: The White House Whiz Kids." *Rolling Stone,* May 19, 1977.

Kramer, Michael. "Blacks and Jews." *New York,* February 4, 1985.

Lathan, Aaron. "Hamilton Jordan: Slob in the White House." *Esquire,* March 1977.

Luce, Clare Booth. "The Light at the End of the Tunnel of Love: Jimmy Carter's Christian Socialism." *National Review,* November 12, 1976.

MacPherson, Myra. "Trilateralists to Abound in Carter's White House." *Washington Post,* January 16, 1977.

Mailer, Norman. "The Search for Carter." *New York Times,* September 26, 1976.

"The Man in Tempo." *Time,* January 11, 1954.

McDonald, Darren J. "Blessed Are the Policy Makers: Jimmy Carter's Faith-Based Approach to the Arab-Israeli Conflict." *Diplomatic History,* June 2015, pp. 452–76.

Moe, Richard. "Health Care for All: A Cautionary Tale from the 1970s." History News Network, April 14, 2019.

———. "The Making of the Modern Vice Presidency." *Carter-Mondale Letter* 10, no. 2 (Winter 2015).

Mohr, Charles. "Carter Credibility Issue: Calley and Vietnam War." *New York Times,* May 21, 1976.

Morris, Willie. "Of Northern Fears, Southern Realities and Jimmy Carter." *New York Times,* July 8, 1976.

Moss, Robert. "Eugene Talmadge and the Art of Political Barbecue." Southern Foodways Alliance, southernfoodways.blogspot.com, November 11, 2013.

Parry, Robert. "Second Thoughts on October Surprise." *Consortium News,* June 8, 2013.

Polner, Murray. "Four Hours in My Lai." *Washington Monthly,* May 1, 1992.

"The President's Boys." *Time,* June 6, 1977.

Quinn, Sally. "The Carter Style: Of the People, For the People." *Washington Post,* January 22, 1977.

———. "Making Capital Gains." *Washington Post,* November 15, 1992.

———. "Where Did All the Good Times Go?" *Washington Post,* December 18, 1977.

Randolph, Eleanor. "Carter Has a Hare-Raising Experience on Plains Trip." *Los Angeles Times,* August 30, 1979.

Raviv, Shaun. "The Ghosts of My Lai." *Smithsonian,* January 2018. https://www .smithsonianmag.com/history/ghosts-my-lai-180967497/.

Reeves, Richard. "Shhh, Don't Wake the Democrats." *New York,* July 26, 1976.

Roper Center for Public Opinion Research. "How Groups Voted in 1980." https:// ropercenter.cornell.edu/how-groups-voted-1980.

Rossiter, Caleb, with Anne-Marie Smith. "Human Rights: The Carter Record, the Reagan Reaction." *International Policy Report,* September 1984, pp. 6–18.

Sanders, Randy. "The Sad Duty of Politics: Jimmy Carter and the Issue of Race in His 1970 Gubernatorial Campaign." *Georgia Historical Quarterly* 76, no. 3 (Fall 1992).

Scheer, Robert. "Jimmy, We Hardly Know Y'all." *Playboy,* November 1976.

Schindler, Alexander M. "The Jews and Carter." *New York Times,* May 8, 1978.

Shapiro, Harvey. "A Conversation with Jimmy Carter." *New York Times Book Review,* June 17, 1977.

Shapiro, T. Rees. "Wesley A. Brown, First Black Naval Academy Graduate." *Washington Post,* May 25, 2012.

Sherrill, Robert. "Hostages." *Grand Street,* Autumn 1985.

Shrum, Robert. "Bert Lance: Jimmy's Bad Risk." *New Times,* September 2, 1977.

Smith, Terence. "Why Carter Admitted the Shah." *New York Times,* May 17, 1981.

Stern, Mark Joseph. "Carter's Quiet Revolution." *Slate,* July 14, 2019.

Stone, I. F. "The Hope." *New York Review of Books,* October 26, 1978.

Swanberg, Wendy. "The Gossip Makes the News: Washington Reporting in the Carter Years." Master's thesis, University of Wisconsin–Madison, 2005.

Thompson, Hunter. "Jimmy Carter and the Great Leap of Faith." *Rolling Stone,* June 3, 1976.

Weiss, Leonard. "Flash from the Past: Why an Apparent Israeli Nuclear Test in 1979 Matters Today." *Bulletin of Atomic Scientists,* September 8, 2015.

Will, George. "A 1946 Lynching Is Still Haunting Us." *Washington Post,* June 6, 2020.

Wills, Garry. "Reading the Carter Riddle." *New York Review of Books,* April 28, 1977.

Wolfe, Alan. "The Two Faces of Carter." *The Nation,* December 18, 1976.

Wooten, James T. "Carter's Georgia Guru." *New York Times Magazine,* March 20, 1977.

Young, Andrew. "Why I Support Jimmy Carter." *The Nation,* April 3, 1976.

INTERVIEWS CONDUCTED BY THE AUTHOR

Aaron, David. April 12, 2016.

Adamson, Terry. December 8, 2015; June 25, 2017; January 9, 2020.

Beard, Tom. February 18, 2016.

Beck, Jay. February 9, 2016; June 30, 2018.

Blum, Barbara. November 4, 2016.

Bolling, Landrum. May 10, 2016.

Bourne, Peter. October 17, 2016.

Brzezinski, Zbigniew. May 4, 2016; June 21, 2016; June 25, 2016.

Burnett, Scott. June 30, 2018.

Butler, Landon. January 13, 2016; April 21, 2016.

Carp, Bertram. January 12, 2016.

Carter, Chip. January 24, 2017; June 30, 2018.

Carter, Jimmy. February 11, 2016; June 24–25, 2016; June 23–24, 2017; September 14, 2017; July 29–30, 2018; June 28, 2019.

Claybrook, Joan. May 9, 2016.

Cleland, Max. May 7, 2016.

Coffey, Shelby. June 27, 2016.

Cohen, Roberta. December 13, 2015.

Dalton, John. June 30, 2018.

Dine, Tom. January 7, 2016.

Doolittle, Jerome. January 31, 2018.

Eizenstat, Stuart. April 27, 2018.

Fallows, James. March 29, 2016.

Fitzpatrick, William. January 29, 2016.

Francis, Les. June 24, 2016.

Free, Jim. April 18, 2016.

Giddins, Gary. December 6, 2018.

Gotbaum, Josh. January 11, 2016.

Granum, Rex. December 16, 2015.

Greenstein, Robert. January 27, 2016.

Harman, Jane. May 5, 2016.

Hertzberg, Hendrik. March 31, 2016.

Hochman, Steve. August 5, 2019.

Hunter, Robert. August 24, 2016.

Kraft, Tim. June 27, 2016.

Lewis, Finlay. December 15, 2015.

MacPherson, Myra. August 7, 2017.

Mathews, Jessica Tuchman. March 29, 2016.

McCleary, Joel. March 23, 2016; May 3, 2016.

McCloy, John J. December 3, 1985.

McHenry, Donald. January 5, 2016.

Miller, William. May 3, 2016.

Mitchell, Bunny. July 31, 2017; August 21, 2017.

Moe, Richard. December 17, 2015; May 2, 2016; December 22, 2017.

Mondale, Walter. June 23, 2016; September 13, 2016.

Moore, Frank. June 23, 2016; June 25, 2016.

Moses, Alfred. March 25, 2016.

Nimitz, Matthew. March 6, 2020.

Onek, Joseph N. April 28, 2016.

Osnos, Peter. March 6, 2020.

Padgett, Dorothy. June 25, 2016.

Parry, Robert. March 25, 2016.

Pertschuk, Michael. August 21, 2019.

Peters, Charles. May 7, 2016.

Pottinger, Stan. February 11, 2020.

Powell, Nan. June 28, 2019.

Rabhan, David. September 14, 2019; October 17, 2019.

Rafshoon, Gerald. December 7, 2015; February 11, 2016; June 23, 2016; June 24, 2016; June 25–26, 2016; October 7, 2016; June 16, 2017; January 10, 2020; August 24, 2020.

Randolph, Eleanor. October 27, 2018.

Rendon, John. December 15, 2015.

Rogoff, Alice. May 5, 2016; May 13, 2016.

Rowe, James. October 20, 2018.

Rubenstein, David. April 29, 2016; June 19, 2016.

Salzberg, John. March 23, 2018.

Schneider, Mark. January 11, 2016.

Schneiders, Greg. April 18, 2016.

Shaw, Jack. May 25, 2013.

Sick, Gary. August 5, 1985; May 24, 2018.

Smith, Alicia. April 15, 2016.

Vance, Cyrus, Jr. March 21, 2017.

Vanden Heuvel, William. October 28, 2019.

Wellford, Harrison. June 22, 2016; October 10, 2016; October 17, 2016.

Wides, Burt. December 4, 2015.

Wise, Phil. February 9, 2016.

Young, Andrew. August 6, 2019.

Zein, Mustafa. October 8, 2012.

ORAL HISTORIES, INTERVIEWS, AND SPEECHES

Brzezinski, Zbigniew. Oral history, February 18, 1982. Presidential Oral Histories, Miller Center of Public Affairs, University of Virginia. https://miller center.org/the-presidency/presidential-oral-histories/zbigniew-brzezinski -oral-history-assistant-president.

Califano, Joseph. Oral history by Edward Berkowitz, August 31, 1995. Donated Historical Materials, Jimmy Carter Presidential Library.

Carter, Chip. Interview by Bob Short, June 23, 2008. Reflections on Georgia Politics, Oral History Collection, University of Georgia. https://kaltura .uga.edu/media/t/1_mjtxebqx.

Carter, Jack. Oral history, June 25, 2003. Jimmy Carter Presidential Library.

Carter, Jimmy. Oral history, February 18, 1982. Presidential Oral Histories, Miller Center of Public Affairs, University of Virginia.

———. Oral history, May 11, 1988. National Park Service Interview, Jimmy Carter Presidential Library.

Carter, Jimmy, and Kim Carter. Seminar discussion, Carter Reunion, June 30, 2018. Recorded by the author.

Carter, Jimmy and Rosalynn. Oral history, 1985. National Park Service, Jimmy Carter Presidential Library.

———. Oral history, May 11, 1988. National Park Service Interview, Jimmy Carter Presidential Library.

Cooks, Stoney. Interview by Tom Dent, July 28, 1981. Tulane University. https:// digitallibrary.tulane.edu/islandora/object/tulane%3A48372.

Eizenstat, Stuart. Oral history, January 29–30, 1982. Presidential Oral Histories, Miller Center of Public Affairs, University of Virginia. https://millercenter .org/the-presidency/presidential-oral-histories/stuart-eizenstat-oral -history.

English, Ida. Oral history, December 21, 1985. National Park Service Interview, Jimmy Carter Presidential Library.

Fallows, James. Exit interview, November 14, 1978. Jimmy Carter Presidential Library.

Hertzberg, Hendrik. Exit interview, December 10, 1980. Jimmy Carter Presidential Library.

Hoyt, Mary Finch. Exit interview, undated (circa December 1980). Jimmy Carter Presidential Library.

Ignatius, David. Eulogy for Zbigniew Brzezinski, June 9, 2017.

Jackson, Ruth. Oral history, December 20, 1985. National Park Service Interview, Jimmy Carter Presidential Library.

Kahn, Alfred E. Oral history, December 10–11, 1981. Presidential Oral Histories, Miller Center of Public Affairs, University of Virginia. https://millercenter .org/the-presidency/presidential-oral-histories/alfred-e-kahn-oral-history.

Kirbo, Charles. Oral history, January 5, 1983. Presidential Oral Histories, Miller Center of Public Affairs, University of Virginia. https://millercenter.org /the-presidency/presidential-oral-histories/charles-kirbo-oral-history -advisor-close-friend.

Kraft, Tim. Exit interview by Marie Allen, August 31, 1979. Jimmy Carter Presidential Library.

Lance, Bert. Oral history, May 12, 1982. Presidential Oral Histories, Miller Center of Public Affairs, University of Virginia. https://millercenter.org/the -presidency/presidential-oral-histories/bert-lance-oral-history.

Maynes, Charles William. Oral history, August 14, 1998. Library of Congress.

Metrinko, Michael. Oral history, August 26, 1999. Association for Diplomatic Studies and Training Foreign Affairs Oral History Project, Georgetown University. https://www.adst.org/OH%20TOCs/Metrinko,%20Mike.toc.pdf ?_ga=2.140164021.707592957.1575482293-350211411.1574618593.

Moore, Frank. Oral history, 1980, 2002. Jimmy Carter Presidential Library.

———. Oral history, September 18–19, 1981, Presidential Oral Histories, Miller Center of Public Affairs, University of Virginia. https://millercenter.org /the-presidency/presidential-oral-histories/frank-moore-oral-history.

———. Oral history, July 30–31, 2002, Jimmy Carter Presidential Library.

Onek, Joseph N. Oral history interviews by Edward Berkowitz, August 10, 1995. Donated Historical Material, Jimmy Carter Presidential Library.

Powell, Jody. Oral history, December 17–18, 1981. Presidential Oral Histories, Miller Center of Public Affairs, University of Virginia. https://millercenter .org/the-presidency/presidential-oral-histories/jody-powell-oral-history.

Rafshoon, Gerald M. Oral history, April 8, 1983.

———. Presidential Oral Histories, Miller Center of Public Affairs, University of Virginia. https://millercenter.org/the-presidency/presidential-oral-histories /gerald-m-rafshoon-oral-history.

Rubenstein, David. Exit interview, December 3, 1980. Jimmy Carter Presidential Library.

Spann, Gloria Carter. Oral history, December 7, 1988. National Park Service Interview, Jimmy Carter Presidential Library.

Talmadge, Herman, with Jack Nelson, July 15 and 24, 1975. Southern Oral History Collection, no. 4007.

Thompson, Hunter S. CBC interview, 1977.

Watson, Jack, Jr. Oral history, April 17–18, 1981. Presidential Oral Histories, Miller Center of Public Affairs, University of Virginia. https://miller center.org/the-presidency/presidential-oral-histories/jack-h-watson-jr -oral-history.

Williams, Jan. Oral history, December 20, 1985. National Park Service Interview, Jimmy Carter Presidential Library.

Wise, David. Oral history, December 17, 1985. National Park Service Interview, Jimmy Carter Presidential Library.

Wise, P. J. Oral history, December 20, 1985. National Park Service Interview, Jimmy Carter Presidential Library.

Young, Andrew. Transcript of videotaped interview by Dan Shilon, August 14, 1979. Jerusalem Domestic Television. "Andrew Young, 1/20/79–8/17/79" folder, box 16, Special Advisor to the President. Moses Papers. Jimmy Carter Presidential Library.

DIARIES, UNPUBLISHED PAPERS, VIDEOS

Butler, Landon. Unpublished diary, 1976–1980.

Carter, Jimmy. Daily diary. https://www.jimmycarterlibrary.gov/assets/docu ments/diary/.

———. Unpublished portions of Camp David diary.

Demme, Jonathan, dir. *Jimmy Carter, Man from Plains*. Sony Pictures, 2007.

Doolittle, Jerome. Unpublished diary.

Jordan, Hamilton. Unprocessed papers, Jimmy Carter Presidential Library.

Kirbo, Charles. Unprocessed papers, Jimmy Carter Presidential Library.

Kopple, Barbara, dir. *Desert One*. History Channel, September 2019.

Kraft, Tim. Unpublished diary and notebooks.

PBS NewsHour. "Former President Jimmy Carter Addresses Cancer and Treatment." YouTube, August 20, 2015. https://www.youtube.com/watch?v=CfOz WiJWg20.

Race for the White House 1976: Jimmy Carter vs. Gerald Ford. Aired September 2020 on CNN.

Saunders, Andrew, dir. *Race for the White House 1980: Ronald Reagan vs. Jimmy Carter*. Aired February 2020 on CNN.

Thompson, Hunter S. "Hunter S. Thompson Remembers Jimmy Carter's Capti-
   vating Bob Dylan Speech (1974)." CBC. http://www.openculture.com/2012
   /07/hunter_s_thompson_remembers_jimmy_carters_captivating_bob
   _dylan_speech_1974.html.
Wharton, Mary, dir. *Jimmy Carter: Rock & Roll President*. CNN, 2020.

GOVERNMENT ARCHIVES

George H. W. Bush Presidential Library.
Jimmy Carter Presidential Library.
National Archives.
U.S. Office of the Historian. Foreign Relations of the United States: Jimmy Carter
   Administration (1977–1980). https://history.state.gov/historicaldocuments
   /carter.

   1. Foundations of Foreign Policy
   2. Human Rights and Humanitarian Affairs
   3. Foreign Economic Policy
   4. National Security Policy
   5. European Security, 1977–1983
   6. Soviet Union
   7. Poland, 1977–1981
   8. Arab-Israeli Dispute, January 1977–August 1978
   9. Arab-Israeli Dispute, August 1978–December 1980
   10. Arab-Israeli Dispute, August 1978–December 1980, 2nd rev. ed.
   14. Afghanistan
   15. China
   17. Central America
   18. Southern Africa
   19. Horn of Africa
   20. Sub-Saharan Africa
   21. North Africa
   22. Middle East Region; Arabian Peninsula
   23. South Asia
   24. Eastern Europe
   25. Cyprus; Turkey; Greece
   26. Southeast Asia and the Pacific
   27. Mexico, Cuba, and the Caribbean
   28. South America; Latin America Region
   30. Arms Control and Nonproliferation

32. Organization and Management of Foreign Policy
33. Panama
34. Public Diplomacy

OTHER SOURCES

Richard V. Allen Papers, Hoover Institution Archives, Stanford University.

Camp David Accords. September 17, 1978. http://avalon.law.yale.edu/20th_cen
tury/campdav.asp.

The Carter Center home page: www.cartercenter.org.

Jimmy Carter Presidential Library. Office of Staff Secretary collection, Presidential Files series, folder 10/1/79, container 132. https://www.jimmycarter
library.gov/digital_library/sso/148878/132/SSO_148878_132_16.pdf.

William Casey Papers, Hoover Institution Archives, Stanford University.

CREST (Central Intelligence Agency Records Search Tool): The CREST system is
the publicly accessible repository of the subset of CIA records reviewed
under the twenty-five-year program in electronic format (manually reviewed
and released records are accessioned directly into the National Archives in
their original format). Over eleven million pages have been released in
electronic format and reside on the CREST database, www.cia.gov/library
/readingroom/collection/crest-25-year-program-archive.

In re Hamilton Jordan, 745 F.2d 1574 (D.C. Cir. 1984). https://law.justia.com
/cases/federal/appellate-courts/F2/745/1574/128691/.

John J. McCloy Papers, Amherst College.

National Security Archive. "The Pentagon and the CIA Sent Mixed Message to
the Argentine Military." March 28, 2003. http://nsarchive.gwu.edu/NSAEBB
/NSAEBB85/.

"The Vela Flash: Forty Years Ago," National Security Archive, September 22,
2019, https://nsarchive.gwu.edu/briefing-book/nuclear-vault/2019-09-22
/vela-flash-forty-years-ago.

Notes

PROLOGUE

3 **"Tight as bark on a tree"** Nicholas Dawidoff, "Riddle of Jimmy Carter," *Rolling Stone.*

3 **nonimperial presidency** Bruce Mazlish and Edwin Diamond, *Jimmy Carter,* p. 246.

4 **"She was innocent"** Kai Bird, recorded conversation, February 14, 2016, Plains, Georgia.

4 **a home bought for her** Gerald Rafshoon interview, June 16, 2017.

5 **"utter failure as a national leader"** Dominic Sandbrook, *Mad as Hell,* p. 400.

5 **"mediocre presidency"** Burton I. Kaufman and Scott Kaufman, *The Presidency of James Earl Carter, Jr.,* p. 250.

5 **"a decent man if an inept"** Gore Vidal, *Palimpsest,* p. 73.

5 **"killer rabbit"** Brooks Jackson, "Killer Rabbit Attacks Carter in Canoe—Loses," AP, *Los Angeles Times,* August 29, 1979.

5 **"inordinate fear of communism"** *New York Times,* May 23, 1977.

5 **"first American president to take"** Garry Wills, *Under God,* p. 250.

7 **"Jimmy Carter really does"** Thomas Frank, *The People, No,* p. 205.

8 **"too many of us now"** Mattson, *"What the Heck Are You Up To, Mr. President?"* p. 159.

9 **"whip his ass"** Carter diary, June 12, 1979, and June 20, 1979, *White House Diary,* pp. 326 and 332.

9 **"meanest men"** Hunter S. Thompson, CBC interview, 1977; www.openculture .com/2012/07/hunter_s_thompson_remembers_jimmy_carters_captivating _bob_dylan_speech_1974.html.

9 **"government is not the solution"** Rick Perlstein, *Reaganland,* p. 914.

10 **"These wounds are very deep"** Mattson, *"What the Heck Are You Up To, Mr. President?"* pp. 207–17.

10 **"The American Negro"** James Baldwin, *The Fire Next Time,* p. 101.

11 **"Our society is steadily growing"** Jimmy Carter, *Living Faith,* p. 111.

CHAPTER 1: THE PAST IS NEVER DEAD

15 **360-acre farm** E. Stanly Godbold, Jr., *Jimmy & Rosalynn Carter*, p. 18.

16 **blew a smoke ring** Jimmy Carter oral history, May 11, 1988, p. 130.

16 **"The greatest day in my life"** Jimmy Carter oral history, May 11, 1988, p. 139.

16 **"Daddy was a very aggressive"** Jimmy Carter oral history, May 11, 1988, p. 4; Jimmy Carter, *An Hour Before Daylight*, pp. 238–39.

16 **"I remember a man named"** Jimmy Carter oral history, May 11, 1988, p. 215.

17 **"Everything Earl Carter touched"** Hugh Carter, *Cousin Beedie and Cousin Hot*, p. 51. Earl's farm store sold goods exclusively to his tenants. Locals called these little groceries "commissaries." See also David Wise oral history, p. 19, box 2.

17 **thought them boring** Carter, *Cousin Beedie and Cousin Hot*, p. 44.

17 **"very accomplished tennis player"** Jimmy Carter oral history, May 11, 1988, p. 167.

17 **net worth was a quarter million dollars** Carter, *Cousin Beedie and Cousin Hot*, p. 91; Godbold, *Jimmy & Rosalynn Carter*, p. 17; Kenneth E. Morris, *Jimmy Carter, American Moralist*, p. 29.

17 **"There was always an argument"** Jimmy Carter oral history, May 11, 1988, p. 218.

18 **"Jimmy and them"** Peter Goldman, "Sizing Up Carter," *Newsweek*. Decades later, A. D. Davis was convicted of manslaughter. Jonathan Alter, *His Very Best*, p. 41.

18 **William Decker Johnson** Godbold, *Jimmy & Rosalynn Carter*, p. 22.

18 **"like a puppy dog"** Carter, *An Hour Before Daylight*, p. 36.

18 **"aristocrat"** and a **"queen"** Godbold, *Jimmy & Rosalynn Carter*, p. 22.

19 **"She was nice and gentle"** Jimmy Carter oral history, May 11, 1988, pp. 229–30.

19 **"More than anyone else"** Carter, *An Hour Before Daylight*, p. 53.

19 **"She more or less raised us"** Gloria Carter Spann oral history, December 7, 1988, p. 21, box 2.

19 *Amos 'n' Andy:* Jimmy Carter, *Living Faith*, p. 10.

20 **"deep South dead since"** Curtis Wilkie, *Dixie*, p. 18. Wilkie is quoting William Faulkner's *Absalom, Absalom!*

20 **"good and evil"** Godbold, *Jimmy & Rosalynn Carter*, pp. 80 and 226; Harvey Shapiro, "A Conversation with Jimmy Carter," *New York Times Book Review*.

20 **"The past is never dead"** William Faulkner, *Requiem for a Nun*, p. 73.

20 **"We deliberately set ourselves"** Wilkie, *Dixie*, p. 18.

20 **462,000 slaves** John C. Inscoe, "Georgia in 1860," *New Georgia Encyclopedia*.

20 **"I grew up in one"** Carter, *An Hour Before Daylight*, pp. 17 and 19.

20 **"was an accepted fact"** Carter, *An Hour Before Daylight*, p. 20.

21 **50 percent of the residents** Andrew Young, "Why I Support Jimmy Carter," *The Nation*.

21 **"Jimmy Carter's daddy"** Nicholas Dawidoff, "The Riddle of Jimmy Carter," *Rolling Stone*.

21 **"Oh, he said things"** Kandy Stroud, *How Jimmy Won*, pp. 121–22; Miss Lillian herself was known to have used the n-word, once in the presence of the journalist Eleanor Randolph. Randolph, "The Carter Complex," *Esquire*, November 1, 1977.

21 "We didn't have electricity" Jimmy Carter oral history, p. 182. National Park Service Interview, May 11, 1988.

22 "the South is another land" W. J. Cash, *The Mind of the South,* p. xlvii.

22 "attachment to fictions" Cash, *Mind of the South,* pp. 428–29.

22 "unthinking sadism" Willie Morris, *North Toward Home,* p. 90.

22 "manners and morals" James Conaway, "Willie Morris in the Land of Faulkner," *Washington Post.*

23 "After my brother passed" Ruth Jackson oral history, p. 9, box 2.

23 "My Daddy was not a carpenter" Gloria Carter Spann oral history, December 7, 1988, p. 72, box 2.

23 "We in the South love" William Anderson, *The Wild Man from Sugar Creek,* pp. 209–10.

23 Talmadge spent the night Godbold, *Jimmy & Rosalynn Carter,* p. 17.

23 "I can carry any county" Herman Talmadge oral history with Jack Nelson; Robert Moss, "Eugene Talmadge and the Art of Political Barbecue."

24 the scene of 589 lynchings AJC Staff, "Hundreds More Were Lynched in the South Than Previously Known," AJC.com.

24 "He turned against Roosevelt" Jimmy Carter oral history, May 11, 1988, p. 140.

24 sharing a meal with a Black man Carter, *Living Faith,* p. 53.

24 The sanitarium paid her $4 Jimmy Carter oral history, May 11, 1988, p. 4.

24 "She was the first white lady" Ruth Jackson oral history, p. 9.

24 "It seems to me" Jimmy Carter, *A Remarkable Mother,* p. 69.

25 "I didn't care" Jimmy Carter and Kim Carter, transcribed seminar discussion, June 30, 2018, p. 3.

25 shared a bourbon nightcap Godbold, *Jimmy & Rosalynn Carter,* p. 16.

25 "We had too much money" Godbold, *Jimmy & Rosalynn Carter,* p. 14.

25 "She was considered the most" Carter, *Cousin Beedie and Cousin Hot,* p. 202.

25 "even lie on his bed" Carter, *Cousin Beedie and Cousin Hot,* p. 31.

25 "But the strong memory" Jimmy Carter oral history, May 11, 1988, p. 200.

25 "We weren't allowed to talk" Gloria Carter Spann oral history, December 7, 1988, p. 30, box 2.

25 "Every Christmas when I was asked" Jimmy Carter oral history, May 11, 1988, p. 211.

26 Tolstoy's *War and Peace* Jimmy Carter oral history, December 8, 1988, p. 75.

26 "I would study my plate" Carter, *Cousin Beedie and Cousin Hot,* p. 42.

26 "We could take a running" Gloria Carter Spann oral history, December 7, 1988, p. 8, box 2.

26 "I saw the bus coming" Jimmy Carter oral history, May 11, 1988, p. 205, box 1.

26 "I scream, you scream" Jimmy Carter oral history, May 11, 1988, p. 124.

26 "We would mix the meat" Jimmy Carter oral history, May 11, 1988, p. 121.

27 renting out the shacks for $2 Jimmy Carter oral history, May 11, 1988, p. 126.

27 "We'd go in there" Jimmy Carter oral history, May 11, 1988, pp. 193–94.

27 peach tree switch Norman Mailer, "The Search for Carter," *New York Times;* Stroud, *How Jimmy Won,* p. 125.

27 "Daddy's spankings were not" Jimmy Carter oral history, May 11, 1988, p. 185.

Earl "was kind of hot tempered." One evening the family was sitting at dinner and Earl grew angry because his salt shaker wouldn't work. "He picked that salt shaker up and threw it over on the fireplace and busted all over everything, just scared the fool out of all of us" (p. 196).

27 "This is a pain" Jimmy Carter, *A Full Life,* p. 14.

28 "At eight o'clock" Jimmy Carter oral history, May 11, 1988, p. 199.

28 "You would dip your mop" Jimmy Carter oral history, May 11, 1988, pp. 227–28.

29 "Jimmy, I got something" Jimmy Carter oral history, May 11, 1988, p. 209.

29 "I refused because I hadn't" Jimmy Carter oral history, May 11, 1988, p. 71.

29 "I went to school" P. J. Wise oral history, p. 8, box 2.

30 "I don't care how black" Ida English oral history, p. 9.

30 "She was always challenging me" Jimmy Carter oral history, May 11, 1988, p. 7.

30 "a nagging degree of skepticism" Carter, *Living Faith,* pp. 18–21.

30 "that the time had come" Carter, *A Full Life,* p. 24.

31 "So if anyone asked me" Jimmy Carter oral history, May 11, 1988, p. 9.

31 "After Jimmy's noon departure" Godbold, *Jimmy & Rosalynn Carter,* p. 49.

32 "My main trouble" Godbold, *Jimmy & Rosalynn Carter,* p. 51.

32 "I ran with you" T. Rees Shapiro, "Wesley A. Brown, First Black Naval Academy Graduate."

32 "goddamn nigger lover" Robert J. Schneller, Jr., *Breaking the Color Barrier,* p. 218. Brown was the first African American to graduate from the Naval Academy; he served twenty-five years in the navy, retiring in 1969 as a lieutenant commander.

32 "I think I was kin" Jimmy and Rosalynn Carter oral history, p. 345.

32 "She was remarkably beautiful" Carter, *A Full Life,* p. 38.

32 They were both virgins Alter, *His Very Best,* p. 68.

33 "With her heart-shaped face" Mailer, "Search for Carter."

33 "first experience with impending death" Carter, *A Full Life,* p. 48.

33 "Oh, Rosalynn, my darling" Alter, *His Very Best,* p. 75.

33 "I didn't think he had" Jimmy Carter oral history, May 11, 1988, p. 148.

34 "Either choose the navy or politics" Carter, *Living Faith,* pp. 92–93.

34 "Jimmy, it's too soon" Carter, *A Full Life,* p. 61.

34 "disagreed so much" Jimmy Carter oral history, May 11, 1988, p. 148.

34 "Sharp-tongued Hyman Rickover" "The Man in Tempo," *Time,* January 11, 1954.

35 "Why not?" Carter, *A Full Life,* pp. 62–63.

35 "We feared and respected him" Peter G. Bourne, *Jimmy Carter,* p. 76.

36 "Being right was" Bourne, *Jimmy Carter,* p. 77.

36 "excellent progress in learning" Godbold, *Jimmy & Rosalynn Carter,* p. 68.

36 "longest and most thorough conversations" Carter, *A Full Life,* p. 65.

36 first school for African American children Godbold, *Jimmy & Rosalynn Carter,* p. 71.

36 "last tortured breath" Carter, *A Full Life,* p. 66.

CHAPTER 2: A PECULIAR HERITAGE

37 "one of the strangest" Jimmy Carter, *A Full Life,* p. 66.

37 "I argued" Rosalynn Carter, *First Lady from Plains,* p. 33.

38 "She almost quit me" Peter G. Bourne, *Jimmy Carter,* p. 81; E. Stanly Godbold, Jr., *Jimmy & Rosalynn Carter,* p. 75.

38 "God did not intend" Bourne, *Jimmy Carter,* p. 81. Kandy Stroud reports that a Carter aide told her that Carter had once said that he had quit the navy because "the Lord didn't want him making weapons of war anymore" (Kandy Stroud, *How Jimmy Won,* p. 133).

38 "He had to come back" Bourne, *Jimmy Carter,* p. 81.

38 "I had the most over-whelming sense" Willie Morris, *North Toward Home,* p. 176.

38 "the most brutal part of America" Morris, *North Toward Home,* p. 391.

39 "President Truman was horrified" *New York Times,* July 31, 1946, p. 1.

39 "reluctance of Walton County citizens" *New York Times,* August 4, 1946, p. 77.

40 "It's okay—Ol' Gene Will Be" The Herblock cartoon was reprinted by *The New York Times* on August 4, 1946.

40 Talmadge allegedly offered immunity Laura Wexler, *Fire in a Canebrake,* pp. 128 and 190; George Will, "A 1946 Lynching Is Still Haunting Us," *Washington Post*; Greg Bluestein, "Ex-Governor Investigated in 1946 Lynchings," NBC News.com.

40 "When the mob gangs can take" Wexler, *Fire in a Canebrake,* p. 204.

41 "We love it and we hate it" Willie Morris, *Terrains of the Heart,* p. 75.

41 "the one-horse farmer" C. Vann Woodward, *The Burden of Southern History,* pp. 18–19.

42 a mere $280 Jimmy Carter oral history, May 11, 1988, p. 163; Carter, *A Full Life,* p. 72.

42 Klan in business suits H. Brandt Ayers, *In Love with Defeat,* p. 37.

42 "flush it down the toilet" Jimmy Carter, *Turning Point,* p. 23.

42 "I was really worried" James Wooten, *Dasher,* p. 237.

42 "Coons and Carters Go Together" Carter, *A Full Life,* p. 79.

43 a regular Birch Society column Jimmy Carter, *Living Faith,* p. 67.

43 "He was a gentle man" Dallas Lee, *The Cotton Patch Evidence,* p. 1; Hamilton Jordan, *A Boy from Georgia,* p. 209.

43 "It was shocking" Jordan, *A Boy from Georgia,* p. 208; Tracy Elaine K'Meyer, *Interracialism and Christian Community in the Postwar South,* pp. 150 and 156–57.

44 pecan trees were chopped down Bruce Mazlish and Edwin Diamond, *Jimmy Carter,* p. 134.

44 he tape-recorded the conversation Lee, *Cotton Patch Evidence,* pp. 147–55.

46 "brain-washed peonage" K'Meyer, *Interracialism and Christian Community,* pp. 90–91 and 97; "Grand Jury Strongly Believes That Koinonia Is a Communist Front," *Americus Times-Recorder,* April 5, 1957.

46 "I am delighted to see" Bourne, *Jimmy Carter,* p. 100.

46 "About a third" Jim Auchmutey, *The Class of '65,* pp. 40–41.

46 **Rosalynn liked Jordan** Godbold, *Jimmy & Rosalynn Carter*, p. 89. Inexplicably, James Wooten later reported in his 1978 book, *Dasher*, that Carter had told Hamilton Jordan in 1966 that he knew of his Uncle Clarence, "but I don't think I've ever met him" (Wooten, *Dasher*, p. 260).

46 **"He'd heard that there were"** Wooten, *Dasher*, p. 233; Mazlish and Diamond, *Jimmy Carter*, p. 135.

46 **"They said it was Communist"** Auchmutey, *Class of '65*, p. 41.

46 **"I went there several times"** Robert Scheer, "Jimmy, We Hardly Know Y'all," *Playboy*; Bourne, *Jimmy Carter*, p. 98; Mazlish and Diamond, *Jimmy Carter*, p. 135.

46 **"He has never come over here"** Mazlish and Diamond, *Jimmy Carter*, p. 137.

47 **"fringe elements"** Scheer, "Jimmy, We Hardly Know Y'all," *Playboy*; Bourne, *Jimmy Carter*, p. 98; Mazlish and Diamond, *Jimmy Carter*, p. 136.

47 **"We never did anything heroic"** Hamilton Jordan, *No Such Thing as a Bad Day*, p. 206; Godbold, *Jimmy & Rosalynn Carter*, p. 89.

47 **The Koinonians filed suit** Lee, *Cotton Patch Evidence*, p. 161–62; Godbold, *Jimmy & Rosalynn Carter*, p. 89.

47 **certain financial ruin** Bourne, *Jimmy Carter*, p. 99.

47 **"His ambition caused him to miss"** Nicholas Dawidoff, "The Riddle of Jimmy Carter," *Rolling Stone*.

47 **"Peculiar Institution"** Woodward, *The Burden of Southern History*, p. 22.

47 **"a man who had great influence"** Jimmy Carter, *The Personal Beliefs of Jimmy Carter*, pp. 220–21.

47 **In 1968, Millard Fuller** Jimmy Carter and Rosalynn Carter, *Everything to Gain*, pp. 99–100; Randall Balmer, *Redeemer*, p. 163.

47 **"I am proud to be a neighbor"** Douglas Brinkley, *The Unfinished Presidency*, p. 150.

48 **"the black sheep of the family"** Jordan, *A Boy from Georgia*, p. 207.

48 **"When Rosalynn and I talked"** Jimmy Carter oral history, May 11, 1988, p. 42.

48 **John F. Kennedy in 1960** Jon Ward, *Camelot's End*, p. 56.

48 **"It was a cut and dried"** Jimmy Carter oral history, May 11, 1988, p. 49.

48 **"It was a hard time for us"** Rosalynn Carter oral history, May 11, 1988, pp. 48–49, National Park Service Interview, JC Library.

49 **He hung a bright fluorescent light** Norman Mailer, "The Search for Carter," *New York Times*; Carter and Carter, *Everything to Gain*, p. 81.

49 **"It seems inconceivable"** Carter, *A Full Life*, p. 81.

49 **"How can you, as a Christian"** Carter, *Living Faith*, p. 9.

49 **motivated by his boredom** Godbold, *Jimmy & Rosalynn Carter*, p. 92.

50 **never left Georgia** Griffin Bell III, "Citizen Lawyer," *Journal of Southern Legal History*, pp. 30 and 33.

50 **"was not a shock"** Carter, *Turning Point*, p. 41.

50 **"I don't know"** Bell, "Citizen Lawyer," p. 29.

51 **"Jimmy is so naïve"** Carter, *A Full Life*, p. 83; Kenneth E. Morris, *Jimmy Carter*, p. 136.

51 **"He was followed"** Carter, *First Lady from Plains*, p. 48.

51 **French Alsace-Lorraine** Betty K. Carter to Charles Kirbo, August 20, 1991, unprocessed Charles Kirbo Papers, Jimmy Carter Presidential Library.

51 **"When I was a little boy"** Stroud, *How Jimmy Won*, p. 200.

52 **grossed $2 million to $3 million** Stroud, *How Jimmy Won*, pp. 199–200.

52 **"Trial work is his ace"** James T. Wooten, "Carter's Georgia Guru," *New York Times Magazine*.

52 **One friend compared** Gerald Rafshoon interviews, December 7, 2015, and June 16, 2017.

52 **"No one speaks more slowly"** Carter, *Turning Point*, p. 149.

52 **"He appeared to have just"** Carter, *Turning Point*, pp. 125–26.

52 **"I recollect that he"** Wooten, "Carter's Georgia Guru."

53 **"he didn't have much"** Charles Kirbo oral history, p. 3.

53 **"just like chicken thieves"** Godbold, *Jimmy & Rosalynn Carter*, p. 99; Carter, *Turning Point*, p. 151.

53 **"I know your normal practice"** Carter, *Turning Point*, p. 153.

53 **in honor of Judge Crow** Godbold, *Jimmy & Rosalynn Carter*, p. 99; Carter, *Turning Point*, p. 156.

53 **"Now," Kirbo said** Wooten, "Carter's Georgia Guru," p. 18.

53 **"After it was all over"** Charles Kirbo oral history, p. 3.

54 **Kirbo's legal fee was $2,500** Wooten, "Carter's Georgia Guru."

54 **workaholic and playaholic** Peter Goldman, "Sizing Up Carter," *Newsweek*.

54 **"they wouldn't get mad at him"** Charles Kirbo oral history, pp. 3–4.

54 **"Going to see Charlie Kirbo"** Wooten, "Carter's Georgia Guru."

54 **"Now, I regard the mule"** Wooten, "Carter's Georgia Guru."

55 **"She liked the entire"** Carter, *A Full Life*, p. 89; Carter, *First Lady from Plains*, p. 50.

55 **"brilliant and very liberal"** Bourne, *Jimmy Carter*, p. 141.

56 **"I learned," he later said** Patrick Anderson, *Electing Jimmy Carter*, pp. 8–9.

56 **"That's good!"** Bourne, *Jimmy Carter*, p. 140.

56 **"I got beat up every day"** Chip Carter interview by Bob Short.

56 **"People hated Johnson down here"** Jimmy Carter, *A Remarkable Mother*, p. 81; Godbold, *Jimmy & Rosalynn Carter*, p. 109.

57 **"It hurt to lose"** Anderson, *Electing Jimmy Carter*, p. 12.

57 **"accustomed to accomplishing"** Carter, *A Full Life*, pp. 92–93.

57 **"abandon my faith altogether"** Carter, *Living Faith*, p. 26.

57 **"an acute reactive depression"** Balmer, *Redeemer*, p. 25.

57 **"cried like a baby"** Goldman, "Sizing Up Carter."

57 **"taken aback because the man"** Balmer, *Redeemer*, p. 25.

58 **"sawdust Christianity"** Goldman, "Sizing Up Carter."

58 **Billy Graham and Oral Roberts** Chip Carter interview by Bob Short.

58 **"She advised me"** Carter, *A Full Life*, p. 92.

58 **"What about all political ambitions?"** Jules Witcover, *Marathon*, p. 270–71.

58 **"accurate, basically"** Witcover, *Marathon*, p. 271; Goldman, "Sizing Up Carter."

58 **"bemoaned my misfortune"** Carter, *Living Faith*, p. 202.

59 **"no flashing lights"** Carter, *First Lady from Plains*, p. 62; Godbold, *Jimmy & Rosalynn Carter*, p. 130; Goldman, "Sizing Up Carter."

59   "If you were arrested" Leo P. Ribuffo, *Right, Center, Left,* p. 224.

59   had already decided to make Carter, *First Lady from Plains,* p. 57.

59   "remained an idiosyncratic believer" Darren J. McDonald, "Blessed Are the Policy Makers," *Diplomatic History.*

59   "my continuing doubts" Carter, *Living Faith,* p. 25.

59   "religion is a search" Stroud, *How Jimmy Won,* p. 169.

60   *Reinhold Niebuhr: On Politics:* Godbold, *Jimmy & Rosalynn Carter,* p. 131.

60   "political Bible" Bourne, *Jimmy Carter,* p. 171.

60   "One of my greatest regrets" Anderson, *Electing Jimmy Carter,* p. 73. Carter persuaded Niebuhr's widow to send him a collection of his published essays.

60   "the sad duty of politics" Haynes Johnson, "Boom," *Washington Post,* May 10, 1978.

60   "I was nervous" Carter, *A Full Life,* pp. 93–94.

60   "There was no wave" Witcover, *Marathon,* p. 271.

60   "Being born again is a new life" Carter, *Living Faith,* p. 20; McDonald, "Blessed Are the Policy Makers."

60   "Some people relate religion" Goldman, "Sizing Up Carter."

61   "I have a tendency to exalt myself" Hugh Carter, *Cousin Beedie and Cousin Hot,* p. 117.

61   "modicum of humility" Ribuffo, *Right, Center, Left,* p. 224.

61   "the teachings of Christ" Carter, *Living Faith,* p. 225.

61   "love must be translated into justice" Anderson, *Electing Jimmy Carter,* p. 58; June Bingham, *Courage to Change,* p. 15.

61   "I had adopted" Jimmy Carter oral history, February 18, 1982.

CHAPTER 3: THE POPULIST FROM PLAINS

62   multimillion-dollar operation Kenneth E. Morris, *Jimmy Carter,* p. 151.

63   "where it's warm, people have" Jimmy Carter, *A Remarkable Mother,* pp. 87–88.

63   "what life is all about" Carter, *A Remarkable Mother,* pp. 121–22; E. Stanly Godbold, Jr., *Jimmy & Rosalynn Carter,* p. 133.

63   "In my view" Jack Carter oral history, p. 5; Joshua Kendall, *First Dads,* p. 63.

64   "conservative progressive" Godbold, *Jimmy & Rosalynn Carter,* p. 137.

64   "I believe that I'm a more" Randy Sanders, "The Sad Duty of Politics," *Georgia Historical Quarterly,* p. 613; Morris, *Jimmy Carter,* pp. 183 and 356; *Atlanta Constitution,* June 14, 1966.

64   "the big-shots that own" Sanders, "Sad Duty of Politics," p. 622.

64   "He's not that bad" William Lee Miller, *Yankee from Georgia,* p. 63. Young tells the same story in his 1996 memoir, *An Easy Burden,* on p. 169—but in his telling of it he cites Sheriff Chappell, who served under Police Chief Laurie Pritchard.

64   "I drove all over Georgia" Nicholas Dawidoff, "The Riddle of Jimmy Carter," *Rolling Stone.*

64   "Dad really isn't an orator" Jack Carter oral history, p. 21.

64 "Captain Midnight" Office of Staff Secretary, 1976 Campaign Transition File, 1970 Campaign folder, box 2, Jimmy Carter Presidential Library.

65 $8,600 to Carter's campaign William Safire, "Jimmy's Friend Erwin Deserves Close Scrutiny," *New York Times,* December 8, 1976; Godbold, *Jimmy & Rosalynn Carter,* p. 165.

65 "I do not know how" Peter G. Bourne, *Jimmy Carter,* p. 181.

65 "He's an unbelievable pilot" Godbold, *Jimmy & Rosalynn Carter,* p. 167.

65 "packed his father's head" Bourne, *Jimmy Carter,* p. 181.

66 "Black people were not" David Rabhan interviews, September 14, 2019, and October 17, 2019.

66 "Over the objections" Charles Kirbo oral history, p. 4.

66 "disgrace" and a "shame" Bourne, *Jimmy Carter,* p. 183.

66 "close connections with" Godbold, *Jimmy & Rosalynn Carter,* p. 147.

66 "I believe I know white people" Charles Kirbo, "People" (undated memo), unprocessed Charles Kirbo papers, Jimmy Carter Presidential Library.

67 "I liked this guy Carter" Gerald M. Rafshoon oral history, April 8, 1983; Morris, *Jimmy Carter,* p. 143.

67 drinking beer together Kandy Stroud, *How Jimmy Won,* p. 207; Hugh Carter, *Cousin Beedie and Cousin Hot,* p. 150.

67 "Let's take a camera" Gerald M. Rafshoon oral history, April 8, 1983.

67 "I think there's a flaw" Gerald M. Rafshoon oral history, April 8, 1983.

68 "He could not stand to work" Gerald M. Rafshoon oral history, April 8, 1983.

68 "almost Elizabethan in its inflections" Paul Hendrickson, "Jimmy Carter, Casting Back," *Washington Post,* May 22, 1988.

68 "It's not nervous" Gerald M. Rafshoon oral history, April 8, 1983.

68 "This is the door" Bourne, *Jimmy Carter,* pp. 189–90.

69 "intellectual red-neck" Howard Norton and Bob Slosser, *The Miracle of Jimmy Carter,* p. 48.

69 "I am convinced" Godbold, *Jimmy & Rosalynn Carter,* p. 150.

69 "I have a son in Vietnam" Godbold, *Jimmy & Rosalynn Carter,* p. 137.

69 "no trouble pitching" Morris, *Jimmy Carter,* p. 184.

69 "I told people" Bruce Mazlish and Edwin Diamond, *Jimmy Carter,* p. 183.

69 "Jimmy can and does" Sanders, "Sad Duty of Politics," p. 621.

69 "Charlie doesn't care much" Morris, *Jimmy Carter,* p. 176.

69 "He was a moderate to moderates" Morris, *Jimmy Carter,* p. 178.

69 "He could charm" Bourne, *Jimmy Carter,* p. 188.

69 "fact sheets" Sanders, "Sad Duty of Politics," p. 628; Stephen Brill, "Jimmy Carter's Pathetic Lies," *Harper's,* March 1976.

70 "You won't like my campaign" William Lee Miller, *Yankee from Georgia,* p. 107; Godbold, *Jimmy & Rosalynn Carter,* p. 152. Carter later told Jonathan Alter that he regretted being associated with Roy Harris—but if he had publicly refuted Harris, "that would have been the end of my political career" (Alter, *His Very Best,* p. 162).

70 "to establish and maintain" James Wooten, *Dasher,* pp. 288–89 and 292.

70 "He's somebody who was willing" Dawidoff, "Riddle of Jimmy Carter."

70 "Good grief, this campaign" Dorothy Padgett, *Jimmy Carter,* p. 38.

71 "things had been falling apart" Jordan, *A Boy from Georgia,* p. 12.

71 "I felt real shame" Jordan, *A Boy from Georgia,* p. 136.

71 "Change came hard" Jordan, *A Boy from Georgia,* p. 141.

72 "I was not proud" Jordan, *A Boy from Georgia,* p. 202.

72 "political animal" Randall Balmer, *Redeemer,* p. 38.

72 who initiated the introduction Bourne, *Jimmy Carter,* p. 155.

72 "killing insects was more important" Jordan, *A Boy from Georgia,* p. ix.

72 "We were the class" "The President's Boys," *Time,* June 6, 1977.

72 "He is a nice fella" Hamilton Jordan, *No Such Thing as a Bad Day,* p. 138.

73 "We have made progress" Jordan, *No Such Thing as a Bad Day,* p. 139.

73 "no doctor would risk" Jordan, *No Such Thing as a Bad Day,* p. 140.

73 "great man I had barely known" Jordan, *A Boy from Georgia,* p. 219. Sitting in his White House office, Jordan told authors Bruce Mazlish and Edwin Diamond that his uncle Clarence Jordan was "the greatest man I've ever known" (Mazlish and Diamond, *Jimmy Carter,* p. 133).

73 she understood that racial segregation Reverend Dr. Robert L. Maddox, "Parents Provided Rich Home Life in Vienna, Ga.," *Carter-Mondale Letter* 6, no. 2 (Summer 2010), Carter Center.

73 handful of white teachers "President's Boys," *Time.*

73 "the most important things" Adam Bernstein, *Washington Post,* cited in *Carter-Mondale Letter* 6, no. 2 (Summer 2010), Carter Center. Chip Carter once saw Jody shoot one hundred out of one hundred skeets at the Camp David skeet range (Chip Carter interview by Bob Short).

74 "You don't know what loneliness is" "President's Boys," *Time.*

74 "Jody was a serious" Peter Bourne interview.

74 "My part of the state" Mazlish and Diamond, *Jimmy Carter,* p. 186.

74 "We soon found that" Jimmy Carter, eulogy for Jody Powell, Cambridge, Md., December 17, 2009.

74 "we worked out a better arrangement" Padgett, *Jimmy Carter,* p. 408.

75 "understanding that people are complicated" Padgett, *Jimmy Carter,* p. 407.

75 a single shot of Chivas Peter Goldman, "Sizing Up Carter," *Newsweek;* Stroud, *How Jimmy Won,* p. 217.

75 gnaw his fingernails down "President's Boys," *Time.*

75 "totally disorganized" Stroud, *How Jimmy Won,* p. 218.

75 "Outside of Rosalynn" Stroud, *How Jimmy Won,* p. 223.

75 "This is a mistake" Charles Kirbo to Jimmy Carter, May 22, 1970, unprocessed Charles Kirbo papers, Jimmy Carter Presidential Library.

75 Carter spent $700,000 Godbold, *Jimmy & Rosalynn Carter,* p. 165.

75 "If we had lost" Rosalynn Carter, *First Lady from Plains,* p. 68.

76 "stunning upset" Godbold, *Jimmy & Rosalynn Carter,* p. 156.

76 "Lester Maddox is the embodiment" Wooten, *Dasher,* p. 293.

76 "unprincipled grinning chameleon" Balmer, *Redeemer,* p. 31.

76 "more of a class distinction" Sanders, "Sad Duty of Politics," p. 622.

76 **only 5 percent of the Black vote** Bourne, *Jimmy Carter,* p. 196; Godbold, *Jimmy & Rosalynn Carter,* p. 160.

76 **"To win in politics"** Jerome Doolittle, unpublished diary, August 7, 1978.

77 **"The time for racial discrimination"** Carter, *A Full Life,* p. 101; Bourne, *Jimmy Carter,* p. 199; Carter, *First Lady from Plains,* p. 68; Godbold, *Jimmy & Rosalynn Carter,* p. 166.

77 **"I told Jimmy"** Douglas Brinkley, "What It Takes," *New Yorker.*

77 **"I think you should be careful"** Kirbo memo to Carter, November 23, 1970; Charles Kirbo Papers, Jimmy Carter Presidential Library.

78 **"I realize that the *test of a leader*"** Wooten, *Dasher,* pp. 299–300.

78 **"Being called a liar"** Joe Klein, "Hamilton Jordan and Jody Powell," *Rolling Stone;* Dawidoff, "Riddle of Jimmy Carter."

78 **"He's cold, cunning and cruel"** "The Coming of Carter," *Newsweek,* July 19, 1976.

78 **"I always thought"** Sanders, "Sad Duty of Politics," p. 634.

78 **"lacked the experience to tear"** Sanders, "Sad Duty of Politics," p. 634.

78 **"he would never go through"** Norton and Slosser, *Miracle of Jimmy Carter,* p. 48; Wooten, *Dasher,* pp. 295–96.

79 **"It is important that you retain"** Charles Kirbo memo to Jimmy Carter, November 23, 1970, Charles Kirbo unprocessed papers, Jimmy Carter Presidental Library.

79 **"give the little people"** Charles Kirbo memo to Jimmy Carter, December 28, 1970, Charles Kirbo unprocessed papers, Jimmy Carter Presidential Library.

79 **"ghettos, law enforcement, rapid transit"** Kirbo memo to Carter, December 28, 1970.

CHAPTER 4: JIMMY WHO?

80 **"a 45-year-old peanut farmer"** "New Governor of Georgia Urges End of Racial Bias," *New York Times,* January 13, 1971. (Actually, Carter was forty-six years old, not forty-five.)

81 **"Dixie Whistles a Different Tune"** Jimmy Carter, *A Full Life,* p. 101; Peter G. Bourne, *Jimmy Carter,* p. 201; Gerald Rafshoon interview, June 26, 2016.

81 **"promoting you for all kinds of damned jobs"** Charles Kirbo to Jimmy Carter, November 13, 1970, unprocessed Charles Kirbo papers, Jimmy Carter Presidential Library.

81 **"Mother raised vegetables"** Clare Crawford, "A Story of Love and Rehabilitation," *People.*

82 **"I saw him twice"** Crawford, "A Story of Love and Rehabilitation."

82 **"She was young, black and penniless"** Rosalynn Carter, *First Lady from Plains,* p. 96.

82 **"She was just three"** Crawford, "A Story of Love and Rehabilitation." Other accounts of Mary Fitzpatrick's murder case include: Carter, *A Full Life,* p. 103; Jimmy Carter, *Keeping Faith,* p. 30; Carter, *First Lady from Plains,* p. 96; Douglas Brinkley, *The Unfinished Presidency,* p. 256.

82 **"She convinced us of her innocence"** Carter, *A Full Life,* p. 103. In 1982, Carter wrote, "We were convinced that she was innocent of this charge" (*Keeping Faith,* p. 30). Carter also noted that the judge who had sentenced Mary to life imprisonment was local Superior Court judge Tom Marshall, the same magistrate who in 1962 had ruled that Carter's name should be stricken from the ballot. Carter clearly had a low opinion of Judge Marshall—who by 1976 was chief justice of the Georgia Supreme Court. Carter reported, "Eventually, a retrial was ordered, and the authorities were persuaded that Mary was innocent. She was granted a full pardon" (Carter, *A Full Life,* pp. 85 and 103).

82 **"with faint praise"** Peter Goldman, "Sizing Up Carter," *Newsweek.*

82 **"I usually know"** Charles Kirbo oral history, p. 40.

82 **"Kirbo speaks only to Carter"** Patrick Anderson, *Electing Jimmy Carter,* p. 39.

83 **canceled any religious services** Leo P. Ribuffo, *Right, Center, Left,* p. 216.

83 **"People wouldn't know"** Charles Kirbo oral history, p. 40.

83 **"It was a sound move"** Charles Kirbo memo to Jimmy Carter, July 16, 1971, Charles Kirbo unprocessed papers, Jimmy Carter Presidential Library.

83 **"He had a policy"** Charles Kirbo oral history, p. 5.

84 **"I don't use numbers"** Robert Shrum, "Bert Lance," *New Times.*

84 **"You know, every once"** Shrum, "Bert Lance."

84 **"zero-based"** Carter had become enamored with the notion of zero-based budgeting after reading an article about it in the *Harvard Business Review.* Goldman, "Sizing Up Carter."

84 **"Don't pay any attention"** Bourne, *Jimmy Carter,* p. 218.

84 **"took full advantage"** Carter, *A Full Life,* p. 104.

84 **"He was always so right"** James Wooten, *Dasher,* p. 328.

85 **"I have never seen a man"** Curtis Wilkie, *Dixie,* p. 219.

85 **"Hell, I couldn't wait"** Goldman, "Sizing Up Carter."

85 **Georgia parolees doubled** E. Stanly Godbold, Jr., *Jimmy & Rosalynn Carter,* p. 196.

85 **"It is important for Baptists"** Godbold, *Jimmy & Rosalynn Carter,* p. 195.

85 **"to see my own county"** Godbold, *Jimmy & Rosalynn Carter,* p. 194.

86 **first Jewish judge** Godbold, *Jimmy & Rosalynn Carter,* p. 195.

86 **"personal intervention"** "Blacks and Whites Stop Weapons Race in Georgia," *New York Times,* October 2, 1971; Godbold, *Jimmy & Rosalynn Carter,* pp. 205–6; "'Arms Race' Over in Georgia Area," *New York Times,* October 17, 1971.

86 **"Here were these 25-year-old kids"** Joe Klein, "Hamilton Jordan and Jody Powell," *Rolling Stone,* p. 65.

86 **"Jody—and Jimmy—really enjoyed"** Klein, "Hamilton Jordan and Jody Powell," p. 65.

87 **"I never thought Calley"** Carter continued, "And I thought he should be punished and still do. I never expressed any contrary opinion." But he added that he had felt "at the time of Calley's trial which was held in Georgia, that it was not right to equate what Calley did with what other American servicemen were doing in Vietnam." Charles Mohr, "Carter Credibility Issue," *New York Times.*

87 "scapegoat" Duane Riner, "Carter Decrees Day of Tribute," *Atlanta Constitution,* April 2, 1971.

87 "American Fighting Men's Day" Some accounts of Carter's press conference quoted him urging Georgians to "honor the flag as Rusty [Calley] had done" (Murray Polner, "Four Hours in My Lai," *Washington Monthly,* and Shaun Raviv, "The Ghosts of My Lai"). Carter denied in 1976 that he had said this. *The New York Times* reported that Governor Carter claimed that Calley's conviction had lowered the morale of U.S. soldiers fighting in Vietnam: "Opposition to Calley's Conviction and Sentence Grows in Nation," *New York Times,* April 2, 1971.

88 "It was a skillful and successful ploy" Bourne, *Jimmy Carter,* p. 214.

88 "While I disagree with your position" Charles Kirbo memo to Jimmy Carter, undated (circa April 1971), unprocessed Charles Kirbo papers, Jimmy Carter Presidential Library.

88 Vietnam as a "mistake" Charles Kirbo to Jimmy Carter, May 27, 1971, Charles Kirbo Papers, Jimmy Carter Presidential Library.

88 "ridiculous or irresponsible to criticize" Charles Kirbo memo to Jimmy Carter, June 18, 1971, unprocessed Charles Kirbo papers, Jimmy Carter Presidential Library.

88 "a bit conservative" Charles Kirbo memo to Jimmy Carter, undated (circa April 1971), unprocessed Charles Kirbo papers, Jimmy Carter Presidential Library.

89 To Carter's surprise James "Chip" Earl Carter III oral history interview, June 23, 2008, Reflections on Georgia Politics Oral History Collection, University of Georgia.

89 "remain moderate and progressive" Charles Kirbo memo to Jimmy Carter, June 27, 1972, unprocessed Charles Kirbo Papers, Jimmy Carter Presidential Library; Godbold, *Jimmy & Rosalynn Carter,* p. 232.

89 Bourne and Bond failed Bourne, *Jimmy Carter,* p. 231; Julian Bond, "Why I Don't Support Jimmy Carter," *The Nation.*

89 "it was important to make it" Jody Powell to Jimmy Carter, July 19, 1972, "Correspondence from Jody Powell to Jimmy Carter [1] folder," box 14, Subject Files, Jody Powell Papers, Jimmy Carter Presidential Library.

90 "Once you have made a decision" Goldman, "Sizing Up Carter." Bourne's memo was dated July 25, 1972, and is reproduced in whole in Kandy Stroud's book *How Jimmy Won,* p. 23.

90 "The son of a bitch" Godbold, *Jimmy & Rosalynn Carter,* p. 255; Jules Witcover, *Marathon,* p. 110.

90 "She wants to be first lady" Anderson, *Electing Jimmy Carter,* p. 12. See also Stroud, *How Jimmy Won,* p. 92.

91 "a strong surprise showing" Witcover, *Marathon,* p. 114.

91 "In my opinion" Witcover, *Marathon,* pp. 110–11.

91 "I think we are sort of" Charles Kirbo memo to Jimmy Carter, December 1, 1972, unprocessed Charles Kirbo papers, Jimmy Carter Presidential Library.

91 "its liberal orientation" Randall Balmer, *Redeemer,* p. 43.

91   **"President of *what*?"** Jimmy Carter, *A Remarkable Mother,* p. 138.

92   **"I'll be damned"** Witcover, *Marathon,* p. 115.

92   **"benevolent conservatism"** Charles Kirbo memo to Jimmy Carter, February 6, 1973, unprocessed Charles Kirbo Papers, Jimmy Carter Presidential Library.

92   **"believes in or will implement"** Charles Kirbo memo to Jimmy Carter, March 13, 1973, unprocessed Charles Kirbo Papers, Jimmy Carter Presidential Library.

92   **"know that you are a businessman"** Charles Kirbo to Jimmy Carter, "Comments—Yale Speech," April 11, 1973, Charles Kirbo Papers, Jimmy Carter Presidential Library.

93   **"the peace we have"** Charles Kirbo memo to Jimmy Carter, February 6, 1973, unprocessed Charles Kirbo Papers, Jimmy Carter Presidential Library.

93   **"The Watergate fuss"** Charles Kirbo memo to Jimmy Carter, May 23, 1973, unprocessed Charles Kirbo Papers, Jimmy Carter Presidential Library.

94   **"kind of pretended to be reluctant"** Kathryn J. McGarr, *The Whole Damn Deal,* p. 141.

94   **"I personally cannot afford"** Hamilton Jordan memo to Jimmy Carter, December 3, 1973, unprocessed Charles Kirbo Papers, Jimmy Carter Presidential Library.

94   **"Bob was an innocent victim"** Charles Kirbo oral history, p. 7.

94   **"the Trojan peanut"** "The President's Boys," *Time.*

94   **"Is this yours?"** McGarr, *Whole Damn Deal,* p. 141.

95   **Carter attended his first** Godbold, *Jimmy & Rosalynn Carter,* p. 253; Holly Sklar, ed., *Trilateralism,* p. 81.

95   **"studied those things like a Bible"** Jimmy Carter interview, September 14, 2017.

95   **"My homeland was denied to me"** Charles Gati, "The World According to Zbig," *Politico.*

96   **"Any further delay"** Kai Bird, *The Chairman,* p. 530.

96   **"solid as a rock"** Hamilton Jordan, *Crisis,* p. 40.

97   **"overoptimistic"** Zbigniew Brzezinski, *Power and Principle,* p. 37; David S. McLellan, *Cyrus Vance,* p. 25; George Packer, *Our Man,* p. 179.

97   **"Mr. Secretary, would you mind"** Bourne, *Jimmy Carter,* p. 241.

97   **"Then I started to listen"** Stroud, *How Jimmy Won,* p. 148.

97   ***Blonde on Blonde*** Anderson, *Electing Jimmy Carter,* p. 8.

98   **"First thing he did"** Jonathan Alter, *His Very Best,* p. 209; *Jimmy Carter: Rock and Roll President,* directed by Mary Wharton, CNN, 2020.

98   **"painfully timid"** Jeff Cochran, "When Jimmy Carter Met Bob Dylan," *Like the Dew.*

98   **"I thought I was going to get"** Gregg Allman with Alan Light, *My Cross to Bear,* p. 265. Some of these quotes are slightly different in a speech by President Bill Underwood, Mercer University, January 17, 2017.

98   **"Gregory—can I call you"** Underwood speech, January 17, 2017.

99   **"Everyone thought he was"** Bourne, *Jimmy Carter,* p. 241.

99   **"just very bland"** Jack Carter oral history, p. 21.

99   **"Jimmy Carter baffled me"** Edward M. Kennedy, *True Compass,* pp. 352–53.

99 "the relaxed and confident way" Hunter S. Thompson, *The Great Shark Hunt,* pp. 470–71.

99 "was basically the same speech" Bourne, *Jimmy Carter,* p. 242.

99 "salvage part of my ego" Garry Wills, "Reading the Carter Riddle," *New York Review of Books.*

100 "I don't know, it may be" Thompson, *Great Shark Hunt,* p. 492.

100 "The other source" Thompson, *Great Shark Hunt,* p. 487.

100 "It was the anger in his voice" Thompson, *Great Shark Hunt,* p. 476.

100 "There is no transcript" Thompson, *Great Shark Hunt,* p. 478.

100 "I went in and just" Bourne, *Jimmy Carter,* p. 242.

100 "I get chill bumps" Godbold, *Jimmy & Rosalynn Carter,* p. 263; Jack Carter oral history, p. 22.

100 "a king hell bastard of a speech" Bourne, *Jimmy Carter,* p. 242; Hunter Thompson, "Jimmy Carter and the Great Leap of Faith," *Rolling Stone;* Thompson, *Great Shark Hunt,* p. 485.

101 "functional meanness" Hunter S. Thompson interview, CBC, 1977.

101 "political genius" Norman Mailer, "The Search for Carter," *New York Times.*

101 "Carter cut him down that day" Wills, "Reading the Carter Riddle."

101 Jordan's 137 questions Unprocessed Hamilton Jordan Papers, Jimmy Carter Presidential Library.

103 "Stu, I have already decided to run" Stuart E. Eizenstat, *President Carter,* p. 35.

104 "a Southern Kennedy" Godbold, *Jimmy & Rosalynn Carter,* p. 271.

104 "You're going to lose" Gerald Rafshoon interview, December 7, 2015.

104 "The reason he says" "The Coming of Carter," *Newsweek,* July 19, 1976.

104 "Well, maybe a little" Carter, *A Remarkable Mother,* pp. 146–47; Dorothy Padgett, *Jimmy Carter,* p. 126. Steve Hochman email to the author, September 18, 2020.

104 "He recited this sequence" Witcover, *Marathon,* p. 198.

104 "disgrace to the human race" Eizenstat, *President Carter,* p. 49.

104 "as revenues permit" Eizenstat, *President Carter,* p. 47.

105 "Carter is not just complex" Stroud, *How Jimmy Won,* p. 130.

105 "He never had a sleepless night" Stroud, *How Jimmy Won,* p. 150.

105 "Certain politicians feel" Goldman, "Sizing Up Carter."

105 "I am a Southerner" William Lee Miller, *Yankee from Georgia,* p. 74.

106 contempt for Carter Gregg Herken, *The Georgetown Set,* p. 374.

106 "He can't be president" Gerald Rafshoon interview, December 7, 2015.

106 "I tend to regard Carter" Arthur M. Schlesinger, Jr., *Journals,* pp. 406–7.

106 "seems to me a humorless" Andrew Schlesinger and Stephen Schlesinger, eds., *The Letters of Arthur Schlesinger, Jr.,* pp. 439–40.

106 "cold, tough, terrifyingly" Schlesinger, *Journals,* p. 409.

106 "I don't know exactly" Mailer, "Search for Carter."

107 "The conventional image" Witcover, *Marathon,* p. 211.

107 "I am not sure what" Witcover, *Marathon,* pp. 320–24.

107 one-third of Americans claimed " 'Born-Again' Experience Not Rare," *Washington Post,* September 22, 1976.

107 "**very considerable intelligence**" Schlesinger, *Journals,* p. 413.

107 "**sexual conservative**" Mailer, "Search for Carter."

108 "**Ted is quite clearly prepared**" Schlesinger, *Journals,* p. 415.

108 "**the liberals' pet Cracker**" Carl T. Rowan, "That's Enough of Those 'Hillbilly' Jokes," *Washington Star,* November 19, 1976.

108 "**I was not thinking**" Miller, *Yankee from Georgia,* p. 93.

108 "**Do you think northerners**" Greg Schneiders interview.

108 "**They think there's a place**" Stroud, *How Jimmy Won,* pp. 36–37; Jimmy Carter, *White House Diary,* pp. 164–65.

109 "like a father to me" Carter, *White House Diary,* p. 164.

109 "**well-meaning people**" Willie Morris, "Of Northern Fears, Southern Realities and Jimmy Carter," *New York Times.*

109 "**The real wonder about Carter**" Jerome Doolittle, unpublished diary, March 1, 1978.

110 "**It was so damned hard**" Wendy E. Swanberg, "The Gossip Makes the News," p. 124.

110 "**Even if we win**" Goldman, "Sizing Up Carter."

110 "**We'll be getting to know**" Richard Reeves, "Shhh, Don't Wake the Democrats," *New York.*

110 "**like a couple of raw-boned**" Bourne, *Jimmy Carter,* p. 337; Anderson, *Electing Jimmy Carter,* p. 68.

110 "**Our candidate may have been**" Anderson, *Electing Jimmy Carter,* p. 2.

110 "**That country-boy act**" Klein, "Hamilton Jordan and Jody Powell."

110 "**There's just one more**" Anderson, *Electing Jimmy Carter,* p. 12.

110 "**A lot of people in Washington**" Ken Auletta, "The Waiting-for-Jimmy Blues," *New York.*

111 "**But then I overheard**" Gerald Rafshoon interview, June 26, 2016.

111 "**If, after the inauguration**" McLellan, *Cyrus Vance,* p. 24.

111 "**I've got one sister**" Carter, *A Remarkable Mother,* p. 31; Wilkie, *Dixie,* p. 226.

112 "**a sorry son of a bitch**" Wilkie, *Dixie,* p. 227.

112 "**Billy drinks too much**" Stroud, *How Jimmy Won,* pp. 42–47.

112 "**Some people are just dumb**" Carter, *A Remarkable Mother,* p. 145.

112 "**I hate to use the word ruthless**" Goldman, "Sizing Up Carter"; Clare Booth Luce, "The Light at the End of the Tunnel of Love," *National Review.*

112 "**Sometimes,**" she told one Carter, *A Remarkable Mother,* p. 148.

112 "**his soul stare**" Stroud, *How Jimmy Won,* p. 133.

113 "**Behind that big smile**" Wilkie, *Dixie,* p. 218.

113 "**I suppose he felt**" Wilkie, *Dixie,* p. 232.

113 "**nuclear physicist**" Wilkie, *Dixie,* p. 224.

113 "**Here,**" Carter said Wilkie, *Dixie,* p. 230.

113 "**Maybe it was better**" Wilkie, *Dixie,* pp. 225 and 230.

114 "**Jesus Christ, if we had**" Anderson, *Electing Jimmy Carter,* pp. 30–31.

114 "**Both Carter and his wife**" Thompson, *Great Shark Hunt,* p. 484.

114 "**Hunter Thompson was a delightful**" "Dr. Hunter S. Thompson Remembered,"

Thrasher's Blog, March 11, 2005, http://www.thrashersblog.com/2005/03/dr-hunter-s-thompson-remembered.html.

114 "an almost totally unknown ex-governor" Thompson, *Great Shark Hunt,* p. 481.

115 he ate black-eyed peas with Rosalynn Eizenstat, *President Carter,* p. 386.

115 "We didn't need any" Gerald Rafshoon interview, August 24, 2020.

115 "My name is Jimmy Carter" Witcover, *Marathon,* pp. 368–69.

115 "populist in tone" Dominic Sandbrook, *Mad as Hell,* p. 157.

116 "If you and I make a mistake" Stroud, *How Jimmy Won,* pp. 339–41.

116 "I found him in jockey shorts" Anderson, *Electing Jimmy Carter,* p. 133.

117 "The thing that is drummed" Robert Scheer, "Jimmy, We Hardly Know Y'all," *Playboy;* Bourne, *Jimmy Carter,* p. 347.

117 "weirdo factor" Bruce Mazlish and Edwin Diamond, *Jimmy Carter,* p. 225.

117 "They can't kill you for lookin'" Ribuffo, *Right, Center, Left,* p. 222.

117 "Jimmy talks too much" Carter, *First Lady from Plains,* p. 132.

117 "open with everything" Charles Kirbo oral history, p. 5.

117 "quit that stuff about never telling" Goldman, "Sizing Up Carter."

118 "destroyed his lead" Anderson, *Electing Jimmy Carter,* p. 113.

118 Carter blamed Powell Anderson, *Electing Jimmy Carter,* p. 113. Robert Scheer later pointed out that after he completed the article, "I could never get Jody or anyone else on the staff to look at it" (Stroud, *How Jimmy Won,* p. 219).

118 "If I should ever decide" Stroud, *How Jimmy Won,* p. 381.

118 "Jimmie and I used to" Stroud, *How Jimmy Won,* p. 407.

118 "I'm going to hold you to it" Eizenstat, *President Carter,* p. 386.

118 Fanta laced with Jack Daniel's Stroud, *How Jimmy Won,* p. 411.

118 "We have waited" Bourne, *Jimmy Carter,* p. 355.

119 If fewer than ten thousand citizens Mazlish and Diamond, *Jimmy Carter,* p. 227; Witcover, *Marathon,* p. 643.

119 "least acceptable among Northern liberals" Wooten, *Dasher,* p. 38.

119 amounted to $21.8 million Reeves, "Shh, Don't Wake the Democrats."

119 "a good and decent man" Stroud, *How Jimmy Won,* p. 411.

119 "Governor," he said, "congratulations" Wilkie, *Dixie,* p. 234.

119 "I came all the way through" Miller, *Yankee from Georgia,* pp. 85 and 87.

120 "He really seems to me" Schlesinger, *Journals,* pp. 423–24.

CHAPTER 5: MR. CARTER GOES TO WASHINGTON

124 "By this time" Greg Schneiders interview.

124 "an extraordinary fellow" Charles Kirbo oral history, January 5, 1983.

125 "Watson had a real staff" David Rubenstein interview, June 19, 2016; Jack Watson, Jr., oral history.

125 "All of a sudden we found" Stuart E. Eizenstat, *President Carter,* p. 68.

125 "What about us?" David Rubenstein interviews, April 29, 2016, and June 19, 2016.

125 "JC is unhappy" Landon Butler, unpublished diary, November 13–15, 1976.

125 "Welcome to Washington" Sally Quinn, "Making Capital Gains," *Washington Post*.

126 "improper and inconsistent" Burton I. Kaufman and Scott Kaufman, *The Presidency of James Earl Carter*, p. 30.

126 "It was an over-reaction to Watergate" Gerald M. Rafshoon oral history, April 8, 1983.

126 "Hamilton and Jody were young boys" Charles Kirbo oral history, pp. 17–18.

127 "felt a little guilty" Charles Kirbo oral history, pp. 17–18.

127 "Governor, I thought I could" Eizenstat, *President Carter*, p. 92.

127 "Why didn't I think of Charlie?" Charles Kirbo oral history, p. 16.

127 "hasn't got the judgment" Charles Kirbo oral history, p. 40.

127 "natural selection" Jimmy Carter, *Keeping Faith*, pp. 50–52.

128 "specific goals and priorities" Cyrus Vance, *Hard Choices*, p. 29.

128 "outspokenness on the Middle East" Douglas Brinkley, "Out of the Loop," *New York Times*. Carter showed Brinkley relevant passages on Ball from the unpublished sections of his diary.

128 "I felt a growing rapport" Cyrus Vance, *Hard Choices*, pp. 30–33.

129 "too much of an advocate" Clark Clifford with Richard Holbrooke, *Counsel to the President*, p. 621; Betty Glad, *An Outsider in the White House*, p. 26.

129 "I feel at ease with you" George Packer, *Our Man*, p. 168.

129 "Governor, I don't think" George Packer, *Our Man*, pp. 171.

129 "I like hearing different opinions" Eizenstat, *President Carter*, p. 66.

129 "I was an eager student of Zbig's" Justin Vaïsse, *Zbigniew Brzezinski*, pp. 244 and 273.

130 "A schematic portrait of Brzezinski" Vaïsse, *Zbigniew Brzezinski*, pp. 264–68.

130 "Zbig would be my favorite" Carter, *Keeping Faith*, p. 54.

130 "Zbig represented his boldness" Hamilton Jordan, *Crisis*, p. 38.

131 "balanced team" Zbigniew Brzezinski, *Power and Principle*, p. 10; Vaïsse, *Zbigniew Brzezinski*, p. 272.

131 "more idealistic views" Brzezinski, *Power and Principle*, pp. 10 and 13.

132 "I have been told" Charles Gati, ed., *Zbig*, p. 17.

133 "We were country bumpkins" Chip Carter interview by Bob Short.

133 "greatly illuminating" James Fallows exit interview, pp. 3 and 6.

134 Lunching on boxed fried chicken William Lee Miller, *Yankee from Georgia*, p. 93.

134 "Oliphant Flap" Carl T. Rowan, "That's Enough of Those 'Hillbilly' Jokes," *Washington Star*, November 19, 1976.

134 "What's it like?" Walter F. Mondale and Dave Hage, *The Good Fight*, p. 176.

134 "Yes, ma'am, we've been fixing" Jimmy Carter, *White House Diary*, p. 10.

135 "Frank Moore is my man" Barbara Blum interview. Blum was a witness to the phone call.

135 "spear carrier" Frank Moore oral history, December 17, 1980.

135 "I saw these children" Frank Moore oral history, July 30–31, 2002.

136 "Tell him Sam Brown" Butler, unpublished diary, December 13, 1976.

136 "feeling particularly cocky" Butler, unpublished diary, November 12, 1976.

136 **bonds worth more than $170,000** Fred Barbash, "Most White House Aides Have Little Wealth," *Washington Post,* June 1, 1979.

136 "Landon was very competent" Gerald M. Rafshoon oral history, April 8, 1983.

136 "The transition is a complete bummer" Butler, unpublished diary, December 21, 1976.

136 "I am overwhelmed" Butler, unpublished diary, November 10, 1976.

137 "shaping up as defacto chief" Butler, unpublished diary, December 14, 1976.

137 "keeps things moving" Butler, unpublished diary, December 13, 1976.

137 "is a very unpredictable and secretive" Butler, unpublished diary, December 28, 1976.

137 "on the verge of some bad press" Butler, unpublished diary, December 16, 1976.

137 "a perfect name for someone" Butler, unpublished diary, November 16, 1976.

137 "Boy Scout" Tim Kraft interview.

137 "He was in town" Butler, unpublished diary, November 29–December 12, 1976; Tim Kraft interview.

137 **trying to have a child** Butler, unpublished diary, December 14, 1976.

137 "Somehow staffers are assumed" Butler, unpublished diary, December 31, 1976.

138 "He treated Nancy terribly" Peter Bourne interview.

138 "I'm neat, he's not" *People,* February 28, 1977.

138 "We'll never be able" Peter Bourne interview.

139 "He was not my cup of tea" Bunny Mitchell interviews.

139 "For these Black men" Bunny Mitchell interviews.

140 "didn't want anything like that" Mondale, *Good Fight,* p. 162; Richard Moe email to the author, July 26, 2020.

140 "This is fine" Mondale, *Good Fight,* p. 172.

140 **Carter gave Mondale a West Wing** Joel K. Goldstein, *The White House Vice Presidency,* p. 63.

140 "wasted national asset" Richard Moe, "The Making of the Modern Vice Presidency," *Carter-Mondale Letter,* p. 18.

140 "Stu, now you have two deputies" Eizenstat, *President Carter,* p. 99.

141 **Susan Clough had been** Clare Crawford, "Rosalynn and I Pick My Secretary," *People,* May 9, 1977.

141 "Dear Hamilton, beware the spokes" Eizenstat, *President Carter,* p. 75.

141 "It's amazing," **Butler jotted** Butler, unpublished diary, January 5, 1977.

142 "I like to think" Robert Reinhold, "Young Lawyer Helped Carter Get Past Many Shoals," *New York Times,* December 7, 1976.

142 "perpetually worried Stu was" Patrick Anderson, *Electing Jimmy Carter,* p. 77.

142 "Stu was not fun" David Rubenstein interviews, April 29, 2016, and June 19, 2016.

142 "He knew everything" Frank Moore oral history, December 17, 1980; Les Francis interview, June 24, 2016.

142 **encrusted with ice** David Rubenstein interview, June 19, 2016.

142 "The thing that's so surprising" Jerome Doolittle, unpublished diary, December 16, 1977.

143 **propose to his wife, Betty** Jimmy Carter note to Robert Lipshutz, October 1, 1979, folder, box 132, Office of Staff Secretary, Presidential Files, Jimmy Carter Presidential Library.

143 **"My being unqualified"** Myra MacPherson, "Trilateralists to Abound in Carter's White House," *Washington Post,* January 16, 1977.

143 **"Midge, you're going to keep"** Doreen J. Mattingly, *A Feminist in the White House,* p. 124 (manuscript).

143 **"Midge is a live-wire"** Butler, unpublished diary, January 4, 1977.

143 **"loud-mouthed pushy little broad"** Mattingly, *Feminist in the White House,* p. 139 (manuscript).

143 **"kind of fell in love with her"** Mattingly, *Feminist in the White House,* p. 104 (manuscript).

144 **"he can be exacting with staff"** Tim Kraft, unpublished diary, January 4, 1977.

144 **"a whole series of minor infractions"** Butler, unpublished diary, January 3, 1977.

145 **"I think the Carter cabinet"** Gerald Rafshoon interview, December 7, 2015.

145 **Kirbo was one of seven people** Jimmy Carter to Mail Room & Staff, January 25, 1977, Charles Kirbo Papers, Jimmy Carter Presidential Library.

146 **"I had confidence in Bert"** Charles Kirbo oral history.

146 **"assembled a strong team"** "The Cabinet Choices," *New York Times,* December 22, 1976.

146 **"I must say"** Butler, unpublished diary, December 19, 1976.

147 **"No, that's not the job for me"** Ted Sorensen, *Counselor,* p. 486.

147 **"Of course, political history"** Jimmy Carter oral history, December 8, 1988, National Park Service Interview, Jimmy Carter Presidential Library, p. 4.

147 **Ironically, even Senator Ted Kennedy** Sorensen, *Counselor,* p. 495.

148 **Sorensen's sworn testimony** Testimony of Theodore C. Sorensen, July 21, 1975, Church Committee Hearings, National Archives record no. 157-10005-10253.

148 **"about as well received"** Sorensen, *Counselor,* p. 493.

148 **"Honestly, I'm not sure"** Sorensen, *Counselor,* p. 500.

148 **"personal, catty, sniping stuff"** *New York Times,* February 2, 1977.

149 **"I'll always wonder"** Sorensen, *Counselor,* p. 501. Kirbo may also have been sent to persuade Sorensen to withdraw. (Terry Adamson interview, June 25, 2017.)

149 **"a rare defeat"** *New York Times,* February 2, 1977.

149 **"Well, it was a disaster"** Joel McCleary interview, March 23, 2016. McCleary served as treasurer of the Democratic Party from 1977 to 1978 and then as a deputy assistant to the president from 1978 to 1980.

150 **"I thought, frankly"** Kathryn J. McGarr, *The Whole Damn Deal,* p. 210.

150 **"If you want something"** McGarr, *Whole Damn Deal,* p. 202.

150 **"I believe he's one of the best"** McGarr, *Whole Damn Deal,* p. 218.

150 **"opportunistic"** Peter Bourne interview.

150 **"I was a pain in the ass"** McGarr, *Whole Damn Deal,* p. 216.

150 **"Kraft," Strauss said** Tim Kraft, unpublished diary, 1977, p. 1; Tim Kraft interview.

150 **"false modesty, indecision"** Tim Kraft, unpublished diary, 1977, p. 1.

150 **"a running discourse on pecans"** Tim Kraft, unpublished diary, January 11, 1977.

151 **"I could be killed"** Tim Kraft, unpublished diary, January 13, 1977.

151 **"Incredible. Just like my old man"** Tim Kraft, unpublished diary, January 19, 1977.

152 **"strangely calm"** Carter, *Keeping Faith,* p. 19.

152 **"to walk humbly with thy God"** Carter, *Keeping Faith,* pp. 20–21.

152 **"Tim, if we're going to"** Tim Kraft, unpublished diary, January 20, 1977. Chip Carter says the decision to walk ostentatiously down Pennsylvania Avenue was made in Plains on the previous Thanksgiving holiday. (Chip Carter interview with Bob Short.)

152 **It was a coat** Gerald Rafshoon interview, February 11, 2016.

153 **"Mother, I'm going to be fine"** Jan Williams oral history, p. 26, box 2.

153 **"Frank knows everybody"** Jim Galloway, *Atlanta Journal-Constitution,* January 14, 2017.

153 **"I'll admit that walkin'"** Miller, *Yankee from Georgia,* p. 109.

153 **"Many people along the parade"** Carter, *White House Diary,* p. 10.

153 **"one of those few perfect moments"** Carter, *Keeping Faith,* p. 17.

153 **"Stay close together"** Jimmy Carter, *A Remarkable Mother,* p. 155.

CHAPTER 6: WHITE HOUSE LIFE

154 **"I'm just going to the Oval Office"** Jimmy Carter, *Keeping Faith,* p. 23.

155 **"I thought he had no chance"** Max Cleland interview, May 16, 2016.

155 **booed Carter for three** Peter G. Bourne, *Jimmy Carter,* p. 341; Jules Witcover, *Marathon,* p. 526. According to Paul Sullivan, Carter's campaign director in Illinois, Carter had promised another campaign aide, Bill Dickson, that he would issue an amnesty.

156 **210,000 Vietnam-era draft evaders** Allen Pusey, "Jan. 21, 1977: Carter Pardons Vietnam-Era Draft Dodgers," *ABA Journal,* January 1, 2014, http://www.aba journal.com/magazine/article/jan._21_1977_carter_pardons_vietnam-era _draft_dodgers.

156 **"the most disgraceful thing"** Bourne, *Jimmy Carter,* p. 366.

156 **"Dasher" to "Deacon"** Tim Kraft, unpublished diary, January 21, 1977, Kraft Diary folder, Kraft Papers, Kai Bird.

157 **"nonflamboyant style"** Nina S. Hyde, "Rosalynn Carter's Fashion," *Washington Post,* January 30, 1977.

157 **"There is nothing royal"** Sally Quinn, "The Carter Style: Of the People, For the People," *Washington Post.*

157 **"Sally insinuated"** Jimmy Carter interview, September 14, 2017.

157 **"Sally makes me want to commit suicide"** Wendy Swanberg, "The Gossip Makes the News: Washington Reporting in the Carter Years," p. 48; Hamilton Jordan, *Crisis,* p. 171.

157 **"Dear Hot"** Lillian Carter to Jimmy Carter, January 21, 1977, box 4, Office of Staff Secretary, Presidential Files, Jimmy Carter Presidential Library.

158 "constant access to me" Jimmy Carter, *White House Diary,* p. 12.

158 "I got into a few heated exchanges" Tim Kraft exit interview by Marie Allen, "Transition" folder, Kraft Papers, Kai Bird.

158 five hours each week Tim Kraft memo to Jimmy Carter, March 11, 1977, Presidential Time Analysis 1977 folder, box 1, Donated Historical Materials, Tim Kraft Collection, Subject Files, Jimmy Carter Presidential Library.

158 "Frankly, I think that" Tim Kraft memo to Zbigniew Brzezinski, July 28, 1977, 1977 folder, Tim Kraft Papers, courtesy of Tim Kraft.

158 "This note is outrageous" Tim Kraft memo to Zbigniew Brzezinski, July 28, 1977, 10 Memos, 1977 folder, box 1, Donated Historical Materials, Tim Kraft Collection, Jimmy Carter Presidential Library.

158 "I need more time alone" Jimmy Carter to Tim Kraft, January 25, 1977, 1977 folder, Tim Kraft Papers, courtesy of Tim Kraft.

158 "I don't think Carter" Tim Kraft, unpublished diary, January 21, 1977, Kraft Diary folder, Tim Kraft Papers, courtesy of Tim Kraft.

158 "I always looked forward" Jimmy Carter oral history, February 18, 1982.

159 A *Flag Day* painting Tim Kraft handwritten note, Tim Kraft unpublished diary, February 6, 1977, Kraft Diary folder, Tim Kraft Papers, courtesy of Tim Kraft.

159 eight or ten hours a day Jimmy Carter, *White House Diary,* p. 12.

159 "Recuerdos de la Alhambra" Bourne, *Jimmy Carter,* p. 209.

159 "So much for foreign policy" Tim Kraft handwritten note to Tim Smith, undated, White House Support folder, Tim Kraft Papers, courtesy of Tim Kraft.

159 "I'd say, 'Mr. President'" Tim Kraft interview.

159 "also felt strange occupying" Carter, *White House Diary,* p. 12. The Carters eventually watched 480 movies in the White House theater, about two a week—though many of them were screened for Amy and her school friends. (Jimmy Carter, *A Full Life,* p. 121.)

159 "sell or buy without discussion" Robert J. Lipshutz memo to White House Staff, February 12, 1977, 1977 folder, Tim Kraft Papers, courtesy of Kraft.

160 "It doesn't sound like" Rosalynn Carter, *First Lady from Plains,* p. 144; Kate Andersen Brower, *The Residence,* p. 64.

160 "I couldn't believe it" Carter, *First Lady from Plains,* p. 157.

160 Jimmy relented only Stuart E. Eizenstat, *President Carter,* p. 109.

160 "no need for the extra guard" Jimmy Carter to Dick Keiser, November 2, 1977, Susan Clough file, box 45, White House Staff Papers, Jimmy Carter Presidential Library.

160 "Jimmy Carter is a wonderfully sweet" Alice Rogoff interview, May 5, 2016.

160 "more frugality, less ostentation" Carter, *Keeping Faith,* p. 26.

161 battered, eleven-year-old blue Volkswagen Nan Powell email to the author, July 6, 2017. *Time* magazine reported that the Volkswagen was a 1966 model ("The President's Boys," *Time*).

161 "depomping the Presidency" Hedrick Smith, "Carter So Far: Mix of Symbol and Substance," *New York Times,* March 6, 1977.

161 "If I'd only learned" Patrick Anderson, *Electing Jimmy Carter,* p. 82.

161 **"His weapon of choice"** David Broder, *Washington Post,* cited in *Carter-Mondale Letter* 5, no. 2 (Summer 2010), Carter Center.

161 **"I am specifically authorized"** "President's Boys," *Time.*

161 **an outright lie** On the eve of the April 1980 hostage rescue mission, Powell felt compelled to lie when he told the journalist Jack Nelson that the White House was not considering a military operation. Powell felt this was virtually the only time he had to tell an outright lie.

161 **"Beat that one to death"** Press Conference at the White House with Jody Powell, #319, June 28, 1978, p. 8, "News Conference Transcripts and Press Releases 1978 (5)" folder, box 16, Press Office–Media Liaison Office, Marc Henderson's Subject Files, Jimmy Carter Presidential Library.

161 **"Demagoguery in the Congress"** Press Conference at the White House with Jody Powell, #268, April 5, 1978, p. 11, "News Conference Transcripts and Press Releases folder," box 15, Press Office–Media Liaison Office, Marc Henderson's Subject Files, Jimmy Carter Presidential Library.

162 **"the first major threat"** Joe Klein, "Hamilton Jordan and Jody Powell," *Rolling Stone.*

162 **"Carter is always offering himself up"** Jerome Doolittle, unpublished diary, April 11, 1978.

162 **"If he is a success"** "President's Boys," *Time.*

162 **"Why should I spend all this time"** Gerald Rafshoon interview, June 23, 2016.

162 **"wanted me to express"** Nancy Collins, "President's Regrets," *Washington Post,* May 1, 1978.

162 **"completely irresponsible and unnecessarily"** Carter, *White House Diary,* p. 192.

163 **325 television sets** Carter, *First Lady from Plains,* p. 154.

163 **"all the cuts and frills"** Landon Butler, unpublished diary, February 14, 1977; Laura Foreman, "Carter's Cousin Hugh Brings Thrifty Ways to White House," *New York Times,* April 8, 1977; Karen De Witt, "Cousin Cheap," *Washington Post,* May 17, 1977. Previously, Hugh Carter, Jr., had been operations manager for the Harland Company, an Atlanta check-printing firm.

163 **"Since you are in touch"** Hugh Carter memo to Jody Powell, January 22, 1977, "Jody Powell Memoranda 1/21/77–7/18/77" folder, box 36, Jimmy Carter Presidential Library.

163 **"I would never use"** Carter, *White House Diary,* p. 56; Hugh Carter, Jr., memo to Jimmy Carter, March 23, 1977, "Memoranda: Carter, Hugh, Jr., 2/1/77–8/1/77" folder, box 41, CF, O/A 2, Staff Offices, Press, Powell, Jimmy Carter Presidential Library.

163 **"We just want to keep"** De Witt, "Cousin Cheap."

163 **in search of a cab home** Matthew Nimitz interview.

163 **"stereotype that we never lived down"** Eizenstat, *President Carter,* p. 113.

164 **He called it his "Shangri-La"** "Camp History," Camp David folder, box 6, Staff Offices, Counsel Lipshutz, Jimmy Carter Presidential Library.

164 **"The wall opens"** Chip Carter interview by Bob Short.

164 **"It's secluded," Carter noted** Jimmy Carter, *White House Diary,* p. 28.

164 **$800,000 to operate** Michael Kernan, "Inside the Mountain Hideaway," *Washington Post,* September 6, 1978.

164 **"I cannot accept so valuable a gift"** Jimmy Carter to Muhammad Ali, September 14, 1977, folder A, box 45, Susan Clough File, White House Staff Papers, Jimmy Carter Presidential Library.

164 **"Carter family habit"** Joshua Kendall, *First Dads,* p. 66; *New York Times,* June 7, 1977.

165 **"Amy's been much happier"** Carter, *White House Diary,* p. 25.

165 **"I said that if I got my parole"** B. Drummond Ayres, Jr., "For Amy Carter's Ex–Baby Sitter, Inaugural Trip Was a Fairy Tale," *New York Times,* January 25, 1977.

165 *Saturday Night Live* The episode aired on March 12, 1977.

165 **"Come on in!"** Brower, *Residence,* p. 187.

165 **"Welcome, I hope you have"** Chip Carter interview, January 24, 2017.

166 **"I would regularly have to"** Brower, *Residence,* p. 98.

166 **"experimented"** Kendall, *First Dads,* p. 63, Norman Mailer, "The Search for Carter," *New York Times.*

166 **"with a beer in one hand"** Kim Kelly, "Willie Nelson Definitely Smoked Weed on the Roof of the White House with Jimmy Carter's Son," Vice.com, September 1, 2015, https://noisey.vice.com/en_us/article/willie-nelson-weed-jimmy-carters-son. (See also Willie Nelson, with Bud Shrake, *Willie: An Autobiography* [New York: Simon & Schuster, 1988], pp. 195–96: "I guess the roof of the White House is the safest place I can think of to smoke dope.")

166 **"I like them very much"** Carter, *White House Diary,* p. 465.

166 **"There was something ghostly about it"** Paul Hendrickson, "Jimmy Carter, Casting Back," *Washington Post.*

167 **"offered to denounce him"** "Castro, Praising Carter, Sees a Prospect of Ties," *New York Times,* February 10, 1977.

167 **"all for Moyers"** Butler, unpublished diary, February 1, 1977.

167 **"I decided right then"** Carter, *White House Diary,* pp. 16–17 and 32; "Carter Is Reported to Weigh Moyers as Head of CIA," *New York Times,* January 27, 1977; Butler, unpublished diary, February 1, 1977.

167 **"Firing so many people"** Chris Whipple, *The Spy Masters,* p. 92.

168 **"There are limits to indecency"** Doolittle, unpublished diary, April 12, 1977.

168 **"All of the inner circle"** Jane Frank memo to Jack Watson, June 4, 1977, 1977 folder, Tim Kraft Papers, courtesy of Tim Kraft. Jane Frank later married Sidney Harman and became Congresswoman Jane Harman.

168 **"the real wonder about Carter"** Doolittle, unpublished diary, March 1, 1978.

168 **"Picture the second most powerful"** Sally Quinn, "The Number Two Man," *Washington Post,* January 16, 1977; Wendy Swanberg, "The Gossip Makes the News: Washington Reporting in the Carter Years," p. 47.

169 **"Hamilton was the poster child"** Alice Rogoff interview, May 5, 2016.

169 **"You'd never know it"** Les Francis interview. Francis recalls attending the ballet with Jordan several times at the Kennedy Center.

169 **"Ham's thumbing his nose"** Butler, unpublished diary, January 27, 1977.

169 **"Ham is letting his desk"** Butler, unpublished diary, February 10, 1977.

169   "If this was all there was" Butler, unpublished diary, February 1, 1977.

169   "He has a way" Carter, *White House Diary,* p. 16.

170   "None of us would be any good" Jimmy Carter note to Bob Lipshutz, February 2, 1977, for distribution to nineteen White House staffers, 1977 folder, Tim Kraft Papers; Butler, unpublished diary, February 3, 1977.

170   seventy-one hours each week Tim Kraft memo to Jimmy Carter, March 11, 1977, Presidential Time Analysis 1977 folder, box 1, Donated Historical Materials, Tim Kraft Collection, Subject Files, Jimmy Carter Presidential Library.

170   "I enjoy it" "Interview with the President for UPI Advisory Board, Cabinet Room," April 27, 1979, News Conference Transcripts folder, box 15, Press Office–Media Liaison Office, Marc Henderson's Subject Files, Jimmy Carter Presidential Library.

170   blood pressure of 120/80 Dr. William Lukash, "President Carter's Annual Physical Examination," April 5, 1979, "Jody Powell Briefings 1979 (1)" folder, box 22, Press Office–Media Liaison Office, Marc Henderson's Subject Files, Jimmy Carter Presidential Library.

170   "He was a solitary man" Kati Marton, *Hidden Power,* p. 223.

170   "Carter's Style Making Aides" James Wooten, "Carter's Style Making Aides Apprehensive," *New York Times,* April 25, 1977.

171   "Jody," asked one reporter "Jody Powell White House Press Briefing," April 25, 1977, Jimmy Carter Presidential Library; also found in 1977 folder, Tim Kraft Papers, courtesy of Tim Kraft.

172   "I wish he were my son" Clare Crawford, "The Tie That Binds Hamilton Jordan to Carter Isn't Around His Neck," *People,* February 6, 1978.

172   "Watch the typos!" Jimmy Carter to Susan Clough, undated memo, "Memos Between President Carter and Susan Clough, 3/3/77–12/13/78," box 41, Susan Clough File, Jimmy Carter Presidential Library.

172   "genital" Terry Adamson interview, December 8, 2015.

172   "I came in on time" Butler, unpublished diary, January 22, 1979.

173   "You're fired" Butler, unpublished diary, March 2, 1977.

173   "I'm out of here by noon" Tim Kraft interview.

173   "Stupid idea" Butler, unpublished diary, February 25, 1977.

173   "Maybe," noted Carter Carter, *White House Diary,* p. 24.

173   "fairly constant level" Carter, *White House Diary,* p. 39.

173   "But his biggest problem" David Rubenstein interview, June 19, 2016.

173   "I'm here at 5:30" Tim Kraft, unpublished notebook, July 13–Sept 27, 1977, courtesy of Tim Kraft.

174   "The Carters don't have friends" Marton, *Hidden Power,* p. 229.

174   "Friends aren't necessary" Nicholas Dawidoff, "The Riddle of Jimmy Carter," *Rolling Stone.*

174   "I tell him what I think" *New York Times,* March 10, 1977.

174   "If you ask me" Marton, *Hidden Power,* p. 217.

174   "I think the Carters" Mary Finch Hoyt exit interview.

174   "driving, pragmatic" Mary Finch Hoyt exit interview.

174   "I loved the politics" Marton, *Hidden Power,* p. 224.

174 "politically risky" Carter, *First Lady from Plains*, pp. 156–58.

175 "I hated to make speeches" James Wooten, "Mrs. Carter Sees Role Widening," *New York Times*, March 15, 1977.

175 "to remove the stigma" *New York Times*, March 10, 1977.

175 "I'll try to convince Jimmy" Marjorie Hunter, "Mrs. Carter's Mental Health Drive Has Tight Budget," *New York Times*, April 22, 1977.

175 "tough lady" John Leonard, Books of the Times, *New York Times*, March 8, 1977.

175 "She may be soft-spoken" Kandy Stroud, "Rosalynn's Agenda in the White House," *New York Times*, March 20, 1977.

176 David Rubenstein was delegated David Rubenstein exit interview.

176 brown leather folder Eizenstat, *President Carter*, p. 107.

176 "That would explain his edginess" Butler, unpublished diary, April 27, 1977.

176 "I was determined" Marton, *Hidden Power*, p. 230.

176 "I really can't think" "President's Boys," *Time*.

176 "Twelve days is just too long" Carter, *White House Diary*, p. 64.

177 "It was a challenge" Carter, *First Lady from Plains*, p. 184.

177 "Who elected her?" Marton, *Hidden Power*, p. 231.

177 "What irritates me" Marton, *Hidden Power*, p. 231.

177 "There's no way" Marton, *Hidden Power*, p. 233.

177 "I do not condemn" Douglas Brinkley, *The Unfinished Presidency*, p. 5.

177 "Thinking how stupid it was" Katharine Graham, *Personal History*, p. 610.

178 "If there is one thing" Eizenstat, *President Carter*, p. 112.

178 "I failed to make" Jimmy Carter interview, September 14, 2017.

178 eight hundred people to the South Lawn Carter, *White House Diary*, p. 202.

178 "Whatever the political future" Gary Giddins, "Jazz at Jimmy's," *Village Voice*.

179 "I've never seen anyone play" George Wein, "A Great Day in Washington," *Jazz Times*, June 1, 2003, https://jazztimes.com/features/george-wein-a-great-day-in-washington/.

179 "I might have to after tonight" National Public Radio recording of White House Jazz Festival, June 18, 1978.

179 "the best party we've ever had" Carter, *White House Diary*, p. 202.

179 James Baldwin and Albert Murray Jacqueline Trescott and Joseph McLellan, "A Who's Who of Jazz on the South Lawn," *Washington Post*, June 19, 1978.

CHAPTER 7: LIFE IS UNFAIR

180 "You shouldn't have said" Kenneth E. Morris, *Jimmy Carter*, p. 242.

180 "Everybody has warned me" Peter G. Bourne, *Jimmy Carter*, p. 373.

181 Rosalynn tried to persuade him Stuart E. Eizenstat, *President Carter*, p. 165.

181 deregulate *new* natural gas Eizenstat, *President Carter*, p. 144.

182 "masterful in ways he intended" "The Chat by the Fire," *New York Times*, February 4, 1977.

182 65 percent approval rating Morris, *Jimmy Carter*, p. 242; Dominic Sandbrook, *Mad as Hell*, p. 226.

182 **"We've made some mistakes"** James T. Wooten, "Carter, Telling of Woes, Sympathizes with Lincoln," *New York Times,* February 9, 1977.

182 **"I felt completely at ease"** Jimmy Carter, *White House Diary,* p. 17.

182 **"Carter at his best"** James Reston, "Carter and the Press," *New York Times,* February 9, 1977.

182 **"In his first two months"** James Fallows, "The Passionless Presidency," *The Atlantic.*

183 **"The attacks on him"** Carter, *White House Diary,* p. 23.

183 **"great choice"** Butler, unpublished diary, March 2, 1977.

183 **"To a surprising degree"** Richard Holbrooke, draft *Newsweek* column, January 27, 1977, "Correspondence, F-J" folder, box 12, Subject Files, Jody Powell Papers, Jimmy Carter Presidential Library.

183 **"We cannot measure"** Nancy Hicks, "Feminists Critical of Carter on Jobs," *New York Times,* February 8, 1977.

184 **"Well, as you know"** Laura Foreman, "President Defends Court's Action Curbing Federal Aid for Abortion," *New York Times,* July 13, 1977.

184 **"During the campaign"** Martin Tolchin, "A Ban on Abortions Paid for by Medicaid Criticized as Unfair," *New York Times,* June 2, 1977.

184 **"Carter Discovers 'Life Is Unfair'"** Rick Perlstein, *Reaganland,* p. 128.

184 **"Democratic power grab"** Perlstein, *Reaganland,* p. 95.

185 **"Appalling," said a Chrysler** Ernest Holsendolph, "Lobbyist for Nader to Head Safety Unit," *New York Times*, March 19, 1977.

185 **"dragon-lady"** Judith Weinraub, "The Tiger in the Consumers' Tank," *Washington Post*, May 5, 1977.

185 **"I can't underline"** Bourne, *Jimmy Carter,* p. 364.

185 **sixty consumer activists** David Bollier, "Chapter 3: The Office of Citizen," in *Citizen Action and Other Big Ideas.*

185 **"They're not going to be"** *New York Times,* April 20, 1977.

186 **nine thousand lives annually** *New York Times,* July 1, 1977.

186 **Claybrook persuaded Carter** Joan Claybrook interview.

186 **"furious about our proposals"** Carter, *White House Diary,* p. 42.

186 **"cowardly defector from"** *Washington Post,* December 1, 1977; Joan Claybrook interview; Michael R. Lemov, *Car Safety Wars,* p. 139.

186 **"I would never have dreamed"** Eizenstat, *President Carter,* p. 390.

187 **"I really don't know one plane"** Robert D. Hershey, Jr., "Alfred Kahn Dies at 93," *New York Times,* December 28, 2010.

187 **"antitrust immunity"** Alfred Kahn to Jimmy Carter, July 27, 1977, NLC-126-8-25-1-5, Jimmy Carter Presidential Library.

187 **"expend whatever energy"** Tom Beebe to Jimmy Carter, August 8, 1977, "Aviation-Airline Regulatory Reform (2)" folder, box 148, Staff Offices, Domestic Policy Staff, Eizenstat, Jimmy Carter Presidential Library.

187 **"After we'd notched this victory"** Stuart Eizenstat speech, Lake Tahoe, June 23, 2017.

188 **Greenstein had ditched** *New York Times,* April 20, 1977.

190 **"It was certainly"** Robert Greenstein interview.

190   **nineteen of these projects** Eizenstat, *President Carter,* p. 256.

190   **"They are raising Cain"** Jimmy Carter, *Keeping Faith,* p. 78.

190   **"In a democracy"** John A. Farrell, *Tip O'Neill and the Democratic Century,* p. 458; Eizenstat, *President Carter,* p. 258.

190   **a "real mud fight"** Eizenstat, *President Carter,* p. 258; Jim Free interview, April 18, 2016.

191   **"the battle left deep scars"** Eizenstat, *President Carter,* p. 263; Carter, *Keeping Faith,* p. 79.

191   **"great waste of federal funds"** Gus Speth and Charles Warren memo to Jimmy Carter, undated, "Water Policy (Decision Memo and Backup) [2]" folder, box 314, Domestic Policy Staff, Eizenstat, Jimmy Carter Presidential Library.

191   **"Many of our wild rivers"** Jimmy Carter, *A Full Life,* p. 184.

192   **"The problem is that Jimmy"** Martin Schram, "Living with Congress: Carter Should Study LBJ's Way," *Newsday,* circa 1977.

192   **"It fed the emerging narrative"** Les Francis interview.

192   **"White male workers' income"** Jefferson Cowie, *Stayin' Alive,* p. 12.

193   **"I'm becoming more concerned"** Carter, *White House Diary,* p. 39.

193   **"One always knew"** Cowie, *Stayin' Alive,* p. 266.

193   **"neglecting social programs"** Carter, *White House Diary,* pp. 45–46.

194   **"Carter will adopt"** Alan Wolfe, "The Two Faces of Carter," *The Nation.*

194   **"just didn't understand Irish"** Julian E. Zelizer, *Jimmy Carter,* p. 58.

194   **"Tip,"** Carter later recalled Farrell, *Tip O'Neill and the Democratic Century,* p. 444.

194   **$66 billion** Bourne, *Jimmy Carter,* p. 375.

195   **"Jack doesn't get mad"** Farrell, *Tip O'Neill and the Democratic Century,* p. 449.

195   **"could have slugged"** Eric Alterman and Kevin Mattson, *The Cause,* p. 305; Bourne, *Jimmy Carter,* pp. 370–71; Bourne, *Jimmy Carter,* p. 366.

195   **"Carter used to think"** Sally Quinn, "Making Capital Gains," *Washington Post.*

196   **"Hannibal Jerkin"** Bourne, *Jimmy Carter,* p. 371; Farrell, *Tip O'Neill and the Democratic Century,* p. 452.

196   **"What can I do for you"** Jimmy Carter eulogy for Hamilton Jordan, May 23, 2008, C-Span, https://www.c-span.org/video/?205630-1/hamilton-jordan -memorial-service.

196   **"They say it's that we're inept"** Schram, "Living with Congress."

196   **"That ought to last"** Farrell, *Tip O'Neill and the Democratic Century,* p. 450.

196   **"They ran against"** Farrell, *Tip O'Neill and the Democratic Century,* p. 446.

197   **"a couple of good, strong drinks"** Carter, *White House Diary,* p. 183.

197   **"This is not something"** Carter, *White House Diary,* p. 60.

197   **"He's so supportive"** Carter, *White House Diary,* p. 183.

197   **"command widespread acceptance"** Edward M. Kennedy, *True Compass,* p. 356.

198   **seventy-nine senators or congressmen** Trey Flynn memo to Jay Beck, May 19, 2016, courtesy of Jay Beck.

198   **"He would never call"** Farrell, *Tip O'Neill and the Democratic Century,* p. 456.

198   "We had them over" Farrell, *Tip O'Neill and the Democratic Century,* p. 456.

198   "Carter thought politics" Bourne, *Jimmy Carter,* p. 420.

198   "The worst thing you could say" Bourne, *Jimmy Carter,* p. 420.

198   "told them in a nice way" Carter, *White House Diary,* p. 75.

198   "Stick to policy" Richard Moe interview, December 17, 2015.

198   "He's just not a politician" Bourne, *Jimmy Carter,* p. 421.

198   "JC not a politician" Eizenstat legal pad #39, September 20, 1978; Eizenstat, *President Carter,* p. 223.

199   "I'm going to be much more" Carter, *White House Diary,* p. 35.

199   "Whenever you have to make" Hamilton Jordan to Jimmy Carter, Personal and Confidential memo, undated, "Early Months Performance, HJ Memos to Pres., 1977," box 34a, Office of the Chief of Staff, Hamilton Jordan Confidential Files, Jimmy Carter Presidential Library.

200   "a crisis soon forgotten" Carter, *Keeping Faith,* p. 91.

200   2.3 times the average per capita Robert A. Strong, "Jimmy Carter: Domestic Affairs," undated, MillerCenter.org, https://millercenter.org/president/carter /domestic-affairs.

201   "I can't understand it" Carter, *Keeping Faith,* pp. 96–97.

201   "Tonight I want to have" Eizenstat, *President Carter,* p. 166.

201   "moral equivalent of war" Burton I. Kaufman and Scott Kaufman, *The Presidency of James Earl Carter, Jr.,* p. 38.

201   suggested to him by Admiral Rickover Carter, *Keeping Faith,* p. 91.

201   "For the first time" Kaufman and Kaufman, *Presidency of James Earl Carter,* p. 38.

201   "moral equivalent of war" Eizenstat, *President Carter,* p. 167.

201   "driving people out" *New York Times,* April 30, 1977.

201   "asinine bill" Jim Free memo, "Congressional Telephone Call Proposal," April 19, 1977, "PR 5-2, 4/14/77–4/20/77" folder, box PR-14, White House Central File, Jimmy Carter Presidential Library.

202   "The influence of the oil and gas" Carter, *White House Diary,* p. 110.

202   "You have not been a failure" "Phone call from Admiral Rickover," December 14, 1977, "Memos Between President Carter and Susan Clough, 3/3/77–12/13/78" folder, box 41, Susan Clough File, Jimmy Carter Presidential Library.

202   "It's a bitch!" Rosalynn Carter, *First Lady from Plains,* p. 158.

203   1.8 million barrels per day Strong, "Jimmy Carter."

203   "nothing less than a disgrace" Kaufman and Kaufman, *Presidency of James Earl Carter,* p. 71.

204   "superficial" Carter, *White House Diary,* p. 53; Kaufman and Kaufman, *Presidency of James Earl Carter,* p. 72.

204   "you will have to instruct" Carter, *White House Diary,* p. 53; Kaufman and Kaufman, *Presidency of James Earl Carter,* p. 72.

204   "insidious game" Carter, *Keeping Faith,* p. 84.

204   "a pack of powerful and ravenous wolves" Carter, *Keeping Faith,* p. 84. See also Carter, *White House Diary,* p. 142.

204 "I don't appreciate" Carter, *White House Diary,* pp. 142 and 145.

205 "The Business [Roundtable] group" Butler, unpublished diary, January 15, 1978.

205 "to tackle the vested interests" Charles Kirbo memo to Jimmy Carter, May 31, 1977, Charles Kirbo Papers, Jimmy Carter Presidential Library.

205 "His words were softer" Jimmy Carter, 1996 memorial service for Charles Kirbo; Charles Kirbo, Jr., "Dear Brother Tom: Words, Letters and Memos of Charles H. Kirbo" (unpublished manuscript, undated), unprocessed Charles Kirbo papers, Jimmy Carter Presidential Library.

206 "but I was much impressed" Kirbo memo, "Discuss with President Carter," undated, circa 1977, unprocessed Charles Kirbo papers.

207 "to find at least one black" Judge Griffin Bell speech, Charlotte, North Carolina, April 12, 1988, courtesy of Terry Adamson.

207 Carter's success rate Strong, "Jimmy Carter."

208 "You have proposed so much" Eizenstat, *President Carter,* p. 190.

208 public financing of congressional Kaufman and Kaufman, *Presidency of James Earl Carter,* p. 64.

208 "If you could start over" Joseph Califano, "Welfare Reform: A Dream That Was Impossible," *Washington Post,* May 22, 1981, excerpted from Joseph Califano, *Governing America.*

208 "Are you telling me" Kaufman and Kaufman, *Presidency of James Earl Carter,* p. 66.

208 "humanly possible" Bourne, *Jimmy Carter,* p. 418.

209 "worse than we thought" *New York Times,* May 3, 1977.

209 "It's so complicated" Carter, *White House Diary,* p. 75.

209 "the Middle East of domestic politics" Califano, "Welfare Reform."

209 1.4 million public-sector jobs Ronald Brownstein, "Social Programs: Clinton's Welfare Reforms Shaped by Predecessors' Frustrated Efforts," *Los Angeles Times,* June 14, 1994.

209 "No legislative struggle" Califano, "Welfare Reform."

210 "This was a world" Joseph A. Califano, Jr., *Inside,* p. 369.

210 "He's not our kind of person" Califano, *Inside,* p. 326.

210 more than $505,000 annually Califano, *Inside,* p. 326.

210 "I wanted to prove" Joseph Califano oral history by Edward Berkowitz, Joseph Califano folder, box 2, Oral History Interviews, Papers of Edward D. Berkowitz, Donated Historical Materials, Jimmy Carter Presidential Library.

210 "The trouble with Califano" Eleanor Randolph, "Califano Charges Through," *Chicago Tribune,* March 26, 1978.

210 hired a personal chef Randolph, "Califano Charges Through."

210 "Well, I've got some advice" Califano, *Inside,* p. 332.

211 "slow-motion suicide" Califano, *Inside,* p. 355.

211 six million people died Califano, *Inside,* p. 356.

211 "Joe, about smoking" Califano, *Inside,* p. 368.

211 "Califano does very well" Carter, *White House Diary,* p. 145.

212 "I'm very high on Joe" Califano, *Inside,* p. 334.

212 "a strong man in a tough place" Charles Kirbo oral history.

212 "Califano was a prick" Les Francis interview.

212 "Joe—I don't feel" Hamilton Jordan handwritten note to Joseph Califano, undated, "Califano, Joseph" folder, box 33, Chief of Staff Jordan, Jimmy Carter Presidential Library.

212 "This can't go on" Alter, *His Very Best*, p. 313.

213 "Some mornings he would wake" Charles Kirbo oral history, p. 11.

213 "I enjoyed talking with Kirbo" Carter, *White House Diary*, p. 59.

213 "working on an arrangement" Charles Kirbo memo to Jimmy Carter, May 16, 1977, Charles Kirbo Papers, Jimmy Carter Presidential Library.

213 18 percent Charles Kirbo memo to Jimmy Carter, May 11, 1977, Charles Kirbo Papers, Jimmy Carter Presidential Library.

213 "I feel confident" Charles Kirbo memo to Jimmy Carter, April 14, 1977, Charles Kirbo Papers, Jimmy Carter Presidential Library.

213 "We've talked about it" Eizenstat, *President Carter*, p. 25.

214 "Charlie," he exclaimed Terry Adamson interview, December 8, 2015. Adamson heard this story from Jack Nelson, the Washington bureau chief for the *Los Angeles Times*.

CHAPTER 8: LANCEGATE

215 "size of an elephant" Jimmy Carter, *Keeping Faith*, p. 128.

215 "Our conversations are wide-ranging" *New York Times*, April 18, 1977; Stuart E. Eizenstat, *President Carter*, p. 117.

216 "a friendly bear of a guy" Robert Shrum, "Bert Lance," *New Times; New York Times*, April 18, 1977; Dom Bonafede, *The National Journal*.

216 "He knew how to deal" Charles Kirbo oral history, p. 20.

216 "an easy, boyish way" Carter, *Keeping Faith*, p. 128.

217 never more than $60,000 John F. Berry, "Unraveling a Lance Bank's Finances," *Washington Post*, October 16, 1977.

217 $11.9 million to $54.1 million Bert Lance with Bill Gilbert, *The Truth of the Matter*, p. 139.

217 sixty-room mansion Eizenstat, *President Carter*, p. 121.

217 "Country banks are different" Lance, *Truth of the Matter*, p. 145.

217 "the economy needs to be stimulated" Lance, *Truth of the Matter*, p. 82.

218 "He did owe a good deal" Charles Kirbo oral history, p. 18.

218 "If you and Bert want to buy" Charles Kirbo to Jimmy Carter, July 25, 1977, Charles Kirbo Papers, Jimmy Carter Presidential Library.

218 "shocked and frightened" Hamilton Jordan memo to Jimmy Carter, "Lance, Bert, 1977" folder, box 35, Hamilton Jordan's Confidential Files, Jimmy Carter Presidential Library, https://www.jimmycarterlibrary.gov/digital_library /cos/142099/35/cos_142099_35_17-Lance_Bert.pdf; Rick Perlstein, *Reaganland*, p. 146.

219 "never stuck it in his own pocket" Eizenstat, *President Carter*, p. 128.

219 "Bert Lance enjoys" *New York Times*, August 19, 1977.

219 "Bert, I'm proud of you" Carter, *Keeping Faith,* p. 130.

219 "I almost died" Eizenstat, *President Carter,* p. 128.

220 "was run like a piggy bank" Shrum, "Bert Lance." According to Stu Eizenstat, Lance's bank made a $4.7 million loan to Carter's peanut warehouse in 1975— a loan that was quickly repaid. (Eizenstat, *President Carter,* p. 121.)

220 $25,000 to $110,000 *New York Times,* August 19, 1977.

220 "Bert, we're going to have" *New York Times,* August 19, 1977.

220 "Bert had a chance" Landon Butler, unpublished diary, September 4, 1977.

220 "Nothing Lance did was illegal" Connie Evans memo to Senator Charles Percy, August 22, 1977, courtesy of Ken Ackerman.

220 "He thought they were mistreating Bert" Charles Kirbo oral history, p. 21.

220 "The *Washington Post* is conducting" Carter, *Keeping Faith,* p. 132.

221 "Even some members" Lance, *Truth of the Matter,* pp. 140 and 142.

221 "Bert Lance has done nothing" Lance, *Truth of the Matter,* p. 136.

221 "I defended Bert early on" Landon Butler, unpublished diary, September 4, 1977.

222 "could not bring myself" Carter, *Keeping Faith,* p. 132.

222 "oversight in campaign bookkeeping" Fred Barnes, "Carter to Reimburse Bank for Providing Plane Trips," *Washington Star,* August 23, 1977.

222 net worth of $2.6 million *New York Daily News,* September 15, 1977.

222 "At this point in time" Connie Evans memo to Senator Percy, August 22, 1977, courtesy of Ken Ackerman.

222 "Lance is clearly on the ropes" Landon Butler, unpublished diary, September 8–9, 1977.

222 their knees, praying together Zbigniew Brzezinski interview, May 4, 2016; Eizenstat, *President Carter,* p. 130.

223 "Rosalynn and I both decided" Carter, *Keeping Faith,* p. 134, citing Carter's diary of September 17, 1977.

223 "I will fire anyone" Eizenstat, *President Carter,* p. 130.

223 "I talked to Kirbo" Jimmy Carter diary, September 17–18, 1977, quoted in Carter, *Keeping Faith,* p. 134. See also https://www.jimmycarterlibrary.gov/digital_library /cos/142099/35/cos_142099_35_17-Lance_Bert.pdf.

223 "Well, Bert, my primary responsibility" Charles Kirbo oral history, p. 22.

223 "For one of the rare times" Carter, *Keeping Faith,* p. 134.

224 "that red-eyed campaign-fatigue look" Tim Kraft, unpublished notebook, July 13–September 27, 1977, courtesy of Tim Kraft.

224 "I didn't argue with him" Carter, *Keeping Faith,* p. 135; Lance, *Truth of the Matter,* p. 148.

224 "probably one of the worst" Carter, *Keeping Faith,* p. 135.

224 "All that was untrue" LaBelle Lance, *This Too Shall Pass,* p. 9; Berry, "Unraveling a Lance Bank's Finances."

225 "adamantly opposed" Carter, *Keeping Faith,* p. 136.

225 "in bitter terms" Carter, *Keeping Faith,* p. 136; Jimmy Carter, daily diary, September 21, 1977, Jimmy Carter Presidential Library; Lance, *Truth of the Matter,* pp. 130 and 150; Jimmy Carter, *White House Diary,* p. 103.

225 **"right down the tube"** Tim Kraft, unpublished notebook no. 4, 1977, September 21, 1977, courtesy of Tim Kraft.

225 **"has shaken my belief"** Lance, *Truth of the Matter,* p. 150.

225 **"You are a great group"** Bert Lance handwritten note "To All the OMB People," courtesy of Ken Ackerman.

225 **The president's poll numbers** Eizenstat, *President Carter,* p. 134.

226 **"The Lance affair has"** George Will, *Newsweek,* September 19, 1977.

226 **"Some of the things"** Charles Kirbo oral history, p. 21.

226 **"I understand why he went"** Charles Kirbo oral history, p. 21.

226 **"should never have been named"** Eizenstat, *President Carter,* p. 120.

226 **"fortitude to tell the president"** Eizenstat, *President Carter,* p. 134.

227 **"You really don't know?"** Lance, *Truth of the Matter,* p. 155.

CHAPTER 9: DEPARTURES IN FOREIGN POLICY

228 **"If you want a magnolia"** Adam Bernstein, "Patricia Derian, Activist Who Was President Carter's Human Rights Chief, Dies at 86," *Washington Post,* May 20, 2016; Betty Glad, *An Outsider in the White House,* p. 23; William Michael Schmidli, *The Fate of Freedom Elsewhere,* p. 95.

229 **"tyranny of those little towns"** *New York Times,* June 23, 1977.

229 **"I don't tap-dance"** Hodding Carter, eulogy for Patt Derian, June 2016.

229 **"beat the bureaucracy"** Iain Guest, *Behind the Disappearances,* p. 156.

229 **"wasn't looking so much"** Paul Vitello, "Patricia Derian, Diplomat Who Made Human Rights a Priority, Dies at 86," *New York Times*, May 20, 2016.

229 **"the NSC [Brzezinski] frequently is"** Patricia Derian memo to the Secretary, October 22, 1979, "Next Seventeen Months—mtgs. with A/S" folder, box 18, Records of Anthony Lake, 1977–1981, RG 59, entry P9, Records of the State Department, National Archives.

229 **"adversarial relationship with much"** Paul H. Kreisberg memo to Deputy Secretary [Warren Christopher], October 23, 1979, "Next Seventeen Months— mtgs. with A/S" folder, box 18, Records of Anthony Lake, 1977–1981, RG 59, entry P9, Records of the State Department, National Archives.

230 **"It sickened me"** Martin Edwin Andersen, "Kissinger and the 'Dirty War,'" *The Nation.*

230 **"sending a dangerous and double"** Patt Derian notes, early April 1977, National Security Archive, http://nsarchive.gwu.edu/NSAEBB/NSAEBB85/.

230 **"I'm going to tell you"** Schmidli, *Fate of Freedom Elsewhere,* p. 83.

231 **"It's possible that they're"** Guest, *Behind the Disappearances,* pp. 161–63.

231 **"If the Argentine situation"** Schmidli, *Fate of Freedom Elsewhere,* p. 50.

232 **"moderately repressive autocratic"** Guest, *Behind the Disappearances,* p. 247.

232 **stacked with unpacked boxes** Roberta Cohen interview.

232 **"I thought she was smart"** Mark Schneider interview.

232 **"our country to be the focal"** Peter G. Bourne, *Jimmy Carter,* p. 384.

232 **"There has to be a homeland"** *New York Times,* March 18, 1977.

232 "Being confident of our own" *New York Times,* May 23, 1977; Bourne, *Jimmy Carter,* p. 385.

233 Hendrik "Rick" Hertzberg Hendrik Hertzberg interview.

233 Fallows passed Doolittle's memo Robert Schlesinger, *White House Ghosts,* p. 275; Jerry Doolittle memo to Jim Fallows, undated, "Speechwriters 5/3/77–5/27/77" folder, Jimmy Carter Presidential Library.

234 "suggest that a major motivation" Vice President Mondale memo to President Carter, May 12, 1977, document 43, Foreign Relations of the United States, 1977–1980, vol. 2, Human Rights and Humanitarian Affairs.

234 "reflected Carter's priorities" Jessica Tuchman Mathews interview.

234 "Brzezinski is better informed" Charles Kirbo oral history, p. 40.

234 "Human rights," Tuchman said Jessica Tuchman Mathews interview.

235 "deep disagreements" *New York Times,* April 12, 1979. Jessica Tuchman later married and became known as Jessica Tuchman Mathews. She was president of the Carnegie Endowment for International Peace from 1997 to 2015.

235 Brzezinski deftly used Caleb Rossiter with Anne-Marie Smith, "Human Rights: The Carter Record, the Reagan Reaction," *International Policy Report.*

235 "At the time" Jessica Tuchman Mathews interview.

235 "I saw human rights" Glad, *An Outsider in the White House,* p. 72.

235 "I liked him personally" Jimmy Carter interview, September 14, 2017.

235 "I recognized Zbig's strengths" Jimmy Carter oral history, February 18, 1982.

236 "We had a good time" Zbigniew Brzezinski interview, May 4, 2016.

236 "immaculately dressed, trim" David Ignatius, eulogy for Zbigniew Brzezinski.

236 "Woody Woodpecker" Jerome Doolittle, unpublished diary, November 18, 1977; Hamilton Jordan, *Crisis,* p. 41.

236 "Most of the people" Landon Butler, unpublished diary, June 1, 1978.

236 "didn't like Brzezinski" Doolittle, unpublished diary, March 1, 1978.

236 "bland, disingenuous and a double-dealer" Rick Hertzberg diary, December 19–21, 1977; Schlesinger, *White House Ghosts,* p. 282.

237 "contractual," focused on "negotiating agreements" Brzezinski memo to the President, April 21, 1978, "NSC Weekly Reports, 1–5/78" folder, box 29, Plains Subject File, Jimmy Carter Presidential Library.

238 "was just the CIA" Doolittle, unpublished diary, November 18, 1977.

238 "without delay" President Carter to Soviet General Secretary Brezhnev, January 26, 1977, Foreign Relations of the United States, 1977–1980, vol. 6, Soviet Union.

238 "much greater reductions" President Carter to Soviet General Secretary Brezhnev, February 14, 1977, document 7, Foreign Relations of the United States, 1977–1980, vol. 6, Soviet Union, p. 21.

238 "putting forward deliberately unacceptable" Soviet General Secretary Brezhnev to President Carter, February 25, 1977, document 12, Foreign Relations of the United States, 1977–1980, vol. 6, Soviet Union.

239 "obviously severe in tone" Cyrus Vance memo to the president, March 3, 1977, NLC-128-4-24-7-2, Jimmy Carter Presidential Library.

239 "brutal, cynical, sneering" Glad, *An Outsider in the White House,* p. 53.

239 **He knew the Soviets were unlikely** "I expect the Soviets will not accept our proffered offer." (Brzezinski diary, March 25, 1977, cited in David S. McLellan, *Cyrus Vance*, p. 40.)

239 **Brzezinski was quite cynically** Glad, *An Outsider in the White House*, pp. 16, 45, and 48.

240 **"Surely the Soviets"** Burton I. Kaufman and Scott Kaufman, *The Presidency of James Earl Carter, Jr.*, p. 48.

240 **"The tables have been turned"** Glad, *An Outsider in the White House*, p. 53.

240 **ambitious covert operation** Glad, *An Outsider in the White House*, p. 51.

240 **"marginal value to our national interest"** Butler, unpublished diary, May 3, 1977.

240 **"underestimating the Soviets' displeasure"** Glad, *An Outsider in the White House*, p. 54.

240 **"Brzezinski, however, never accepted"** Carter, "Life Inside the Carter State Department," p. 214.

241 **"When it comes to the Panama Canal"** Jimmy Carter, *Keeping Faith*, p. 154; *New York Times*, February 29, 1976.

241 **"It's obvious that we cheated"** Jimmy Carter, *White House Diary*, p. 86.

241 **"These were not easy decisions"** Carter, *Keeping Faith*, pp. 154–55; Carter, *White House Diary*, p. 30.

242 **"There's a lot of natural opposition"** Carter, *White House Diary*, p. 73.

242 **"a few nuts"** Carter, *White House Diary*, p. 80.

242 **"After all we've been through"** Butler, unpublished diary, September 4, 1977.

242 **"an unbelievable show of strength"** Butler, unpublished diary, September 4, 1977.

242 **"we were doing the right thing"** Carter, *White House Diary*, p. 90; Carter, *Keeping Faith*, p. 161.

243 **a Gallup poll indicated** Carter, *Keeping Faith*, p. 162; Carter, *White House Diary*, p. 96.

243 **"move away from it"** Carter, *White House Diary*, p. 88.

243 **"The opposition has a 'cause'"** David McCullough to Jimmy Carter, October 21, 1977, "Panama Canal, 1977–78 [1]" folder, box 67, Staff Offices, Press, Powell, Jimmy Carter Presidential Library.

243 **"Frankly, I'm just as sure"** Butler, unpublished diary, September 4, 1977.

243 **"I recognize clearly"** Jimmy Carter to Barry Goldwater, September 10, 1977, folder G, 1977–81, box 45, Jimmy Carter Personal, Susan Clough file, Jimmy Carter Presidential Library.

244 **"He's a helluv'a lot better actor"** "Is This the Same Duke?" undated newspaper clip, "Assignments, Presidential 1977" folder, box 33, Office of the Chief of Staff, Hamilton Jordan Confidential Files, Jimmy Carter Presidential Library.

244 **"Now I have taken your letter"** *New York Times*, March 16, 1987; Scott Eyman, *John Wayne* (New York: Simon & Schuster, 2014), p. 537.

244 **"shakedown"** William Safire, "Panama Townhouse," *New York Times*, January 2, 1978.

244 **"Strauss was trying to make"** Butler, unpublished diary, January 20, 1977, January 1, 1978, and January 3, 1978.

245 "It's hard to concentrate" Carter, *Keeping Faith*, p. 171.

245 "soft on foreign affairs" Carter, *Keeping Faith*, p. 175. Hayakawa had once said that America should keep the Panama Canal because "we stole it fair and square" (Rick Perlstein, *Reaganland*, p. 140).

246 "This has been one" Carter, *Keeping Faith*, 171; Carter, *White House Diary*, p. 177.

246 "I had never been more tense" Carter, *White House Diary*, p. 178; Carter, *Keeping Faith*, p. 173.

246 "This time last year" Hedrick Smith, *New York Times*, April 20, 1978.

246 "We would have started our" Carter, *Keeping Faith*, p. 178.

246 "sentimental journey back" Adam Clymer, *New York Times*, April 19, 1978.

247 "might hold his nose" Carter, *White House Diary*, p. 166.

247 carefully on June 6, 1977 Carter, *White House Diary*, p. 61; Jimmy Carter, *A Full Life*, p. 147.

247 "a gross waste of money" Carter, *Keeping Faith*, p. 81.

248 "He seemed to be relieved" Carter, *White House Diary*, p. 66; Carter, *Keeping Faith*, p. 82.

248 "It was an easy and logical" Carter, *White House Diary*, p. 66.

248 Senator Barry Goldwater *New York Times*, June 29, 1977; *New York Times*, June 30, 1977.

248 "great surprise and excitement" Doolittle, unpublished diary, June 30, 1977.

248 "They are breaking open" *New York Times*, July 3, 1977.

248 "himself a statesman" Editorial, *New York Times*, June 29, 1977.

248 "the finest moment of his brief" Tom Wicker, *New York Times*, July 3, 1977.

248 "The adverse reaction" Carter, *White House Diary*, p. 67.

249 "exciting display of professional competence" Carter, *White House Diary*, p. 179.

249 "We prevailed against" Carter, *White House Diary*, p. 179.

249 Pentagon's budget increased annually Eizenstat, *President Carter*, p. 607.

CHAPTER 10: "ISRAEL TRUSTS NO ONE"

251 "Palestinian entity federated" Brookings Middle East Study Group, "Toward Peace in the Middle East"; Salim Yaqub, *Imperfect Strangers*, p. 174.

251 "PLO Chairman Arafat is seeking" William Quandt and Samuel Hoskinson memo to Zbigniew Brzezinski, February 9, 1977, Secret (declassified November 11, 2008), NLC-7-49-3-2-8, Jimmy Carter Presidential Library.

251 "I was infatuated with the Holy Land" Jimmy Carter, *Palestine*, p. 22.

251 "this homeland for the Jews" Jimmy Carter, *Keeping Faith*, p. 274.

251 Mondale was surprised Lawrence Wright, *Thirteen Days in September*, p. 6.

252 "resolve the underlying problems" Carter, *Keeping Faith*, pp. 276–77.

252 "only to be told" Carter, *Keeping Faith*, p. 279.

252 "I've put in an awful lot" Jimmy Carter, *White House Diary*, p. 31; Wright, *Thirteen Days in September*, p. 8.

252 **"one of the most ineffective persons"** Carter, *White House Diary*, p. 71.

253 **"At first, he was a little"** Carter, *White House Diary*, pp. 38–39.

253 **"complexion was much darker"** Carter, *Keeping Faith*, p. 282.

253 **"On borders, I do not think"** Memorandum of Conversation, April 4, 1977, Top Secret (declassified October 31, 2013), NLC-25-109-8-2-3, Jimmy Carter Presidential Library.

255 **When Kissinger vetoed** Kai Bird, *The Good Spy*, p. 181.

256 **"Israel trusts no one"** Memorandum of Conversation, April 4, 1977, Top Secret (declassified October 31, 2013), NLC-25-109-8-2-3, Jimmy Carter Presidential Library.

256 **"a shining light"** Carter, *Keeping Faith*, p. 282.

256 **"Not in my lifetime!"** Carter, *Keeping Faith*, p. 283.

256 **"my best day as president"** Carter, *Keeping Faith*, p. 284.

257 **"favorably impressed with the Arab leaders"** Yaqub, *Imperfect Strangers*, p. 243.

257 **"My own judgment"** Carter, *White House Diary*, p. 44.

257 **"It was frightening"** Carter, *White House Diary*, pp. 56–57; Jimmy Carter daily diary, April 4, 1977.

257 **"Begin, by his extremism"** Yaqub, *Imperfect Strangers*, p. 244.

258 **"to repair my damaged political base"** Carter, *Keeping Faith*, p. 290.

258 **White House office safe** Wright, *Thirteen Days in September*, p. 7.

258 **"I would compare"** Hamilton Jordan memo, June 1977, "Middle East 1977" folder, box 35, Hamilton Jordan Confidential Files, Jimmy Carter Presidential Library. See also Wright, *Thirteen Days in September*, p. 7.

258 **25 percent of campaign contributions** Jeremy Sharon, "US Jews Contribute Half of All Donations to the Democratic Party," *Jerusalem Post*, September 27, 2016, https://www.jpost.com/US-Elections/US-Jews-contribute-half-ofsall-donations -to-the-Democratic-party-468774; J. J. Goldberg, *Jewish Power*, p. 276. Goldberg reports that traditionally about half of the funding for the Democratic National Committee comes from Jewish American donors.

260 **"It was a paradox"** Wright, *Thirteen Days in September*, pp. 7–8.

260 **"dire predictions"** Carter, *White House Diary*, p. 71.

260 **"quite congenial, dedicated"** This quote is not reprinted in Carter's *White House Diary* but can be found in his memoir, *Keeping Faith*, p. 290.

261 **"to keep an open mind"** Carter, *Keeping Faith*, pp. 290–91.

261 **"proceed aggressively"** Carter, *White House Diary*, p. 82.

261 **"sooner or later there would"** Henry Brandon diary, August 31, 1977, cited in Yaqub, *Imperfect Strangers*, p. 251.

262 **"I would come with a one-page"** Landrum Bolling interview.

262 **"only a promise"** Yaqub, *Imperfect Strangers*, p. 248.

263 **"code-words for Israel's destruction"** Yaqub, *Imperfect Strangers*, p. 252.

263 **"the screams arise"** Carter, *White House Diary*, p. 111.

263 **"appalled"** Rabbi Alexander Schindler, "The Jews and Carter," *New York Times*.

263 **"The Israelis are absolutely shameless"** Landon Butler, unpublished diary, October 11, 1977.

263 "felt particularly embattled" Carter, *Keeping Faith*, p. 294.

263 "I'd rather commit political suicide" Yaqub, *Imperfect Strangers*, p. 252; Carter, *White House Diary*, p. 115.

263 "He was obviously quite nervous" Carter, *Keeping Faith*, p. 294; Carter, *White House Diary*, p. 112.

264 idea of a unified delegation Yaqub, *Imperfect Strangers*, pp. 252–53.

264 "I need your help" Carter, *Keeping Faith*, p. 295.

264 "he's going to take bold action" Carter, *White House Diary*, p. 126.

264 "bold initiative" Carter, *Keeping Faith*, p. 296.

264 "seriously complicate, rather" Jimmy Carter rough draft of letter to Anwar Sadat, undated, declassified June 2, 2008, NLC-128-11-18-1-7, CREST, Jimmy Carter Presidential Library.

264 "I haven't done anything" Carter, *Keeping Faith*, p. 297; Carter, *White House Diary*, p. 138. Oddly, Carter doesn't include the words "I haven't done anything . . . that each of them wanted peace" in his published diary. These words are quoted only in *Keeping Faith*.

265 "As you know" Anwar Sadat undated handwritten note to Jimmy Carter, declassified June 2, 2008, NLC-128-11-18-23-3, CREST, Jimmy Carter Presidential Library.

265 "There is the need" Memorandum of Telephone Conversation, Jimmy Carter and Menachem Begin, November 17, 1977, Secret (declassified June 16, 2008), NLC-128-6-2-1-0, CREST, Jimmy Carter Presidential Library.

265 "danger to Sadat's life" Carter, *White House Diary*, p. 138.

265 "Stu, I think I am going" Stuart E. Eizenstat, *President Carter*, p. 474.

265 "disappointed with Begin's speech" Carter, *White House Diary*, p. 139.

265 "still hope that Israel can have" Anthony Lake memo to the Secretary, November 25, 1977, "TL Sensitive 10/1–12/31/77" folder, box 17, Records of Anthony Lake, 1977–1981, RG 59, entry P9, National Archives.

266 "Although Sadat's visit" Carter, *White House Diary*, pp. 139–41.

266 "to protect Israel" *New York Times*, October 5, 1977.

266 "I'm really troubled" Koch's October 3, 1977, letter suggested that Carter intended to force Israel "to negotiate with the PLO. . . . We must not and will not tolerate the abandonment of the state of Israel to those dedicated to her destruction." (Ed Koch to Jimmy Carter, October 3, 1977, "Keefe to Krueger" folder, box 45, Susan Clough File, Jimmy Carter Presidential Library.)

267 "catering to Arab demands" *New York Times*, October 5, 1977.

267 "in a pre-publicized but friendly way" Carter, *White House Diary*, p. 112.

267 "Ed Koch was seriously hurt" Carter, *White House Diary*, p. 119.

267 "a real mensch" Jerome Doolittle, unpublished diary, August 9, 1978.

267 "The Jews and Jimmy Carter" *New York Times*, November 6, 1977.

268 "a failure of nerve" Yaqub, *Imperfect Strangers*, p. 260.

268 "Bye-bye PLO" *New York Times*, December 30, 1977.

268 "inadequate" Jimmy Carter handwritten note, December 16, 1977, folder 25, President's Personal Foreign Affairs File, Plains File, Jimmy Carter Presidential Library.

268 **"I am very disappointed"** Memorandum of Conversation, Anwar Sadat and Jimmy Carter, January 18, 1978, Secret (declassified June 9, 2008), NLC-128-11-18-3-5, CREST, Jimmy Carter Presidential Library.

269 **"true Pole and a righteous man"** Carter, *White House Diary*, p. 155.

269 **"I asked him if he"** Jimmy Carter, *A Full Life*, p. 133.

269 **"delightful banquet"** Carter, *White House Diary*, p. 156.

270 **his speechwriter, Jim Fallows** Andrew Scott Cooper, *The Fall of Heaven*, p. 282.

270 **"If the misery of others"** Carter, *Keeping Faith*, p. 437; Carter, *White House Diary*, p. 156.

270 **"Allahu Akbar"** Julian E. Zelizer, *Jimmy Carter*, p. 72.

270 **"was for us that rarest"** Henry Kissinger, *White House Years*, p. 1261.

270 **"It was," he later noted** Carter, *White House Diary*, p. 135.

271 **"One thing I can say"** Chris Whipple, *The Spymasters*, p. 97.

271 **"Salt Peanuts"** Jimmy Carter diary, November 15, 1977, *White House Diary*, p. 136. Carter noted that the short concert "brought back old times when I was an avid jazz fan."

271 **"he was quite embarrassed"** Carter, *White House Diary*, p. 137.

271 **"No, there is nothing I can do"** Carter, *Keeping Faith*, pp. 436–37.

271 **"even a prerevolutionary situation"** Carter, *Keeping Faith*, p. 438; Rick Perlstein, *Reaganland*, p. 433.

272 **3,087 political prisoners** Cooper, *Fall of Heaven*, p. 237.

272 **"SAVAK worked very well"** Cooper, *Fall of Heaven*, p. 239.

272 **"displayed megalomaniacal tendencies"** Zbigniew Brzezinski, *Power and Principle*, pp. 360.

273 **"Complaints after the revolution"** James A. Bill, *The Eagle and the Lion*, p. 219.

273 **"no more than an ignorant peasant"** Asadollah Alam, *The Shah and I*, p. 500.

CHAPTER 11: WASHINGTON DISTRACTIONS

274 **"The bloom is off"** Landon Butler, unpublished diary, December 10, 1977.

275 **"Its thrust was to argue"** Butler, unpublished diary, December 16, 1977.

275 **"There is not a person"** Hamilton Jordan memo to President Carter, first draft, December 1977, "Administrative Review, Goals & Priorities" folder, box 33, Office of the Chief of Staff, Hamilton Jordan Confidential Files, Jimmy Carter Presidential Library.

275 **"but in addition, it is more"** "The Freshman" (editorial), *New York Times*, November 3, 1977.

275 **"Carter terribly tired"** Peter G. Bourne, *Jimmy Carter*, p. 524.

275 **"You find it difficult"** Hamilton Jordan memo to President Carter, first draft, December 1977, "Administrative Review, Goals & Priorities" folder, box 33, Office of the Chief of Staff, Hamilton Jordan Confidential Files, Jimmy Carter Presidential Library.

276 **"If you were a guest"** Edward M. Kennedy, *True Compass*, pp. 360–61.

276 **"He was an outsider"** Kennedy, *True Compass*, p. 353.

276 "One hundred and sixteen days" Peter S. Canellos, ed., *Last Lion*, p. 200.

277 "a substantial tax increase" Jimmy Carter, *White House Diary*, p. 152.

277 "largest peacetime tax increase" Julian E. Zelizer, *Jimmy Carter*, p. 71.

277 "gave Senator Kennedy his word" Butler, unpublished diary, December 21, 1977; Jimmy Carter, daily diary, December 20, 1977. Kennedy and Carter talked for thirty minutes about healthcare.

277 "unselfish and also politically competent" Carter, *White House Diary*, p. 171.

277 "I just wasn't sure with Carter" Kennedy, *True Compass*, p. 358.

278 "Hubert seemed to be in good spirits" Jimmy Carter, diary, December 10–11, 1978, *White House Diary*, pp. 146–47; Jimmy Carter, *A Full Life*, pp. 162–63.

278 "It has been a rocky year" "The Freshman" (editorial), *New York Times*, November 3, 1977.

278 "Name any inflammable" James Reston, *New York Times*, April 5, 1978.

279 "1977 was a good year" Carter, *White House Diary*, p. 163.

279 "Carter offered to rid us" Russell Baker, *New York Times*, December 18, 1977.

279 "I cheer myself with the thought" Calvin Trillin, "Variations," *The Nation*, April 22, 1978.

279 "I admit nothing" Curtis Wilkie, *Dixie*, p. 239.

280 "There's a hell of a lot more" Edward Walsh, "White House Disassociates Itself from Billy's Remarks," *Washington Post*, January 12, 1979.

280 "He is seriously ill" Wilkie, *Dixie*, p. 240.

280 "about the dumbest bastard" Walsh, "White House Disassociates Itself."

280 "became an apparently hopeless alcoholic" Jimmy Carter, *Living Faith*, p. 244.

280 "the most inaccurate periodical" Carter, *White House Diary*, p. 211.

280 "would have tried less" Hedrick Smith, "Problems of a Problem Solver," *New York Times*, January 8, 1978.

281 "My God, I've been set up" Hamilton Jordan, *No Such Thing as a Bad Day*, p. 67.

281 "Where Did All the Good Times Go?" Sally Quinn, "Where Did All the Good Times Go?" *Washington Post*.

282 "didn't exactly have a honeymoon" Tim Kraft, handwritten note cards, nos. 14–15, courtesy of Tim Kraft.

283 "blonde, very pretty and single" Sally Quinn, "Peach Frost and Soft Talk of the President's Secretary," *Washington Post*, November 6, 1977.

283 "My wife was also less" Jody Powell, *The Other Side of the Story*, p. 113.

283 "I'd like to punch Sally Quinn" Diana McLellan, *Ear on Washington*, p. 235; Swanberg, "Gossip Makes the News," p. 49; Joseph A. Califano, Jr., *Governing America*, p. 416.

284 "White House Biggie" Diana McLellan, The Ear, *Washington Star*, December 15, 1977.

284 "That story was crap" Powell, *Other Side of the Story*, p. 131.

284 "Ham had a wild streak" Les Francis interview.

284 "I'm just hurt" Wendell Rawls, Jr., "Slur to Envoy's Wife Tied to Carter Aide," *New York Times*, December 19, 1977.

284 "I talked to Jody" Carter, *White House Diary*, p. 152.

285 **"bringing together two men"** William Safire, "Barbara's Dinner Party," *New York Times,* December 22, 1977.

285 **"Ham was more relaxed"** Butler, unpublished diary, December 20, 1977.

285 **"I put up a brave front"** Jordan, *No Such Thing as a Bad Day,* pp. 68–71.

286 **"You ought to get out"** Jordan, *Crisis,* p. 173.

286 **"My overreaction became"** Powell, *Other Side of the Story,* p. 130; Swanberg, "Gossip Makes the News," pp. 95–96; Dan Morgan, "The Jordan Encounter," *Washington Post,* February 21, 1978.

286 **former college roommate** Maxine Cheshire, *Washington Post,* September 26, 1980.

287 **"Jody said Hamilton kind of"** Jerome Doolittle, unpublished diary, February 20, 1978, and March 6, 1978.

287 **"bare-chested, peanut-feeding yahoos"** Swanberg, "Gossip Makes the News," pp. 93–94.

287 **"Well, what have they screwed up"** The *Post*'s John Goshko related this to Doolittle. (Doolittle, unpublished diary, March 29, 1978.)

287 **"General disillusionment with JC"** Doolittle, unpublished diary, July 26, 1978.

287 **"Carter himself was not fun"** Swanberg, "Gossip Makes the News," p. 93.

287 **"There is something about Jimmy Carter"** Gary Wills, "Reading the Carter Riddle," *New York Review of Books.*

287 **"Slob in the White House"** Aaron Lathan, "Hamilton Jordan: Slob in the White House," *Esquire;* Garret Epps, "The Myth of Hamilton Jordan," *Washington Post Magazine.*

288 **"His marriage is on the rocks"** Butler, unpublished diary, December 10, 1977.

288 **"his work was clearly a problem"** Butler, unpublished diary, January 9, 1978.

288 **Chip Carter sold Kraft a jukebox** Tim Kraft interview.

288 **"I'm the same slob"** Clare Crawford, "The Tie That Binds Hamilton Jordan to Carter Isn't Around His Neck," *People,* February 6, 1978.

288 **"Suffice it to say"** Butler, unpublished diary, January 18, 1978, and January 22, 1978.

CHAPTER 12: TROUBLES WITH LIBERALS

290 **"breaking his word of honor"** Jimmy Carter, *White House Diary,* pp. 167 and 161.

290 **"was an obstacle to peace"** Carter, *White House Diary,* p. 162.

290 **"I think we ought to move"** Carter, *White House Diary,* p. 168.

290 **"The president is damned mad"** Landon Butler, unpublished diary, February 13, 1978.

290 **"I spelled out the relative"** Carter, *White House Diary,* p. 171.

290 **"he did not want Jerusalem"** Carter, *White House Diary,* p. 170.

290 **"With the exception of Alex"** Carter, *White House Diary,* p. 171.

291 **"feeling that the administration"** Ronald I. Rubin, "The Most Powerful Rabbis in New York," *New York,* January 22, 1979; Ron Rubin, *A Jewish Professor's Political Punditry* (Syracuse, N.Y.: Syracuse University Press, 2013), pp. 208–9.

291 "appalled" Alexander M. Schindler, "The Jews and Carter," *New York Times.*

291 "given away everything" Kathleen Teltsch, "U.S. Rabbi Tells of Talk with Sadat," *New York Times,* January 21, 1978.

291 "We know some Jewish leaders" Terence Smith, "Jews in U.S. Aren't Sure Just How to Take Sadat," *New York Times,* February 12, 1978.

292 "We felt we shouldn't intrude" Smith, "Jews in U.S. Aren't Sure."

292 "My feeling is that" Smith, "Jews in U.S. Aren't Sure."

292 "act like an ass" Carter, *White House Diary,* p. 171.

292 "Zbig is clearly tilted" Butler, unpublished diary, February 12, 1978.

292 "the Brzezinski meeting was" Bernard Gwertzman, "Jewish Leader Says Mideast Policy Makes a 'Question Mark' of Carter," *New York Times,* March 10, 1978.

293 resignation of Mark A. Siegel Mark Siegel to Jimmy Carter, March 8, 1978, folder 10, box 20, MS-630, American Jewish Archives, Cincinnati, Ohio.

293 "as an American, Jew" Terence Smith, "Carter Liaison Aide with Jews to Quit White House," *New York Times,* March 9, 1978.

293 "Mark is getting the classic" Butler, unpublished diary, February 5, 1978.

293 "Mark Siegel is a fine young man" "Transcript of the President's News Conference on Foreign and Domestic Matters," *New York Times,* March 10, 1978.

293 "will fan the concern" Gwertzman, "Jewish Leader Says Mideast Policy."

294 "probably had two purposes" Zbigniew Brzezinski top secret memo to Jimmy Carter, March 15, 1978, NLC-1-5-5-63-1, CREST, Jimmy Carter Presidential Library.

294 "cowardly and senseless attack" Carter, *White House Diary,* p. 178.

294 "Ever since 1948" David Rubenstein interview, June 19, 2016.

295 "There is a clear possibility" Butler, unpublished diary, February 13, 1978, and February 14, 1978.

295 not been consulted by Carter Butler, unpublished diary, May 12, 1978.

295 "Carter saw unions as just another" Jefferson Cowie, *Stayin' Alive,* p. 265.

295 "Stu, I will never do this again" Stuart E. Eizenstat, *President Carter,* p. 299.

295 "The president simply doesn't" Butler, unpublished diary, January 15, 1978, and May 10, 1978.

295 "Jimmy Carter doesn't understand" Butler, unpublished diary, January 15, 1978.

296 "I have really developed" Butler, unpublished diary, September 11, 1978, and September 13, 1978.

296 "The labor law reform breakfast" Butler, unpublished diary, May 9, 1978.

296 25 percent of the country's workers Judith Stein, *Pivotal Decade,* p. 182.

296 "The truth is that the AFL-CIO" Butler, unpublished diary, May 12, 1978.

297 "wave of hysteria" Butler, unpublished diary, May 10, 1978.

297 "the Israeli lobby" Carter, *White House Diary,* p. 195.

297 "I think we have done" Butler, unpublished diary, May 15, 1978.

297 "I feel more at home" Jimmy Carter, *White House Diary,* p. 164.

297 "found that Russell Long had filled" Ira Shapiro, *The Last Great Senate,* p. 180.

297 "always a waste of time" Jimmy Carter, *White House Diary,* p. 164.

298   **"New Foundations"** Hendrik Hertzberg oral history exit interview, December 10, 1980, Jimmy Carter Presidential Library.

298   **"If you propose an urban policy"** Peter G. Bourne, *Jimmy Carter,* p. 420.

298   **"pompous, prickly, disrespectful,"** Eizenstat, *President Carter,* p. 397; Jimmy Carter diary, February 2, 1978, *White House Diary,* p. 168.

299   **"Spending tended to go up"** Lawrence J. McAndrews, *The Presidents and the Poor,* p. 97.

299   **"I wish you could have seen"** Bourne, *Jimmy Carter,* pp. 416–17.

299   **"The world had changed"** Bourne, *Jimmy Carter,* p. 417.

300   **"very caustic, no true believer"** Jerome Doolittle, unpublished diary, November 29, 1978.

300   **"The citizens' movement creates"** David Bollier, "Chapter 3: The Office of Citizen," in *Citizen Action and Other Big Ideas.*

300   **"It was a cheap"** Bollier, "Chapter 3: The Office of Citizen."

301   **"enough White House muscle"** Ralph Nader, "Esther Peterson 1906–1997," *In the Public Interest,* December 26, 1997.

301   **"too abrasive and aggressive"** Myra MacPherson, "Trilateralists to Abound in Carter's White House," *Washington Post,* January 16, 1977.

301   **"a pain in the neck"** Carter diary, January 12, 1979, *White House Diary,* p. 277; Eizenstat, *President Carter,* p. 842.

302   **"I supported you on ERA"** Maggie Doherty, "Bella Abzug's Fight for a Broader Feminism," *New York Review of Books,* November 5, 2020.

302   **"used as a scapegoat"** Terence Smith, "Carter, in Angry Exchange, Ousts Bella Abzug from Women's Unit," *New York Times,* January 13, 1979.

302   **"Costanza was given an impossible job"** Doreen Mattingly, *A Feminist in the White House,* p. 183; *Ms.,* January 1979, p. 56.

302   **"made it plain that [Carter]"** Charles Kirbo memo to President Carter, October 25, 1978, unprocessed Charles Kirbo papers, Jimmy Carter Presidential Library.

303   **"How many law review articles"** Terry Adamson, "Hardworking Bell Leaves a Legacy to Be Appreciated," *Journal of Southern Legal History,* p. 312.

303   **"excessively liberal"** Carter, *White House Diary,* p. 397.

303   **Carter appointed fifty-seven minorities** Mark Joseph Stern, "Carter's Quiet Revolution," *Slate,* July 14, 2019.

303   **"Ted Kennedy is running for president"** Carter, *White House Diary,* p. 167.

303   **"no philosophical differences"** Jimmy Carter handwritten note to Benjamin E. Mays, October 31, 1979, box 46, Susan Clough File.

303   **"I would think it"** Charles Kirbo memo, May 10, 1979, unprocessed Charles Kirbo papers, Jimmy Carter Presidential Library.

304   **Twenty-six million Americans** Eizenstat, *President Carter,* p. 821.

304   **"We have an abominable system"** Jimmy Carter, *Keeping Faith,* p. 85.

304   **"We can't get this overnight"** Eizenstat, *President Carter,* p. 821.

304   **"I will move it myself"** Eizenstat, *President Carter,* p. 822.

305   **"too deep to reverse myself"** Carter, *White House Diary,* p. 175.

305 "heated meeting" Carter, *White House Diary,* p. 183.

305 "it would be years" Carter, *White House Diary,* p. 203; Carter, *Keeping Faith,* p. 86.

305 "It is ridiculous" Eizenstat, *President Carter,* p. 825.

305 "a recipe for failure" Edward M. Kennedy, *True Compass,* p. 359.

306 "at least $100 billion" Carter, *Keeping Faith,* p. 86.

306 "that they do not have at present" "Summary Fact Sheet: President Carter's National Health Plan Legislation," June 12, 1979, "National Health Insurance" folder, box 24, CF, O/A 729 1, Eizenstat, Staff Offices, Domestic Policy Staff, Jimmy Carter Presidential Library.

306 $15 billion to $27 billion Joe Califano memo to Jimmy Carter, May 22, 1978, "National Health Insurance" folder, 4/78, box 24, Staff Offices, Domestic Policy Staff, Eizenstat, Jimmy Carter Presidential Library.

306 "a good chance to succeed" Carter, *Keeping Faith,* p. 86.

307 "You've slid on so many timetables" Eizenstat, *President Carter,* p. 827.

307 "we could not win" Eizenstat, *President Carter,* p. 827.

307 "slipped on timing" Eizenstat, *President Carter,* p. 828.

308 "This is the beginning" Joseph N. Onek interview.

308 "We'll just have to hang tough" Carter, *White House Diary,* p. 208.

308 "long enough for him to study" Carter, *Keeping Faith,* p. 87.

308 "catastrophic" Philip Shabecoff, "Kennedy Assails Carter on Health," *New York Times,* July 29, 1978.

308 "betrayed my trust" Carter, *White House Diary,* p. 209.

308 "a mere down-payment" "Health Insurance in Installments" (editorial), *New York Times,* August 1, 1978.

308 "In effect," Carter later wrote Carter, *Keeping Faith,* p. 86.

308 Eizenstat estimated that an additional Eizenstat, *President Carter,* p. 833.

309 Dick Gephardt of Missouri fought Carter Alicia Smith interview.

309 "comprehensive plan now or nothing" Jody Powell memo to Jimmy Carter, May 18, 1979, "National Health Insurance" folder, box 24, CF, O/A 729 1, Eizenstat, Staff Offices, Domestic Policy Staff, Jimmy Carter Presidential Library.

309 "The truth is hospital" Joseph N. Onek oral history by Edward Berkowitz, box 2, Jimmy Carter Presidential Library.

309 "less of a chance of passing" Eizenstat, *President Carter,* p. 832.

309 "I urge the Congress" White House Press statement on National Health Plan, June 12, 1979, "National Health Plan" folder, box 35, Office of Anne Wexler, Jimmy Carter Presidential Library; Rick Perlstein, *Reaganland,* p. 561.

310 "bore a striking resemblance" Richard Moe, "Health Care for All: A Cautionary Tale from the 1970s," History News Network.

310 "The missed opportunity" Eizenstat, *President Carter,* p. 818.

310 "The president had to decide" Doolittle, unpublished diary, August 9, 1978.

310 "This, of course" Carter, *White House Diary,* p. 211.

310 "the traditional idea of" "Interview with the president by John Chancellor," January 13, 1979, "News Conference Transcripts and Press Releases (1)" folder,

box 18, Marc Henderson Subject Files, Press Office, Jimmy Carter Presidential Library.

311 **"You told me to play tennis"** Eizenstat, *President Carter,* pp. 678–79.

CHAPTER 13: TROUBLES WITH A SPEECHWRITER

312 **"He is in trouble now"** James Reston, *New York Times,* April 5, 1978.

313 **"I thought I'd never"** Charles Peters interview.

313 **"Speeches were not something"** James Fallows exit interview.

313 **Nixon had more than a dozen** Jim Fallows memo to Jody Powell, February 9, 1977, "Administrative Information" folder, box 1, Staff Offices, Speechwriters, Fallows, Speechwriters staff, 1977, Jimmy Carter Presidential Library.

313 **"We in the speechwriting"** Jim Fallows memo to Hugh Carter, August 30, 1977, "Administrative Information" folder, box 1, Staff Offices, Speechwriters, Fallows, Speechwriters staff, 1977, Jimmy Carter Presidential Library.

314 **"Jody Powell was much less"** Fallows interview; Hendrik Hertzberg interview.

314 **serious tennis since high school** Fallows exit interview.

314 **"I didn't experience that"** Hendrik Hertzberg interview.

314 **"has a wooden ear"** Fallows exit interview.

315 **"His editing," said Doolittle** Jerome Doolittle interview.

315 **"Carter doesn't seem to want writers"** Jerome Doolittle, unpublished diary, March 22, 1977.

315 **"tamper with his unvarnished, natural style"** Fallows exit interview.

315 **"profound mistake"** Fallows exit interview.

315 **"They don't want a president"** Doolittle, unpublished diary, June 7, 1977.

315 **"they couldn't afford Billy's fee"** Doolittle, unpublished diary, July 21, 1977.

315 **"Very poor. Next time"** James Fallows memo to the president, January 25, 1977, with Carter handwritten comment, "Memoranda: Eizenstat, Stu, 6/10/77–7/19/77" folder, box 42, Staff Offices, Press, Powell, Jimmy Carter Presidential Library.

316 **"thinking JC could be"** Doolittle, unpublished diary, January 26, 1977; "Carter and Byrd Vie to Get Laughs at Reception," *New York Times,* January 28, 1977.

316 **"my one moment of success"** Fallows exit interview; Carter, *White House Diary,* p. 193. Doolittle had a different take in his diary—where he reported that Carter, after complaining about his speechwriters, had nevertheless used the original draft: "It's like a dog pissing on a tree to mark his territory. JC had now convinced himself that he had done the speeches, after regrettably inadequate performances by his speechwriters." (Doolittle, unpublished diary, April 13, 1978.)

316 **"I kept trying to tell them"** James Fallows interview.

317 **"We exist to construct Potemkin villages"** Doolittle, unpublished diary, January 31, 1978.

317 **16 percent in 1978** Dominic Sandbrook, *Mad as Hell,* p. 234.

317 **"This kind of thing"** Jim Fallows to Gerald Rafshoon, June 29, 1978, "Memo-

randa, Fallows, Jim" folder, box 42, Staff Offices, Press, Powell, Jimmy Carter Presidential Library.

317 **as early as March** Doolittle, unpublished diary, March 8, 1978.

317 **"The mood toward Carter"** Doolittle, unpublished diary, August 7, 1978.

318 **"I feel great personal loyalty"** Jim Fallows to President Carter, June 21, 1978; Jimmy Carter to Jim Fallows, June 27, 1978, "Fallows-Freeman" folder, box 45, Susan Clough File, Jimmy Carter Presidential Library; Fallows exit interview.

318 **"If there is a single grievous"** Fallows exit interview.

318 **"before pissing in the punchbowl"** Doolittle, unpublished diary, December 12, 1978.

318 **"Mingled feelings, sad at leaving"** Doolittle, unpublished diary, January 9, 1979.

318 **"The Passionless Presidency"** James Fallows, "The Passionless Presidency: The Trouble with Jimmy Carter's Administration," *The Atlantic,* May 1979.

318 **"I thought it would be a useful"** Charles Peters interview.

318 **"save the Carter presidency"** James Fallows interview.

320 **"I contributed the Marshal Pétain line"** Charles Peters interview.

321 **"He lied, he lied"** Stuart E. Eizenstat, *President Carter,* p. 711.

321 **"he'd turn around and go back"** Eizenstat, *President Carter,* p. 711.

321 **"the responsibility for coordinating"** Eizenstat, *President Carter,* p. 712; Susan Clough, letter to *New York Times,* June 22, 1986.

321 **"I hope you will be able"** James Fallows to Carter, April 4, 1979, with Carter handwritten note, "Fallows-Freeman" folder, box 45, Susan Clough File, Jimmy Carter Presidential Library.

321 **"I was disappointed"** Jimmy Carter interview, September 14, 2017.

322 **"angry exchanges"** James Fallows interview.

322 **"Goddammit, Jim,"** Jody told Caryl Conner, "For a Passionless Presidency Feelings About Jim Fallows Run Pretty High in the White House," *People,* May 28, 1979. A former speechwriter for the late Senator Hubert Humphrey, Conner himself had left the Carter speechwriting staff at the same time as Fallows. In 1999, Fallows criticized George Stephanopoulos for having written *All Too Human,* an insider's account of the Clinton presidency. Fallows wrote, "This is an interesting book that should not have been written. . . . No normal person likes to be seen as disloyal. But I felt justified, even compelled to write those articles at the time." The optics were worse for Stephanopoulos, if only because he had been paid $3 million for his tell-all book—while Fallows had turned down a lucrative book advance. Another difference, Fallows thought, was that Stephanopoulos was truly a top aide to the president, equivalent to Jody Powell—and by contrast, "I was a nobody in the Carter administration." (James Fallows, "History vs. Loyalty," *Washington Monthly,* June 1999.)

322 **"I have a hard time"** Jody Powell oral history.

322 **"the recent controversy"** James Fallows to Hamilton Jordan, April 27, 1979, and Jordan's undated reply, Hamilton Jordan Papers, Jimmy Carter Presidential Library.

322 **"more harmful than Fallows intended"** James Reston, "Leaders of Men," *New York Times,* April 27, 1979.

322 **"Some of your old associates"** Conner, "For a Passionless Presidency."

322 **"That *Atlantic* essay was a knife"** Alice Rogoff interview, May 5, 2016.

322 **"I was appalled"** Landon Butler interview, January 13, 2016; Alice Rogoff interview, May 13, 2016; Tim Kraft, handwritten note card no. 34, Tim Kraft Papers, courtesy of Kraft.

CHAPTER 14: TRIUMPH AT CAMP DAVID

324 **"city of tomorrow"** Robert I. Friedman, "The Settlers," *New York Review of Books,* June 15, 1989.

324 **"In a few weeks or months"** Ned Temko, *To Win or to Die,* p. 198.

325 **"I don't think anyone made"** Hamilton Jordan to Jimmy Carter, undated but attached to Carter notes dated January 2, 1978, "Egypt, 11/77–11/81" folder, President's Personal Foreign Affairs, Plains File, Jimmy Carter Presidential Library.

325 **"Sadat-Begin talks have broken"** Jimmy Carter, *White House Diary,* p. 165.

325 **"I then read to Begin"** Carter, *White House Diary,* p. 180.

326 **"the six noes"** Lawrence Wright, *Thirteen Days in September,* p. 42.

326 **"When the meal was over"** Jimmy Carter, *Keeping Faith,* p. 311.

326 **"Begin is solely holding up"** Stuart E. Eizenstat, *President Carter,* p. 488. Eizenstat is citing his yellow-pad notes from April 3, 1978.

326 **"He's a small man"** Jimmy Carter, diary, May 1, 1978; *White House Diary,* p. 193.

326 **"Dear friend," Sadat wrote** Anwar Sadat handwritten letter to Jimmy Carter, April 24, 1978, "Sadat (Anwar) Communications, 1/77–11/80" folder, box 35, Plains File, Jimmy Carter Presidential Library.

327 **"It's so beautiful here"** Rosalynn Carter, *First Lady from Plains,* p. 226.

327 **"almost one of desperation"** Jimmy Carter, *Palestine,* p. 45.

327 **"Are you willing to be"** Carter, *First Lady from Plains,* p. 226.

327 **"losing proposition"** Carter, *First Lady from Plains,* p. 227.

327 **"If you fail, we're done"** Wright, *Thirteen Days in September,* p. 45.

327 **"the president simply cannot"** Zbigniew Brzezinski, *Power and Principle,* p. 251.

327 **"It was a daring stroke"** Cyrus Vance, *Hard Choices,* p. 217.

327 **"During recent weeks"** Jimmy Carter to Anwar Sadat, August 3, 1978, "Sadat (Anwar) Communications, 1/77–11/80" folder, box 35, Plains File, Jimmy Carter Presidential Library.

328 **"We got word that Israel"** Carter, *White House Diary,* p. 214.

328 **"nothing for nothing"** Wright, *Thirteen Days in September,* p. 42.

329 **"Sadat cannot afford a failure"** Brzezinski, *Power and Principle,* p. 253.

329 **"With Sadat, the problem"** Cyrus Vance memo to Jimmy Carter, "Camp David Talks," undated (declassified November 15, 2013), NLC-6-52-7-6-5, CREST, Jimmy Carter Presidential Library.

330 **"Carter made a precise list"** Jimmy Carter, handwritten notes, "Preparation for Mtg," September 5, 1978, "Mid East: Camp David Summit" folder, President's Working Papers, 10/22/73–9/12/78, box 28, Plains File, Jimmy Carter Presiden-

tial Library. Carter reproduces a similar list with slightly different language in his presidential memoir, *Keeping Faith,* pp. 325–27.

331 "**somewhat ill at ease**" Carter, *Keeping Faith,* pp. 329–30.

331 "**In general,**" **he dictated** Jimmy Carter, unpublished Camp David diary, p. 6.

331 "**I don't believe he has any intention**" Carter, *First Lady from Plains,* p. 231.

331 "**Unless our proposals**" Carter, unpublished Camp David diary, p. 6.

332 "**I want this**" Carter, unpublished Camp David diary, p. 7.

332 "**I saw for the first time**" Carter, *Keeping Faith,* pp. 340–41; Wright, *Thirteen Days in September,* pp. 66–67.

332 "**Begin's successors might be forced**" Carter, unpublished Camp David diary, p. 8.

333 "**the incarnation of masculine elegance**" Ezer Weizman, *The Battle for Peace,* p. 344.

333 "**I could not understand**" Carter, *Keeping Faith,* pp. 345–46.

333 "**We adjourned in good spirits**" Carter, unpublished Camp David diary, p. 11.

334 "**bulldog persistence and his ability**" Weizman, *Battle for Peace,* p. 362.

334 "**What do you actually want**" Carter, unpublished Camp David diary, p. 14.

334 "**My reelection is not nearly as important**" Carter, unpublished Camp David diary, p. 13.

334 "**I wanted them to address**" Carter, *Keeping Faith,* pp. 350–51.

334 "**no compatibility between**" Carter, *Keeping Faith,* p. 355.

334 "**It was mean**" Carter, *First Lady from Plains,* pp. 234–35.

335 "**Barbara, will you please come out**" Gerald Rafshoon interview, December 7, 2015. See also Eizenstat, *President Carter,* p. 526.

335 "**If sovereignty is to mean**" Carter, *Keeping Faith,* p. 360.

336 "**I will never** *personally* **recommend**" Carter, *Keeping Faith,* p. 365; Wright, *Thirteen Days in September,* p. 115.

336 "**Begin was just now**" Carter, *Keeping Faith,* pp. 365–66; Wright, *Thirteen Days in September,* p. 116.

337 "**I will not sign a Sinai agreement**" Carter, *Keeping Faith,* p. 345.

337 "**modifying the text**" Jimmy Carter, *A Full Life,* p. 155.

338 "**Necessary elements of an agreement**" Jimmy Carter, handwritten notes, September 9, 1978, "Mid East: Camp David Summit" folder, President's Working Papers, 10/22/73–9/12/78, box 28, Plains File, Jimmy Carter Presidential Library. A summary of these notes can be found in Carter, *Keeping Faith,* p. 371, and Wright, *Thirteen Days in September,* p. 153.

339 "**His textual criticisms**" Brzezinski, *Power and Principle,* p. 259.

339 "**is always willing to accommodate**" Brzezinski, *Power and Principle,* p. 259.

339 "**Rapid granting of full autonomy**" Carter, *Keeping Faith,* p. 371.

340 "**Poles apart,**" **quipped** Wright, *Thirteen Days in September,* p. 160.

340 "**Menachem just loves to play chess!**" Brzezinski, *Power and Principle,* p. 259.

340 "**Do me a favor**" Weizman, *Battle for Peace,* p. 347; Wright, *Thirteen Days in September,* p. 160.

341 "**then we will go home**" Wright, *Thirteen Days in September,* p. 164.

341 "**He did so with great emotion**" Moshe Dayan, *Breakthrough,* p. 171; Wright,

Thirteen Days in September, p. 172. Littleberry Carter was shot dead in 1873 during a gunfight with his business partner.

341 **His voice was at first soft** Wright, *Thirteen Days in September,* pp. 172–73.

341 **"The war of 1967 gives Israel"** Brzezinski, *Power and Principle,* p. 260; Wright, *Thirteen Days in September,* p. 173.

342 **"No self-respecting Arab"** Carter, unpublished Camp David diary, p. 35; Brzezinski, *Power and Principle,* pp. 260–61; Carter, *Keeping Faith,* p. 375–76; Wright, *Thirteen Days in September,* pp. 174–76.

342 **"We will not accept that!"** Wright, *Thirteen Days in September,* p. 176.

342 **"It's becoming clearer"** Carter, unpublished Camp David diary, p. 41.

343 **"described Begin as a psycho"** Brzezinski, *Power and Principle,* p. 262; Wright, *Thirteen Days in September,* p. 177; Carter, *First Lady from Plains,* p. 241.

343 **"I had become a master"** Carter, *Keeping Faith,* p. 396.

343 **fifteen feet by twenty-two feet** Wright, *Thirteen Days in September,* p. 191.

343 **"never seen a man more tenacious"** "Carter the Tenacious," *Washington Star,* November 1, 1978.

343 **"This is the most serious talk"** Carter, *Keeping Faith,* p. 385.

344 **"my position represent[s] the Israeli people"** Carter, *Keeping Faith,* p. 386; Wright, *Thirteen Days in September,* p. 197.

344 **"It was a fairly heated discussion"** Carter, unpublished Camp David diary, p. 49.

344 **nearly eleven hours** Carter, *Keeping Faith,* p. 388.

344 **the Sinai settlements were such a stickler** Wright, *Thirteen Days in September,* p. 186.

345 **"Zbig," said Carter, "I am very much"** Zbigniew Brzezinski, *Power and Principle,* p. 265.

345 **"I think it's all coming together"** Carter, *First Lady from Plains,* p. 247.

345 **"Good heavens," Mondale was heard** Wright, *Thirteen Days in September,* p. 244.

346 **"in a rather peremptory"** Brzezinski, *Power and Principle,* p. 266.

346 **"had a humdinger of an argument"** Brzezinski, *Power and Principle,* p. 266.

347 **"Sadat is leaving"** Carter, *Keeping Faith,* p. 391.

347 **"prayed fervently for a few"** Carter, *Keeping Faith,* p. 392; Brzezinski, *Power and Principle,* p. 271.

347 **"I didn't say anything"** Brzezinski, *Power and Principle,* p. 272.

347 **"We are wasting our time"** Wright, *Thirteen Days in September,* p. 233.

348 **"I will make it very clear"** Brzezinski, *Power and Principle,* p. 272.

348 **"You know, the implication"** Brzezinski, *Power and Principle,* p. 272.

348 **"If you give me this statement"** Carter, *Keeping Faith,* p. 393.

349 **"I thought the discussion"** Carter, *Keeping Faith,* p. 396.

349 **"ultimatum"** Carter, unpublished Camp David diary, p. 59.

349 **"breakthrough"** Carter, *Keeping Faith,* p. 396.

349 **"surprisingly amicable discussion"** Carter, *Keeping Faith,* p. 396.

349 **"On the West Bank settlements"** Carter, unpublished Camp David diary, p. 60.

349 **"Finally, we agreed on the exact language"** Jimmy Carter memo, "Settlements in

West Bank and Gaza," September 20, 1978, "Mid-East: Camp David Summit" folder, President's Working Papers, 9/13/78–9/27/78, box 28, Plains File, Jimmy Carter Presidential Library. Carter's secretary, Susan Clough, sent copies of this note to Prime Minister Begin, Secretary Vance, Zbigniew Brzezinski, and Jody Powell. This document can also be found as "Note Prepared by President Carter" (document 54) in U.S. Office of the Historian, *Foreign Relations of the United States, 1977–1980*, vol. 9, *Arab-Israeli Dispute, August 1978–December 1980*, 2nd rev. ed.

350 **"After the signing"** Carter, unpublished Camp David diary, p. 60, courtesy of Gerald Rafshoon.

350 **"What Sadat Gets"** Carter, unpublished Camp David diary, p. 68, courtesy of Gerald Rafshoon.

350 **"recognize the legitimate rights"** Camp David Accords. See also Weizman, *Battle for Peace,* p. 372.

351 **"I got the settlement freeze"** Wright, *Thirteen Days in September,* p. 254.

351 **"differed substantially from that"** Jimmy Carter memo, "Settlements in West Bank and Gaza," September 20, 1978, "Mid-East: Camp David Summit" folder, President's Working Papers, 9/13/78–9/27/78, box 28, Plains File, Jimmy Carter Presidential Library.

351 **"Go back and get the right letter"** Wright, *Thirteen Days in September,* p. 261.

351 **"Barak confirmed that my"** Carter, *Keeping Faith,* p. 400.

351 **"My notes are clear"** Carter, *Keeping Faith,* p. 397.

351 **"This is the exact language"** Carter, *Keeping Faith,* p. 401.

352 **"would *not* commence until after"** Carter, *Keeping Faith,* p. 400.

352 **"a very unpleasant session"** Carter, *Keeping Faith,* p. 398.

353 **At 3:26 P.M. he found** Jimmy Carter, daily diary, September 17, 1978, Jimmy Carter Presidential Library.

353 **"I wanted to be able to say"** Wright, *Thirteen Days in September,* p. 259.

353 **breaking his promise to Sadat** Carter, *Keeping Faith,* p. 399; Wright, *Thirteen Days in September,* p. 260.

353 **"I will accept the letter"** Carter, *Keeping Faith,* p. 399; Carter, daily diary, September 17, 1978.

354 **"That's it. I think we have it"** Brzezinski, *Power and Principle,* p. 270; Carter, daily diary, September 17, 1978; Wright, *Thirteen Days in September,* p. 262.

354 **"rather tired, with a wistful smile"** Brzezinski, *Power and Principle,* pp. 270–71.

354 **Begin was withholding the side letter** Just two days later, on September 19, 1978, Jody Powell held a press conference in which he flatly explained, "Well, the language that was agreed upon was quite specific that night. That was agreed upon—the language was originally, as they sat down that evening, a part of, I believe, the final paragraph, or one of the two or three final paragraphs, in the comprehensive agreement. Okay? I remember that because it happened to be on the same page and right below it began a section that was headed 'Egypt and Israel.' The language was agreed upon. . . . We agreed to take it out and that that language reflecting that agreement would be placed in a letter." ("News Conference at the White House with Jody Powell, #358," September 19, 1978, "1978 [7]"

folder, box 16, Press Office–Media Liaison Office, Marc Henderson's Subject Files, Jimmy Carter Presidential Library.)

354 **"Because of the Jerusalem issue"** Cyrus Vance, *Hard Choices*, p. 225.

354 **"a darn shame"** Hugh Sidey, *Washington Star*, September 24, 1978.

355 **"the Jimmy Carter conference"** Wright, *Thirteen Days in September*, pp. 264–65.

355 **"I have just signed the greatest document"** Temko, *To Win or to Die*, p. 231.

355 **"The Israelis," he told Hussein** "Memo for the Record: President's Telephone Conversation with King Hussein of Jordan," September 18, 1978, document no. 58, in U.S. Office of the Historian, Foreign Relations of the United States, 1977–1980, vol. 9, Arab-Israeli Dispute, August 1978–December 1980, 2nd rev. ed.

355 **"It became obvious"** Carter, diary, September 18, 1978, *White House Diary*, pp. 245–46.

355 **"After the signing"** Wright, *Thirteen Days in September*, p. 268.

355 **"He's trying to welsh on the deal"** Carter, diary, September 19, 1978, *White House Diary*, pp. 246–47.

356 **"denying the agreement"** Carter, diary, September 21, 1978, *White House Diary*, p. 247.

356 **"extremely upset over Begin's"** Telegram 12849 from Tel Aviv, September 20, 1978, RG 59, Central Foreign Policy File, P840153-2618, National Archives, cited in document 65, U.S. Office of the Historian, Foreign Relations of the United States, 1977–1980, vol. 9, Arab-Israeli Dispute, August 1978–December 1980, 2nd rev. ed.

356 **"Begin promised me"** Wright, *Thirteen Days in September*, p. 320.

356 **"Personal for the President's Eyes Only"** Menachem Begin to Jimmy Carter, October 29, 1978 (declassified June 16, 2008), NLC-128-3-3-18-4, CREST, Jimmy Carter Presidential Library.

357 **"as flexible as possible"** "Memo for the Record, Telephone Conversation Between President Carter and Prime Minister Begin," November 12, 1978 (declassified June 16, 2008), NLC-128-3-3-17-5, Jimmy Carter Presidential Library.

357 **"very abusive"** Carter, diary, November 12, 1978, *White House Diary*, p. 259. See also Jimmy Carter handwritten letter to Menachem Begin, November 11, 1978 (declassified June 2, 2008), NLC-128-3-3-15-7, CREST, Jimmy Carter Presidential Library.

357 **"quoting Dayan saying"** and **"he couldn't negotiate for Israel"** Carter diary, October 31, 1978, and November 1, 1978, *White House Diary*, pp. 256–57.

357 **"President Carter's emergence as the peacemaker"** James R. Dickenson, "Hill Greets Peacemakers with Emotional Tidal Wave," *Washington Star*, September 19, 1978, p. 1.

357 **"tremendous achievement"** *Washington Star*, September 24, 1978.

357 **"We all owe a great debt"** Hugh Sidey, "Carter Shows He Can Play the Game of Making Things Go," *Washington Star*, September 24, 1978.

358 **"So now, what do we say"** Richard L. Strout, *TRB: Views and Perspectives on the Presidency*.

358 **"delightful, full of fun"** Jimmy Carter, diary, September 19, 1978, *White House Diary*, p. 247; Carter, *Keeping Faith*, p. 405. Included in this meeting were such

influential Jewish leaders as Theodore Mann, president of the Conference of Presidents of Major American Jewish Organizations, and Lawrence Weinberg, president of the American Israel Public Affairs Committee.

358 **criticize Begin's behavior** Edward Sanders memo for the president, September 21, 1978, "Memos, Presidential, 8/8/78–2/1/79" folder, box 10, Special Advisor to the President, Moses, Jimmy Carter Presidential Library.

358 **"You will live to regret this agreement"** Mohamed Ibrahim Kamel, *The Camp David Accords,* p. 376.

359 **"The process is underway"** I. F. Stone, "The Hope," *New York Review of Books,* October 26, 1978.

359 **Begin did not want a peace** For more on Salameh's assassination, see Kai Bird, *The Good Spy,* p. 215.

359 **eighteen to twenty new settlements** William B. Quandt memo to Zbigniew Brzezinski, October 31, 1978, document 120, U.S. Office of the Historian, Foreign Relations of the United States, 1977–1980, vol. 9, Arab-Israeli Dispute, August 1978–December 1980, 2nd rev. ed.

359 **"There is no other explanation"** Jimmy Carter handwritten comment on cable from Jerusalem to White House, declassified June 2, 2008, CREST, NLC-128-3-20-1-3, Jimmy Carter Presidential Library.

360 **"Begin wanted to keep two things"** Carter, *Keeping Faith,* p. 405.

360 **"I do not believe he would"** Eizenstat, *President Carter,* p. 534.

361 **5,000 to 24,000 under his tenure** "Begin Visits Elon Moreh, Other West Bank Settlements," Jewish Telegraphic Agency, March 2, 1981.

CHAPTER 15: "A WEIRD PERIOD FOR LIBERALS"

362 **miserable 38 percent approval** Betty Glad, *An Outsider in the White House,* p. 153; William Greider, "Poll Finds Carter Popularity Soars," *Washington Post,* September 24, 1978.

362 **"The women are very happy"** Jimmy Carter, diary, October 20, 1978, *White House Diary,* p. 253.

363 **"The next step"** Carter, diary, October 26, 1978, *White House Diary,* p. 256.

363 **"so watered down"** and **"would play a cruel hoax"** Jefferson Cowie, *Stayin' Alive,* p. 284.

364 **"He didn't tell me the truth"** John A. Farrell, *Tip O'Neill and the Democratic Century,* pp. 516–17.

364 **"you [Carter] simply do not enjoy"** Farrell, *Tip O'Neill and the Democratic Century,* p. 518.

364 **"Tip is working hard"** Farrell, *Tip O'Neill and the Democratic Century,* p. 518.

364 **"cast a pall over everybody"** Carter diary, October 3, 1978, *White House Diary,* p. 249.

365 **refused to include a windfall-profits tax** Julian E. Zelizer, *Jimmy Carter,* p. 86.

365 **an alarming 8 percent** Joe Califano, "Memorandum for the President," September 18, 1978, "Anti-Inflation, 9/78 (2)" folder, box 145, Staff Offices, Domestic Policy Staff, Eizenstat, Jimmy Carter Presidential Library.

365 **"practical dreamers"** Terence Smith, "Carter Asks Party Support," *New York Times,* December 9, 1978.

365 **"There could be few more"** Edward M. Kennedy, *True Compass,* p. 363; Stuart E. Eizenstat, *President Carter,* p. 830.

366 **"The son of a bitch"** Peter S. Canellos, ed., *Last Lion,* p. 212.

366 **"share equally" in any reductions** Adam Clymer, "Kennedy Assails Carter," *New York Times,* December 10, 1978.

366 **"following my guidelines re zero-based"** Carter diary, December 4, 1978, *White House Diary,* p. 263.

367 **"to rebuild our long-neglected military"** Jimmy Carter, *Keeping Faith,* p. 222.

367 **"If there is any purpose"** Adam Cymer, "Carter's Inflation Plan Draws Fire," *New York Times,* December 9, 1978.

367 **"This is one group"** Carter, diary, October 21, 1978, *White House Diary,* p. 254.

367 **"He owes us the presidency"** Peter G. Bourne, *Jimmy Carter,* p. 431.

368 **"I'm discouraged at the differences"** Carter, diary, June 11, 1978, *White House Diary,* p. 199.

368 **"tolerate a plan that provides"** Rick Perlstein, *Reaganland,* p. 335.

368 **"I am hoping"** Eizenstat, *President Carter,* pp. 316 and 320.

369 **"I deserved the rebuke"** Ibid.

369 **"It's a weird period for liberals"** Bourne, *Jimmy Carter,* p. 431; *Washington Post,* December 11, 1978.

369 **"Inflation has hit us hardest"** Tom Wicker, "Big Four Inflation," *New York Times,* July 26, 1977.

370 **"our most serious domestic problem"** Jimmy Carter, "Remarks of the President in His Address to the Nation on Inflation," October 24, 1978, "Inflation #1 of 2: Presidential Memorandum and Statements, 9/78–3/79" folder, box 21, Staff Offices, Counsel Lipshutz, Jimmy Carter Presidential Library; Eizenstat, *President Carter,* p. 323.

370 **"the most conservative president"** Perlstein, *Reaganland,* pp. 380 and 383.

370 **"Budget deficits do not cause inflation"** Secretary Marshall, "Memorandum for the Economic Policy Group," April 8, 1977, "Anti-Inflation" folder, box 144, Staff Offices, Domestic Policy Staff, Eizenstat, Jimmy Carter Presidential Library.

370 **deficit of only about $25 billion** Carter, diary, November 14, 1977, *White House Diary,* p. 134.

370 **"Please present to me"** Jimmy Carter to Alfred Kahn, October 25, 1978, "Inflation #1 of 2: Presidential Memorandum and Statements, 9/78–3/79" folder, box 21, Staff Offices, Counsel Lipshutz, Jimmy Carter Presidential Library.

371 **"kumquat"** Robert D. Hershey, Jr., "Alfred E. Kahn Dies at 93," *New York Times,* December 28, 2010.

371 **"have lunch with Amy at McDonald's"** Alfred E. Kahn memo to the presi-

dent, October 11, 1979, "Presidential File, 10/79–1/2/80" folder, box 34, Special Advisor–Inflation Kahn, Jimmy Carter Presidential Library.

372 **"a couple of blind spots"** Alfred E. Kahn oral history.

372 **"huge gasoline tax"** Kahn oral history.

372 **"I can't figure out"** Hershey, "Alfred E. Kahn Dies at 93."

372 **"seduced"** Carter, *Keeping Faith*, p. 196; Carter diary, May 26, 1978, *White House Diary*, p. 196.

372 **"He almost fainted"** Carter, *Keeping Faith*, p. 200; Carter diary, December 16, 1978.

373 **"It is obvious that"** Carter, diary, November 8, 1978, *White House Diary*, p. 258; *Keeping Faith*, p. 409.

373 **"Yes, but I agree with you"** Zbigniew Brzezinski, *Power and Principle*, p. 276.

373 **"I would be willing to lose"** Brzezinski, *Power and Principle*, p. 278.

373 **"Stu," said the president one day** Eizenstat, *President Carter*, p. 542.

373 **"would prefer Carter not"** Brzezinski, *Power and Principle*, p. 279.

374 **"made some very combative comments"** Carter, diary, March 1, 1979, *White House Diary*, p. 297.

374 **"still wants to destroy Israel"** Carter, *Keeping Faith*, p. 415.

374 **"If he hadn't been my guest"** Brzezinski, *Power and Principle*, p. 281.

374 **sat alone on the Truman Balcony** Carter, *Keeping Faith*, p. 415.

374 **"If we're not successful"** Carter, diary, March 2, 1979, *White House Diary*, p. 298.

374 **"the whole thing was doomed"** Carter, *Keeping Faith*, pp. 415–16.

374 **"terrific political gamble"** Farrell, *Tip O'Neill and the Democratic Century*, p. 510.

374 **"I told Sadat this"** Carter, diary, March 9, 1979, *White House Diary*, p. 300; Jimmy Carter oral history, February 18, 1982.

375 **"I have rarely been so disgusted"** Carter, diary, March 10, 1979, *White House Diary*, p. 301.

375 **"He aked me first"** Carter, diary, March 11, 1979, *White House Diary*, p. 301.

375 **"goal of completing the negotiations"** William B. Quandt, *Camp David*, pp. 305, 313, and 404.

375 **"some rather earthy comments"** Brzezinski, *Power and Principle*, pp. 284–85.

375 **"there was quite a buzz"** Carter, diary, March 12, 1979, *White House Diary*, p. 302.

376 **"I've always liked the King David Hotel"** Eizenstat, *President Carter*, p. 546. Gerald Rafshoon told this story to Eizenstat, April 4, 2014.

376 **"refusing to budge"** Carter, diary, March 13, 1979, *White House Diary*, p. 303.

376 **"I pressed him hard"** Carter, *Keeping Faith*, p. 424.

376 **"self-governing authority"** Quandt, *Camp David*, pp. 403–4; Brzezinski, *Power and Principle*, p. 285.

377 **"Carter had no stomach"** Quandt, *Camp David*, pp. 403–4.

378 **"The last two weeks"** Landon Butler, unpublished diary, March 18, 1979.

378 **"It was a remarkable evening"** Zbigniew Brzezinski, *Power and Principle*, pp. 287–88.

CHAPTER 16: AN AYATOLLAH'S REVOLUTION

380 **"truly massive riots"** Gary Sick, *All Fall Down,* p. 35.

380 **"successful revolutions were historical rarities"** Zbigniew Brzezinski, *Power and Principle,* p. 355.

380 **"Chip was attacked"** Jimmy Carter diary, October 28, 1978, *White House Diary,* p. 252.

381 **oil revenues to decline by two-thirds** Andrew Scott Cooper, *The Fall of Heaven,* p. 427.

381 **"We encouraged him to hang firm"** Carter diary, November 2, 1978, *White House Diary,* p. 257.

381 **"Iran is not in a revolutionary"** Sick, *All Fall Down,* p. 92.

381 **losing side of a revolution** James A. Bill, *The Eagle and the Lion,* p. 252.

381 **Former vice president Nelson Rockefeller** Sick, *All Fall Down,* p. 68; Bill, *Eagle and the Lion,* p. 251.

382 **"evils of the Carter administration"** James E. Akins to Zbigniew Brzezinski, December 6, 1978 (declassified May 4, 1989), FO8, CO128, CO71, ND16/COI-7, Kissinger, Henry, Mandatory Review MR-NLC-88-10, WH Central File, Subject File, Executive, Jimmy Carter Presidential Library.

382 **"poisoning the well"** Hodding Carter III, "Life Inside the Carter State Department," *Playboy,* p. 161.

382 **"Iran became the crown jewel"** Kai Bird, *The Chairman,* pp. 642 and 752n2.

383 **$500 million in outstanding loans** Bird, *Chairman,* p. 642; David D. Kirkpatrick, "Bank's Secret Campaign to Win Entry to U.S. for Shah of Iran," *New York Times.*

383 **"risks were too high relating"** Kirkpatrick, "Bank's Secret Campaign."

383 **fine beluga caviar** John J. McCloy interview; Bird, *Chairman,* p. 642.

383 **"shared view"** Bird, *Chairman,* p. 642; Bill, *Eagle and the Lion,* p. 436.

383 **"I'm increasingly concerned about Iran"** Carter diary, December 2, 1978, *White House Diary,* p. 263.

383 **"Our reporting from Iran"** Akins to Brzezinski, December 6, 1978.

384 **"without reservation"** Sick, *All Fall Down,* p. 68.

384 **"professional anti-communist polemicist"** Sick, *All Fall Down,* p. 106; Robert Moss, "Who's Meddling in Iran?" *The New Republic,* December 2, 1978.

385 **"did not have a real sense"** Cooper, *Fall of Heaven,* p. 418.

385 **"Dictatorship," he said** Sohrab Ahmari, "My Family's Iranian Revolution," *Wall Street Journal,* February 2, 2019.

385 **millions of Iranians** Abbas Milani, *The Shah,* p. 394.

385 **"We made the shah"** Milani, *Shah,* p. 395; Jimmy Carter, *Keeping Faith,* p. 442 (Carter diary, December 14, 1978).

386 **"tell another head of state"** Sick, *All Fall Down,* p. 116.

386 **"with all due respect"** Bill, *Eagle and the Lion,* p. 253.

386 **"a painful experience"** Cyrus Vance, *Hard Choices,* p. 328; Carter, *White House Diary,* p. 267. Brzezinski admits in his memoir, *Power and Principle,* published in the same year as Vance's 1983 memoir, that he had "four or five telephone

conversations" with Zahedi—but he claims that Carter told Zahedi to keep in touch with Brzezinski. (Brzezinski, *Power and Principle*, p. 370.)

386 "I don't know. I hope so" Sick, *All Fall Down*, p. 110.

386 "I fully expect the shah" Bill, *Eagle and the Lion*, p. 259.

386 "I think that what's happening" *New York Times*, December 25, 1978.

387 popping ten milligrams of Valium Milani, *The Shah*, p. 400.

387 "The patient was almost" Cooper, *Fall of Heaven*, p. 475.

387 "Try feeding them cake" Cooper, *Fall of Heaven*, p. 234.

388 "Cy wanted us to stay" Carter, *Keeping Faith*, p. 444.

389 According to Carter's diary notes Jimmy Carter, daily diary, January 5, 1979, CREST NLC-128-4-12-3-9, #5A, declassified June 16, 2008. Carter's published diary contains only a portion of this diary entry. (Carter, *White House Diary*, p. 273.)

389 "We should have encouraged" Brzezinski, *Power and Principle*, p. 378. Note that Brzezinski is quoting directly from his personal diary.

389 to approve Huyser's meetings Sick, *All Fall Down*, p. 132.

389 "social democrats" William H. Sullivan, *Obbligato*, p. 263.

390 "Sullivan's plan," Gary Sick later wrote Sick, *All Fall Down*, p. 135.

390 "insane" and "incomprehensible" Carter, *Keeping Faith*, p. 446; William Sullivan, Eyes Only Telegram for the Secretary, January 10, 1979, document 11, "Iran's 1979 Revolution Revisited," National Security Archive, February 11, 2019, https://nsarchive.gwu.edu/briefing-book/iran/2019-02-11/irans-1979-revolution-revisited-failures-few-successes-us-intelligence-diplomatic-reporting.

390 "but Cy said he was just hot-tempered" Jimmy Carter diary, January 10, 1979, *White House Diary*, p. 276; Sick, *All Fall Down*, p. 138; Brzezinski, *Power and Principle*, p. 381.

391 "I got stern and noisy" Kirkpatrick, "Bank's Secret Campaign."

391 "Sullivan thought we ought to permit" Carter diary, February 5, 1979, *White House Diary*, p. 288.

391 "My own simple view" Cooper, *Fall of Heaven*, p. 477.

391 "We are giving up" Cooper, *Fall of Heaven*, p. 479, citing NSC Weekly Report no. 84, January 12, 1979, Jimmy Carter Presidential Library.

391 "Zbig—After we make" Brzezinski, *Power and Principle*, p. 382.

392 "He was worried" Milani, *Shah*, p. 414.

392 "This suits me fine" Carter, *Keeping Faith*, pp. 447–48.

393 "we will sell our oil" Kambiz Fattahi, "Two Weeks in January: America's Secret Engagement with Khoemini," BBC.com, June 3, 2016, https://www.bbc.com/news/world-us-canada-36431160.

393 "Nothing could be worse" Butler, unpublished diary, January 23, 1979.

393 "Khomeini returned to Iran" Carter diary, February 1, 1979, *White House Diary*, p. 287.

393 "We should be careful" Cooper, *Fall of Heaven*, p. 490, citing Brzezinski memorandum to the president, NSC Weekly Report no. 87, February 2, 1979, Jimmy Carter Presidential Library.

394 "I laid down the law" Carter diary, February 6, 1979, *White House Diary*, p. 289.

394 **"the shah feels betrayed"** Carter diary, February 7, 1979, *White House Diary,* p. 289.

394 **"a sort of Bonapartist counter-revolution"** Kirkpatrick, "Bank's Secret Campaign."

395 **"playing a lonely hand"** Sick, *All Fall Down,* p. 156.

395 **"10,000 of the best U.S. troops"** General Robert E. Huyser, *Mission to Tehran,* pp. 283–84; Brzezinski, *Power and Principle,* p. 393.

395 **"Tell Brzezinski to fuck off"** Ken Follett, *On Wings of Eagles,* p. 285; William H. Sullivan, *Mission to Iran,* p. 253; Brzezinski, *Power and Principle,* p. 392. See also David Newsom secret memo to Warren Christopher, September 10, 1980, recounting this February 11, 1979, phone conversation with Sullivan, "Telcon with Amb. Sullivan" folder, box 1, entry 14, Records of Warren Christopher, 1977–1980, National Archives, College Park, Md. See also Scott Armstrong, "U.S. Urged Crackdown on Opposition," *Washington Post,* October 27, 1980.

396 **"The President looked tired"** Butler, unpublished diary, February 12, 1979.

396 **"It is possible to say"** William Sullivan cable to Secstate, March 8, 1979, "Telcon w/Amb Sullivan" folder, box 1, entry 14, Records of Warren Christopher, 1977–1980, National Archives, College Park, Md.

396 **"A depressing story"** Brzezinski, *Power and Principle,* p. 393.

397 **"The shah was reproached"** Ryszard Kapusciniski, *Shah of Shahs,* p. 117.

397 **"It was difficult to know"** Bill, *Eagle and the Lion,* p. 257.

397 **"second-rate thinker"** *New York Times,* January 2, 1981; Hodding Carter III, "Life Inside the Carter State Department," *Playboy,* p. 214.

398 **$2 billion to $4 billion worth of assets** Ann Crittenden, "Bankers Say Shah's Fortune Is Well Above a Billion," *New York Times,* January 10, 1979.

398 **"I authorized Vance"** Carter diary, March 15, 1979, *White House Diary,* p. 304.

398 **code-named "Project Alpha"** Bird, *Chairman,* p. 644.

398 **$40,000 to write a short book** Bird, *Chairman,* p. 644; "Memo for the Record re: Professor George Lenczowski," December 10, 1979, folder 2, box SH 1, John J. McCloy Papers, Amherst College. The book in question was apparently never published.

399 **"personal and confidential" memos** Bird, *Chairman,* p. 644; Joseph V. Reed memo to "Volunteer Team on the Project Eagle," October 23, 1979; John J. McCloy memo to Mr. Reilly, May 7, 1980, folder 2, box SH 1, John J. McCloy Papers, Amherst College. In the spring of 1980, Reed informed members of Project Alpha that he had just discovered that his phone lines at One Chase Plaza were being wiretapped. There is no indication in McCloy's papers whether it was later determined who was responsible.

399 **"outrage"** Zbigniew Brzezinski interview, May 4, 2016.

399 **"I said," Kissinger recalled** Bird, *Chairman,* p. 645; Brzezinski, *Power and Principle,* p. 473; William Shawcross, *The Shah's Last Ride,* p. 153.

399 **"Circumstances had changed"** Bird, *Chairman,* p. 645; Carter, *Keeping Faith,* p. 452; Shawcross, *Shah's Last Ride,* p. 154.

400 **"It makes no sense to bring"** Bird, *Chairman,* p. 645; Hamilton Jordan, *Crisis,* p. 29.

400 "a man who for 37 years" Bird, *Chairman,* pp. 645–46; Bill, *Eagle and the Lion,* p. 335; Shawcross, *Shah's Last Ride,* p. 13.

400 "We can't get away" Rosalynn Carter, *First Lady from Plains,* p. 292; Bird, *Chairman,* p. 646.

400 "track me down" Gary Sick interview, August 5, 1985; Bird, *Chairman,* p. 648.

401 "Enjoyed having lunch with you today" Bird, *Chairman,* p. 649.

401 "Fuck the shah" Brzezinski, *Power and Principle,* p. 474; Bird, *Chairman,* pp. 648–49.

401 Khomeini's seventy-four-page blueprint Cooper, *Fall of Heaven,* p. 493. Khomeini's "velayat-e faqih" (guardianship of the jurist) thesis became the philosophical justification for the Islamic Republic.

402 twelve thousand Iranians Cooper, *Fall of Heaven,* p. 493.

CHAPTER 17: TILTING AGAINST AMERICAN EXCEPTIONALISM

404 "irresponsible scare tactics" Jimmy Carter, *White House Diary,* p. 310.

404 "primarily to demonstrate the safety" Jimmy Carter diary, March 31, 1979, and April 1, 1979, *White House Diary,* p. 310.

404 "We were getting about one-third" Carter diary, April 1, 1979, *White House Diary,* p. 310.

404 "I voted against a general" Jessica Tuchman Mathews interview.

405 "Although this accident" Transcript of Carter speech on April 5, 1979, *New York Times,* April 6, 1979.

405 $13 per barrel in mid-1979 Samantha Gross, "What Iran's 1979 Revolution Meant for US and Global Oil Markets," Brookings.edu.

406 stood at 42 percent Gerald Rafshoon memo to Jimmy Carter, February 1979, cited by J. William Holland, "The Great Gamble: Jimmy Carter and the 1979 Energy Crisis," *Prologue.*

406 a CBS/*New York Times* poll Stuart E. Eizenstat, *President Carter,* p. 668; Patrick Caddell memo to Jimmy Carter, June 11, 1979, "Patrick Caddell [3]" folder, box 33, Chief of Staff, Jordan, Jimmy Carter Presidential Library.

406 "We were in deep shit" Eizenstat, *President Carter,* p. 666.

406 "big and fleshy" Patrick Anderson, *Electing Jimmy Carter,* p. 51.

406 "Swarthy and slightly oafish" Kandy Stroud, *How Jimmy Won,* p. 190.

406 "style" Elizabeth Drew, "Phase: In Search of a Definition," *New Yorker.*

407 "This is my pollster" Eizenstat, *President Carter,* p. 667; Patrick Caddell interview by Stuart Eizenstat, April 1 and 17, 1993.

407 "While we would go home" Eizenstat, *President Carter,* p. 664; Gerald Rafshoon interview by Stuart Eizenstat, February 26, 1990.

407 "Of Crisis and Opportunity" Holland, "Great Gamble," p. 65.

407 "hyperbolic" and "historically reckless" Eizenstat, *President Carter,* pp. 672–73; Holland, "Great Gamble," p. 65.

407 "basic deep-seated and growing" Carter diary, April 28, 1979, *White House Diary,* p. 316; Jimmy Carter, daily diary, 10:35 A.M.–11:45 A.M., April 28, 1979.

408 "almost a Rasputin" Eizenstat, *President Carter,* p. 673.

408 "foul mood about everything" Eizenstat, *President Carter,* p. 668; Caddell interview by Eizenstat, April 1, 1993; Carter, daily diary, 6:56 P.M.–9:00 P.M., May 20, 1979.

408 "an experienced outsider" Carter diary, May 22, 1979, *White House Diary,* p. 321.

408 "Brandy, what can we do?" H. Brandt Ayers, *In Love with Defeat,* p. 224.

408 "We had a strange private dinner" Carter, *White House Diary,* p. 323.

409 destroy the Protestant work ethic Daniel Bell obituary, *The Economist,* February 3, 2011.

409 "the most level-headed and constructive" Carter diary, May 30, 1979, *White House Diary,* p. 323; Eizenstat, *President Carter,* p. 669.

409 "very interesting. . . . No one" Charles Peters interview.

410 "What I found most refreshing" Daniel Bell to Jody Powell, June 2, 1979, Jody Powell Papers, Jimmy Carter Presidential Library.

410 "the situation is desperate" Eizenstat, *President Carter,* pp. 668–69.

410 50 percent increase in oil prices Steven M. Gillon, *The Democrats' Dilemma,* p. 255.

410 "Mondale could see" Gillon, *Democrats' Dilemma,* p. 257.

411 "bunch of crap" Eizenstat, *President Carter,* p. 668.

411 "It'll be better if you quit" Gillon, *Democrats Dilemma,* p. 259. Gillon is citing an interview with Joan Mondale and her diary entry.

411 "accommodation with a totalitarian superpower" Rick Perlstein, *Reaganland,* p. 595.

412 "the gross waste of money" Carter diary, June 4, 1979, *White House Diary,* p. 323.

412 "a total waste" Eizenstat, *President Carter,* p. 613.

412 "Kennedy, continuing his irresponsible and abusive" Carter diary, June 12, 1979, *White House Diary,* p. 325.

413 "I'll whip his ass" Carter diary, June 12, 1979, and June 20, 1979, *White House Diary,* pp. 326 and 332.

413 "it was the best thing" Carter diary, June 20, 1979, *White House Diary,* p. 332.

413 "A generation from now" "Carter Welcomes Solar Power," *New York Times,* June 21, 1979; David Biello, "Where Did the Carter White House Solar Panels Go?" *Scientific American,* August 6, 2010.

413 "Our luncheon was bitter" Carter diary, June 27, 1979, *White House Diary,* p. 335.

414 "All the news from home was bad" Carter diary, June 29, 1979, *White House Diary,* p. 336.

414 "come back right away" Eizenstat, *President Carter,* p. 670.

414 "I do not need to detail" Holland, "Great Gamble," p. 67.

414 "I couldn't get any damn gas" Stuart Eizenstat oral history.

414 "to shift the cause" Holland, "Great Gamble," p. 67.

415 "one of the most brilliant" Carter diary, July 4, 1979, *White House Diary,* p. 340.

415 "Nobody wants to hear it" Rosalynn Carter, *First Lady from Plains,* p. 286.

416 "Carter is very tired" Eizenstat, *President Carter*, pp. 674–75.

416 "his body seems shrunken" Drew, "Phase."

416 7.6 minutes per mile Carter diary, December 12, 1978, *White House Diary*, p. 265.

416 "a showdown with Caddell" Eizenstat, *President Carter*, p. 677.

416 "Stu and Fritz were adamantly against" Carter diary, July 5, 1979, *White House Diary*, p. 341; Eizenstat, *President Carter*, p. 677.

416 "Don't panic and overreact" Jimmy Carter handwritten notes, July 5, 1979, "Camp David Domestic Summit: President's Notes, 7/79" folder, box 19, Camp David Domestic Summit, Plains File, Jimmy Carter Presidential Library.

417 "not enough fingers" Carter handwritten notes, July 5, 1979.

417 "was the craziest goddamn thing" Eizenstat, *President Carter*, pp. 679–81. Carter's own handwritten notes had Mondale telling him, "Pres dead tired." (Carter handwritten notes, July 5, 1979.)

417 "frank discussion" Carter diary, July 5, 1979, *White House Diary*, p. 341.

418 "has decided to cancel the speech" Hedrick Smith, "President Cancels Address on Energy; No Reason Offered," *New York Times*, July 5, 1979; Drew, "Phase."

418 "An air of mystery" Terence Smith, "Decision by Carter to Put Off Speech Has a Broad Effect," *New York Times*, July 6, 1979.

418 "end the vacillation" Smith, "Decision by Carter to Put Off Speech."

419 "It brought the conversation" Richard Moe email to the author, August 16, 2020.

419 "as unusual a weekend" Eizenstat, *President Carter*, pp. 684–85; Jimmy Carter, daily diary, July 7, 1979, https://www.jimmycarterlibrary.gov/assets/documents/diary/1979/d070779t.pdf.

419 "We sat on the floor" Charles Kirbo oral history.

420 "Mr. President, don't just preach" Eizenstat, *President Carter*, p. 686.

420 "Camp David is serene and lovely" Landon Butler, unpublished diary, July 11, 1979. (This diary entry was written on July 11 but covers Butler's observations from Camp David earlier in the week.)

420 "degenerate into a bitch session" Hamilton Jordan handwritten note to Jimmy Carter, undated, "Camp David, 1979 (Changes, etc)" folder, box 34A, Chief of Staff, Jordan, Jimmy Carter Presidential Library.

420 "a waste of time" Kevin Mattson, "*What the Heck Are You Up To, Mr. President?*," p. 141.

421 "God squad" Mattson, "*What the Heck Are You Up To*," p. 141.

421 "We have passed from an era" Mattson, "*What the Heck Are You Up To*," pp. 142–43.

422 "The best meeting" Carter diary, July 10, 1979, *White House Diary*, p. 343.

422 "He said the president had said" Butler, unpublished diary, July 11, 1979.

423 "Good evening. This is a special" Mattson, "*What the Heck Are You Up To*," pp. 207–17.

425 "almost a sermon" Mattson, "*What the Heck Are You Up To*," p. 159.

425 11 percent overnight Mattson, "*What the Heck Are You Up To*," p. 161; Eizenstat, *President Carter*, p. 691.

425 **"went over spectacularly well"** Mattson, *"What the Heck Are You Up To,"* p. 170; Stuart Eizenstat oral history.

425 **"Jimmy Carter got his voice"** Eizenstat, *President Carter,* p. 691.

426 **"boldly and correctly"** "Riding Casually to War" (editorial), *New York Times,* July 17, 1979.

426 **"give the American people"** *New York Times,* July 17, 1979, p. 14.

426 **"bring us all together"** Drew, "Phase," p. 56.

426 **"a dramatic proposal"** Meg Jacobs, *Panic at the Pump,* p. 224.

427 **"I cannot quarrel"** Jacobs, *Panic at the Pump,* p. 229.

427 **"counterproductive to what"** Jacobs, *Panic at the Pump,* p. 227.

CHAPTER 18: "YOU SHOULD FIRE PEOPLE"

429 **"In all the years"** Stuart E. Eizenstat, *President Carter,* p. 695.

429 **"I may ask all"** Eizenstat, *President Carter,* p. 695.

429 **"harshest words"** Richard Moe email to the author, August 16, 2020.

429 **"They [the cabinet members]"** Jimmy Carter diary, July 17, 1979, *White House Diary,* p. 344.

429 **"Maybe we should offer our resignations"** Eizenstat, *President Carter,* p. 697.

430 **"You should fire people"** Eizenstat, *President Carter,* p. 694; Stuart Eizenstat, pad 58, July 5, 1979, Jimmy Carter Presidential Library.

430 **"sashaying around the world"** Ambassador Rodney Kennedy-Minott eyes-only letter to Hamilton Jordan, June 13, 1979, unprocessed Charles Kirbo papers, Jimmy Carter Presidential Library.

430 **"the only way you could get"** Gerald Rafshoon interview, June 24, 2016. Rafshoon said something similar as well to Stuart Eizenstat. (Eizenstat, *President Carter,* p. 702.)

431 **"he'll cut you up"** Eizenstat, *President Carter,* p. 698.

431 **"dreaded this duty"** Jimmy Carter, *Keeping Faith,* p. 121.

431 **"slight distrust"** Jimmy Carter interview, September 14, 2017.

432 **"We can't go with quotas"** Eizenstat, *President Carter,* pp. 865–66; Eizenstat is quoting from his yellow legal pad no. 24, September 12, 1977.

432 **without any explicit quotas** Peter G. Bourne, *Jimmy Carter,* p. 425; Carter, *White House Diary,* p. 88.

432 **"I want the two of you"** Rodger D. Citron, "A Life in the Law: An Interview with Drew Days," *Touro Law Review,* July 14, 2013, http://www.tourolawreview.com/2013/07/a-life-in-the-law-an-interview-with-drew-days/.

433 **eager to resign** Jimmy Carter diary, September 5, 1979, *White House Diary,* p. 354; Jimmy Carter interview, September 14, 2017. Rosalynn Carter was annoyed that Bell had felt compelled in the spring of 1979 to appoint a "special counsel" to investigate whether monies from the Carter peanut warehouse had been illegally siphoned into the Carter presidential campaign in 1975–76. Special counsel Paul Curran issued a report in October 1979 that exonerated the

Carters, but Rosalynn thought Bell never should have allowed the investigation to go forward.

433 **told Adams he should resign** Eizenstat, *President Carter,* p. 699.

433 **"as though he was interviewing"** Carter diary, July 19, 1979, *White House Diary,* pp. 345–46.

434 **"Edgy Capital Sifting Rumors"** Hedrick Smith, "Edgy Capital Sifting Rumors," *New York Times,* July 19, 1979.

434 **"slaughterhouse, a purge"** Eizenstat, *President Carter,* p. 700.

434 **"Everyone around here is very"** *New York Times,* July 20, 1979, p. 1.

434 **"The President basked in the applause"** Kevin Mattson, *"What the Heck Are You Up To, Mr. President?,"* p. 168.

434 **approval rating at 25 percent** Elizabeth Drew, "Phase," *New Yorker,* August 27, 1979.

434 **"I handled the Cabinet changes"** Carter, *Keeping Faith,* p. 121.

434 **"bad idea"** Eizenstat, *President Carter,* p. 700.

435 **Powell was calling Califano a liar** Drew, "Phase."

435 **"There's no doubt"** Drew, "Phase."

435 **"The past two weeks"** Mattson, *"What the Heck Are You Up To,"* p. 172.

436 **"But two or three people"** Richard Moe interview, May 2, 2016.

436 **Miller hastily walked Moe** Richard Moe interview, May 2, 2016; Jimmy Carter, daily diary, July 24, 1979.

437 **"Volcker was sitting"** Eizenstat, *President Carter,* pp. 337–38.

437 **"I would advocate tighter policies"** Paul A. Volcker, *Keeping At It,* p. 103.

437 **"I need to get somebody"** Eizenstat, *President Carter,* p. 338.

437 **"intelligent, highly trained"** Carter diary, July 24, 1979, *White House Diary,* p. 347.

437 **"I just blew any chance"** Volcker, *Keeping At It,* p. 103.

437 **"I want you to tell him"** Bourne, *Jimmy Carter,* p. 448.

437 **"Well, let me ask my wife"** Richard Moe interview, May 2, 2016. Moe had stepped out of the room, but Miller later told him of Carter's conversation with Clausen. Moe was astonished that Clausen would put the president of the United States on hold.

438 **his usual wake-up call at 5:30** Carter, daily diary, July 25, 1979.

438 **"Isn't there any way"** Eizenstat, *President Carter,* p. 341.

438 **"practical monetarism"** Volcker, *Keeping At It,* p. 106.

438 **interest rates ballooned to 18 percent** Volcker, *Keeping At It,* p. 108.

439 **"We had to live with that"** Stuart Eizenstat oral history.

439 **"ill-advised"** Volcker, *Keeping At It,* p. 111.

439 **"This will hurt us politically"** Carter diary, September 25, 1979, *White House Diary,* p. 468.

439 **2.4 million manufacturing jobs** Rick Perlstein, *Reaganland,* p. 634.

439 **"I always give him a lot"** Eizenstat, *President Carter,* p. 353; Eizenstat interview of Volcker, July 31, 1989.

CHAPTER 19: FOREIGN POLICY IMBROGLIOS

441 **"like a hot wire"** John Dinges and Saul Landau, *Assassination on Embassy Row,* pp. 208–9.

442 **"By what right"** Robert Pastor memo to Zbigniew Brzezinski, October 11, 1979, document 234, U.S. Office of the Historian, Foreign Relations of the United States: Jimmy Carter Administration (1977–1980), vol. 28, South America, Latin America Region. See also "The Letelier/Moffitt Assassinations: Policy Toward Chile," dissent channel cable by Robert Steven, former Chile desk officer, and three other State Department officials, October 1, 1979, doc. no. C06480661, Peter Kornbluh, September 20, 1979, National Security Archive.

442 **"the secret police of Chile"** Patricia Derian memo to the Secretary, October 12, 1979, box 1, ARC ID 1487627 P, entry 14, Office of the Deputy Secretary Warren Christopher, Note to Researcher to Letelier-Moffitt, National Archives.

443 **"did not wish to break relations"** Carter handwritten marginal note, Memorandum from Acting Secretary Warren Christopher to President Carter, October 2, 1979, document 232, U.S. Office of the Historian, Foreign Relations of the United States: Jimmy Carter Administration (1977–1980), vol. 28, South America, Latin America Region.

443 **"egregious act of international terrorism"** Dinges and Landau, *Assassination on Embassy Row,* pp. 380–81; Secretary Vance memo to Jimmy Carter, October 19, 1979, document 235, U.S. Office of the Historian, Foreign Relations of the United States: Jimmy Carter Administration (1977–1980), vol. 28, South America, Latin America Region.

443 **"the U.S. putting J. Edgar Hoover"** President Carter et al., Memorandum of Conversation, July 1, 1980, document 237, U.S. Office of the Historian, Foreign Relations of the United States: Jimmy Carter Administration (1977–1980), vol. 28, South America, Latin America Region.

444 **"what we regard as convincing"** George P. Shultz memo to Jimmy Carter, October 6, 1987, Briefing Book no. 560, September 23, 2016, National Security Archive.

445 **"the question was not if Somoza"** Presidential Review Committee, Secret, June 11, 1979, NLC-33-10-9-3-2, Jimmy Carter Presidential Library.

445 **"Ok, but before we provide support"** President's Assistant for National Security Affairs (Brzezinski) memo to President Carter, June 23, 1979, document 223, U.S. Office of the Historian, Foreign Relations of the United States: Jimmy Carter Administration (1977–1980), vol. 17, Central America.

446 **"into play looks like"** Telegram from the Embassy in Nicaragua to the Department of State, June 28, 1979, document 239, U.S. Office of the Historian, Foreign Relations of the United States: Jimmy Carter Administration (1977–1980), vol. 17, Central America.

446 **"on the grounds that the U.S."** Memorandum for the Record, July 10, 1979, document 263, U.S. Office of the Historian, Foreign Relations of the United States: Jimmy Carter Administration (1977–1980), vol. 17, Central America.

446 **"assist democratic elements"** Summary of Conclusions of a Special Coordina-

tion Committee (Intelligence) Meeting, July 17, 1979, document 286, U.S. Office of the Historian, *Foreign Relations of the United States: Jimmy Carter Administration (1977–1980), vol. 17, Central America.*

447 **"the Carter administration not only"** Jeane J. Kirkpatrick, "Dictatorships and Double Standards," *Commentary.*

447 **"I have concluded that"** Presidential Directive NSC-6, March 15, 1977, document 9, U.S. Office of the Historian, *Foreign Relations of the United States: Jimmy Carter Administration (1977–1980), vol. 23, Mexico, Cuba and the Caribbean.*

447 **"The second round of talks"** Briefing Memorandum, May 2, 1977, document 15, U.S. Office of the Historian, *Foreign Relations of the United States: Jimmy Carter Administration (1977–1980), vol. 23, Mexico, Cuba and the Caribbean.*

447 **a settlement worth $600 million** Secretary of the Treasury Blumenthal memo to President Carter, August 12, 1977, document 21, U.S. Office of the Historian, *Foreign Relations of the United States: Jimmy Carter Administration (1977–1980), vol. 23, Mexico, Cuba and the Caribbean.*

447 **"trusted friend and advisor"** President Carter letter to Dr. Fidel Castro Ruz, February 7, 1978 (declassified September 25, 2014), "Cuba, 2/78–9/80" folder, CREST, NLC-128R-1-18-62-3, Jimmy Carter Presidential Library.

448 **"it appears we have gone"** John M. Goshko, "Expanded Cuban Presence Decried by U.S.," *Washington Post,* November 18, 1977.

448 **"We are getting sucked in"** Zbigniew Brzezinski, *Power and Principle,* p. 182.

448 **"Everyone otherwise was against me"** Brzezinski, *Power and Principle,* p. 183.

449 **"We will end up losing SALT"** Brzezinski, *Power and Principle,* p. 186.

449 **"I could sense"** Brzezinski, *Power and Principle,* p. 182.

449 **"SALT lies buried in the sands"** Brzezinski, *Power and Principle,* p. 189.

449 **"abusive against the Soviets"** Carter diary, May 29, 1978, *White House Diary,* p. 197.

449 **"Zbig is too competitive"** Carter diary, February 7, 1979, *White House Diary,* p. 289.

450 **"Extraordinarily frank and helpful"** Peter Tarnoff and Robert Pastor memo to the President, "Discussions with Fidel Castro," January 16–17, 1980 (declassified 2008), "Cuba, 2/78–9/80" folder, box 19, Plains File, NLC-128-1-18-6-3, Jimmy Carter Presidential Library.

450 **his communist "paradise"** Stuart E. Eizenstat, *President Carter,* p. 873.

451 **"face to face summit meeting"** Peter Tarnoff, "Account of Mr. Paul Austin's Conversation with Cuban President Fidel Castro," September 8, 1980, "Cuba, 2/78–9/80" folder, box 19, Plains File, Jimmy Carter Presidential Library.

452 **"I don't have guilt feelings"** George Packer, *Our Man,* p. 179.

452 **"You need to choose"** Packer, *Our Man,* p. 186.

452 **"Zbig, you have a tendency"** Zbigniew Brzezinski to Jimmy Carter, October 13, 1978, "Weekly Reports 9/78–12/78" folder, Subject File, box 42, Brzezinski Donated Materials, Jimmy Carter Presidential Library; Kenton Clymer, "Jimmy Carter, Human Rights, and Cambodia," *Diplomatic History,* April 2003, p. 255.

452 **"worst violator of human rights"** Clymer, "Jimmy Carter, Human Rights, and Cambodia," p. 246.

452 **"the Soviet-backed"** Clymer, "Jimmy Carter, Human Rights, and Cambodia," p. 257.

453 **"It ran counter to"** Packer, *Our Man,* p. 198.

453 **"the situation in Cambodia"** Carter, *White House Diary,* p. 190.

453 **"incomprehensible"** Patricia Derian briefing memo to Secretary Vance, October 22, 1979, document 194, U.S. Office of the Historian, Foreign Relations of the United States: Jimmy Carter Administration (1977–1980), vol. 2, Human Rights and Humanitarian Affairs; Cyrus Vance, *Hard Choices,* p. 126.

453 **"Are you telling me"** Packer, *Our Man,* p. 202.

454 **"Rosalynn Carter walked through"** Henry Kamm, "Mrs. Carter Visits Thai Camp," *New York Times,* November 10, 1979.

454 **"looked like a tiny monkey"** Rosalynn Carter, *First Lady from Plains,* p. 280.

454 **"There was an indication"** Jimmy Carter diary, September 22, 1979, *White House Diary,* p. 357.

454 **Brzezinski briefed the president** Carter, daily diary, September 22, 1979.

454 **"every known atmospheric nuclear explosion"** "Report on Possible Nuclear Explosion of September 22, 1979," Anthony Lake Papers, RG 59, P9, box 17, National Archives. See also Thomas O'Toole, "Experts Explore Cause of Flash," *Washington Post,* November 2, 1979.

455 **"Israeli–South African relationship"** State Department cable, "Possible Israeli–South African Nuclear Connection," November 23, 1977 (declassified November 19, 2013), CREST NLC-16-108-2-13-9, National Archives.

455 **"Do not let any allegation leak"** "Summary of Conclusions of a Mini-Special Coordination Committee Meeting," September 23, 1979, document 362, U.S. Office of the Historian, Foreign Relations of the United States: Jimmy Carter Administration (1977–1980), vol. 16, Southern Africa.

455 **dinner at the Brzezinski home** Carter, daily diary, September 22, 1979.

455 **"a nuclear explosion (1-3 KT)"** "Summary of Conclusions of a Mini-Special Coordination Committee Meeting."

455 **"There was sheer panic"** Seymour Hersh, *The Samson Option,* p. 274.

456 **"bet 2 to 1 in favor"** Document 11, Spurgeon Keeny, Deputy Director, Arms Control and Disarmament Agency, to Ambassador Henry Owen, "Transmittal of Letter from Richard Garwin," October 19, 1979, sending letter from Richard Garwin to Harold M. Agnew and Stephen J. Lukasik, October 18, 1979, Secret, cited by William Burr and Avner Cohen, eds., "New Evidence on 22 September 1979 Vela Event," National Security Archive, Briefing Book #570.

456 **"an unbiased outside study"** Hersh, *Samson Option,* p. 273.

457 **"We knew something happened"** Zbigniew Brzezinski interview, June 21, 2016.

457 **"We have a growing belief"** Jimmy Carter diary, February 27, 1980, *White House Diary,* p. 405.

457 **a small flotilla of Israeli naval vessels** Hersh, *Samson Option,* p. 278.

457 **Admiral Stansfield Turner** In the 1990s, Turner told the historian Avner Cohen

that he knew the Israelis were responsible. See also CIA report, "The 22 September 1979 Event," January 21, 1980 (declassified June 2004). A cover note stated, "Its conclusions rest largely on circumstantial evidence and on the assumption that there was a nuclear explosion on 22 September 1979." https://nsarchive2 .gwu.edu/NSAEBB/NSAEBB190/03.pdf.

457 **Dan Raviv, who claimed** *CBS Evening News,* February 21, 1980. Among Raviv's sources were Eliyahu Speiser, a Knesset member who told Raviv that the Vela event was an Israeli test "with the assistance and cooperation of South Africa."

457 **"unique to nuclear shots"** Robert A. Martin memo to Paul Hare, June 17, 1980, Department of State, Secret, Declassified NND66817, RG 59, National Archives.

458 **a deep hole had been discovered** Frances D. Cook memo to Richard Moose, June 10, 1980, Department of State, Declassified NND66817, RG 59, P9, box 18, National Archives.

458 **"white wash, due to political considerations"** Burr and Cohen, eds. "New Evidence on 22 September 1979 Vela Event."

458 **former Israeli government officials** Hersh, *Samson Option,* p. 271. See also "The Vela Flash: Forty Years Ago," National Security Archive, September 22, 2019, https://nsarchive.gwu.edu/briefing-book/nuclear-vault/2019-09-22/vela -flash-forty-years-ago.

458 **"more and more information revealed"** Leonard Weiss, "Flash from the Past," *Bulletin of Atomic Scientists.*

CHAPTER 20: MUCH ADO ABOUT NOTHING

461 **"Peter was not Jody's"** Patrick Anderson, *Electing Jimmy Carter,* p. 67.

461 **"We had a pleasant evening"** Jimmy Carter diary, March 10, 1978, *White House Diary,* p. 176.

461 **"about the closest friend"** Michael Massing, *The Fix,* p. 139; Stuart Auerbach, "There's More to Carter's 'Closest Friend' Than 'Flaky Accent,'" *Washington Post,* June 21, 1976.

461 **"one of the few people"** Edward Walsh and Ronald Shaffer, "Carter Drug Adviser Put on Leave," *Washington Post,* July 20, 1978.

461 **"I wrote a real prescription"** Walsh and Shaffer, "Carter Drug Adviser Put on Leave."

462 **"But when I got up"** Fred Barbash, "The Quaalude Affair," *Washington Post,* July 21, 1978.

462 **"unaccountable lapse of judgment"** "The Departure of Dr. Bourne," *Washington Post,* July 21, 1978.

462 **liberalization of marijuana laws** Massing, *Fix,* pp. 140–42.

462 **They viewed** *Elmer Gantry* Jimmy Carter, daily diary, December 1, 1978.

462 **"What's so funny?"** David A. Kaplan email to the author, November 21, 2018.

463 **"gotten himself into serious trouble":** Carter, *White House Diary,* p. 351.

463 **"practically invented racism"** Graham Hovey, "Young's Fall Attributed to Deception on Meeting," *New York Times,* August 17, 1979.

463 **Carter always backed** In the spring of 1977, Charlie Kirbo wrote to Carter, "I feel confident that after being bumped about a bit he [Young] will settle down and do the job you expect of him." (Charles Kirbo memo to President Carter, April 14, 1977, unprocessed Charles Kirbo papers, Jimmy Carter Presidential Library.)

464 **"Carter wanted him there"** Zbigniew Brzezinski interview, May 4, 2016.

464 **According to Stu Eizenstat** Stuart E. Eizenstat, *President Carter,* p. 849.

464 **"Well, I wish you'd try"** Andrew Young, transcript of videotaped interview by Dan Shilon.

465 **"absolutely ridiculous"** Carter, *White House Diary,* p. 352.

465 **"not talking to the enemy"** Eizenstat, *President Carter,* p. 849.

465 **"I mean, he said it"** Stoney Cooks interview by Tom Dent.

466 **"Of course we were talking"** Donald McHenry interview.

466 **"Andy had grown up"** Charles William Maynes oral history.

466 **"Ambassador Young has had"** State Department transcript, August 13, 1979, "Young, Andrew—Meeting with PLO, 8/79" folder, box 82, Staff Offices, Press, Powell, Jimmy Carter Presidential Library.

467 **"Andy was actually covering"** Stoney Cooks interview by Tom Dent.

467 **"truth about the exact nature"** Wolf Blitzer, "Andy Young's Undoing," *Jerusalem Post,* September 15, 1979 (on file in "Young, Andrew" folder, box 16, Special Advisor to the President, Moses, Jimmy Carter Presidential Library).

467 **"The sharks are out"** Donald McHenry interview.

467 **"one of the most heart-wrenching"** Carter, *White House Diary,* p. 352.

468 **"Andy must go"** Eizenstat, *President Carter,* p. 851.

468 **Jody Powell actually wept** Carter diary, August 15, 1979, *White House Diary,* p. 352; *New York Times,* August 18, 1979.

468 **"Andy was not penitent at all"** Carter diary, August 15, 1979, *White House Diary,* p. 352.

468 **"I really don't feel a bit sorry"** *New York Times,* August 16, 1979.

469 **"I have never been sure"** Jimmy Carter, *A Full Life,* p. 142.

469 **an Israeli listening device** Stanley W. Cloud, "Israeli Agents Bugged Young, Sources Insist," Time-Life News Service, August 23, 1979.

469 **"much evidence points to the Israelis"** Eizenstat, *President Carter,* p. 850.

469 **"There was an intercept"** Anonymous diplomat, January 5, 2016.

469 **national security adviser claimed** Zbigniew Brzezinski interview, May 4, 2016.

469 **"I don't know how they got it"** Don Oberdorfer, "Young Criticizes Israeli Chieftains, U.S. PLO Policy," *Washington Post,* August 20, 1979.

469 **"You would think"** Donald McHenry interview.

470 **"indeed did talk"** Editorial, *Washington Post,* September 10, 1979.

470 **"and we realized the significance"** Carl Gershman, "The Andrew Young Affair," *Commentary.*

470 **"deplorable act"** Eizenstat, *President Carter,* p. 852.

470 **"The perception on the street"** Gershman, "Andrew Young Affair."

470 **"our former allies"** Gershman, "Andrew Young Affair."

470 **Milton A. Wolf, had not even** *New York Times,* August 17, 1979.

470 **"stubborn and intransigent"** Brian Kates, "Young Slams Israel," *New York Daily News,* August 20, 1979.

471 **"There are some who attribute"** "Black-Jewish Relations," *Afro-American,* August 28–September 1, 1979.

471 **"their own homeland"** Eizenstat, *President Carter,* p. 853.

471 **"we cannot work with"** "11 Jewish Groups Reject Criticism from Blacks," *New York Times,* August 24, 1979.

471 **"The Young affair has been"** John Herbers, "Aftermath of the Andrew Young Affair: Blacks, Jews and Carter All Could Suffer Greatly," *New York Times,* September 6, 1979.

472 **"a pure and simple exploitation"** Michael Kramer, "Blacks and Jews," *New York.*

472 **"I was sure the president"** "Black Votes, Jewish Votes," *Washington Post,* September 10, 1979.

472 **"much of the animosity"** William Safire, "Of Blacks and Jews," *New York Times,* September 27, 1979.

472 **"American Jewish leaders or anyone else"** Edward Cowan, "President Asserts Jewish Leaders Did Not Pressure Him to Dismiss Young," *New York Times,* September 24, 1979.

472 **had Young remained in his post** Garry Wills, *Under God,* p. 253.

473 **"When we looked at the photograph"** "Remarks of the President in a Meeting with Florida Newspaper Editors," August 31, 1979, "News Conference Transcripts, 1979 (8)" folder, box 19, Press Office Media Liaison, Marc Henderson Subject Files, Jimmy Carter Presidential Library.

473 **"Brzezinski will go to any extreme"** Don Irwin, "President Splits a Few Hares in Telling of Pond Encounter," *Los Angeles Times,* September 1, 1979.

473 **"A 'killer rabbit' attacked"** Brooks Jackson, "Killer Rabbit Attacks Carter in Canoe—Loses," *Los Angeles Times;* Jody Powell, *The Other Side of the Story,* p. 105.

474 **"parrying and thrusting"** Eleanor Randolph, "Carter Has a Hare-Raising Experience on Plains Trip," *Los Angeles Times,* August 30, 1979.

474 **"Bunny Goes Bugs"** Brooks Jackson, "Bunny Goes Bugs: Rabbit Attacks President,"*Washington Post,* August 30, 1979.

474 **"Oh, by the way"** "Informal Q and A on the Outskirts of Plains, Georgia," August 31, 1979, News Conference Transcripts, folder, box 19, Press Office, Marc Henderson's Subject Files, Jimmy Carter Presidential Library.

475 **"bashing a bunny in the head"** "Carter Attacked by 'Killer Senator,'" *Los Angeles Times,* August 31, 1979; *Washington Post,* September 1, 1979.

475 **"the rabbit controversy"** Charles Goodwin to Press Office Staff, "Jody's Briefing This Date," September 4, 1979, "Jody Powell Briefings, 1979 [2]" folder, box 22, Press Office, Marc Henderson's Subject Files, Jimmy Carter Presidential Library. For an explanation of the rooster pepper sausage story, see Marion Burros, "Bell's Pepper, the Spur of the Moment," *Washington Post,* July 29, 1979; Marion Burros, *Washington Post,* November 2, 1978.

475 **"*rooster pepper sausage*"** The supposed aphrodisiac sausage was indeed a hoax, concocted by Judge Bell and Kirbo. See "Conversations with Judge Bell," *Journal of Southern Legal History,* 18, nos. 1 and 2 (2010), pp. 227–28.

475 **"It was a nightmare"** Powell, *Other Side of the Story,* p. 108.

476 **"It was the most magical club"** Alan Light, "Studio 54, the Other Magical Kingdom," *New York Times,* October 7, 1918.

476 **"I'll stay aloof"** Carter diary, August 24, 1979, *White House Diary,* p. 353.

477 **"did not like Jimmy Carter"** Jason Breslow, "The Frontline Interview: Roger Stone," *Frontline,* PBS, September 27, 2016.

477 **"I saw him [Jordan]"** "I Got No Kick from Studio 54," *People,* September 10, 1979; Carter B. Horsley, "Figure in Jordan Case Arrested at Studio 54," *New York Times,* October 7, 1979.

477 **"Maybe this will be"** Hamilton Jordan, *No Such Thing as a Bad Day,* pp. 73–74.

477 **"Everybody knows Hamilton"** "I Got No Kick from Studio 54," *People,* September 10, 1979.

478 **"The person who made the latest charge"** Wendy E. Swanberg, "The Gossip Makes the News," p. 117.

478 **According to Bob Woodward** Douglas Martin, "Arthur H. Christy, Special Prosecutor, Is Dead at 86," *New York Times,* March 17, 2010; Swanberg, "Gossip Makes the News," p. 118.

478 **$175,000 in legal fees** Swanberg, "Gossip Makes the News," p. 121.

478 **salary at the time was $56,000** "The President's Boys," *Time.*

478 **Chip Carter went to see** Chip Carter interview, June 30, 2018. Steven Brill, editor of *The American Lawyer,* quoted an unnamed Justice Department official explaining why they had refused to negotiate a plea deal with Rubell and Schrager: "If we took a plea, everyone would say we did it to keep them quiet about more information on Jordan or other people. I've already heard a rumor that we're trying to protect one of the president's children." (Steven Brill, "How a Legal Ploy Backfired," *American Lawyer,* reprinted in *Washington Post.*)

479 **"because he was bathed"** Diana McLellan, *Ear on Washington,* p. 146; Swanberg, "Gossip Makes the News," p. 123.

CHAPTER 21: FATEFUL DECISIONS

481 **a pathetic 19 percent** Jon Ward, *Camelot's End,* pp. 125 and 146.

481 **Kennedy came to the White House** Jimmy Carter, daily diary, September 7, 1979; Ward, *Camelot's End,* p. 153; Peter G. Bourne, *Jimmy Carter,* p. 450.

481 **"It's true that Jimmy Carter"** Charles Kirbo, speech, Harvard Law School Forum, October 17, 1979, unprocessed Charles Kirbo Papers, Jimmy Carter Presidential Library.

481 **"must be aware"** Rick Perlstein, *Reaganland,* p. 524; Arthur M. Schlesinger, Jr., *Journals,* p. 461.

481 **"There are no philosophical"** Bourne, *Jimmy Carter,* p. 450.

481 **"The President's speech at the Kennedy"** Ward, *Camelot's End,* p. 153.

481 **"convinced me that I do not"** Jimmy Carter diary, September 8, 1979, *White House Diary,* p. 355.

482 **injected nearly a quart** *Time,* October 15, 1979.

482 **"President Carter, wobbling"** B. Drummond Ayres, Jr., "Carter, Exhausted and Pale, Drops Out of Six Mile Race," *New York Times*, September 16, 1979.

482 **"A weakened America"** Editorial, *New York Times*, September 16, 1979.

482 **"evangelist on running"** B. Drummond Ayres, Jr., "Carter, Exhausted and Pale, Drops Out of Six Mile Race," *New York Times*, September 16, 1979.

482 **"If you get in it"** Ayres, "Carter, Exhausted and Pale, Drops Out."

483 **"more forthcoming attitude"** Kai Bird, *The Chairman*, p. 650; Zbigniew Brzezinski, *Power and Principle*, p. 474.

483 **"Zbig bugged me on it every day"** Brzezinski, *Power and Principle*, p. 474.

484 **"politically it's devastating to SALT"** Carter, daily diary, September 5, 1979, Jimmy Carter, *Keeping Faith*, p. 263.

484 **"this status quo is not acceptable"** Carter, *Keeping Faith*, pp. 263–64.

484 **"Anatoly, were those troops"** Betty Glad, *An Outsider in the White House*, p. 191.

485 **"inappropriate for a mighty nation"** Glad, *An Outsider in the White House*, p. 192.

485 **"to revive the Cold War"** Glad, *An Outsider in the White House*, p. 193; handwritten notes, September 28, 1979, "Cuba, 2/7/8–9/80" folder, box 19, Plains File, Jimmy Carter Presidential Library.

485 **they made it clear** Bird, *Chairman*, pp. 650–51; Bernard Gwertzman, "President Gets Wide-Ranging Advice on Soviet Troops from 15 Experts," *New York Times*, September 30, 1979.

485 **Pushed by Kirbo** Charles Kirbo memo to Jimmy Carter, September 21, 1979, unprocessed Charles Kirbo papers, Jimmy Carter Presidential Library.

485 **"no reason for a return"** Brzezinski, *Power and Principle*, p. 351.

486 **"the most disagreeable comments"** Brzezinski, *Power and Principle*, p. 351.

486 **"Maybe he thought of firing me"** Zbigniew Brzezinski oral history.

486 **"a surprising affinity"** Brzezinski, *Power and Principle*, p. 21.

487 **"I ask President Carter directly"** Memo for the Record, September 9, 1979, folder 2, box SH 1, John J. McCloy Papers, Amherst College.

487 **"Mr. President," Jordan argued** Bird, *Chairman*, pp. 651 and 754; Hamilton Jordan, *Crisis*, p. 31. Carter thought he was being told that the shah was near death and that the only possible treatment existed in New York. Dr. Benjamin Kean in fact had only said that the shah needed treatment in a few weeks—and listed a number of hospitals outside the United States that could handle the case.

488 **"What are you guys"** Bird, *Chairman*, p. 652; Jordan, *Crisis*, p. 32; Carter diary, October 20, 1979, *White House Diary*, p. 364.

488 **"she flinched away ostentatiously"** Ward, *Camelot's End*, p. 152. Carter recollected this in a 2015 interview with Ward.

488 **"seemed startled at first"** *Boston Globe*, October 21, 1979.

489 **"In a few minutes"** "Carter's Remarks," *Boston Globe*, October 21, 1979.

489 **"inform our embassy in Tehran"** Carter diary, October 20, 1979, *White House Diary*, p. 364.

489 **"Our 'mission impossible'"** Bird, *Chairman*, p. 652; Joseph Reed memo to Vol-

unteer Team on the "Project Eagle," October 23, 1979, folder 2, box SH 1, John J. McCloy Papers, Amherst College.

490 **"I was told the shah"** Terence Smith, "Why Carter Admitted the Shah," *New York Times.*

490 **a series of medical mishaps** Jeffrey Fleishman, "Documentary Examines . . . ," *Los Angeles Times,* November 11, 2017; *A Dying King: The Shah of Iran,* directed by Bobak Kalhor, 2017; William Shawcross, *The Shah's Last Ride;* Lawrence K. Altman, M.D., "The Shah's Health," *New York Times.*

490 **"We want to advise you"** Jordan, *Crisis,* p. 18.

490 **"I could picture the revolutionaries"** John Kifner, "Putting the Hostages' Lives First," *New York Times.*

491 **"They'll be released before tonight"** Jordan, *Crisis,* p. 19.

491 **"The biggest political story"** Jordan, *Crisis,* p. 21.

491 **"I thought [it] was devastating"** Carter diary, November 4, 1979, *White House Diary,* p. 367.

492 **"the idiot Khomeini"** Carter diary, November 5, 1979, *White House Diary,* p. 368.

492 **"about 90 Americans"** *New York Times,* November 5, 1979.

492 **had no knowledge of their plans** Mark Bowden, *Guests of the Ayatollah,* p. 14.

493 **"almost impossible to deal"** Carter diary, November 6, 1979, *Keeping Faith,* p. 458.

493 **punish Iran militarily** Edward C. Keefer, *Harold Brown,* p. 299.

493 **Beirut "back channel"** Kifner, "Putting the Hostages' Lives First."

494 **"the detention of the hostages"** David E. Mark secret memo to the Secretary, November 12, 1979, "Iran misc. Nov 1979" folder, box 19, Records of Anthony Lake, 1977–1981, National Archives.

494 **"We all agreed"** Brzezinski, *Power and Principle,* pp. 535–36.

494 **"student mob in Tehran"** Brzezinski, *Power and Principle,* p. 481.

494 **"When he comes back"** Brzezinski, *Power and Principle,* p. 481.

495 **"swayed by emotions"** Brzezinski, *Power and Principle,* p. 481.

495 **"I told him"** Carter diary, November 14, 1979, *White House Diary,* p. 370.

495 **$4.05 million interest due** James A. Bill, *The Eagle and the Lion,* pp. 341–48.

496 **"When the dust had cleared"** Mark Hulbert, *Interlock,* pp. 156, 171–72, and 174; Bird, *Chairman,* p. 654.

497 **"terrible mistake"** Stuart E. Eizenstat, *President Carter,* p. 774.

497 **"If we seize Kharg Island"** Kifner, "Putting the Hostages' Lives First."

497 **"I know that"** Eizenstat, *President Carter,* p. 776.

497 **"mine the entrances to all"** Carter, *Keeping Faith,* p. 466.

497 **"to notify Khomeini through sure channels"** Carter diary, November 23, 1979, *White House Diary,* p. 372.

497 **"He gave a ridiculous reason"** Carter diary, November 29, 1979, *White House Diary,* p. 374.

498 **"I stood there about ten"** Carter diary, November 29, 1979, *White House Diary,* p. 374.

498   "with the unbelievable news" Carter diary, November 29, 1979, *Keeping Faith*, p. 468.

498   "The situation is that" Carter diary, December 1, 1979, *Keeping Faith*, p. 469.

498   "a most disagreeable conversation" Brzezinski, *Power and Principle*, p. 481.

499   "Zbig and Cy have not" Carter diary, December 1–2, 1979, *White House Diary*, p. 375.

499   "Things were better" Carter, *Keeping Faith*, p. 470; Carter diary, December 13, 1979, *White House Diary*, p. 379.

499   "had it not been for Mr. Kissinger" Bill, *Eagle and the Lion*, pp. 335–36.

500   "I gave him my best wishes" Carter diary, December 15, 1979, *White House Diary*, p. 380.

500   "I have made some mistakes" *New York Times*, December 5, 1979, p. 1.

500   "surprisingly good for me" Carter diary, December 8, 1979, *White House Diary*, p. 377.

500   "time was not working" Brzezinski, *Power and Principle*, p. 484.

500   "a bloodless act of war" Brzezinski, *Power and Principle*, p. 484.

501   "I am not going to take any" Bernard Gwertzman, "Carter Says He Plans . . . ," *New York Times*, December 8, 1979; Kifner, "Putting the Hostages' Lives First"; Robert McFadden, Joseph B. Treaster, and Maurice Carroll, *No Hiding Place*, p. 197.

501   "serious mistake" Eizenstat, *President Carter*, p. 776.

501   "I never placed the hostages' lives first" Kifner, "Putting the Hostages' Lives First."

502   "It's relatively lonely at Camp David" Carter diary, December 24, 1979, *White House Diary*, p. 382.

503   "They [the Soviets] have had 215 flights" Carter, *White House Diary*, p. 382.

503   "The entry of our troops" Charles Cogan, "Partners in Time: The CIA and Afghanistan Since 1979," *World Policy Journal*, pp. 73–82.

504   "detailed maps showing" Carter diary, April 4, 1979, *White House Diary*, p. 311.

504   "pushed a decision" Brzezinski, *Power and Principle*, p. 427.

504   "It was in our interest" Zbigniew Brzezinski interview, June 21, 2016.

504   "access to the Indian Ocean" Brzezinski, *Power and Principle*, p. 427.

504   tribesmen of Baluchistan Lawrence Lifschultz, "Pakistan's Prisoner," *New York Times*, December 13, 1979.

505   authorizing $500,000 in cash Presidential finding, July 3, 1979, "CIA Charter: 2/9–25/80" folder, box 60, Counsel's Office, Staff Offices, Jimmy Carter Presidential Library; Justin Vaïsse, *Zbigniew Brzezinski*, p. 310; Robert Gates, *From the Shadows*, p. 146.

505   "that in my opinion" Vincent Jauvert, "Les révélations d'un ancien conseiller de Carter," *Le Nouvel Observateur*.

505   "most of the countryside" Glad, *An Outsider in the White House*, pp. 198–99; Eizenstat, *President Carter*, p. 637; Gates, *From the Shadows*, pp. 146–47.

505   "Had we been tougher" Brzezinski, *Power and Principle*, pp. 432 and 429.

506   "We didn't really trap them" Vaïsse, *Zbigniew Brzezinski*, pp. 307–8.

506   "There goes SALT II" Rosalynn Carter, *First Lady from Plains*, p. 314.

506 **"impossible task"** Carter, *Keeping Faith,* p. 265.

506 **"No," Carter replied, "unless"** Jordan, *Crisis,* p. 88.

CHAPTER 22: AN UNHAPPY SPRING

508 **"Dear Cy," wrote Thomas** Betty Glad, *An Outsider in the White House,* p. 215.

509 **"more assertive"** Glad, *An Outsider in the White House,* p. 204.

509 **"My opinion of the Russians"** Document 133, "Editorial Note," U.S. Office of the Historian, Foreign Relations of the United States: Jimmy Carter Administration (1977–1980), vol. 1; *New York Times,* January 1, 1980, p. 1.

509 **"Perhaps it was just"** Landon Butler, unpublished diary, January 7, 1980.

510 **"The implications of the Soviet invasion"** Glad, *An Outsider in the White House,* p. 200.

510 **"regional security framework"** Zbigniew Brzezinski, *Power and Principle,* p. 445.

510 **increased spending on defense** Stuart E. Eizenstat, *President Carter,* p. 9.

511 **optics of PD-59** Jimmy Carter diary, August 10, 1980, *White House Diary,* p. 456; "Jimmy Carter's Controversial Nuclear Targeting Directive PD-59 Declassified," National Security Archive Electronic Briefing Book no. 390, September 14, 2012, https://nsarchive2.gwu.edu/nukevault/ebb390/; Justin Vaïsse, *Zbigniew Brzezinski,* pp. 312–13.

511 **"He's a genuine hawk"** Butler, unpublished diary, January 3, 1980.

511 **administration "had come off track"** Kai Bird, "Citizen Carter," *The Nation;* Averell Harriman to Edmund Muskie, Harriman private archives.

512 **"I must say that I find"** Charles Kirbo memo to Jimmy Carter, February 12, 1980, unprocessed Charles Kirbo Papers, Jimmy Carter Presidential Library.

512 **"just kicked up dust everywhere"** Charles Kirbo oral history.

512 **"We have evidence that the Politburo"** Carter diary, February 28, 1980, *White House Diary,* p. 406.

512 **"The scary part"** A. S. Chernyaev, *The Diary of Anatoly S. Chernyaev,* National Security Archive, https://nsarchive.gwu.edu/anatoly-chernyaev-diary. Chernyaev was the deputy director of the international department of the Communist Party's Central Committee. "I'm going through a very tough time morally," he wrote in his diary. "Everyone around me, if they do not ask me directly, the expression in their eyes is demanding an answer: 'Whose idea was this [Afghanistan]? What for? Who is supposed to answer for this to the nation and to the world?'"

512 **"For almost ten years"** Vincent Jauvert, "Les révélations d'un ancien conseiller de Carter," *Le Nouvel Observateur.*

513 **"Thus the general effect"** George Kennan, "Who Won the Cold War? Ask Instead, What Was Lost?" *International Herald Tribune,* October 29, 1992; Charles Cogan, "Partners in Time," *World Policy Journal,* pp. 77–82.

513 **"low-level . . . insurgency"** Vaïsse, *Zbigniew Brzezinski,* p. 309.

513 **the rifle slipped and nearly fired** "Brzezinski at the Pass: Bonhomie, Bullets," *New York Times,* February 4, 1980.

514 **48 percent to 40 percent** Jon Ward, *Camelot's End,* p. 179.

514 **"one of the most violent regimes"** Ward, *Camelot's End,* p. 180.

514 **"might endanger the lives"** Ward, *Camelot's End,* p. 181; Dominic Sandbrook, *Mad as Hell,* p. 366.

514 **"We all support our country's efforts"** Ward, *Camelot's End,* p. 181.

515 **"Ted Kennedy leads a cheater's life"** Ward, *Camelot's End,* p. 185.

515 **"I don't think there's any way"** Ward, *Camelot's End,* p. 184.

515 **59 percent to 31 percent** Ward, *Camelot's End,* p. 194.

515 **"I could not believe it"** Ward, *Camelot's End,* p. 194.

515 **"President's hand is hot"** Butler, unpublished diary, December 31, 1979–January 1, 1980.

515 **"Rumors are that Kennedy"** Carter diary, January 25–27, 1980, *White House Diary,* p. 395.

515 **"Republican inflation"** Ward, *Camelot's End,* p. 203.

516 **"He has been freed"** Ward, *Camelot's End,* p. 205.

516 **"If we beat Kennedy"** Hamilton Jordan, *Crisis,* p. 201.

517 **"it's embarrassing to admit a mistake"** Carter diary, March 3, 1980, *White House Diary,* p. 406.

517 **"If you don't mind, Ed"** Ed Koch, quoted in *New York Times,* February 5, 1984.

517 **"about the distrust of American Jews"** Carter diary, March 8, 1980, *White House Diary,* p. 408.

517 **"I don't believe I ever met"** Jody Powell, *The Other Side of the Story,* p. 242.

517 **"Gang of Five"** "Carter Aides Ripped by Koch as Pro-Arab," *New York Daily News,* March 12, 1980.

518 **"Ed Koch was a bastard"** Donald F. McHenry interview.

518 **"disgraceful"** Carter diary, March 10, 1980, *White House Diary,* p. 409.

518 **Seventy-five percent of Jewish voters** Ward, *Camelot's End,* p. 218; Jimmy Carter, daily diary, March 25, 1980.

518 **"It's the U.N. vote"** Jordan, *Crisis,* p. 234.

519 **"There seems to be two White Houses"** Butler, unpublished diary, January 2, 1980.

520 **"un-Islamic"** Mark Bowden, *Guests of the Ayatollah,* p. 328.

521 **"like a make-believe 007"** Jordan, *Crisis,* pp. 155–57.

521 **"I appreciate the great risk"** Jordan, *Crisis,* p. 163.

522 **"Ham, they are crazy. J."** Jordan, *Crisis,* pp. 190–91.

523 **"a fresh incentive"** Jordan, *Crisis,* p. 230.

523 **"I know he's had a difficult week"** Carter diary, March 21–23, 1980, *White House Diary,* p. 411.

523 **"We should allow them"** Eizenstat, *President Carter,* p. 799.

524 **"would undoubtedly result"** Carter diary, March 21–23, 1980, *White House Diary,* p. 411.

524 **"Mine the harbors"** Eizenstat, *President Carter,* p. 781.

524 **Rosalynn was deeply frustrated** Rosalynn Carter unpublished diary, March 31, 1980, quoted by Jonathan Alter, *His Very Best,* p. 561.

524 **"I don't know what we do now"** Jordan, *Crisis,* p. 246.

524 Operation Eagle Claw Paul B. Ryan, *The Iranian Rescue Mission*, pp. 1–2.

525 60 percent of the hostages would be killed Glad, *An Outsider in the White House*, pp. 265–66.

525 "Getting the Hostages Free" Brzezinski, *Power and Principle*, p. 492. (Brzezinski was so gung ho on the plan that he confided to an aide that he wanted to ride along in one of the rescue helicopters. His colleague told him that would be highly inappropriate. (See Rick Perlstein, *Reaganland*, p. 766.)

526 "Gentlemen," Carter announced Jordan, *Crisis*, p. 233.

526 "What do you think?" Jordan, *Crisis*, p. 234.

526 "at this meeting we made" Jimmy Carter, *Keeping Faith*, p. 507.

526 "stunned and angry" Cyrus Vance, *Hard Choices*, p. 409.

527 "Cy has some concerns" Jordan, *Crisis*, p. 235; see also Glad, *An Outsider in the White House*, pp. 263–64.

527 "But they are Americans, Mr. President!" Jordan, *Crisis*, p. 236.

527 "we needed to lance the boil" Brzezinski, *Power and Principle*, p. 494.

527 "I will stick with the decisions" Brzezinski, *Power and Principle*, p. 494.

528 "Even better, Mr. President" Jordan, *Crisis*, p. 238.

528 "Kill 'em all" Ryan, *Iranian Rescue Mission*, p. 28.

528 "we decided to increase" Brzezinski, *Power and Principle*, p. 495.

529 "we could have gotten out" Jordan, *Crisis*, p. 243; Ryan, *Iranian Rescue Mission*, p. 39; Zbigniew, *Power and Principle*, p. 500.

529 "Cy is the ultimate example" Jordan, *Crisis*, p. 246.

529 "Vance has been extremely despondent" Carter diary, April 17, 1980, *White House Diary*, p. 419.

530 "I sensed in my bones" Brzezinski, *Power and Principle*, p. 496.

530 "I stood up, and the three" Carter, *Keeping Faith*, p. 513; Carter, daily diary, April 21, 1980.

530 one of the "worst" days Carter, *Keeping Faith*, p. 514.

531 "I got a disturbing call" Jordan, *Crisis*, p. 253.

531 "two helicopters may be down" Carter, *Keeping Faith*, p. 514.

531 Holloway III criticized the decisions Robert Sherrill, "Hostages," *Grand Street*, Autumn 1985, p. 144.

531 "I think we have an abort situation" Carter, *Keeping Faith*, p. 515.

532 "back him all the way" and "Damn, damn" Brzezinski, *Power and Principle*, p. 498.

532 "Give me a couple of seconds" Ryan, *Iranian Rescue Mission*, p. 84.

532 "I felt extraordinarily sad for him" Brzezinski, *Power and Principle*, p. 498.

532 "What did Beckwith think?" Jordan, *Crisis*, p. 254.

532 "At least there were no" Jordan, *Crisis*, p. 254.

533 "a sense of relief" Vance, *Hard Choices*, p. 411.

533 "That's unbelievable, isn't it?" Carter-Jones audio transcript, in Barbara Kopple, *Desert One*.

534 Also killed was an Iranian agent Ryan, *Iranian Rescue Mission*, pp. 89–90.

534 "The President looked as if" Brzezinski, *Power and Principle*, p. 499.

534 "Mr. President, I'm very, very sorry" Jordan, *Crisis*, p. 255.

534　**Bay of Pigs fiasco** Ryan, *Iranian Rescue Mission,* p. 94.

534　**"I ducked into the President's"** Jordan, *Crisis,* p. 255.

534　**he was really angry with Vance** Jordan, *Crisis,* pp. 256 and 265.

534　**"I still cannot understand"** George Packer, *Our Man,* p. 193.

534　**"The rescue operation is a disaster"** Stanley Hoffman, "Carter's Fiasco in Iran," *New York Times,* April 26, 1980.

535　**"one of the most stupidly planned"** Michael Metrinko oral history, p. 131.

535　**"the election was over"** Eizenstat, *President Carter,* p. 804.

535　**"I almost cried"** Charles Kirbo oral history interview.

535　**"One of the few voices"** Arthur Schlesinger, Jr., "Where Do We Go Now?" *New York Times,* April 26, 1980.

535　**"I am still haunted by memories"** Carter, *Keeping Faith,* p. 518.

535　**"I think the issue would"** John Kifner, "Putting the Hostages' Lives First." *New York Times,* May 17, 1981; Terence Smith, "Why Carter Admitted the Shah." *New York Times,* May 17, 1981.

CHAPTER 23: WHIPPING KENNEDY'S ASS

537　**"There is a deeper failure"** Betty Glad, *An Outsider in the White House,* p. 267.

537　**"they just aren't buying that anymore"** Hamilton Jordan, *Crisis,* p. 268.

538　**"The Ayatollah Khomeini doesn't"** Glad, *An Outsider in the White House,* p. 269.

538　**"manageable enough"** *New York Times,* May 1, 1980.

538　**"We'll catch hell for that"** Jordan, *Crisis,* p. 269.

538　**"mild and short"** *New York Times,* May 1, 1980; *New York Times,* May 3, 1980.

538　**"The gig is up"** Landon Butler, unpublished diary, January 5, 1980.

538　**"It isn't just a campaign"** Jon Ward, *Camelot's End,* p. 224.

538　**"What happened?"** Jordan, *Crisis,* p. 281; Edward M. Kennedy, *True Compass,* p. 379; Jimmy Carter diary, June 5, 1980, *White House Diary,* p. 435; Ward, *Camelot's End,* p. 229.

539　**"more than a prayer"** *New York Times,* June 6, 1980.

539　**"kamikaze mission"** Jordan, *Crisis,* pp. 275–76.

540　**"I've lost all respect for Kennedy"** Butler, unpublished diary, May 13, 1980.

540　**"It's been a long, tough"** Carter diary, June 3, 1980, *White House Diary,* p. 435.

540　**"Carter was a moderately conservative"** Stuart E. Eizenstat, *President Carter,* p. 835.

540　**"Ham is taking less and less"** Butler, unpublished diary, May 5, 1980.

540　**"incredibly disorganized"** Butler, unpublished diary, May 14, 1980, and May 16, 1980.

540　**"Pat and I have been thinking"** Jordan, *Crisis,* pp. 278–79.

541　**"He is right effective"** Kirbo memo to President Carter, July 22, 1980, unprocessed Charles Kirbo papers, Jimmy Carter Presidential Library.

541　**"a geriatric marvel"** Robert Steed to Charles Kirbo, July 21, 1989, unprocessed Charles Kirbo papers, Jimmy Carter Presidential Library.

541 "Hamilton, don't make the same mistake" Jordan, *Crisis,* pp. 284–85.

541 "The Kennedy challenge hurt us" Jordan, *Crisis,* pp. 287–92.

542 "propaganda campaign" Robert Pear, "Billy Carter Settles Charges by U.S. and Registers as an Agent of Libya," *New York Times,* July 15, 1980.

542 "I do not believe" Ward, *Camelot's End,* p. 241.

542 "colorful personality" Terence Smith, "Reports to Congress," *New York Times,* August 5, 1980.

543 "Billy and I have" White House Press Release, January 13, 1979, "News Conference Transcripts, 1979" folder, box 18, Press Office, Marc Henderson's Subject Files, Jimmy Carter Presidential Library.

543 "I told him and Zbig" Lloyd Cutler and Joe Onek memorandum for the president, December 16, 1980, NLC-43-138-4-1-7, Jimmy Carter Presidential Library.

544 "All in all" Carter diary, August 2, 1980, and August 4, 1980, *White House Diary,* pp. 453–54; *New York Times,* August 5, 1980.

544 "You know," Caddell responded Jordan, *Crisis,* p. 295.

544 earnings actually fell Dominic Sandbrook, *Mad as Hell,* p. 374.

544 "We absolutely felt we could" Ward, *Camelot's End,* p. 252.

545 "I have a lot of problems" Carter diary, July 31, 1980, *White House Diary,* p. 452.

545 "We'll either take it out" Carter diary, August 10, 1980, *White House Diary,* p. 456.

545 "Look at him" Jordan, *Crisis,* p. 304.

545 "seemed to be in a good mood" Carter diary, August 11, 1980, *White House Diary,* p. 457.

545 "I didn't press him, Ham" Jordan, *Crisis,* p. 305; Ward, *Camelot's End,* p. 256.

546 "What the fuck are you doing?" Ward, *Camelot's End,* pp. 258–59.

547 "a stirring and emotional speech" Carter diary, August 12, 1980, *White House Diary,* p. 457.

547 "I was amazed and disconcerted" Carter diary, August 14, 1980, *White House Diary,* p. 457.

548 "Hubert Horatio Hornblower" Ward, *Camelot's End,* p. 265; Jordan, *Crisis,* p. 314; *New York Times,* August 15, 1980.

548 "We want Teddy" Jordan, *Crisis,* pp. 314–15; Ward, *Camelot's End,* pp. 267–71; Kennedy, *True Compass,* p. 381.

549 "Don't forget" Peter S. Canellos, ed., *Last Lion,* p. 230.

549 "I think," observed ABC-TV Ward, *Camelot's End,* p. 272.

549 "He was loaded" Ward, *Camelot's End,* pp. 6–7.

549 "seemed to have had a few" Carter diary, August 14, 1980, *White House Diary,* p. 457.

549 "We neglected to take" Ward, *Camelot's End,* p. 258; Jody Powell, *The Other Side of the Story,* p. 245.

550 "That's the worst thing" Bert Lance oral history.

550 "If he had gotten out" Charles Kirbo oral history.

550 "I'm going to go work" Craig Shirley, *Rendezvous with Destiny,* p. 416.

CHAPTER 24: THE OCTOBER SURPRISE

552 "I liked Casey. He was nuts" Kai Bird, *The Good Spy*, p. 253.

552 "We expect Carter will" Francis X. Clines, "About Politics: Reagan's Quiet Campaign Chief," *New York Times*, April 22, 1980; October Surprise Task Force, *Joint Report of the Task Force to Investigate Certain Allegations Concerning the Holding of American Hostages by Iran in 1980*, p. 184.

552 "This campaign is ours" Gary Sick, *October Surprise*, p. 73.

552 "If we could do all that" October Surprise Task Force, *Joint Report of the Task Force*, p. 187.

553 "I have given my all" David D. Kirkpatrick, "Bank's Secret Campaign to Win Entry to U.S. for Shah of Iran," *New York Times*.

553 "Shaheen confirmed to me" Bird, *Good Spy*, pp. 245–46. This account is based on interviews with both Mustafa Zein and Jack Shaw.

554 "said he wanted the PLO" Sick, *October Surprise*, pp. 74–75.

554 "Mr. President, there is something" Bird, *Good Spy*, p. 247. I am citing the historian Douglas Brinkley, who was present at the encounter between Carter and Arafat in Gaza in 1996.

554 off-the-books private diplomacy Kai Bird, "Some 'October Surprise' Conspiracies Turn Out to Be True," *Los Angeles Times*, June 20, 2017.

555 dinner with George H. W. Bush October Surprise Task Force, *Joint Report of the Task Force*, p. 90.

555 a volume entitled *Master of Deception* October Surprise Task Force, *Joint Report of the Task Force*, p. 135 and n254.

556 "He was elegantly turned out" Robert Parry, *Trick or Treason*, p. 77.

556 "Hashemi appears to be in contact" Harold Saunders and David Newsom Secret Action Memorandum to Secretary Vance, December 5, 1979 (declassified June 9, 2008), NLC-128-8-10-3-7, CREST documents, Jimmy Carter Presidential Library.

557 "has contacts with a lawyer" Harold Saunders and David Newsom Secret Briefing Memorandum to Secretary Vance, December 8, 1979 (declassified June 6, 2008), NLC-128-8-10-3-7, CREST documents, Jimmy Carter Presidential Library.

557 "a liberal, secular man" Stan Pottinger interview.

558 Cyrus returned $290,000 October Surprise Task Force, *Joint Report of the Task Force*, pp. 37–38; Jim Drinkard, "Probe of 1980 GOP Hostage Dealings Reveals Covert CIA Operation," Associated Press, November 24, 1992; Parry, *Trick or Treason*, pp. 80–81. Stan Pottinger says he was the middleman who passed the CIA's check on to Hashemi. (Pottinger interview.)

558 "Casey wanted to discuss political matters" Parry, *Trick or Treason*, p. 81; Sick, *October Surprise*, pp. 76–77. Furmark was formerly employed by John Shaheen.

558 "It demonstrated beyond any doubt" Sick, *October Surprise*, p. 81. Coincidentally, Casey himself flew on the Concorde to London on July 1, had a meeting with Prime Minister Margaret Thatcher on July 2, and then traveled on to Paris. He was back in New York by July 5. (Richard V. Allen memo on "Itinerary, such

as it is, July 1–July 5, 1980," "Iran Hostage Crisis, Allen/Casey Travel, 1980" folder, box 55, Richard V. Allen Papers, Hoover Institution Archives, Stanford University.) The folder title is itself suggestive, but there is nothing in the folder about his trip to London in late July. But it does indicate the ease with which Casey could fly to Europe, even as he was juggling his responsibilities as Reagan's campaign manager. (Note: Pasandideh's impending July 2 visit to Madrid was also known to Assistant Secretary Harold Saunders. See Saunders memo to the Secretary, June 27, 1980, NLC-128-2-3-21-1, Jimmy Carter Presidential Library.)

559 **Hashemi checked in to the luxurious** Plaza hotel tax records, in October Surprise Task Force, *Joint Report of the Task Force,* p. 74.

559 **"Cyrus asked me to bring"** Parry, *Trick or Treason,* p. 81.

559 **"good when Republicans were"** October Surprise Task Force, *Joint Report of the Task Force,* pp. 72–78.

560 **"Casey said the Iranians should"** October Surprise Task Force, *Joint Report of the Task Force,* p. 72.

560 **"treated as guests"** Sick, *October Surprise,* pp. 86–87; October Surprise Task Force, *Joint Report of the Task Force,* p. 73.

561 **was decidedly complex** Admittedly, many other strands of the alleged "October surprise" story—such as the allegation that vice presidential candidate Bush had flown to Paris in October to meet with some Iranians—were discredited.

561 **Casey was in California that weekend** October Surprise Task Force, *Joint Report of the Task Force,* p. 85.

561 **"Case Closed"** Lee Hamilton, "Case Closed," *New York Times,* January 24, 1993.

561 **some loony conspiracy story** Steven Emerson and Jesse Furman, writing in *The New Republic,* concluded that the "conspiracy as currently postulated is a total fabrication and that none of the evidence cited to support the October Surprise stood up to scrutiny." ("The Conspiracy That Wasn't," *New Republic,* November 18, 1991, p. 16.)

561 **Casey's Bohemian Grove alibi** Robert Parry, "October Surprise Cover-up Unravels," *Consortium News,* August 6, 2010.

561 **Casey's calendar diaries** October Surprise Task Force, *Joint Report of the Task Force,* p. 21.

561 **"had not responded negatively"** October Surprise Task Force, *Joint Report of the Task Force,* p. 207.

561 **totaled just over $180 million** October Surprise Task Force, *Joint Report of the Task Force,* p. 213.

561 **"then–Secretary of State Alexander M. Haig"** October Surprise Task Force, *Joint Report of the Task Force,* p. 61.

562 **"material relevant to the October Surprise"** Paul Beach Memorandum for the Record, November 4, 1991, courtesy of Robert Parry, FOIA request to George H.W. Bush Presidential Library; Robert Parry, "Second Thoughts on October Surprise," *Consortium News.*

562 **"of special interest to the President"** C. Boyden Gray, "October Surprise Interagency Meeting," November 6, 1991, courtesy of Robert Parry's FOIA request,

memo from George H.W. Bush Presidential Library; Parry, "Second Thoughts on October Surprise."

562 **"If the White House knew"** Parry, "Second Thoughts on October Surprise." Congressman Hamilton was so concerned that he wrote to Secretary of State John Kerry, asking him to search for the Madrid embassy cable concerning Casey's presence in Madrid. (Congressman Lee Hamilton to Secretary of State John Kerry, December 1, 2016, copy in the author's files.)

562 **"Would I be surprised"** Stuart E. Eizenstat, *President Carter,* p. 829 (2020 paperback edition).

563 **private diary of his chief of staff** John A. Farrell, *Richard Nixon,* p. 342.

CHAPTER 25: THE DEFEAT

564 **"I think we are in tough shape"** Tim Kraft memo to Jimmy Carter and Rosalynn Carter, June 26, 1980, Memos, Subject Files, box 1, Tim Kraft Collection, Donated Historical Materials, Jimmy Carter Presidential Library.

564 **"I am not a strong leader"** Jimmy Carter diary, August 24, 1980, *White House Diary,* p. 460.

565 **"could have been written by a Klansman"** Carter diary, August 6, 1980, *White House Diary,* p. 454; Joseph Crespino, "Did David Brooks Tell the Full Story About Reagan's Neshoba County Fair Visit?" History News Network, no date, https://historynewsnetwork.org/article/44535.

565 **"black from white, Jew from Christian"** Dominic Sandbrook, *Mad as Hell,* p. 386.

565 **"A recession is when"** Sandbrook, *Mad as Hell,* p. 386.

565 **"Most of Anderson's supporters"** Carter diary, August 24, 1980, *White House Diary,* p. 460.

566 **"In the past, one could"** Terence Smith, "President Meets Prominent Jews but Wins No Pledge for Support," *New York Times,* September 8, 1980.

566 **"primarily a creation of the press"** *New York Times,* September 10, 1980.

566 **"I take the suitcase"** Matt Labash, "Roger Stone, Political Animal," *Weekly Standard,* November 5, 2007. For more on Cohn's and Stone's roles in the 1980 election, see Nicholas von Hoffman, *Citizen Cohn,* p. 377.

567 **$1.7 million debt** *New York Times,* September 12, 1980. Carter actually took time on October 19, 1980, to attend a fundraising dinner where all the proceeds went to retiring Kennedy's campaign debt. (Jimmy Carter, daily diary, October 19, 1980.)

567 **Carter was "dismayed"** Jimmy Carter, *Living Faith,* pp. 34–35.

567 **"I am absolutely convinced"** Randall Balmer, *Redeemer,* p. 118.

567 **"the true Negro . . . does not want"** Rick Perlstein, *Reaganland,* p. 468.

568 **"really right-wing: against ERA"** Carter diary, January 22, 1980, *White House Diary,* p. 394; *New York Times,* January 24, 1980; Leo P. Ribuffo, *Right, Center, Left,* p. 241.

568 **"He (Falwell) just lied about it"** Dudley Clendinen, "White House Says Minister Misquoted Carter Remarks," *New York Times,* August 8, 1980; Balmer, *Redeemer,* p. 122.

569 **"What is a secular humanist?"** Balmer, *Redeemer,* p. 123; Carter diary, August 7, 1980, *White House Diary,* p. 455.

569 **"abortion, pornography, the drug epidemic"** Balmer, *Redeemer,* p. 146.

569 **"traitor to the South"** Stuart E. Eizenstat, *President Carter,* p. 869.

569 **"My religious beliefs"** Steven R. Weisman, "Appeals Backing GOP Said to Portray Views as Contrary to Bible," *New York Times,* November 1, 1980; Balmer, *Redeemer,* p. 146.

569 **"Although he [Moyers] condemned"** Carter, daily diary, September 26, 1980; *White House Diary,* pp. 468–69.

569 **"What galvanized the Christian community"** Frances Fitzgerald, *The Evangelicals,* p. 304.

570 **"The biggest hang-up"** Carter diary, September 17, 1980, *White House Diary,* p. 465.

570 **$240 million in military equipment** Bernard Gwertzman, "U.S. Ready to Release Arms to Iran When Hostages Have Been Freed," *New York Times,* October 30, 1980.

570 **"this was the first time"** Jimmy Carter, *White House Diary,* p. 466; Klaus Wiegrefe, "Iranian Hostage Crisis: Germany's Secret Role in Ending the Drama," *Spiegel,* August 4, 2015, https://www.spiegel.de/international/zeitgeist/how-gerhard-ritzel -helped-end-the-iranian-hostage-crisis-a-1045268.html.

570 **"except they are crazy"** National Security Council Meeting, September 24, 1980, CREST, NLC-128-12-3-8-6, Jimmy Carter Presidential Library.

571 **"the American proposal has fallen"** Carter, daily diary, October 9, 1980; Jimmy Carter, *Keeping Faith,* p. 560.

571 **agree to ship an inventory** Carter diary, October 11, 1980, *White House Diary,* p. 472.

571 **"The Imam [Khomeini] has taken"** Arafat/Rafsanjani transcript, Arafat to Secretary of State, October 9, 1980, document NLC-131-1-1-25-7, Jimmy Carter Presidential Library.

572 **"it became increasingly obvious"** Abol Hassan Bani-Sadr, *My Turn to Speak,* p. 31.

572 **"So what if Reagan wins?"** Bani-Sadr, *My Turn to Speak,* pp. 32–33.

572 **"The Iranians are still making"** Carter diary, October 24, 1980, *White House Diary,* p. 475.

573 **necessary two-thirds quorum** "Iranian Legislators Delay on Hostages," *New York Times,* October 28, 1980.

573 **"an Iranian banker in New York"** Harold Saunders briefing memorandum to the Secretary, October 22–23, 1980, NLC-128-2-9-6-2, Jimmy Carter Presidential Library.

574 **45 percent to 42 percent** Adam Clymer, "Carter and Reagan to Meet Tonight," *New York Times,* October 28, 1980. A *New York Times*/CBS News poll taken be-

tween October 16 and 20, 1980, rendered similar results: 43 percent for Carter, 41 percent for Reagan, and 9 percent for Anderson, with 13 percent undecided. (*New York Times,* October 23, 1980.)

574 **"Here is something"** Craig Shirley, *Rendezvous with Destiny,* pp. 420 and 438. The conservative columnist George Will confessed in 1983 that he used the briefing books to prep Reagan—and then publicly praised his performance without revealing his role in the debate preparation. He called the briefing books "excruciatingly boring." (*New York Times,* July 9, 1983; Eric Alterman, *Sound & Fury,* pp. 100–101.)

574 **Cheney later phoned Baker** Shirley, *Rendezvous with Destiny,* p. 440.

575 **"The papers were left"** Shirley, *Rendezvous with Destiny,* p. 439.

575 **"didn't help us"** Eizenstat, *President Carter,* pp. 882–83.

575 **"I don't think there's any doubt"** Shirley, *Rendezvous with Destiny,* p. 610.

575 **"There you go again"** *New York Times,* October 29, 1980.

575 **"made a better impression"** Carter diary, October 28, 1980, *White House Diary,* p. 476.

575 **"When people realized"** Eizenstat, *President Carter,* p. 881.

575 **"If I'm re-elected"** Carter diary, October 1, 1980, *White House Diary,* p. 469.

576 **"My hands are getting scratched up"** Carter diary, October 31, 1980, *White House Diary,* p. 478.

576 **"absolutely silenced them"** Eizenstat, *President Carter,* p. 885.

577 **"overruled everybody"** Harold Saunders memo to the Secretary, October 31, 1980, NLC-128-9-1-1-8, Jimmy Carter Presidential Library.

577 **"Why don't you stay?"** Eizenstat, *President Carter,* p. 886.

577 **"political purposes"** Eizenstat, *President Carter,* p. 886.

577 **"1. The American people resent"** Eizenstat, *President Carter,* p. 886.

578 **"confiscate the shah's property"** Carter diary, November 2, 1980, *White House Diary,* p. 478.

578 **"grim and portentous as this"** Eizenstat, *President Carter,* p. 887.

578 **"I'd tell them to go fuck"** Eizenstat, *President Carter,* p. 888, citing an interview with Gerald Rafshoon.

578 **rest of the afternoon** Jimmy Carter, daily diary, November 2, 1980.

578 **"With only two days"** "U.S. Gets Iran Terms on Hostages; Carter Calls Them 'Positive Basis' for Achieving Captives' Freedom," *New York Times,* November 3, 1980.

579 **"helps the president just a bit"** *New York Times,* November 4, 1980.

580 **"The sky has fallen in"** Hamilton Jordan, *Crisis,* pp. 346–48.

580 **"Mr. President, we have let you"** Eizenstat, *President Carter,* p. 889.

580 **"We're going to lose"** Rosalynn Carter, *First Lady from Plains,* p. 322.

581 **"we were not doing well"** Carter, diary, November 4, 1980, *Keeping Faith,* p. 569.

581 **"Pat knows"** Carter, *First Lady from Plains,* p. 323.

581 **"I promised you four years ago"** Eizenstat, *President Carter,* p. 891.

581 **"hurt me deeply"** Carter, *Keeping Faith,* p. 571.

581 **Two-thirds of Jerry Falwell's** Garry Wills, "The Pious President," *New York Times Book Review,* April 26, 2018.

581 **"the Jews didn't even give me"** Carter diary, November 15, 1980, *White House Diary,* p. 485.

582 **white voters by 56 percent** Roper Center for Public Opinion Research, "How Groups Voted in 1980."

CHAPTER 26: WHITE HOUSE TWILIGHT

584 **"I know you all"** "Remarks of the President to Reporters," November 5, 1980, "Subject Files, Presidential Campaign, 1980" folder, box 2, Memos, Tim Kraft Collection, Donated Historical Materials, Jimmy Carter Presidential Library.

584 **"All of us consider"** Jimmy Carter to Ansel Adams, November 9, 1979, folder A, box 45, Susan Clough File, Jimmy Carter Presidential Library.

585 **Stu Eizenstat supported the gambit** Stuart E. Eizenstat, *President Carter,* pp. 269–70.

585 **throw an empty Coke bottle** Jimmy and Rosalynn Carter oral history, 1985, p. 265.

586 **He loved inspecting maps** Jimmy and Rosalynn Carter oral history, 1985, p. 264.

586 **"He knows more about Alaska"** Frank Moore oral history, July 30–31, 2002; Eizenstat, *President Carter,* p. 272.

586 **"Everybody told us we were crazy"** Frank Moore oral history, September 18–19, 1981.

586 **157 million acres of protected wilderness** Eizenstat, *President Carter,* p. 268.

586 **"splendid beauty undiminished"** Jimmy Carter, *Keeping Faith,* p. 583. The bill designated more than 43 million acres as national park land, 54 million acres as national wildlife refuge, 56 million acres as wilderness, and 1.3 million acres as national wild and scenic rivers. (White House press release, August 19, 1980, "Alaska Lands (2)" folder, box 141, Domestic Policy Staff (Eizenstat), Jimmy Carter Presidential Library.)

587 **four very complicated little fly-line** Jimmy Carter diary, November 6, 1980, *White House Diary,* p. 481.

587 **Carter was ready to sign** Gary Sick, *All Fall Down,* pp. 321–22.

588 **Brzezinski characterized the Iranian message** Sick, *All Fall Down,* p. 324; Zbigniew Brzezinski, *Power and Principle,* p. 506; Carter diary, November 26, 1980, *White House Diary,* p. 489.

588 **"My greatest fear"** Hamilton Jordan "Eyes Only" memo to President Carter, undated, "Iran, 11/1–23/80" folder, box 24, Plains File, Jimmy Carter Presidential Library.

589 **"We still don't have"** Carter diary, November 29, 1980, *White House Diary,* p. 489.

589 **"It was obvious"** Kai Bird, *The Chairman,* p. 654.

589 **senior Milbank, Tweed partners, Francis D. Logan** Bird, *Chairman,* p. 654.

589 **"to push the American banks hard"** Carter diary, January 15, 1981, *White House Diary,* p. 508.

589 **"The Bank of America and one"** Carter diary, January 16, 1981, *White House Diary,* p. 509.

589 **"nearly fell off their chairs"** Bird, *Chairman,* p. 654; James B. Stewart, *The Partners,* pp. 36 and 344; Paul Hoffman, *Lions of the Eighties,* p. 313.

589 **"worked out very well"** David D. Kirkpatrick, "Bank's Secret Campaign to Win Entry to the U.S. for the Shah of Iran," *New York Times.*

590 **"Pottinger has briefed us"** Harold Saunders secret memo to the Secretary, November 19, 1980 (declassified May 30, 2008), NLC-128-9-1-13-6, Jimmy Carter Presidential Library.

590 **"obviously ridiculous and unacceptable"** Carter diary, December 19, 1980, *White House Diary,* p. 497; Hamilton Jordan, *Crisis,* p. 362.

590 **"Will the hostages be released"** Sick, *All Fall Down,* p. 329.

590 **refused to be briefed** Carter, *White House Diary,* pp. 487 and 504.

591 **"very envious"** Carter diary, November 20, 1980, *White House Diary,* p. 487.

591 **a copy of the notes** Carter, *Keeping Faith,* p. 577.

591 **"the group of jerks"** Carter diary, January 14, 1981, and January 20, 1981, *White House Diary,* pp. 508 and 513.

591 **"Polly was complaining"** Landon Butler interview, January 13, 2016.

591 **"I enjoyed being with them"** Carter diary, December 25, 1980, *White House Diary,* p. 499.

591 **$1 million in debt** Carter, *White House Diary,* p. 498.

592 **"to see the end of 1980"** Carter diary, December 31, 1980, *White House Diary,* p. 500.

592 **"very close to an acceptance"** Carter diary, January 6, 1981, *White House Diary,* p. 504.

593 **"a few greedy bankers"** Carter, *White House Diary,* p. 506.

593 **"I don't see how they"** Carter diary, January 15, 1981, *White House Diary,* p. 508.

594 **"Why, Jimmy! These are the reasons"** Douglas Brinkley, *The Unfinished Presidency,* p. 32. Brinkley got this story from an interview with speechwriter Chris Matthews.

594 **Carter did not sleep** Carter, *White House Diary,* p. 511; Carter, *Keeping Faith,* p. 595.

594 **"They're going to screw around"** Jordan, *Crisis,* p. 375.

595 **"Have them sign the agreement"** Carter, *White House Diary,* p. 511.

595 **"was not to be disturbed"** Jordan, *Crisis,* p. 377; Carter, *White House Diary,* p. 512.

595 **"Jimmy, the Reagans will be here"** Carter, *White House Diary,* p. 512.

595 **"Well, I better go put on"** Jordan, *Crisis,* p. 379.

596 **"I looked in the mirror"** Carter, *White House Diary,* p. 512.

596 **Thomas Jefferson quote** Carter, *Keeping Faith,* p. 596.

596 **"seemed somewhat disconcerted"** Carter, *White House Diary,* p. 513.

596 **Jordan had two phone lines open** Eizenstat, *President Carter,* p. 896.

597 **"Reagan really did get elected"** Jordan, *Crisis,* p. 380.

CHAPTER 27: KEEPING FAITH

601 **"one of the happiest moments"** Jimmy Carter diary, January 20, 1981, *White House Diary,* p. 513.

601 **Their "involuntary" departure** Douglas Brinkley, *The Unfinished Presidency,* p. xii.

602 **"We're free, we're free"** Terence Smith, "A Weary Carter Returns to Plains," *New York Times,* January 21, 1981.

602 **"a country-western band launched"** Brinkley, *Unfinished Presidency,* p. 40; Smith, "A Weary Carter Returns to Plains."

603 **"I was going to be facing"** Carter diary, January 21, 1981, *White House Diary,* pp. 515–17; Brinkley, *Unfinished Presidency,* p. 41.

604 **"What so many people don't know"** Paul Hendrickson, "Jimmy Carter, Casting Back," *Washington Post.*

604 **"all our debts—a great relief"** Carter diary, March 6, 1981, *White House Diary,* p. 521; "Reports Carter Sells Peanut Business," United Press International, March 6, 1981.

604 **"No one could accuse me"** Jimmy Carter and Rosalynn Carter, *Everything to Gain,* p. 11.

604 **$900,000 book advance** Carter diary, March 6, 1981, *White House Diary,* p. 521.

604 **"*Keeping Faith* was written"** Hendrickson, "Jimmy Carter, Casting Back."

604 **"It's expensive"** Carter diary, February 16, 1981, *White House Diary,* p. 520.

605 **"I guess I was almost a fanatic"** Hendrickson, "Jimmy Carter, Casting Back."

605 **"I realized many years ago"** Jimmy Carter, *A Full Life,* p. 232; Jimmy Carter, *The Paintings of Jimmy Carter.*

605 **"I don't want a monument"** Carter and Carter, *Everything to Gain,* pp. 29 and 31.

606 **"There is life after"** Carter and Carter, *Everything to Gain,* p. 33.

606 **"I never felt deceived"** "Carter Discusses B.C.C.I.," *New York Times,* August 9, 1991.

606 **"may have snookered me"** Brinkley, *Unfinished Presidency,* p. 225.

606 **grown to $100 million** Carter, *A Full Life,* p. 208. By 2015 the Carter Center had an endowment of $600 million.

606 **"We don't go into areas"** Kai Bird, "Citizen Carter," *The Nation.*

607 **"Are you honest people"** Bird, "Citizen Carter."

607 **"I can tell you from my own"** Julian E. Zelizer, *Jimmy Carter,* p. 135.

607 **"He's a pure Calvinist"** Bird, "Citizen Carter."

607 **"extremely competent, a fabulous"** Brinkley, *Unfinished Presidency,* p. 97.

607 **turned this Habitat gig** Jimmy Carter, *Living Faith,* p. 182.

608 "Daddy, when I grow up" Jimmy Carter, eulogy for President Gerald Ford, January 2, 2007, Grand Rapids, Mich., https://www.cartercenter.org/news/editorials _speeches/ford_eulogy.html.

608 "Jimmy Carter is my very best" Brinkley, *Unfinished Presidency*, p. 106.

608 "How do you make" Brinkley, *Unfinished Presidency*, pp. 71–72.

609 "may be more embarrassing" Phil Gailey, "Carter Intent on Suing Washington Post on Rumor," *New York Times*, October 15, 1981.

609 "We now believe the story" Brinkley, *Unfinished Presidency*, p. 74.

610 "What did Christ do with lepers?" Art Harris, "Citizen Carter," *Washington Post*, February 22, 1990.

610 "There were dozens" Brinkley, *Unfinished Presidency*, p. 223.

611 "All had worms emerging" Brinkley, *Unfinished Presidency*, p. 460.

611 a mere twenty-eight individuals Centers for Disease Control and Prevention, "Guinea Worm Disease Frequently Asked Questions (FAQs)," no date, https:// www.cdc.gov/parasites/guineaworm/gen_info/faqs.html.

612 "That's the only way" Brinkley, *Unfinished Presidency*, pp. 263–64.

612 called the mayor a "jerk" Brinkley, *Unfinished Presidency*, p. 152.

612 "has caused both of us" Zelizer, *Jimmy Carter*, p. 130.

612 "Israel is the problem" Brinkley, *Unfinished Presidency*, p. 116.

612 "I know that when any statement" Brinkley, *Unfinished Presidency*, p. 323.

613 "His face was flushed" Brinkley, *Unfinished Presidency*, pp. 327–29.

613 "done everything possible" Bird, "Citizen Carter"; "Carter Meets Arafat in Paris," *New York Times*, April 5, 1990.

614 "Remember, Ken, only one of us" Ken Stein, "My Problem with Jimmy Carter's Book," *Middle East Quarterly*, Spring 2007.

614 "I've been hurt, and so has" Jimmy Carter, *Man from Plains*, directed by Jonathan Demme (Sony Pictures, 2002).

614 "Israeli leaders have embarked" Jimmy Carter, *Palestine: Peace Not Apartheid*, p. 189.

615 "slippery slope toward apartheid" Allison Kaplan Sommer, "Ehud Barak Warns: Israel Faces 'Slippery Slope' Toward Apartheid," *Haaretz*, June 21, 2017.

615 "pariah diplomacy" Jimmy Carter, "Pariah Diplomacy," *New York Times*, April 28, 2008.

615 "Writing it was just plain wrong" Brinkley, *Unfinished Presidency*, p. 339.

615 "Carter is someone" Zelizer, *Jimmy Carter*, p. 129.

616 "We were amazed to discover" Brinkley, *Unfinished Presidency*, p. 408.

616 "horrified" Brinkley, *Unfinished Presidency*, pp. 409–10.

617 "Our marriage survived" Carter, *A Full Life*, p. 226.

617 "Happy Birthday!" Carter and Carter, *Everything to Gain*, pp. 89–90.

617 "decades of untiring effort" "Nobel Peace Prize Awarded to Carter, with a Jab at Bush," *New York Times*, October 12, 2002.

618 "If only for his efforts" Alan Riding, "Praise and Blame for Prize to Carter," *New York Times*, October 12, 2002.

618 "I just thought I had" Richard Fausset and Alan Blinder, "Ailing Jimmy Carter 'At Ease with Whatever Comes,'" *New York Times*, August 21, 2015; *PBS News-*

Hour, "Former President Jimmy Carter Addresses Cancer and Treatment," August 20, 2015.

EPILOGUE

621 **"stepping-stone"** Kai Bird, "Citizen Carter," *The Nation.*

622 **"Obviously, it's the most"** Jimmy Carter oral history, February 18, 1982.

622 **"We obeyed the law"** Jimmy Carter, *White House Diary,* p. 525; Jimmy Carter, *A Full Life,* p. 2.

623 **"Being confident of our own future"** Bourne, *Jimmy Carter,* p. 385.

626 **"is bottomed upon the profound conviction"** C. Vann Woodward, *The Burden of Southern History,* p. 128.

626 **"power cannot be wielded without guilt"** Woodward, *The Burden of Southern History,* p. 162.

627 **"the fallibility of human beings"** Harvey Shapiro, "A Conversation with Jimmy Carter," *New York Times Book Review.*

627 **"chastening experience of being"** Woodward, *Burden of Southern History,* pp. 26–27.

627 **"the buildup in the South"** Harvey Shapiro, "A Conversation with Jimmy Carter," *New York Times,* June 19, 1977.

Index

READ ON FOR AN EXCERPT FROM
THE GOOD SPY BY KAI BIRD

"One of the best accounts we have of how espionage really works."
—Mark Mazzetti, *The New York Times Book Review*

NEW YORK TIMES BESTSELLER

عبد القاصر في مراحل حياته

THE GOOD SPY

THE LIFE AND DEATH OF
ROBERT AMES

KAI BIRD

"A well-researched, engagingly presented biography . . . *The Good Spy* is a fascinating book that sheds much-needed light on one of the murkier corners of CIA—and Middle Eastern—history." *–THE WALL STREET JOURNAL*

CROWN
NEW YORK

Available wherever books are sold

Prologue

Monday, September 13, 1993

It was a bright blue, cloudless September day in Washington, D.C., a day of hope for the peoples of the Middle East after decades of cyclical wars, massacres, and spectacular acts of terrorism. But Frank Anderson—the Central Intelligence Agency's ranking clandestine officer in the Arab world—was nevertheless somehow annoyed that morning. He knew something extraordinarily good was about to happen. At fifty-one, Anderson had spent half his life working on the Middle East. After joining the CIA in 1968, Anderson had risen rapidly in the ranks of the Agency's clandestine services, learning Arabic in Beirut and specializing in the war-torn Middle East. By 1993, he was chief of the Near East and South Asia Division of the CIA's Directorate of Operations. That morning he had every reason to believe that peace was finally coming to a region to which he had dedicated his entire career. He should have felt elated, but he was quietly miffed.

Israeli prime minister Yitzhak Rabin and Yasir Arafat, the chairman of the Palestine Liberation Organization, were about to sign a peace accord at the White House. President Bill Clinton had invited three thousand people to witness the historic moment on the South Lawn of the White House—and Anderson suspected that not a single CIA officer had been invited. Anderson thought that was wrong. Someone in the White House had forgotten how this peace process had started as an intelligence operation. Anderson believed the CIA, through its careful cultivation of clandestine sources, had created the opportunity for the Oslo Accords, which were to be signed that morning. He knew it had all started decades earlier when a young CIA officer named Robert Clayton Ames had cultivated the first highly secret contacts between the United

States and the Palestinians. Ames had paved the way for the peace accords—and for his dedication to his spy craft and his work as an intelligence officer, he'd been murdered in Beirut on April 18, 1983, in the first truck-bomb assault on a U.S. embassy. He had happened to be in the wrong place at the wrong time. The horrifying attack had killed sixteen other Americans—including seven other CIA officers—and forty-six Lebanese civilians. Anderson thought that on this special day someone should remember what Ames had done for the peace process.

So when he arrived at his office at Langley's CIA headquarters that morning, Anderson convened a regular 9:00 A.M. meeting of his top officers. "It was noted that this was a big day for the peace process," recalled Charles Englehart, another clandestine officer, who'd worked with Ames. "We were all quite optimistic in those days that *this* time the Israelis and the Palestinians would get it right. Someone asked who was representing the CIA on the occasion: the director? A quick check indicated that there was no CIA representation at the ceremony."

After an awkward moment of silence, Anderson turned to his assistant, Bob Bossard, and said, "Okay, let's get a bus and go visit our dead." Anderson quickly spread the word that he wanted to take dozens of young, newly minted clandestine officers—and a few analysts—out to Arlington National Cemetery. They would walk to Ames's gravestone and say a few words in his memory. "I'm proud to say that it was my idea," Anderson said many years later. It was a spur-of-the-moment decision. By 10:30 A.M. a CIA bus was waiting at the southwest entrance. "We filled the bus," said Anderson, "probably thirty or forty people." Anderson wanted the younger officers there because he thought of the visit as a "values transmission opportunity."

When they arrived at Ames's gravesite on a gentle hill near a clump of oak trees, Anderson and his colleagues stared across the Potomac River toward the White House. They knew that at that moment, at 11:43 A.M., Israeli and Palestinian officials were signing a Declaration of Principles on Palestinian self-government in the Israeli-occupied territories of Gaza and the West Bank. Rabin said in his formal remarks, "We the soldiers who have returned from the battle stained with blood, we who have fought against you, the Palestinians, we say to you today in a loud and clear voice: 'Enough of blood and tears! Enough!'"

The *New York Times*'s correspondent Thomas Friedman reported that as soon as the documents were signed, President Clinton "took Mr. Arafat in his left arm and Mr. Rabin in his right arm and gently coaxed them together, needing to give Mr. Rabin just a little extra nudge in the back. Mr. Arafat reached out his hand first, and then Mr. Rabin, after a split second of hesitation and with a wan smile on his face, received Mr. Arafat's hand. The audience let out a simultaneous sigh of relief and peal of joy, as a misty-eyed Mr. Clinton beamed away." It was an awkward moment, but "hope" had seemingly "triumphed" over history.

"We were at Bob's gravesite," Anderson later recalled, "at the moment of the handshake—as planned." The chalky white gravestone read simply, "Robert Clayton Ames, Central Intelligence Agency of the United States of America, March 6, 1934–April 18, 1983." Nearby were the graves of veterans from the Civil War and America's wars in Europe, Korea, and Vietnam. A rear admiral born in 1876 was buried behind Ames. But Ames's was then the only gravestone in Arlington to identify a clandestine officer of the CIA. Standing near the grave, Frank Anderson spoke briefly of Ames's career and how Bob's clandestine relationship with Arafat's intelligence chief, Ali Hassan Salameh, had brought the Palestinians in from the cold. Ames, Anderson explained to the novice officers, was one of the CIA's fallen heroes, a man who was good at forming clandestine relationships in a dangerous part of the world. "He was no Lawrence of Arabia," said Henry Miller-Jones, another clandestine officer. "He had little patience with pretentiousness or patronizing 'Arabophiles' and fanatic adventurers. He was never naïve about the Middle East, a cockpit of power politics. He understood the personalities and motivations of the revolutionary left in the Arab world as much as he appreciated the rituals of the Sheiks."

Ames had understood that a good CIA officer must have a curiosity about the foreign other—and a certain degree of empathy for their struggles. As Miller-Jones put it, "He came to know kings, emirs and princes as well as revolutionaries and terrorists, goat herders and penthouse commandos." He was adroit at making his way through the wilderness of mirrors that was the Middle East. He was naturally reserved, a man who easily kept secrets. He inspired trust, even in the company of men with bloody pasts. But he was also an intellectual, who later in his career could brief a president or a secretary of state about the intricacies of Middle Eastern politics and history. He was a model intelligence officer. "Everyone credited Ames with getting the peace process started," recalled Lindsay Sherwin, a CIA analyst.

"There was a moment of silent prayer," recalled Englehart, "as we all stood on the grass around the grave. I remember wondering why, after all we had done for this, President Clinton would not recognize our contribution—but it wasn't politically expedient. We should have known that, but it still stung."

After a few minutes, Anderson led his colleagues over to the nearby grave of William Buckley, the CIA Beirut station chief who'd been kidnapped in March 1984; he had been severely mistreated in captivity and had died fifteen months later, probably of pneumonia. Next they visited the gravesites of James and Monique Lewis, both of whom had died with Ames on that terrible day in April 1983. Both were CIA employees. And then they walked to the gravesite of Kenneth Haas, the CIA station chief in Beirut at the time. He too had died with Ames. Finally, they found the gravesite of Frank Johnston, yet another CIA officer who'd died that day in Beirut. All had been buried in Arlington. It had been a heavy toll— the worst in the Agency's history.

The visit to the cemetery was a sobering moment. But there was also a feeling of exhilaration—as if these sacrifices had been vindicated. "We were all quietly excited," Englehart recalled. "For those of us who spent our working lives in the Arab-Israeli firestorm, it was positive. After all, everybody would get what they wanted [with the Oslo peace accords], or what they thought they wanted. I had a definite feeling at the time that the sacrifices of our dead were not in vain, that the Israeli people and the Palestinian people could at last let go of each other's throats and understand that they are all brothers and sisters."

It was not to be.

PHOTO: © JOSHUA BIRD

KAI BIRD is an award-winning historian and journalist. Executive Director of the Leon Levy Center for Biography, he is the acclaimed author of biographies of John J. McCloy and of McGeorge and William Bundy. He won the Pulitzer Prize for Biography for *American Prometheus: The Triumph and Tragedy of J. Robert Oppenheimer* (co-authored with Martin J. Sherwin). His work includes critical writings on the Vietnam War, Hiroshima, nuclear weapons, the Cold War, the Arab-Israeli conflict, and the CIA. He lives in New York City and Washington, D.C., with his wife, Susan Goldmark.

About the Type

This book was set in Minion, a 1990 Adobe Originals typeface by Robert Slimbach. Minion is inspired by classical, old-style typefaces of the late Renaissance, a period of elegant and beautiful type designs. Created primarily for text setting, Minion combines the aesthetic and functional qualities that make text type highly readable with the versatility of digital technology.

Available from Pulitzer Prize–winning author

KAI BIRD

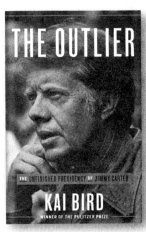
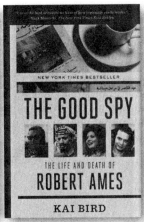

"Kai Bird writes well enough to be a
novelist, too, but his sentences have the
additional virtue of being true."

—*The Times Literary Supplement*